D1288636

More critical praise for *Technical Analysis* . . .

"Long live *Technical Analysis!* Jack has done a phenomenal job of applying it to the markets of the '90s!"

> —Linda Bradford Raschke
> President, The LBR Group

"In his latest *Schwagers on Futures* volume, Jack Schwager provides a *thorough* examination of technical analysis. From the tyro to the tycoon, all market participants will find valuable information in *Technical Analysis*."

> —Patrick A. Arbor
> Chairman, Chicago Board of Trade

"Jack has had more impact than any other author in the futures industry during this century. With the *Schwager on Futures* series, his name will be spoken for centuries to come."

> —Thomas F. Basso
> President, Trendstat Capital Management

Schwager on Futures

Technical
Analysis

Challenges just come into your life to help you grow.
Because if there were no challenges,
we would all be so mediocre.

Wally ("Famous") Amos

Schwager on Futures

Technical
Analysis

Jack D. Schwager

John Wiley & Sons, Inc.

New York • Chichester • Brisbane • Toronto • Singapore

With love to my son Zachary,
who has touched me with his affection,
impressed me with his creativity,
and delighted me with his sense of humor.

This text is printed on acid-free paper.

Copyright © 1996 by Jack D. Schwager.
Published by John Wiley & Sons, Inc.

All rights reserved. Published simultaneously in Canada.

This publication is designed to provide accurate and authoritative
information in regard to the subject matter covered. It is sold
with the understanding that the publisher is not engaged in
rendering legal, accounting, or other professional services. If
legal advice or other expert assistance is required, the services
of a competent professional person should be sought. *From a
Declaration of Principles jointly adopted by a committee of the
American Bar Association and a committee of publishers.*

Library of Congress Cataloging-in-Publication Data:

ISBN 0-471-02051-6

Printed in the United States of America

10 9 8 7 6 5 4 3 2 1

Preface

Trading success cannot be capsulized in a simple indicator, formula, or system—the pronouncements of countless books, advertisements, and brochures notwithstanding. This book is written by a trader, from a trader's perspective, rather than being yet another compendium of analytical techniques, indicators, or systems, using idealized illustrations.

In explaining various analytical techniques and methods, I have tried to keep in the forefront key questions that are often ignored by writers of books on technical analysis: How can the methods described be applied in actual trading? What works and doesn't work in the real world? What are the implications of a method's failure? How can trading systems be designed and tested to maximize their *future* performance rather than their *past* performance?

This is a practical book. I have used many of the methods described in this volume to construct a very profitable trading approach—yes, with real money. Why then am I willing to share this information? Because, to use a building metaphor, I am supplying the tools, but not the architectural design—that is left to the individual reader. I believe that readers who are serious about using technical analysis to become more successful traders and who understand that this goal requires individual work will find much here that is useful.

JACK D. SCHWAGER

New York, New York
October 1995

Acknowledgments

In my early years of involvement with the futures markets, I was a pure fundamentalist and held technical analysis in complete disdain—an opinion, I might add, based on presumptions rather than any knowledge or experience. At the time, I was a research director for a major brokerage firm. One of the analysts in my department was a technician, and I began to notice something odd: He was frequently right in his market calls. We became good friends, and he taught me the rudiments of chart analysis. As I gained experience in applying technical analysis, my opinion of the technique changed 180 degrees from my original skepticism. The technical analyst who first introduced me to the methodology and had such a great impact on my career is Steve Chronowitz. Without Steve, this book would probably never have come into existence.

During the past seven years, I have worked very closely with Louis Lukac, who is my partner in a commodity trading advisory firm. Louis is not only an extraordinarily skilled programmer, but also possesses expert knowledge on system design and testing. Louis has programmed a multitude of the systems I have developed over the years and worked with me in combining these systems into a highly complex computerized trading methodology. Without Louis, I would not have experienced the contentment (and monetary rewards) of seeing my ideas work in the real world.

There were a few subject areas that I wanted to include in this book, but felt that I lacked the appropriate expertise to author to my own satisfaction. I therefore recruited a few select contributing authors for these chapters. These contributing authors and their subjects included Tom Bierovic on oscillators, Richard Mogey on cyclical analysis, and Steve Nison on candlestick charts.

All the foregoing were important, but I owe my greatest thanks to my wife, Jo Ann. Jo Ann understood my need, perhaps even my compulsion, to write the series of which this book is part—to commit these books that were inside of me to the written page. I thank her for supporting me in this project, despite her full knowledge that this endeavor would severely encroach on our time together and on our activities as a family. And on a related note, I thank my children Daniel, Zachary, and Samantha for gracefully bearing my reduced presence in their lives.

Unless otherwise indicated, the charts in this book are reproduced courtesy of Prudential Securities Inc.

J. D. S.

Contents

PART TWO: REAL-WORLD CHART ANALYSIS

PART THREE: OSCILLATORS AND CYCLES

Schwager on Futures

Technical
Analysis

Part One
CHART ANALYSIS

1 Charts: Forecasting Tool or Folklore?

Common sense is not so common.

—Voltaire

There is a story about a speculator whose desire to be a winner was intensified by each successive failure. Initially he tried basing his trading decisions on fundamental analysis. He constructed intricate models that provided price forecasts based on an array of supply/demand statistics. Unfortunately, his models' predictions were invariably upset by some unexpected event, such as a drought or a surprise export sale.

Ultimately, in exasperation, he gave up on the fundamental approach and turned to chart analysis. He scrutinized price charts, searching for patterns that would reveal the secrets of trading success. He was the first to discover such unusual formations as shark-tooth bottoms and Grand Teton tops. But alas, the patterns always seemed reliable until he started basing his trades on them. When he went short, top formations proved to be nothing more than pauses in towering bull markets. Equally distressing, steady uptrends had an uncanny tendency to reverse course abruptly soon after he went long.

"The problem," he reasoned, "is that chart analysis is too inexact. What I need is a computerized trading system." So he began testing various schemes to see if any would have been profitable as a trading system in the past. After exhaustive research, he found that buying pork bellies, cocoa, and Eurodollars on the first Tuesday of months with an odd number of days and then liquidating these positions on the third Thursday of the month would have yielded extremely profitable results during the preceding five years. Inexplicably, this carefully researched pattern failed to hold once he began trading. Another stroke of bad luck.

The speculator tried many other approaches—Elliot waves, Fibonacci numbers, Gann squares, the phases of the moon—but all proved equally unsuccessful. It was at this point that he heard of a famous guru who lived on a remote mountain in the Himalayas and who answered the questions of all pilgrims who sought him out. The trader boarded a plane to Nepal, hired guides, and set out on a two-month trek. Finally, completely exhausted, he reached the famous guru.

"Oh Wise One," he said, "I am a frustrated man. For many years I have sought the key to successful trading, but everything I have tried has failed. What is the secret?"

The guru paused for only a moment, and, staring at his visitor intently, answered, "BLASH." He said no more.

"Blash?" The trader did not understand the answer. It filled his mind every waking moment, but he could not fathom its meaning. He repeated the story to many, until finally one listener interpreted the guru's response.

"It's quite simple," he said, "Buy low and sell high."

The guru's message is apt to be disappointing to readers seeking the profound key to trading wisdom. BLASH does not satisfy our concept of an insight, because it appears to be a matter of common sense. However, if, as Voltaire suggested, "Common sense is not so common," neither is it obvious. For example, consider the following question: What are the trading implications of a market reaching new highs? The "common-sense" BLASH theory would unambiguously indicate that subsequent trading activity should be confined to the short side.

Very likely, a large percentage of speculators would be comfortable with this interpretation. Perhaps the appeal of the BLASH approach is tied to the desire of most traders to demonstrate their brilliance. After all, any fool can buy the market after a long uptrend, but it takes genius to fade the trend and pick a top. In any case, few trading responses are as instinctive as the bias toward buying when prices are low and selling when prices are high.

As a result, many speculators have a strong predilection toward favoring the short side when a market trades in new high ground. There is only one thing wrong with this approach: it doesn't work. A plausible explanation is readily available. A market's ability to reach and sustain new highs is usually evidence of powerful underlying forces that often push prices much higher. Common sense? Certainly. But note that the trading implications are exactly opposite to those of the "common-sense" BLASH approach.

The key point of all of this is that many of our common-sense instincts about market behavior are wrong. Chart analysis provides a means of acquiring common sense in trading—a goal far more elusive than it sounds. For example, if prior to beginning trading an individual exhaustively researched historical price charts to determine the consequences of a market's reaching new highs, he would have a strong advantage in avoiding one of the common pitfalls that await the novice trader. Similarly, other market truths can be gleaned through a careful study of historical price patterns.

It must be acknowledged, however, that the usefulness of charts as an indicator of *future* price direction is a fiercely contested subject. Rather than list the pros and cons of this argument, we note that a recent episode of a popular TV series on the financial markets succinctly highlighted some of the key issues in this debate. The transcript from this program is presented:

MODERATOR: Hello, I'm Louis Puneyser of Wallet Street Week. Tonight we will depart from our normal interview format to provide a forum for a debate on the usefulness of commodity price charts. Can all those wiggly lines and patterns really predict the future? Or is Shakespeare's description of life also appropriate to chart analysis: " . . . a tale told by an idiot, full of sound and fury, signifying nothing"? Our guests tonight are Faith N. Trend, a renowned technical analyst with the Wall Street firm of Churnum & Burnum, and Phillip A. Coin, a professor at Ivory Tower University and the author of *The Only Way to Beat the Market—Become a Broker.* Mr. Coin, you belong to a group called the Random Walkers. Is that some sort of hiking club that decides its destinations by throwing darts at a trail map? (He smiles smugly into the camera.)

PROFESSOR COIN: Well no, Mr. Puneyser. The Random Walkers are a group of economists who believe that market price movements are random. That is, one can no more devise a system to predict market prices than one can devise a system to predict the sequence of colors that will turn up on a roulette wheel. Both events are strictly a matter of chance. Prices have no memory, and what happened yesterday has nothing to do with what will happen tomorrow. In other words, charts can only tell you what has happened in the past; they are useless in predicting the future.

MS. TREND: Professor, you overlook a very important fact: daily prices are not drawn out of a bowl, but rather are the consequence of the collective activity of all market participants. Human behavior may not be as predictable as the motion of planets as governed by the laws of physics, but neither is it totally random. If this is not the case, your profession—economics—is doomed to the same fate as alchemy. (Professor Coin squirms uncomfortably in his seat upon this reference.) Charts reveal basic behavioral patterns. Insofar as similar interactions between buyers and sellers will result in similar price patterns, the past can indeed be used as a guideline for the future.

PROFESSOR COIN: If past prices can be used to predict future prices, why have a myriad of academic studies concluded that tested technical rules failed to outperform a simple buy-and-hold policy once commissions were taken into account?

MS. TREND: The rules used in those studies are generally oversimplified. The studies demonstrate that those particular rules don't work. They don't prove that a richer synthesis of price information, such as chart analysis, or a more complex technical system, cannot be successfully exploited for making trading decisions.

PROFESSOR COIN: Why then are there no studies that conclusively demonstrate the viability of chart analysis as a forecasting tool?

MS. TREND: Your argument merely reflects the difficulties of quantifying chart theories rather than the deficiencies of the chartist approach. One man's top formation is another man's congestion area. An attempt to define anything but the simplest chart pattern mathematically will be unavoidably arbitrary. The problems become even more tangled when one realizes that at any given time, the chart picture may exhibit conflicting patterns. Thus, in a sense, it is not really possible to test many chart theories objectively.

PROFESSOR COIN: That's rather convenient for you, isn't it? If these theories can't be rigorously tested, of what use are they? How do you know that trading on charts will lead to better than a 50/50 success rate—that is, before commissions?

MS. TREND: If you mean that blindly following every chart signal will only make your broker rich, I don't disagree. However, my point is that chart analysis is an art, not a science. A familiarity with basic chart theories is only the starting point. The true usefulness of charts depends on the individual trader's ability to synthesize successfully his own experience with standard concepts. In the right hands, charts can be extremely valuable in anticipating major market trends. There are many successful traders who base their decisions primarily on charts. What would you attribute their success to—a lucky streak?

PROFESSOR COIN: Yes. Exactly that, a lucky streak. If there are enough traders, some of them will be winners, whether they reach their decisions by reading charts or throwing darts at the commodity price page. It's not the method, just the laws of probability. Even in a casino, some percentage of the people are winners. You wouldn't say that their success is due to any insights or system.

MS. TREND: All that proves is that superior performance by some chartists *could* be due to chance. It doesn't disprove the contention that the skillful chartist is onto something that gives him an edge.

MODERATOR: I sense a lot of resistance here, and I think we could use some more support. Have either of you brought any evidence along that would tend to substantiate your positions?

PROFESSOR COIN: Yes! (At this point, Professor Coin pulls a thick manuscript from his briefcase and thrusts it into Mr. Puneyser's hands. The moderator flips through the pages and shakes his head as he notices a profusion of funny little Greek letters.)

MODERATOR: I had something a little less mathematical in mind. Even educational TV is not ready for this.

PROFESSOR COIN: Well, I also have this. (He pulls out a sheet of paper and hands it to Ms. Trend.) How would you interpret this chart, Ms. Trend? (He unsuccessfully attempts to suppress a smirk.)

MS. TREND: I'd say this looks like a chart based on a series of coin tosses. You know, heads one box up, tails one box down.

PROFESSOR COIN: (Whose smirk has turned into a very visible frown.) How did you know that?

MS. TREND: Lucky guess.

PROFESSOR COIN: Well anyway, that doesn't affect my argument. Look at this chart. Here's a trend. And this here—isn't that what you people call a head and shoulders formation?

MODERATOR: Speaking of head and shoulders, do either of you have an opinion on Procter & Gamble?

PROFESSOR COIN: (Continuing.) The same chart patterns you are so quick to point to on your price charts also show up in obviously random series.

MS. TREND: Yes, but that line of reasoning can lead to some odd conclusions. For instance, would you agree that the fact that working economists tend to have advanced degrees is not a chance occurrence?

PROFESSOR COIN: Of course.

MS. TREND: Well then, a random sample of the population is also likely to turn up some people with advanced degrees. Do you then conclude that the fact that an economist has an advanced degree is a coincidence?

PROFESSOR COIN: I still don't see any difference between price charts and my randomly generated chart.

MS. TREND: You don't? Does this look like a randomly generated chart? (Ms. Trend holds up a July 1980 silver chart— see Figure 1.1).

PROFESSOR COIN: Well, not exactly, but . . .

MODERATOR: You might say that not every silver chart has a cloudy trend line.

MS. TREND: (On the attack.) Or this. (She holds up the December 1994 coffee chart—see Figure 1.2.) I could go on.

Figure 1.1
JULY 1980 SILVER

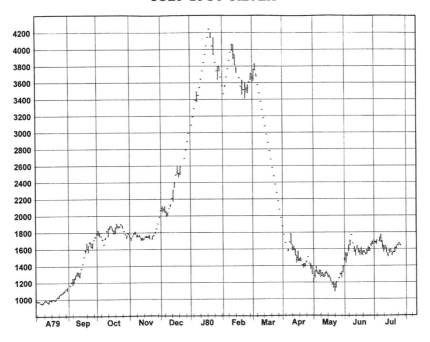

Figure 1.2
DECEMBER 1994 COFFEE

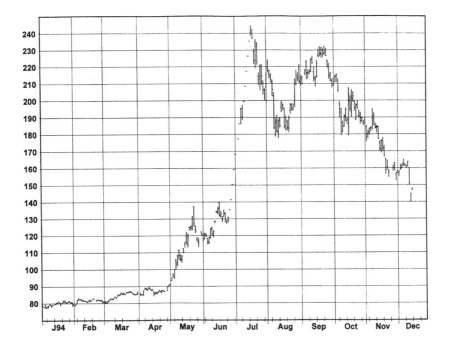

MODERATOR: (To Professor Coin.) Ms. Trend really seems to be percolating. Are there any grounds for dismissing her examples?

PROFESSOR COIN: Well, I admit those examples are pretty extreme, but they still don't prove that past prices can predict future prices.

MODERATOR: Before our time reaches limit-up, so to speak, I would like to rechart our course. I wonder what your opinions are about fundamental analysts?

PROFESSOR COIN: Well, they're better than chartists since they can at least *explain* price moves. But I'm afraid their attempts to *forecast* prices are equally futile. You see, at any given moment, the market discounts all known information, so there is no way they can project prices unless they can anticipate unforeseen future developments such as droughts or export embargoes.

MS. TREND: Well, first I would like to address the implication that chart analysts ignore fundamentals. Actually we believe that the price chart provides an unambiguous and immediate summary of the net impact of all fundamental and psychological factors. In contrast, accurate fundamental models, if they could be constructed at all, would be extremely complex. Furthermore, the fundamental data for the forecast period would have to be estimated, thereby making the price projections extremely vulnerable to error.

MODERATOR: Then you might say you both agree with the statement that fundamentalists end up with holes in their shoes.

MS. TREND: Yes.

PROFESSOR COIN: Yes.

MODERATOR: Well, on that upbeat note of agreement, we end tonight's program.

In a sense, the argument between the "random walkers" and the chartists can never be clearly resolved. It must be understood that it is impossible to prove randomness; all that one can prove is that a given pattern does not exist. Since there is no consensus as to the precise mathematical definition of many chart patterns, the viability of these patterns as price indicators can neither be proven nor disproven.

For example, if one wanted to test the contention that breakouts from trading ranges represent valid trade signals, the first requirement would be to formulate a concise definition of a trading range and a breakout. Assume that the following definitions are adopted: (1) that the *trading range* is a price band that completely encloses all daily price changes during the past six-week period and that is no wider than 5 percent of the median price during that period;[1] and (2) that a *breakout* is a closing price above the six-week trading range. Although the validity of breakouts as trading signals could be tested for these specific definitions, the definitions themselves will be challenged by many. Some of the objections might include the following:

1. The price band is too narrow.
2. The price band is too wide.
3. The six-week period is too long.
4. The six-week period is too short.
5. No allowance is made for isolated days beyond the confines of the range—an event that most chart analysts would agree does not disturb the basic pattern.
6. The direction of the trend prior to the trading range is not considered—a factor many chartists would view as a critical input in interpreting the reliability of a breakout.
7. The breakout should be required to exceed the boundary of the trading range by a minimum amount (e.g., 1 percent of the price level) in order to be viewed as valid.
8. Several closes above the trading range should be required to indicate a breakout.
9. A time lag should be used to test the validity of the breakout; for example, are prices still beyond the trading range one week after the initial penetration of the range?

The preceding list represents only a partial itemization of the possible objections to our hypothetical definitions of a trading range and breakout, and all of this for one of the most basic chart patterns. Imagine the ambiguities and complications in specifically defining a pattern such as a confirmed head and shoulders.

For their part, the chartists cannot win the argument either. Although

---

[1] The specification of maximum price width is deliberately intended to exclude periods of wide-swinging prices from being defined as trading ranges.

chart analysis is based on general principles, its application depends on individual interpretation. The successful chart-oriented trader might not have any doubts about the viability of chart analysis, but the "random walk" theoreticians would dismiss his success as a consequence of the laws of probability, since even a totally random trade selection process would yield a percentage of winners. In short, the debate is not about to be concluded.

It is also important to realize that even if conclusive tests were possible, the conflicting claims of the random walkers and the chartists need not necessarily be contradictory. One way of viewing the situation is that markets may witness extended periods of random fluctuation, interspersed with shorter periods of nonrandom behavior. Thus, even if the price series as a whole appears random, it is entirely possible that there are periods within the data that exhibit definite patterns. The goal of the chart analyst is to identify those periods (i.e., major trends).

The time has come to admit my own biases. Personal experience has convinced me that charts are a valuable, if not essential, trading tool. However, such perceptions do not prove anything. The random walkers would argue that my conclusions could be based on selective memory—that is, a tendency to remember the successes of chart analysis and forget the failures—or just pure luck. And they are right. Such explanations *could* indeed be correct.

The bottom line is that each trader must evaluate chart analysis independently and draw his own conclusions. However, it should be strongly emphasized that charts are considered to be an extremely valuable trading tool by many successful traders, and therefore, the new trader should be wary of rejecting this approach simply on the basis of intuitive skepticism. Some of the principal potential benefits of using charts are listed below. Note that a number of these uses remain valid even if one totally rejects the possibility that charts can be used to forecast prices.

1. Charts provide a concise price history—an essential item of information for any trader.
2. Charts can provide the trader with a good sense of the market's volatility—an important consideration in assessing risk.
3. Charts are a very useful tool to the fundamental analyst. Long-term price charts enable the fundamentalist to isolate quickly the periods of major price moves. By determining the fundamental conditions or events that were peculiar to those periods, the fundamentalist can identify the key price-influencing factors. This information can then be used to construct a price behavior model.
4. Charts can be used as a timing tool, even by traders who formulate their trading decisions on the basis of other information (e.g., fundamentals).

5. Charts can be used as a money management tool by helping to define meaningful and realistic stop points.
6. Charts reflect market behavior that is subject to certain repetitive patterns. Given sufficient experience, some traders will uncover an innate ability to use charts successfully as a method of anticipating price moves.
7. An understanding of chart concepts is probably an essential prerequisite for developing profitable technical trading systems.
8. Cynics take notice: under specific circumstances, a contrarian approach to classical chart signals can lead to very profitable trading opportunities. The specifics of this approach are detailed in Chapter 11.

In short, charts have something to offer everyone, from cynics to believers. The chapters of this section review and evaluate the key concepts of classical chart theory, as well as address the all-important question of how charts can be used as an effective trading tool.

2   Types of Charts

You don't need a weatherman to know which way the wind blows.
—Bob Dylan

BAR CHARTS

Bar charts are by far the most common type of price charts. In a bar chart, each day is represented by a vertical line that ranges from the daily low to the daily high. The day's closing value is indicated by a horizontal protrusion. Figure 2.1 is a daily bar chart of the March 1995 soybean contract.

The daily bar chart is most useful for trading purposes, but bar charts for longer data periods provide extremely important perspective. These longer-period bar charts (e.g., weekly, monthly) are entirely analogous to the daily bar chart, with each vertical line representing the price range and final price level for the period. Figure 2.2 is a weekly bar chart for soybean futures. The segment within the rectangle corresponds to the period depicted by Figure 2.1. Figure 2.3 is a monthly bar chart for soybean futures. The large and small rectangles enclose the periods depicted by Figure 2.2 and Figure 2.1, respectively.

Used in combination, the monthly, weekly, and daily bar charts provide a telephoto-type effect. The monthly and weekly charts would be used to provide a broad market perspective and to formulate a technical opinion regarding the potential long-term trend. The daily chart would then be employed to determine the timing of trades. If the long-term technical picture is sufficiently decisive, by the time the trader gets to the daily charts, he may already have a strong market bias. For example, if he interprets the monthly and weekly charts as suggesting the likelihood that the market has witnessed a major long-term top, he will only monitor the daily charts for sell signals.

The difference in perspective between daily and weekly charts can be striking. For example, the daily bar chart for the March 1995 silver contract (Figure 2.4) is dominated by a very bearish, massive top pattern. The weekly silver chart (Figure 2.5), however, provides a very different picture. Although in this chart the late 1993–1994 price pattern still looks toppy, the chart also reveals that prices are near the low end of a broad historical range and that a

Figure 2.1
DAILY BAR CHART: MARCH 1995 SOYBEANS

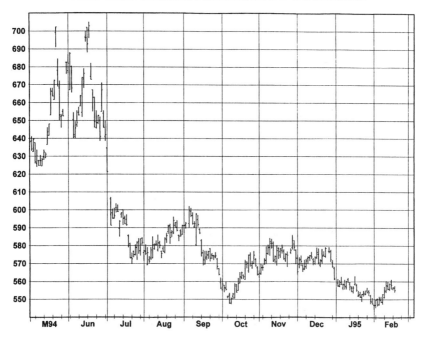

Figure 2.2
WEEKLY BAR CHART: SOYBEANS (NEAREST FUTURES)

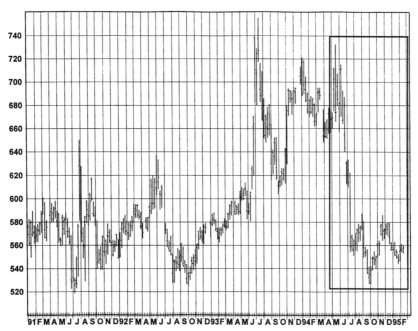

Figure 2.3
MONTHLY BAR CHART: SOYBEANS (NEAREST FUTURES)

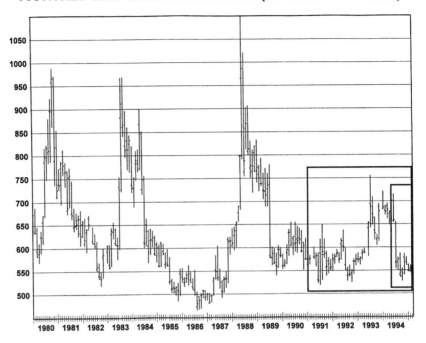

Figure 2.4
DAILY BAR CHART PERSPECTIVE: MARCH 1995 SILVER

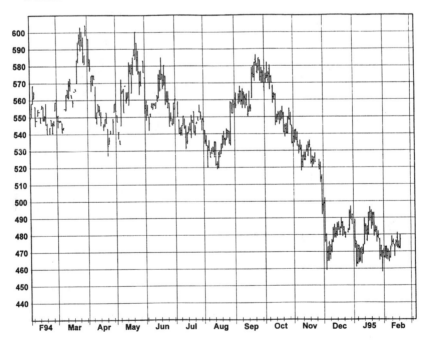

Figure 2.5
WEEKLY BAR CHART PERSPECTIVE: SILVER
NEAREST FUTURES

major price base was apparently formed during the 1991–early 1993 period. Thus, while both charts seem to imply a near-term bearish bias, the weekly chart provides strong reasons for viewing another price downswing as a potential major buying opportunity, whereas there is not even a hint of such a conclusion in the daily chart. The basic point is that longer-term charts may suggest very different interpretations of price patterns than those indicated by daily charts; hence, both types of charts should be examined.

LINKED CONTRACT SERIES: NEAREST FUTURES VERSUS CONTINUOUS FUTURES

The time period covered by the typical weekly or monthly bar chart requires the use of a series of contracts. Normally, these contracts are combined using the *nearest futures* approach: a contract is plotted until its expiration and then the subsequent contract is plotted until its expiration, and so on. The trader should be aware that a nearest futures chart may reflect significant distortions due to the price gaps between the expiring month and the subsequent contract.

Figure 2.6 provides a lucid example of this type of distortion. Note the pattern of consolidations interspersed by single-week, sharp rallies that materialized every three months like clockwork. Was the Euromark during this period subject to some bullish event that occurred every three months? In reality, these regularly spaced, single-week "rallies" were not true price advances at all, but rather an illusory consequence of the transition from the nearest futures contract to the next contract, which during the period depicted consistently traded at a wide premium to the nearby month.

In fact, throughout almost the entire period shown in Figure 2.6, prices actually declined, in the sense that a continuously held long position that was rolled over to the next contract as each expiration approached would have lost money! This point is illustrated by Figure 2.7, which depicts the continuous futures chart for the same market during the same time period. (Price swings in a continuous futures chart, which is defined later in this section, will exactly parallel the equity fluctuations in a continuously held long position.) The gains implied by the fixed interval, sharp upswings in Figure 2.6 could

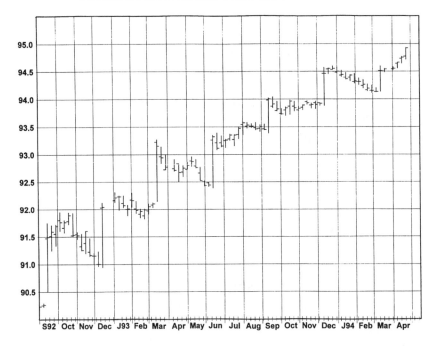

Figure 2.6
DISTORTION IN NEAREST FUTURES CHART:
EUROMARK WEEKLY NEAREST FUTURES

Figure 2.7
CONTINUOUS FUTURES CHART AS ACCURATE
REFLECTION OF EQUITY FLUCTUATIONS:
EUROMARK WEEKLY CONTINUOUS FUTURES

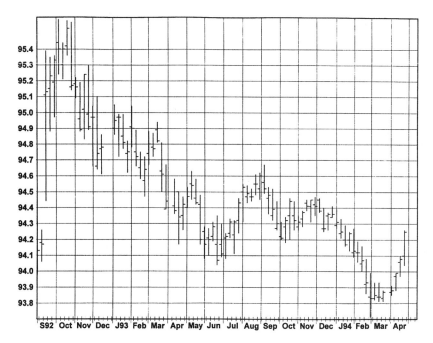

not have been realized by a trader, since he would have liquidated a position in one month and replaced that position in another month that was much higher priced. In fact, it is this price difference between months that is responsible for the *phantom* price moves evident in the nearest futures chart at three-month intervals.

The fact that a nearest futures chart is vulnerable to great distortion, in the sense that price moves depicted in the chart may contrast dramatically with the results realized by an actual trader (as was the case in the Euromark illustration just provided), makes it necessary to consider an alternative linked-contract representation that does not share this defect. The continuous futures chart provides such an alternative approach.

Continuous futures is a series that links together successive contracts in such a way that price gaps are eliminated at rollover points. Although continuous futures will precisely reflect price *swings,* past continuous levels will not match actual historical *levels.* (In contrast, nearest futures will accurately reflect actual historical *levels,* but not price *swings.*) The appropriate series depends on the intended purpose. Nearest futures should be used to indicate the actual price levels at which a market traded in the past. However, continuous futures should be used to illustrate the results that would have been realized by a trader. For a more detailed explanation, see Chapter 12.

CLOSE-ONLY CHARTS

As the name implies, close-only charts are based on closing values and ignore high and low price information. Some price series can only be depicted in close-only chart formats because intraday data are not readily available. Two examples are (1) cash price series (Figure 2.8) and (2) spreads (Figure 2.9). (A spread chart depicts the price *difference* between two contracts.)

Some chart traders may prefer close-only charts even when high/low/close data are available, because they feel a clearer price picture can be obtained by using only the close. In their view, the inclusion of high/low data only

Figure 2.8
CASH PRICE CHART: WHEAT

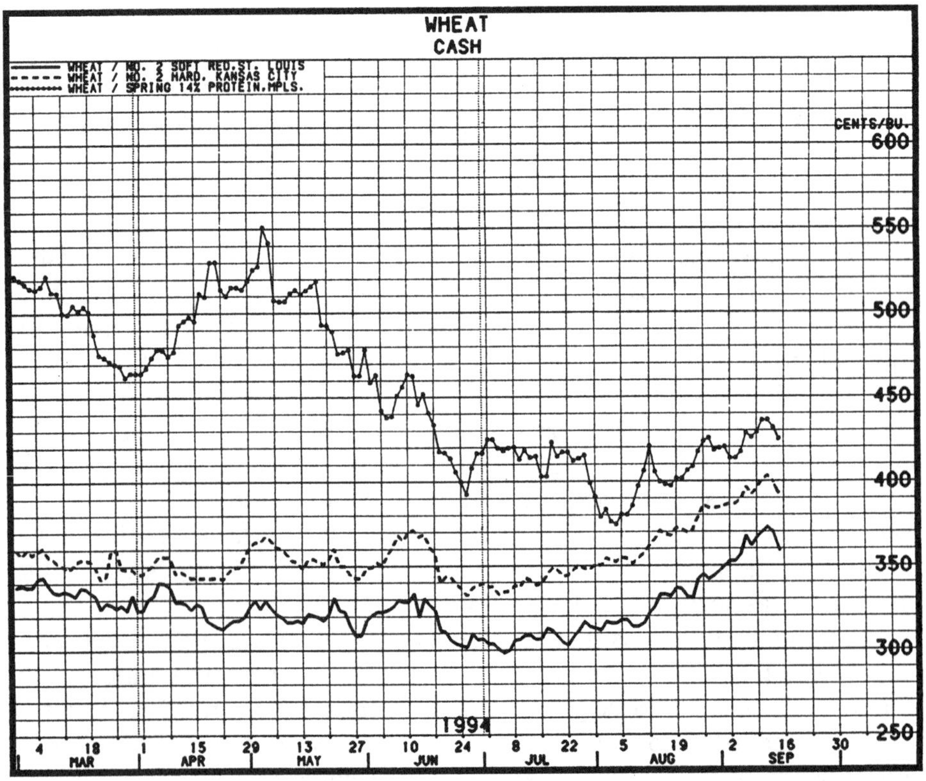

Source: Reprinted with permission, © 1995 Knight-Ridder Financial, 30 South Wacker Drive, Suite 1810, Chicago, Illinois 60606.

Figure 2.9
SPREAD CHART: OCTOBER/DECEMBER COTTON

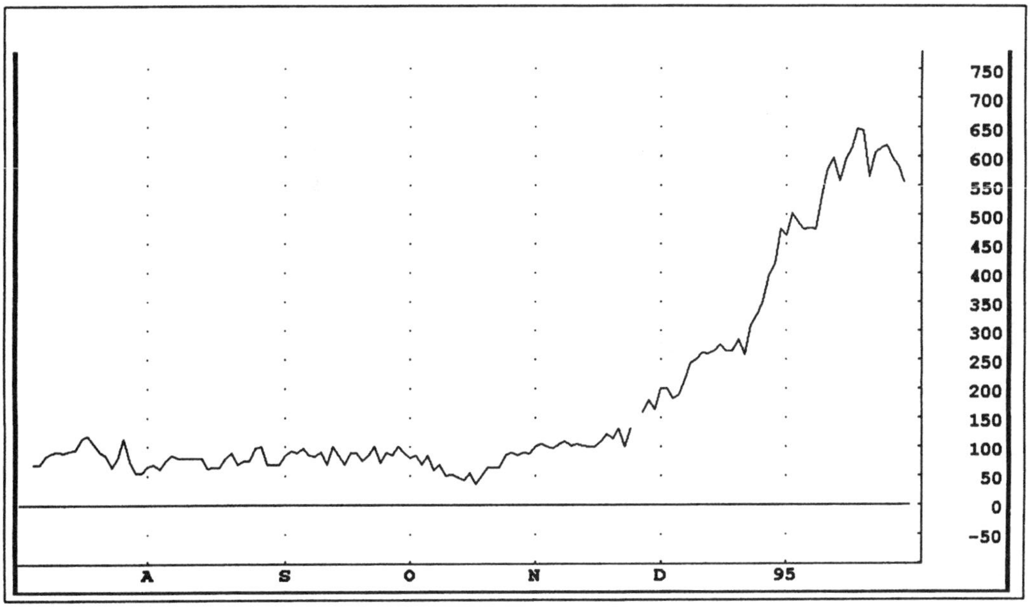

Source: FutureSource; copyright © 1986–1994; all rights reserved.

serves to obfuscate the price chart. There is much to be said for the emphasis on the closing value as the embodiment of the day's essential price information. Nevertheless, many important chart patterns depend on the availability of high/low data and one should think twice before ignoring this information. Furthermore, as a practical matter, bar charts are far more readily available than close-only charts.

POINT AND FIGURE CHARTS

The essential characteristic of the point and figure chart is that it views all trading as a single continuous stream and hence ignores time. A point and figure chart is illustrated in Figure 2.10. As can be seen, a point and figure chart consists of a series of columns of *X*'s and *O*'s. Each *X* represents a price move of a given magnitude called the *box size.* As long as prices continue to rise, *X*'s are added to a column for each increment equal to the box size. However, if prices decline by an amount equal to or greater than the *reversal size* (usually quoted as a multiple of the box size), a new column of *O*'s is initiated and plotted in descending fashion. The number of *O*'s will be dependent on the magnitude of the reversal, but by definition must at least equal the reversal size.

Figure 2.10
POINT AND FIGURE CHART: MARCH 1995 T-BOND

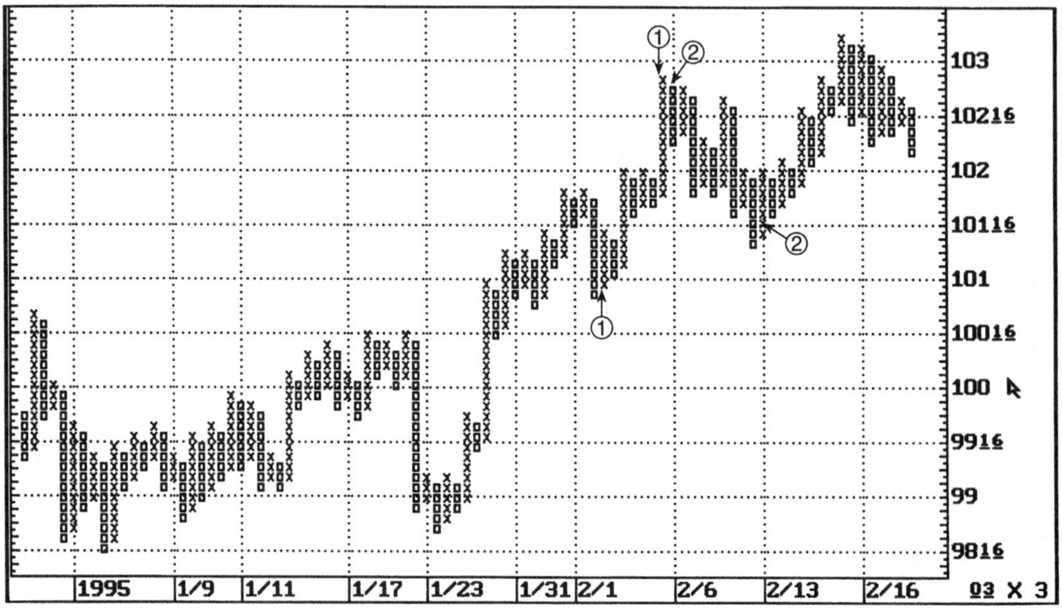

Source: CQG Inc.; copyright © 1994 by CQG Inc.

By convention, the first *O* in a column is always plotted one box below the last *X* in the preceding column. An analogous description would apply to price declines and upside reversals. The choice of box and reversal size is arbitrary.

Figure 2.10 is a point and figure chart with a box size of 3 points and a reversal size of 3 boxes, or 9 points. In other words, as long as a price decline of 9 or more points does not occur, *X*'s continue to be added in a single column. When a price decline of 9 or more points occurs, a new column of *O*'s is begun, with the first *O* placed one box below the last *X*.

As stated previously, the point and figure chart does not reflect time. One column may represent one day or two months. For example, Figure 2.11 is a bar chart corresponding to the point and figure chart in Figure 2.10. The single day on the bar chart, denoted by the symbol "1," and the immediately subsequent six-day period on the bar chart, bracketed by the arrows labeled with the "2" symbol, correspond to the similarly marked intervals on the point and figure chart. Note that whereas the single day occupies seven columns on the point and figure chart, the six-day period accounts for only a slightly greater nine and a fraction columns.

Figure 2.11
BAR CHART CORRESPONDING TO POINT AND FIGURE CHART IN
FIGURE 2.10: MARCH 1995 T-BOND

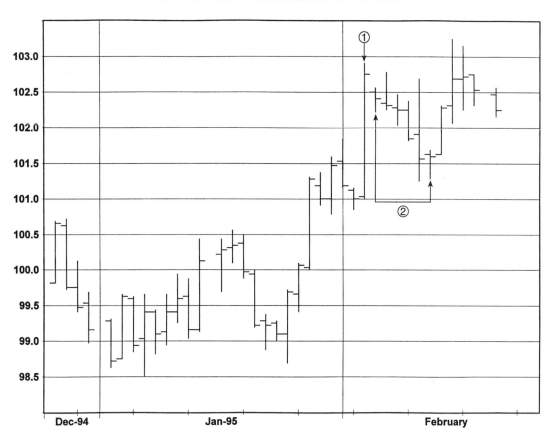

Figure 2.12
CANDLESTICK CHART:
WHITE REAL BODY

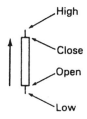

Figure 2.13
CANDLESTICK CHART:
BLACK REAL BODY

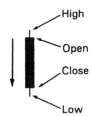

23

CANDLESTICK CHARTS

Candlestick charts add dimension and color to the simple bar chart. The segment of the bar that represents the range between the open and close is represented by a two-dimensional "real body," while the extensions beyond this range to the high and low are shown as lines (called "shadows"). A day on which the open and close are near opposite extremes of the daily range will have a large real body, whereas a day on which there is little net change between the open and close will have a small real body. The color of the real body indicates whether the close was higher than the open (white—Figure 2.12) or lower than the open (black—Figure 2.13). Candlestick charts are discussed in detail in Chapter 13.

3 Trends

The trend is your friend except at the end when it bends.

—Ed Seykota

DEFINING TRENDS BY HIGHS AND LOWS

One standard definition of an uptrend is a succession of higher highs and higher lows. For example, in Figure 3.1, during the March–September period, each relative high (RH) is higher than the preceding high and each relative low (RL) is higher than the preceding low. In essence, an uptrend can be considered intact until a previous reaction low point is broken. A violation of this condition serves as a warning signal that the trend *may* be over. For example, in Figure 3.1, the October penetration of the September relative low proves to be a harbinger of an ensuing decline. It should be emphasized, however, that the disruption of the pattern of higher highs and higher lows (or lower highs and lower lows) should be viewed as a clue, not a conclusive indicator, of a possible long-term trend reversal. Figure 3.2 provides another example of an uptrend defined by successively higher highs and higher lows.

In similar fashion, a downtrend can be defined as a succession of lower lows and lower highs (see Figure 3.3). A downtrend can be considered intact until a previous rally high is exceeded.

Uptrends and downtrends are also often defined in terms of trend lines. An uptrend line is a line that connects a series of higher lows (see Figures 3.4 and 3.5); a downtrend line is a line that connects a series of lower highs (see Figure 3.6). Trend lines can sometimes extend for many years. For example, Figures 3.7 and 3.8 illustrate near decade-long downtrend lines for cocoa in both the nearest and continuous futures charts.

It is not uncommon for reactions against a major trend to begin near a line parallel to the trend line. Sets of parallel lines that enclose a trend are called *trend channels*. Figures 3.9 and 3.10 illustrate extended uptrend and downtrend channels.

Figure 3.1
UPTREND AS SUCCESSION OF HIGHER HIGHS AND
HIGHER LOWS: DECEMBER 1992 EURODOLLAR

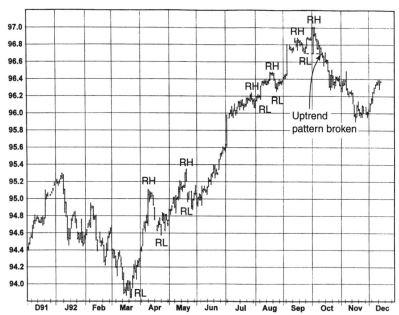

Note: RH = relative high; RL = relative low.

Figure 3.2
UPTREND AS SUCCESSION OF HIGHER HIGHS
AND HIGHER LOWS: DECEMBER 1992 T-BOND

Note: RH = relative high; RL = relative low.

Figure 3.3
DOWNTREND AS SUCCESSION OF LOWER HIGHS
AND LOWER LOWS: DECEMBER 1992 COFFEE

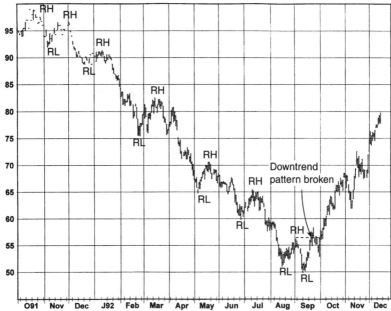

Note: RH = relative high; RL = relative low.

Figure 3.4
UPTREND LINE: JULY 1993 SILVER

Figure 3.5
UPTREND LINE: JUNE 1991 EURODOLLAR

Figure 3.6
DOWNTREND LINE: MATIF NOTIONAL BOND
CONTINUOUS FUTURES

28

Figure 3.7
DOWNTREND LINE: COCOA NEAREST FUTURES

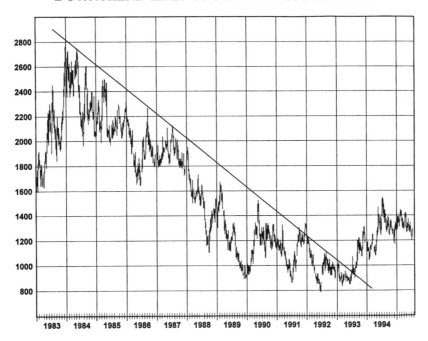

Figure 3.8
DOWNTREND LINE: COCOA CONTINUOUS FUTURES

29

Figure 3.9
UPTREND CHANNEL: JUNE 1991 EURODOLLAR

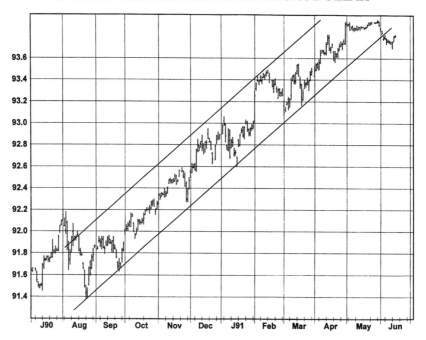

Figure 3.10
DOWNTREND CHANNEL: SEPTEMBER 1992 COCOA

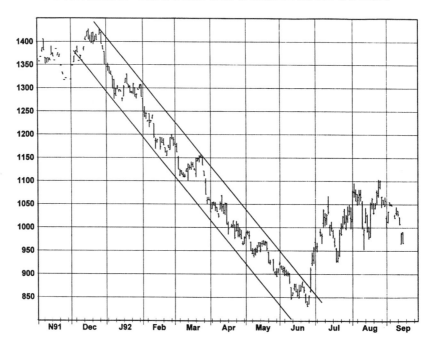

The following rules are usually applied to trend lines and channels:

1. Declines approaching an uptrend line and rallies approaching a down-trend line are often good opportunities to initiate positions in the direction of the major trend.
2. The penetration of an uptrend line (particularly on a closing basis) is a sell signal; the penetration of a downtrend line is a buy signal. Normally, a minimum percentage price move or a minimum number of closes beyond the trend line is required to confirm a penetration.
3. The lower end of a downtrend channel and the upper end of an uptrend channel represent potential profit-taking zones for short-term traders.

Trend lines and channels are useful, but their importance is often overstated. It is easy to overestimate the reliability of trend lines when they are drawn with the benefit of hindsight. A consideration that is frequently overlooked is that trend lines often need to be redrawn as a bull or bear market is extended. Thus, although the penetration of a trend line will sometimes offer an early warning signal of a trend reversal, it is also common that such a development will merely require a redrawing of the trend line. For example, Figure 3.11 is identical to Figure 3.4, except the period depicted is extended by two months. The lower line in Figure 3.11 represents the uptrend line that would have been drawn with the benefit of hindsight. The higher line is reproduced from Figure 3.4 and represents the uptrend line that was indicated until June. The June penetration of the trend line did not result in a trend reversal, but merely necessitated a redrawing of the trend line. It is worth noting that the pattern of higher lows and higher highs remained intact even after the June penetration of the then-existing uptrend line.

Similarly, Figure 3.12 is identical to Figure 3.5, except the period depicted is extended by five months. The lower line in Figure 3.12 represents the uptrend line that would have been drawn with the benefit of hindsight. The higher line is reproduced from Figure 3.5 and represents the uptrend line that was indicated until January. The January penetration of the trend line did not result in a trend reversal, but merely necessitated a redrawing of the trend line.

Figure 3.13 provides an analogous example for a downtrend. This figure is identical to Figure 3.6, except the period depicted is extended by two months. The higher line in Figure 3.13 represents the downtrend line that would have been drawn with the benefit of hindsight. The lower line is reproduced from Figure 3.6 and represents the downtrend line that was indicated until May. The May penetration of the trend line did not result in a trend reversal, but merely necessitated a redrawing of the trend line. In similar fashion, Figure 3.14 is identical to both Figure 3.6 and Figure 3.13, except the period depicted is extended by an additional four months (relative to Figure 3.13). The lower lines are reproduced from Figure 3.6 and Figure 3.13 and

Figure 3.11
UPTREND LINE REDEFINED: JULY 1993 SILVER

Figure 3.12
UPTREND LINE REDEFINED: JUNE 1991 EURODOLLAR

Figure 3.13
DOWNTREND LINE REDEFINED: MATIF
NOTIONAL BOND CONTINUOUS FUTURES

Figure 3.14
DOWNTREND LINE REDEFINED TWICE: MATIF
NOTIONAL BOND CONTINUOUS FUTURES

33

represent the downtrend lines that were indicated until May and July, respectively. The penetration of these trend lines did not result in trend reversals, but merely necessitated the redrawing of the trend line. This example illustrates that trend lines may sometimes have to be redrawn several times.

The preceding examples are meant to drive home the point that the penetration of trend lines is more the rule than the exception. The simple fact is that trend lines tend to be penetrated, sometimes repeatedly, during their evolution, which is equivalent to saying that trend lines are frequently redefined as they extend. The important implications of this observation are that trend lines work much better in hindsight than in real time and that penetrations of trend lines often prove to be false signals. This latter consideration will be revisited in Chapter 11.

TD LINES

In his book, *The New Science of Technical Analysis*,[1] Thomas DeMark accurately notes that the drawing of trend lines is a highly arbitrary process. Presented with the same chart, different people will draw different trend lines. In fact, presented with the same chart at different times, even the same person might well draw the trend line differently.

It is easy to see the reason for this lack of precision. A trend line is typically intended to connect several relative highs or relative lows. If there are only two such points, the trend line can be drawn precisely. If, however, the trend line is intended to connect three or more points—as is frequently the case—a precise line will only exist in the rare circumstance that the relationship between all the points is exactly linear. In most cases, the trend line that is drawn will only exactly touch at most one or two of the relative highs (or lows), while bisecting or missing the other such points. The trend line that provides the best fit is truly in the eye of the beholder.

DeMark recognizes that in order for a trend line to be defined precisely and unambiguously, it must be based on exactly two points. DeMark also notes that contrary to convention, trend lines should be drawn from right to left because "recent price activity is more significant than historical movement." These concepts underlie his approach of drawing trend lines. DeMark's methodology for defining trend lines is explained by the following definitions:[2]

>   **Relative High.** A daily high that is higher than the high on the *N* prior and *N* succeeding days, where *N* is a parameter value that must be

---

[1]John Wiley & Sons Inc., New York, 1994.

[2]The following definitions and terminology differ from those used by DeMark, but the implied method of identifying trend lines is exactly equivalent. I simply find the following approach clearer and more succinct than DeMark's own presentation of the same concept.

defined. For example, if $N = 5$, the relative high is defined as a high that is higher than any high in the prior five days and succeeding five days. (An analogous definition could be applied for data expressed in any time interval. For example, in a 60-minute bar chart, the relative high would be a high that is higher than the high on the prior or succeeding N 60-minute bars.)

Relative Low. A daily low that is lower than the low on the N prior and N succeeding days.

TD Downtrend Line. The prevailing downtrend line is defined as the line connecting the most recent relative high and the most recent preceding relative high that is *also* higher than the most recent relative high. The latter condition is essential to assure that the trend line connecting the two relative highs indeed slopes down. Figure 3.15 illustrates the prevailing TD downtrend line, assuming an $N = 3$ parameter value is used to define relative highs.

TD Uptrend Line. The prevailing uptrend line is defined as the line connecting the most recent relative low and the most recent preceding relative low that is *also* lower than the most recent relative low. Figure 3.16 illustrates the prevailing TD uptrend line, assuming an $N = 8$ parameter value is used to define relative lows.

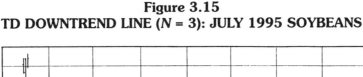

Figure 3.15
TD DOWNTREND LINE ($N = 3$): JULY 1995 SOYBEANS

Figure 3.16
TD UPTREND LINE (*N* = 8): DECEMBER 1994 SWISS FRANC

Figure 3.17
SUCCESSION OF TD UPTREND LINES (*N* = 10):
OCTOBER 1992 SUGAR

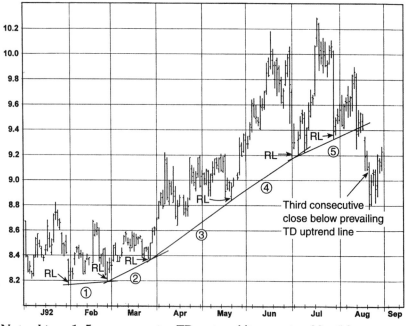

Note: Lines 1–5 are successive TD uptrend lines, using *N* = 10 to define relative lows (RL).

By basing trend line definitions on the most recent relative highs and relative lows, trend lines will be continually redefined as new relative highs and relative lows are defined. For example, Figure 3.17 shows the succession of TD uptrend lines that would be implied as new relative lows are defined ($N = 10$) until a trend reversal signal is received. In this chart it is assumed that a trend reversal signal is defined as three consecutive closes below the prevailing uptrend line. In similar fashion, Figure 3.18 illustrates the succession of TD downtrend lies that would be implied as new relative highs are defined ($N = 8$) until a trend reversal signal is received (again, based on three consecutive closes beyond the trend line).

Different values for N will yield very different trend lines. For example, Figures 3.19–3.21 contrast the TD downtrend lines implied by three different

Figure 3.18
SUCCESSION OF TD DOWNTREND LINES ($N = 8$):
DECEMBER 1992 CORN

Note: Lines 1–3 are successive TD downtrend lines, using $N = 8$ to define relative highs (RH).

Figure 3.19
SUCCESSION OF TD DOWNTREND LINES (N = 2): JUNE 1994 T-BOND

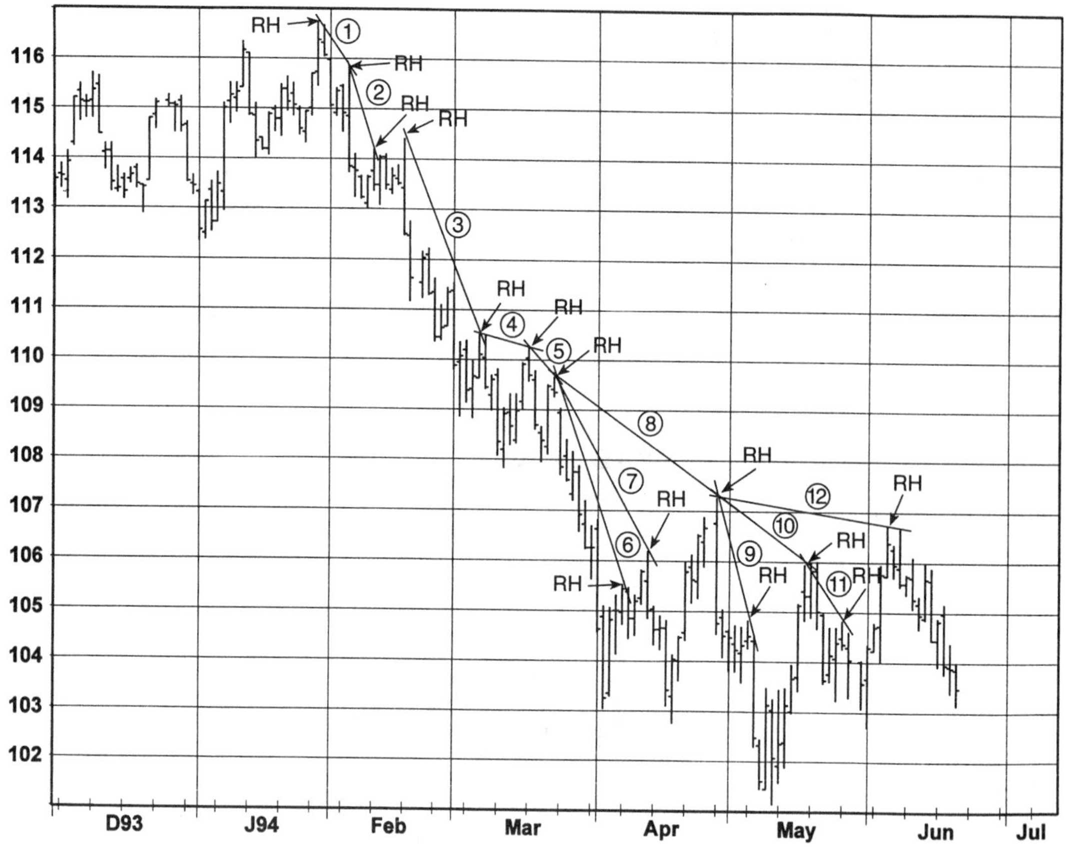

Note: Lines 1–12 are successive TD downtrend lines, using N = 2 to define relative highs (RH).

values of N for the same chart. The lower the value of N, the more frequently the downtrend line is redefined and the more sensitive the line is to penetration. For example, contrast the dozen trend lines generated by the N = 2 definition, versus the mere three lines that result if an N = 10 definition is used.

Similarly, Figures 3.22–3.24 contrast the TD uptrend lines implied by three different values of N for the same chart. As can be seen in Figure 3.22, when the value of N is low (e.g., N = 2), the prevailing uptrend line is redefined frequently and tends to be very sensitive. In fact, during the uptrending period (August–December), 16 different trend lines are generated. For N = 5 the number of uptrend lines is reduced to three during the same period, while for N = 10 there is only a single uptrend line. As these illustrations make clear, the choice of a value for N will make a tremendous difference in the trend lines that are generated and the resulting trading implications.

Figure 3.20
SUCCESSION OF TD DOWNTREND LINES (*N* = 5): JUNE 1994 T-BOND

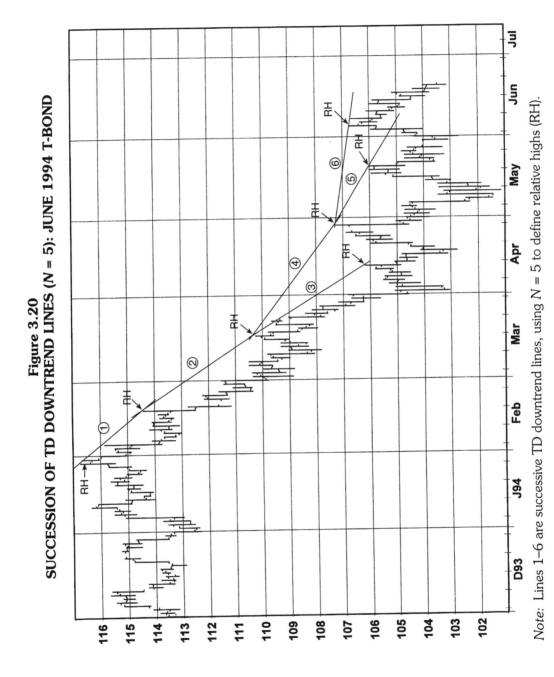

Note: Lines 1–6 are successive TD downtrend lines, using *N* = 5 to define relative highs (RH).

Figure 3.21

SUCCESSION OF TD DOWNTREND LINES ($N = 10$): JUNE 1994 T-BOND

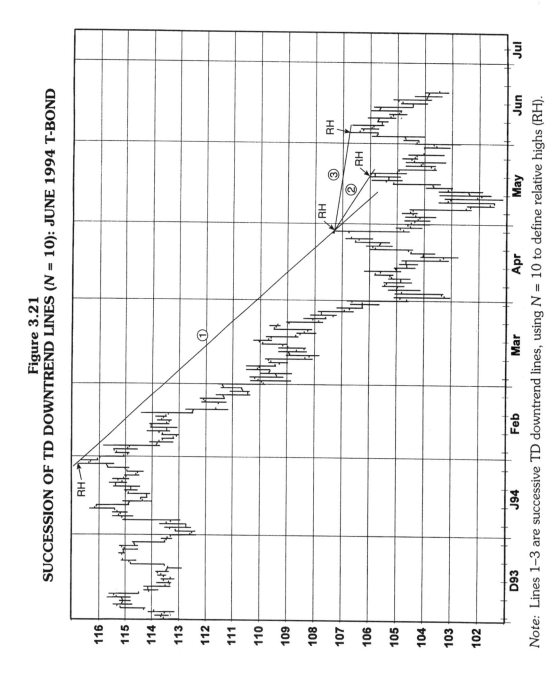

Note: Lines 1–3 are successive TD downtrend lines, using $N = 10$ to define relative highs (RH).

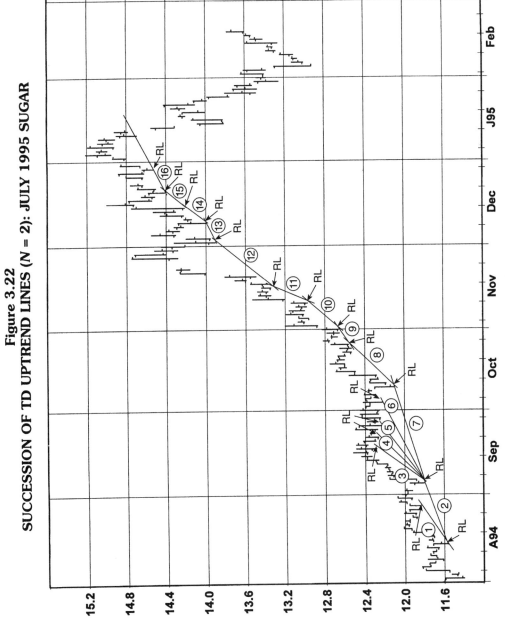

Figure 3.22
SUCCESSION OF TD UPTREND LINES (N = 2): JULY 1995 SUGAR

Note: Lines 1–16 are successive TD uptrend lines, using $N = 2$ to define relative lows (RL).

41

Figure 3.23
SUCCESSION OF TD UPTREND LINES (N = 5): JULY 1995 SUGAR

Note: Lines 1–3 are successive TD uptrend lines, using N = 5 to define relative lows (RL).

DeMark's basic definition of trend lines is equivalent to the aforementioned definitions with N = 1. Although he acknowledges that trend lines can be defined using higher values of N—"TD lines of higher magnitude," in his terminology—his stated preference is for trend lines drawn using the basic definition. Personally, my own preference is quite the opposite. Although it is a truism that using an N = 1 definition for trend lines will yield earlier signals for valid trend line breakouts, the critical tradeoff is that such an approach will tend to provide very tight trend lines that are prone to far more false breakout signals. As a general principle, I think it is far more critical to avoid bad signals than to get the jump on good signals; hence, I strongly favor using higher values of N (e.g., N = 3 to N = 12) to define trend lines.

There is, however, no "right" or "wrong" choice for a value for N; it is strictly a matter of subjective preference. The reader is encouraged to experi-

Figure 3.24
SINGLE TD UPTREND LINE (*N* = 10): JULY 1995 SUGAR

Note: TD uptrend line, using *N* = 10 to define relative lows (RL).

ment drawing trend lines using different values of *N*. Each trader will feel comfortable with certain values of *N* and uncomfortable with others. Generally speaking, short-term traders will gravitate to low values of *N* and long-term traders to higher values.

As a fine-tuning point, which becomes particularly important if trend lines are defined using *N* = 1, it is preferable to define relative highs and relative lows based on true highs and true lows rather than nominal highs and lows. These terms are defined as:

> **True High.** The high or previous close, whichever is higher.
> **True Low.** The low or previous close, whichever is lower.

For most days, the true high will be identical to the high and the true low will be identical to the low. The differences will occur on downside gap days (days on which the entire trading range is below the previous day's close) and upside gap days (days on which the entire trading range is above the previous day's close). The use of true highs and true lows yields relative highs and relative lows that are more in line with our intuitive concept of what these points should represent.

Figure 3.25
NOMINAL HIGHS AND LOWS VERSUS TRUE HIGHS
AND LOWS: DECEMBER 1993 GOLD

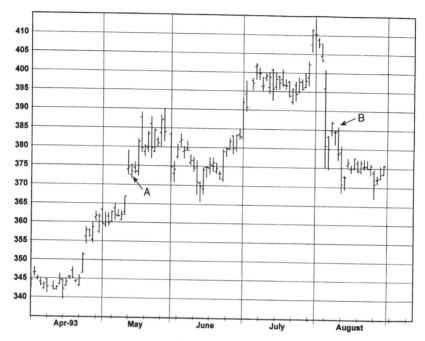

For example, in Figure 3.25, using an $N = 1$ definition, Point A would be identified as a relative low based on the nominal low. This point is only identified as a relative low, however, because of the sharp upside gap on the prior day and hardly fits the intuitive concept of a relative low. Similarly, Point B would be identified as a relative high using nominal highs but not true highs (since the prior day, which witnessed a downside gap, had a higher true high). In both cases, using true highs and lows instead of nominal highs and lows yields intuitively more sensible identifications of relative highs and lows.

INTERNAL TREND LINES

Conventional trend lines are typically drawn to encompass the extreme highs and lows. An argument can be made, however, that the extreme highs and lows represent aberrations due to emotional excesses in the market, and that, as such, these points may be unrepresentative of the dominant trend in the market. An internal trend line does away with the implicit requirement of having to draw trend lines based on extreme price excursions. An internal

Figure 3.26
INTERNAL TREND LINE VERSUS CONVENTIONAL
TREND LINE: MARCH 1991 COTTON

trend line is a trend line drawn so as to best approximate the majority of relative highs or relative lows without any special consideration being given to extreme points. In a rough sense, an internal trend line can be thought of as an approximate best-fit line of relative highs and relative lows. Figures 3.26–3.37 provide a wide range of examples of internal uptrend and downtrend lines, encompassing individual contract charts, daily continuous futures charts, and weekly nearest futures charts. For comparison, these charts also depict conventional trend lines,[3] which are shown as dashed lines.

One shortcoming of internal trend lines is that they are unavoidably arbitrary, perhaps even more so than conventional trend lines, which at least are anchored by the extreme high or low. In fact, there is often more than one plausible internal trend line that can be drawn on a chart—see, for example, Figures 3.38, 3.39, and 3.40. Nevertheless, in my experience, internal trend lines are far more useful than conventional trend lines in defining potential support and resistance areas. An examination of Figures 3.26–3.37 will

---

[3]To avoid cluttering the charts, in most cases, only one or two of the conventional trend lines that would have been implied in the course of the price move are shown.

Figure 3.27
INTERNAL TREND LINE VERSUS CONVENTIONAL TREND LINES: CANADIAN DOLLAR CONTINUOUS FUTURES

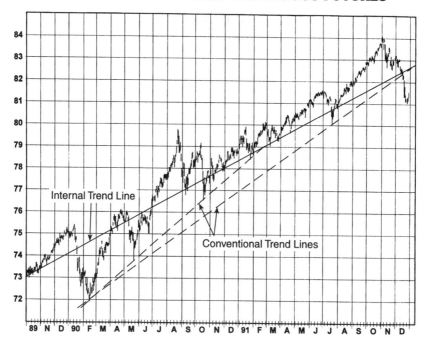

Figure 3.28
INTERNAL TREND LINE VERSUS CONVENTIONAL TREND LINE: JAPANESE YEN CONTINUOUS FUTURES

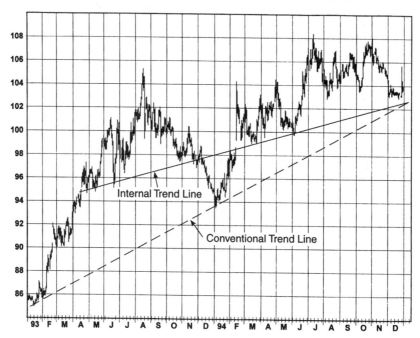

Figure 3.29
INTERNAL TREND LINE VERSUS CONVENTIONAL
TREND LINE: T-BOND NEAREST FUTURES

Figure 3.30
INTERNAL TREND LINE VERSUS CONVENTIONAL
TREND LINE: SUGAR NEAREST FUTURES

47

Figure 3.31
INTERNAL TREND LINE VERSUS CONVENTIONAL
TREND LINE: LUMBER NEAREST FUTURES

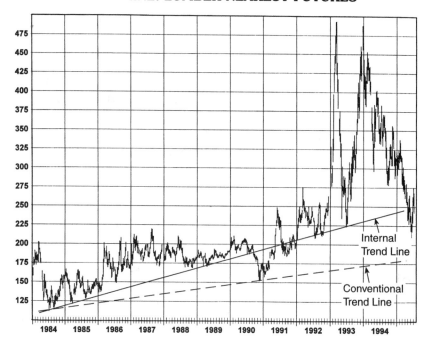

Figure 3.32
INTERNAL TREND LINE VERSUS CONVENTIONAL
TREND LINES: DECEMBER 1994 EURODOLLAR

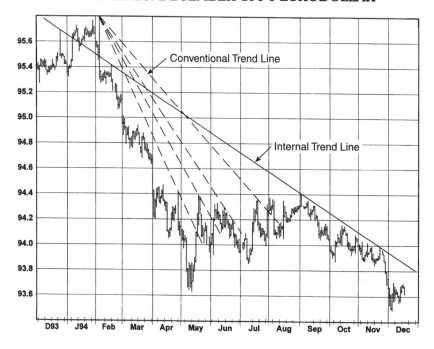

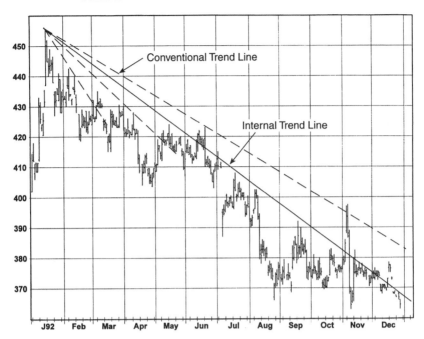

Figure 3.33
INTERNAL TREND LINE VERSUS CONVENTIONAL TREND LINES: DECEMBER 1992 SILVER

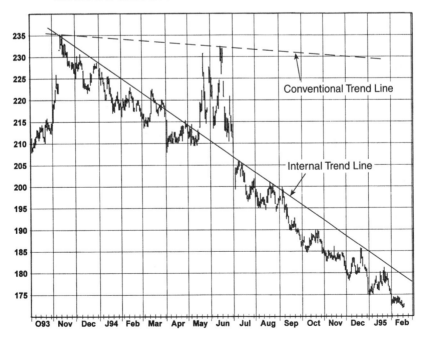

Figure 3.34
INTERNAL TREND LINE VERSUS CONVENTIONAL TREND LINE: SOYBEAN MEAL CONTINUOUS FUTURES

49

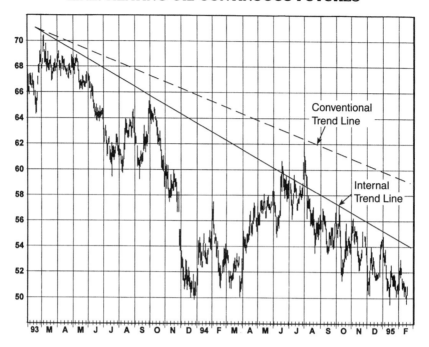

Figure 3.35
INTERNAL TREND LINE VERSUS CONVENTIONAL TREND LINE: HEATING OIL CONTINUOUS FUTURES

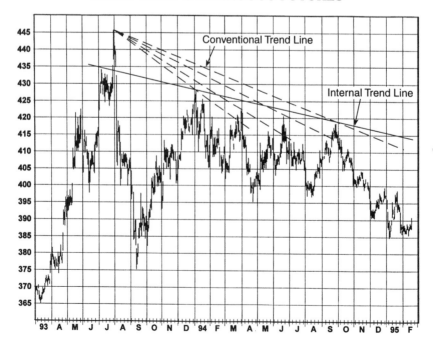

Figure 3.36
INTERNAL TREND LINE VERSUS CONVENTIONAL TREND LINES: GOLD CONTINUOUS FUTURES

Figure 3.37
INTERNAL TREND LINE VERSUS CONVENTIONAL
TREND LINES: HEATING OIL NEAREST FUTURES

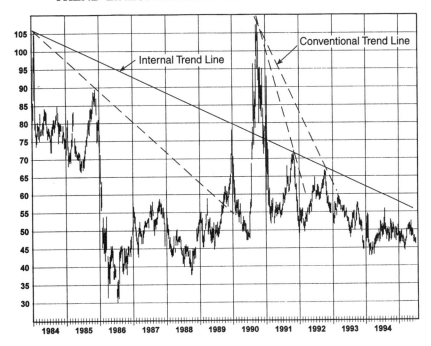

Figure 3.38
ALTERNATIVE INTERNAL TREND LINES:
DECEMBER 1991 COFFEE

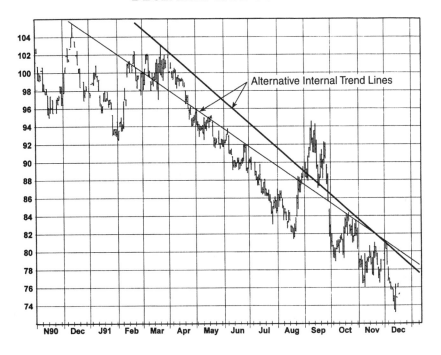

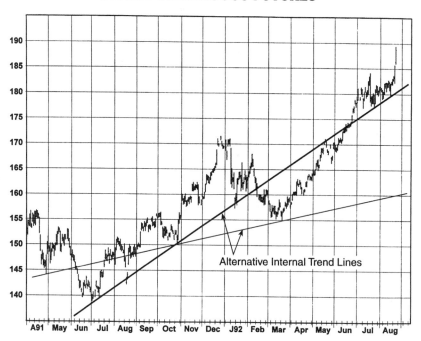

Figure 3.39
ALTERNATIVE INTERNAL TREND LINES: BRITISH POUND CONTINUOUS FUTURES

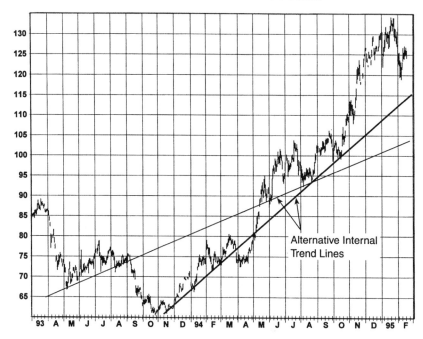

Figure 3.40
ALTERNATIVE INTERNAL TREND LINES: COPPER CONTINUOUS FUTURES

reveal that the internal trend lines depicted in these charts generally provided a better indication of where the market would hold in declines and stall in advances than did the conventional trend lines. Of course, this sample of illustrations does not prove the superiority of internal trend lines over conventional trend lines, since it is always possible to find charts that appear to validate virtually any contention, and such a proof is certainly not intended or implied. Rather, the comparisons in these charts are only intended to give the reader a sense of how internal trend lines *might* provide a better indication of potential support and resistance areas.

The fact that I personally find internal trend lines far more useful than conventional trend lines proves nothing—the anecdotal observation of a single individual hardly represents scientific proof. In fact, given the subjective nature of internal trend lines, a scientific test of their validity would be very difficult to construct. My point, however, is that internal trend lines are a concept that should certainly be explored by the serious chart analyst. By doing so, I am sure many readers will also find internal trend lines more effective than conventional trend lines, or at least a worthwhile addition to the chart analyst's tool kit.

MOVING AVERAGES

Moving averages provide a very simple means of smoothing a price series and making any trends more discernible. A simple moving average is defined as the average close of the past N days, ending in the current day. For example, a 40-day moving average would be equal to the average of the past 40 closes[4] (including the current day). The term *moving average* refers to the fact that the set of numbers being averaged is continuously moving through time. Figure 3.41 illustrates a 40-day moving average superimposed on a price series. Note that the moving average clearly reflects the trend in the price series and smoothes out the meaningless fluctuations in the data. In choppy markets moving averages will tend to oscillate in a general sideways pattern (see, for example, the October 1993–May 1994 period in Figure 3.42).

One very simple method of using moving averages to define trends is based on the direction of change in a moving average's value relative to the previous day. For example, a moving average (and by implication the trend) would be considered to be *rising* if today's value was higher than yesterday's value and *declining* if today's value was lower.

Note that the basic definition of a rising moving average is equivalent to the simple condition that today's close is higher than the close N days ago.

---

[4]Typically, moving averages are calculated using daily closes. However, moving averages could also be based on opens, highs, lows, or an average of the daily open, high, low, and close. Also, moving averages can be calculated for time intervals of data other than daily, in which case the "close" would refer to the final price quote in the given time interval.

Figure 3.41
MOVING AVERAGE (40-DAY) IN TRENDING
MARKET: DECEMBER 1994 NATURAL GAS

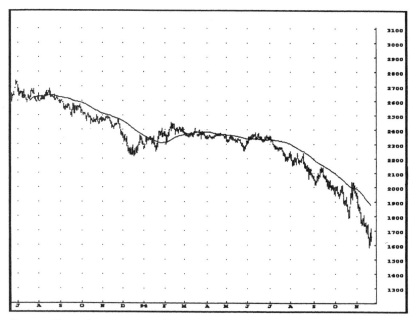

Figure 3.42
MOVING AVERAGE (40-DAY) IN SIDEWAYS
MARKET: MARCH 1995 COCOA

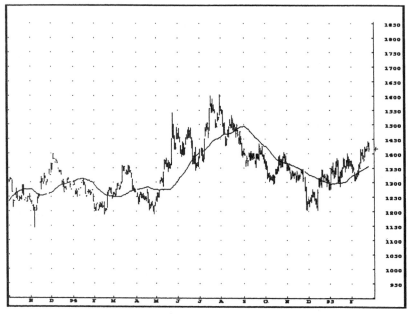

Why? Because yesterday's moving average is identical to today's moving average with the exception that it includes the close N days ago and does not include today's close. Therefore if today's close is higher than the close of N days ago, then today's moving average will be higher than yesterday's moving average. Similarly, a declining moving average is equivalent to the condition that today's close is lower than the close N days ago.

The smoothing properties of moving averages are achieved at the expense of introducing lags in the data. By definition, since moving averages are based on an average of past prices, turning points in moving averages will always lag the corresponding transitions in the raw price series. This characteristic is readily evident in both Figures 3.41 and 3.42.

In trending markets, moving averages can provide a very simple and effective method of identifying trends. Figure 3.43 duplicates Figure 3.41, denoting buy signals at points at which the moving average reversed to the upside by at least 10 ticks and sell signals at points at which the moving average turned down by the same minimum amount. (The reason for using a minimum threshold reversal to define turns in the moving average is to keep trend signals from flipping back and forth repeatedly at times when the mov-

Figure 3.43
MOVING-AVERAGE-BASED SIGNALS IN TRENDING
MARKET: DECEMBER 1994 NATURAL GAS

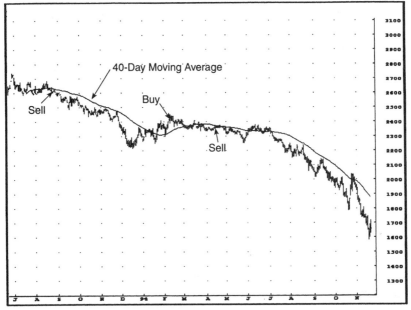

Notes: Buy = 10-tick rise in moving average off its low. Sell = 10-tick decline in moving average off its high.

Source: FutureSource; copyright © 1986–1994; all rights reserved.

Figure 3.44
MOVING-AVERAGE-BASED SIGNALS IN SIDEWAYS MARKET: MARCH 1995 COCOA

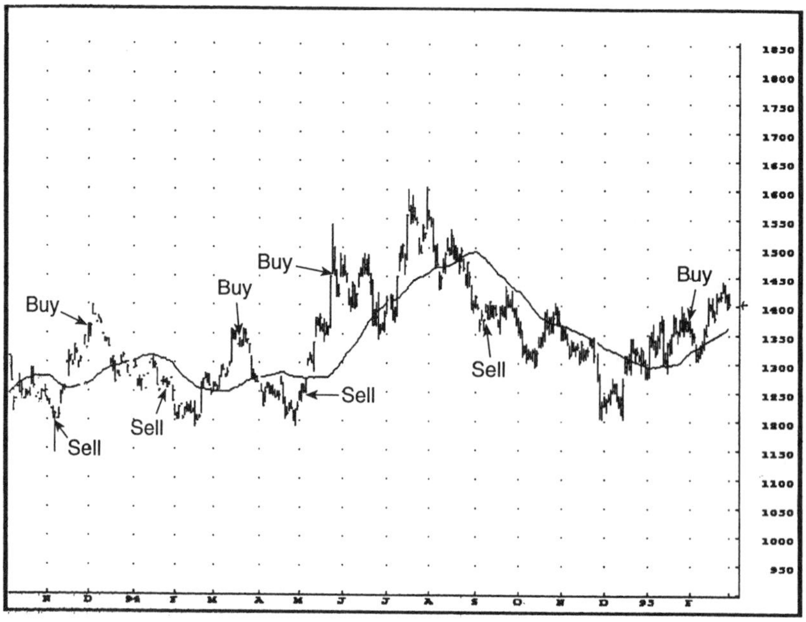

Notes: Buy = 10-tick rise in moving average off its low. Sell = 10-tick decline in moving average off its high.

Source: FutureSource; copyright © 1986–1994; all rights reserved.

ing average is near zero.) As can be seen in Figure 3.43, this extremely simple technique generated superb trading signals. During the 17-month period shown, this method generated only three signals: the first signal captured a major portion of the August–December decline; the second resulted in only a slight loss; and the third caught virtually the entire massive 1994 price slide. You can't ask for much more than that.

The problem is that while moving averages will do well in trending markets, in choppy, sideways markets, moving averages are apt to generate many false signals. For example, Figure 3.44 duplicates Figure 3.42, indicating buy signals at points at which the moving average turned up by at least 10 ticks and sell signals at points witnessing equivalent downside reversals in the moving average. The exact same method that worked so well in Figure 3.43—buying on upturns in the moving average and selling on downturns in the moving average—proves to be a disastrous strategy in this market, yielding six consecutive losses and one break-even trade.

There are many other ways of calculating a moving average besides the simple moving average described in this section. Some of these other methods, as well as the application of moving averages in trading systems, are discussed in Chapter 17.

4 Trading Ranges

There is the plain fool, who does the wrong thing at all times everywhere, but there is the Wall Street fool, who thinks he must trade all the time.

—Edwin Lefèvre

TRADING RANGES: TRADING CONSIDERATIONS

A trading range is a horizontal corridor that contains price fluctuations for an extended period. Generally speaking, markets tend to spend most of their time in trading ranges. Unfortunately, however, trading ranges are very difficult to trade profitably. In fact, most technical traders will probably find that the best strategy they can employ for trading ranges is to minimize their participation in such markets—a procedure that is easier said than done.

Although there are methodologies that can be profitable in trading ranges—oscillators, for example (see Chapter 15)—the problem is that these same approaches are disastrous for trending markets, and while trading ranges are easily identifiable for the past, they are nearly impossible to predict. Also it should be noted that most chart patterns (e.g., gaps, flags, etc.) are relatively meaningless if they occur within a trading range. (Chart patterns are discussed in Chapter 6.)

Trading ranges can often last for years. For example, at the time of this writing, the silver market was in a trading range that was over four years old and still growing (see Figure 4.1). Figure 4.2 depicts a four-year trading range in the soybean meal market. Figures 4.3 and 4.4 show multiyear trading ranges in the lumber market. Note in these latter two illustrations that trading range periods will differ in nearest and continuous futures charts, although there will typically be some significant overlap.

Once a trading range is established, the upper and lower boundaries tend to define support and resistance areas. This topic is discussed in greater detail in the next chapter. Breakouts from trading ranges can provide important trading signals—an observation that is the subject of the next section.

Figure 4.1
MULTIYEAR TRADING RANGE: SILVER CONTINUOUS FUTURES

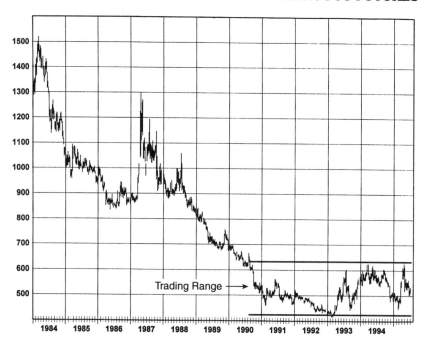

Figure 4.2
**MULTIYEAR TRADING RANGE: SOYBEAN MEAL
NEAREST FUTURES**

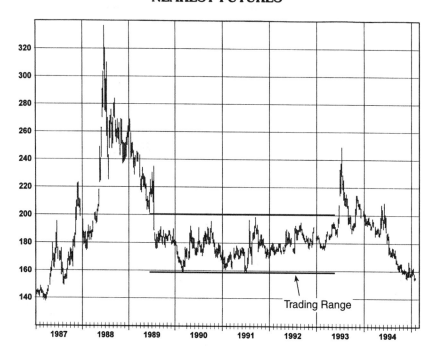

Figure 4.3
MULTIYEAR TRADING RANGE: LUMBER NEAREST FUTURES

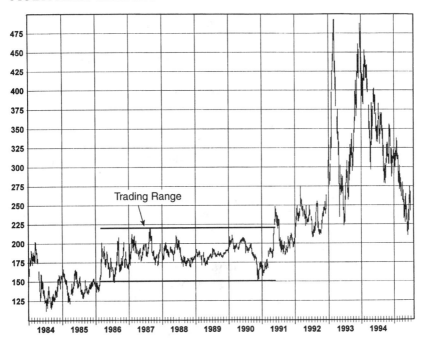

Figure 4.4
MULTIYEAR TRADING RANGE: LUMBER
CONTINUOUS FUTURES

TRADING RANGE BREAKOUTS

A *breakout* from a trading range (see, for example, Figures 4.5 and 4.6) suggests an impending price move in the direction of the breakout. The significance and reliability of a breakout are often enhanced by the following factors:

1. ***Duration of the Trading Range.*** The longer the duration of a trading range, the more potentially significant the eventual breakout. This point is illustrated using a weekly chart example in Figure 4.7 and a daily chart example in Figure 4.8.
2. ***Narrowness of Range.*** Breakouts from narrow ranges tend to provide particularly reliable trade signals (see Figures 4.9 and 4.10). Furthermore, such trades can be especially attractive since the meaningful stop point implies a relatively low dollar risk.
3. ***Confirmation of Breakout.*** It is rather common for prices to break out from a trading range by only a small amount, or for only a few days, and then fall back into the range. One reason for this is that stop orders are frequently clustered in the region beyond a trading range. Consequently, a move slightly beyond the range can sometimes trigger a string of stops. Once this initial flurry of orders is filled, the breakout will fail unless there are solid fundamental reasons and underlying buying (or overhead selling in the case of a downside breakout) to sustain the trend.

In view of these behavioral considerations, the reliability of a breakout from a trading range as a signal for an impending trend is significantly improved if prices are still beyond the range after a number of days (e.g., 5). Other types of confirmation can also be used—minimum percent penetration, given number of thrust days (discussed in Chapter 6), and so on. Although waiting for a confirmation following breakouts will lead to worse fills on some valid signals, it will help avoid many "false" signals. The net balance of this tradeoff will depend upon the confirmation condition used and must be evaluated by the individual trader. The key point, however, is that the trader should experiment with different confirmation conditions, rather than blindly follow all breakouts. This advice is perhaps even more valid now (1995) than a decade ago, as the increased use of technical analysis seems to have resulted in an increased frequency of false breakouts.

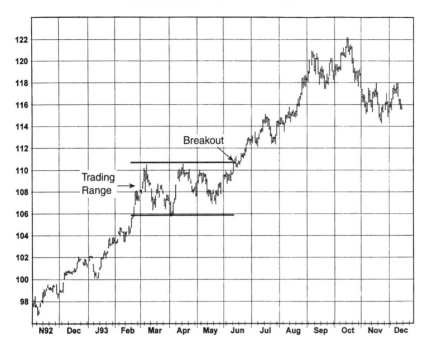

Figure 4.5
UPSIDE BREAKOUT FROM TRADING RANGE:
DECEMBER 1993 T-BOND

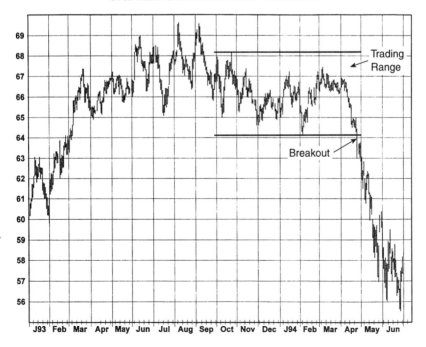

Figure 4.6
DOWNSIDE BREAKOUT FROM TRADING RANGE:
CATTLE CONTINUOUS FUTURES

61

Figure 4.7
UPSIDE BREAKOUT FROM EXTENDED TRADING RANGE: COPPER NEAREST FUTURES

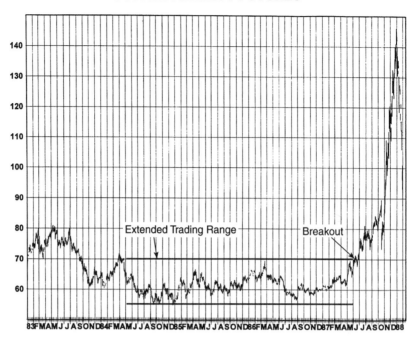

Figure 4.8
UPSIDE BREAKOUT FROM EXTENDED TRADING RANGE: JULY 1993 MEAL

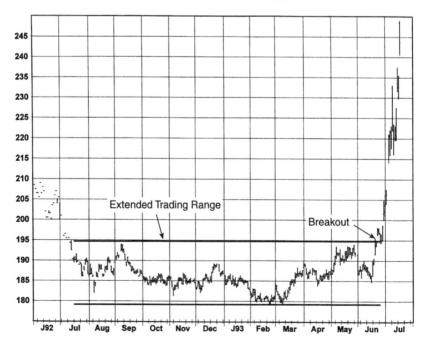

Figure 4.9
UPSIDE BREAKOUTS FROM NARROW TRADING RANGES: SEPTEMBER 1990 BRITISH POUND

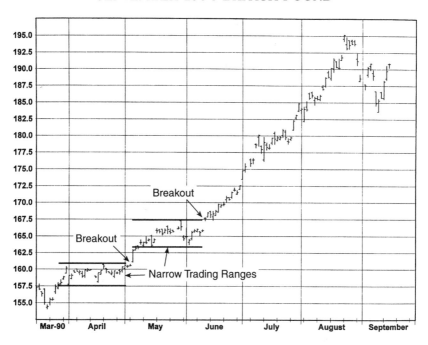

Figure 4.10
UPSIDE BREAKOUT FROM NARROW TRADING RANGE: OCTOBER 1990 UNLEADED GAS

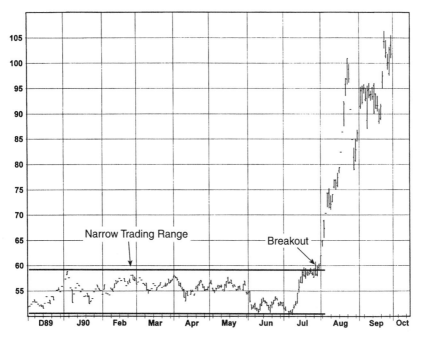

5 Support and Resistance

*In a narrow market, when prices are not getting anywhere to
speak of but move in a narrow range, there is no sense in trying
to anticipate what the next big movement is going to be—up or
down.*

—Edwin Lefèvre

TRADING RANGES

Once a trading range is established (at least one to two months of sideways
price movement), prices will tend to meet resistance at the upper end of the
range and support at the lower end of the range. Although chart analysis is best
suited as a tool to signal trend-following trades, some agile traders adopt a
strategy of selling rallies and buying declines in a trading range situation. Generally speaking, such a trading approach is difficult to pull off successfully. Furthermore, it should be emphasized that fading minor trends within a trading
range can lead to disaster unless losses are limited (e.g., liquidation of position if
prices penetrate range boundary by a specified minimum amount, or the market trades beyond the range for a minimum number of days, or both).

After prices break out from a trading range, the interpretation of support
and resistance is turned on its head. Specifically, once prices witness a sustained breakout above a trading range, the upper boundary of that range
becomes a zone of price support. The extended lines in Figures 5.1 and 5.2
indicate the support levels implied by the upper boundaries of the prior trading ranges. In the case of a sustained breakout below a trading range, the
lower boundary of that range becomes a zone of price resistance. The extended lines in Figures 5.3 and 5.4 indicate the resistance levels implied by
the lower boundaries of preceding trading ranges.

PRIOR MAJOR HIGHS AND LOWS

Normally, resistance will be encountered in the vicinity of previous major highs
and support in the vicinity of major lows. Figures 5.5, 5.6, and 5.7 each illus-

64

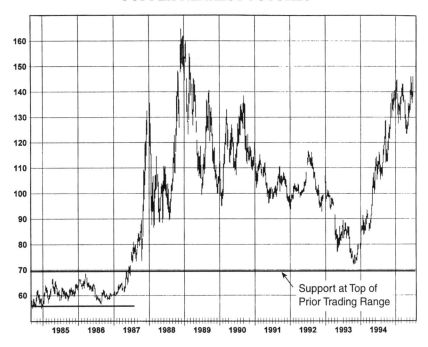

Figure 5.1
SUPPORT NEAR TOP OF PRIOR TRADING RANGE:
COPPER NEAREST FUTURES

Support at Top of
Prior Trading Range

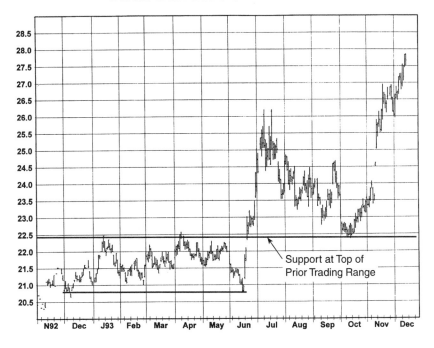

Figure 5.2
SUPPORT NEAR TOP OF PRIOR TRADING RANGE:
DECEMBER 1993 SOYBEAN OIL

Support at Top of
Prior Trading Range

Figure 5.3
RESISTANCE NEAR BOTTOM OF PRIOR TRADING RANGE: DECEMBER 1992 CANADIAN DOLLAR

Figure 5.4
RESISTANCE NEAR BOTTOM OF PRIOR TRADING RANGE: UNLEADED GAS CONTINUOUS FUTURES

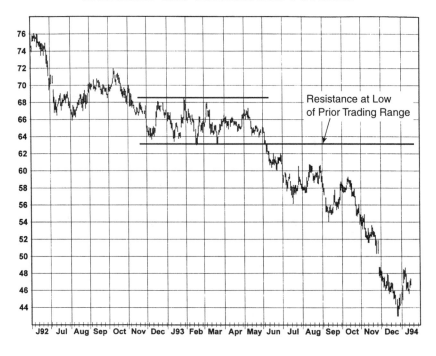

trate both behavioral patterns. For example, in Figure 5.5 note that the major 1988 peak formed just below the 1985 high, while the 1989 low provided a support level that held both the 1991 and 1992 lows. In Figure 5.6 the late 1990 low held just below the 1986 bottom, while the 1992 reversal formed just above the early 1989 peak. Although the concept of resistance near prior peaks and support near prior lows is perhaps most important for weekly charts, such as Figures 5.5 and 5.6, the principle also applies to daily charts, such as Figure 5.7. In this chart, note that the May 1994 and December 1994 price reversals occurred just above the January 1994 peak, while the October 1994 low formed just slightly above the July 1994 low.

It should be emphasized that a prior high does not imply that subsequent rallies will fail *at or below* that point, but rather that resistance can be anticipated in the *general vicinity* of that point. Similarly, a prior low does not imply that subsequent declines will hold *at or above* that point, but rather that support can be anticipated in the *general vicinity* of that point. Some

Figure 5.5
RESISTANCE AT PRIOR HIGH AND SUPPORT AT
PRIOR LOW: SOYBEAN OIL NEAREST FUTURES

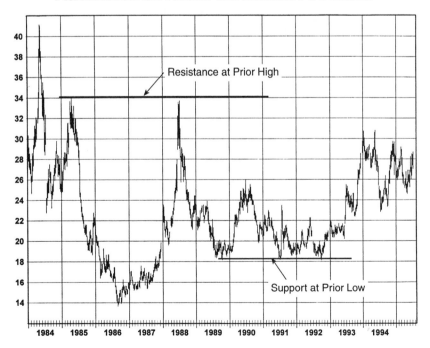

Figure 5.6
RESISTANCE AT PRIOR HIGH AND SUPPORT AT PRIOR LOW: WHEAT NEAREST FUTURES

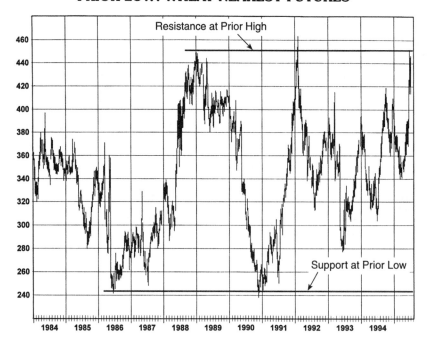

Figure 5.7
RESISTANCE AT PRIOR HIGH AND SUPPORT AT PRIOR LOW: SOYBEAN OIL CONTINUOUS FUTURES

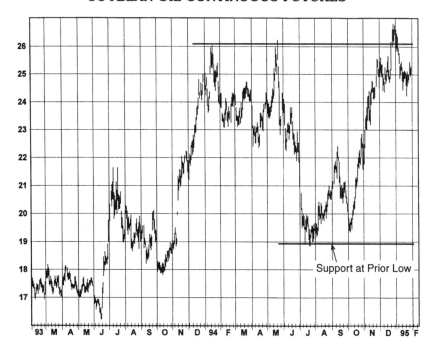

practitioners of technical analysis treat prior highs and lows as points endowed with sacrosanct significance. If a prior high was 1078, then they consider 1078 to be major resistance, and if, for example, the market rallies to 1085, they consider resistance to be broken. This is nonsense. Support and resistance should be considered approximate areas, not precise points. Note that although prior major highs and lows proved highly significant as resistance and support in all three charts—Figures 5.5, 5.6, and 5.7—only in Figure 5.5 did subsequent price rallies and breaks actually reverse *at or before* reaching these points. The type of price action represented by these charts is fairly typical.

The penetration of a previous high can be viewed as a buy signal, and the penetration of a prior low can be viewed as a sell signal. Similar to the case of breakouts from trading ranges, however, to be viewed as trading signals, penetrations of highs and lows should be significant in terms of price magnitude, time duration, or both. Thus, for example, as should be clear following the preceding discussion regarding Figures 5.6 and 5.7, a one-period (one-day for daily chart, one-week for weekly chart) modest penetration of a prior high or low would not prove anything. A stronger confirmation than a mere penetration of a prior high or low should be required before assuming such an event represents a buy or sell signal. Some examples of possible confirmation conditions include a minimum number of closes beyond the prior high or low, a minimum percent price penetration, or both requirements.

Figures 5.8 and 5.9 illustrate examples of penetrations of previous highs as buy signals, assuming a confirmation condition of three closes above the high. Similarly, Figures 5.10 and 5.11 provide examples of penetrations of previous lows as sell signals, using an analogous confirmation condition. Incidentally, note that Figure 5.8 also provides a good example of a prior high acting as resistance (before it is actually penetrated) and a previous low holding as support, while Figure 5.11 offers a classic example of a previous high representing major resistance.

Following a *sustained* penetration of a prior high or low, the interpretation of support and resistance is turned on its head. In other words, the area of a prior high becomes support and the area of a previous low becomes resistance. For example, in Figure 5.12, which reproduces Figure 5.9, the February 1991 high, which is penetrated in July 1992, successfully holds as a support area at the September 1992 low. The September low, which is subsequently penetrated in October, then proves to be a resistance area that stops the late November–early December rebound. In Figure 5.13, which reproduces Figure 5.10, the 1987 low, which is penetrated in 1989, proves to be a potent resistance area that stems repeated rally attempts in 1990 and 1991. (Incidentally, note that this chart also provides an excellent example of resistance at a prior high, with the major 1994 rally stalling only moderately below the early 1986 peak.) Finally, in Figure 5.14, which reproduces Figure

Figure 5.8
PENETRATION OF PREVIOUS HIGH AS BUY SIGNAL:
DEUTSCHE MARK CONTINUOUS FUTURES

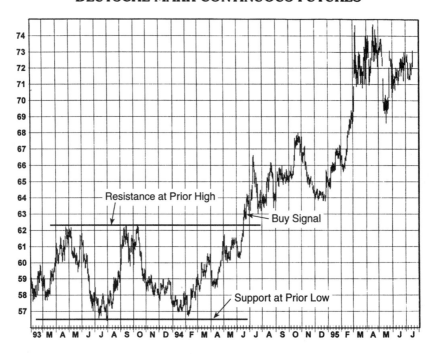

Figure 5.9
PENETRATION OF PREVIOUS HIGH AS BUY SIGNAL:
DEUTSCHE MARK CONTINUOUS FUTURES

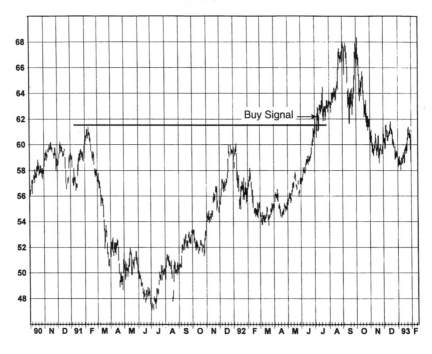

Figure 5.10
PENETRATION OF PREVIOUS LOW AS SELL
SIGNAL: COFFEE NEAREST FUTURES

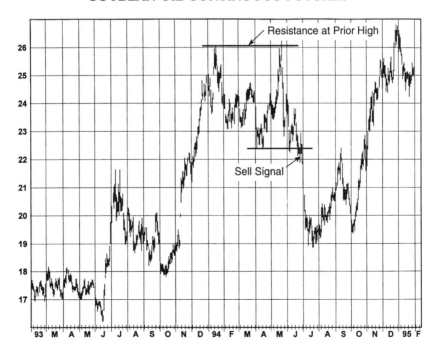

Figure 5.11
PENETRATION OF PREVIOUS LOW AS SELL SIGNAL:
SOYBEAN OIL CONTINUOUS FUTURES

Figure 5.12
SUPPORT AT PRIOR RELATIVE HIGH AND RESISTANCE AT PRIOR RELATIVE LOW: DEUTSCHE MARK CONTINUOUS FUTURES

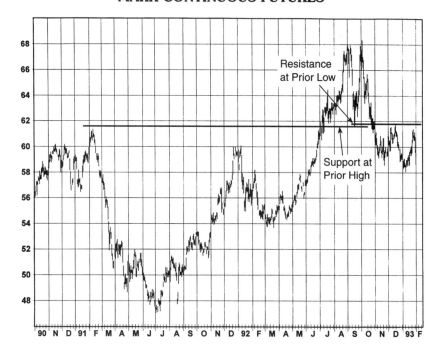

Figure 5.13
RESISTANCE AT PRIOR RELATIVE LOW: COFFEE NEAREST FUTURES

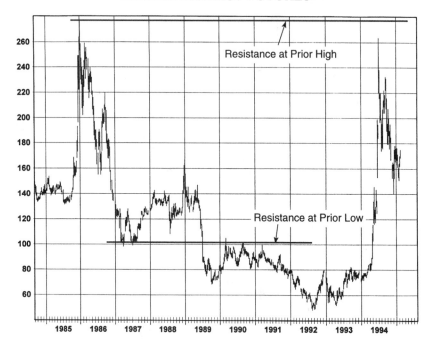

Figure 5.14
RESISTANCE AT PRIOR RELATIVE LOW:
SOYBEAN OIL CONTINUOUS FUTURES

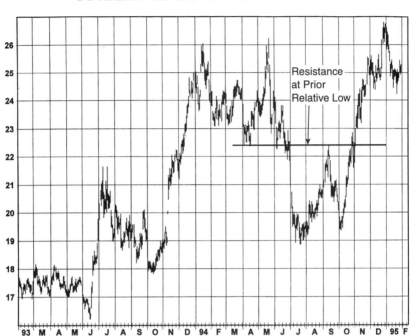

5.11, the April 1994 low, which is penetrated in June, proves to be a major resistance area that leads to a price reversal in September.

CONCENTRATIONS OF RELATIVE HIGHS AND RELATIVE LOWS

The previous section dealt with support and resistance at prior major highs and lows—single peaks and nadirs. In this section we are concerned with support and resistance at price zones with concentrations of relative highs and relative lows rather than absolute tops and bottoms. Specifically, there is often a tendency for relative highs and relative lows to be concentrated in relatively narrow zones. These zones imply support regions if current prices are higher and resistance areas if current prices are lower. This approach is particularly useful for anticipating support and resistance areas in long-term charts. Figures 5.15–5.19 provide weekly chart examples of support being encountered at prior concentrations of relative lows and relative highs (or relative lows alone). Figures 5.20 and 5.21 provide weekly chart examples of

Figure 5.15
SUPPORT ZONE DEFINED BY CONCENTRATION OF PRIOR RELATIVE LOWS AND HIGHS: SWISS FRANC NEAREST FUTURES

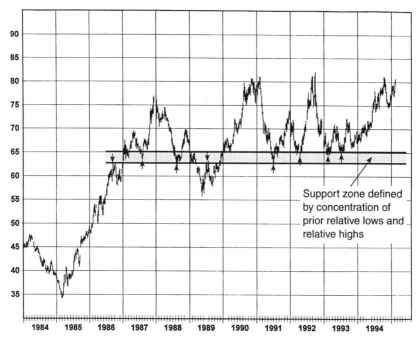

Note: ↑ = relative low; ↓ = relative high.

Figure 5.16
SUPPORT ZONE DEFINED BY CONCENTRATION OF PRIOR RELATIVE LOWS AND HIGHS: GOLD NEAREST FUTURES

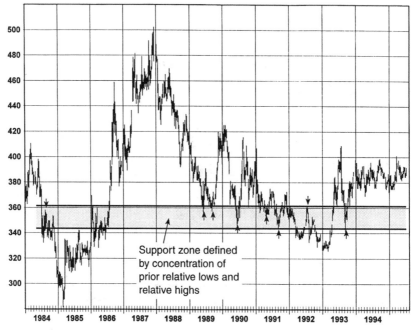

Note: ↑ = relative low; ↓ = relative high.

Figure 5.17
SUPPORT ZONE DEFINED BY CONCENTRATION OF PRIOR RELATIVE LOWS: COTTON NEAREST FUTURES

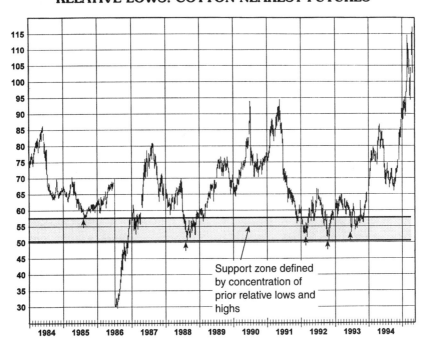

Note: ↑ = relative low.

Figure 5.18
SUPPORT ZONE DEFINED BY CONCENTRATION OF PRIOR RELATIVE LOWS: SOYBEAN NEAREST FUTURES

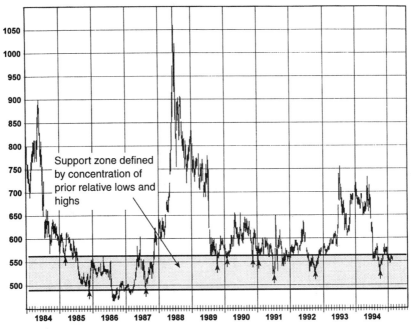

Note: ↑ = relative low.

Figure 5.19
SUPPORT ZONE DEFINED BY CONCENTRATION OF PRIOR RELATIVE LOWS AND HIGHS: CORN NEAREST FUTURES

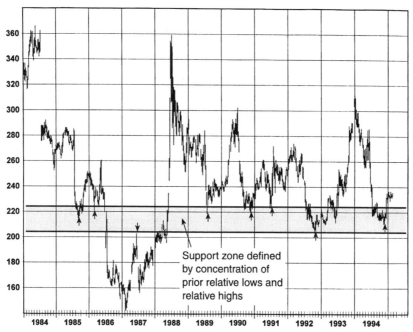

Note: ↑ = relative low; ↓ = relative high.

Figure 5.20
RESISTANCE ZONE DEFINED BY CONCENTRATION OF PRIOR RELATIVE HIGHS AND LOWS: CRUDE OIL NEAREST FUTURES

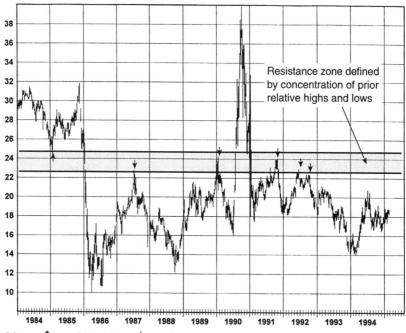

Note: ↑ = relative low; ↓ = relative high.

Figure 5.21
RESISTANCE ZONE DEFINED BY CONCENTRATION OF PRIOR RELATIVE HIGHS AND LOWS: SILVER NEAREST FUTURES

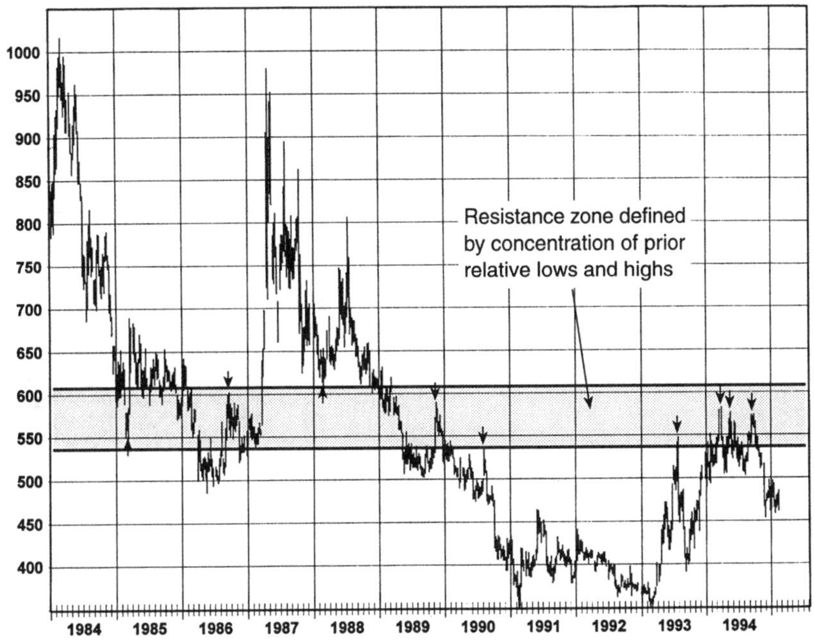

Note: ↑ = relative low: ↓ = relative high.

resistance being encountered at prior concentrations of relative highs and relative lows (or relative highs alone).

The approach of using concentrations of prior relative highs and lows to define support and resistance can also be applied to daily continuous futures charts of sufficient duration (e.g., two years). (The life span of most individual contract charts is too short for this method to be effectively applied.) For example, Figures 5.22, 5.23, and 5.24 show daily continuous futures charts with resistance zones defined by prior relative highs and lows.

TREND LINES, CHANNELS, AND INTERNAL TREND LINES

The concept that trend lines, channel lines, and internal trend lines indicate areas of potential support and resistance has already been detailed in Chapter 3. Again, as previously discussed, based on personal experience, I believe that internal trend lines are more reliable in this regard than conventional

Figure 5.22
RESISTANCE ZONE DEFINED BY CONCENTRATION OF PRIOR RELATIVE HIGHS AND LOWS: DEUTSCHE MARK CONTINUOUS FUTURES

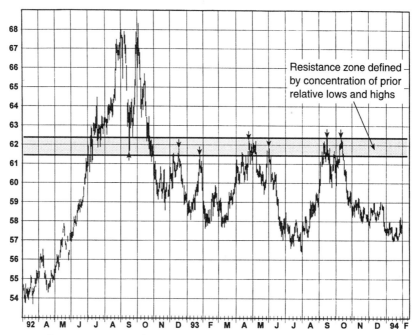

Note: ↑ = relative low; ↓ = relative high.

Figure 5.23
RESISTANCE ZONE DEFINED BY CONCENTRATION OF PRIOR RELATIVE HIGHS: GOLD CONTINUOUS FUTURES

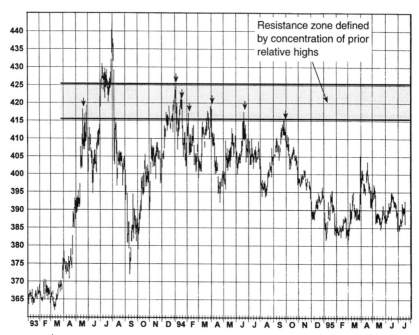

Note: ↓ = relative high.

Figure 5.24
RESISTANCE ZONE DEFINED BY CONCENTRATION
OF PRIOR RELATIVE HIGHS AND LOWS: SOYBEAN
CONTINUOUS FUTURES

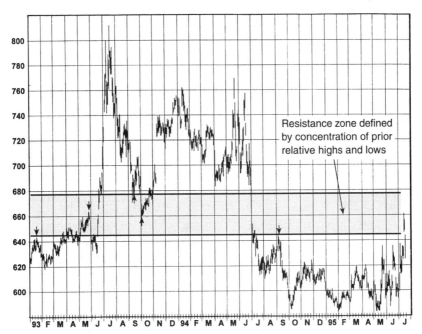

Note: ↑ = relative low; ↓ = relative high.

trend lines. However, the question of which type of trend line is a better indicator is a highly subjective matter, and some readers may well reach the opposite conclusion. In fact, there is not even a mathematically precise definition of a trend line or internal trend line, and how these lines are drawn will vary from individual to individual.

PRICE ENVELOPE BANDS

A price envelope band can be derived from a moving average. The upper band of the price envelope is defined as the moving average plus a given percent of the moving average. Similarly, the lower band of the price envelope is defined as the moving average minus a given percent of the moving average. For example, if the current moving average value is 600 and the percent value is defined as 3 percent, the upper band value would be 618 and the lower band value would be 582. By selecting an appropriate percent boundary for a given moving average, an envelope band can be defined so that it encompasses most of the price activity, with the upper boundary approximately coinciding with relative highs and the lower boundary approximately coinciding with relative lows.

Figure 5.25 illustrates a price envelope band for the March 1994 T-bond contract using a 20-day moving average and a 2.5 percent value. As can be seen, the price envelope provides a good indication of support and resistance levels. An alternative way of expressing the same concept is that the price envelope indicates overbought and oversold levels. Price envelope bands can also be applied to data for other than daily time intervals. For example, Figure 5.26 illustrates a 1.2 percent price envelope band applied to 90-minute bars for the same market shown in Figure 5.25 (but of course for a shorter time period).

It should be noted, however, that the price envelope is not as effective a tool as it might appear to be. Although it provides a reasonably good indication of when the market may be nearing a turning point, during extended trends, prices can continue to hug one end of the price envelope. This pattern, for example, is evident in Figure 5.25 during the late February–April 1994 period. During this time, the price envelope repeatedly suggested that

Figure 5.25
**PRICE ENVELOPE BAND AS INDICATION OF SUPPORT AND
RESISTANCE IN DAILY BAR CHART: MARCH 1995 T-BOND**

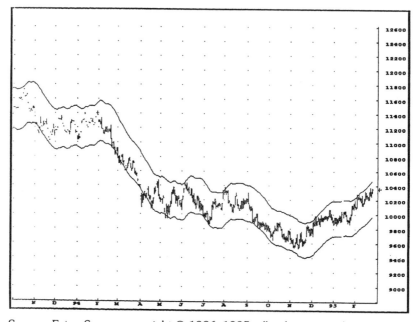

Figure 5.26
PRICE ENVELOPE BAND AS INDICATION OF
SUPPORT AND RESISTANCE IN 90-MINUTE
BAR CHART: MARCH 1995 T-BOND

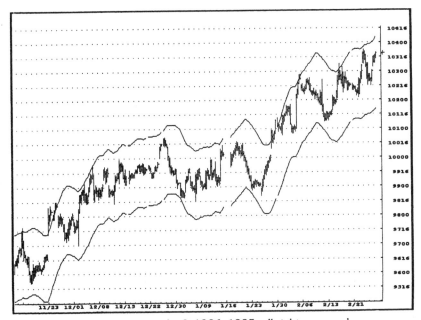

Source: FutureSource; copyright © 1986–1995; all rights reserved.

prices were oversold, while prices continued to slide steadily lower. Thus while it is true that price excursions beyond the price envelope band tend to be limited and temporary, the fact that prices are near one of the boundaries of the envelope does not necessarily mean that a price turning point is imminent. On balance, the price envelope provides one means of gauging potential areas of support and resistance, but it is by no means infallible.

6   Chart Patterns

Never confuse brilliance with a bull market.

—Paul Rubin

ONE-DAY PATTERNS

Gaps

A gap day is one in which the low is above the previous day's high or the high is below the previous day's low. There are four basic types of gaps:

1. ***Common Gap.*** This type of gap occurs within a trading range and is not particularly significant. Figures 6.1, 6.2, and 6.3 show a few of the common gaps occurring in these charts.
2. ***Breakaway Gap.*** This type of gap occurs when prices surge beyond the extreme of a trading range, leaving an area in which no trading activity has occurred (see Figures 6.1 and 6.2). A breakaway gap that is not filled within a few days is one of the most significant and reliable chart signals.
3. ***Runaway Gap.*** This type of gap occurs when a trend accelerates and is a characteristic of strong bull and bear markets. In particularly powerful bull and bear markets a series of runaway gaps can occur on consecutive days (see Figures 6.1, 6.2, and 6.3).
4. ***Exhaustion Gap.*** This type of gap occurs after an extended price move and is soon followed by a trend reversal (see Figures 6.1 and 6.2). The exhaustion gap may sound like a particularly useful technical signal until one realizes that the difference between an exhaustion gap and a runaway gap is hindsight. However, in some instances, an exhaustion gap can be recognized at a very early point in the trend reversal—see discussion of *island reversals* in the section entitled "Top and Bottom Formations."

Figure 6.1
PRICE GAPS: DECEMBER 1994 COFFEE

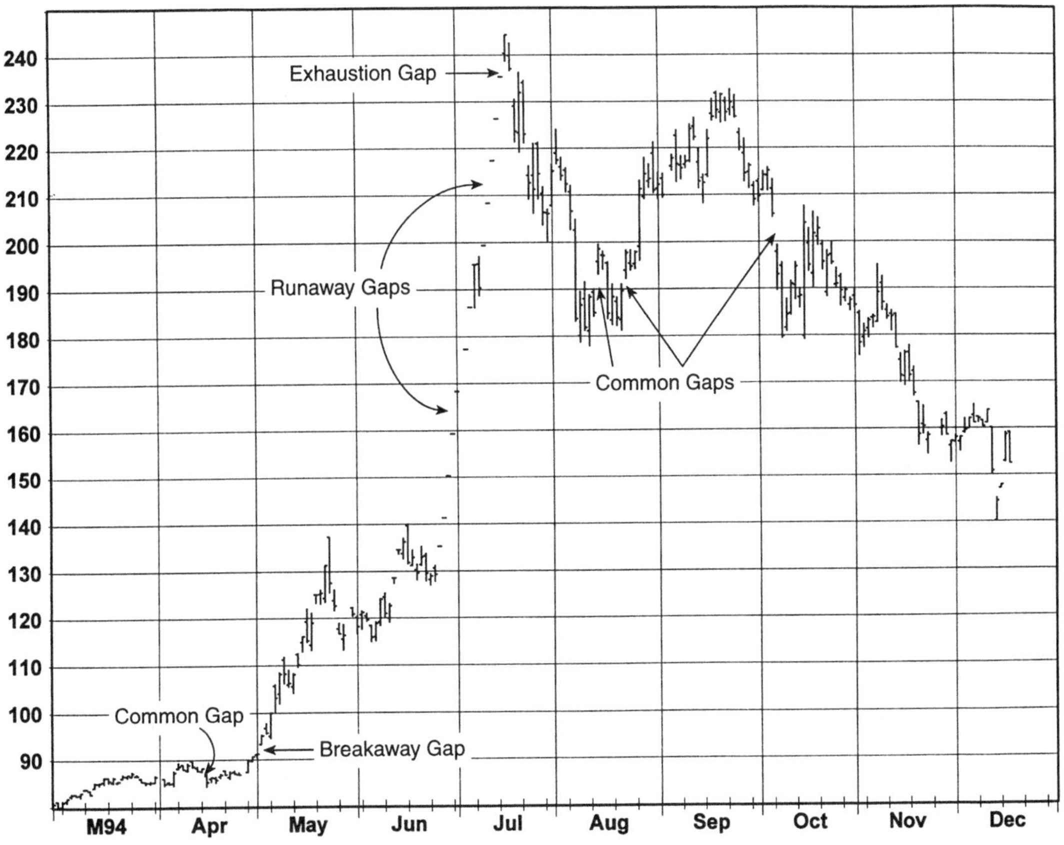

Spikes

A spike high is a day whose high is sharply above the high of the preceding and succeeding days. Frequently, the closing price on a spike high day will be near the lower end of the day's trading range. A spike high is only meaningful if it occurs after a price advance, in which case it can often signify at least a temporary climax in buying pressure, and hence can be viewed as a potential relative high. Sometimes spike highs will prove to be a major top.

Generally speaking, the significance of a spike high will be enhanced by the following factors:

> **1.** A wide difference between the spike high and the highs of the preceding and succeeding days.

Figure 6.2
PRICE GAPS: FEBRUARY 1995 HOGS

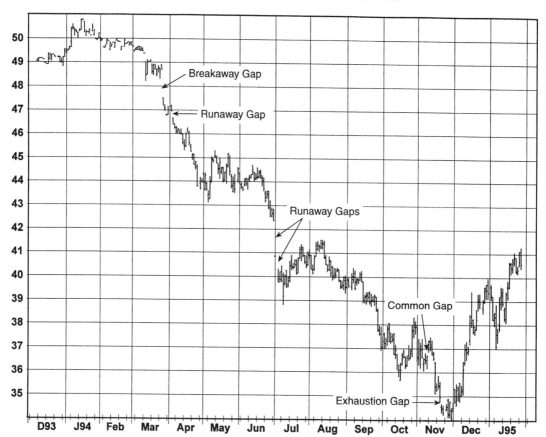

2. A close near the low of the day's range.
3. A substantive price advance preceding the spike's formation.

The more extreme each of these conditions, the greater the likelihood that a spike high will prove to be an important relative high or even major top.

In analogous fashion, a spike low is a day whose low is sharply below the low of the preceding and succeeding days. Frequently, the closing price on a spike low day will be near the upper end of the day's trading range. A spike low is only meaningful if it occurs after a price decline, in which case it can often signify at least a temporary climax in selling pressure, and hence can be viewed as a potential relative low. Sometimes spike lows will prove to be a major bottom.

Generally speaking, the significance of a spike low will be enhanced by the following factors:

Figure 6.3
PRICE GAPS: MARCH 1992 FCOJ

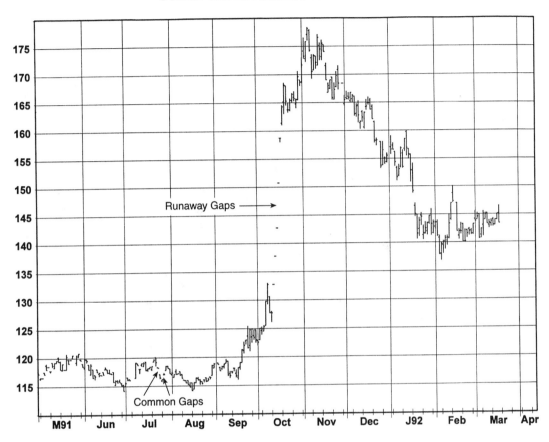

1. A wide difference between the lows of the preceding and succeeding days and the spike low.
2. A close near the high of the day's range.
3. A substantive price decline preceding the spike's formation.

The more extreme each of these conditions, the greater the likelihood that a spike low will prove to be an important relative low or even major bottom.

Figures 6.4–6.6 contain several illustrations of spike highs and spike lows. Figure 6.4 shows an example of three spike highs occurring within an approximate two-month time span, the first defining a relative high and the latter two occurring in close proximity with near-equal highs and combining to form a major top. Figures 6.5 and 6.6 each contain examples of both a relative high and relative low formed by spikes.

Figure 6.4
SPIKE HIGHS: MARCH 1995 COCOA

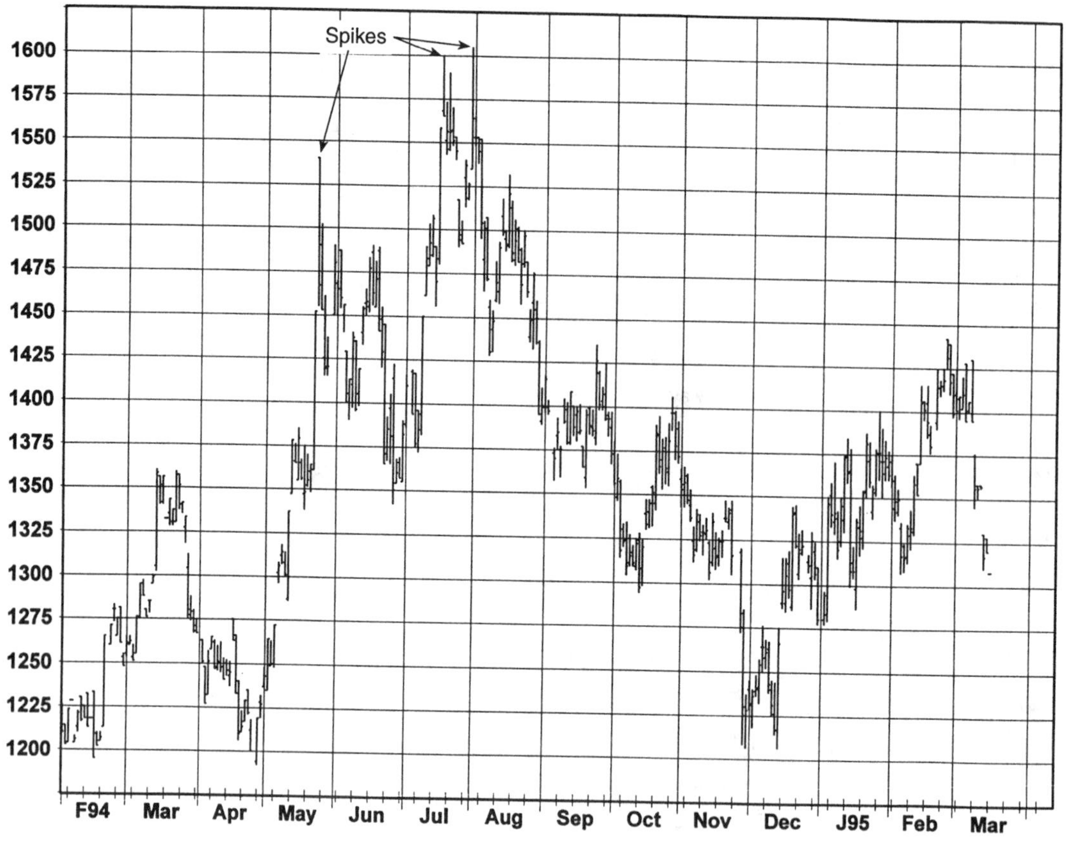

The preceding descriptions of spike highs and lows listed three essential characteristics that typify such days. However, the definition of these conditions was somewhat imprecise. Specifically, how great must the difference be between a day's high (low) and the highs (lows) of the preceding and succeeding days in order for it to qualify as a spike high (low)? How close must the close be to the low (high) for a day to be considered a spike high (low)? How large must a preceding advance be for a day to be viewed as a possible spike high? The answer to these questions is that there are no precise specifications; in each case, the choice of a qualifying condition is a subjective one. However, Figures 6.4–6.6 should provide an intuitive sense of the types of days that qualify as spikes.

It is possible, though, to construct a mathematically precise definition for spike days. An example of such a definition for a spike high might be a day that fulfilled all of the following conditions (the definition for a spike low day would be analogous):

Figure 6.5
SPIKE LOW AND SPIKE HIGH: JULY 1991 COFFEE

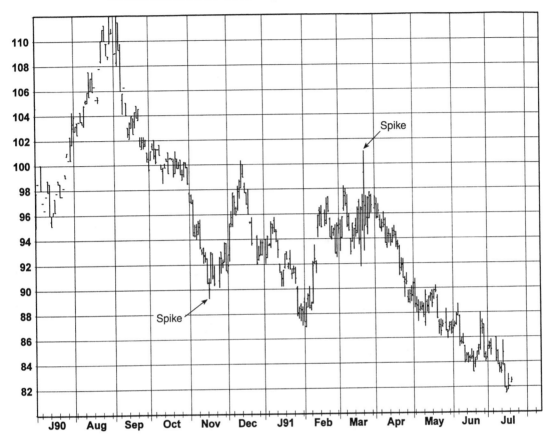

1. $H_t - \text{Max}(H_{t-1}, H_{t+1}) > k \cdot \text{ADTR}$,

where
H_t = high on given day
H_{t-1} = high on preceding day
H_{t+1} = high on succeeding day
k = multiplicative factor that must be defined (e.g., k = 0.75)
ADTR = average daily true range during past 10 days[1]

2. $H_t - C_t > 3 \cdot (C_t - L_t)$,

where
C_t = close on given day
L_t = low on given day

---

[1]The true range is equal to the true high minus the true low. The true high is the maximum of the current day's high and the previous day's close. The true low is the minimum of the current day's low and the previous day's close. (The true high and true low were defined in Chapter 3.)

Figure 6.6
SPIKE HIGH AND SPIKE LOW: MARCH 1991 COTTON

3. $H_t >$ maximum high during past N days, where N = constant that must be defined (e.g., N = 50).

The first of the preceding conditions assures us that the spike high will exceed the surrounding highs by an amount at least equal to three-quarters of the past 10-day average true range (assuming the value of k is defined as 0.75). The second condition assures us that the day's low will be in the lower quartile. The third condition, which requires that the day's high exceed the highest high during the past 50 days (assuming N = 50), guarantees that the day was preceded by an upswing. (Generally speaking, higher values of N will require larger prior advances.)

The three-part definition just provided for a spike high day is only intended to offer an example of how a mathematically precise definition can be constructed. Many other definitions are possible.

Reversal Days

The standard definition of a reversal high day is a day that witnesses a new high in an upmove and then reverses to close below the preceding day's close. Analogously, a reversal low day is a day that witnesses a new low in a decline and then reverses to close above the preceding day's close. The following discussion focuses on reversal high days, but mirror-image comments would apply to reversal low days.

Similar to spike highs, a reversal high day is generally interpreted as suggesting a buying climax and hence a relative high. However, the condition required for a reversal high day by the standard definition is a relatively weak one, meaning that reversal high days are fairly common. Hence, while many market highs are reversal days, the problem is that the majority of reversal high days are not highs. Figure 6.7, which illustrates this point, is fairly typical. Note that a reversal high day occurred at almost the exact peak of a massive bull market and would have provided an excellent sell signal. Note also, however, that this reversal day was preceded by six other reversal days that would have provided sell signals of varying degrees of extreme prematurity. Figure 6.8 depicts another example of the commonplaceness of premature reversal day signals. In this case, a reversal day actually occurred at the exact peak of a huge bull market. This incredible sell signal, however, was also preceded by five other reversal days that occurred far earlier in the advance. Anyone who might have traded this market based on reversal signals would probably have thrown in the towel well before the valid signal finally materialized.

In the examples just provided, at least a reversal day signal occurred at or near the actual high. Frequently, however, an uptrend will witness a number of reversal highs that prove to be false signals and then fail to register a reversal high near the actual top. It can be said that reversal high days successfully call 100 out of every 10 highs. In other words, reversal days provide occasional excellent signals, but far more frequent false signals.

In my opinion, the standard definition of reversal days is so prone to generating false signals that it is worthless as a trading indicator. The problem with the standard definition is that merely requiring a close below the prior day's close is much too weak a condition. Instead, I suggest defining a reversal high day as a day that witnesses a new high in an upmove and then reverses to close below the preceding day's *low*. (If desired, the condition can be made even stronger by requiring that the close be below the low of the prior two days.) This more restrictive definition will greatly reduce the number of false reversal signals, but it will also knock out some valid signals. For example, this revised definition would have eliminated all six false signals in Figure 6.7. Unfortunately, it would also have excluded the one valid signal. In Figure 6.8, however, the more restrictive definition for a reversal day would have avoided all five premature reversal day signals, while leaving the single valid signal intact.

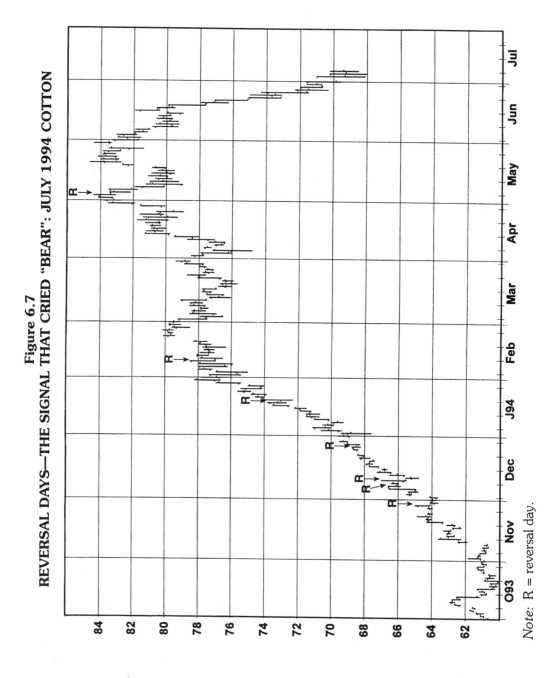

Figure 6.7
REVERSAL DAYS—THE SIGNAL THAT CRIED "BEAR": JULY 1994 COTTON

Note: R = reversal day.

90

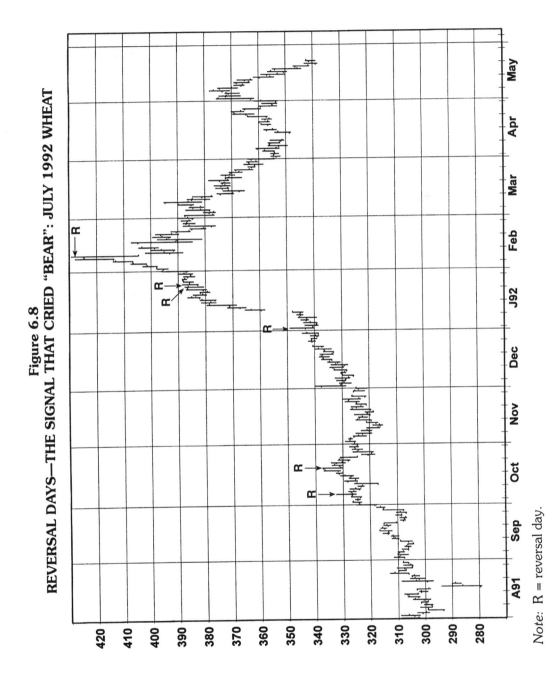

Figure 6.8
REVERSAL DAYS—THE SIGNAL THAT CRIED "BEAR": JULY 1992 WHEAT

Note: R = reversal day.

A reversal day may sound somewhat similar to a spike day, but the two patterns are not equivalent. A spike day will not necessarily be a reversal day, and a reversal day will not necessarily be a spike day. For example, a spike high day may not witness a close that is below the previous day's low (or even below the previous day's close—as specified by the standard definition), even if the close is at the day's low. As an example of the reverse case, a reversal high day may not *significantly* exceed the prior day's high, as required by the spike high definition, or exceed to the subsequent day's high at all, since the subsequent day's price action is not part of the reversal day definition. Also, it is possible that a reversal day's close may not be near the low, a standard characteristic of a spike day, even if it is below the previous day's close.

Occasionally, a day will be both a reversal day and a spike day. Such days are far more significant than days that are only reversal days. An alternative to using the more restrictive definition for a reversal day is using the standard definition, but requiring that the day also fulfill spike day conditions. (Although

Figure 6.9
SPIKE REVERSAL DAYS: SEPTEMBER 1994 COFFEE

a day that met both the strong reversal day condition and the spike day conditions would be most meaningful of all, such days are fairly rare.) Figure 6.9 provides an example of a major bull market that witnessed two days that met both spike and reversal high day conditions. The first of these days was a relative high that proved to be a highly premature signal. The second such day, however, marked the precise peak of the towering advance.

Thrust Days

An upthrust day is a day in which the close is above the previous day's high. A downthrust day is a day in which the close is below the previous day's low. The significance of thrust days is tied to the concept that the close is by far the most important price of the day. A single thrust day is not particularly meaningful, since thrust days are quite common. However, a series of upthrust days (not necessarily consecutive) would reflect pronounced strength. Similarly, a series of downthrust days would reflect pronounced market weakness.

During bull markets upthrust days significantly outnumber downthrust days. See, for example, the March–July period in Figure 6.10. Conversely, in bear markets downthrust days significantly outnumber upthrust days. See, for example, the February–March period in Figure 6.11. And, as should come as no surprise, in sideways markets, upthrust and downthrust days tend to be in rough balance. See, for example, the April–June period in Figure 6.11.

Run Days

A run day is a strongly trending day. Essentially, a run day is a more powerful version of a thrust day (although it is possible for a run day to fail to meet the thrust day condition). Run days are defined as follows.

Up Run Day. A day that meets the following two conditions:

1. The true high of the run day is greater than the maximum true high of the past N days (e.g., $N = 5$).[2]
2. The true low on the run day is less than the minimum true low on the subsequent N days.[3]

Down Run Day. A day that meets the following two conditions:

---

[2] The true high, which was defined in Chapter 3, is the maximum of the current day's high and the previous day's close.

[3] The true low, which was defined in Chapter 3, is the minimum of the current day's low and the previous day's close.

Figure 6.10
UPTHRUST AND DOWNTHRUST DAYS IN BULL
MARKET: AUGUST 1993 GOLD

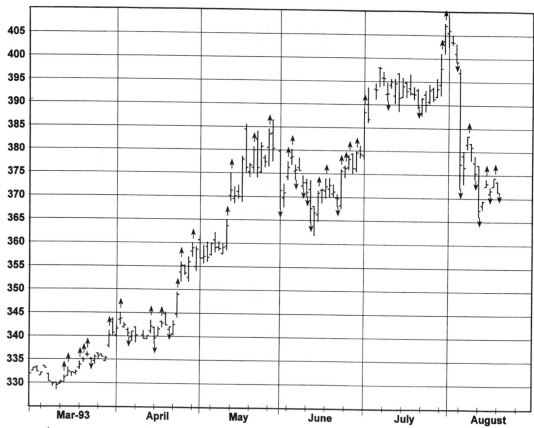

Note: ↑ = upthrust day; ↓ = downthrust day.

1. The true low of the run day is less than the minimum true low of the past *N days.*
2. The true high on the run day is greater than the maximum true high on the subsequent *N* days.

As can be seen by these definitions, run days cannot be defined until *N* days after their occurrence. Also, note that although most run days are also thrust days, it is possible for the run day conditions to be met on a day that is not a thrust day. For example, it is entirely possible for a day's low to be lower than the past five-day low, its high to be higher than the subsequent five-day high, and its close to be *higher* than the previous day's low.

Figures 6.12 and 6.13 provide examples of run days (based on a defini-

Figure 6.11
UPTHRUST AND DOWNTHRUST DAYS IN
BEAR MARKET: JUNE 1994 T-BOND

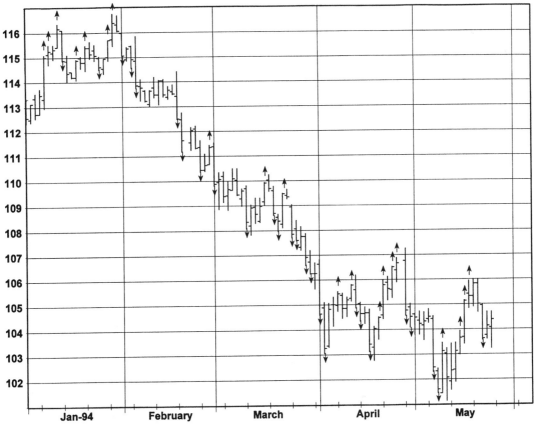

Note: ↑ = upthrust day; ↓ = downthrust day.

tion of $N = 5$). As can be seen, run days tend to occur when the market is in a trend run—hence the name. The materialization of up run days, particularly in clusters, can be viewed as evidence that the market is in a bullish phase (see Figure 6.12). Similarly, a predominance of down run days provides evidence that the market is in a bearish state (see Figure 6.13). In Chapter 18, we use the concept of run days to construct trading systems.

Wide-Ranging Days

A wide-ranging day is a day whose volatility significantly exceeds the average volatility of recent trading days. Wide-ranging days are defined as follows:

Figure 6.12
RUN DAYS IN BULL MARKET: MARCH 1993 T-BOND

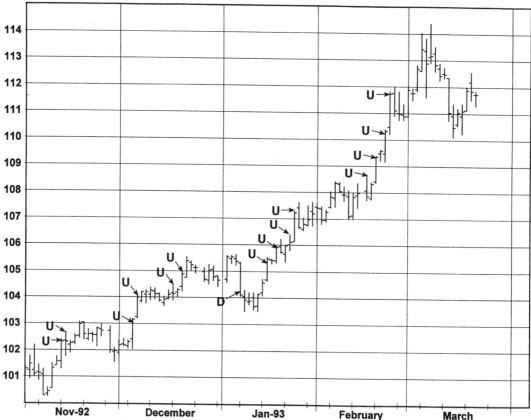

Note: U = up run day; D = down run day.

Wide-Ranging Day. A day on which the *volatility ratio* (VR) is greater than *k* (e.g., *k* = 2.0). The VR is equal to today's true range divided by the true range of the past *N*-day period (e.g., *N* = 15).

Wide-ranging days can have special significance. For example, a wide-ranging day with a strong close that materializes after an extended decline is often a signal of an upside trend reversal. Figures 6.14–6.16 provide examples of wide-ranging up days that materialized following extended declines and heralded major advances. In Figure 6.16 there are actually two back-to-back wide-ranging days that developed just above the low of the prior bear market.

Figure 6.13
RUN DAYS IN BEAR MARKET: MARCH 1991 SUGAR

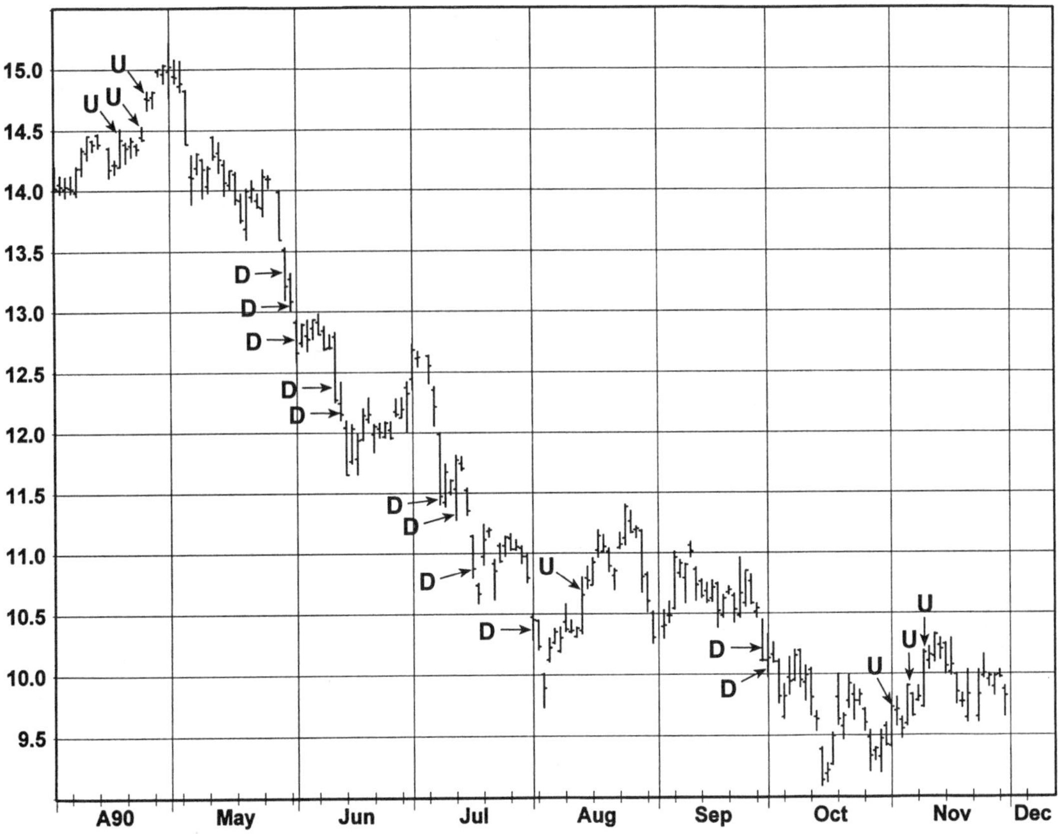

Note: U = up run day; D = down run day.

Similarly, a wide-ranging day with a weak close that occurs after a major advance can often signal a downside trend reversal. Figures 6.17 and 6.18 show monster wide-ranging down days that occurred near the peaks of prior major advances, which each offset weeks' worth of upward price movement. Such huge wide-ranging days should be viewed as serious warning flags that a previous major trend has been reversed. Figure 6.19 shows an incredible succession of four wide-ranging days that retraced the equivalent of four months of prior upmovement. The first of these days emerged fairly close to what effectively was the top of a seven-year bull market. In Chapter 18, the concept of wide-ranging days is used as the primary element in constructing a sample trading system.

Figure 6.14
WIDE-RANGING UP DAY: AUGUST 1994 CRUDE OIL

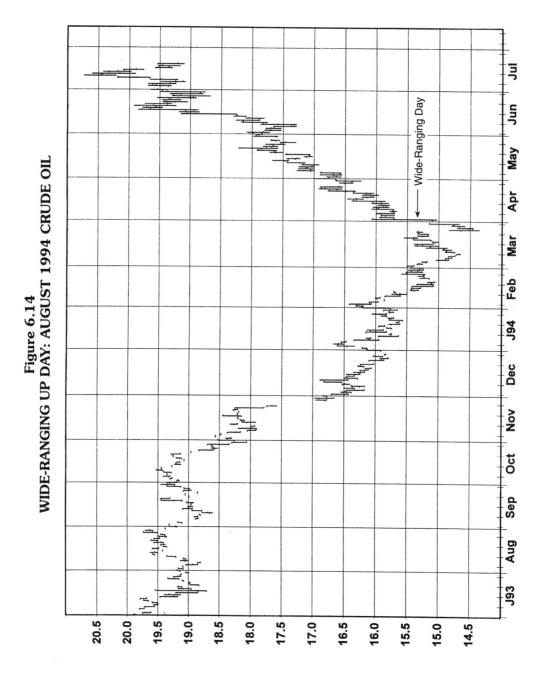

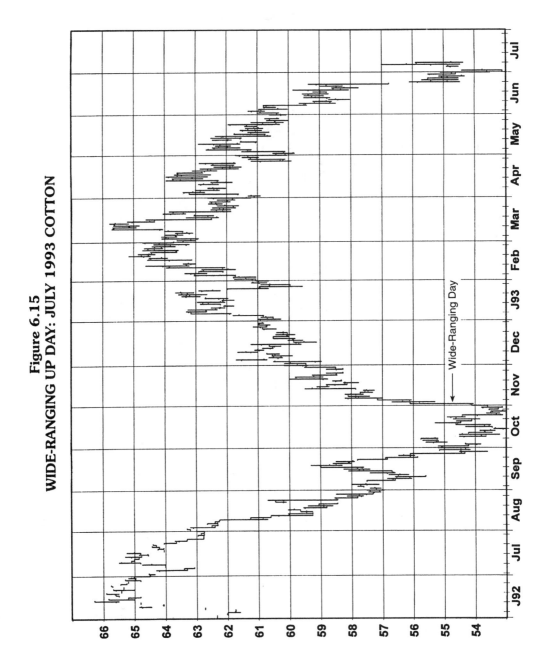

Figure 6.15
WIDE-RANGING UP DAY: JULY 1993 COTTON

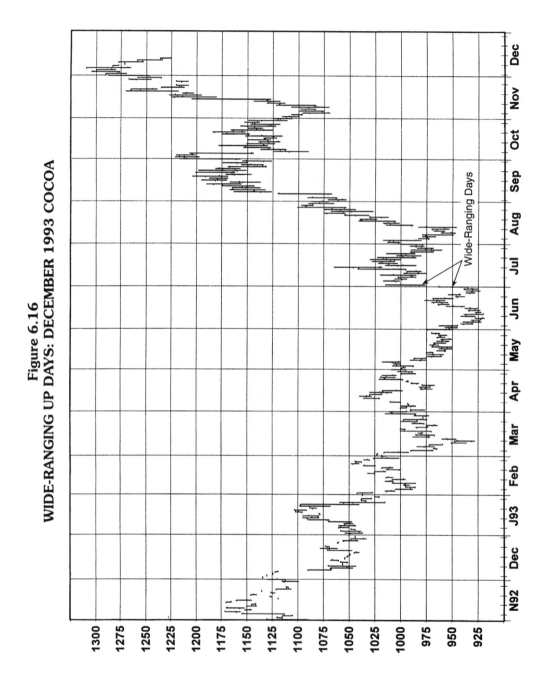

Figure 6.16
WIDE-RANGING UP DAYS: DECEMBER 1993 COCOA

Figure 6.17
WIDE-RANGING DOWN DAY: CANADIAN DOLLAR CONTINUOUS FUTURES

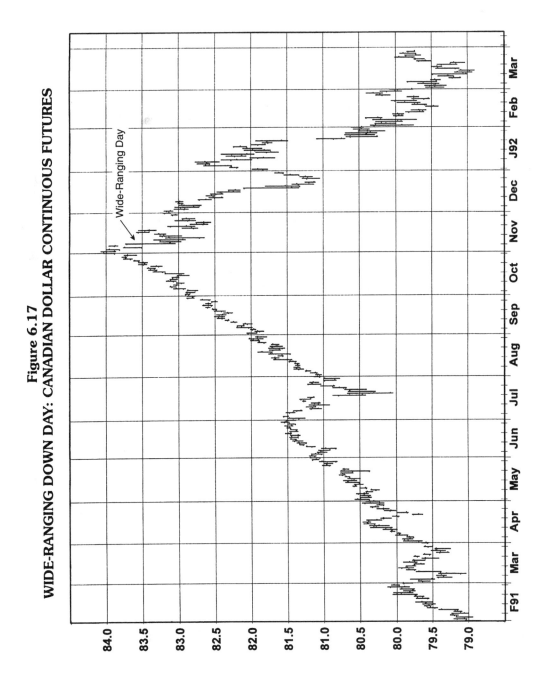

Figure 6.18
WIDE-RANGING DOWN DAY: DECEMBER 1993 GOLD

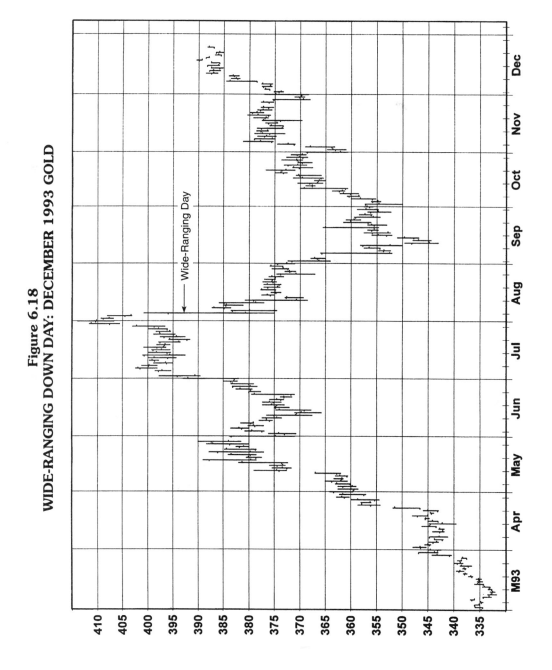

Figure 6.19
WIDE-RANGING DOWN DAYS: BRITISH POUND CONTINUOUS FUTURES

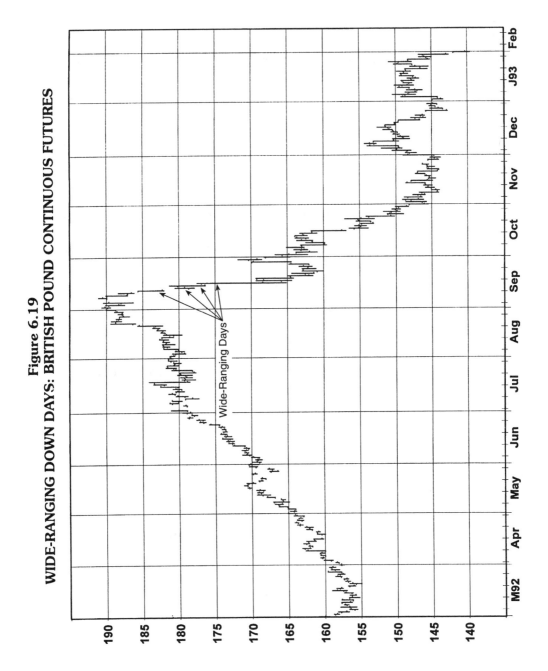

CONTINUATION PATTERNS

Continuation patterns are various types of congestion phases that materialize within long-term trends. As the name implies, a continuation pattern is expected to be resolved by a price swing in the same direction that preceded its formation.

Triangles

There are three basic types of triangle patterns: symmetrical (see Figures 6.20 and 6.21), ascending (see Figures 6.22 and 6.23), and descending (see Figures 6.24 and 6.25). A symmetrical triangle is usually followed by a continuation of the trend that preceded it, as in Figures 6.20 and 6.21. Conventional chart wisdom suggests that nonsymmetrical triangles will yield to a trend in the direction of the slope of the hypotenuse, as is the case in Figures 6.22–6.25. However, the direction of the breakout from a triangle formation is more important than the type. For example, in Figure 6.26, although the April–August 1994 congestion pattern is an ascending triangle, the breakout is on the downside and is followed by a sharp decline.

Figure 6.20
SYMMETRICAL TRIANGLE: FCOJ CONTINUOUS FUTURES

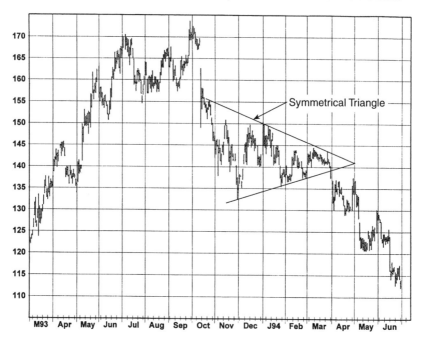

Figure 6.21
SYMMETRICAL TRIANGLE: SWISS FRANC
CONTINUOUS FUTURES

Symmetrical Triangle

Figure 6.22
ASCENDING TRIANGLE: SEPTEMBER 1992 EURODOLLAR

Ascending Triangle

105

Figure 6.23
ASCENDING TRIANGLE: OCTOBER 1992 SUGAR

Figure 6.24
DESCENDING TRIANGLE: SOYBEAN OIL
CONTINUOUS FUTURES

106

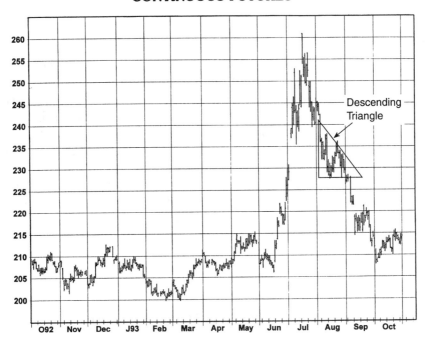

Figure 6.25
DESCENDING TRIANGLE: SOYBEAN MEAL
CONTINUOUS FUTURES

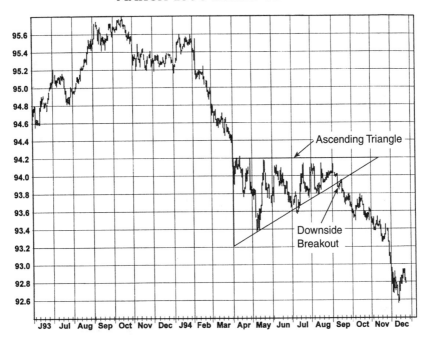

Figure 6.26
ASCENDING TRIANGLE WITH DOWNSIDE BREAKOUT:
MARCH 1995 EURODOLLAR

Flags and Pennants

Flags and pennants are narrow-band, short-duration (e.g., one to three weeks) congestion phases within trends. The formation is called a flag when it is enclosed by parallel lines and a pennant when the lines converge. Figures 6.27 and 6.28 illustrate both types of patterns. Pennants may appear to be similar to triangles, but they differ in terms of time: the triangle has a longer duration.

Flags and pennants typically represent pauses in a major trend. In other words, these patterns are usually followed by price swings in the same direction as the price swings that preceded their formation.

A breakout from a flag or pennant can be viewed as a confirmation that the trend is continuing and a trading signal in the direction of the trend. Since breakouts are usually in the direction of the main trend, however, I prefer to enter positions during the formation of the flag or pennant, anticipating the

Figure 6.27
FLAGS AND PENNANTS: MARCH 1995 SUGAR

Figure 6.28
FLAGS AND PENNANTS: JULY 1992 COCOA

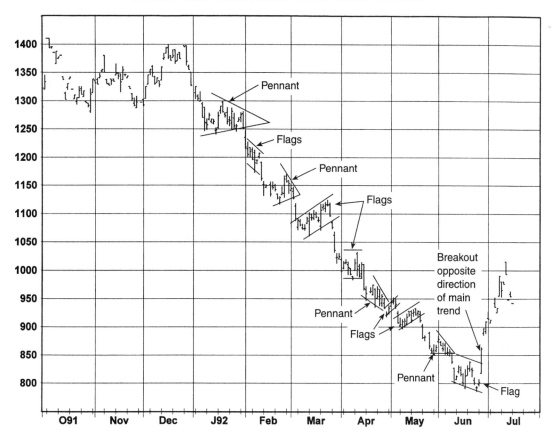

probable direction of the breakout. This approach allows for more advantageous entries of trades, without a significant deterioration in the percentage of correct trades, since reversals following breakouts from flags and pennants are about as common as breakouts in the counter-to-anticipated direction. Following a breakout from a flag or pennant, the opposite extreme of the formation can be used as an approximate stop-loss point.

A significant penetration of a flag or pennant in the opposite-to-anticipated direction—that is, counter to the main trend—can be viewed as a signal of a potential trend reversal. For example, in Figure 6.28 note that after a long string of flags and pennants that were resolved by breakouts in the direction of the main trend, the opposite direction penetration of the flag formed in June led to a sharp rally.

Flags and pennants typically point in the opposite direction of the main trend. This characteristic is exhibited by the majority of flags and pennants illustrated in Figures 6.27 and 6.28, which are fairly representative charts. The direction in which a flag or pennant points, however, is not an important consideration. In my experience, I have not found any significant difference in reliability between flags and pennants that point in the same direction as the main trend as opposed to the more usual opposite slope.

Flags or pennants that form near the top or just above a trading range can be particularly potent bullish signals. In the case where a flag or pennant forms near the top of a trading range, it indicates that the market is not backing off despite having reached a major resistance area—the top of the range. Such price action has bullish implications and suggests that the market is gathering strength for an eventual upside breakout. In the case where the flag or pennant forms above the trading range, it indicates that prices are holding above a breakout point, thereby lending strong confirmation to the breakout. Generally speaking, the more extended the trading range, the greater the potential significance of a flag or pennant that forms near or above its top. Figures 6.29–6.32 provide four examples of flags or pennants that materialized near the top or above trading ranges and proved to be precursors of explosive advances.

For similar reasons, flags or pennants that form near the bottom or just below trading ranges are particularly bearish patterns. Figures 6.33–6.36 provide four examples of flags or pennants that materialized near the bottom or below trading ranges and proved to be harbingers of steep price declines.

TOP AND BOTTOM FORMATIONS

V Tops and Bottoms

The "V" formation is a turn-on-a-dime type of top (see Figure 6.37) or bottom (see Figure 6.38). One problem with a V top or bottom is that it is frequently difficult to distinguish from a sharp correction unless accompanied by other technical indicators (e.g., prominent spike, significant reversal day, wide gap, wide-ranging day). The V bottom in Figure 6.38 did contain such a clue—an extreme spike—whereas the V top in Figure 6.37 was unaccompanied by any other evidence of a trend reversal.

Double Tops and Bottoms

Double tops and bottoms are exactly what their names imply. Of course, the two tops (or bottoms) that make up the pattern need not be exactly the same, only in the same general price vicinity. Double tops and bottoms that materialize after large price moves should be viewed as strong indicators of a major

Figure 6.29
FLAG NEAR TOP OF TRADING RANGE AS BULLISH SIGNAL:
OCTOBER 1990 HEATING OIL

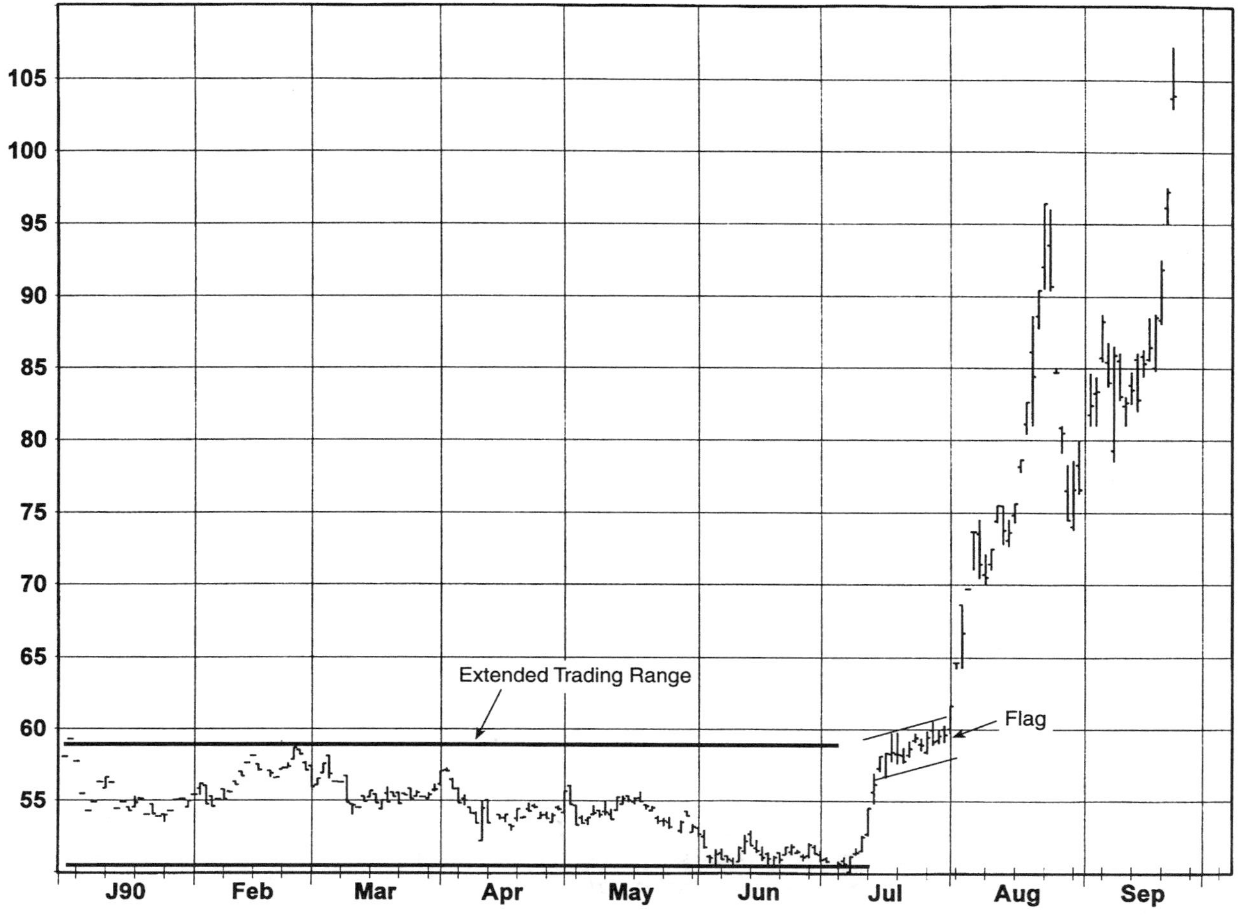

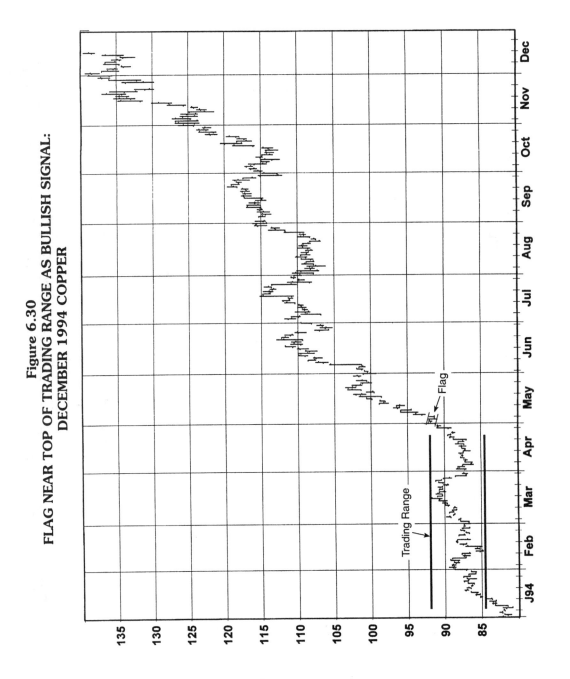

Figure 6.30
FLAG NEAR TOP OF TRADING RANGE AS BULLISH SIGNAL:
DECEMBER 1994 COPPER

112

Figure 6.31
PENNANT ABOVE TOP OF TRADING RANGE AS BULLISH
SIGNAL: JULY 1993 SOYBEANS

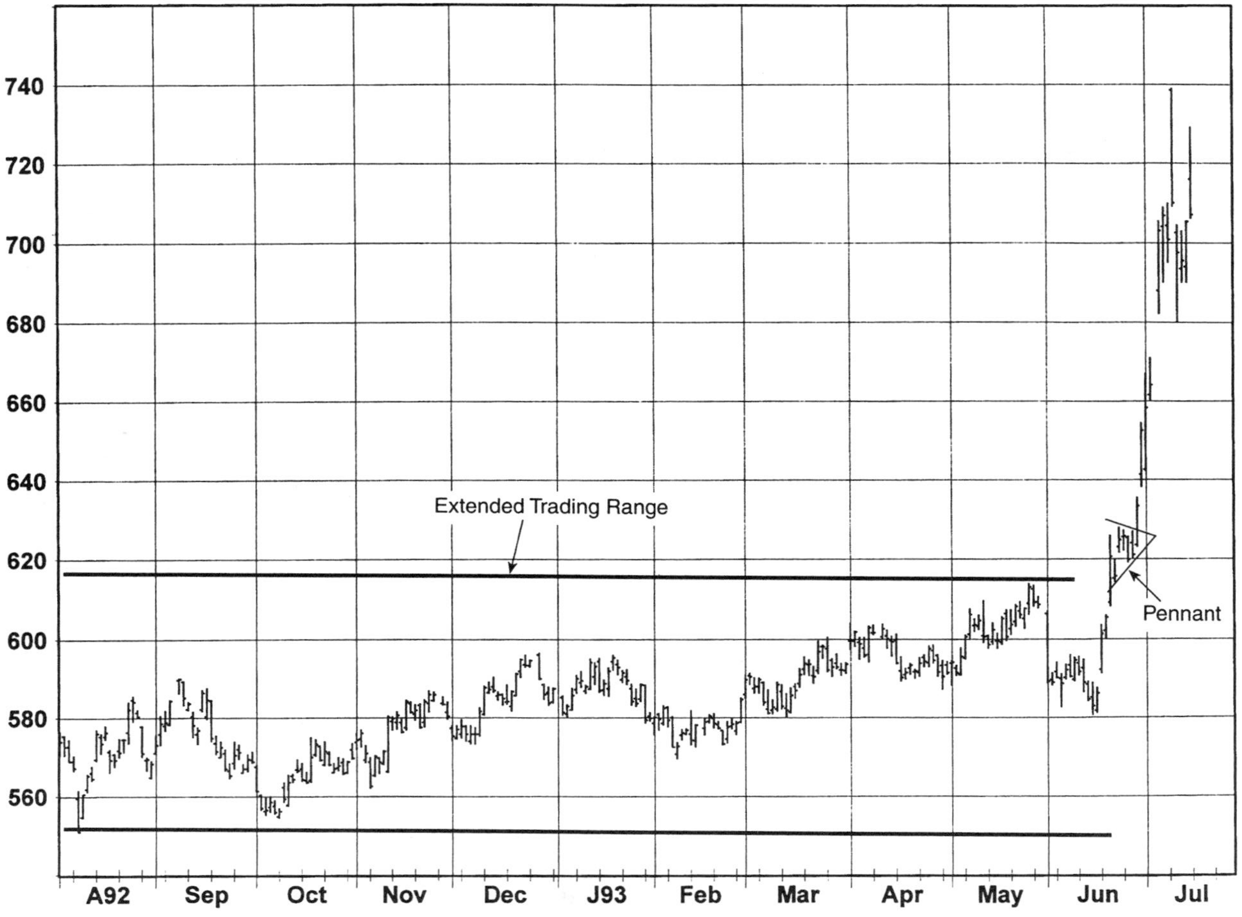

Figure 6.32
FLAG ABOVE TOP OF TRADING RANGE AS BULLISH SIGNAL:
JULY 1993 SOYBEAN MEAL

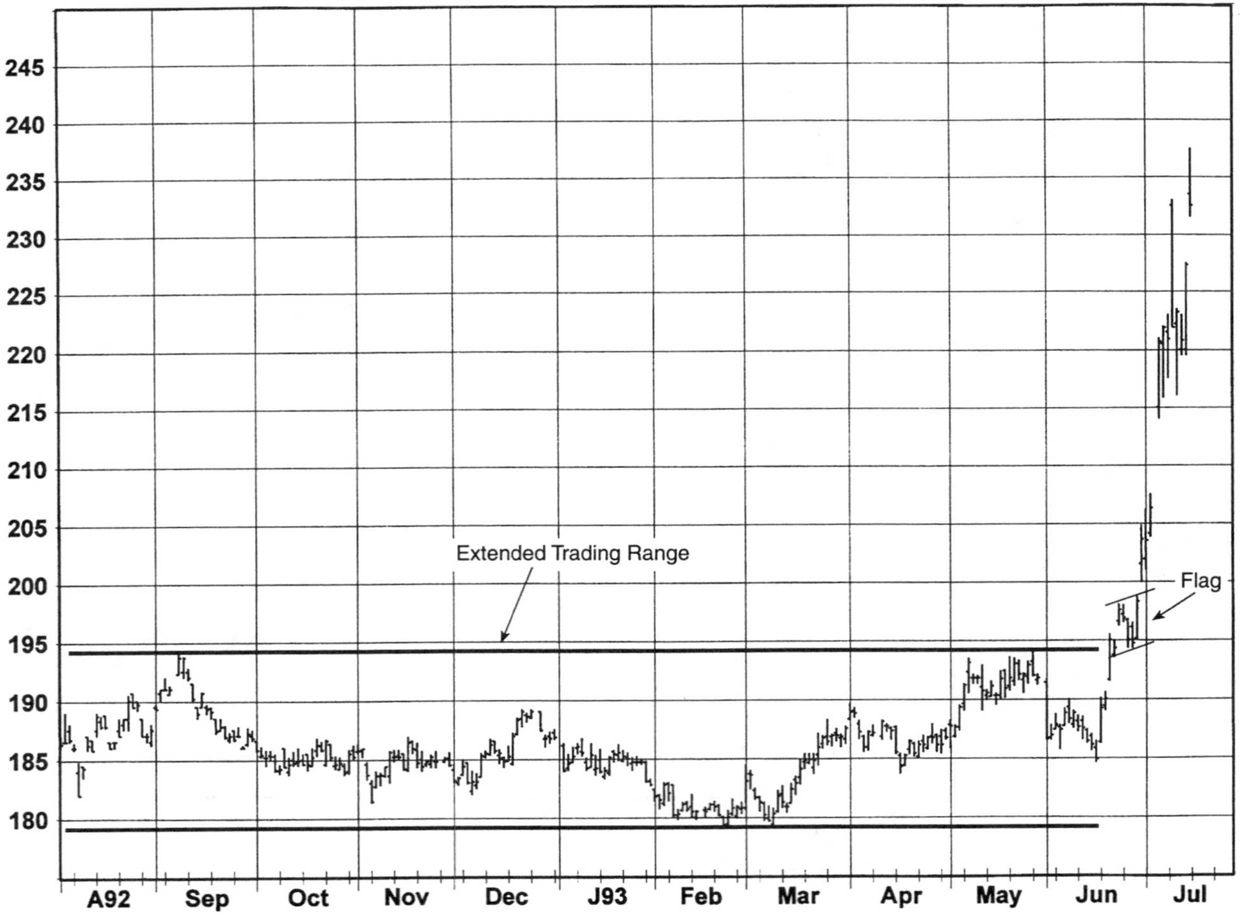

114

Figure 6.33
FLAG BELOW BOTTOM OF TRADING RANGE AS BEARISH
SIGNAL: PLATINUM CONTINUOUS FUTURES

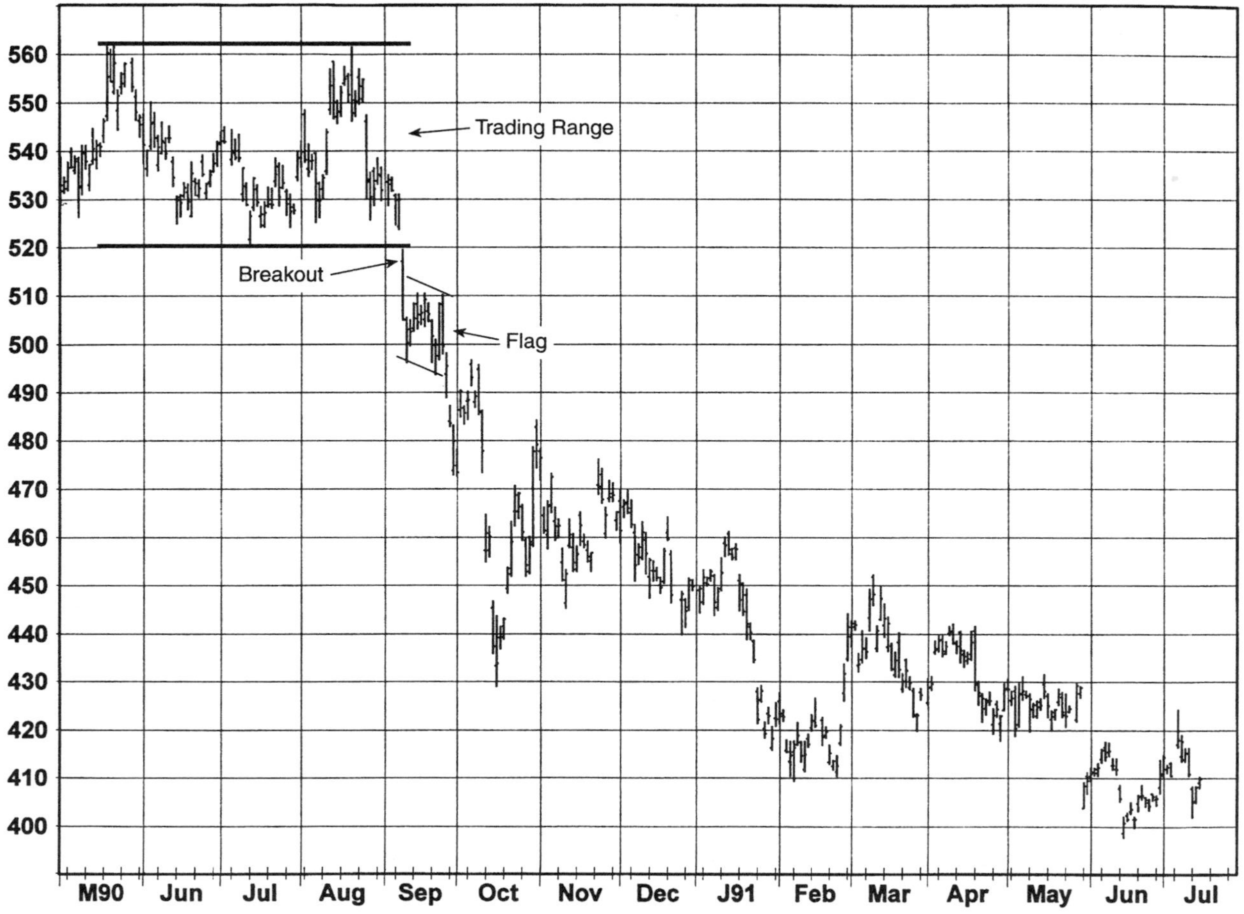

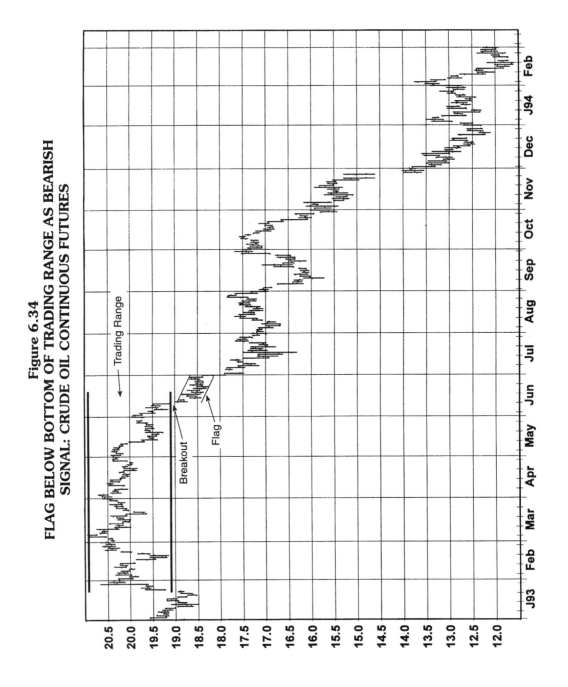

Figure 6.34
FLAG BELOW BOTTOM OF TRADING RANGE AS BEARISH
SIGNAL: CRUDE OIL CONTINUOUS FUTURES

Figure 6.35
FLAG NEAR BOTTOM OF TRADING RANGE AS BEARISH
SIGNAL: JUNE 1994 EURODOLLAR

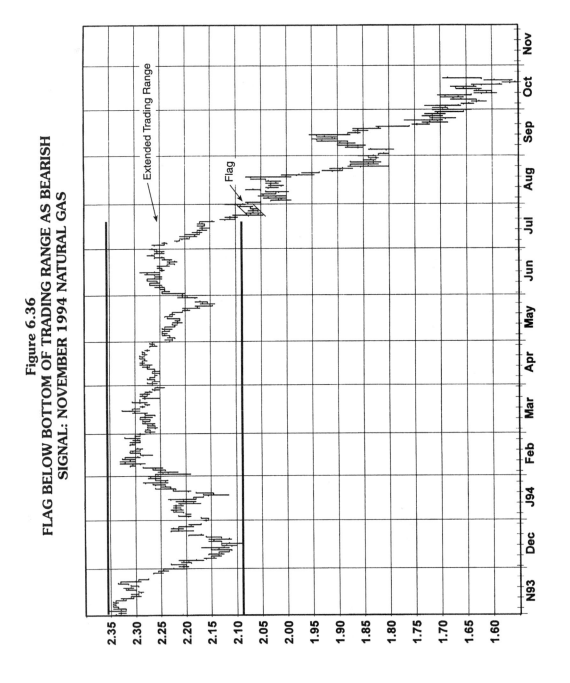

Figure 6.36
FLAG BELOW BOTTOM OF TRADING RANGE AS BEARISH
SIGNAL: NOVEMBER 1994 NATURAL GAS

Figure 6.37
"V" TOP: CANADIAN BOND CONTINUOUS FUTURES

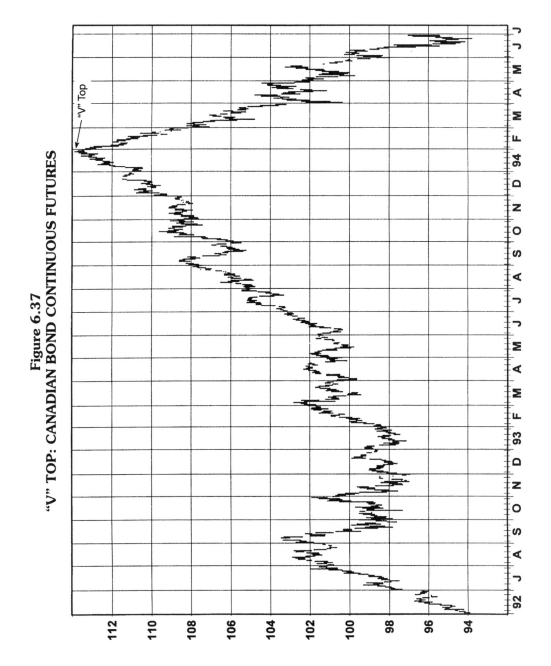

Figure 6.38
"V" BOTTOM: ITALIAN BOND CONTINUOUS FUTURES

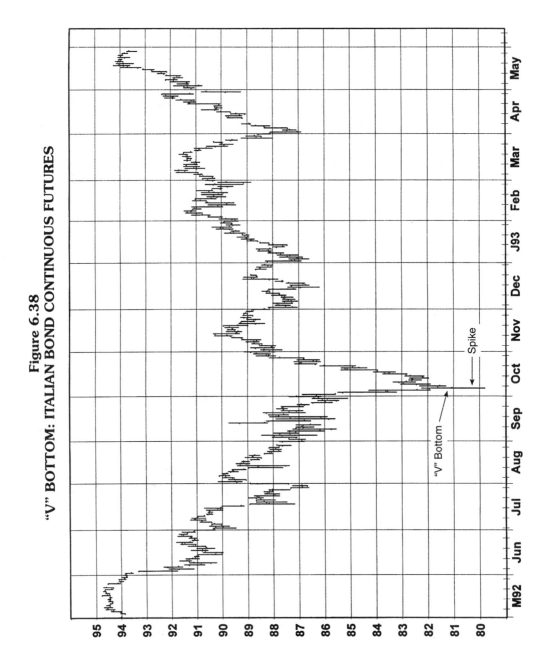

trend reversal. Figure 6.39 illustrates a major double top in the deutsche mark. (Continuous futures are used for all of the charts illustrating double tops and bottoms because the liquid trading period for most individual contracts is not sufficiently long to display the time span encompassing these patterns and the preceding and succeeding trends.)

A double top (bottom) is considered completed when prices move below (above) the reaction low (high) between the two tops (bottoms) of the formation. When the intervening reaction is very deep, as for example in Figure 6.39, it is impractical to wait for such an "official" confirmation, and the trader may have to anticipate that the pattern has formed based on other evidence. For example, in Figure 6.39 the confirmation of the double top does not occur until the market has surrendered nearly half of the entire April–August advance. However, the spike high that developed at the second top and the flag pattern that formed after the initial downswing from that high implied that the next price swing would also be down. Based on these clues, a trader could have reasonably concluded that a double top was in place, even though the pattern had not yet been completed in terms of the standard definition.

Figure 6.40 depicts the double top that capped the early 1990s imposing bull market in the Australian 10-year bond. Note that a weekly chart is used in order to show the full extent of the prolonged advance that preceded this formation. This chart provides a perfect example of the double top (or bottom) as a major trend transition pattern. In this instance, the pullback between the two tops is very shallow, and as a result, in sharp contrast to Figure 6.39, the double-top pattern is confirmed very close to the actual peak.

Figures 6.41 and 6.42 illustrate double-bottom patterns. Figure 6.43 shows a single chart containing both a double bottom and a double top. Top and bottom formations with more repetitions (e.g., triple top or bottom) occur rather infrequently, but would be interpreted in the same fashion. Figure 6.44 displays a rare, classic triple bottom, with all three lows nearly identical. Figure 6.45 provides an example of a triple top.

Head and Shoulders

The head and shoulders is one of the best known chart formations. The head-and-shoulders top is a three-part formation in which the middle high is above the high points on either side (see Figure 6.46). Similarly, the head-and-shoulders bottom is a three-part formation in which the middle low is below the low point on either side (see Figure 6.47). Perhaps one of the most common mistakes made by novice chartists is the premature anticipation of the head-and-shoulders formation. The head and shoulders is not considered complete until the neckline is penetrated (see Figures 6.46 and 6.47). Furthermore, a valid

Figure 6.39
DOUBLE TOP: DEUTSCHE MARK CONTINUOUS FUTURES

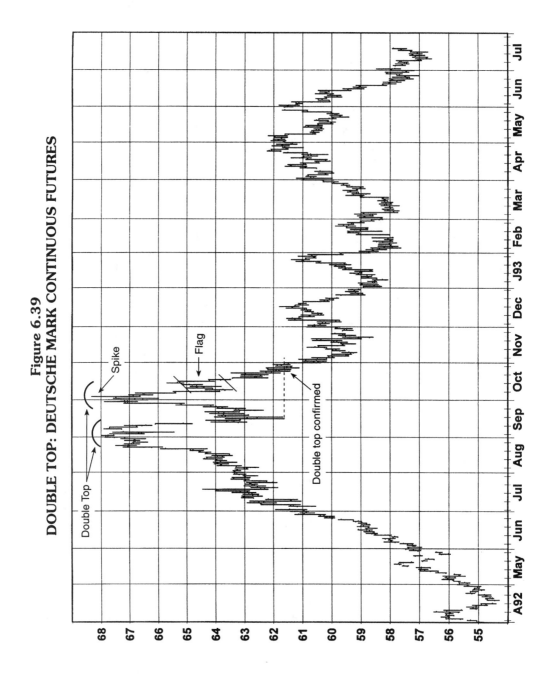

Figure 6.40

DOUBLE TOP: AUSTRALIAN 10-YEAR BOND WEEKLY CONTINUOUS FUTURES

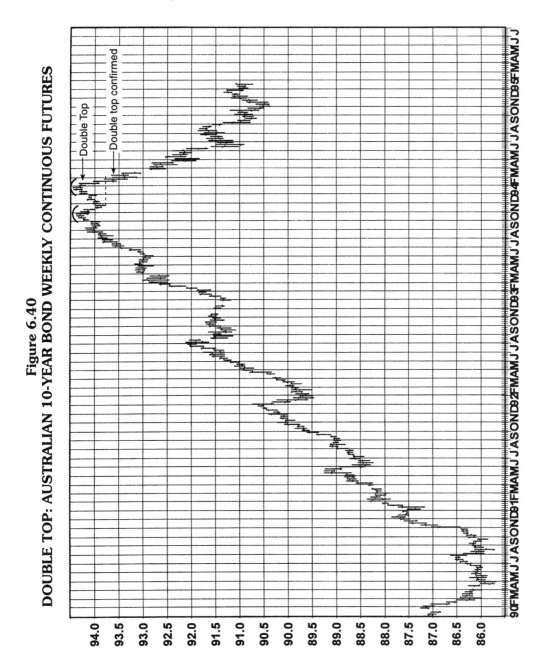

Figure 6.41
DOUBLE BOTTOM: UNLEADED GAS CONTINUOUS FUTURES

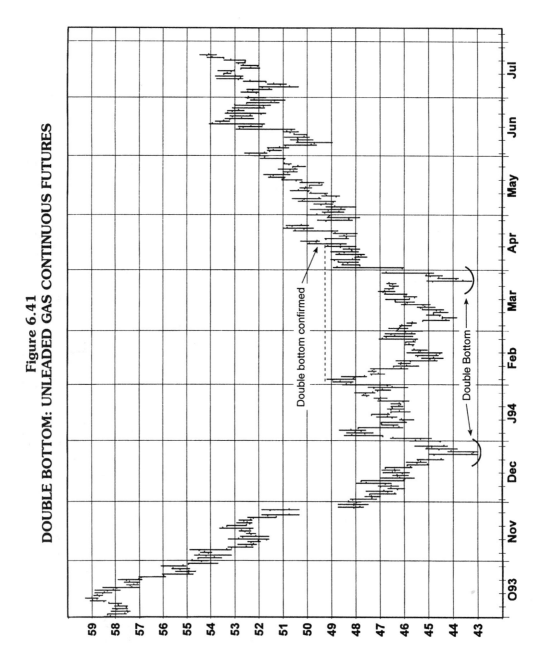

Figure 6.42
DOUBLE BOTTOM: SOYBEANS CONTINUOUS FUTURES

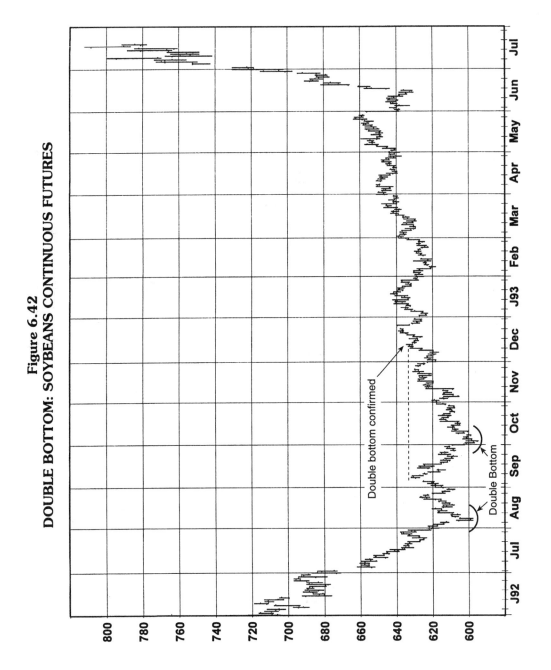

Figure 6.43
DOUBLE TOP AND DOUBLE BOTTOM: JAPANESE YEN CONTINUOUS FUTURES

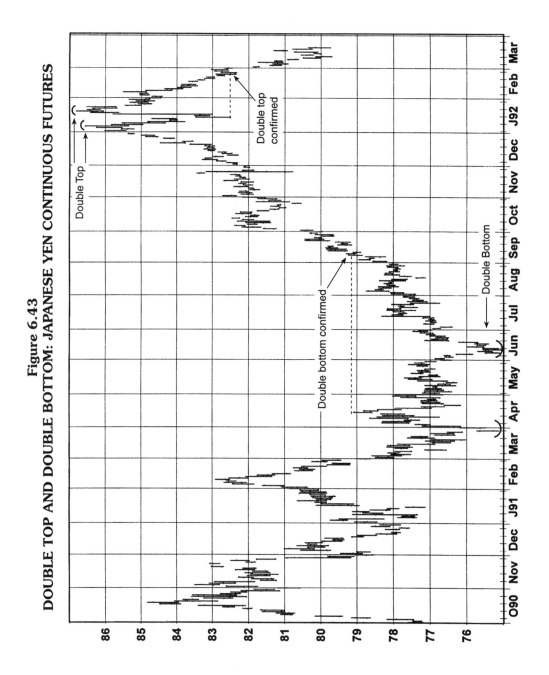

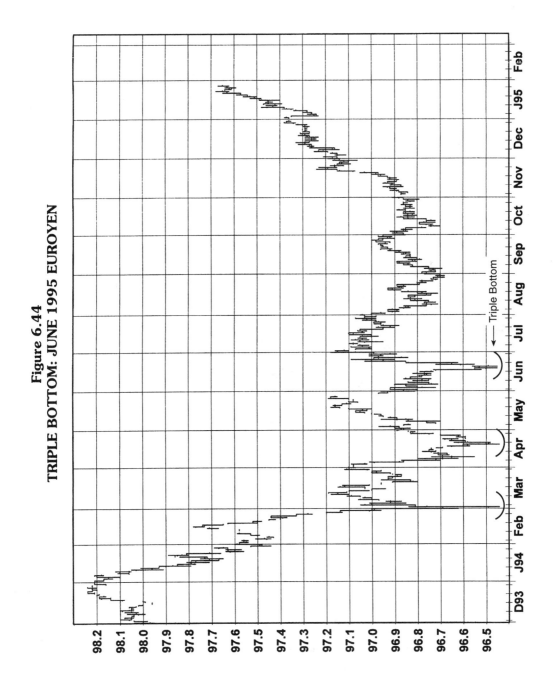

Figure 6.44
TRIPLE BOTTOM: JUNE 1995 EUROYEN

127

Figure 6.45
TRIPLE TOP: DECEMBER 1993 COTTON

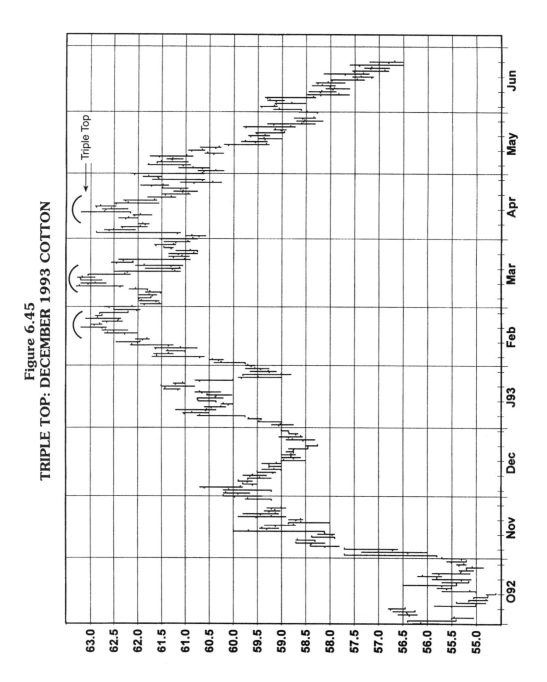

128

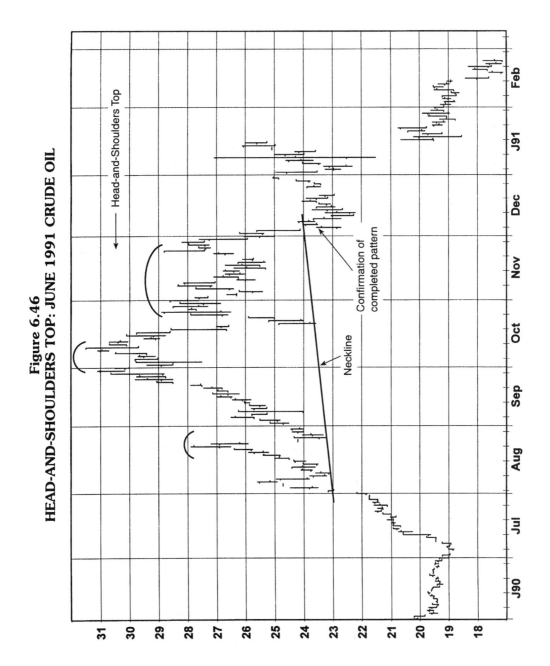

Figure 6.46
HEAD-AND-SHOULDERS TOP: JUNE 1991 CRUDE OIL

Figure 6.47
HEAD-AND-SHOULDERS BOTTOM: DECEMBER 1992 COFFEE

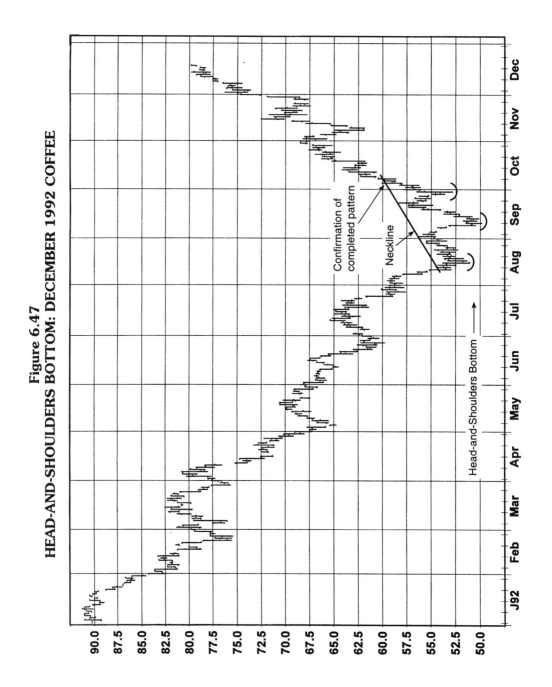

head and shoulders is only formed after a major price move has occurred. Patterns that bear the shape of a head-and-shoulders formation, but lack this requirement, can be misleading.

Rounded Tops and Bottoms

Rounded tops and bottoms (also called *saucers*) occur somewhat infrequently, but are among the most reliable top and bottom formations. Figure 6.48 shows a continuous futures chart with a rounding top that marked the transition between a major uptrend and an even more imposing downtrend. Ideally, the pattern would not contain any jags, as this chart does; however, I consider the main criterion to be whether the outer perimeter conforms to a rounding shape, which it does. Figure 6.49 depicts a rounding-top pattern for an individual contract chart. Figure 6.50 displays another individual contract chart exhibiting a rounding-top pattern, with the interesting phenomenon that the secondary high also reflects a rounding-top pattern. Figure 6.51 shows a rounding top that was itself part of a double-top formation. This pattern marked a dramatic trend transition. (Incidentally, Figure 6.51 also contains some excellent examples of symmetrical triangles as continuation patterns, which were discussed earlier in this chapter.) Finally, Figures 6.52 and 6.53 provide some examples of rounding-bottom formations.

Triangles

Triangles, which are among the most common continuation patterns, can be top and bottom formations as well. Figures 6.54 and 6.55 illustrate triangle tops. As in the case of the continuation pattern, the key consideration is the direction of the breakout from the triangle.

Wedge

In a rising wedge, prices edge steadily higher in a converging pattern (see Figures 6.56 and 6.57). The inability of prices to accelerate on the upside despite continued probes into new high ground suggests the existence of strong scale-up selling pressure. A sell signal occurs when prices break below the wedge line. Figure 6.58 provides an example of a declining wedge. Wedge patterns can sometimes take years to complete. Figures 6.59 and 6.60 depict a multiyear declining wedge in the gold market, shown in terms of both nearest and continuous futures. Although the nearest and continuous futures charts reflect significant differences, they both exhibit declining wedge patterns.

Figure 6.48
ROUNDING TOP: MATIF NOTIONAL BOND
CONTINUOUS FUTURES

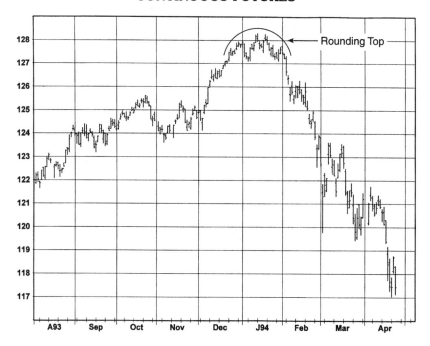

Figure 6.49
ROUNDING TOP: AUGUST 1994 HOGS

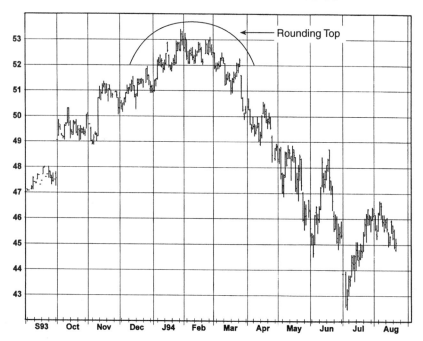

Figure 6.50
TWO ROUNDING TOPS: MAY 1995 WHEAT

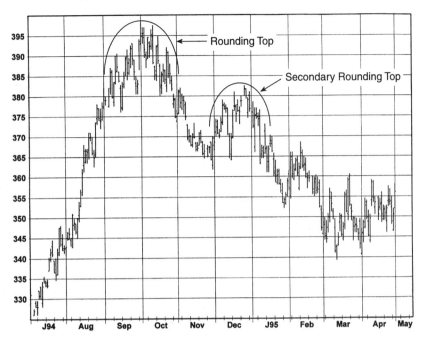

Figure 6.51
ROUNDING TOP AS PART OF DOUBLE TOP: ITALIAN BOND CONTINUOUS FUTURES

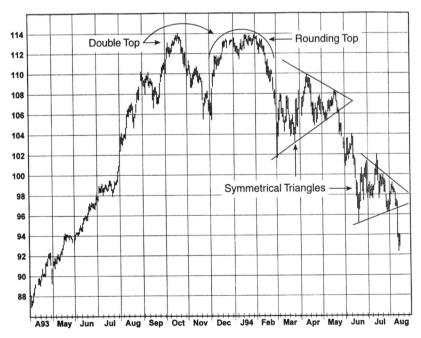

Figure 6.52
ROUNDING BOTTOM: MAY 1994 COPPER

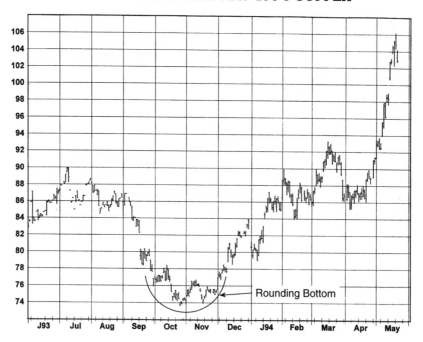

Figure 6.53
ROUNDING BOTTOM: AUGUST 1992 NATURAL GAS

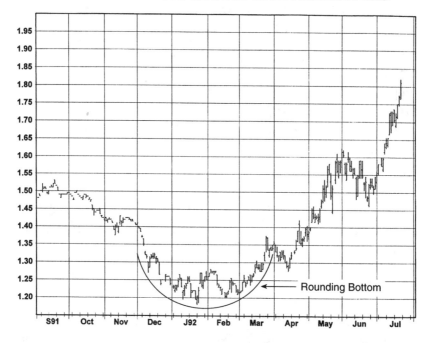

Figure 6.54
TRIANGLE TOP: SEPTEMBER 1991 SILVER

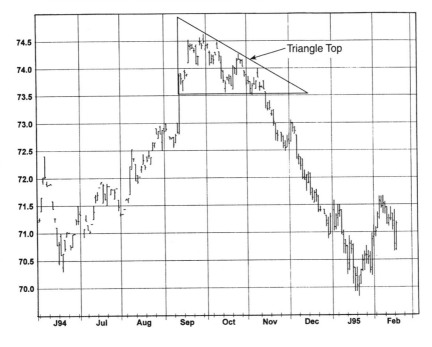

Figure 6.55
TRIANGLE TOP: MARCH 1995 CANADIAN DOLLAR

Figure 6.56
RISING WEDGE: JULY 1993 COTTON

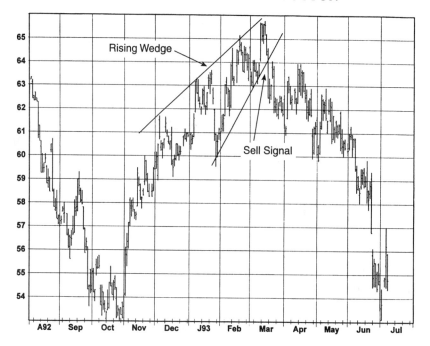

Figure 6.57
RISING WEDGE: UNLEADED GASOLINE
CONTINUOUS FUTURES

136

Figure 6.58
DECLINING WEDGE: CRUDE OIL CONTINUOUS FUTURES

Figure 6.59
MULTIYEAR DECLINING WEDGE: GOLD WEEKLY
NEAREST FUTURES

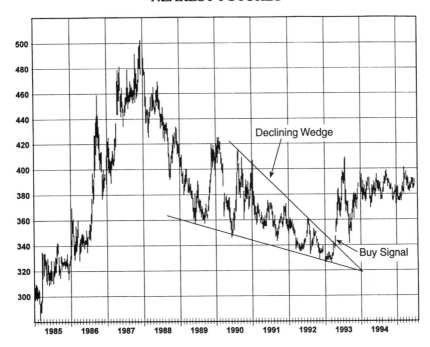

137

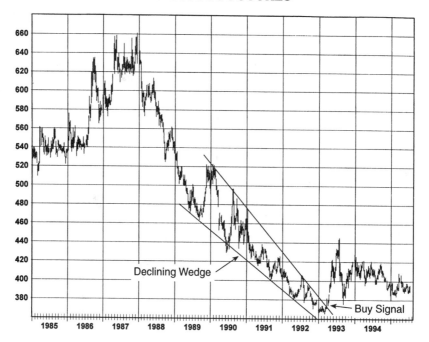

Figure 6.60
MULTIYEAR DECLINING WEDGE: GOLD WEEKLY
CONTINUOUS FUTURES

Island Reversal

An island top is formed when prices gap higher after an extended advance, trade one or more days leaving the gap open, and then gap lower. Figures 6.61 and 6.62 show examples of island tops in which the "island" portion of the formation consists of a single day, while Figure 6.63 illustrates an island top in which the market traded above the initial gap for several days before gapping lower. Figure 6.64 depicts an island bottom. Sometimes the market can trade for several weeks before a second gap in the opposite direction completes the formation (see, for example, the island top in Figure 6.65).

The sequence of a climactic gap up (down) without any follow-through and a subsequent gap down (up) is a potent combination. Island reversals can often signal major trend transitions and should be given significant weight unless the gap is eventually filled.

An island reversal signal would remain in force as long as the more recent gap of the formation is not filled. It should be noted that false island reversal signals are common—that is, island reversals are often filled within the first few days of their formation. Consequently, it is usually a good idea to wait for

Figure 6.61
ISLAND TOP: NOVEMBER 1994 HEATING OIL

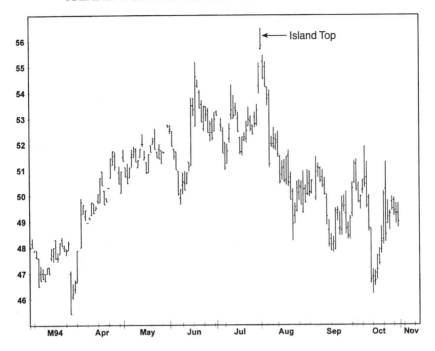

Figure 6.62
ISLAND TOP: DECEMBER 1994 SOYBEAN OIL

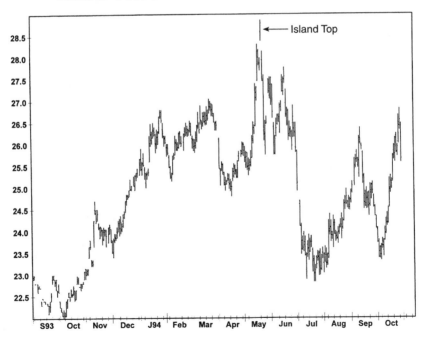

Figure 6.63
ISLAND TOP: JANUARY 1994 PLATINUM

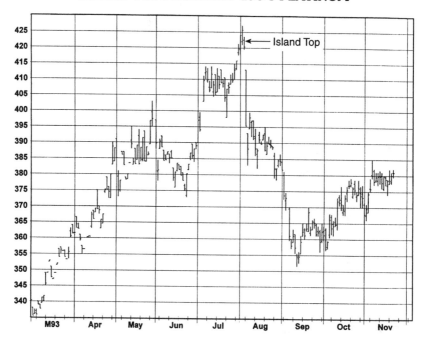

Figure 6.64
ISLAND BOTTOM: MARCH 1992 SUGAR

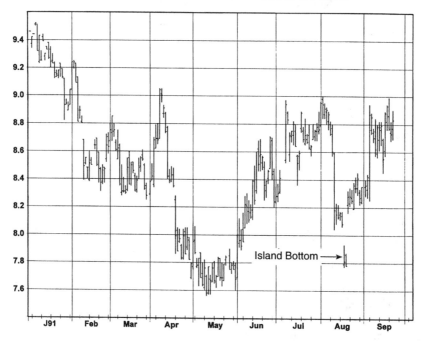

Figure 6.65
ISLAND TOP: DECEMBER 1992 BRITISH POUND

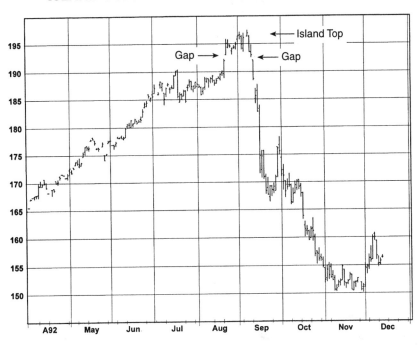

at least 3 to 5 days after the island reversal's initial formation before concluding that it is a valid reversal signal. The tradeoff, however, is that such a wait for confirmation will often result in a worse entry level when the island reversal signal is valid.

Spikes and Reversal Days

These one-day patterns, which often mark relative highs and relative lows, and sometimes major peaks and bottoms, are discussed in an earlier section of this chapter.

7 Is Chart Analysis Still Valid?

I always laugh at people who say, "I've never met a rich techni-cian." I love that! It is such an arrogant, nonsensical response. I used fundamentals for nine years and got rich as a technician.

—Marty Schwartz

Most traders who have never used chart analysis (and even some who have) are quite skeptical about this approach. Some of the commonly raised objections include: "How can such a simple analytical approach work?" "Since key chart points are hardly a secret, won't floor traders sometimes push the market enough to trigger chart stops artificially?" Even if chart analysis worked before it was detailed in scores of books, isn't the method too well publicized to still be effective?"

Although the points raised by these questions are basically valid, a number of factors explain why chart analysis remains an effective trading approach:

1. Trading success does not depend on being right more than half the time, or for that matter, even half the time, as long as losses are rigidly controlled and profitable trades are permitted to run their course. For example, consider a trader who in March 1991 assumes that September 1992 Eurodollars have entered another trading range (see Figure 7.1) and decides to trade in the direction of any subsequent closing breakout. Figure 7.2 indicates the initial trade signals and liquidation points that would have been realized as a result of this strategy. The implicit assumption is that stops are placed at the midpoint of the trading range. (The relevant considerations in choosing a stop point are discussed in detail in Chapter 9.) As can be seen in Figure 7.2, the first two trades would have resulted in immediate losses. Figure 7.3, however, illustrates that the third signal proved to be the real thing, indicating a long position in time to benefit from a major price advance that far exceeded the combined price swings on the prior two

Figure 7.1
TRADING RANGE MARKET: SEPTEMBER 1992 EURODOLLAR

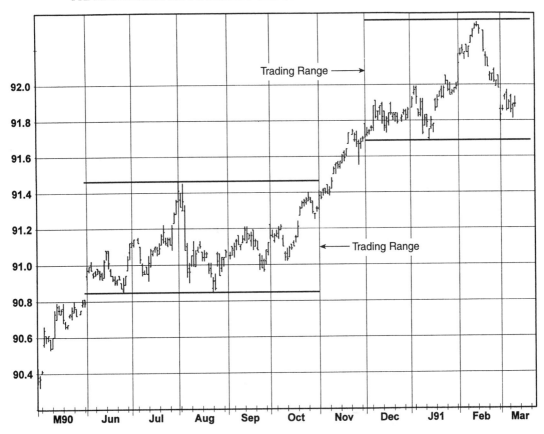

adverse trades. (Note that the relevant trading range is redefined—that is, widened—after each of the false breakouts.)

It is noteworthy that although two out of three trades were losers, on balance, the trader would have realized a large net profit. The key point is that a disciplined adherence to money management principles is an essential ingredient in the successful application of chart analysis to trading.

2. Chart analysis can be made much more effective by requiring confirmation conditions for trade entry, rather than blindly following all technical signals. There is a natural tradeoff in the choice of confirmation rules: the less restrictive the conditions, the greater the number of false signals; the more restrictive the conditions, the greater the surrendered profit potential due to late entry. Some of the key methods that can be used to construct confirmation conditions might include the following:

Figure 7.2
FALSE BREAKOUT SIGNALS: SEPTEMBER 1992 EURODOLLAR

time delays, minimum percent penetration, and specific chart patterns
(e.g., trade must be confirmed by two subsequent thrust days in the
direction of signal).

There is no such thing as a best set of confirmation conditions. In
any list of tested alternatives, the indicated best strategy will vary from
market to market as well as over time. Thus, the ultimate choice of
confirmation rules will depend upon the trader's analysis and experience. In fact, the specific choice of confirmation conditions is one of
the pivotal ways in which chart analysis is individualized.

As an illustration of how confirmation conditions might be used,
consider the following set of rules:

a. Wait three days after signal is received.
b. For a buy signal, enter trade if the close is above the high since
signal was received, or on the first subsequent day fulfilling this
condition. An analogous condition would apply to sell signals.

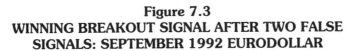

Figure 7.3
WINNING BREAKOUT SIGNAL AFTER TWO FALSE
SIGNALS: SEPTEMBER 1992 EURODOLLAR

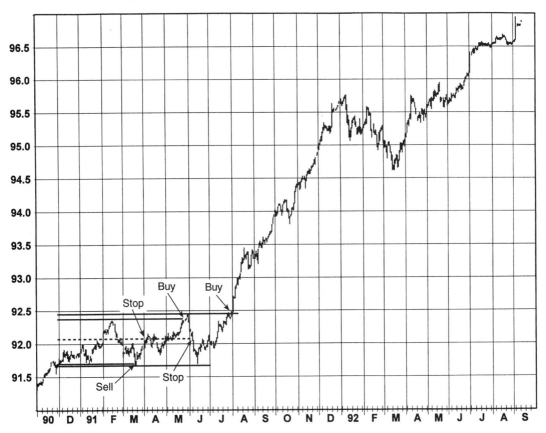

As can be seen in Figure 7.2, these rules would have filtered out the losing March and May signals, while only modestly delaying the entry point for the subsequent highly profitable buy signal. Of course, one could also construct examples in which the use of confirmation conditions is detrimental to the trading results. However, the key point is that the use of confirmation rules is one of the primary means of transforming classical chart concepts into a more powerful trading approach.

3. Chart analysis is more than just the recognition and interpretation of individual patterns. One of the earmarks of the successful chart trader is an ability to synthesize the various components of the overall picture. For example, the trader who recognizes just a trading range in September 1992 Eurodollars (see Figure 7.1) would treat upside and downside breakouts equivalently. However, the more experienced chartist will also consider the broader picture. For example, by examining

Figure 7.4
LONG-TERM CHART AS PART OF COMPREHENSIVE
ANALYSIS: EURODOLLAR CONTINUOUS FUTURES

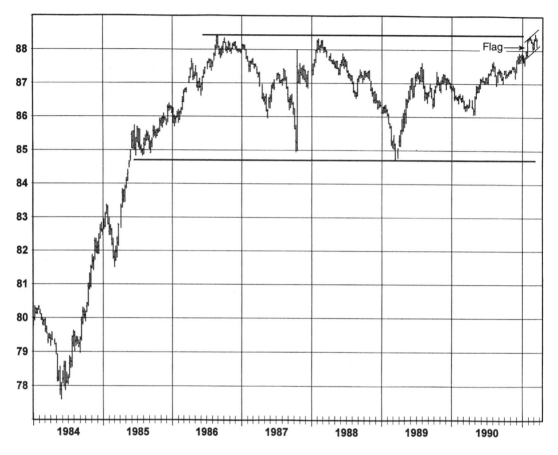

the long-term weekly continuous futures chart in early 1991 (see Figure 7.4), the analyst could have noted that the market had just formed a flag pattern near the top of a five-year trading range. This extremely bullish long-term chart picture would have strongly cautioned against accepting any apparent sell signals on the daily chart. Such a more comprehensive chart analysis could therefore have helped the analyst avert the false sell signal in March (see Figure 7.2) and adopt a much more aggressive trading stance from the long side than would have been warranted if the situation were viewed as just another trading range.

Of course, the preceding example benefits from hindsight. However, the point is not to prove that the application of chart analysis to the Eurodollar market in early 1991 would have conclusively indicated the probable continuation of a long-term bull market, but rather to illustrate the multifaceted analytical process of the experienced chart trader. It should be clear that the skill and subjectivity implied in this approach place chart analysis in the realm of an art that cannot be mimicked by merely following a set of textbook rules. This is a crucial point in understanding how the chartist approach can remain valid despite widespread publicity.

4. Assuming some skill in fundamental forecasting (i.e., a better than 50/50 accuracy rate), chart analysis can be combined with fundamental projections to provide a more effective approach. Specifically, if the long-term fundamental forecast indicates the probability of much higher (lower) prices, only bullish (bearish) chart signals would be accepted. If the fundamental projection was neutral, both buy and sell signals would be accepted. Thus, the chart analyst who is also a competent fundamental analyst would have a decided edge over the majority of traders basing their trading decisions solely on chart-oriented input.

5. The failure of a market to follow through in the direction of a key chart signal is a crucial item of information often overlooked by novice chartists. Recognizing and acting on these situations can greatly enhance the effectiveness of the chartist approach. This subject is discussed in detail in Chapter 11, "The Most Important Rule in Chart Analysis."

In conclusion, the skeptics are probably correct in claiming that a Pavlovian response to chart signals will not lead to trading success. However, this in no way contradicts the contention that a more sophisticated utilization of charts, as suggested by the cited factors, can indeed provide the core of an effective trading plan. In any case, chart analysis remains a highly individualistic approach, with success or failure critically dependent on the trader's skill and experience. It would be unreasonable to expect to play the violin well without some degree of practice and innate talent. Chart analysis is no different—the sour notes of novice practitioners notwithstanding.

8   Midtrend Entry and Pyramiding

Nobody can catch all the fluctuations.

—Edwin Lefèvre

For many reasons, a trader may find herself considering whether to enter a new position after the market has already witnessed a substantial price move. Some examples: (1) she was not previously following the market; (2) in an effort to get a better price, she futilely waited for a price correction that never developed; (3) she was previously skeptical regarding the sustainability of the trend, but has now changed her opinion. Faced with such a situation, many traders will be extremely reluctant to trade the market. This attitude can be easily explained in psychological terms. The act of entering a new position after a trend is already well underway in a sense represents a self-admission of failure. Even if the trade is profitable, the speculator knows that her gains would have been much greater if she had acted earlier. Thus, even when she has a strong sense of probable market direction, the trader may think: "I've missed so much of the move, why bother?"

As an example, consider a chart-oriented trader examining the coffee market in mid-May 1994 (see Figure 8.1) after not having participated in the sharp price advance prior to that time. She would note that the market had penetrated the upside of a prior yearlong trading range, with prices remaining in new high ground for two weeks—a very bullish chart configuration. In addition, she would note that prices had just formed a flag pattern after an upmove—price action indicative of another imminent upswing. However, observing that prices had already advanced over 35 percent since the April low set less than one month earlier, she might be reluctant to enter a new long position belatedly, reasoning that the market was overextended.

Figure 8.2 vividly illustrates the folly of this conclusion. Incredibly, as of mid-May 1994, coffee prices had only completed about one-fifth of their ultimate advance. Moreover, the remaining four-fifths of the price rise was achieved in a mere two months. The moral of this tale is provided by an observation in *Remi-*

Figure 8.1
MISSED PRICE MOVE? (JULY 1994 COFFEE)

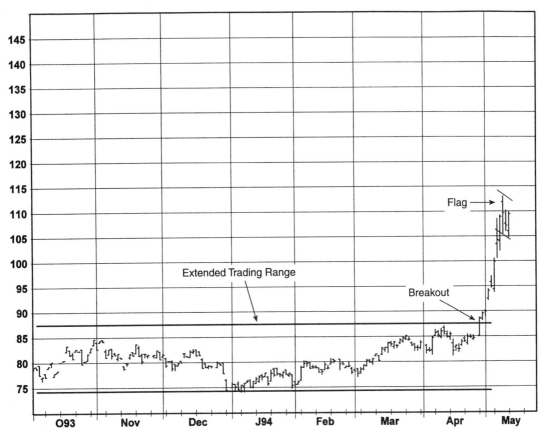

niscences of a *Stock Operator* by Edwin Lefèvre: "[Prices] are never too high to begin buying or too low to begin selling."

The key question is how one enters the market in the midst of a major trend. Actually, the goals in implementing a midtrend position are the same as those for initiating any position: favorable timing of entry and risk control. The following are a few key strategies that could be employed to achieve these objectives:

1. *Percent Retracement.* This approach attempts to capitalize on the natural tendency of a market to partially retrace prior price swings. Generally speaking, one might initiate the position any time the market retraces a given percentage of the price swing from the last relative low or relative high. A reasonable choice for this percentage would be a figure in the 35–65 percent range. A price in the proximity of the relative low or relative high could be used

Figure 8.2
HOW IT TURNED OUT (JULY 1994 COFFEE)

as a stop point on the position. Figure 8.3 illustrates the entry points using this approach, assuming a 50 percent retracement criterion. The main advantage of this method is that it is capable of providing superior entry points (as was the case in the chosen illustration). However, it is also subject to a major disadvantage: frequently, the necessary retracement condition may not be fulfilled until the trend has carried much further, or possibly even reversed.

2. *Reversal of Minor Reaction.* This approach is based on waiting for a minor reaction to materialize and then entering on the first signs of a resumption of the major trend. Of course, the precise method would depend on how a reaction and trend resumption were defined. The choices are virtually limitless. For illustration purposes, we will provide one possible set of definitions.

A "reaction" is identified whenever the *reaction count* reaches 4. The reaction count is initially set to 0. In a rising market, the count would be raised to 1 any day in which the high and low were equal or lower than the corre-

Figure 8.3
BUY SIGNALS ON 50-PERCENT RETRACEMENTS (SEPTEMBER 1994 DEUTSCHE MARK)

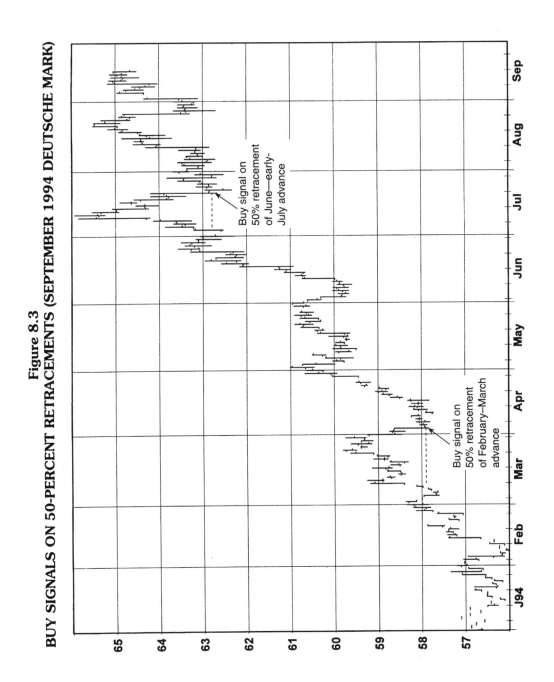

sponding points on the day on which the high of the move was set. The count would be increased by 1 each day the high and low are equal or lower than the high and low of the most recent day on which the count was increased. The count would be reset to 0 any time the market moved to new highs. Analogous conditions would apply to a declining market.

The resumption of the major trend would be indicated whenever the *thrust count* reached 3. The thrust count would initially be set to 0 and would begin being monitored after a reaction was defined. In the case of a reaction in a rising market, the thrust count would increase by 1 on each upthrust day and would be reset to 0 any time the reaction low was penetrated. Once a signal was received, the reaction low could be used as a stop-loss reference point. For example, the position might be liquidated any time the market closed below the reaction low. Once again, an analogous set of conditions could be used for defining a resumption of the trend in a declining market.

Figure 8.4 illustrates the reversal of minor reaction approach using the specific definitions just detailed. The points at which reactions are defined are denoted by the symbol *RD,* with the numbers prior to these points indicating the reaction count values. Buy signals are indicated at the points at which the thrust count equals 3, with the letters prior to these points indicating the thrust count values. For any given entry point, stop-loss liquidation would be signaled by a close below the most recent "stop level," which in the example provided occurs in January 1995. Note that the last RD point is never followed by a buy signal because the market closes below the most recent stop level before the thrust count can build.

3. *Continuation Pattern and Trading Range Breakouts.* The use of continuation patterns and trading ranges for entry signals was discussed in Chapter 6. Since to some extent chart patterns are in the eye of the beholder, this approach will reflect a degree of subjectivity. Figure 8.5 offers one interpretation of continuation patterns (implicit assumption: at least five trading days are required to form a continuation pattern), and the corresponding buy points based on closes above these consolidations. It should be noted, however, that once a trend is considered established, it is not absolutely necessary to wait for penetrations of continuation patterns as confirmation of trade entry signals. By definition, these patterns are expected to be resolved by price swings in the same direction as the price moves that preceded their formation. Thus, for example, in an uptrend, long positions could be established within consolidation patterns based on an expectation of an eventual upside breakout. The low prices in the patterns depicted in Figure 8.5 could be used as reference points for the placement of protective stops.

4. *Reaction to Long-Term Moving Average.* Price retracements to a moving average of the price series can be viewed as signals that the

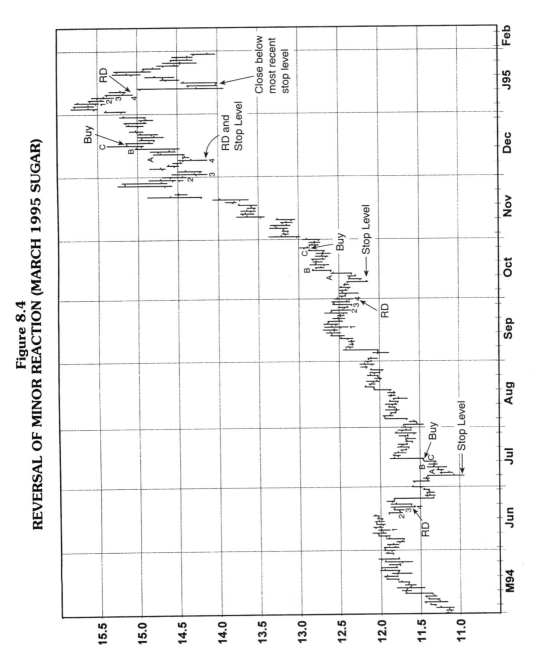

Figure 8.4
REVERSAL OF MINOR REACTION (MARCH 1995 SUGAR)

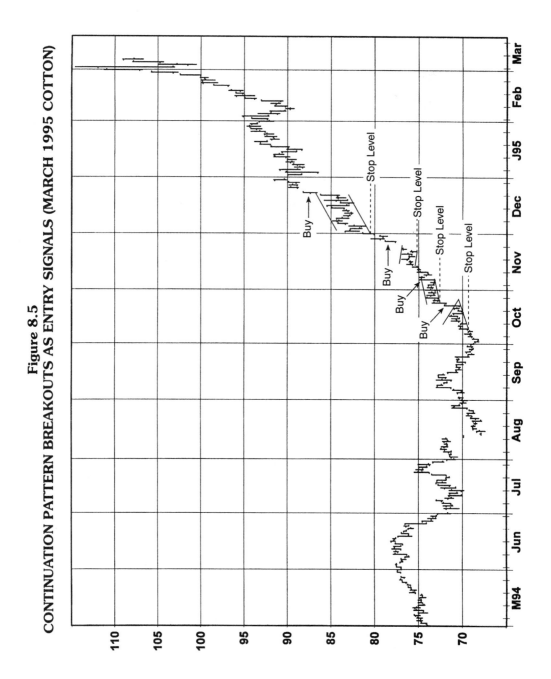

Figure 8.5
CONTINUATION PATTERN BREAKOUTS AS ENTRY SIGNALS (MARCH 1995 COTTON)

Figure 8.6
REACTION TO LONG-TERM MOVING AVERAGE
(SEPTEMBER 1994 DEUTSCHE MARK)

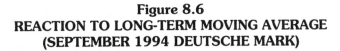

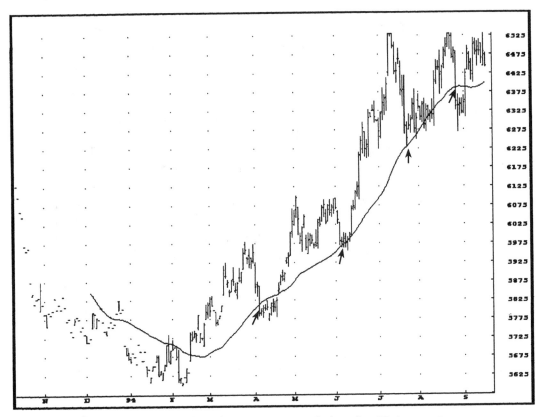

Note: ↑ = buy entry signal based on a reaction to below the 40-day moving average.

reaction to the main trend is near an end. Specifically, if a trader believed that an uptrend was in place, long positions could be entered anytime prices declined to below a specified moving average. Similarly, if a downtrend was believed to be in effect, short positions could be initiated on rallies above the moving average. Figure 8.6, which superimposes a 40-day moving average over the September 1994 deutsche mark contract, provides an illustration of this approach. Assume that a trader decided that the deutsche mark had entered an uptrend. Price pullbacks below the 40-day moving average could be used as entry signals for long positions. The arrows in Figure 8.6 indicate potential buy entry levels based on this approach.

In Chapter 17, we see how crossovers of moving averages can be used as *trend-reversal* signals. In the application just described, we have used moving average crossover points to signal *countertrend* trade entry signals. There is no contradiction. When moving average crossovers are employed for generating trend reversal signals, typically, two moving averages are used so that the smoothing of both data series will reduce false trend-reversal signals. In the method just detailed, we deliberately defined crossover points based on the price series itself, which is more sensitive than a moving average since it contains no smoothing of the data, and one moving average. In other words, we would use more sensitive definitions of moving average crossovers for countertrend applications than we would for trend-identification applications.

It should be noted that the problem of midtrend entry is identical to the problem of pyramiding.[1] Both transactions involve implementing a position after the market has already witnessed a substantial move in a given direction. Consequently, the strategies discussed in this chapter for a midtrend entry could also be applied to the timing of pyramid positions. A few additional guidelines are necessary for pyramiding. First, one should not add to any existing position unless the last unit placed shows a profit. Second, one should not add to an existing position if the intended stop point would imply a net loss for the entire position. Third, pyramid units should be no greater than the base (initial) position size.

---

[1]Pyramiding is the implementation of additional units to an existing position.

9 Choosing Stop-Loss Points

It was the same with all. They would not take a small loss at first but had held on, in the hope of a recovery that would "let them out even." And prices had sunk and sunk until the loss was so great that it seemed only proper to hold on, if need be a year, for sooner or later prices must come back. But the break "shook them out," and prices just went so much lower because so many people had to sell, whether they would or not.

—Edwin Lefèvre

The success of chart-oriented trading is critically dependent on the effective control of losses. A precise stop-loss liquidation point should be determined *before* initiating a trade. The most disciplined approach would be to enter a good-till-canceled (GTC) stop order at the same time the trade is implemented. However, if the trader knows he can trust himself, he could predetermine the stop point and then enter a day order at any time this price is within the permissible daily limit.

How should stop points be determined? A basic principle is that the position should be liquidated at or before the point at which price movement causes a transition in the technical picture. For example, assume a trader decides to sell December T-bonds after the late February downside breakout has remained intact for five days (see Figure 9.1). In this case, the protective buy stop should be placed no higher than the upper boundary of the November–February trading range, since the realization of such a price would totally transform the chart picture. Some of the technical reference points commonly used for placing protective stops include:

1. **Trend Lines.** A sell stop can be placed below an uptrend line; a buy stop can be placed above a downtrend line. One advantage of this approach is that the penetration of a trend line will usually be one of the first technical signals in a trend reversal. Thus, this type of stop point will strongly limit the magnitude of the loss or surrendered open profits.

Figure 9.1
STOP PLACEMENT FOLLOWING TRADING RANGE
BREAKOUT: DECEMBER 1994 T-BOND

However, this attribute comes at a steep price: trend line penetrations are prone to false signals. As discussed in Chapter 3, it is common for trend lines to be redefined in the course of a bull or bear market.

2. **Trading Range.** As illustrated in the preceding December T-bond example, the opposite side of a trading range can be used as a stop point. Frequently, the stop can be placed closer (particularly in the case of broader trading ranges) because if the breakout is a valid signal, prices should not retreat too deeply into the range. Thus, the stop might be placed somewhere in the zone between the midpoint and the more distant boundary of the range. The near end of the trading range, however, would not be a meaningful stop point. In fact, retracements to this area are so common that many traders prefer to wait for such a reaction before initiating a position. (The advisability of this delayed entry strategy following breakouts is a matter of personal choice: in

many instances it will provide better fills, but it will also cause the trader to miss some major moves.)

3. **Flags and Pennants.** After a breakout in one direction of a flag or pennant formation, the return to the opposite end (or some point beyond) can be used as a signal of a price reversal, and by implication a point for placing stops. For example, in Figure 9.2 the sharp downside penetration of a flag pattern in early July was quickly followed by a rebound above the same formation. This price action proved to be a precursor of a major price advance.

4. **Wide-Ranging Days.** Similar to flags and pennants, after a breakout in one direction, the return to the opposite end can be used as a signal of a price reversal, and hence a point for placing stops. For example, in Figure 9.3 note how the return of prices back to below the true low of the wide-ranging up day formed in mid-September (after initially trading above this pattern) led to a major price collapse.

5. **Relative Highs and Relative Lows.** If the implied risk is not too great, the most recent relative high or relative low can be used as a stop point.[1] For example, assume a trader initiated a long position in March cotton in response to the confirmation of a double bottom in early November (see Figure 9.4). In this case, the sell stop could be placed below either the August low or the October low.

Sometimes the risk implied by even the closest technically significant points may be excessive. In this case, the trader may decide to use a *money stop*— that is, a protective stop-loss point with no technical significance that is determined by the desired dollar risk level. For example, consider the plight of a trader early April 1993 who after the swift, steep March 1993 price break is convinced that the lumber market has witnessed a major top (see Figure 9.5). The closest meaningful stop point—the contract high (which is the nearest relative high)—would imply a risk of nearly $15,000 per contract (assuming entry at the midpoint of the April trading range)! Although risk can sometimes be reduced if the trader waits for a reaction before entering the market, such a retracement may not occur until the market moves substantially lower. Thus, in a situation in which the nearest meaningful stop point implies a very large risk, a market order accompanied by a money stop may represent the most viable trading approach.

Stops should be used not only to limit losses but also to protect profits. In the case of a long position, the stop should be raised intermittently as the

---

[1]The specific definition of a relative low (relative high) is somewhat arbitrary. (The following description is in terms of the relative low, but analogous commentary would apply to the relative high.) The general definition of a relative low is a day whose low is below the lows of the preceding and succeeding N days. The specific definition of a relative low will depend on the choice of N. A reasonable range for N is 5–15.

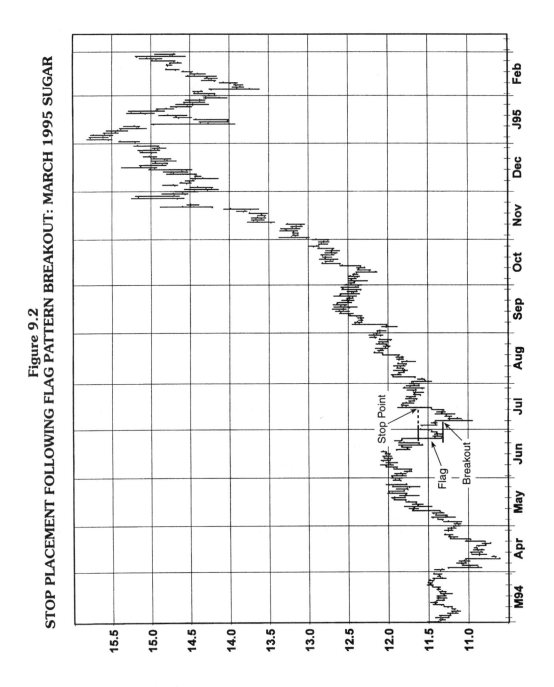

Figure 9.2
STOP PLACEMENT FOLLOWING FLAG PATTERN BREAKOUT: MARCH 1995 SUGAR

Figure 9.3
STOP PLACEMENT FOLLOWING WIDE-RANGING DAY BREAKOUT: DECEMBER 1994 SILVER

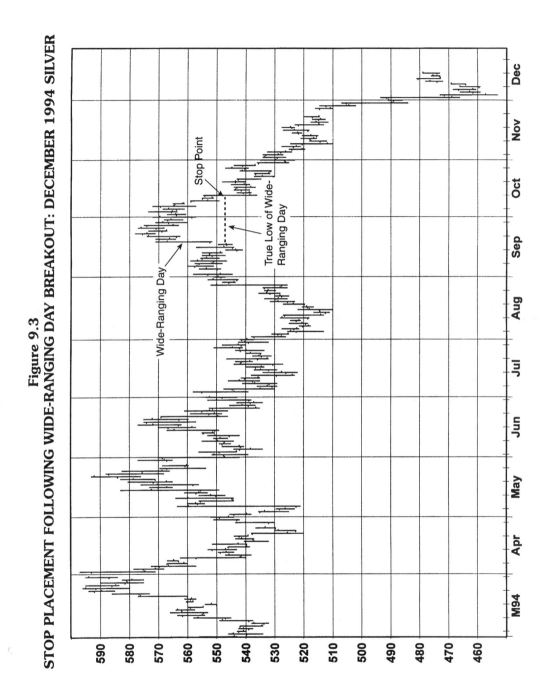

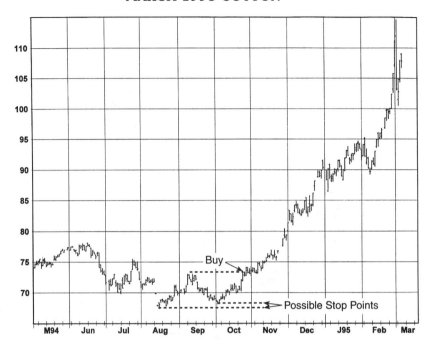

Figure 9.4
STOP PLACEMENT AT RELATIVE LOWS:
MARCH 1995 COTTON

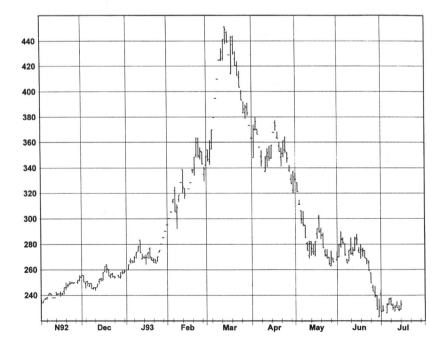

Figure 9.5
EXAMPLE OF MARKET WHERE MONEY STOP
APPROPRIATE: JULY 1993 LUMBER

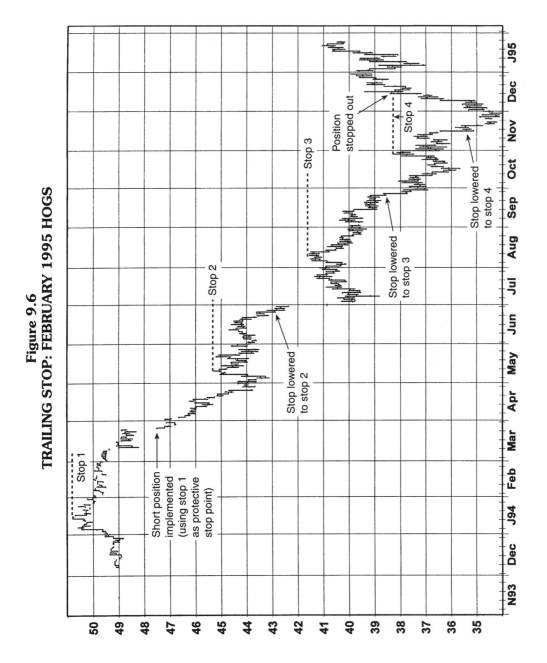

Figure 9.6
TRAILING STOP: FEBRUARY 1995 HOGS

163

market rises. Similarly, in a declining market, the stop should be lowered as the market declines. This type of stop is called a *trailing stop*.

Figure 9.6 illustrates the use of a trailing stop. Assume a trader implements a hog position on the late March downside gap below the December–March trading range, with a stop-loss liquidation plan keyed to relative highs. Specifically, the trader plans to liquidate the long position following a close above the most recent relative high with the reference point being revised each time the market moves to new low ground. (Of course, the stop condition may often be more restrictive. For example, the trader might require a specified number of closes above a previous high, or a minimum penetration of that high to activate the stop.) Thus, the initial stop-loss point would be a close above the January high (stop 1). Following the late June decline to new lows, the stop-loss reference point would be lowered to the May high (stop 2). In similar fashion the stop reference points would be lowered successively to the levels indicated by stop 3 and stop 4. The positions would be stopped out on the rebound above stop 4 in December.

As a general rule, stops should only be changed in order to reduce risk. Some traders who can't stand the thought of getting stopped out at the bottom of a move (top if short) may be diligent in placing a GTC stop order upon initiating the position, but then cancel the order when the market gets within range. This type of order has been derisively, albeit appropriately, referred to as a CIC (cancel if close) order. Revising the stop to allow greater risk defeats the entire purpose of the stop.

10 Setting Objectives and Other Position Exit Criteria

It never was my thinking that made the big money for me. It was always my sitting. Got that? My sitting tight! It is no trick at all to be right on the market.

—Edwin Lefèvre

A trade is like the army—getting in is a lot easier than getting out. Providing the trader is adhering to money management principles, a losing trade presents little ambiguity; that is, liquidation would be indicated by a predetermined stop point. However, the profitable trade presents a problem (albeit a desirable one). How should the trader decide when to take profits? A myriad of solutions have been proposed to this dilemma. The following sections explore some of the primary approaches.

CHART-BASED OBJECTIVES

Many chart patterns are believed to provide clues regarding the magnitude of the potential price move. For example, conventional chart wisdom suggests that once prices penetrate the neckline of a head-and-shoulders formation, the ensuing price move will at least equal the distance from the top (bottom) of the head to the neckline. As another example, many point-and-figure chartists claim that the number of columns that compose a trading range provides an indication of the potential number of boxes in a subsequent trend. (See discussion in Chapter 2 for an explanation of point and figure charting.) Generally speaking, chart patterns are probably considerably less reliable as indicators of price objectives than as trade signals.

MEASURED MOVE

This method is the essence of simplicity. The underlying premise is that markets will move in approximately equal size price swings. Thus if a market rallies 30 cents and then reacts, the implication is that the rally from the reaction low will approximate 30 cents. Although the measured move concept is so simple that it strains credibility, the approach offers reasonable guidelines more frequently than one might expect. When two or more of these objectives nearly coincide, it tends to enhance the reliability of the price area as an important objective zone.

Figure 10.1 provides an excellent example of the application of the measured move technique, with a succession of reasonably accurate price targets occurring on a single chart. A measured move objective based on assuming that the price decline from the January 1994 high would equal the downswing from the October 1993 peak to the November 1993 relative low indicated a downside target of 107–26 (MM1). This price target was in the ballpark of the actual March relative low of 106–16. A measured move objective based on assuming that the price decline from the March 1994 relative high would equal the downswing from the January 1994 high to the March 1994 relative low indicated a downside target of 99–27 (MM2). This price target represented a virtual bull's-eye versus the actual May low of 99–24. Finally, a measured move objective

Figure 10.1
MEASURED MOVES: DECEMBER 1994 T-BOND

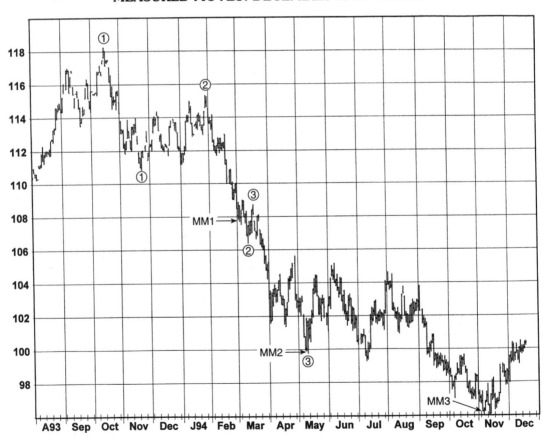

based on assuming that the price decline from the June 1994 high would equal the downswing from the March 1994 relative high to the May 1994 low indicated a downside target of 96–08 (MM3). Again, this price target almost exactly pinpointed the actual market low, which was set in November at 96–01.

Since price swings often span several contracts, it is useful to apply the measured move technique to longer-term price charts that link several contracts. Generally speaking, continuous futures charts are more appropriate than nearest futures charts for measured move analysis because, as was noted in Chapter 2 and is further detailed in Chapter 12, continuous futures accurately reflect price swings, whereas nearest futures do not.

Figure 10.2 illustrates the measured move objective implied by the major price advance from the September 1993 low to the January 1994 peak. The indicated measured move target (MM1) was derived by assuming that the price advance from the July 1994 low would equal this prior price swing. As can be seen, this objective precisely projected the actual 1994 market top.

Figure 10.2
MEASURED MOVE: WHEAT CONTINUOUS FUTURES

Figure 10.3 shows the application of the measured move approach to a corn continuous futures chart. This chart reflects a multitude of surprisingly accurate measured move targets. The measured move objective implied by the initial downswing from the January 1994 market top (MM1) almost exactly coincided with the actual March 1994 relative low. Although the measured move objective implied by the February–early March downswing (MM2) proved a bit wide of the actual May low, the measured move objective indicated by the entire decline from the January 1994 top to the March relative low (MM3) was near perfect in projecting the actual May low. Particularly striking was the fact that the very major measured move objective implied by the entire decline from the January 1994 top to the May 1994 low (MM4) almost exactly projected the November 1994 bottom. Moreover, the September–early October downswing provided a similar reinforcing measured move objective (MM5). Together, these two measured move objectives provided strong evidence that the market was near a potential major bottom in late November 1994.

As was seen in the previous corn chart example, there often will be more than one measured move objective for the same projected low or high. This will occur when there is more than one relevant price swing for deriving a measured move objective. When two or more of these objectives nearly coincide, it tends to enhance the reliability of the projected price area as an important target zone.

Figure 10.4 provides a perfect example of multiple near coinciding measured move price targets. As can be seen, the measured move objectives implied by the late March–late May advance (MM1), the June upswing (MM2), and the late June to mid–July upmove (MM3) all approximately coincided just below the actual market top formed in August. Figure 10.5 provides another example. The measured move objectives implied by the late January–early March decline (MM1) and the mid-March to mid-April downswing (MM2) approximately coincided just above the actual May low.

RULE OF SEVEN

This is an interesting and easy-to-use approach detailed in *Techniques of a Professional Chart Analyst* by Arthur Sklarew. The rule of seven refers to a common set of multipliers used to determine objectives, which are derived by dividing 7 by 5, 4, 3, and 2, respectively. Thus the multipliers are: $7 \div 5 = 1.4$, $7 \div 4 = 1.75$, $7 \div 3 = 2.33$, and $7 \div 2 = 3.5$. The products of each of these multipliers and the magnitude of the first price swing in a bull market are added to the low to obtain a set of price objectives. (In a bear market, the products are subtracted from the high.)

Sklarew suggests using the latter three multipliers (1.75, 2.33, and 3.5) for finding objectives in bull markets and the first three multipliers (1.4, 1.75,

Figure 10.3
MEASURED MOVES: CORN CONTINUOUS FUTURES

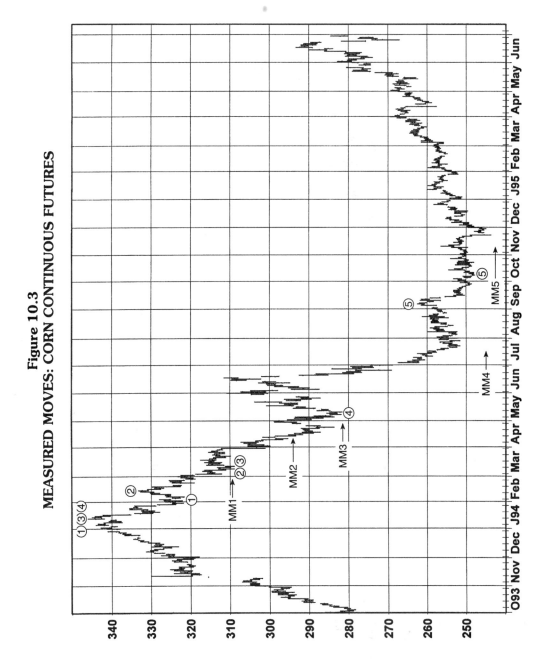

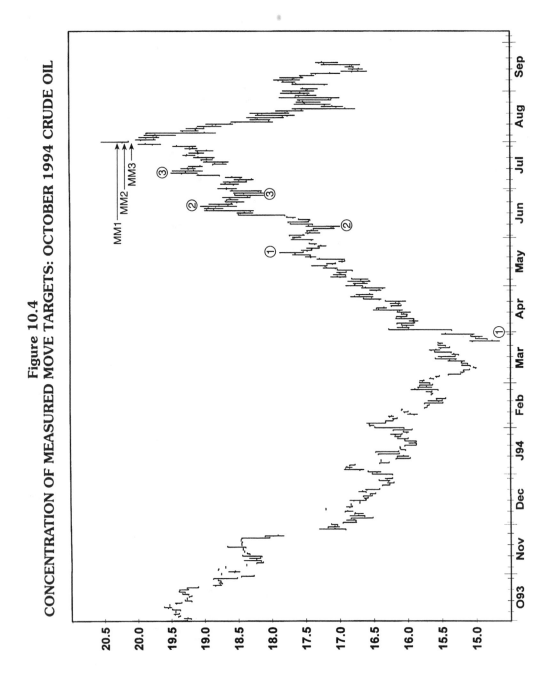

Figure 10.4
CONCENTRATION OF MEASURED MOVE TARGETS: OCTOBER 1994 CRUDE OIL

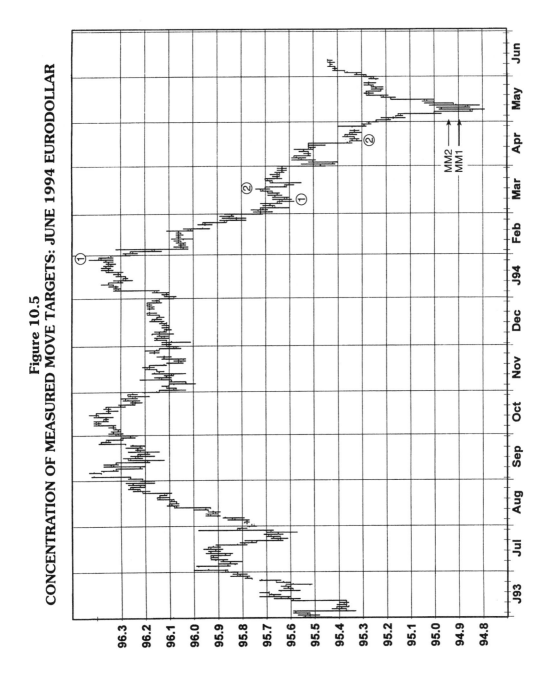

Figure 10.5
CONCENTRATION OF MEASURED MOVE TARGETS: JUNE 1994 EURODOLLAR

and 2.33) for deriving objectives in a bear market. In addition, he indicates that objectives based on the lower multipliers are more meaningful if the reference price move (the price swing multiplied by the multipliers) is of extended duration (i.e., several months) and objectives based on the higher multipliers are more significant if a short-term price swing is used in the calculations. Of course, there will be some degree of subjectivity in this approach, since the perception of what constitutes the first price swing in a trend could vary from trader to trader.

The rule of seven is illustrated in Figure 10.6. (Note that this is the same chart that was used as Figure 10.4 to illustrate measured move objectives. Readers may find it instructive to compare the implications of these two approaches.) The first wave of the bull market that began in late April was equal to 162 points. Following Sklarew's guidelines, since this is a bull market, we use the second through fourth objectives (obtained using the multipliers 1.75, 2.33, and 3.55). The March 28 low, which is used to calculate all the objec-

Figure 10.6
RULE OF SEVEN: OCTOBER 1994 CRUDE OIL

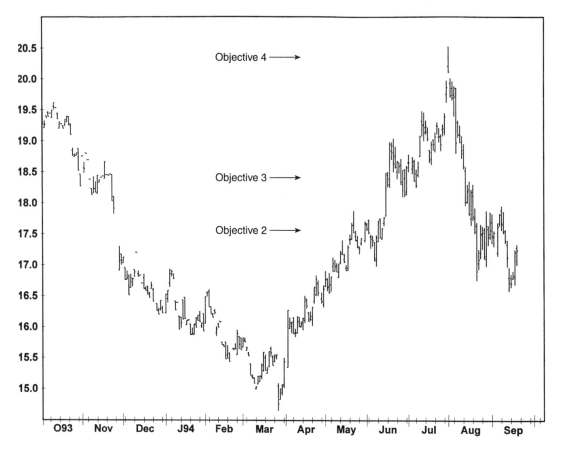

tives, was 1465. The second objective is 1749 [1465 + (1.75 × 162) = 1749]. (Remember, we skip the first objective because this is a bull market.) The third objective is 1843 [1465 + (2.33 × 162)]. The fourth objective is 2032 [1465 + (3.5 × 162)]. These objectives are denoted by arrows in Figure 10.6. Note that objective 2 was modestly below the May 23 high at 1787; objective 3 was moderately below the June 21 high at 1904; and objective 3 was modestly below the August 1 high at 2052. Although the objectives didn't pinpoint any of these highs, they provided reasonably accurate profit-taking targets for long positions.

Figure 10.7 illustrates the rule of seven for a bear market. The first wave of this bear market (shown for a continuous futures contract) was equal to 7–23 points. Following Sklarew's guidelines, since this is a bear market, we use the first through third objectives (obtained using the multipliers 1.4, 1.75, and 2.33). The products of these three multipliers and the initial price swing are subtracted from the high of the move to obtain downside objectives. These

Figure 10.7
RULE OF SEVEN: T-BOND CONTINUOUS FUTURES

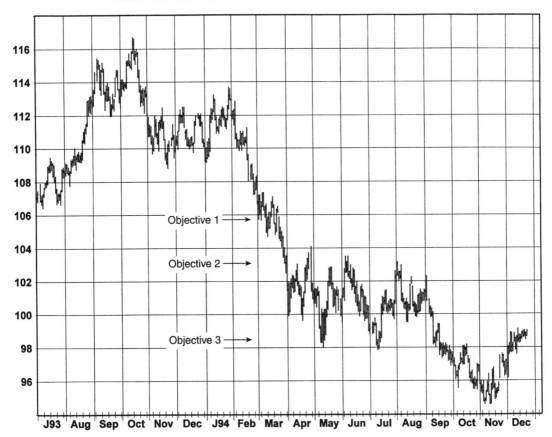

objectives are denoted by arrows in Figure 10.7. As can be seen, the first objective was only modestly above the March 1994 relative low, while the third objective was only slightly higher than the major May 1994 relative low. (Objective 2 did not correspond to any significant relative low.)

It should be noted that hindsight was used in selecting Figures 10.6 and 10.7 to illustrate the rule of seven. In most cases, the correspondence between projected and actual highs and lows will not be as close as in these two examples. Nevertheless, the rule of seven provides one reasonable approach for deriving objectives, and traders may find some experimentation with this method worthwhile.

SUPPORT AND RESISTANCE LEVELS

Points near support levels provide a reasonable choice for setting initial objectives on short positions. For example, the indicated objective zone in Figure 10.8 is based on support anticipated in the area of two prior relative highs. Similarly, prices near resistance levels can be used for setting initial objectives on long positions. For example, the indicated objective zone in Figure 10.9 is based on resistance implied at the lower portion of a prior extended trading range.

Generally speaking, support and resistance levels usually represent only temporary rather than major objectives. Consequently, in using this approach, it is advisable to seek to reenter the position at a better price if a reaction does develop.

OVERBOUGHT/OVERSOLD INDICATORS

Overbought/oversold indicators refer to various technical measures intended to reflect when prices have risen or fallen too sharply and are thus vulnerable to a reaction. Figure 10.10 illustrates the relative strength index (RSI), which provides an example of an overbought/oversold indicator.[1] The RSI has a range of values between 0 and 100. Based on the standard interpretation, levels above 70 suggest an overbought condition, while levels below 30 suggest an oversold condition.

The choice of specific overbought/oversold boundaries is a subjective one. For example, instead of 70 and 30, one might use 75 and 25, or 80 and 20. The more extreme the selected threshold levels, the closer the overbought/oversold signals will be to market turning points, but the more such points that will be missed.

---

[1] The RSI was originally introduced in J. Welles Wilder, Jr., *New Concepts in Technical Trading Systems.* Winston-Salem, North Carolina: Hunter Publishing Co., 1978.

Figure 10.8

DOWNSIDE OBJECTIVE AT SUPPORT ZONE: DECEMBER 1994 WHEAT

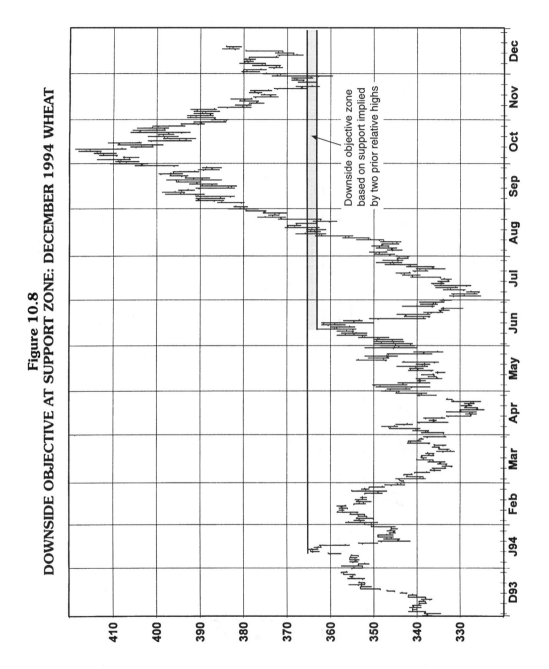

Downside objective zone
based on support implied
by two prior relative highs

175

Figure 10.9
UPSIDE OBJECTIVE AT RESISTANCE ZONE: CATTLE CONTINUOUS FUTURES

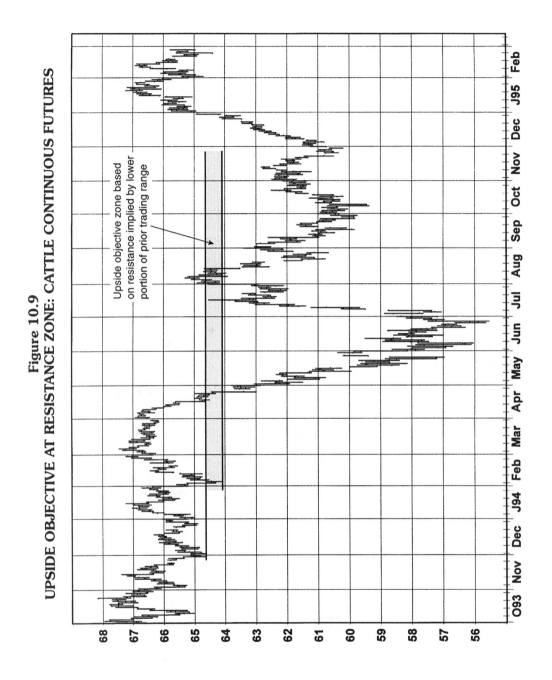

Upside objective zone based on resistance implied by lower portion of prior trading range

Figure 10.10
RELATIVE STRENGTH INDEX IN TRADING RANGE MARKET:
MARCH 1995 SOYBEAN OIL

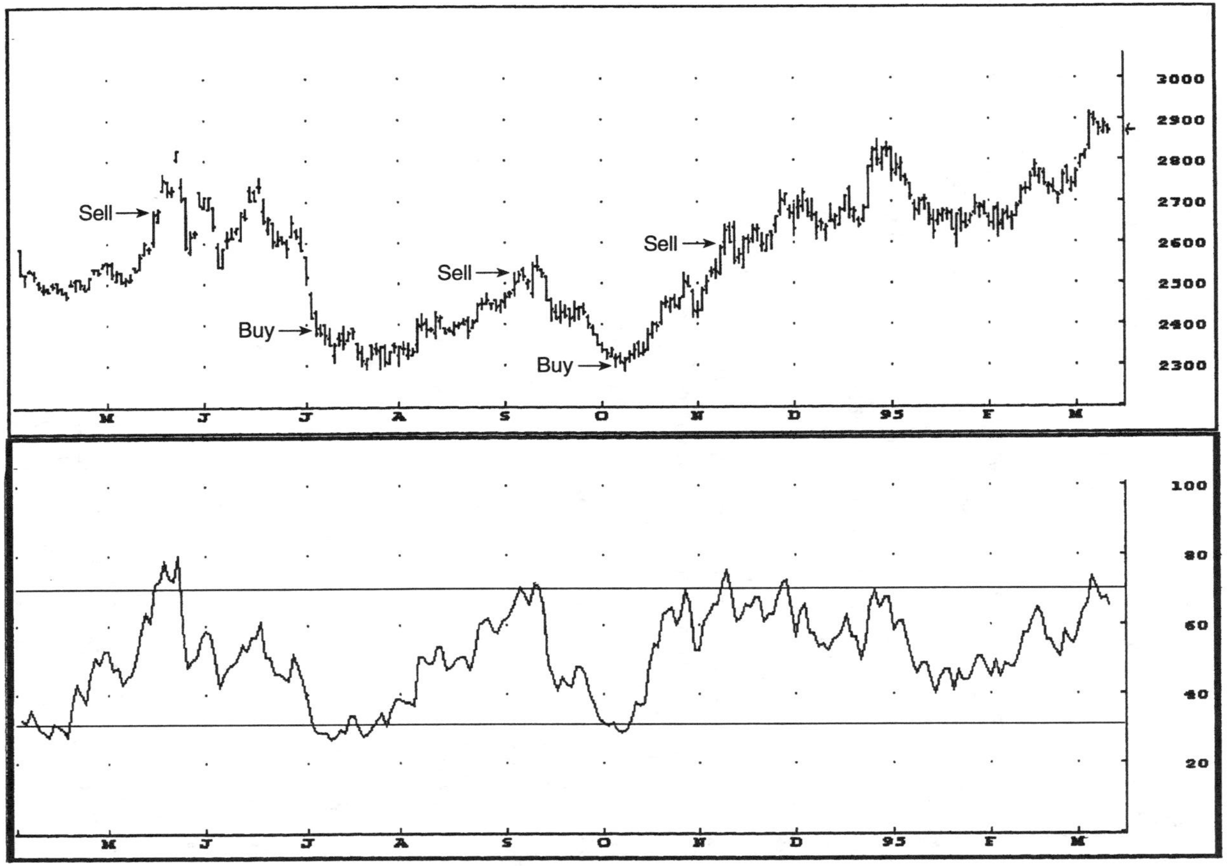

Source: FutureSource; copyright © 1986–1995; all rights reserved.

The buy arrows in Figure 10.10 denote points at which the RSI crosses below 30—that is, reaches an oversold condition that can be viewed as a signal to liquidate short positions. The sell arrows in Figure 10.10 denote points at which the RSI crosses above 70—that is, reaches an overbought condition that can be viewed as a signal to liquidate long positions.

On balance, the overbought/oversold signals in Figure 10.10 provide reasonably good position liquidation signals. The first overbought signal and the first oversold signal come somewhat early, but still occur within the upper and lower quartiles of their respective price swings. The next pair of overbought/oversold signals is particularly timely, especially the oversold signal, which hits the exact low. The final signal, however, is terrible: the oversold signal on November 8, 1994 comes seven weeks and more than 250 points early. This example hints at both the attributes and drawbacks of using overbought/oversold indicators as liquidation signals. The approach will usually work well when the market is in a trading range, but will fail miserably during strong trending phases.

In Figure 10.10, the overbought/oversold signals worked on balance because the illustrated market remained predominantly in a trading range pattern. Figure 10.11 illustrates the application of RSI overbought/oversold signals in a market dominated by a trending phase. The initial oversold signal in Figure 10.11 is perfect, catching the exact low. The first overbought signal is also timely, coming quite close to the subsequent relative high, albeit the ensuing pullback is moderate. The next two signals, however, which are both overbought ones, come drastically early in terms of both time and price movement.

The derivation, interpretation, and application of overbought/oversold indicators are discussed in detail in Chapter 15.

DEMARK SEQUENTIAL

All the popular overbought/oversold indicators (e.g., RSI, MACD, stochastic) are very highly correlated with each other. Tom DeMark's sequential, which is intended to signal points where the market is fully extended and vulnerable to a major trend reversal, represents a completely different and original overbought/oversold indicator. The sequential methodology falls within the domain of pattern recognition. The sequential is fully described in a 48-page chapter in Tom DeMark's book.[2] The following brief summary of the technique is intended to give the reader a general sense of the approach. Readers interested in a fully detailed explanation of sequential, which includes several additional qualifying conditions and a discussion of various alternative trade entry and exit rules, are referred to DeMark's text.

---

[2] *The New Science of Technical Analysis.* New York: John Wiley & Sons, 1994.

Figure 10.11
RELATIVE STRENGTH INDEX IN TRENDING MARKET: MARCH 1995 SUGAR

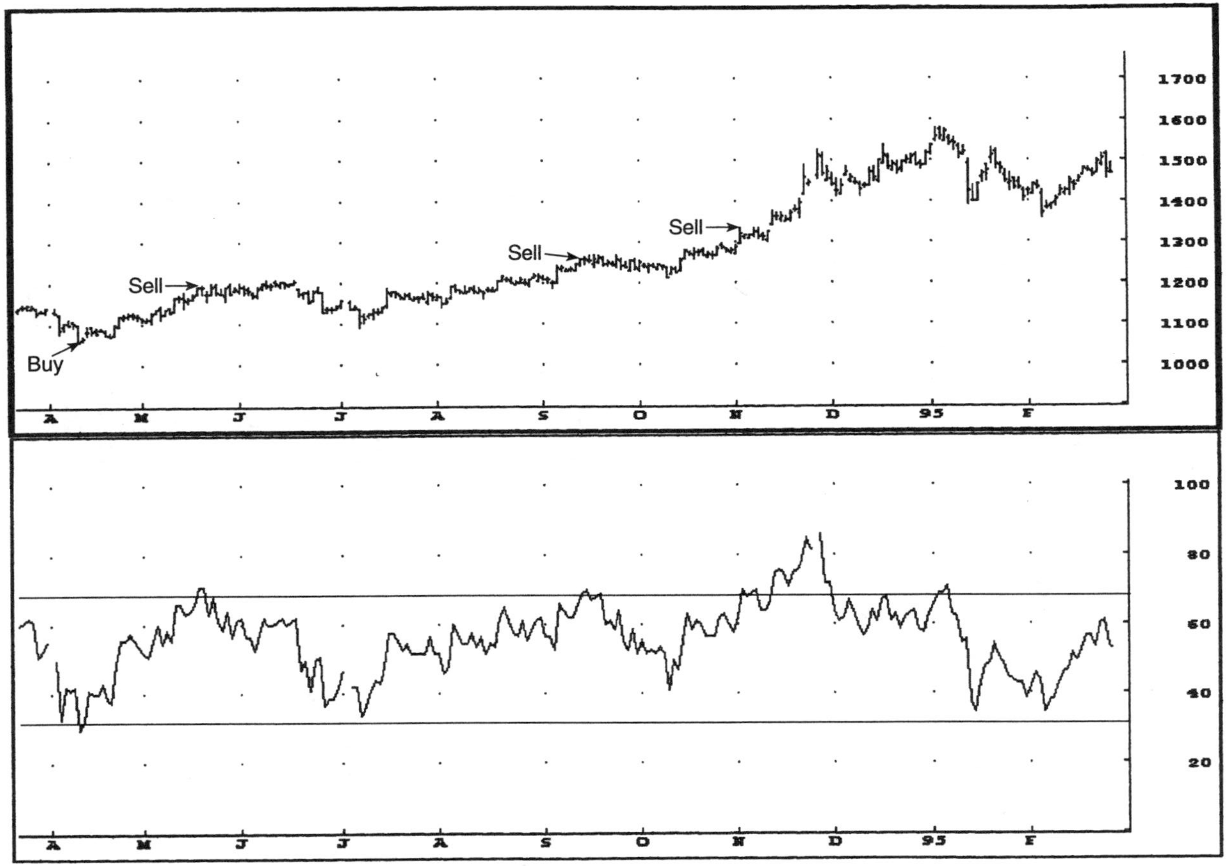

Source: FutureSource; copyright © 1986–1995; all rights reserved.

The fulfillment of the sequential *buy* conditions involves three basic stages:

1. **Setup.** The setup requires nine or more consecutive closes that are lower than the corresponding closes four trading days earlier.
2. **Intersection.** This condition requires that the high of any day on or after the eighth day of the setup exceed the low of any day three or more trading days earlier. Essentially, this is a minimal qualifying condition that assures that the buy setup will not be deemed complete in a "waterfall" price slide.
3. **Countdown.** The countdown stage begins once the previous two conditions have been fulfilled. Starting from 0, the countdown increases by one on each day with a close lower than the low two days earlier. A sequential buy signal is generated once the countdown reaches 13. It should be stressed that in contrast to the setup stage, countdown days do not need to be consecutive. The countdown is canceled if any of the following three conditions arise:
   a. There is a close that exceeds the highest intraday high during the setup stage.
   b. A *sell* setup occurs (that is, nine consecutive closes above the corresponding closes four days earlier).
   c. Another buy setup occurs before the buy countdown is complete. In this situation, the new buy setup takes precedence, and the countdown restarts from 0 once the intersection condition is met.

The fulfillment of the sequential *sell* conditions are analogous:

1. **Setup.** The setup requires nine or more consecutive closes that are higher than the corresponding closes four trading day earlier.
2. **Intersection.** This condition requires that the low of any day on or after the eighth day of the setup is lower than the high of any day three or more trading days earlier. Essentially, this is a minimal qualifying condition that assures that the buy setup will not be deemed complete in a "runaway" rally.
3. **Countdown.** The countdown stage begins once the previous two conditions have been fulfilled. Starting from 0, the countdown increases by one on each day with a close higher than the high two days earlier. A sequential sell signal is generated once the countdown reaches 13. It should be stressed that in contrast to the setup stage, countdown days do not need to be consecutive. The countdown is canceled if any of the following three conditions arise:
   a. There is a close that is below the lowest intraday low during the setup stage.
   b. A *buy* setup occurs (that is, nine consecutive closes below the corresponding closes four days earlier).

c. Another sell setup occurs before the sell countdown is complete. In this situation, the new sell setup takes precedence, and the countdown restarts from 0 once the intersection condition is met.

Figures 10.12–10.16 provide illustrations of markets that fulfilled the complete sequential process. In each case, the setup, intersection, and countdown stages have been marked on the charts. The preceding description will be clearer if read in conjunction with an examination of these charts.

Figure 10.12 provides an illustration of a sequential buy in the December 1994 T-bond market. Note that in this case, the ninth day of the setup stage also fulfilled the countdown condition (close below low two days earlier) and hence also represented day one of the countdown stage. (The intersection condition was fulfilled on day eight of the setup.) The sequential buy conditions were fulfilled in their entirety within four days of the lowest close and at a price very near this close.

Figure 10.13, which depicts the March 1995 cocoa contract, provides another example of a sequential buy. In this case, however, the first day of the countdown does not occur until two days after the setup is complete. Also note the wide gap between day one and day two of the countdown and the fact that the market retraced the entire decline of the countdown stage before resuming its downtrend. (In fact, the first condition for canceling the countdown was almost invoked, but the high close of the rebound just missed closing above the highest intraday high during the setup stage.) In this illustration the sequential rules provide a perfect signal since the countdown stage is completed at the exact low close.

Figure 10.14 provides another example of a sequential buy as it occurred in the January 1994 FCOJ (frozen concentrated orange juice) contract. Note that in this case the setup for the sequential buy follows a completed setup for a sequential sell—one in which the countdown never got off the ground. Here too, the sequential sequence is completed at the precise low close, which in this case also happens to be the day with the lowest low.

Figure 10.15, which depicts the March 1995 dollar index contract, provides an illustration of a sequential sell. Note that the first day of the countdown occurs on the ninth day of the setup. The sequential sell sequence is completed just one day after the high close (as well as high day).

The sequential rules can also be applied to bar charts for time periods other than daily. In Figure 10.16, a sequential buy is illustrated for a monthly nearest futures bar chart in the gold market. The sequential conditions are fulfilled three time periods (i.e., three months) before the lowest monthly close in the five-year decline and at a price only slightly above the low close.

The preceding examples were obviously selected with hindsight to illustrate the methodology. Of course, in real-life trading, the accuracy of the DeMark Sequential will not approach the uniformly near-perfect signals provided by the previous set of examples. If it did, all anyone would need to do

Figure 10.12
DEMARK SEQUENTIAL: DECEMBER 1994 T-BOND

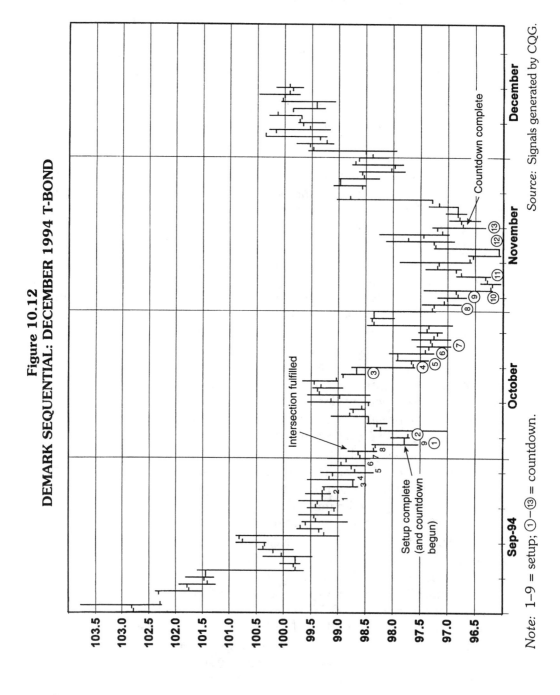

Source: Signals generated by CQG.

Note: 1–9 = setup; ①–⑬ = countdown.

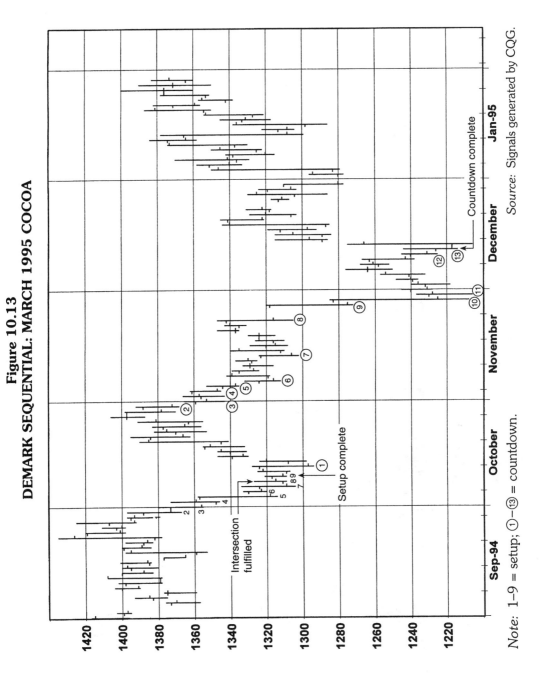

Figure 10.13
DEMARK SEQUENTIAL: MARCH 1995 COCOA

Source: Signals generated by CQG.

Note: 1–9 = setup; ①–⑬ = countdown.

183

Figure 10.14
DEMARK SEQUENTIAL: JANUARY 1994 FCOJ

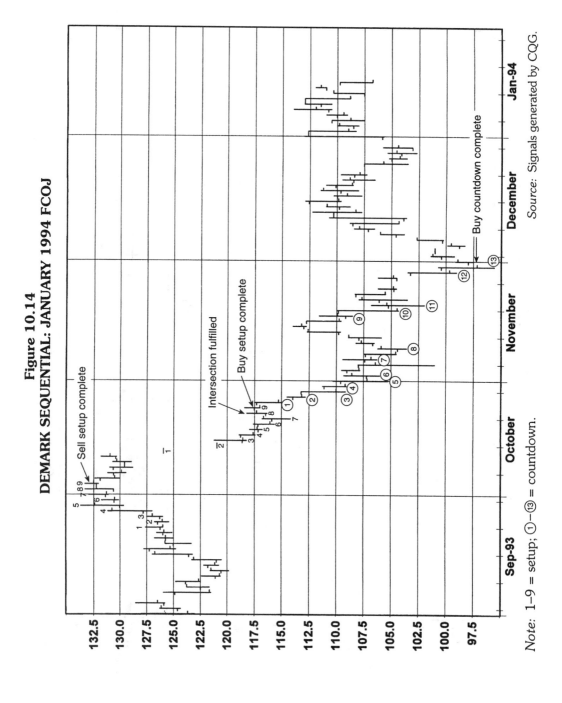

Source: Signals generated by CQG.

Note: 1–9 = setup; ①–⑬ = countdown.

184

Figure 10.15
DEMARK SEQUENTIAL: MARCH 1995 DOLLAR INDEX

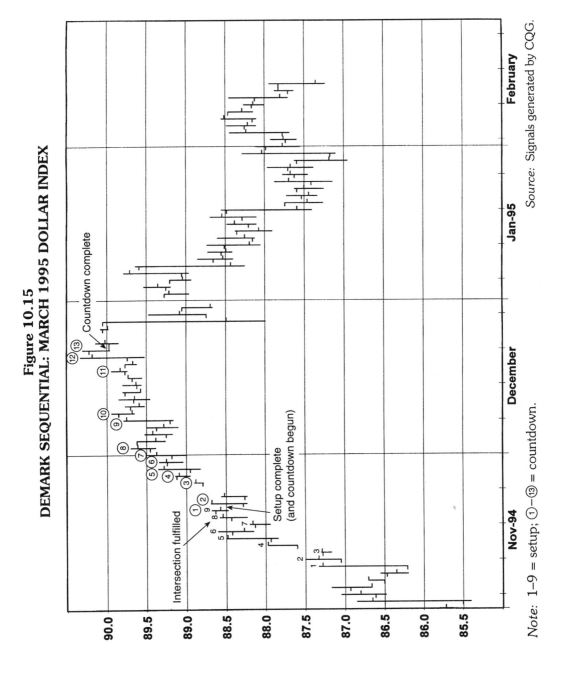

Source: Signals generated by CQG.

Note: 1–9 = setup; ①–⑬ = countdown.

Figure 10.16
DEMARK SEQUENTIAL: GOLD MONTHLY NEAREST FUTURES

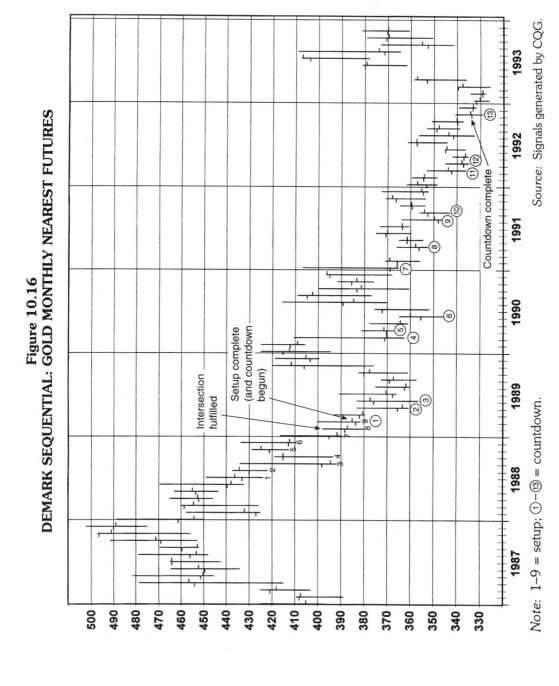

Note: 1–9 = setup; ①–⑬ = countdown.

Source: Signals generated by CQG.

would be to trade all sequential signals and retire a multimillionaire. Nevertheless, these examples should demonstrate that the sequential can be a very powerful tool, with the capability of providing extraordinary timing signals. The sequential also has the advantage of being inversely correlated to trend-following approaches that typically dominate the technical tool bag. For these reasons, many traders might find the DeMark Sequential a very useful addition to their overall trading methodology.

CONTRARY OPINION

The theory of contrary opinion suggests that whenever a large majority of speculators are bullish, those who want to be long are already long. Consequently, there will be a paucity of potential new buyers, and the market will be vulnerable to a downside reaction. An analogous interpretation would apply when the majority of traders are bearish. Contrary opinion measures are either based on surverys of recommendations contained in market letters or on trader surveys, and implicitly assume that these opinions represent a reasonable proxy for overall market sentiment. The overbought and oversold thresholds in contrary opinion indexes will vary with the source.

Although contrary opinion is undoubtedly a sound theoretical concept, the Achilles' heel of this approach is the difficulty of measuring market sentiment accurately. Contrary opinion measures provided by existing services have frequently signaled major turning points. On the other hand, it is also not unusual for a contrary opinion index to stay high while the market continues to climb, or to stay low as the market continues to slide. On balance, this method provides useful information as long as it is not used as the sole trading guideline.

TRAILING STOPS

The use of trailing stops may be among the least glamorous, but most sensible, methods of determining a trade exit point. Although one will never sell the high or buy the low using this method, the approach comes closest to the ideal of permitting a profitable trade to run its course. Trailing stops were detailed in Chapter 9.

CHANGE OF MARKET OPINION

This is another approach with very little flash, but lots of common sense. In this case, the trader sets no predetermined objectives at all, but rather maintains the position until her market opinion changes to at least neutral.

11 The Most Important Rule in Chart Analysis

The market is like a flu virus—as soon as you think you have it pegged, it mutates into something else.

—Wayne H. Wagner

FAILED SIGNALS

A failed signal is among the most reliable of all chart signals. When a market fails to follow through in the direction of a chart signal, it very strongly suggests the possibility of a significant move in the opposite direction. For example, in Figure 11.1 note how the market abruptly reversed course after breaking out above the early-April high and the late-April–early-May consolidation. If the upside penetration signal were valid, the market should not have retreated back to the lower portion of the consolidation and certainly not below its lower boundary. The fact that such a retracement occurs almost immediately following the breakout strongly suggests a "bull trap." Such price action is consistent with the market's rising just enough to activate stop orders lying beyond the boundary of the range, but uncovering no additional buying support after the breakout—an indication of a very weak underlying technical picture. In effect, the immediate failure of the apparent buy signal can be viewed as a strong indication that the market should be sold.

Now that we have established the critical importance of failed signals, the following sections, detail various types of failed signals, along with guidelines as to their interpretation and trading implications.

BULL AND BEAR TRAPS

Bull and bear traps are major breakouts that are soon followed by abrupt, sharp price reversals, in stark contrast to the price continuation patterns that are expected to follow breakouts. In my experience, this type of counter-to-

Figure 11.1
BULL TRAP: OCTOBER 1993 SUGAR

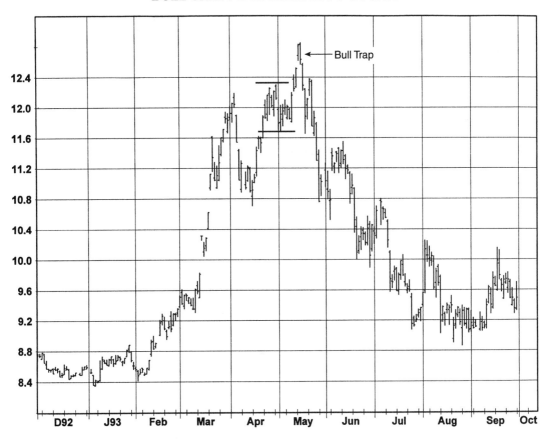

anticipated price action is among the most reliable indicators of major tops and bottoms. An example of a bull trap was provided in the previous section (Figure 11.1). Another classic example of a bull trap was the October 1993 peak of a six-year bull market in T-bonds (see Figure 11.2). Note that the mid-October upside breakout to new record highs above the prior seven-week trading range was immediately followed by a steep price break.

Analogous to the bull trap, in the case of a bear trap, the market falls just enough to trigger resting stops below the low end of a trading range, but fails to uncover any additional selling pressure after the breakout—an indication of substantial underlying strength. In effect, the immediate failure of a sell signal can be viewed as a signal that the market should be bought.

Figure 11.3, which depicts the culmination of a six-year downtrend in the silver market, provides a classic example of a bear trap. In February 1993 the market witnessed a sharp two-day plunge below both the prior very narrow

Figure 11.2
BULL TRAP: JUNE 1994 T-BOND

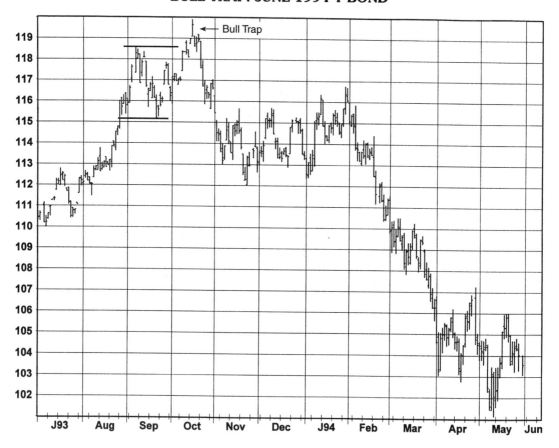

three-month trading range and a broader six-month trading range. Instead of continuing lower, prices held in midair, initially moving sideways and eventually rebounding back into the trading range. This price action proved to be a precursor of a dramatic rally.

Figure 11.4 provides another example of a bear trap. After an extremely steep four-month price slide, in late October 1992 prices fell to a new low for the move, breaking below a trading range formed in the prior month. Prices witnessed no follow-through, however, and within a week had rallied back to the upper half of the prior trading range. The market continued to advance, eventually recapturing nearly the entire July–October decline. (Interestingly, this chart also exhibits a bull-trap top, as the June 1992 peak was formed by a wide upside gap to a new high, which saw absolutely no follow-through and was immediately followed by the aforementioned price slide.)

Figure 11.3
BEAR TRAP: JULY 1993 SILVER

How much of a pullback is required to indicate that a bull or bear trap has occurred? The following are several possible confirmation conditions:

Initial Price Confirmation. A price retracement to the median of the consolidation that preceded the breakout.

Strong Price Confirmation. A price retracement to the more distant boundary (lower for bull trap; upper for bear trap) of the consolidation that preceded the breakout.

Time Confirmation. The failure of the market to return to the extreme price witnessed following the breakout within a specified amount of time (e.g., 4 weeks).

The tradeoff between initial and strong price confirmations is that the former will provide better entry levels in trading bull and bear traps, whereas the latter

Figure 11.4
BEAR TRAP AND BULL TRAP: MARCH 1993 COTTON

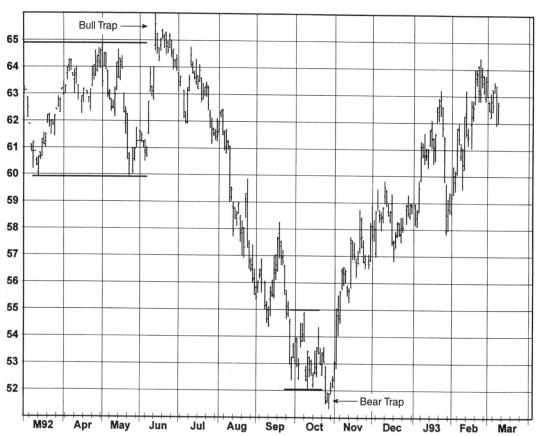

will provide more reliable signals. The time confirmation condition can be used on its own or in conjunction with the two price confirmation conditions. Figures 11.5 and 11.6 repeat Figures 11.2 and 11.3 adding each of the three confirmation conditions (the time confirmation condition is assumed to be four weeks). Note that the time confirmation can occur after both price confirmation conditions (as is the case in Figure 11.5), or before both price confirmation conditions (as is the case in Figure 11.6), or any point between.

A bull-trap signal would be invalidated if the market returned to the breakout high. Similarly, a bear-trap signal would be invalidated if the market returned to the breakout low. More sensitive conditions could be used to invalidate bull- or bear-trap signals once the market has moved sufficiently in the direction of the signal or a specified amount of time has elapsed. An example of such a condition would be the return of prices to the opposite boundary of a consolidation once a strong price confirmation signal was received (e.g., in the case of a bull trap, a

Figure 11.5
BULL TRAP CONFIRMATION CONDITIONS: JUNE 1994 T-BOND

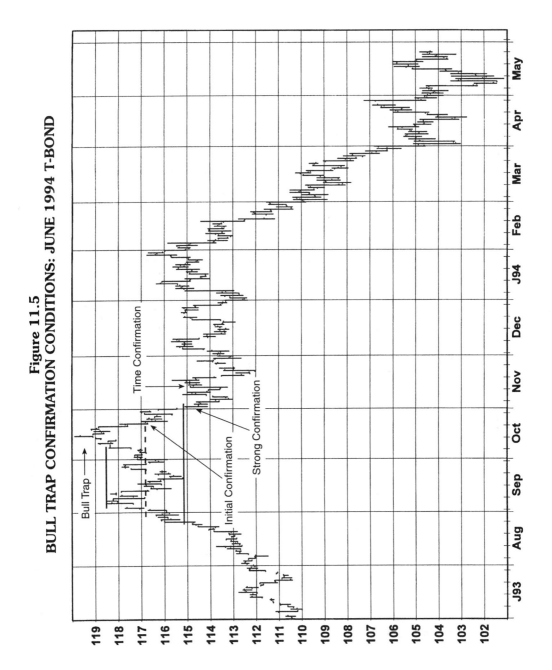

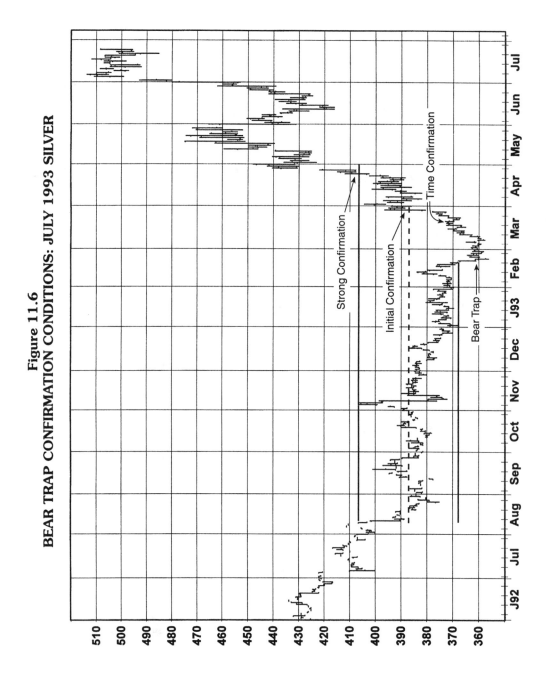

Figure 11.6
BEAR TRAP CONFIRMATION CONDITIONS: JULY 1993 SILVER

194

return to the top of the consolidation after prices broke to below the low end of the consolidation). An example of a more sensitive combined price/time invalidation signal would be the return of prices to the median of a consolidation (i.e., the initial *price* confirmation point for bull- and bear-trap signals) any time four or more weeks after a strong price confirmation was received. The more sensitive the selected invalidation condition, the smaller the loss on an incorrect call of a bull or bear trap, but the greater the chance that a correct trade will be abandoned prematurely.

If the selected invalidation condition does not occur, a trade implemented on a bull- or bear-trap signal would be held until a price objective or other trade liquidation condition was met or until there was evidence of an opposite direction trend reversal.

FALSE TREND-LINE BREAKOUTS

As was discussed in Chapter 3, trend lines are particularly prone to false breakouts. Such false breakouts can be used as signals for trading in the direction opposite to the breakout. In fact, in my opinion, false trend breakout signals are considerably more reliable than conventional trend breakout signals. In the case of a downtrend, a false trend breakout would be confirmed if the market witnessed a specified number of closes (e.g., two, three) below the trend line following an upside breakout. Similarly, in the case of an uptrend, a false trend breakout would be confirmed if the market witnessed a specified number of closes above the trend line following a downside breakout.

Figure 11.7 provides an example of a false breakout of a downtrend line. Note that the June upside breakout of the downtrend line defined by three prior relative highs was soon followed by a break below the line. The indicated failure signal is based on an assumed requirement of two closes below the line for confirmation.

It is quite possible for a chart to yield several successive false trend breakout signals in the process of the trend line being repeatedly redefined. In Figure 11.8 the initial upside penetration of the prevailing downtrend line occurred in mid-December. Prices quickly retreated back below the line, with the indicated failure signal assumed to be triggered by the second close below the line. Another false breakout occurred several weeks later, based on the redefined trend line using the December relative high (trend line II). Once again prices quickly retreated below the downtrend line, yielding another false trend breakout signal. The redrawn trend line incorporating the January relative high (trend line III) was briefly penetrated on the upside in March, leading to a third false trend breakout.

Figure 11.9 illustrates false trend breakouts in the case of an uptrend line. Here too, failure signals are assumed to be confirmed following the second

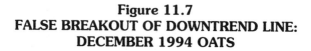

Figure 11.7
FALSE BREAKOUT OF DOWNTREND LINE:
DECEMBER 1994 OATS

close beyond the trend line in the direction of the original trend. Two such false trend breakout buy signals are shown.

FILLED GAPS

As was detailed in Chapter 6, gaps are normally considered patterns that presage a continuation of the trend in the direction of the gap. When a gap is filled, such a development qualifies the original gap as a failed signal. The significance of filled gaps is enhanced if the following additional characteristics apply:

- The filled gap is particularly wide
- The filled gap is a breakaway gap
- Two or more consecutive gaps are filled

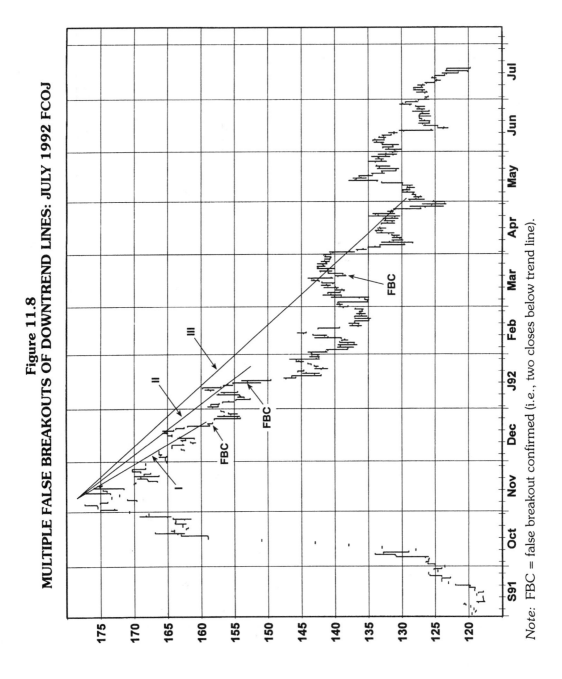

Figure 11.8
MULTIPLE FALSE BREAKOUTS OF DOWNTREND LINES: JULY 1992 FCOJ

Note: FBC = false breakout confirmed (i.e., two closes below trend line).

197

Figure 11.9
MULTIPLE FALSE BREAKOUTS OF UPTREND LINE: JULY 1995 SUGAR

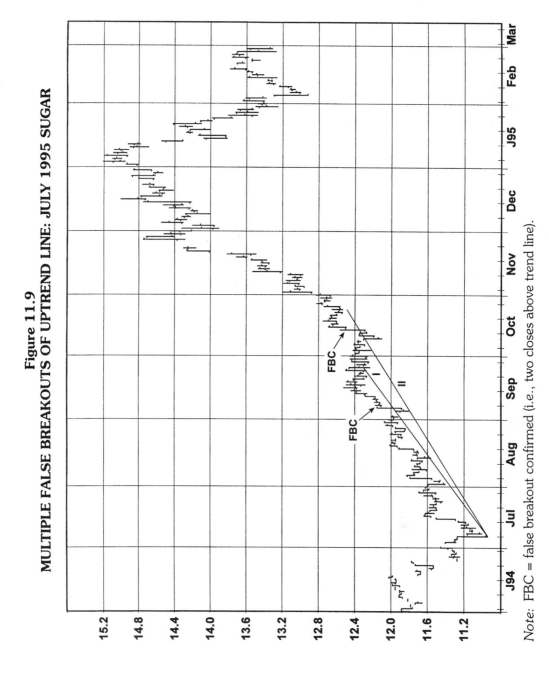

Note: FBC = false breakout confirmed (i.e., two closes above trend line).

Although typically a gap is considered filled if the intraday price reaches the high (low, in the case of a downside gap) on the day prior to the gap, I prefer a more rigid definition requiring a close below (above, in the case of a downside gap) the close on the day prior to the gap day. This more restrictive definition will reduce the number of times a prior gap is interpreted as a failed signal when such a conclusion ultimately proves unwarranted, at the expense of signaling such an event slightly later in cases where it is the correct call.

In Figure 11.10 a breakaway upside gap is filled about one week later. Interestingly, the gap is filled on a wide-ranging day, which is itself a signal that a downside reversal may have occurred. These patterns presaged an extended price slide in sugar futures. In Figure 11.11 an upside gap that formed one day before the extreme high of the bull market was filled two days later, providing a very early signal of what proved to be a major trend reversal. In Figure 11.12 a breakaway gap formed on the precise high day of a near-vertical rally. This gap was filled (using our more restrictive definition) only two days later, providing an early warning signal of an abrupt trend reversal, which would have retraced a substantial portion of the prior advance before it would have been recognized by more conventional trend-identification methods.

Figures 11.13–11.15 provide examples of downside filled gaps as failed signals. In Figure 11.13 a wide downside gap to a new low is filled only two days later (one day after the low), providing an extremely early signal of what ultimately proved to be a very major trend reversal. (Another instance of a downside gap being filled occurred just under three months later.) In Figure 11.14 the day that fills the gap is itself a wide-ranging day, in effect providing a strong dual signal in a single trading session. As can be seen, this combined signal was immediately followed by a steep rally.

Figure 11.15 provides an example of two consecutive downside gaps being filled. Although this price action accurately signaled that a major bottom had been established, note that prices first retreated before beginning a sustained advance. The implied lesson is that even valid indications of a failed signal may first witness a price correction before the anticipated price move materializes. In the case of downside gaps, the failed signal can be considered to remain in force as long as prices do not close below the gap, or lowest gap if there is more than one. (Similarly, in the case of upside gaps, the failed signal can be considered to remain in force as long as prices do not close above the gap, or highest gap if there is more than one.)

RETURN TO SPIKE EXTREMES

As was detailed in Chapter 6, price spikes frequently occur at important price reversals. Consequently, the return of prices to a prior spike extreme can be viewed as transforming the original spike into a failed signal. The more extreme

Figure 11.10
FILLED UPSIDE GAP: MARCH 1991 SUGAR

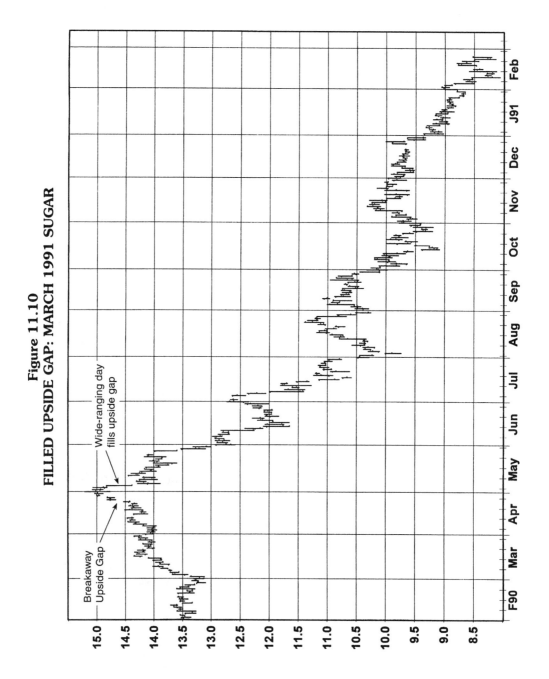

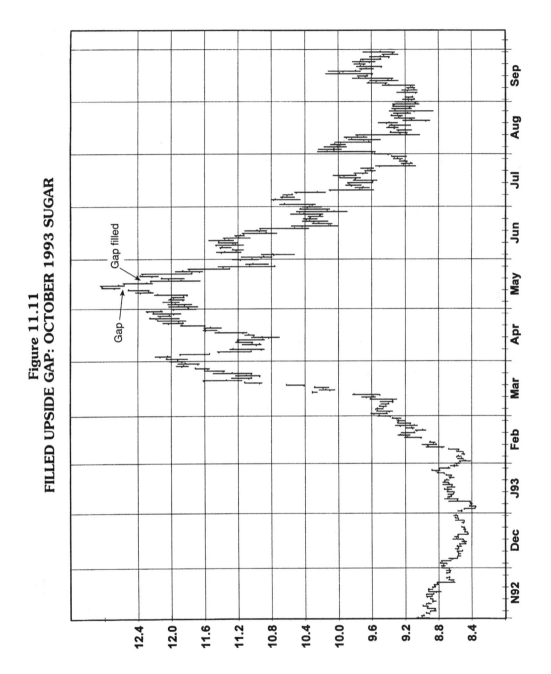

Figure 11.11
FILLED UPSIDE GAP: OCTOBER 1993 SUGAR

Figure 11.12
FILLED UPSIDE GAP: DECEMBER 1993 MEAL

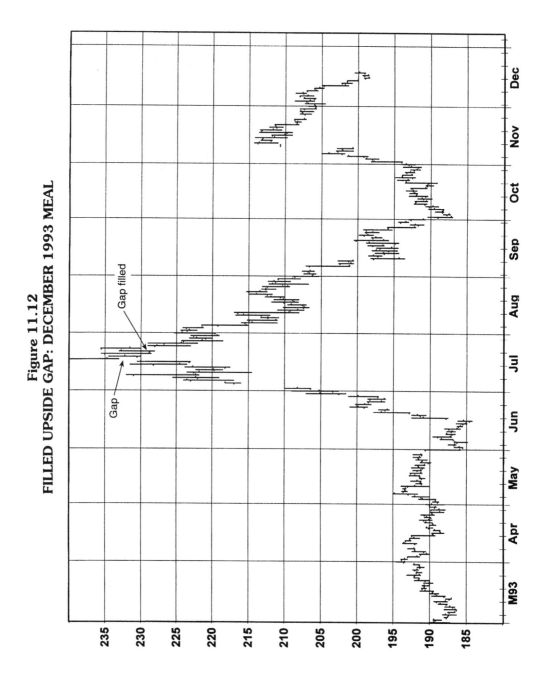

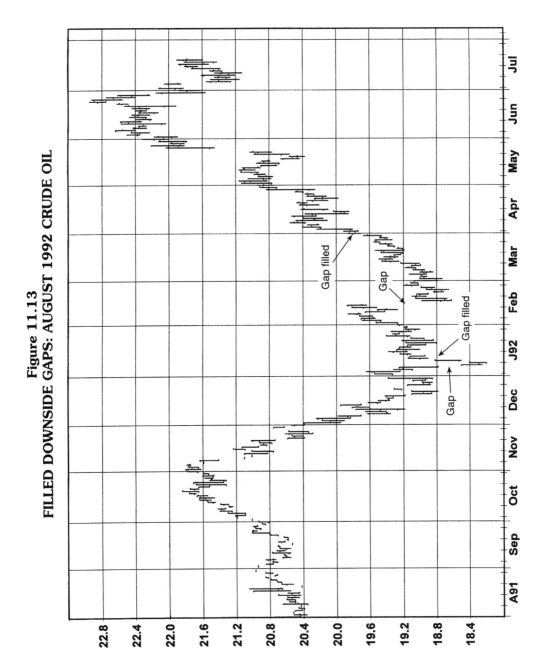

Figure 11.13
FILLED DOWNSIDE GAPS: AUGUST 1992 CRUDE OIL

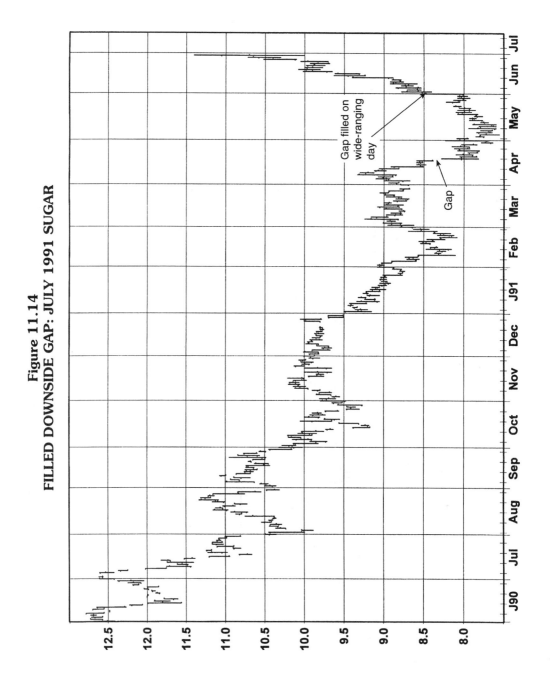

Figure 11.14
FILLED DOWNSIDE GAP: JULY 1991 SUGAR

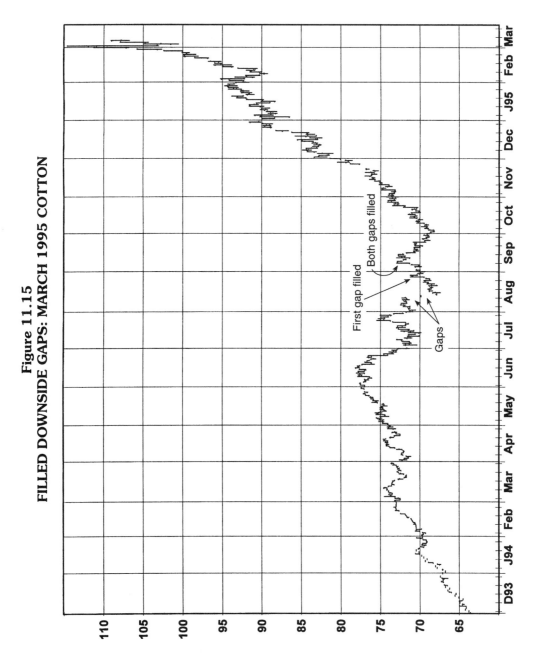

Figure 11.15
FILLED DOWNSIDE GAPS: MARCH 1995 COTTON

the spike (i.e., the greater the magnitude by which the spike high exceeds the highs on the prior and subsequent days or the spike low falls below the lows on the prior and subsequent days), the greater the significance of its penetration. The significance of such failed signals is also enhanced if at least several weeks, and preferably several months, have elapsed since the original spike.

In Figure 11.16 the return to the July spike high four months later led to a substantial extension on the upside. In Figure 11.17 the penetration of the July spike high nearly seven months later also led to a further large advance. Figure 11.18 provides an example of the penetration of a downside gap, with prices sliding sharply following this event. Figure 11.19 contains examples of both the penetration of a major spike high and a major spike low. In each case, the market subsequently witnessed a dramatic price extension.

In Figure 11.20 the penetration of the July spike high a little over a month later leads to the anticipated further advance. Note, however, that the penetration of the October spike low several months later proves misleading—a *failed* failed signal so to speak. Generally speaking, a close beyond the opposite extreme of the spike can be viewed as negating the failed signal. In this case, the market closed above the high of the spike low day four days after the spike was penetrated.

RETURN TO WIDE-RANGING DAY EXTREMES

As was explained in Chapter 6, wide-ranging days with particularly strong or weak closes tend to lead to price extensions in the same direction. Consequently, the close above the high price of a downside wide-ranging day or below the low price of an upside wide-ranging day can be viewed as confirming such days as failed signals.

In Figure 11.21 the very pronounced wide-ranging day formed in late May is penetrated on the upside about two weeks later, leading to an enormous rally. Interestingly, this confirmation of a failed signal occurred the day after an upside wide-ranging day, in effect providing back-to-back signals of a potential trend reversal. In Figure 11.22 two downside wide-ranging days formed in close proximity are each penetrated on the upside in the subsequent period. Moreover, note that an upside wide-ranging day materialized between these two penetrations. This confluence of bullish signals proved to be a precursor of a major rally.

Figures 11.23 and 11.24 provide examples of the downside penetration of upside wide-ranging days. In Figure 11.23 the closing downside penetration of the huge wide-ranging day that formed one day before the top was followed by an enormous price slide. Note that the close below the wide-

Figure 11.16
PENETRATION OF SPIKE HIGH: MARCH 1994 SOYBEAN OIL

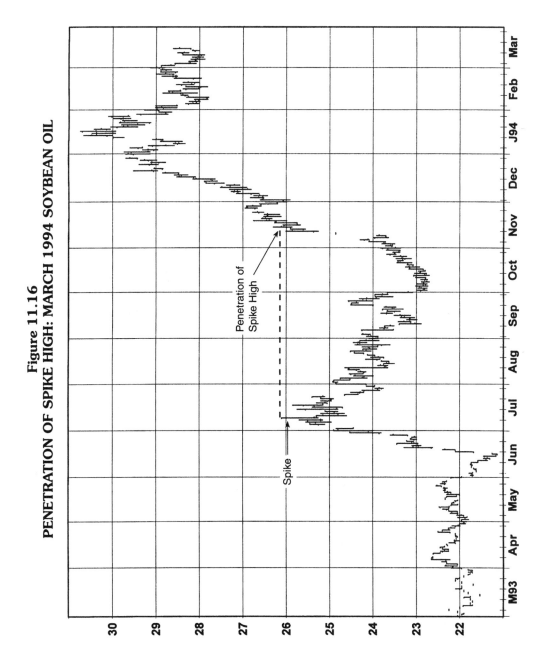

Figure 11.17
PENETRATION OF SPIKE HIGH: JULY 1991 COTTON

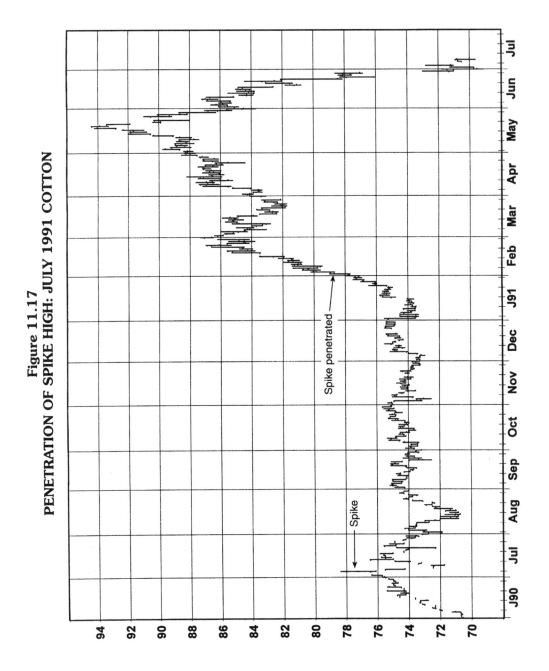

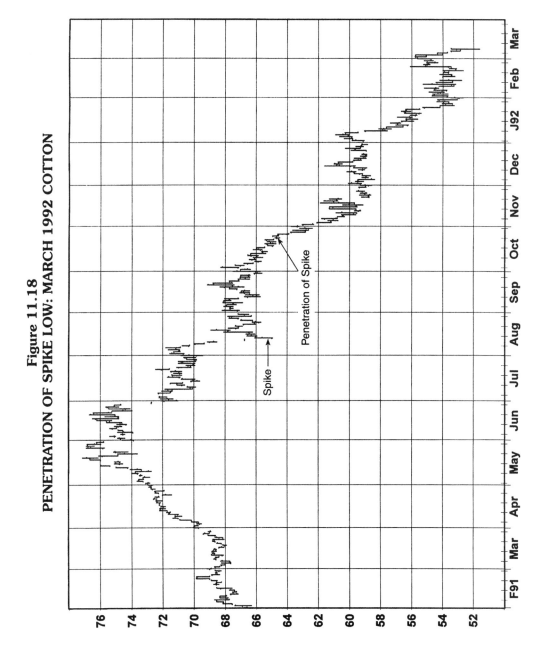

Figure 11.18
PENETRATION OF SPIKE LOW: MARCH 1992 COTTON

209

Figure 11.19
PENETRATION OF SPIKE HIGH AND SPIKE LOW: MARCH 1995 COFFEE

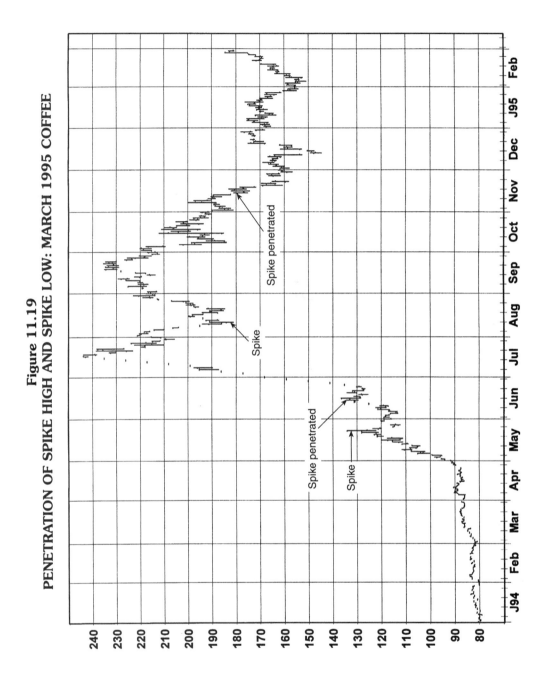

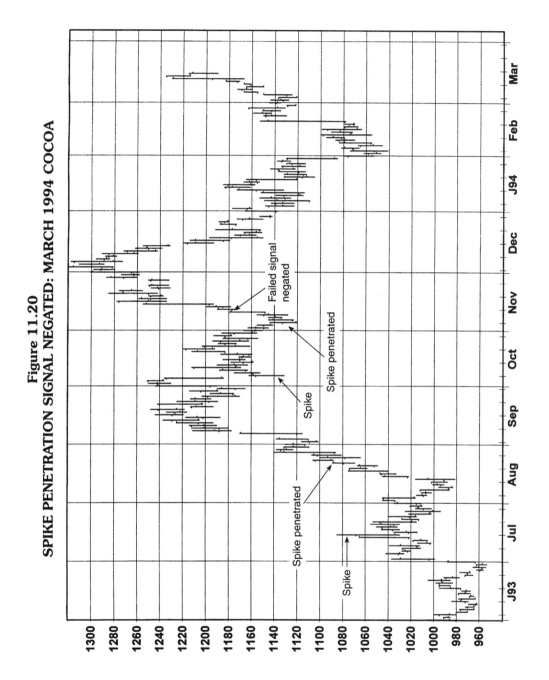

Figure 11.20
SPIKE PENETRATION SIGNAL NEGATED: MARCH 1994 COCOA

211

Figure 11.21
PENETRATION OF DOWNSIDE WIDE-RANGING DAY: NOVEMBER 1993 SOYBEANS

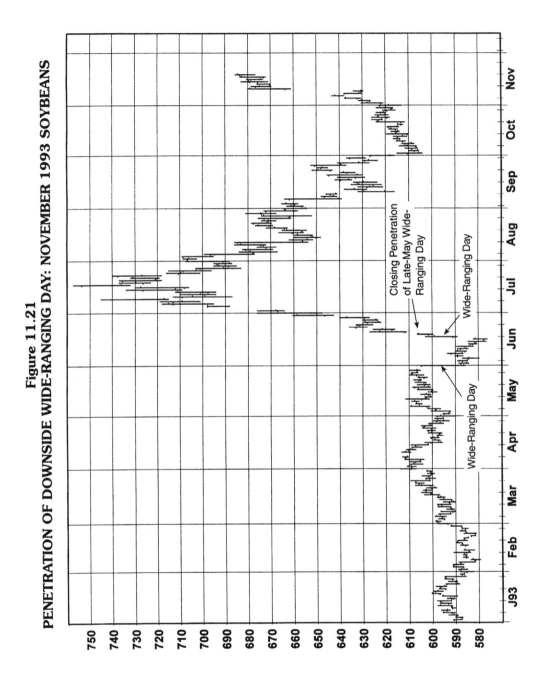

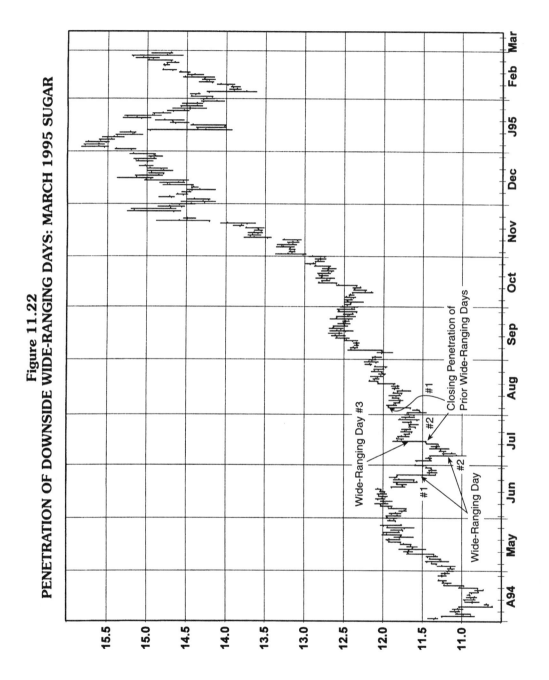

Figure 11.22

PENETRATION OF DOWNSIDE WIDE-RANGING DAYS: MARCH 1995 SUGAR

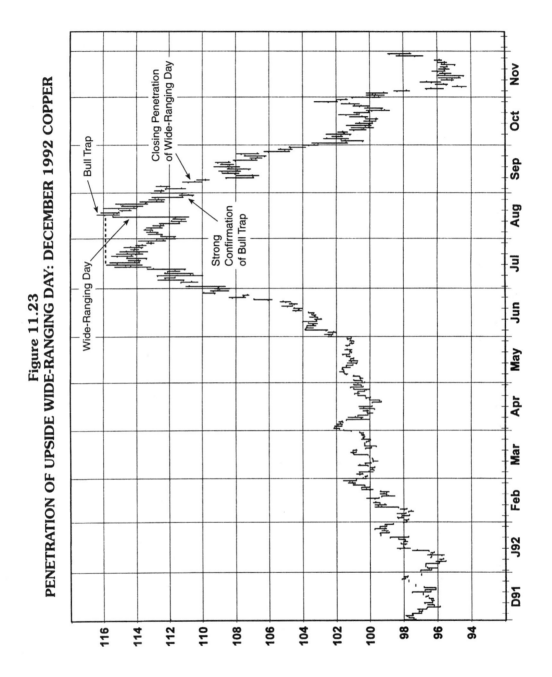

Figure 11.23
PENETRATION OF UPSIDE WIDE-RANGING DAY: DECEMBER 1992 COPPER

214

Figure 11.24
PENETRATION OF UPSIDE WIDE-RANGING DAY: JUNE 1994 EURODOLLAR

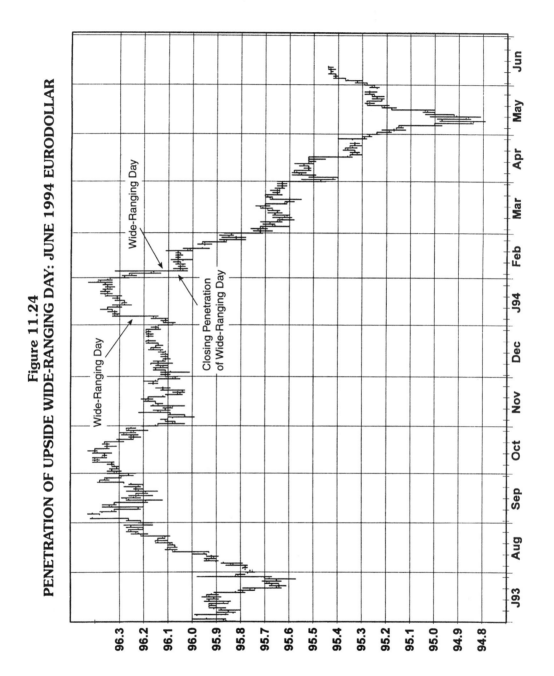

ranging day was preceded by a strong confirmation signal of a bull trap. In Figure 11.24 the closing downside penetration of the early January wide-ranging day was itself a wide-ranging day and proved to be an early signal of an impending massive price decline.

COUNTER-TO-ANTICIPATED BREAKOUT OF FLAG OR PENNANT

As was explained in Chapter 6, typically, flag or pennant consolidations tend to be followed by price swings in the same direction as the price swings that preceded their formation. Therefore, if a flag or pennant formation is followed by a breakout in the opposite direction of the preceding price swing, it would qualify the pattern as a failed signal.

In Figure 11.25, just as would have been implied by the chart interpretation guidelines presented in Chapter 6, the flag and pennant formations that evolved during the illustrated downtrend were generally followed by down-swings. The one exception, however, was the flag that formed following a downside breakout to a new low for the move in March. In this instance, the flag was followed by an upside breakout. This counter-to-anticipated price action augured a significant rebound. In Figure 11.26 note that both the April and October lows were formed by flags that were penetrated by price swings opposite to the expected direction.

Figure 11.27 depicts a major bottom that was established by a flag that was followed by a counter-to-anticipated breakout. In this instance, however, the breakout was itself followed by a pullback before the sharp price advance ensued. The lesson is that the counter-to-anticipated breakout does not need to be followed by an immediate extension of the price move in order to be a valid confirmation of a failed signal. How much of a retracement can be allowed before the interpretation of a failed signal is abandoned? One reasonable approach is to consider the confirmation of a failed signal in force as long as prices do not close beyond the opposite end of the relevant flag or pennant. The retracement in the illustrated example stopped short of such a point.

Figures 11.28–11.30 provide examples of downside breakouts of flags or pennants that formed after price advances. In each of these cases, a flag or pennant formed at or near contract highs—normally, a very bullish development. Instead of leading to renewed advances, however, each of these flags or pennants yielded to a sharp downside breakout. In all three instances, the failed signals implied by the counter-to-anticipated breakouts provided extraordinarily timely indications of major trend reversals. Although prices witnessed immediate, sustained downtrends in Figures 11.28 and 11.29, note that in Figure 11.30, prices first rebounded back to the pennant before plunging. This pullback, however, did not carry above the pennant; therefore according to the

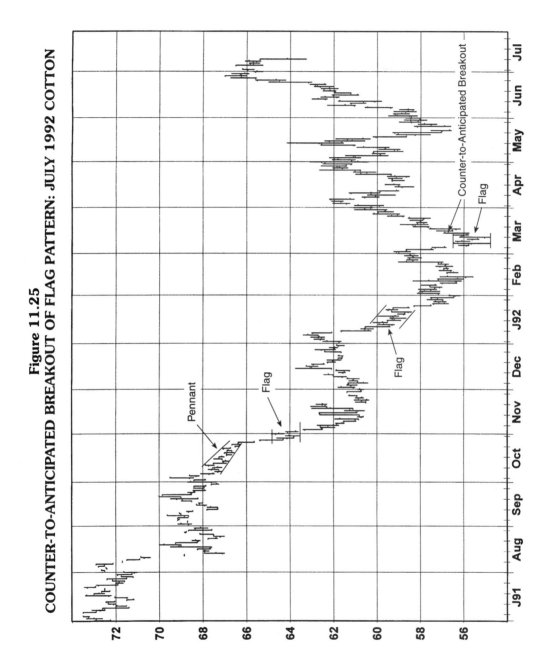

Figure 11.25
COUNTER-TO-ANTICIPATED BREAKOUT OF FLAG PATTERN: JULY 1992 COTTON

Figure 11.26
COUNTER-TO-ANTICIPATED BREAKOUT OF FLAG PATTERNS:
DECEMBER 1994 SOYBEAN OIL

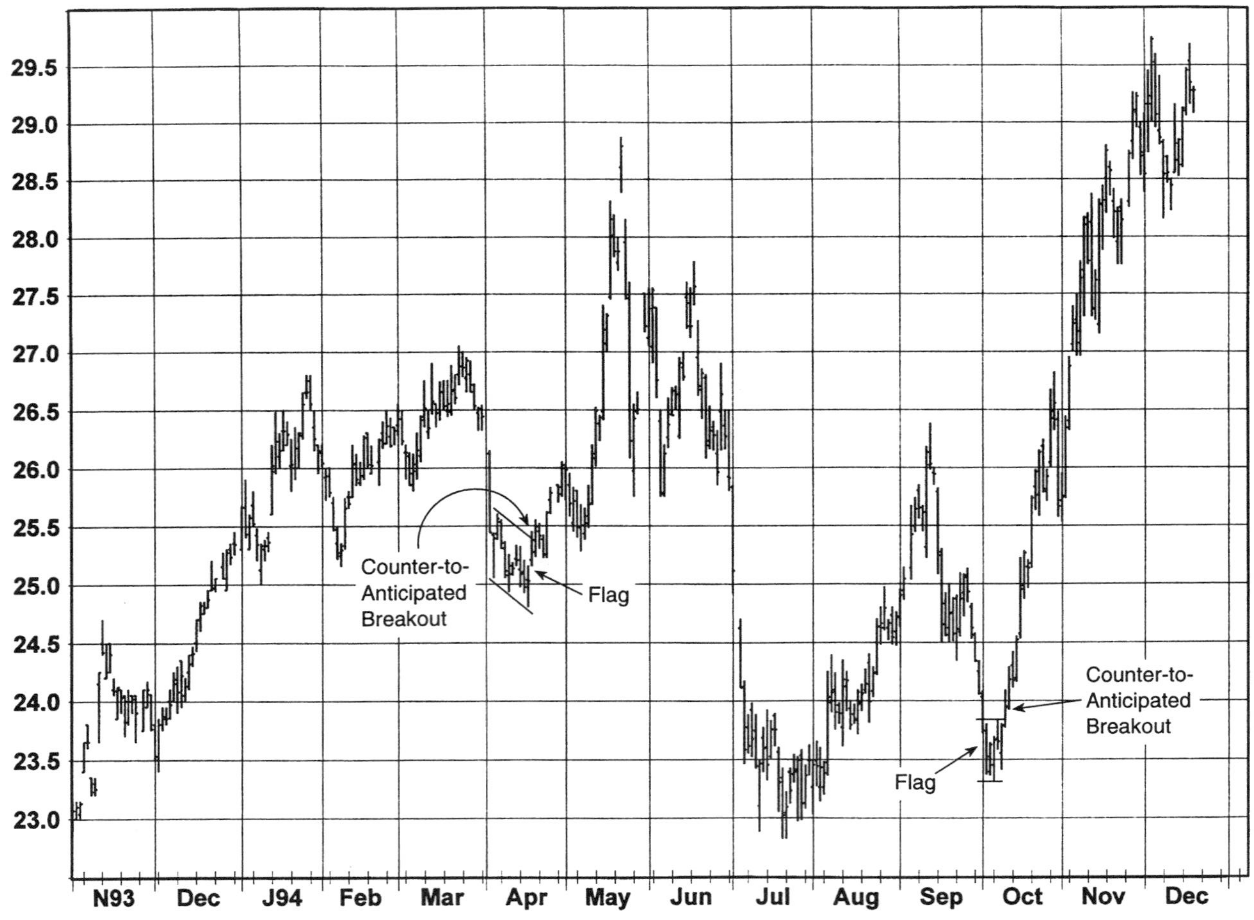

218

Figure 11.27
COUNTER-TO-ANTICIPATED BREAKOUT OF FLAG PATTERN FOLLOWED BY PULLBACK: MARCH 1994 COTTON

Figure 11.28
COUNTER-TO-ANTICIPATED BREAKOUT OF FLAG PATTERN: MARCH 1992 COCOA

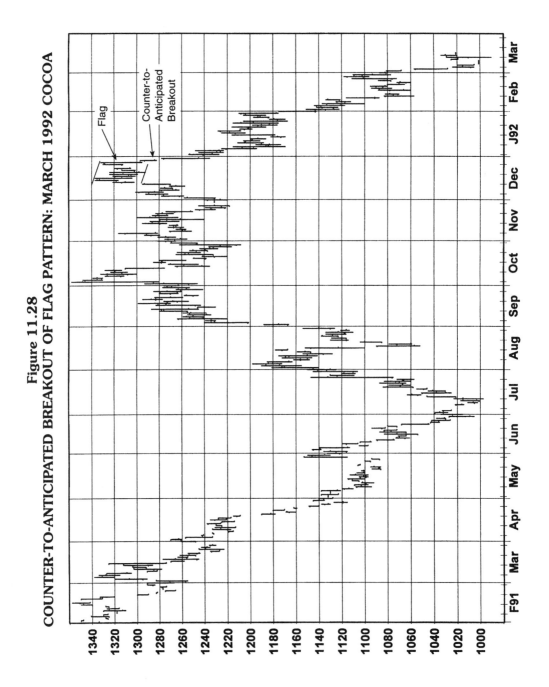

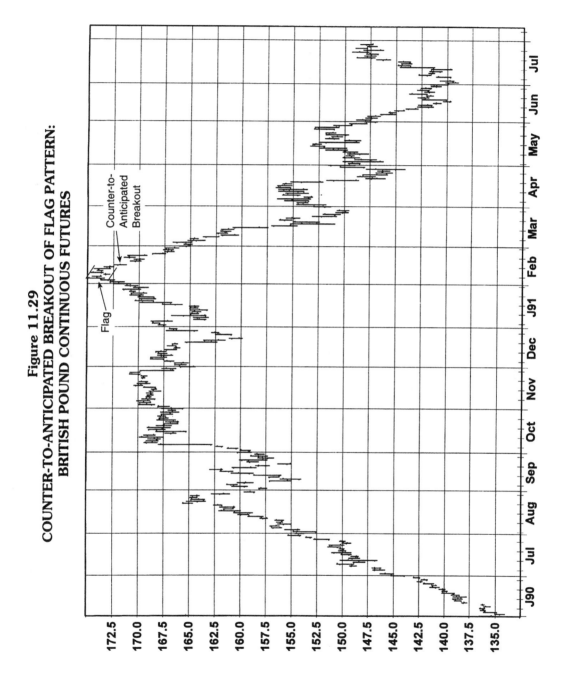

Figure 11.29
COUNTER-TO-ANTICIPATED BREAKOUT OF FLAG PATTERN:
BRITISH POUND CONTINUOUS FUTURES

221

Figure 11.30
COUNTER-TO-ANTICIPATED BREAKOUT OF PENNANT: MARCH 1993 COTTON

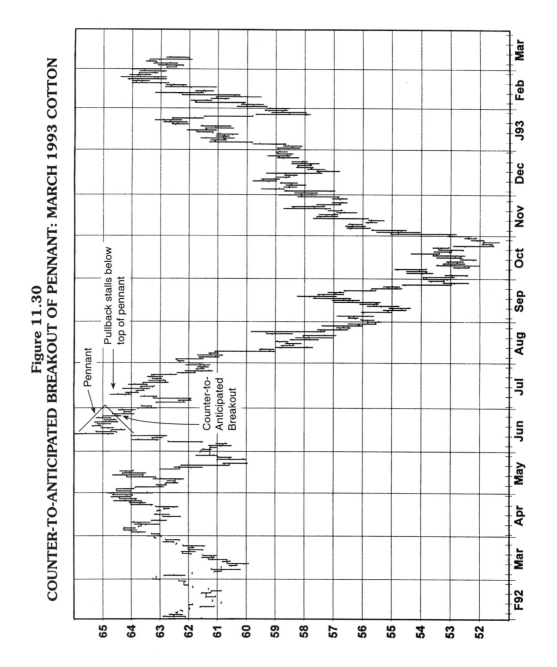

previously provided rule, the implications of the failed signal would still be considered to be in effect.

OPPOSITE DIRECTION BREAKOUT OF FLAG OR PENNANT FOLLOWING A NORMAL BREAKOUT

In some cases, flags and pennants are followed by breakouts in the anticipated direction, but prices then reverse closing beyond the opposite extreme of the flag or pennant. This combined price action provides another example of a failed signal, since the anticipated breakout of the flag or pennant is followed by a price reversal instead of a price follow-through. Note that a *close* beyond the opposite end of the flag or pennant is required to confirm a failed signal, rather than a mere intraday penetration. Although this more restrictive condition will yield slightly less timely confirmations of failed signals in cases when such a conclusion proves valid, it will reduce the number of inaccurate calls of failed signals.

In Figure 11.31 the flag consolidation that formed near the top of a four-month advance was followed by an upside breakout, as might have been anticipated. Instead of witnessing a further sustained advance, however, prices moved higher for only two days and within two weeks had retreated to below the low end of the flag consolidation. This price action qualified the earlier upside breakout above the flag pattern as a failed signal. Figure 11.31 may look familiar. It is the same chart that was presented earlier in this chapter as Figure 11.11, illustrating another failed signal (a filled gap) that occurred in the same time vicinity. Thus the May 1993 peak in sugar was actually marked by two failed signals.

Figure 11.32 provides another illustration of a failed upside penetration of a flag pattern. In this chart, the flag that formed after a huge three-month rally was also followed by an upside breakout and then a retreat below the low end of the flag. In this instance, note that the initial break below the flag was followed by another bounce. This initial penetration below the low end of the flag did not qualify as a confirmation of a failed signal, however, since the market did not close below the flag—a development that did not occur until about a week later.

Figure 11.33 illustrates a failed downside penetration of a pennant that occurred after an extended price slide. This downside breakout led to little further downside movement, and prices soon rebounded back above the top of the pennant, confirming a failed signal and presaging a large advance. Figure 11.34 contains two instances of flags formed after downswings that witnessed initial breakouts in the anticipated direction and fairly immediate rebounds above the top of the patterns. The first such occurrence marked the

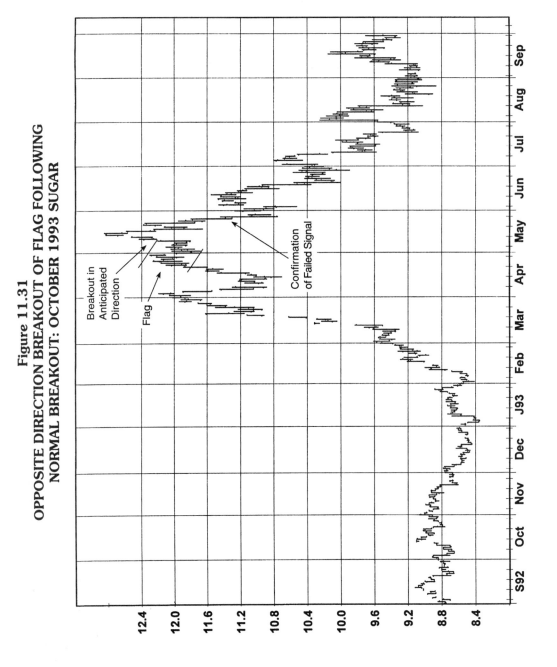

Figure 11.31
OPPOSITE DIRECTION BREAKOUT OF FLAG FOLLOWING
NORMAL BREAKOUT: OCTOBER 1993 SUGAR

224

Figure 11.32
OPPOSITE DIRECTION BREAKOUT OF FLAG FOLLOWING
NORMAL BREAKOUT: JULY 1993 COFFEE

Figure 11.33
OPPOSITE DIRECTION BREAKOUT OF PENNANT FOLLOWING
NORMAL BREAKOUT: DECEMBER 1992 COFFEE

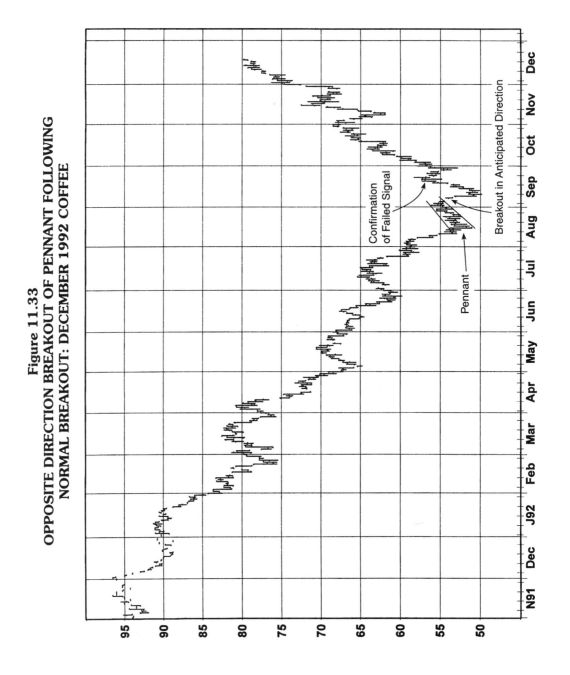

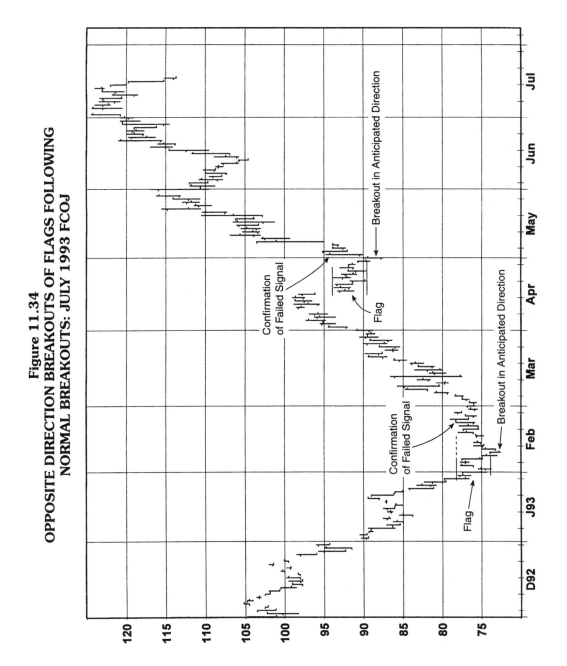

Figure 11.34
OPPOSITE DIRECTION BREAKOUTS OF FLAGS FOLLOWING
NORMAL BREAKOUTS: JULY 1993 FCOJ

major bottom and the second an important relative low. Figure 11.35 provides another example in which a rebound above the top of a flag after an initial downside breakout confirmed a relative low that led to a large advance. Note that this chart also contains an example of a failed signal based on a counter-to-anticipated breakout from a flag—an event that occurred at the market top.

PENETRATION OF TOP AND BOTTOM FORMATIONS

The penetration of patterns that are normally associated with major tops and bottoms represent another important type of failed signal. For example, Figure 11.36 illustrates the double top formed in May 1994 coffee and the penetration of this top about seven months later. Figure 11.37, which depicts the July 1994 contract, shows the immense rally that followed this upside breakout. Although in this chart the July–September 1993 double top looks like nothing more than a squiggle in an extended, narrow trading range, Figure 11.36 makes clear that, at the time, the formation did appear to be a double top. It was only the towering proportions of the subsequent May–July 1994 rally that made the earlier price action look like part of a narrow trading range in comparison. Figure 11.38 provides an example of a downside penetration of a double bottom in the Canadian dollar continuous futures chart—a failed signal that led to an immediate sharp price slide.

Penetrations of double-top and double-bottom patterns provide good signals but are relatively rare. Failed signals involving head-and-shoulders patterns are more common and often provide excellent trading indicators. Although the choice of what condition constitutes a confirmation of a failed head-and-shoulders pattern is somewhat arbitrary, I would use the criterion of prices retracing beyond the most recent shoulder. For example, in Figure 11.39 the rebound above the July shoulder would represent a confirmation of a failed head-and-shoulders top pattern. In this case, the confirmation condition is followed by an immediate, sharp price advance. Frequently, however, prices may first dip back after penetrating the shoulder, even when a substantial advance ultimately ensues. (For example, see Figures 11.40 and 11.41.) Figure 11.42 provides an example of a failed signal involving a *complex* head-and-shoulders top pattern. (A *complex* head-and-shoulders pattern is one that includes two or more shoulders on either side of the head.)

Figures 11.43–11.45 illustrate examples of failed head-and-shoulders bottom patterns. In analogous fashion to the head-and-shoulders top case, the downside penetration of the more recent shoulder is used as the confirmation condition of a failed signal. Note that in all three cases prices first rebounded after the confirmation signal before eventually heading sharply lower. As the

Figure 11.35
OPPOSITE DIRECTION BREAKOUT OF FLAG FOLLOWING
NORMAL BREAKOUT: APRIL 1992 HEATING OIL

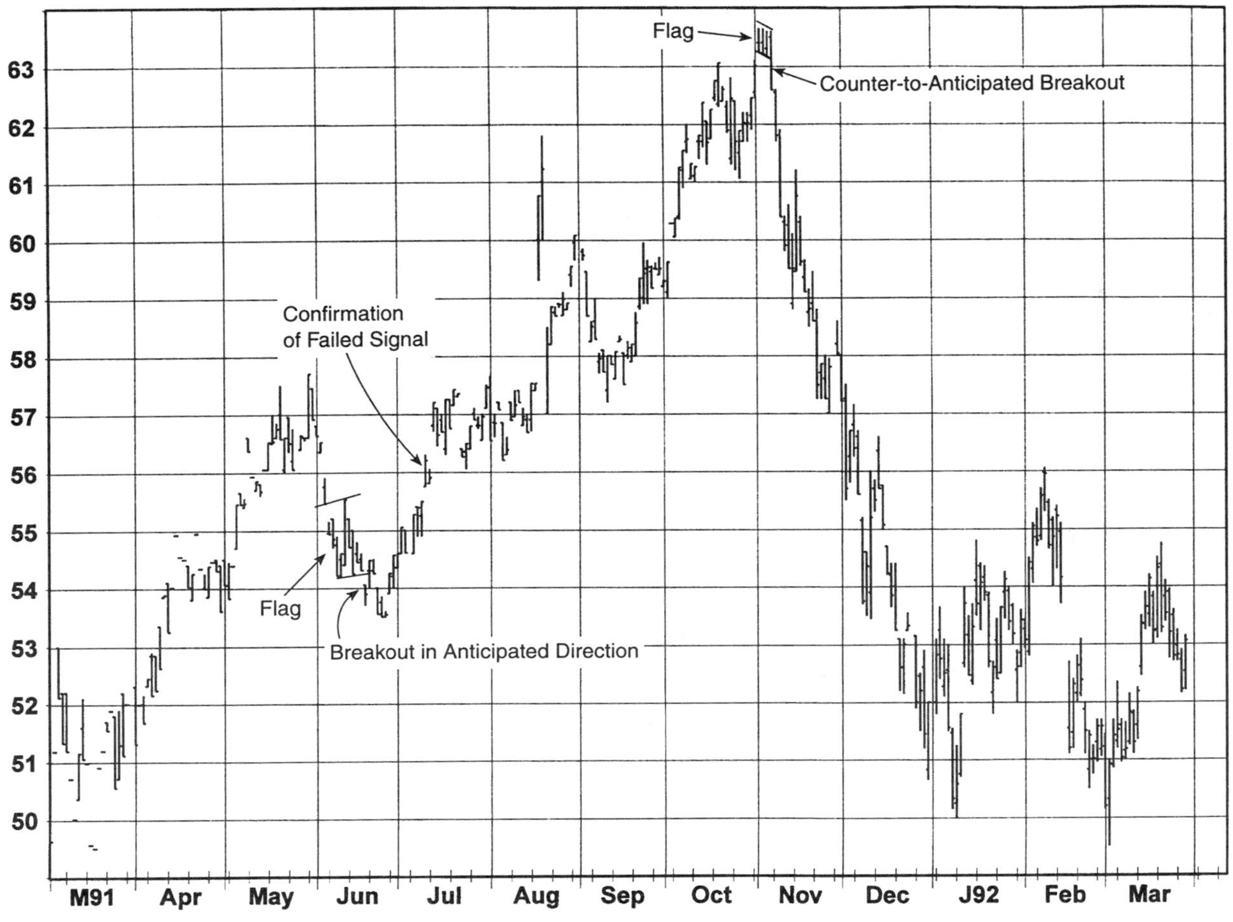

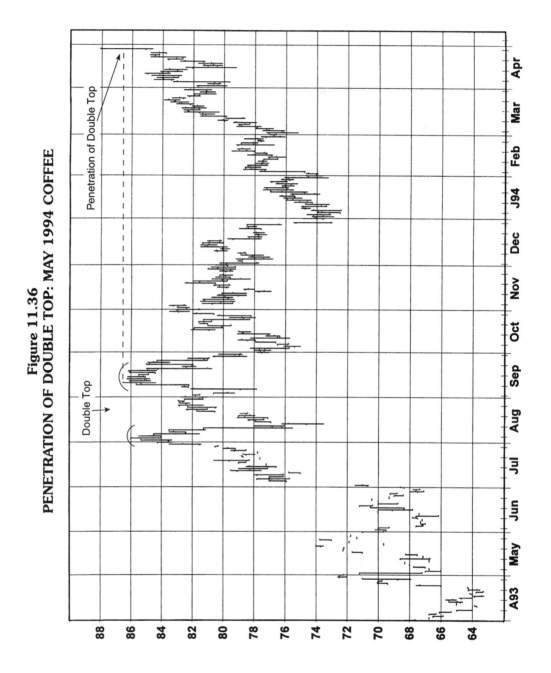

Figure 11.36
PENETRATION OF DOUBLE TOP: MAY 1994 COFFEE

Figure 11.37
PENETRATION OF DOUBLE TOP: JULY 1994 COFFEE

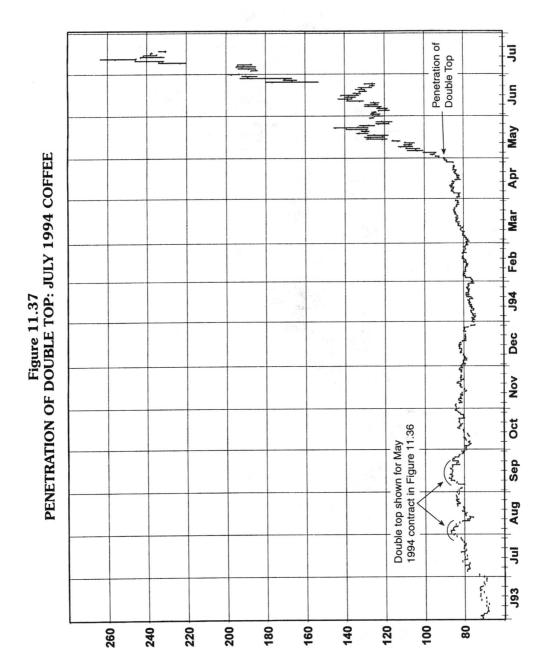

Figure 11.38
PENETRATION OF DOUBLE BOTTOM: CANADIAN DOLLAR CONTINUOUS FUTURES

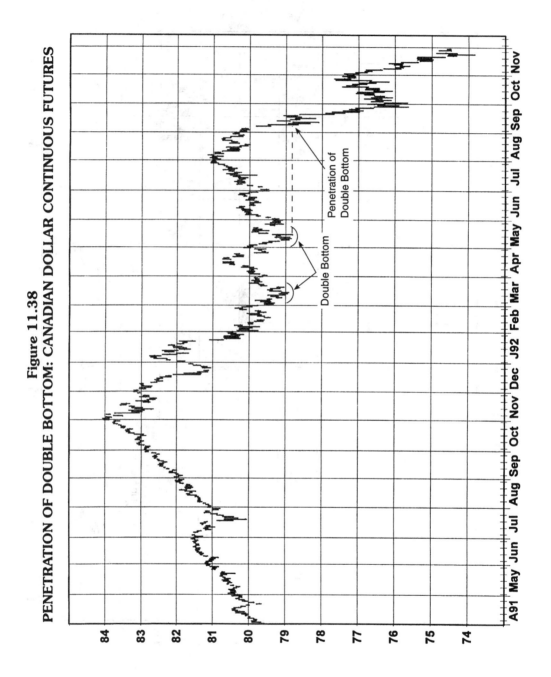

Figure 11.39
FAILED HEAD-AND-SHOULDERS TOP PATTERN: MARCH 1995 COTTON

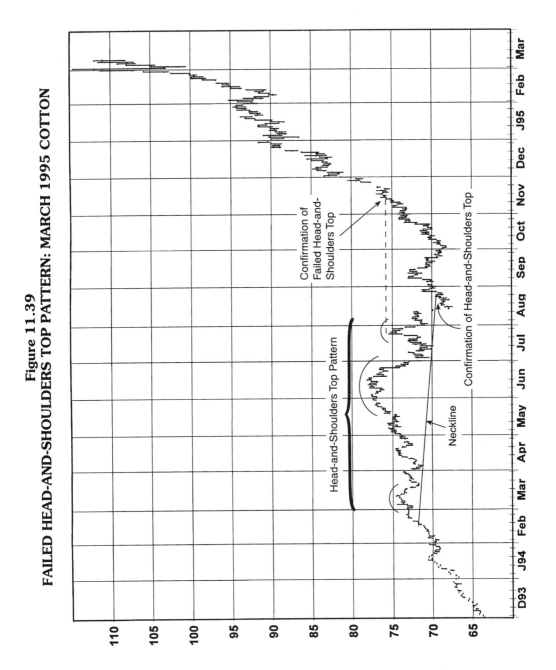

Figure 11.40
FAILED HEAD-AND-SHOULDERS TOP PATTERN: JUNE 1993 T-BOND

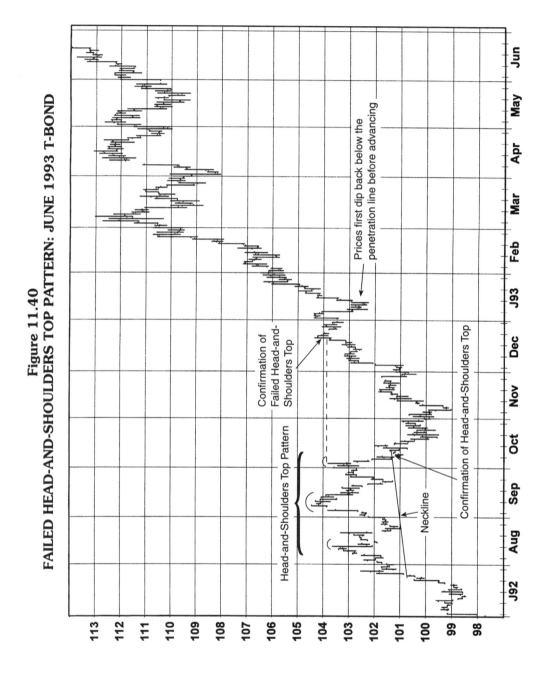

234

Figure 11.41
FAILED HEAD-AND-SHOULDERS TOP PATTERN: BRITISH POUND CONTINUOUS FUTURES

235

Figure 11.42
FAILED COMPLEX HEAD-AND-SHOULDERS TOP
PATTERN: JULY 1993 SOYBEAN OIL

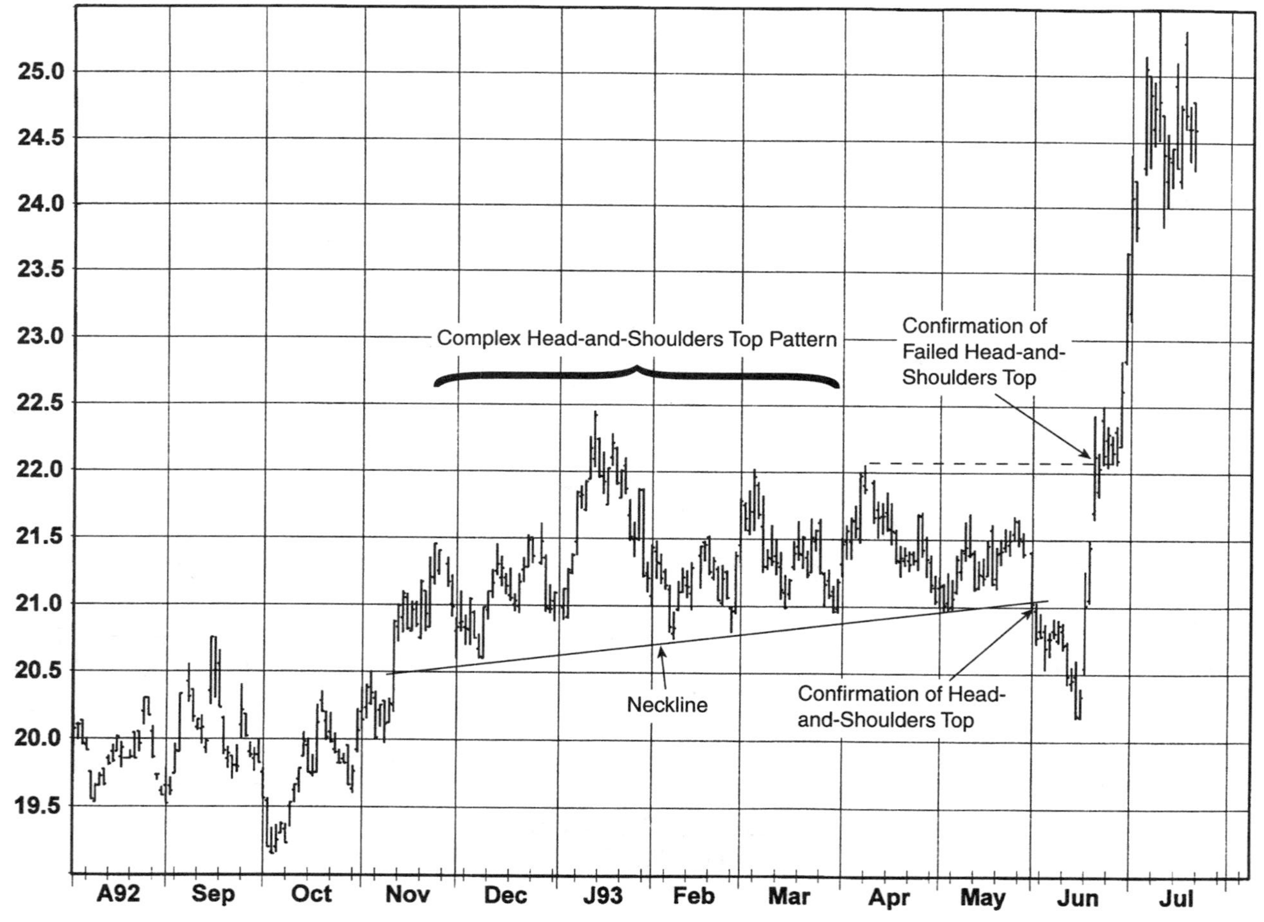

Figure 11.43
FAILED HEAD-AND-SHOULDERS BOTTOM PATTERN: JULY 1991 SOYBEAN OIL

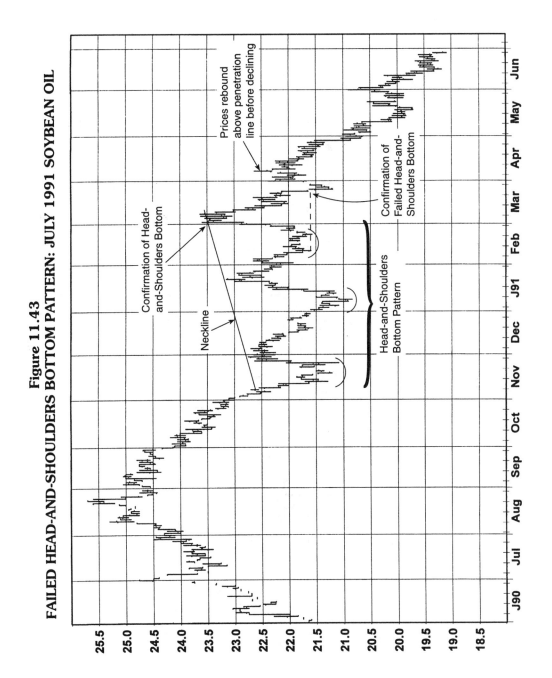

237

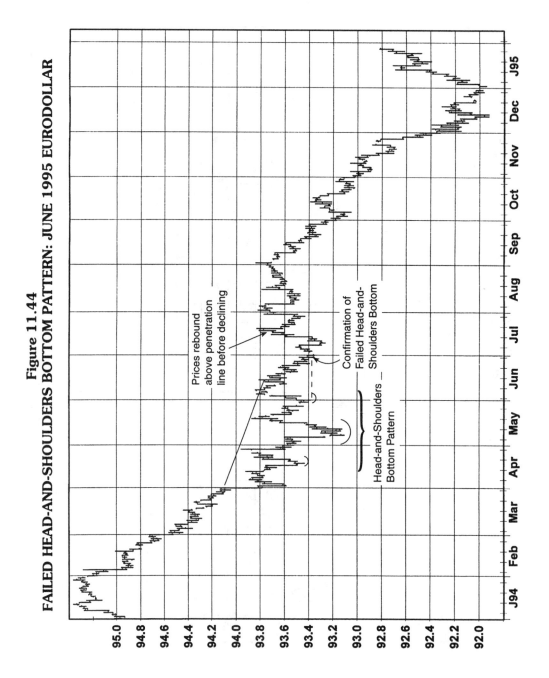

Figure 11.44
FAILED HEAD-AND-SHOULDERS BOTTOM PATTERN: JUNE 1995 EURODOLLAR

238

Figure 11.45
FAILED HEAD-AND-SHOULDERS BOTTOM PATTERN:
CANADIAN DOLLAR CONTINUOUS FUTURES

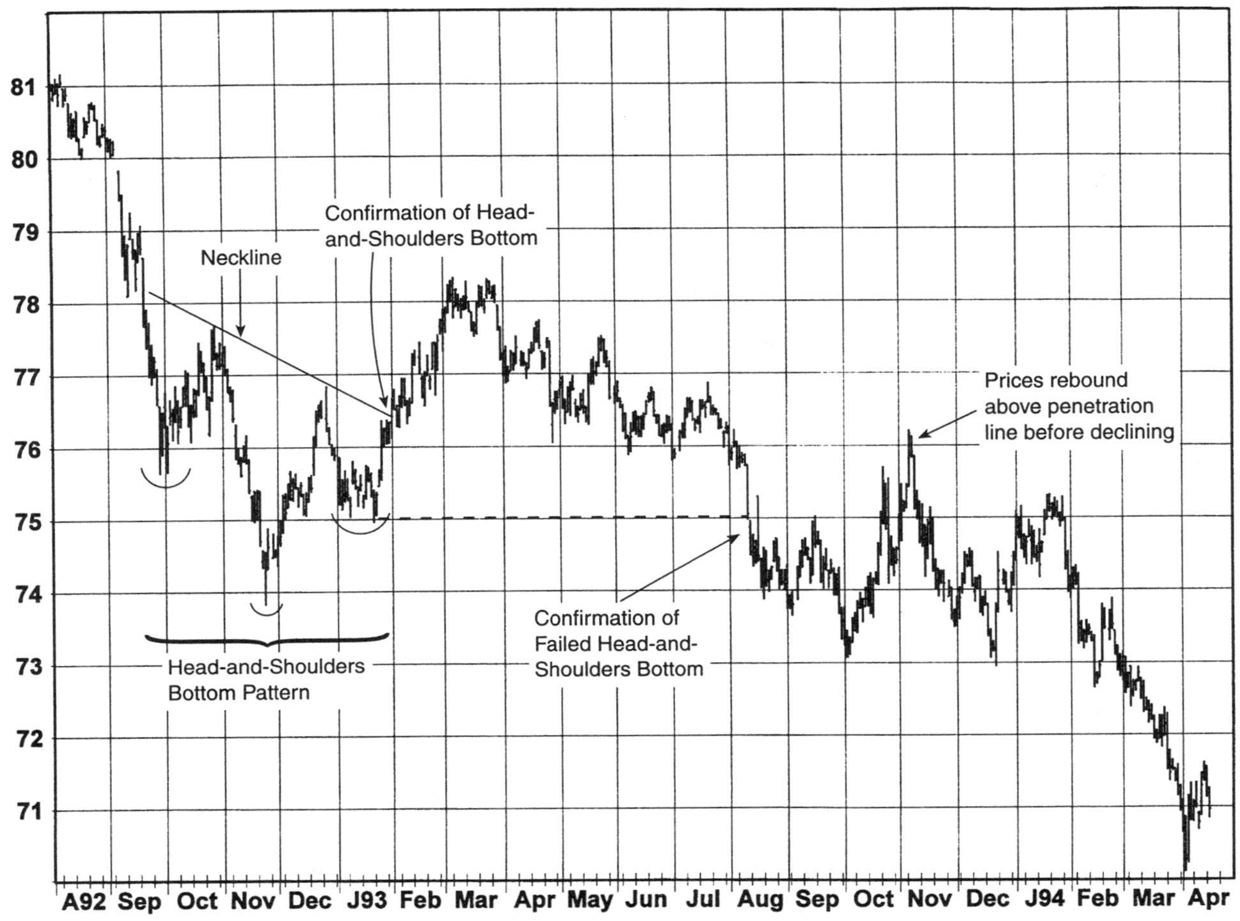

foregoing examples suggest, the trader may often benefit by waiting for a retracement before implementing a position based on the confirmation of a failed head-and-shoulders pattern. The tradeoff is that such a strategy will result in missing very profitable trades in those cases where there is no retracement (for example, Figures 11.39 and 11.42) or only a very modest retracement.

BREAKING OF CURVATURE

As was discussed in Chapter 6, rounding patterns often provide very reliable trading signals. In this sense, the breaking of a curved price pattern can be viewed as transforming the pattern into a failed signal. For example, in Figure 11.46 the breaking of the curvature of what had been an apparent rounding-top pattern represented a bullish signal.

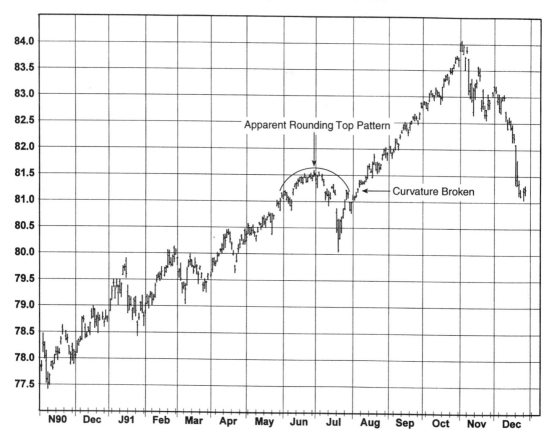

Figure 11.46
BREAKING OF CURVATURE: CANADIAN
DOLLAR CONTINUOUS FUTURES

THE FUTURE RELIABILITY
OF FAILED SIGNALS

There is an inverse relationship between the popularity of an indicator and its efficiency. For example, prior to the 1980s, when technical analysis was used by fewer market practitioners, chart breakouts (price moves above or below prior trading ranges) tended to work relatively well, providing many excellent signals without an abundance of false signals. In my observation, as technical analysis became increasingly popular and breakouts a commonly used tool, the efficiency of this pattern seemed to deteriorate. In fact, it now seems that price *reversals* following breakouts are more often the rule than the exception.

As stated earlier, I find failed signals considerably more reliable than conventional chart patterns. Although the concept of failed signals is certainly not new—in fact, my own book, *A Complete Guide to the Futures Markets,* written in 1984, contains a section on this topic—I am not aware of its usage being strongly emphasized elsewhere. If the use of failed signals were to become significantly more widespread, however, their long-term reliability could be adversely affected.

As a final comment, it should be emphasized that the concept of failed signals in this chapter has been presented in the context of conventional chart analysis as it exists today. In the future—particularly the distant future—what passes for popular chart interpretation may well change. The concept of failed signals, however, can be made dynamic by pegging it to the conventional wisdom. In other words, if a new chart pattern became popular as a technical signal in the future (e.g., in the way breakouts are widely used today), a failure of the pattern could be viewed as more significant than the pattern itself. In this more general sense, the concept of failed signals could prove timeless.

CONCLUSION

The novice trader will ignore a failed signal, riding his position into a large loss while hoping for the best. The more experienced trader, having learned the importance of money management, will exit quickly once it is apparent that he has made a bad trade. However, the truly skilled trader will be able to do a 180-degree turn, reversing his position at a loss if market behavior points to such a course of action. In other words, it takes great discipline to capitalize on failed signals, but such flexibility is essential to the effective synthesis of chart analysis and trading.

12 Linking Contracts for Long-Term Chart Analysis: Nearest Versus Continuous Futures

THE NECESSITY OF LINKED-CONTRACT CHARTS

Many of the chart analysis patterns and techniques detailed in Chapters 3–6 require long-term charts—often charts of multiyear duration. This is particularly true for the identification of top and bottom formations, as well as the determination of support and resistance levels.

A major problem facing the chart analyst in the futures markets is that most futures contracts have relatively limited life spans, and even shorter periods in which these contracts have significant trading activity. For many futures contracts (e.g., currencies, stock indexes) trading activity is almost totally concentrated in the nearest one or two contract months. For example, in Figure 12.1, note that there are only about five months of liquid data for the depicted Swiss franc futures contract, which was the dominant contract for this market at the time (late December 1994). In fact, in some markets almost all trading is concentrated in the nearest position (e.g., most foreign bond futures), with the result that meaningful price data exist for only one to three months, as illustrated by Figures 12.2 and 12.3, which depict the March 1995 Gilt (U.K. bond) and Italian bond contracts in late 1994. Note that there are only about two months of liquid data in these charts, despite the fact that the illustrated contracts were by far the most active in these markets at the time.

The limited price data available for many futures contracts—even those that are the most actively traded contracts in their respective markets—makes it virtually impossible to apply most chart analytical techniques to individual contract charts. Even in those markets in which the individual contracts have

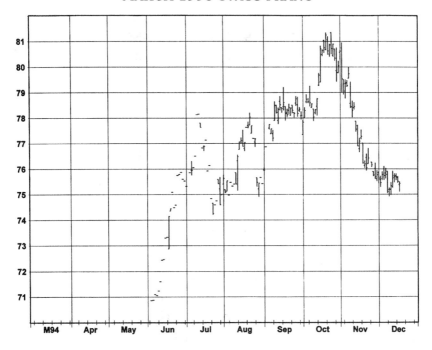

Figure 12.1
MARCH 1995 SWISS FRANC

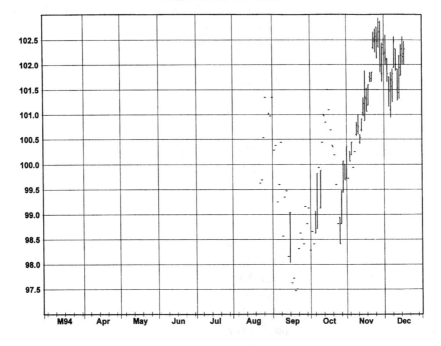

Figure 12.2
MARCH 1995 GILT

243

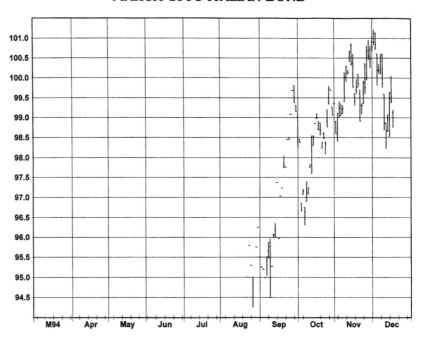

Figure 12.3
MARCH 1995 ITALIAN BOND

a year or more of liquid data, part of a thorough chart study would still encompass analyzing multiyear weekly and monthly charts. Thus, the application of chart analysis unavoidably requires linking successive futures contracts into a single chart. In markets with very limited individual contract data, such linked charts will be a necessity in order to perform *any* meaningful chart analysis. In other markets, linked charts will still be required for analyzing multiyear chart patterns.

METHODS OF CREATING LINKED-CONTRACT CHARTS

Nearest Futures

The most common approach for creating linked-contract charts is typically termed as "nearest futures." This type of price series is constructed by taking each individual contract series until its expiration and then continuing with the next contract until its expiration, and so on.

Although, at surface glance, this approach appears to be a reasonable method for constructing linked-contract charts, the problem with a nearest futures chart is that there are price gaps between expiring and new con-tracts—and quite frequently, these gaps can be very substantial. For example, assume that the October cattle contract expires at 60 cents and that the next nearest contract (December) closes at 63 cents on the same day. Further assume that on the next day December cattle move limit-down from 63 cents to 61 cents. A nearest futures price series will show the following closing levels on these two successive days: 60 cents, 61 cents. In other words, the nearest futures contract would show a one-cent gain on a day on which longs would actually have experienced a limit-down price loss of two cents. This example is by no means artificial. Such distortions—and indeed more ex-treme ones—are quite common at contract rollovers in nearest futures charts.

The vulnerability of nearest futures charts to distortions at contract rollover points makes it desirable to derive alternative methods of constructing linked-contract price charts. One such approach is detailed in the next section.

Continuous (Spread-Adjusted) Price Series

The spread-adjusted price series, which we term "continuous futures," is con-structed by adding the cumulative difference between the old and new con-tracts at rollover points to the new contract series. An example should help clarify this method. Assume we are constructing a spread-adjusted continuous price series for COMEX gold using the June and December contracts.[1] If the price series begins at the start of the calendar year, initially the values in the series will be identical to the prices of the June contract expiring in that year. Assume that on the rollover date (which need not necessarily be the last trad-ing day) June gold closes at $400 and December gold closes at $412. In this case, all subsequent prices based on the December contract would be adjusted downward by $12—the difference between the December and June con-tracts on the rollover date.

Assume that at the next rollover date December gold is trading at $450 and the subsequent June contract is trading at $464. The December contract price of $450 implies that the spread-adjusted continuous price is $438. Thus, on this second rollover date, the June contract is trading $26 above the adjusted series. Consequently, all subsequent prices based on the second June contract would be adjusted downward by $26. This procedure would continue, with the adjustment for each contract dependent on the cumulative

---

[1]The choice of a combination of contracts is arbitrary. One can use any combination of actively traded months in the given market. For example, in the case of COMEX gold, choices range from constructing a series based on all six actively traded contracts—February, April, June, August, October, and December—to a series based on only a single contract—for example, December.

total of the present and prior transition point price differences. The resulting price series would be free of the distortions due to spread differences that exist at the rollover points between contracts.

The construction of a continuous futures series can be thought of as the mathematical equivalent of taking a nearest futures chart, cutting out each individual contract series contained in the chart, and pasting the ends together (assuming a continuous series employing all contracts and using the same rollover dates as the nearest futures chart). Typically, as a last step, it is convenient to shift the scale of the entire series by the cumulative adjustment factor, a step that will set the current price of the series equal to the price of the current contract without changing the shape of the series. The construction of a continuous futures chart is discussed in greater detail in Chapter 19, "Selecting the Best Futures Price Series for Computer Testing."

Comparing the Series

It is important to understand that a linked futures price series can only accurately reflect either price *levels,* as does nearest futures, or price *moves,* as does continuous futures, but not both—much as a coin can either land on heads or tails, but not both. The adjustment process used to construct continuous series means that past prices in a continuous series will not match the actual historical prices that prevailed at the time. However, a continuous series will accurately reflect the actual price movements of the market and will exactly parallel the equity fluctuations experienced by a trader who is continually long (rolling over positions on the same rollover dates used to construct the continuous series), whereas a nearest futures price series can be extremely misleading in these respects.

NEAREST VERSUS CONTINUOUS FUTURES IN CHART ANALYSIS

Given the significant differences between nearest and continuous futures price series, the obvious question in the reader's mind is probably: Which series— nearest futures or continuous futures—would be most appropriate for chart analysis? To some extent, this is like asking, Which factor should a consumer consider before purchasing a new car: price or quality? The obvious answer is both—each factor provides important information about a characteristic that is not measured by the other. In terms of price series, considering nearest futures versus continuous futures, each series provides information that the other doesn't. Specifically, a nearest futures price series provides accurate information about past price *levels,* but not price *swings,* whereas the exact reverse statement applies to a continuous futures series.

Consider, for example, Figure 12.4. What catastrophic event caused the instantaneous 40-cent collapse depicted by the nearest futures chart for cotton in 1986? Answer: absolutely nothing. This "phantom" price move reflected nothing more than a transition from the old crop July contract to the new crop October contract. (The wide price gap between the two contracts in that year was due to a change in the government farm program, which drastically reduced the loan level, and in turn the effective floor price, for the new crop.) In fact, prices were actually in an uptrend during this particular contract transition! Figure 12.5, which depicts the continuous futures price for the same market (and by definition eliminates price gaps at contract rollovers), illustrates the general uptrend in the cotton market during this period—an uptrend that actually began off a major low set in the previous year. Clearly, the susceptibility of nearest futures charts to distortions caused by wide gaps at rollovers can make it difficult to use nearest futures for chart analysis that focuses on price swings.

On the other hand, the continuous futures chart achieves accuracy in depicting price swings at the sacrifice of accuracy in reflecting price levels. In

Figure 12.4
COTTON NEAREST FUTURES

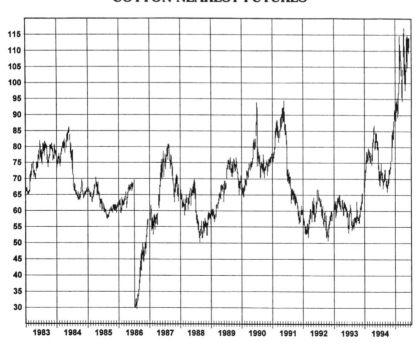

Figure 12.5
COTTON CONTINUOUS FUTURES

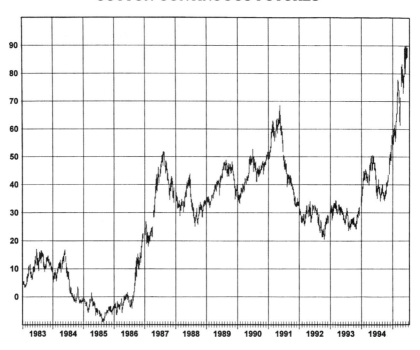

order to accurately show the magnitude of past price swings, historical continuous futures prices can end up being very far removed from the actual historical price levels. In fact, it is not even unusual for historical continuous futures prices to be negative (see Figure 12.6). Obviously, such "impossible" historical prices can have no relevance as guidelines to prospective support levels.

The fact that each type of price chart—nearest and continuous—has certain significant intrinsic weaknesses argues for combining both types of charts in a more complete analysis. Often these two types of charts will provide entirely different price pictures. For example, consider the nearest futures chart for hogs depicted in Figure 12.7. Looking at this chart, it is tempting to conclude that hogs have essentially been in a wide-swinging trading range market for the entire 12-year period shown. Now go back and reexamine Figure 12.6, which is the continuous version of the same market. In this chart, it is evident that the hog market has witnessed a number of major trends—price movements that were completely hidden by the nearest futures chart (and would have been realized in actual trading). It is no exaggeration to say that, without the benefit of the chart labels, it would be virtually impossible to recognize that Figures 12.6 and 12.7 depict the same market.

Figure 12.6
HOGS CONTINUOUS FUTURES

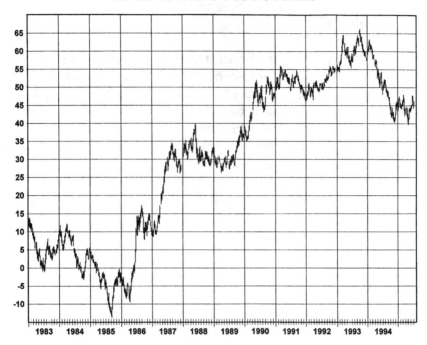

Figure 12.7
HOGS NEAREST FUTURES

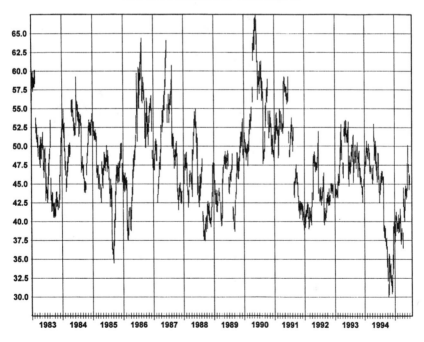

CONCLUSION

In summary, technical analysts should at least experiment in using continuous futures charts as a supplement to conventional nearest futures charts to see whether such an addition enhances the reliability of their analysis. The charts that follow provide comparisons between long-term nearest and continuous charts for key futures markets (other than cotton and hogs, which have already been displayed). Readers are reminded that continuous futures charts generated in the future will show different price scales than those shown in the following pages (although the price moves will remain the same), since it is assumed that the scales will be adjusted to match the prevailing current contract.

T-BOND NEAREST FUTURES

T-BOND CONTINUOUS FUTURES

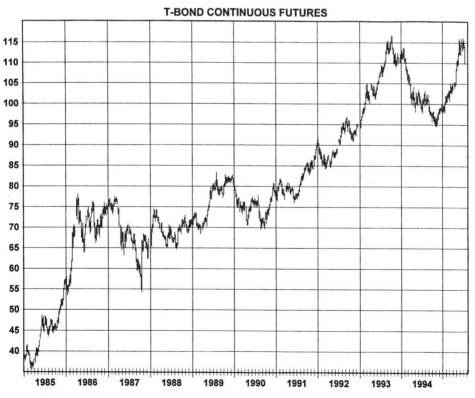

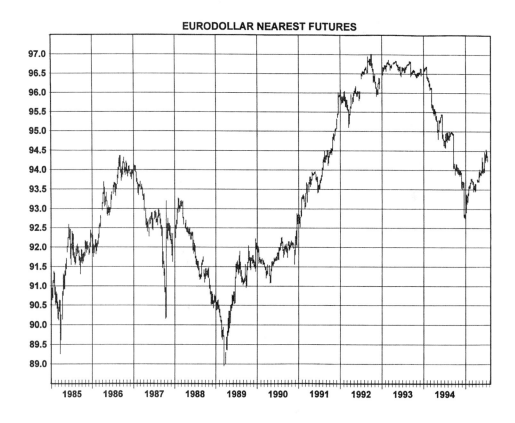

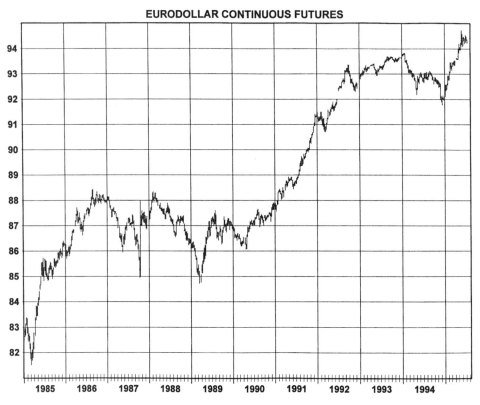

SP500 NEAREST FUTURES

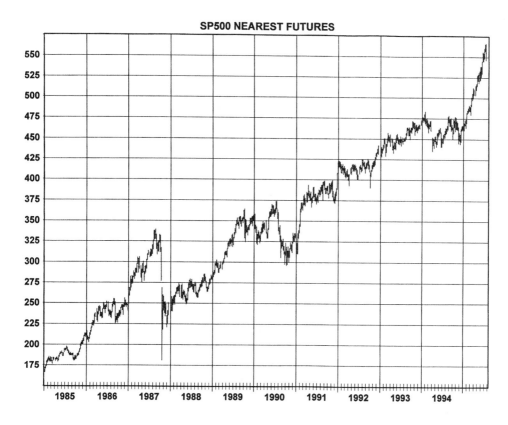

SP500 CONTINUOUS FUTURES

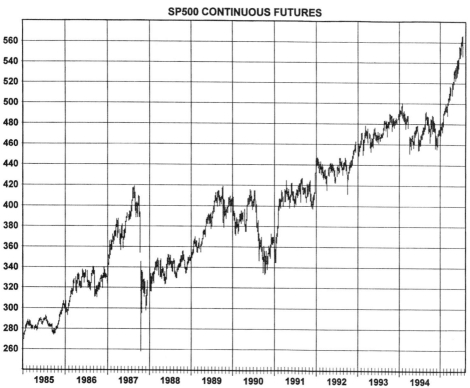

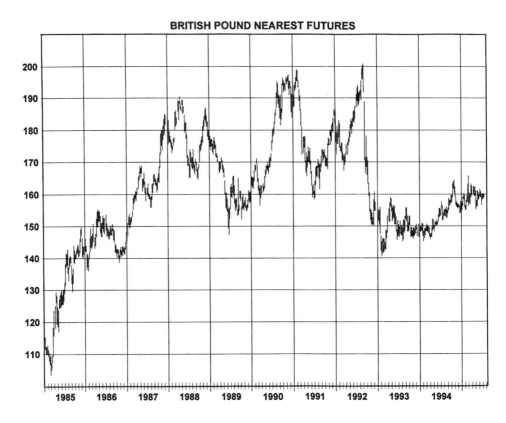

JAPANESE YEN NEAREST FUTURES

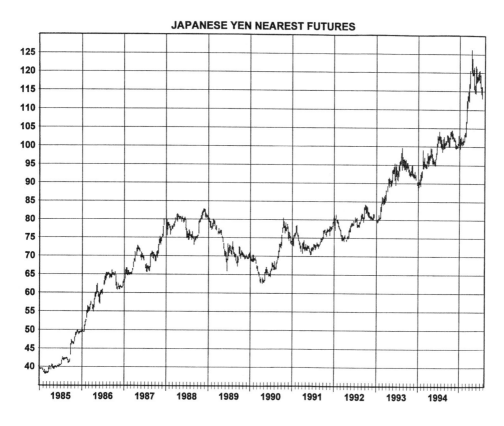

JAPANESE YEN CONTINUOUS FUTURES

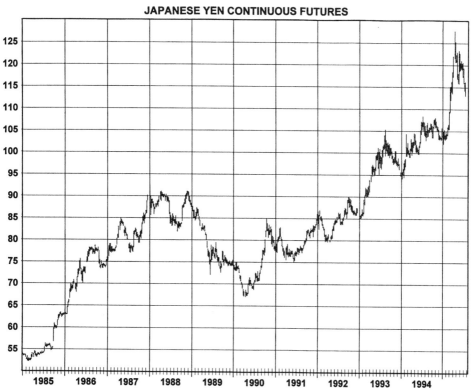

DEUTSCHE MARK NEAREST FUTURES

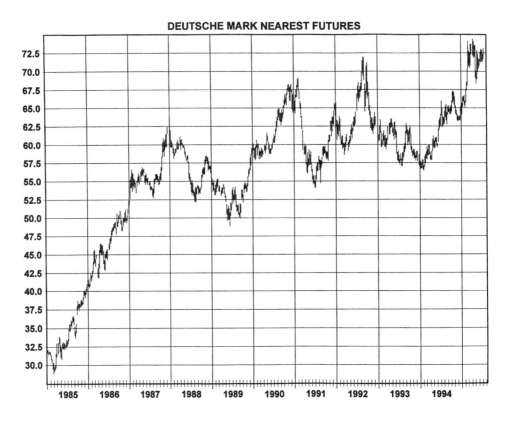

DEUTSCHE MARK CONTINUOUS FUTURES

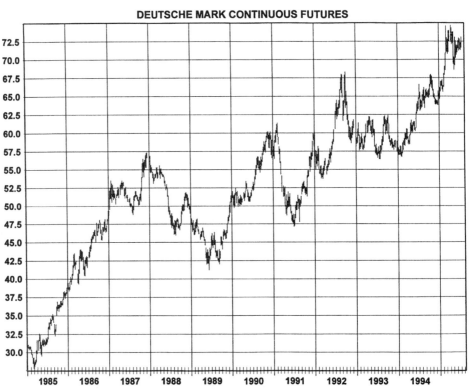

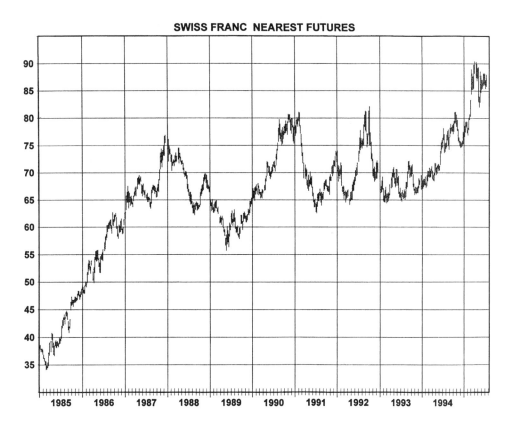

SWISS FRANC NEAREST FUTURES

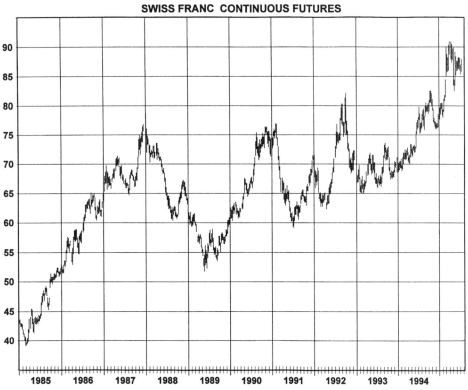

SWISS FRANC CONTINUOUS FUTURES

CANADIAN DOLLAR NEAREST FUTURES

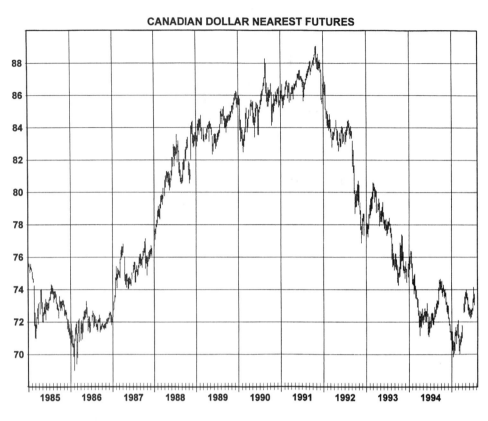

CANADIAN DOLLAR CONTINUOUS FUTURES

GOLD NEAREST FUTURES

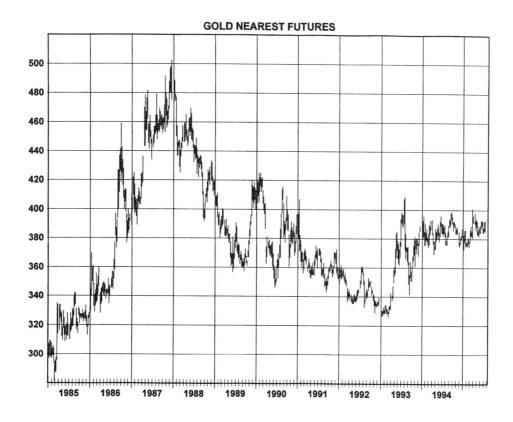

GOLD CONTINUOUS FUTURES

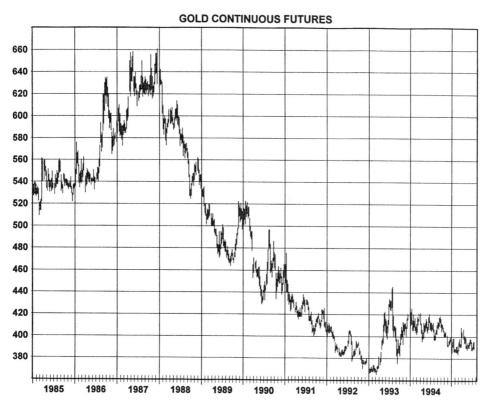

PLATINUM NEAREST FUTURES

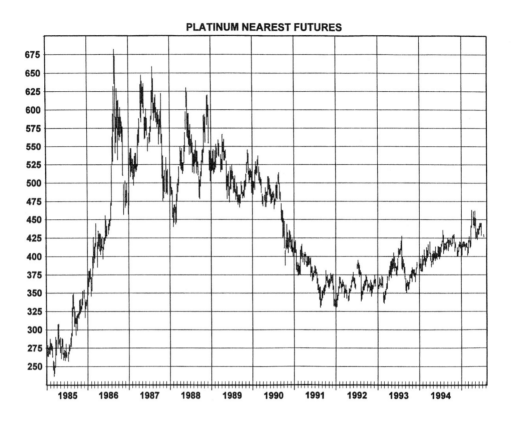

PLATINUM CONTINUOUS FUTURES

SILVER NEAREST FUTURES

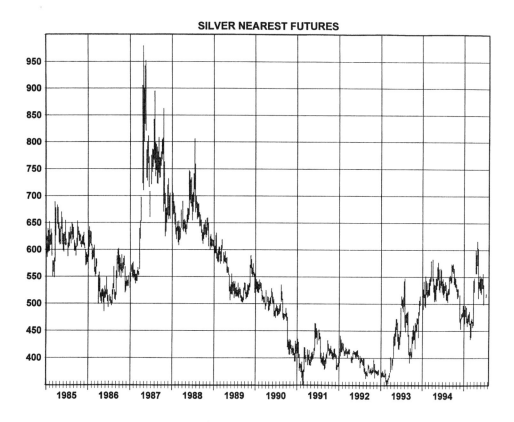

SILVER CONTINUOUS FUTURES

COPPER NEAREST FUTURES

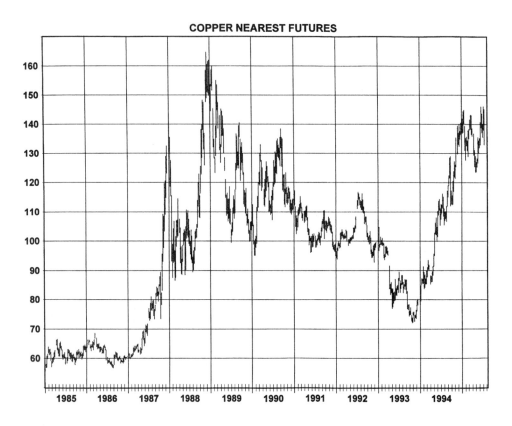

COPPER CONTINUOUS FUTURES

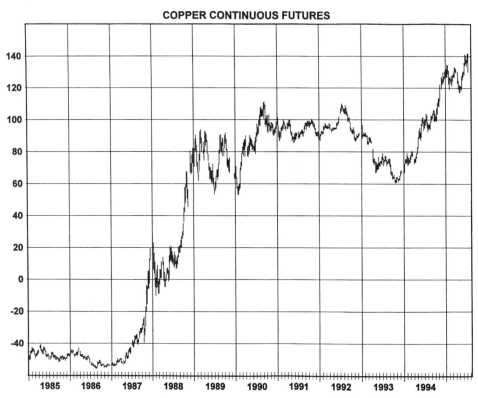

CRUDE OIL NEAREST FUTURES

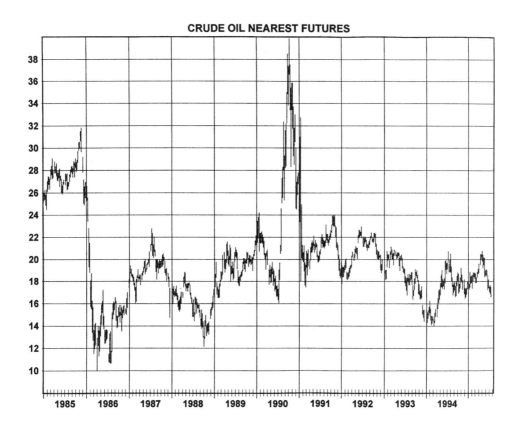

CRUDE OIL CONTINUOUS FUTURES

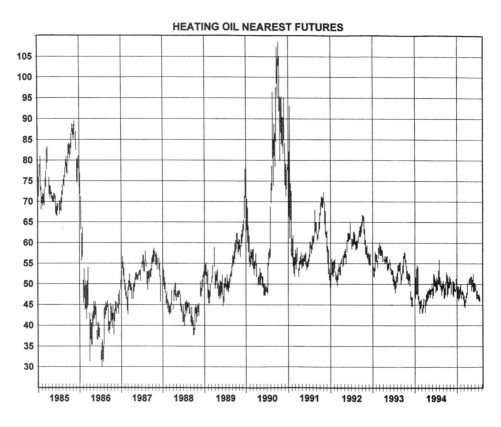

HEATING OIL NEAREST FUTURES

HEATING OIL CONTINUOUS FUTURES

UNLEADED GAS NEAREST FUTURES

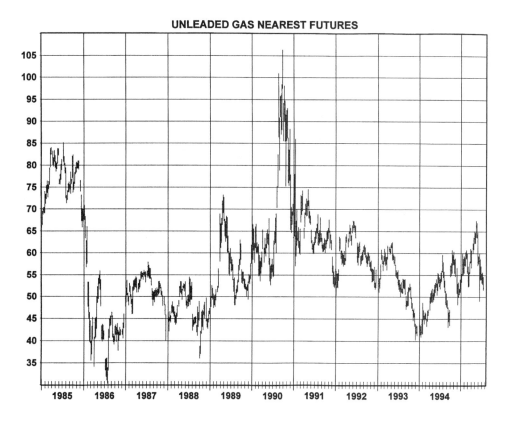

UNLEADED GAS CONTINUOUS FUTURES

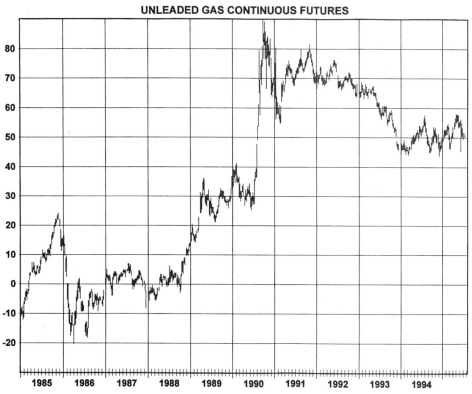

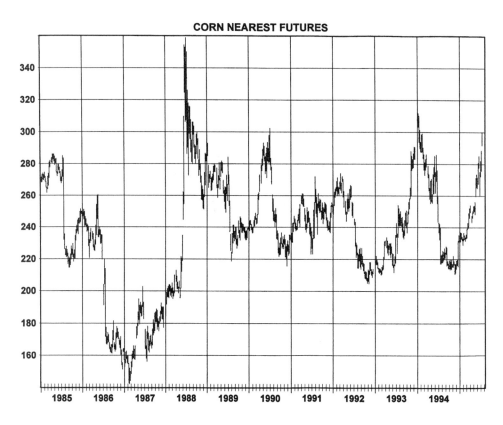

CORN NEAREST FUTURES

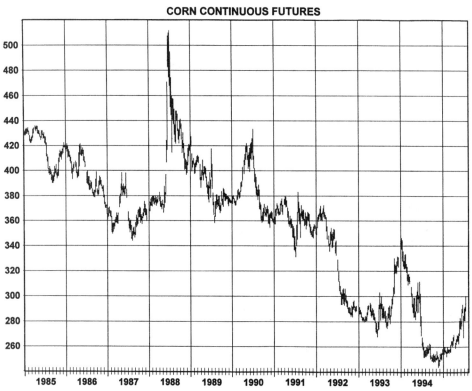

CORN CONTINUOUS FUTURES

WHEAT NEAREST FUTURES

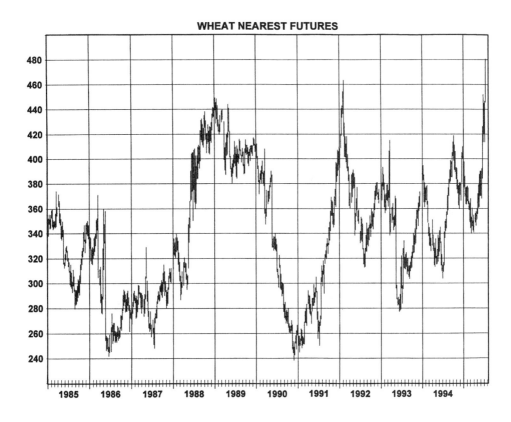

WHEAT CONTINUOUS FUTURES

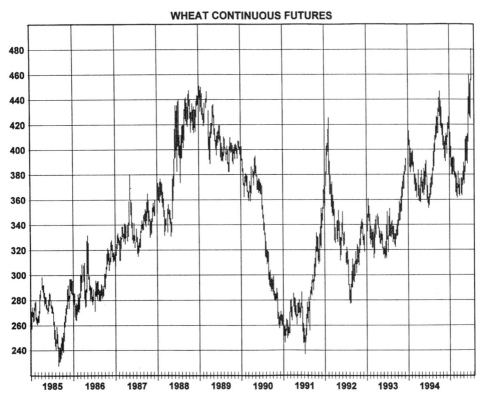

SOYBEANS NEAREST FUTURES

SOYBEANS CONTINUOUS FUTURES

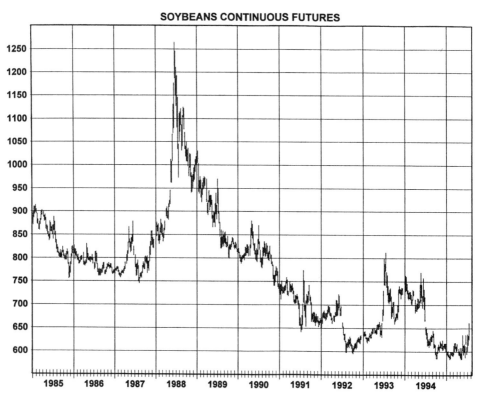

SOYBEAN MEAL NEAREST FUTURES

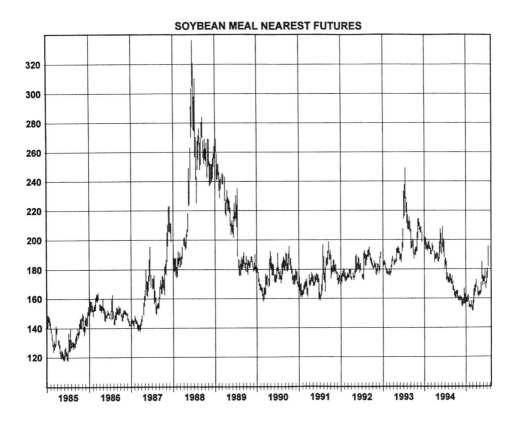

SOYBEAN MEAL CONTINUOUS FUTURES

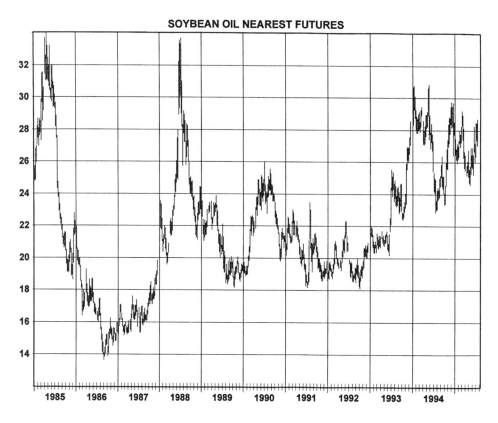

SOYBEAN OIL NEAREST FUTURES

SOYBEAN OIL CONTINUOUS FUTURES

CATTLE NEAREST FUTURES

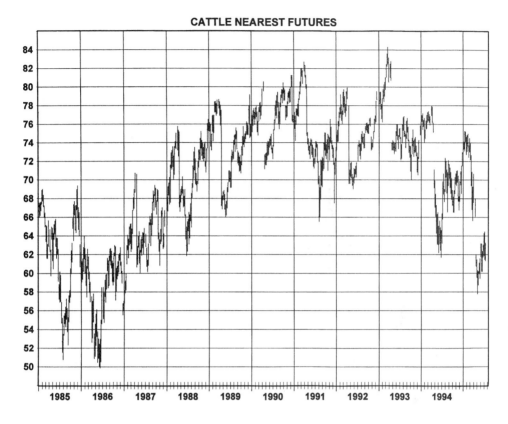

CATTLE CONTINUOUS FUTURES

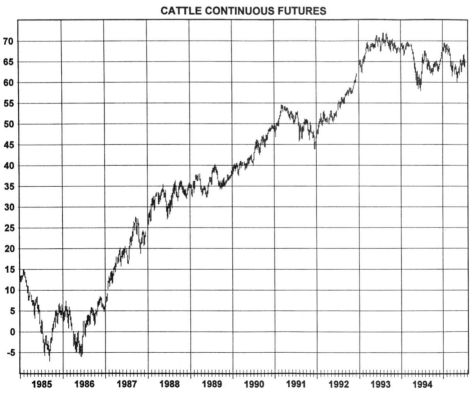

SUGAR NEAREST FUTURES

SUGAR CONTINUOUS FUTURES

COFFEE NEAREST FUTURES

COFFEE CONTINUOUS FUTURES

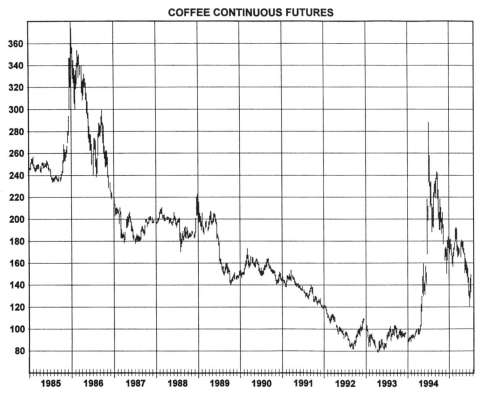

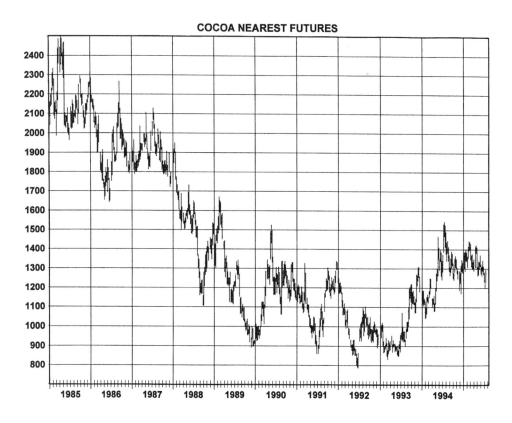

COCOA NEAREST FUTURES

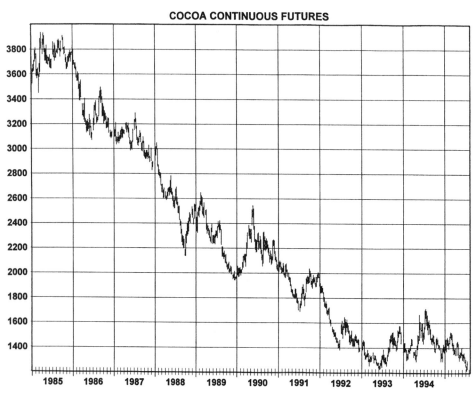

COCOA CONTINUOUS FUTURES

FCOJ NEAREST FUTURES

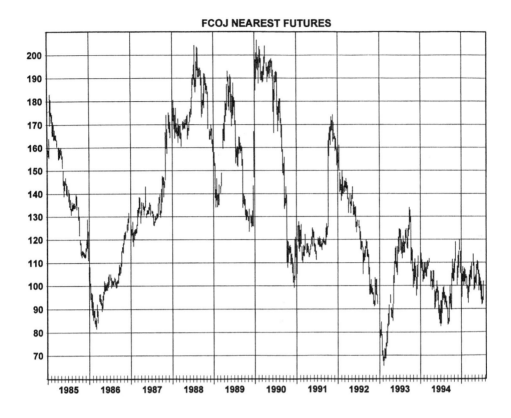

FCOJ CONTINUOUS FUTURES

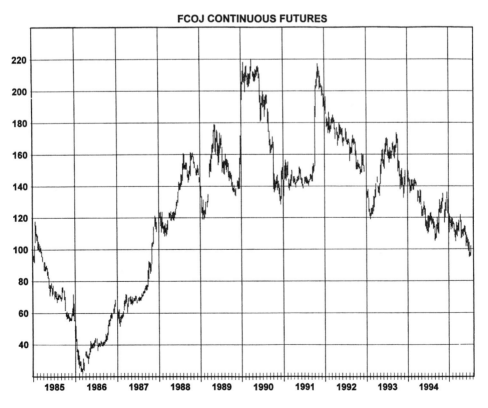

LUMBER NEAREST FUTURES

LUMBER CONTINUOUS FUTURES

13 An Introduction to Japanese Candlestick Charts

Steve Nison

(Edited by Jack Schwager)

Mountain, Wind, Forest, Fire.

Banner carried by the troops of the seventeenth-century Japanese general Shingen to connote that success in battle required knowing when to be:

> as immovable as a **mountain;**
> as quick as the **wind;**
> as patient as the **forest;**
> and when to invade like a **fire.**

Candle charts are Japan's most popular, and oldest, form of technical analysis. Candle charts predate point and figure and bar charts. The Japanese recognized the importance of technical analysis long ago. They were the first to trade futures. In the mid-1600s they traded "empty rice" contracts (that is rice that wasn't there—in other words, rice futures). The main rice futures

---

Mr. Nison is a senior vice president at Daiwa Securities America, Inc., in New York. He is the author of the highly acclaimed book, *Japanese Candlestick Charting Techniques.* His new book is *Beyond Candlesticks—New Japanese Trading Techniques.* Mr. Nison is a world-renowned speaker, and has given highly praised seminars including a special presentation for the World Bank in Washington, D.C. Featured stories about his work have appeared in the *Wall Street Journal, Institutional Investor,* the *L.A. Times, Barron's,* and the *Japan Economic Journal.* He regularly appears as guest technical commentator on CNBC. Mr. Nison, who has an M.B.A. in finance and investments, has been analyzing the financial markets for nearly 20 years. He is a Chartered Market Technician and a member of the Market Technicians Association.

exchange was in Osaka, Japan. Commerce was so important in that city that the traditional greeting was "mokariamakka," which means, "Are you making a profit?"—an expression that has survived to the present day.

In my six years of prying open the "secrets of the Orient," I had over a dozen books translated from Japanese into English. The following fascinating excerpt is taken from one of these books:

> When all are bearish, there is cause for prices to rise. When everyone is bullish, there is cause for the price to fall.

Doesn't this sound like contrary opinion that is used by so many traders? Yet this book, titled *The Fountain of Gold*, was written in 1755. Before America was even a nation, the Japanese were trading with contrary opinion! This book also contains the following advice:

> To learn about the market ask the market—only then can you become a detestable market demon.

What a great expression! Who wouldn't enjoy being a detestable market demon.

Amazingly, candlestick charting techniques, used for generations in the Far East, were virtually unknown in the West until they were revealed in my first book, *Japanese Candlestick Charting Techniques*, published in 1991. Before this time, there were few services offering candlestick charts in the United States and Europe. Now almost every real-time technical service and technical analysis software package supplies candle charts to their clients. The profusion of services offering candlestick charts attests to their popularity and usefulness. It is fascinating that for nearly 100 years the West's two main charting tools have been bar charts and point and figure charts. Yet, within two years of the publication of *Japanese Candlestick Charting Techniques*, candle charts joined bar and point and figure charts as a basic charting tool.

In the early days of fur trading in the United States, there was a company that was known for both its willingness to take risks and for its careful preparation. Trading journeys were undertaken with much excitement, but in case the expedition members forgot anything, on the first night they would camp out just a few miles away from the company's headquarters. In other words, careful preparation spared the travelers potential difficulties.

Similarly, success in trading requires careful preparation. For those new to candlestick analysis, this chapter starts slowly down the road of candles by presenting a primer on basic candle theory and patterns. But even a discussion of the basic candle signals is sufficient to show how candlestick charts open avenues of analysis not available elsewhere. After being exposed to candlestick charts, some traders never go back to bar charts.

WHY HAVE CANDLE CHARTS BECOME SO POPULAR?

Why are flames of interest in candles growing brighter each day? Some reasons include:

1. Candlestick charting tools are so versatile that they can be used with any Western technical tool. As is shown later, candlestick charts are drawn using the same data as conventional bar charts: high, low, open, and close. The significance of this fact is that any of the technical analytical methods used with bar charts (such as moving averages, trendlines, retracements) can be employed with candlestick charts. Moreover—and this is the key point—candlestick charts can provide signals not available on bar charts.

2. Candlestick charts have widespread applicability. Candlestick techniques can be used for speculation, investing, and hedging; they can be used for futures, equities, options. In other words, candlestick charts can be used anywhere technical analysis is applied.

3. Candle charts allow traders to get a jump on those who only use bar charts. Bar chart reversals may take weeks to develop; candlestick chart reversal signals often unfold in a few sessions.

4. Candle charting techniques, while new to the West, have been refined by generations of use in Japan.

5. There is strong interest in how the Japanese use their technical analysis to trade. The Japanese are major players in most of the world's markets, and the Japanese use candle charts to trade in all the markets. The following excerpt from the magazine *Euroweek,* quoting an English trader who works at a Japanese bank, illustrates the importance of candlestick charts to the Japanese.

   > All the Japanese traders here—and that's in the foreign exchange, futures and equity markets—use candles. It might be difficult to work out the billions of dollars traded in London on interpretations of these charts each day, but the number would be significant.

   Think about it. Although billions are traded every day based on candle chart signals, until recently we didn't have a clue as to how the Japanese viewed the market with their technicals. That is unbelievable. The candle chart in Japan is as popular as the bar chart is here. Understanding how the Japanese use their most popular technical tool may help answer the question, "What are the Japanese going to do next?"

6. No doubt, the rapidly growing appeal of candlestick charts has been enhanced by the picturesque terms used to describe the patterns. There are

hammers, evening stars, and *engulfing patterns.* The Japanese terminology gives candlesticks a flavor all their own. Many traders find that
once they get a taste of candlestick charts, they can't do without them.

The Japanese are well versed in Western methods of technical analysis.
Although the books I had translated primarily explained candlestick techniques,
each one contained large sections that discussed American technical tools. The
following quote from one of these books typifies the Japanese perspective on
Western versus Eastern technical techniques:

> To understand stocks it is not enough to know the Japanese chart
> methods . . . one must [also] absorb the best parts of Western technicals.

As this statement demonstrates, the Japanese use a combination of candlestick charting techniques and Western technical tools. Why shouldn't we do
the same? By merging the best of the East and the West, we can achieve a
powerful synergy of technical techniques. The Japanese are very knowledge-
able about the technical tools used in the West. Now it is our turn to learn
from them.

CONSTRUCTING THE CANDLESTICK LINES

Figures 13.1 and 13.2 display some basic candlestick lines. The broad part of
the candlestick line is called the "real body." The real body represents the
range between the session's open and close. If, as in Figure 13.1, the close of
the session is lower than open, then the real body is black (i.e., filled in). If the
close of the session is higher than the open (Figure 13.2), the real body is
white (i.e., empty).

The thin lines above and below the real body are called the "shadows."
These are the session's price extremes. The shadow above the real body is
called the upper shadow, and the shadow under the real body is the lower
shadow. Thus, the peak of the upper shadow is the high of the session, and
the bottom of the lower shadow is the low of the session.

Based on the preceding definitions, Figure 13.1 is a session that opened
near the high and closed near the low. Conversely, Figure 13.2 is a session
that opened near the low and closed near the high. We see why these charts
are named candlestick charts: the individual lines often look like candles with
their wicks.

A powerful insight offered by candlestick charts is that the color and shape
of the candle lines visually display who is winning the battle between the bulls

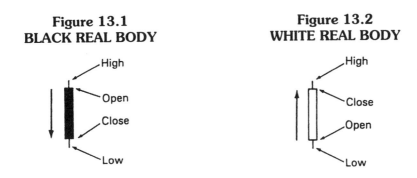

Figure 13.1
BLACK REAL BODY

Figure 13.2
WHITE REAL BODY

and the bears. A long white real body tells us that the bulls are in charge, while a long black real body reflects a session in which the bears are in control. A small real body (white or black) indicates a period in which the bulls and bears are more in balance.

It's important to note that the candle lines can be drawn for all time frames, from intraday to monthly charts. For example, a 60-minute candle line uses the open, high, low, and close of 60-minute periods. A daily chart would use the open, high, low, and close. A candle line in a weekly chart would be based on Monday's open, the high and low of the week, and Friday's close.

Doji

Figure 13.3 provides several examples of doji (pronounced dō-gee). A doji is a candle in which the opening and close are the same. Thus, they have no real bodies. Even if a candle line has an open and close that are not exactly the same, but are extremely close, it can often be viewed as a doji. A doji reflects a market in which the bulls and bears are in equilibrium.

In a laterally trading market, a doji is neutral, because it reinforces the

Figure 13.3
DOJI

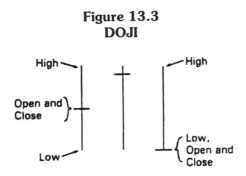

neutral state of the market. However, during an uptrend, a doji session could be an indication of a market turn, since a doji tells us that the bulls have lost control of the market, although it does not reflect that the bears have yet taken over. Doji represent indecision. Indecision, uncertainty, or vacillation by the buyers will not maintain an uptrend. It takes the conviction of buyers to sustain a rally. If the market has had an extended rally and then a doji (read "indecision") surfaces, it could mean that the scaffolding of buyers' support will give way. Consequently, there is increased risk that the market will fall. A doji that follows a tall new high is especially important. The Japanese refer to such a doji as "a symptom of uneasiness at a high price."

In Figure 13.4 a rally that started in mid-December stalled after a doji formed following a tall white candle. The appearance of this doji told of a market in which the bulls and bears were in equilibrium—a very sharp departure from the prior two sessions in which the two tall white candles displayed a vibrant and healthy market in which the bulls were in control. As the Japa-

Figure 13.4
DOJI FOLLOWING TALL, WHITE CANDLE:
MARCH 1994 BRITISH POUND

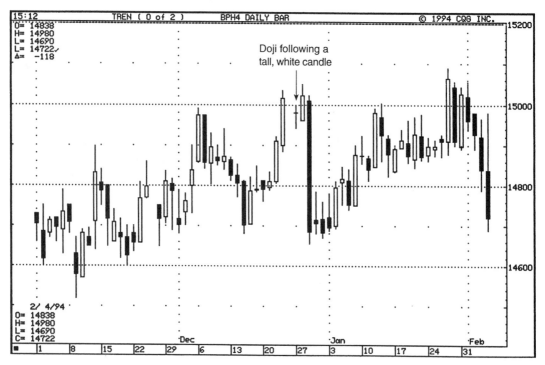

Source: CQG Inc.; copyright © 1994 by CQG Inc.

nese phrase it, the appearance of the doji showed that "the market is separating from its trend."

The Hammer

A candle with a very long lower shadow and small real body (either white or black) near the top end of the trading range is called a "hammer" (see Figure 13.5). This name derives not only from the shape of the pattern, but also refers to the concept that the market is hammering out a base. If this type of candle line emerges during a downtrend, it could signal a reversal in the trend. The hammer can be recognized by three criteria:

1. The real body is at the upper end of the trading range (the color of the real body is unimportant)
2. A long lower shadow that is at least twice the height of the real body
3. A very short or nonexistent upper shadow

The longer the lower shadow, the shorter the upper shadow, and the smaller the real body, the more meaningful the bullish hammer.

A hammer pictorially displays that the market opened near its high, sold off during the session, and then rallied sharply to close at, or near, the high of the session. The hammer is an excellent example of how candlestick charts can reveal a great deal of market information with only a single candle line.

Frequently, if a hammer follows a steep decline, the market retraces to retest the hammer's support area, and by doing so expands the base. Figure 13.6 provides an example of such a situation. Note that the hammer at point 1 was tested shortly afterwards by another hammer at point 2. This second hammer, with its long lower shadow, was followed three sessions later by a candle with a long, white real body at point 3, revealing evidence of strong buying when the market moved to the hammer's support area.

Figure 13.5
HAMMER

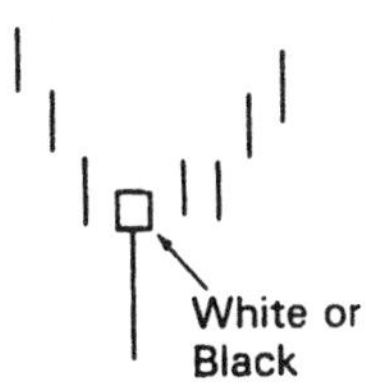

Figure 13.6
HAMMER: MARCH 1994 CORN

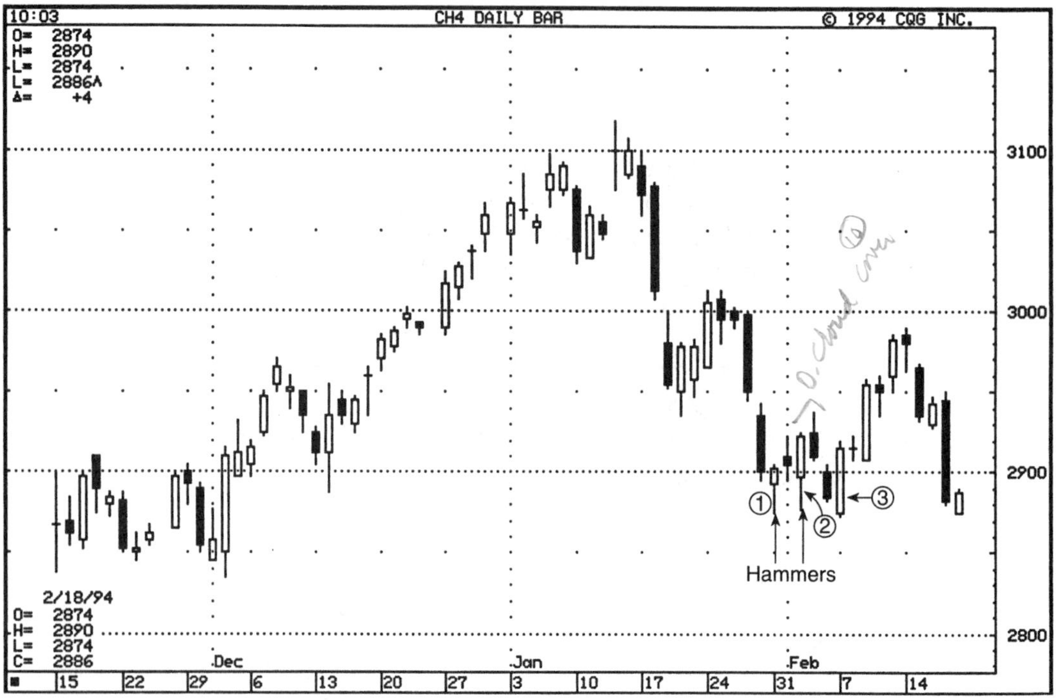

Source: CQG Inc.; copyright © 1994 by CQG Inc.

The Hanging Man

The hanging man (Figure 13.7) has the same shape as the hammer just de-scribed: a long lower shadow and a small real body at the upper end of the candle's range. The distinction between the two is that, whereas the hammer appears after a sell-off, the hanging man appears after a rally. In other words, while both the hammer and hanging man have the same shape, they are referred to by different names depending on the trend preceding the candle line. When the pattern develops after an uptrend (i.e., hanging man), it indicates that the market's advance may be near an end. The name hanging man is derived from the fact that the pattern looks like a hanging man with dangling legs.

It may seem unusual that the same candlestick line can be both bullish and bearish. Yet, the same dichotomy appears in Western charting. For example, the island formation on bar charts is either bullish or bearish depending on the preceding trend. An island after a prolonged uptrend is bearish, while the same island pattern after a downtrend is bullish (see Chapter 6).

Analogous to the hammer, the longer the lower shadow, the shorter the upper shadow, and the smaller the real body, the more meaningful the hang-

Figure 13.7
HANGING MAN

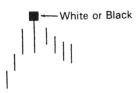

ing man. It is especially important to wait for bearish confirmation with the hanging man, since the pattern's long lower shadow shows that there is still rising power left in the market. An example of such confirmation would be a close below the real body of the hanging man in the next period—a development that would indicate that everyone who bought at the open or close of the hanging man session is now losing money. In this scenario, these longs may decide to liquidate, thereby triggering a further weakening of prices.

In Figure 13.8 a hanging man formed at point 1. However, note the lack of confirmation in the following session when prices moved above the high of the hanging man at point 1. The fact that prices close higher than the hanging man

Figure 13.8
HANGING MAN AND CONFIRMATION: MARCH 1994 COCOA

session voids any of the bearish potential of the hanging man. Point 2, however, is another hanging man, and in this case the next session (point 3) provided confirmation of the pattern, as prices closed below the body of the hanging man.

The Shooting Star

Just as a candle in a downtrend with a long lower shadow (hammer) is potentially bullish, a candle with a long upper shadow after an uptrend has bearish overtones. If a candle with a very long upper shadow and a small real body near the bottom end of the session's range emerges during an uptrend, it is called a "shooting star" (Figure 13.9). A classic shooting star has a real body that gaps away from the prior real body. The color of the real body is unimportant.

The Japanese place the most emphasis on the real body—they refer to the real body (the relationship between the open and close) as the essence of the price movement. However, shadows can play an important part in assessing the market's action. For example, the shooting star's long upper shadow graphically displays that the bears are aggressive enough to drag prices down to near the lows by the close of that session.

As shown in Figure 13.10, a shooting star emerged at January's price peak. This shooting star confirmed the resistance area set by the prior day's high near 118. The shooting star graphically tells us that the market opened near its low on this day, then strongly rallied, and finally backed off to close near the low of the session.

The Engulfing Patterns

A bullish engulfing pattern (Figure 13.11) occurs when the market is in a downtrend, and a white real body engulfs the prior period's black real body. A bearish engulfing pattern (Figure 13.12) occurs when the market is in an uptrend, and a black real body engulfs the prior period's white real body. For an engulfing pattern to be valid, the market has to be in a clearly definable

Figure 13.9
SHOOTING STAR

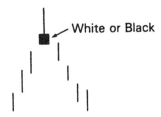

White or Black

Figure 13.10
SHOOTING STAR AND BULLISH ENGULFING
PATTERN: MARCH 1994 T-BONDS

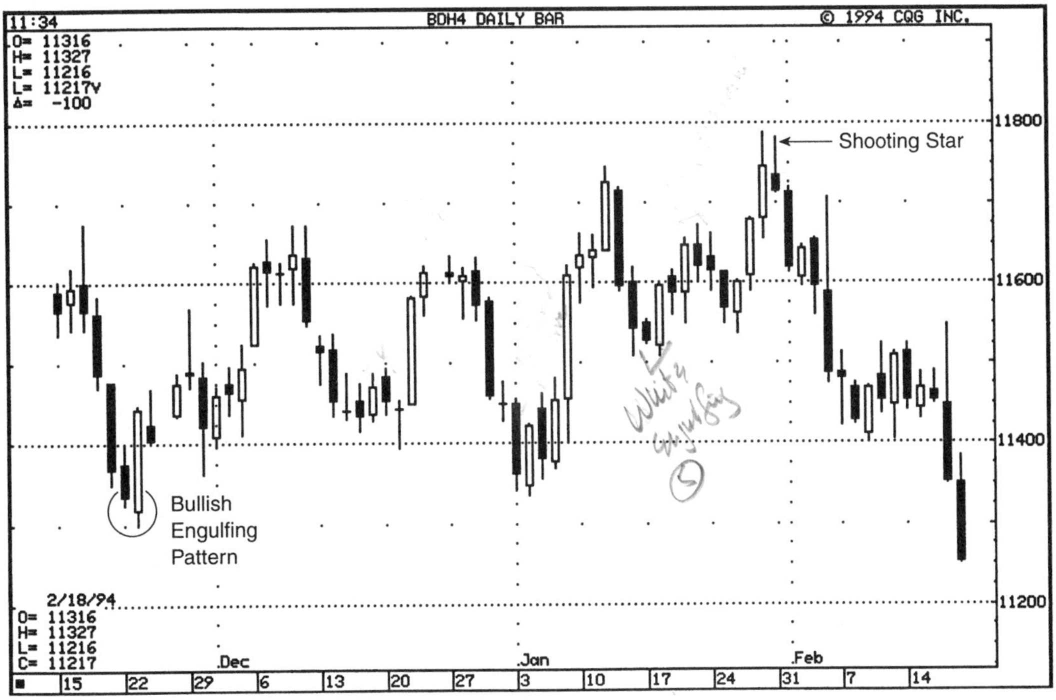

Source: CQG Inc.; copyright © 1994 by CQG Inc.

uptrend or downtrend—even if it is a short-term trend. Because the engulfing pattern requires only that the second real body engulf the prior real body (and not the shadows), this pattern will give a signal not visible on a bar chart. The larger the second body (i.e., the engulfing body) relative to the first, the more significant the pattern.

The engulfing pattern is illustrative of how candles can help provide greater insight into the behavior of the markets. A candle chart, like a bar chart, shows the trend of the market, but, unlike the bar chart, candles also show the force behind the move. If the market is in a downtrend, it means that the bears are in control. If a long white candle then wraps around a black candle after a downtrend (i.e., forms a bullish engulfing pattern), it demonstrates that the bulls have wrested control from the bears.

Looking again at Figure 13.10, we see an example of a bullish engulfing pattern in mid-November. The long white candle following the short black real body shows the force of the bulls wresting control from the bears and represents a classic bullish engulfing pattern. Note how this bullish engulfing pattern became support throughout December and January.

**Figure 13.11
BULLISH ENGULFING
PATTERN**

**Figure 13.12
BEARISH ENGULFING
PATTERN**

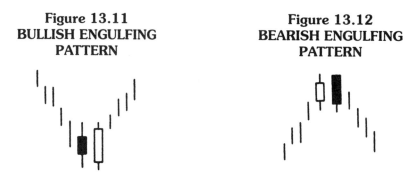

Figure 13.13 provides an example of a bearish engulfing pattern. In early February, the market had broken out above resistance implied by the prior two-month trading range (near $16.00). Shortly thereafter, however, the emergence of a bearish engulfing pattern hinted that the market was in trouble. This was a classic bearish engulfing pattern, as the second black real body was much larger than the prior white real body.

**Figure 13.13
BEARISH ENGULFING PATTERN AND MORNING
STAR: MARCH 1994 CRUDE OIL**

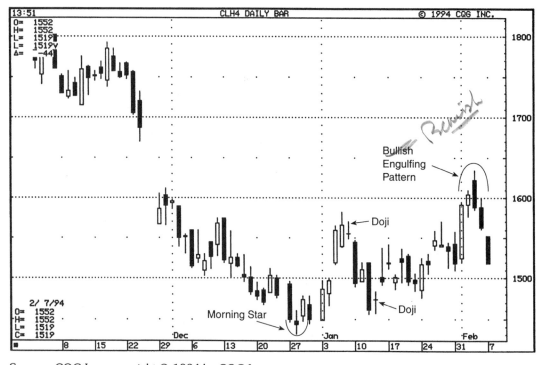

Source: CQG Inc.; copyright © 1994 by CQG Inc.

Figure 13.14
BEARISH ENGULFING PATTERN: MARCH
1994 T-BONDS 60-MINUTE CHART

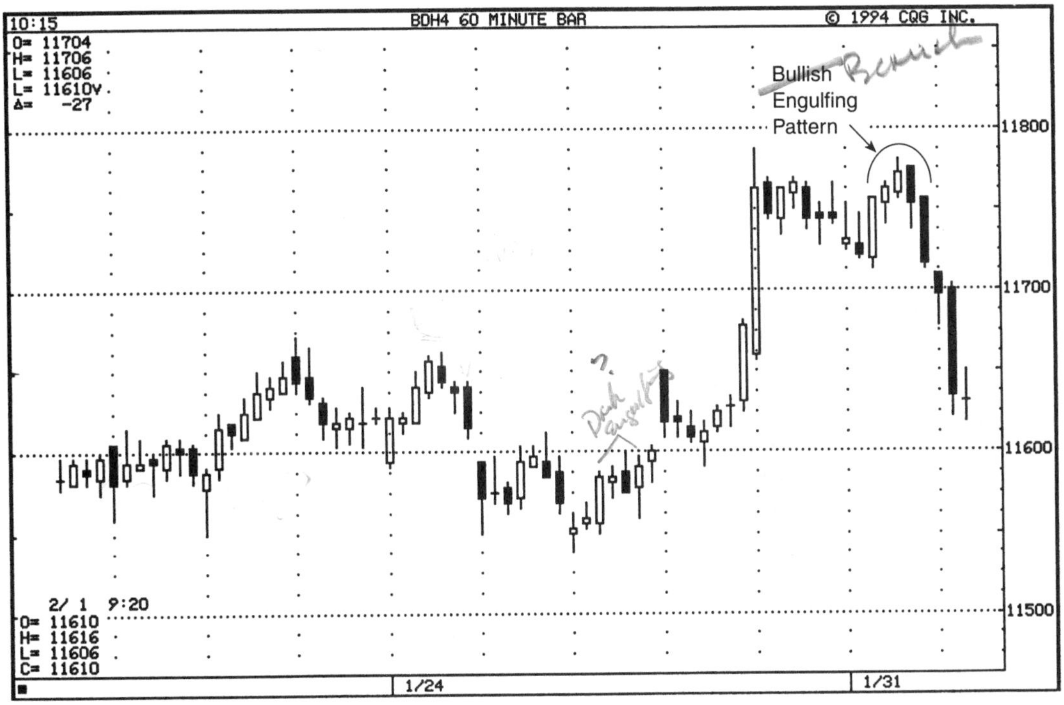

Source: CQG Inc.; copyright © 1994 by CQG Inc.

Figure 13.14 illustrates a bearish engulfing pattern in an intraday chart. Note in this example that the second session of the bearish engulfing pattern does not make a new high. Thus, a bar chart would show no sign of a reversal, which requires a new high and a close below the prior close. However, all that is required for a bearish engulfing pattern is that the second candle's black real body wrap around the prior candle's white real body. Thus, in this instance, the candlestick chart provided a reversal signal—via the bearish engulfing pattern—that was not evident on a bar chart. This is just one example of how candle charts can provide an early reversal signal that is not available to users of bar charts.

The Dark Cloud Cover

The dark cloud cover (Figure 13.15) is a bearish reversal signal. The first session of this two-candlestick pattern is a strong white real body. The second session's price opens above the prior session's high (i.e., above the top of the

Figure 13.15
DARK CLOUD COVER

upper shadow). By the end of the second session, however, the market closes near the low of the session and well within the prior session's white body. The dark cloud cover pictorially illustrates that the market's ability to rise has been immobilized.

The greater the degree of penetration into the white real body, the more valid the signal. Some Japanese technicians require the black real body to penetrate at least 50% into the white real body. If the black candlestick does not close below the halfway point of the white candlestick, it may be best to wait for more bearish confirmation on the session after the dark cloud cover.

Figure 13.16 provides an illustration of a dark cloud cover. On the first session of this pattern, the bulls were still in control. On the next session, the market opened at a new high. The bulls were obviously still content. But then by the end of the second session, prices fell, closing well below the midpoint of the prior session's white real body. With new highs failing, and prices closing well below the prior close, longs may have second thoughts about their positions and decide to liquidate. Also, in seeing the inability of bulls to hold new highs, traders waiting to sell short might step in. It's remarkable how much information can be gleaned from the mere two candle lines that make up the dark cloud cover.

The Morning Star

The morning star (Figure 13.17) is a bottom reversal pattern. Its name is derived from the morning star (the planet Mercury), because just as its name-sake foretells the sunrise, the morning star presages higher prices. The morning star is a three-day pattern that consists of a tall, black real body, followed by a small real body (white or black) that gaps lower, and finally a white real body that moves well within the first period's black real body. This pattern signals that the bulls have seized control.

When the morning star pattern begins, the market is in a downtrend, as evidenced by the tall, black real body in the most recent trading session. At

Figure 13.16
DARK CLOUD COVER: MARCH 1994 HEATING OIL

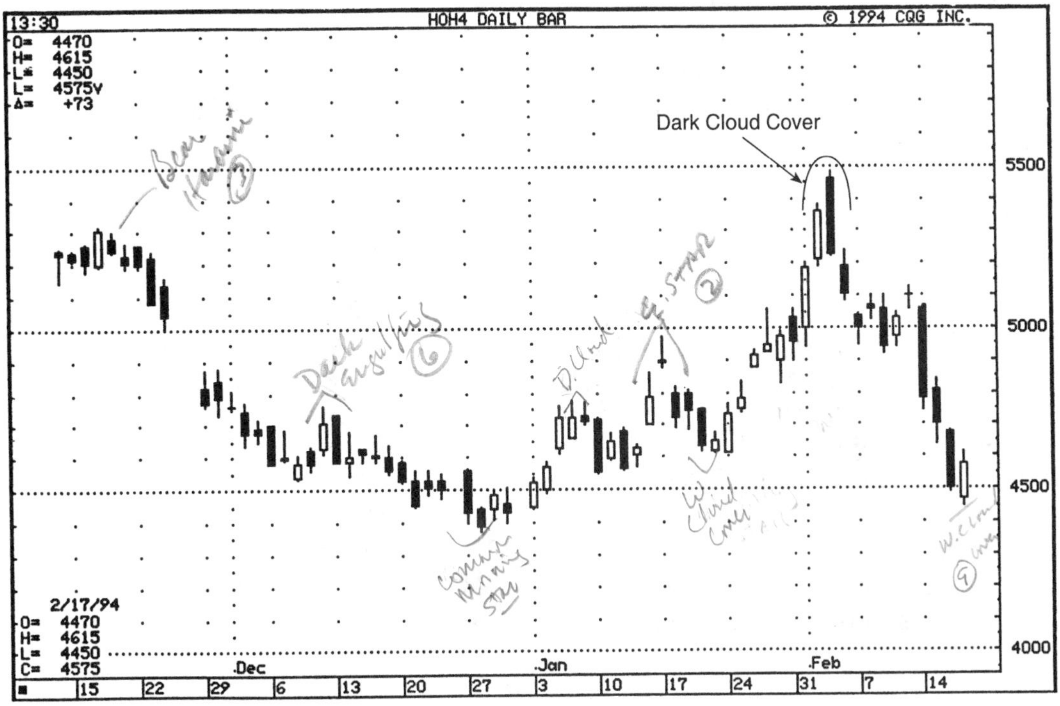

Dark Cloud Cover

Source: CQG Inc.; copyright © 1994 by CQG Inc.

this point, the bears are clearly in command. Then a small real body appears, suggesting that sellers are losing the capability to drive the market lower. Finally, on the third day, the large, white real body demonstrates that the bulls have taken over. An ideal morning star would have a gap before and after the middle line's real body (i.e., the star). The second gap, however, is rare, and its absence does not substantially reduce the significance of the formation.

Referring back to Figure 13.13, we see an example of a morning star

Figure 13.17
MORNING STAR

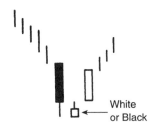

White
or Black

formed at the late-December bottom. Many of the candle patterns, such as the morning star discussed here, become important support or resistance areas. For example, note that the doji that appeared following a large, black real body in mid-January—a formation suggesting an upside reversal—formed just above the support area implied by the morning star. (Interestingly, another doji that appeared four days earlier following a tall white candle in early January, presaged a price decline.)

The Evening Star

The evening star (Figure 13.18) is the bearish counterpart of the morning star pattern. In the evening star, a long, white real body is followed by a small real body (black or white), and finally a black real body that moves sharply into the first session's white real body. The third candle corroborates a top and completes the three-candle pattern of the evening star.

One of the most fascinating aspects of candle charts is the terminology. For example, the previously discussed morning star was named after the planet Mercury, which comes out before the sun rises—a bullish connotation. The evening star is named after the planet Venus, which comes out before darkness sets in, an association with clear bearish overtones. Thus, the names of the candlestick patterns convey the emotional health of the market at the time the pattern is formed.

Just as a morning star can become a support area, the evening star can become a resistance level. As illustrated in Figure 13.19, the evening star formed on the weekly Italian bond chart provided a ceiling for the subsequent rally. A clear failure of the evening star would require a close above the highest upper shadow of the pattern. In this case, it would require a weekly close above the high of the evening star to confirm a breakout from the evening star's resistance area.

**Figure 13.18
EVENING STAR**

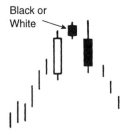

Black or
White

Figure 13.19
EVENING STAR: ITALIAN BOND WEEKLY CHART

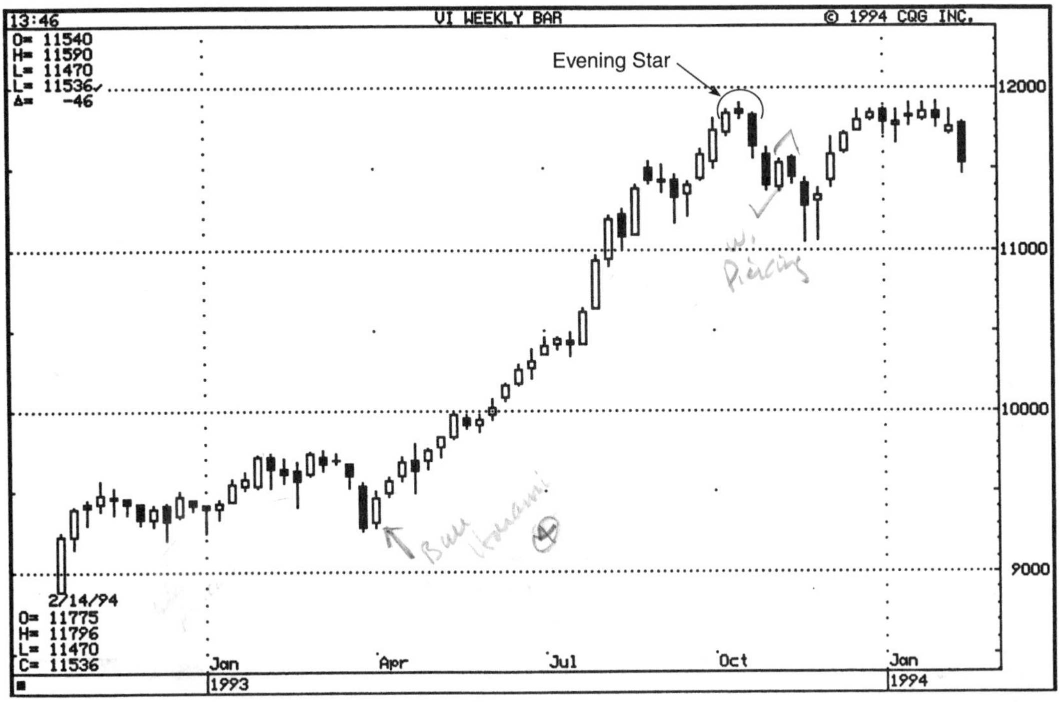

Source: CQG Inc.; copyright © 1994 by CQG Inc.

Windows

The "window" in candlestick charts is the same as a gap in bar charts. Thus a rising window forms when the low of the today's lower shadow is above the high of yesterday's upper shadow (Figure 13.20). A falling window occurs when the top of today's upper shadow is below the low of yesterday's lower shadow (Figure 13.21). Windows provide good visual clues because they display market action and sentiment that is very one-sided.

Windows are continuation patterns in that the market normally resumes the direction of the trend that preceded the pattern. Thus, after a rising window, which is a bullish continuation pattern, the prior uptrend should continue. A falling window has bearish implications, since it implies that the prior downtrend should resume.

A Japanese saying about windows is, "The reaction will go until the window." In other words, the window should be the limit on a reaction. Thus, for a rising window, sell-offs should stop within the window. For a falling window,

**Figure 13.20
RISING WINDOW**

**Figure 13.21
FALLING WINDOW**

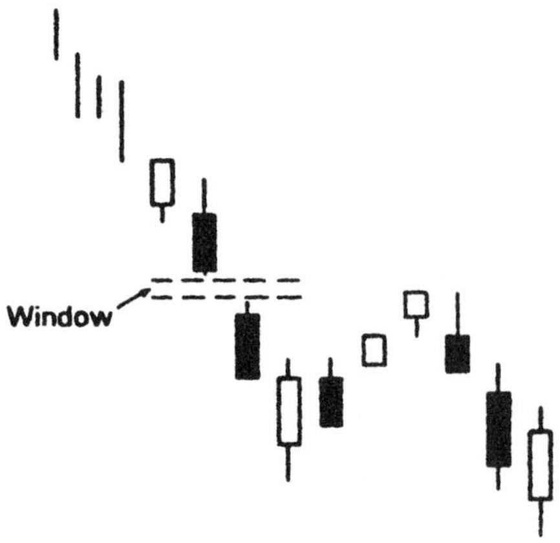

**Figure 13.22
FALLING WINDOW AS RESISTANCE:
MARCH 1994 UNLEADED GAS**

Source: CQG Inc.; copyright © 1994 by CQG Inc.

rallies should stop within the window. Figure 13.22 provides an example of a rally failing at a prior falling window. Note also how this reversal was confirmed by a shooting star.

When using windows as support and resistance indicators, it should be noted that prices may temporarily fall below the bottom of a rising window, or rise above the top of a falling window, before moving back in the direction of the window. For example, in Figure 13.23, note that although the September low held in the vicinity of the prior rising window, it penetrated the low of that window.

As a general rule, a window can be considered voided (in terms of its significance as support or resistance) if prices *close* beyond the window, but not if prices merely penetrate the window intraday (or intraweek for a weekly chart). For example, if there is a rising window between $83 and $85 and then the market closes under the bottom of the window (i.e., under $83), the uptrend can be considered to be over. Conversely, if there is a falling window between $62 and $60, once the bulls close the market above the top of this window (over $62), the downtrend can be considered terminated.

Figure 13.23
RISING WINDOW AS SUPPORT: GOLD WEEKLY CHART

Source: CQG Inc.; copyright © 1994 by CQG Inc.

CONCLUSION

The Japanese say, "The psychology of market participants, the supply and demand equation, and the relative strengths of buyers and sellers are all reflected in the one candlestick or in a combination of candlesticks." This chapter was just an introduction to candlestick chart analysis. There are many more patterns, concepts, and trading techniques. But even this basic introduction should provide a sense of how candles open new doors of analysis. The essential point is that candlestick charts provide an extra dimension that is unavailable in bar charts, and yet allow the trader to use all the same technical devices that can be applied to bar charts. Ideally, candlestick charts would be combined with Western chart analysis techniques.

AFTERWORD (by Jack Schwager)

Most classical chart patterns do not lend themselves to objective, precise mathematical definition. That is, although these patterns can be defined mathematically, different people will come up with significantly different definitions. For example, if 10 competent computer programmers were asked to write code that would identify a head-and-shoulders formation, it is quite likely that all 10 resulting programs would differ somewhat in the segments of data within a price series they identified as pattern occurrences.

Candlestick chart patterns are different, however, in that their simplicity—most require only one, two, or three price bars—generally does allow for specific, objective (or at least near objective) definitions. For example, although different people might come up with different specifications of how long the lower shadow needs to be for a day to be defined as a hammer, there would be a great degree of similarity between varying definitions. Moreover, some candlestick patterns would lend themselves to exact mathematical definitions. For example, a bearish engulfing pattern—a black real body that engulfs the prior period's white real body—can be described by an exact mathematical definition. This quality of candlestick patterns means that it is possible to computer test the predictive accuracy of these patterns. The obvious question is: Can one profit from automatically implementing trades at the occurrence of candlestick patterns?

To answer this question, I turned to Bruce Babcock, the editor and publisher of *Commodity Traders Consumers Report*, who had developed a software program to test candlestick patterns.[1] The test I requested Bruce to run was a simple one: Would a buy-and-hold (or sell-and-hold) strategy following the occurrence of various basic candlestick patterns show a profit over the next 5 to 10 days?

---

[1] The software used was the *Candlestick Professional System Tester,* produced by *Commodity Traders Consumer Report,* 1731 Howe Street, Sacramento, CA 95825.

Six patterns—each in a bullish and bearish equivalent—were tested for a sample of 10 markets, using 5 years of data (1900–1994). At Bruce's suggestion, these patterns were also tested with a five-day momentum filter to assure that the trade was consistent with the short-term trend direction. In each case, $100 was deducted per trade to cover slippage and commissions. The results, which are summarized in Table 13.1, were not encouraging. Only a small minority of pattern/market combinations tested showed profitability in a five-year test. Even the profitable combinations were not good enough to trade, as the drawdowns were much too large in relation to profits. It is worth noting, however, that the filter variations did better, suggesting that taking the trend into account is at least a step in the right direction.

The test just described does not prove that candlestick charts have no value, but rather that a simplistic interpretation of candlestick patterns is not profitable. The implied lesson is that blindly following candlestick patterns is not an effective methodology. However, it is entirely possible that a more complex analysis of candlestick charts, which takes into account the context in which specific candlestick patterns occur (i.e., other prevailing patterns, both candlestick and classical) and incorporates money management strategies, could be useful. (These aspects are discussed in Nison's new book, *Beyond Candlesticks*.) Also, insofar as candlestick charts show more information than bar charts and offer an alternative visual depiction of price data, some traders may find these charts more natural or useful than conventional bar charts. The bottom line is that a determination of whether candlestick charts are a useful tool must be made individually by each trader based on experience and experimentation. In this respect, candlestick chart analysis is similar to classical chart analysis—it is more of an art than a science.

Table 13.1
CANDLE PATTERN TESTS[a]

(a) Hammers and Hanging Man Lines (No Filters, Hold 5 Days)

	Number of Trades	Percent Winners	Maximum Drawdown	Average Trade	Net Profit
T-Bonds	38	47	12,425	−261	−9925
Eurodollars	17	53	1,775	−49	−825
D-Marks	18	61	5,688	97	1,737
J. Yen	21	48	7,213	50	1,050
Gold	26	38	5,830	−119	−3,090
Silver	25	36	6,835	−246	−6,160
Soybeans	13	46	2,513	9	113
Corn	19	26	3,288	−149	−2,838
Crude Oil	17	47	3,180	−14	−230
Sugar	39	31	12,202	−281	−10,945

Table 13.1 (continued)

(b) Hammers and Hanging Man Lines (Momentum Filter, Hold 5 Days)

	Number of Trades	Percent Winners	Maximum Drawdown	Average Trade	Net Profit
T-Bonds	42	50	9,056	–19	–794
Eurodollars	18	56	2,800	–60	–1,075
D-Marks	19	26	8,063	–375	–7,125
J. Yen	21	43	7,937	–193	–4,050
Gold	28	46	3,120	39	1,100
Silver	25	52	2,285	70	1,760
Soybeans	13	38	3,400	–259	–3,363
Corn	18	33	1,538	–76	–1,375
Crude Oil	17	29	5,960	–262	–4,450
Sugar	39	54	2,082	106	4,130

(c) Hammers and Hanging Man Lines (No Filters, Hold 10 Days)

	Number of Trades	Percent Winners	Maximum Drawdown	Average Trade	Net Profit
T-Bonds	32	50	6,588	–38	–1,200
Eurodollars	16	44	2,550	–158	–2,525
D-Marks	18	56	5,425	349	6,287
J. Yen	19	63	8,325	313	5,950
Gold	24	33	4,330	–125	–2,990
Silver	25	44	6,790	–180	–4,510
Soybeans	12	67	1,438	101	1,213
Corn	19	26	5,038	–235	–4,463
Crude Oil	17	59	3,060	106	1,800
Sugar	36	39	13,190	–295	–10,634

(d) Hammers and Hanging Man Lines (Momentum Filter, Hold 10 Days)

	Number of Trades	Percent Winners	Maximum Drawdown	Average Trade	Net Profit
T-Bonds	40	45	13,119	–313	–12,500
Eurodollars	18	44	4,450	–182	–3,275
D-Marks	19	37	8,675	–292	–5,550
J. Yen	21	43	12,100	–275	–5,775
Gold	26	46	4,830	–118	–3,080
Silver	25	52	3,860	89	2,230
Soybeans	12	33	3,475	–271	–3,250
Corn	18	44	1,250	–52	–938
Crude Oil	17	35	6,780	–287	–4,880
Sugar	37	57	2,166	131	4,857

Table 13.1 (continued)

(e) Engulfing Pattern (No Filters, Hold 5 Days)

	Number of Trades	Percent Winners	Maximum Drawdown	Average Trade	Net Profit
T-Bonds	102	37	30,069	−235	−23,950
Eurodollars	49	45	6,600	−111	−5,450
D-Marks	71	44	26,563	−323	−22,925
J. Yen	54	39	16,112	−298	−16,112
Gold	84	37	12,860	−70	−5,920
Silver	93	32	7,705	−83	−7,695
Soybeans	101	35	11,813	−83	−8,400
Corn	65	31	7,563	−116	−7,563
Crude Oil	97	40	14,760	−132	−12,780
Sugar	74	35	7,784	−105	−7,747

(f) Engulfing Pattern (Momentum Filter, Hold 5 Days)

	Number of Trades	Percent Winners	Maximum Drawdown	Average Trade	Net Profit
T-Bonds	40	45	12,169	−253	−10,125
Eurodollars	15	33	3,050	−170	−2,550
D-Marks	27	41	16,225	−601	−16,225
J. Yen	19	26	12,813	−674	−12,813
Gold	29	45	4,570	−12	−350
Silver	32	31	6,270	−95	−3,050
Soybeans	32	53	3,288	93	2,975
Corn	23	43	2,413	−18	−413
Crude Oil	37	38	8,030	−75	−2,760
Sugar	26	35	2,870	−106	−2,757

(g) Engulfing Pattern (No Filters, Hold 10 Days)

	Number of Trades	Percent Winners	Maximum Drawdown	Average Trade	Net Profit
T-Bonds	91	36	35,663	−263	−23,913
Eurodollars	45	38	7,625	−129	−5,825
D-Marks	65	48	27,625	−335	−21,788
J. Yen	51	35	31,513	−618	−31,513
Gold	74	42	15,370	−115	−8,480
Silver	78	33	13,795	−177	−13,770
Soybeans	83	43	10,763	−78	−6,463
Corn	56	30	7,663	−123	−6,888
Crude Oil	89	42	9,920	51	4,510
Sugar	62	34	10,235	−160	−9,896

Table 13.1 (continued)

(h) Engulfing Pattern (Momentum Filter, Hold 10 Days)

	Number of Trades	Percent Winners	Maximum Drawdown	Average Trade	Net Profit
T-Bonds	38	47	14,581	−306	−11,613
Eurodollars	15	40	3,750	−165	−2,475
D-Marks	25	32	26,788	−1,055	−26,363
J. Yen	19	26	17,325	−912	−17,325
Gold	29	52	3,190	116	3,370
Silver	30	43	7,140	−112	−3,360
Soybeans	31	45	5,038	−23	−725
Corn	22	55	1,875	19	425
Crude Oil	36	50	3,790	212	7,650
Sugar	24	38	3,690	−111	−2,669

(i) Shooting Star (No Filters, Hold 5 Days)

	Number of Trades	Percent Winners	Maximum Drawdown	Average Trade	Net Profit
T-Bonds	36	36	14,069	−237	−8,538
Eurodollars	15	33	4,050	−172	−2,575
D-Marks	28	36	8,575	−109	−3,062
J. Yen	28	50	9,612	−146	−4,087
Gold	41	39	6,770	−129	−5,300
Silver	12	25	2,045	−91	−1,095
Soybeans	27	48	3,063	−95	−2,563
Corn	30	37	6,450	−127	−3,813
Crude Oil	24	42	4,980	−85	−2,030
Sugar	36	28	4,518	−126	−4,518

(j) Shooting Star (Momentum Filter, Hold 5 Days)

	Number of Trades	Percent Winners	Maximum Drawdown	Average Trade	Net Profit
T-Bonds	25	44	6,556	−75	−1,875
Eurodollars	13	38	2,700	−73	−950
D-Marks	18	44	4,475	171	3,075
J. Yen	17	47	11,150	−377	−6,412
Gold	26	42	3,980	−135	−3,500
Silver	4	25	850	−138	−550
Soybeans	18	50	1,738	153	2,763
Corn	22	36	3,888	−81	−1,775
Crude Oil	18	33	4,990	−149	−2,680
Sugar	24	42	2,187	−60	−1,448

Table 13.1 (continued)

(k) Shooting Star (No Filters, Hold 10 Days)

	Number of Trades	Percent Winners	Maximum Drawdown	Average Trade	Net Profit
T-Bonds	30	37	17,013	−402	−12,063
Eurodollars	15	40	4,600	−205	−3,075
D-Marks	24	38	14,975	−420	−10,075
J. Yen	26	38	18,137	−440	−11,450
Gold	36	33	5,910	−86	−3,080
Silver	11	64	1,360	152	1,670
Soybeans	26	46	3,925	−11	−275
Corn	26	46	4,788	−37	−950
Crude Oil	21	57	1,350	162	3,410
Sugar	30	33	3,026	−69	−2,070

(l) Shooting Star (Momentum Filter, Hold 10 Days)

	Number of Trades	Percent Winners	Maximum Drawdown	Average Trade	Net Profit
T-Bonds	21	52	10,163	159	3,338
Eurodollars	13	38	4,175	−188	−2,450
D-Marks	17	35	9,150	−272	−4,625
J. Yen	17	41	14,675	−373	−6,337
Gold	23	39	3,340	−106	−2,430
Silver	4	50	665	−51	−205
Soybeans	17	47	1,700	259	4,400
Corn	21	48	4,200	−42	−875
Crude Oil	17	47	2,010	1	10
Sugar	21	48	1,875	119	2,503

(m) Doji (No Filters, Hold 5 Days)

	Number of Trades	Percent Winners	Maximum Drawdown	Average Trade	Net Profit
T-Bonds	23	43	13,581	−590	−13,581
Eurodollars	93	38	7,100	−59	−5,525
D-Marks	22	50	6,012	−98	−2,162
J. Yen	12	25	4,838	−327	−3,925
Gold	25	44	3,530	−128	−3,190
Silver	18	28	3,665	79	1,425
Soybeans	23	39	6,188	−269	−6,188
Corn	60	38	2,463	−39	−2,325
Crude Oil	23	30	8,850	−160	−3,690
Sugar	33	21	7,166	−201	−6,638

Table 13.1 (continued)

(n) Doji (Momentum Filter, Hold 5 Days)

	Number of Trades	Percent Winners	Maximum Drawdown	Average Trade	Net Profit
T-Bonds	8	38	3,819	−416	−3,331
Eurodollars	35	31	4,900	−123	−4,300
D-Marks	9	44	1,362	−35	−312
J. Yen	5	0	1,450	−290	−1,450
Gold	8	38	930	−116	−930
Silver	9	56	815	618	5,560
Soybeans	8	38	1,488	−48	−388
Corn	18	39	688	−9	−163
Crude Oil	7	43	1,170	−144	−1,010
Sugar	13	8	2,622	−202	−2,622

(o) Doji (No Filters, Hold 10 Days)

	Number of Trades	Percent Winners	Maximum Drawdown	Average Trade	Net Profit
T-Bonds	20	25	16,938	−847	−16,938
Eurodollars	79	42	5,000	−26	−2,050
D-Marks	21	52	6,975	−26	−538
J. Yen	12	50	2,662	306	3,675
Gold	24	46	3,300	68	1,630
Silver	18	33	7,605	−103	−1,850
Soybeans	23	30	9,138	−397	−9,138
Corn	56	52	1,825	45	2,513
Crude Oil	23	35	8,550	−313	−7,210
Sugar	29	45	4,689	−70	−2,038

(p) Doji (Momentum Filter, Hold 10 Days)

	Number of Trades	Percent Winners	Maximum Drawdown	Average Trade	Net Profit
T-Bonds	8	25	5,950	−674	−5,394
Eurodollars	32	47	5,150	−127	−4,075
D-Marks	9	56	2,350	532	4,787
J. Yen	5	40	3,350	−365	−1,825
Gold	8	25	1,350	−169	−1,350
Silver	9	56	2,420	533	4,975
Soybeans	8	38	1,638	−77	−613
Corn	18	56	738	55	988
Crude Oil	7	29	2,210	−316	−2,210
Sugar	11	45	2,795	−55	−607

Table 13.1 (continued)

(q) Piercing Line and Dark Cloud Cover (No Filters, Hold 5 Days)[b]

	Number of Trades	Percent Winners	Maximum Drawdown	Average Trade	Net Profit
T-Bonds	15	20	13,938	−929	−13,938
Eurodollars	5	40	1,150	−175	−875
D-Marks	8	63	6,725	−542	−4,338
J. Yen	11	27	6,400	−582	−6,400
Gold	14	43	2,230	−99	−1,380
Silver	14	29	1,820	−56	−790
Soybeans	19	32	5,938	−294	−5,588
Corn	25	32	2,888	−116	−2,888
Crude Oil	25	32	4,490	−144	−3,610
Sugar	13	38	1,463	−60	−785

(r) Piercing Line and Dark Cloud Cover (Momentum Filter, Hold 5 Days)[b]

	Number of Trades	Percent Winners	Maximum Drawdown	Average Trade	Net Profit
T-Bonds	5	40	3,181	−538	−2,688
Eurodollars	3	33	825	−233	−700
D-Marks	3	67	1,088	71	212
J. Yen	8	25	4,275	−534	−4,275
Gold	4	75	410	155	620
Silver	6	50	610	278	1,665
Soybeans	8	13	4,525	−566	−4,525
Corn	12	33	1,163	−94	−1,125
Crude Oil	12	17	3,580	−250	−3,000
Sugar	10	40	1,028	−8	−82

(s) Piercing Line and Dark Cloud Cover (No Filters, Hold 10 Days)[b]

	Number of Trades	Percent Winners	Maximum Drawdown	Average Trade	Net Profit
T-Bonds	15	33	9,344	−623	−9,344
Eurodollars	5	40	1,825	−260	−1,300
D-Marks	8	25	11,250	−813	−6,500
J. Yen	11	36	9,662	−878	−9,662
Gold	14	21	4,380	−269	−3,760
Silver	14	21	5,335	−381	−5,335
Soybeans	19	32	6,375	−336	−6,375
Corn	24	42	4,813	−182	−4,363
Crude Oil	24	21	7,350	−290	−6,970
Sugar	13	46	1,991	8	100

Table 13.1 (continued)

(t) Piercing Line and Dark Cloud Cover (Momentum Filter, Hold 10 Days)[b]

	Number of Trades	Percent Winners	Maximum Drawdown	Average Trade	Net Profit
T-Bonds	5	60	1,475	556	2,781
Eurodollars	3	33	1,200	−375	−1,125
D-Marks	3	0	3,963	−1,321‘	−3,963
J. Yen	8	38	6,200	−775	−6,200
Gold	4	50	630	−2	−10
Silver	6	33	2,350	−152	−915
Soybeans	8	25	1,725	−216	−1,725
Corn	12	42	2,350	−170	−2,038
Crude Oil	12	17	4,380	−365	−4,380
Sugar	10	50	625	155	1,554

(u) Morning and Evening Stars (No Filters, Hold 5 Days)

	Number of Trades	Percent Winners	Maximum Drawdown	Average Trade	Net Profit
T-Bonds	22	59	6,188	−89	−1,950
Eurodollars	9	56	1,700	−136	−1,225
D-Marks	18	44	4,200	−181	−3,262
J. Yen	14	36	11,925	−733	−10,263
Gold	11	27	2,350	−174	−1,910
Silver	21	43	1,660	70	1,465
Soybeans	21	38	7,413	−325	−6,825
Corn	12	33	1,950	−96	−1,150
Crude Oil	17	41	4,050	11	180
Sugar	12	17	3,307	−247	−2,958

(v) Morning and Evening Stars (Momentum Filter, Hold 5 Days)

	Number of Trades	Percent Winners	Maximum Drawdown	Average Trade	Net Profit
T-Bonds	12	67	3,781	−35	−419
Eurodollars	3	33	825	−142	−425
D-Marks	12	42	3,662	−187	−2,250
J. Yen	5	20	2,725	15	75
Gold	5	20	1,760	−352	−1,760
Silver	15	53	1,410	184	2,760
Soybeans	8	50	3,263	−330	−2,638
Corn	5	20	1,650	−208	−1,038
Crude Oil	8	25	2,510	−135	−1,080
Sugar	8	25	2,157	−226	−1,808

Table 13.1 (continued)

(w) Morning and Evening Stars (No Filters, Hold 10 Days)

	Number of Trades	Percent Winners	Maximum Drawdown	Average Trade	Net Profit
T-Bonds	21	24	17,725	−722	−15,163
Eurodollars	9	44	1,850	−178	−1,600
D-Marks	18	56	4,063	351	6,325
J. Yen	13	31	7,738	−319	−4,150
Gold	10	60	1,360	−76	−760
Silver	19	58	3,735	249	4,725
Soybeans	21	38	8,938	−364	−7,638
Corn	12	50	1,338	−64	−763
Crude Oil	16	38	9,900	−366	−5,860
Sugar	12	42	4,034	−336	−4,034

(x) Morning and Evening Stars (Momentum Filter, Hold 10 Days)

	Number of Trades	Percent Winners	Maximum Drawdown	Average Trade	Net Profit
T-Bonds	12	17	8,513	−686	−8,231
Eurodollars	3	33	1,125	−367	−1,100
D-Marks	12	50	3,063	373	4,475
J. Yen	5	20	2,475	−288	−1,438
Gold	4	50	1,080	−170	−680
Silver	13	77	2,575	439	5,710
Soybeans	8	50	3,025	−189	−1,513
Corn	5	40	2,500	−395	−1,975
Crude Oil	7	29	7,890	−950	−6,650
Sugar	8	50	3,489	−401	−3,208

[a]All results include $100 deduction for slippage and commissions.
[b]The piercing line, which is not explicitly mentioned in the foregoing chapter, is the bullish counterpart of the dark cloud cover pattern.

Part Two

REAL-WORLD CHART ANALYSIS

14 Real-World Chart Analysis

The spectator's chief enemies are always boring from within. It is inseparable from human nature to hope and to fear. *In speculation when the market goes against you, you hope that every day will be the last day—and you lose more than you should had you not listened to hope—to the same ally that is so potent a success-bringer to empire builders and pioneers, big and little. And when the market goes your way you become fearful that the next day will take away your profit, and you get out—too soon.* Fear keeps you from making as much money as you ought to. *The successful trader has to fight these two deep-seated instincts. He has to reverse what you might call his natural impulses.* Instead of hoping he must fear; instead of fearing he must hope. *He must fear that his loss may develop into a much bigger loss, and hope that his profit may become a big profit.*

—Edwin Lefèvre

It is always easy to analyze a chart with the benefit of hindsight. It is quite another matter to analyze a chart in real time, with actual trading decisions dependent on the outcome. In order to realistically illustrate the process of using charts to make trading decisions, upon signing the contract to do this book, I started keeping a diary of all the trade recommendations I issued in my role as director of futures research at Prudential Securities. For each trade, I noted the reasons for entry and exit, as well as any lessons provided by the trade after the smoke had cleared.

There were too many recommendations to include all such trades in this volume. Also, because the reasoning for many trades was very similar, it was desirable to exclude a substantial portion of the recommendations issued during this period in order to avoid excessive redundancy. However, an effort was made to include a substantive number of losing trades to keep the overall illustration as realistic as possible. (Although the sample in this chapter contains a smaller *percentage* of losing trades than the full list of all trades—because a large proportion of losing trades were short-lived transactions, resulting in small losses, and largely the same as other trades in the group—this factor is counterbalanced by the fact that the cumulative net profit of the trades illustrated is also substantially less than the total profit realized on all trade recommendations issued during the survey period.)

HOW TO USE THIS CHAPTER

1. Do not read this chapter out of sequence. It is essential that Part One be read before this chapter.
2. For maximum benefit, reading this chapter should be a hands-on experience. It is suggested that the reader first photocopy all the *odd* pages of the charts that follow.
3. Each trade contains the reasons for entering the position. Consider whether you interpret the chart the same way. Even technical analysts using the same patterns may interpret these patterns differently. One man's double top is another man's trading range consolidation, and so on. In short, second-guessing is strongly *encouraged*. Remember, many of these trades turned out to be losers.
4. The illustrations in the following charts are top-heavy with the analytical tools and chart patterns that I tend to rely on most heavily. This by no means implies that these methods are the most important or accurate, only that they are the ones I am most comfortable using. Chart analysis is a very subjective endeavor.

    There are many techniques that have been described in this book that are not applied in the following illustrations. Some readers may find these other analytical tools helpful as supplemental input or even as substitute methodologies. The mix of methods I feel most comfortable with is likely to be quite different from the approach that will be most suitable for each individual reader. In essence, each practitioner of chart analysis must choose an individual set of technical tools and define a personal analytical style.
5. Analyze the chart on each odd page using your favorite approach, specifically detailing your own strategy. If you have made photocopies, you can mark these copies up to your heart's content. Then turn to the next (even) page to see how your analysis (and mine) turned out in the real world. This page contains the reasons for trade exit and observations related to the trade.

By following this procedure instead of passively reading the chapter, you will obtain the maximum learning benefit.

Figure 14.1*a*
SEPTEMBER 1993 T-BOND

Trade Entry Reason

A flag formed near the top of a trading range is usually a bullish pattern. The implication is that the ability of the market to move sideways near major resistance (e.g., the top of a trading range), rather than pulling back, reflects significant underlying strength.

Do you agree or disagree with the analysis?
Evaluate the situation before turning page.

Figure 14.1b
SEPTEMBER 1993 T-BOND

Trade Exit

The trade was liquidated on a raised protective stop. The stop was raised to a very close point because of the proximity of a major measured move objective (MM1).

Comment

This trade provides a good illustration of the principle that a market is never too high to buy. Also note that although entry was near a record high price level, the risk on the trade was kept low by being able to define a relatively close stop: the initial stop was placed just below the low end of the illustrated flag pattern in Figure 14.1a.

Figure 14.2a
DECEMBER 1993 T-BOND

Trade Entry Reasons

1. The breakout above the triangular consolidation implied a continuation of the bull move.
2. The pullback brought prices close to the major support level indicated by both an extended internal trend line and the top of the triangle.

Do you agree or disagree with the analysis?
Evaluate the situation before turning page.

Figure 14.2*b*
DECEMBER 1993 T-BOND

Trade Exit

The significant downside penetration of the lower end of the triangle invalidated the original trade signal.

Comment

A trade should always be liquidated once the primary premise for the trade is violated. In this instance, prices should have held above or near the top of the triangle. Once prices broke meaningfully below the low end of the triangle, the validity of the prior breakout seemed highly questionable. Getting out on the first sign that the market had violated the original trade premise helped keep the loss on the trade relatively small. As can be seen in Figure 14.2*b*, even a small amount of procrastination would have been very costly.

Figure 14.3a
MARCH 1993 T-BOND

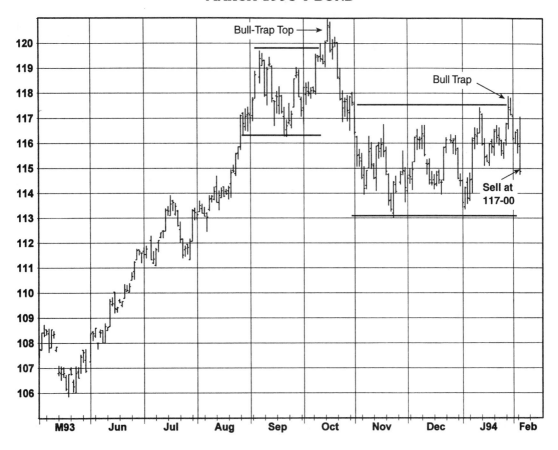

Trade Entry Reasons

1. The October bull-trap top, which formed in record high territory after a very extended price advance, suggested that a major peak had been established. At the time shown, prices had only retraced a small portion of the prior advance, which extended back well before the start of this chart (see, for example, Figure 14.1b), implying substantial further downside potential.

2. The late January upside breakout above the November–January trading range and the subsequent pullback deep into the range represented another bull-trap.

Note that the trade recommendation called for selling on a rebound back to 117-00 as opposed to going short at the market.

Do you agree or disagree with the analysis?
Evaluate the situation before turning page.

Figure 14.3b
MARCH 1993 T-BOND

Comment

As can be seen on the chart, the market failed to rebound to the recommended sell point at 117-00. As shown, the sell point was subsequently lowered on three separate occasions. In each instance, the market failed to reach the recommended sell level. As a result, even though the original trade idea was excellent, with the market witnessing a large and rapid price move in the anticipated direction, the trade opportunity was entirely missed.

In every trade there is a tradeoff between getting a better entry price and assuring that the position is implemented. This trade highlights the potential pitfall in waiting for a better entry level instead of initiating the position at the market. As in this example, such a more cautious approach can result in missing major winning trades. This observation is not intended to imply that one should always implement intended trades at the market, but it does serve to emphasize the attribute of market orders: they assure that trading opportunities will not be missed. In particular, market orders should be favored in long-term trades that are believed to offer a large profit potential—as was the case in this illustration. Even so, the error made in this trade was not the initial use of a limit order, which could have been justified based on the prevailing trading-range pattern, but rather the failure to convert to a market entry approach once the price action (e.g., the flag consolidations formed after the initial recommendation) suggested that a rebound was unlikely.

Figure 14.4a
T-BOND CONTINUOUS FUTURES

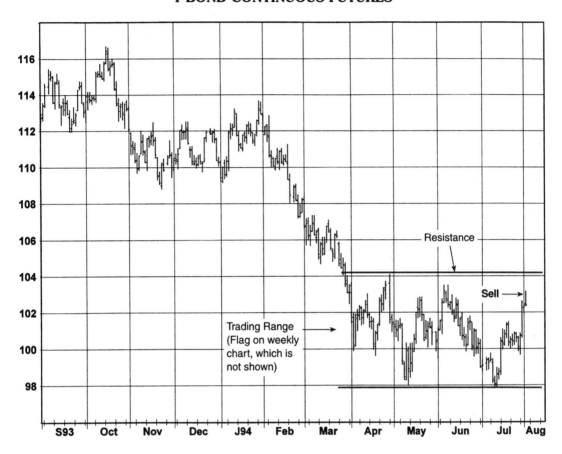

Trade Entry Reasons

1. On a long-term (weekly) chart, the April–July trading range had the appearance of a flag consolidation—a formation that suggests an impending price move in the direction of the preceding price swing.

2. The market was near the resistance level implied by the upper band of the trading range.

Do you agree or disagree with the analysis?
Evaluate the situation before turning page.

Figure 14.4b
T-BOND CONTINUOUS FUTURES

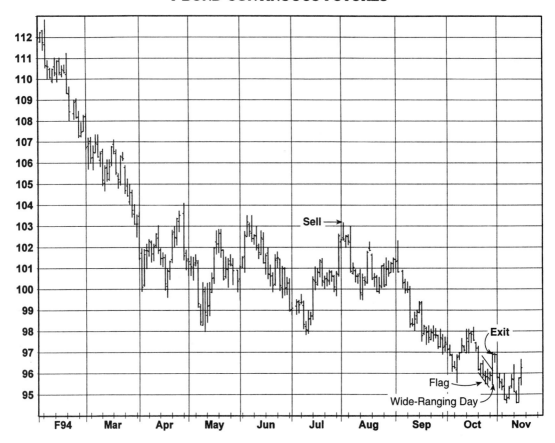

Trade Exit

The trade was liquidated because the short-term price action suggested a possible reversal. Specifically, the exit day witnessed a counter-to-anticipated breakout from a flag consolidation and was also a wide-ranging up day.

Comment

Although on the illustrated daily bar chart for trade entry (Figure 14.4a) it was just as plausible to assume that the prevailing trading range represented a bottom formation as it was to assume that it was a pause in an unfinished downtrend, the long-term weekly chart (not shown) strongly favored the latter interpretation. The point is that it is usually advisable to first examine a longer-term chart to gain a broad perspective before analyzing a shorter-term chart. (As used here, the terms *longer term* and *shorter term* are subjective. For some traders, longer term will mean weekly or monthly and shorter term daily; for other traders, longer term might mean daily and shorter term intraday.)

In regards to the trade liquidation, although the exit day ultimately proved not to be a reversal, the reasoning for liquidation was still sound, especially in view of the substantial favorable price move realized by the trade, which enhanced the chance of at least an intermediate rebound. In fact, prices only extended modestly lower before rebounding above the exit point (see Figure 14.5a).

318

Figure 14.5*a*
T-BOND CONTINUOUS FUTURES

Trade Entry Reasons

1. Upside price gap.
2. Upside breakout of flag consolidation.
3. Wide-ranging up day.

Do you agree or disagree with the analysis?
Evaluate the situation before turning page.

Figure 14.5b
T-BOND CONTINUOUS FUTURES

Trade Exit

The trade was liquidated because of a sustained downside breakout of a triangular consolidation following a failed upside breakout of the same pattern.

Comment

Although in hindsight, the decision to liquidate the trade proved to be wrong, I would not term it a trading mistake, since at the time it had appeared that a price reversal had occurred.

Figure 14.6a
T-BOND CONTINUOUS FUTURES

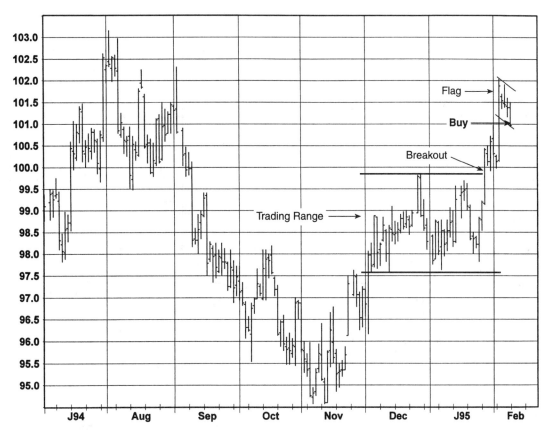

Trade Entry Reasons

1. Sustained upside breakout above prior trading range.
2. Flag consolidation formed above prior trading range.

Do you agree or disagree with the analysis?
Evaluate the situation before turning page.

Figure 14.6b
T-BOND CONTINUOUS FUTURES

Trade Exit

The trade was liquidated on a raised protective stop. The stop had been brought in relatively close because a spike high that had remained intact for nearly two weeks suggested that a top might be in place.

Comment

The exit on this trade proved highly premature, as the market subsequently moved much higher. Although, as cited, the existence of a spike high provided some justification for a close stop, it is noteworthy that the stop had been raised above the closest meaningful point, which was probably the midpoint of the prior trading range. The lesson is that bringing in stop points closer than meaningful levels will often result in exiting good trades far too early.

Figure 14.7a
DECEMBER 1994 EURODOLLAR

Trade Entry Reason

A flag formed above an extended trading range often provides an excellent buy signal, as the ability of the market to hold after a major breakout serves to confirm the breakout.

Do you agree or disagree with the analysis?
Evaluate the situation before turning page.

Figure 14.7*b*
DECEMBER 1994 EURODOLLAR

Trade Exit

The trade was liquidated on a raised money management stop. The stop was kept close because of the magnitude of the preceding advance.

Comment

This trade provides a good illustration of the principle that a market is never too high to buy (or too low to sell). Also note that even though the long position was entered at a record high level, the risk was kept small, because it was possible to define a relatively close meaningful stop. The initial stop was placed a few points below the flag pattern illustrated in Figure 14.7*a*.

Figure 14.8a
DECEMBER 1994 BRITISH POUND

Trade Entry Reasons

1. Sustained upside breakout above triangle consolidation.
2. Pennant consolidation following an upswing

Do you agree or disagree with the analysis?
Evaluate the situation before turning page.

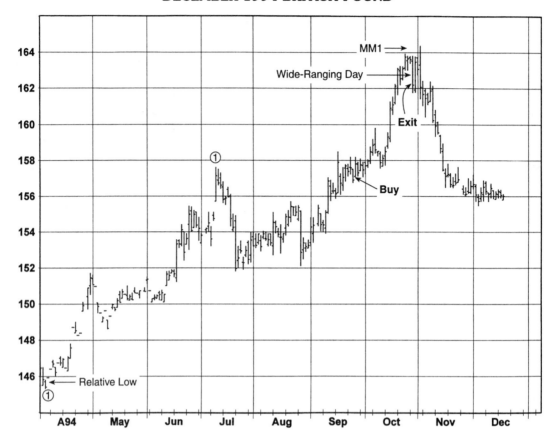

Figure 14.8b
DECEMBER 1994 BRITISH POUND

Trade Exit

The trade was liquidated on the downside wide-ranging day following the approximate attainment of a major measured move objective (MM1).

Comment

This trade had originally been recommended several weeks before the indicated buy point, using a limit order within the triangle consolidation (see Figure 14.8a), in anticipation of an eventual upside breakout from this formation. This buy point was never reached, and eventually a long position was recommended at the market. This action helped salvage the substantial remaining profit potential in the trade. The general lesson illustrated by this trade is that if a market fails to reach a limit entry price and starts to move in the anticipated direction, it often makes sense to enter the trade somewhat belatedly at a less favorable price, as opposed to abandoning the idea as a missed trade.

This trade also illustrates how using the approach of a measured move objective as an indicator to exit a trade on the first sign of failure can help dramatically limit the surrender of large open profits.

Figure 14.9a
MARCH 1995 BRITISH POUND

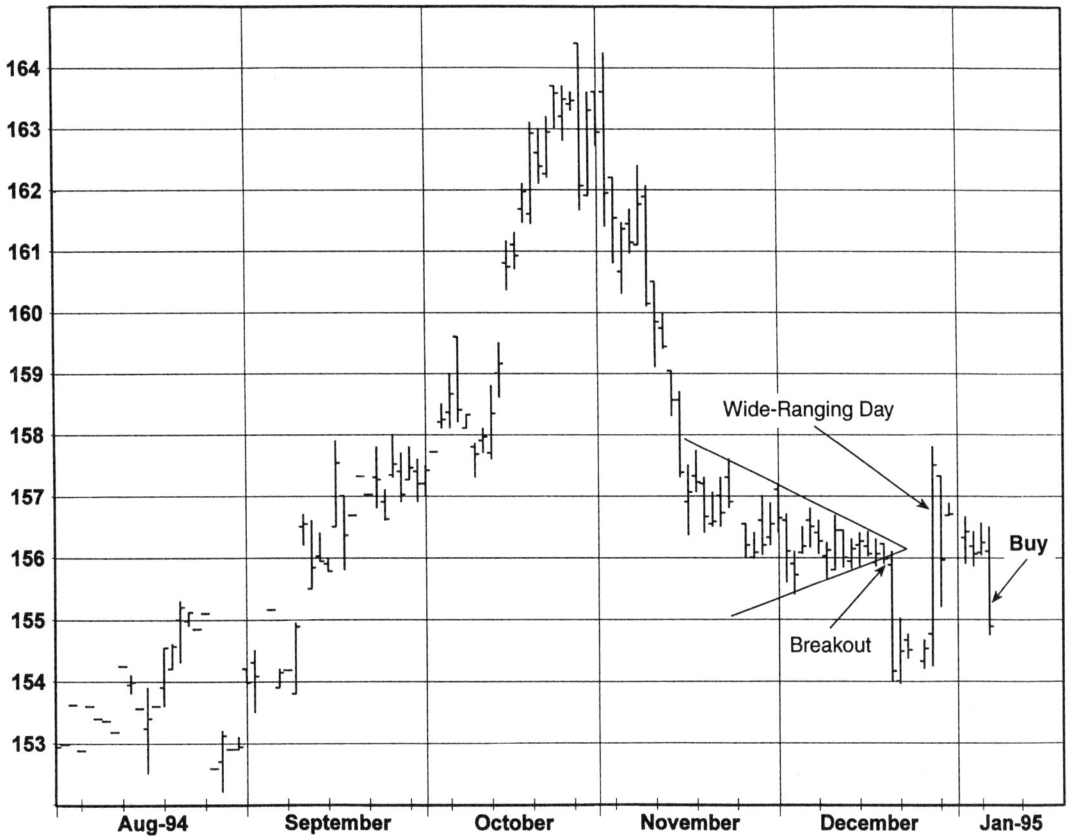

Trade Entry Reason

The upside wide-ranging day, which more than offset a prior downside break-out from a triangle consolidation, suggested that a trend reversal had occurred. Therefore a buy recommendation was issued on the subsequent dip in anticipation that the December low would hold.

Do you agree or disagree with the analysis?
Evaluate the situation before turning page.

Figure 14.9b
MARCH 1995 BRITISH POUND

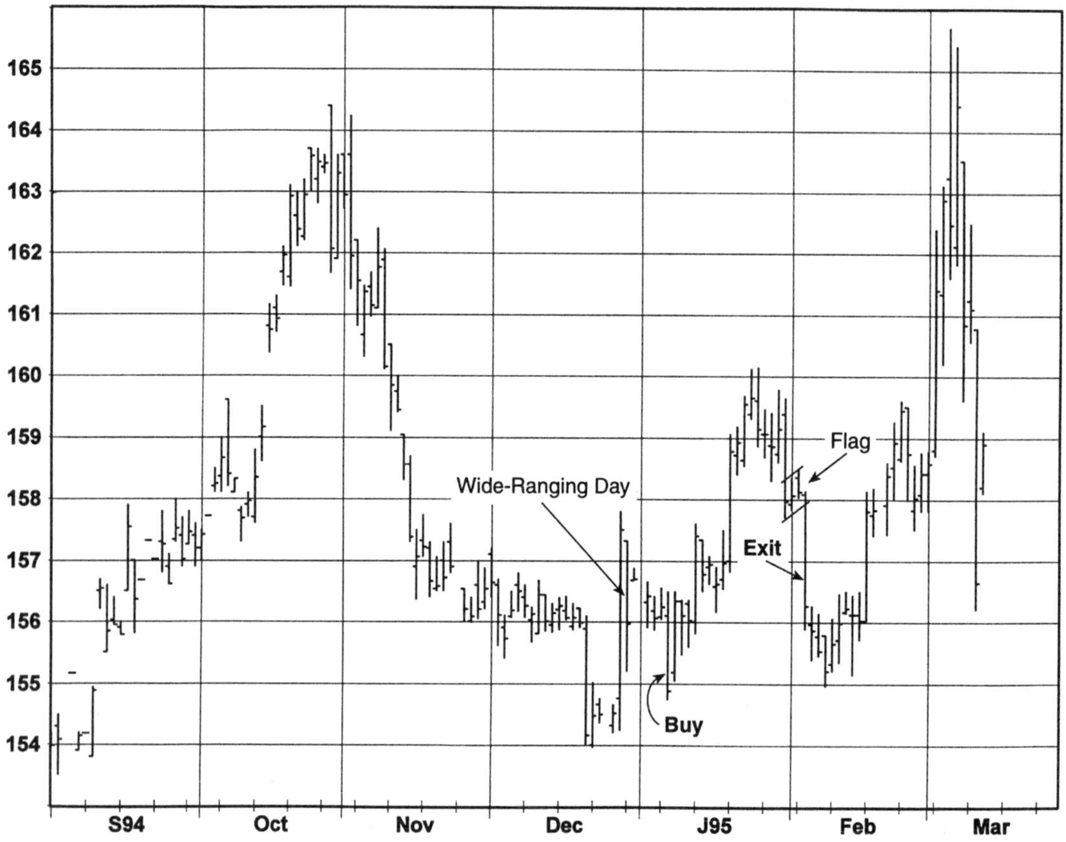

Trade Exit

The trade was liquidated because of the downside penetration of a flag pattern.

Comment

Wide-ranging days that close dramatically counter to a prior trend often provide an early warning signal of a trend reversal.

Figure 14.10a
DECEMBER 1993 JAPANESE YEN

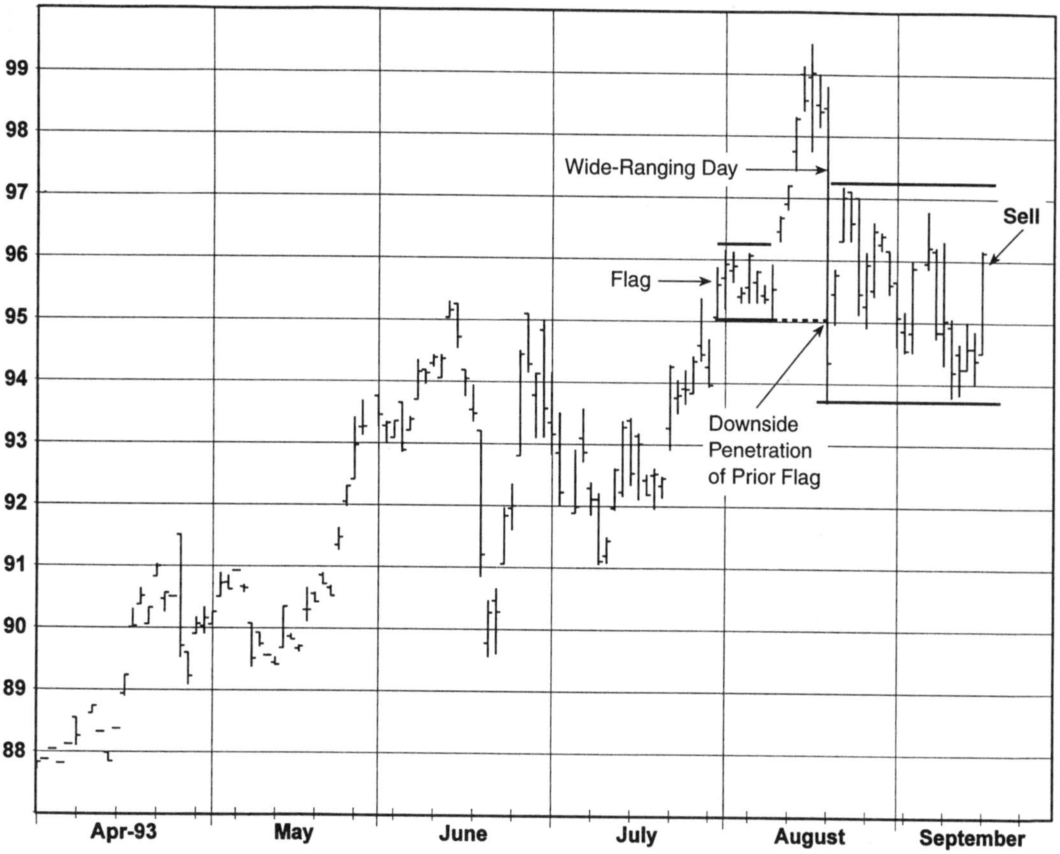

Trade Entry Reasons

1. The failure of prices to recover to the top of a wide-ranging day after a month's time increased the likelihood that a top was in place.

2. The downside penetration of the low end of a prior flag consolidation suggested a price failure.

3. The market consolidated in a sideways pattern following a downswing—price action that usually leads to another downswing.

Do you agree or disagree with the analysis?
Evaluate the situation before turning page.

Figure 14.10b
DECEMBER 1993 JAPANESE YEN

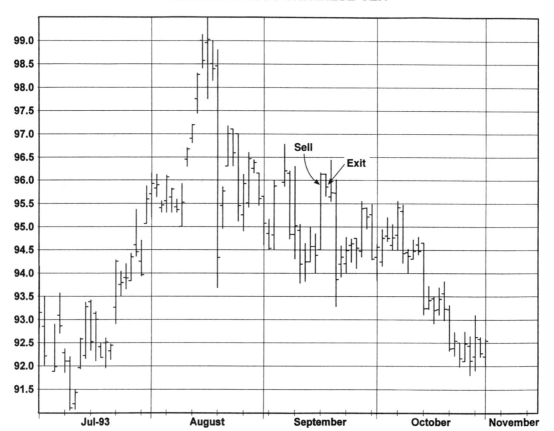

Trade Exit

In order to sharply limit the possible loss on the trade, the close-only stop was lowered to 10 points better than breakeven only one day after entry—a stop that was barely touched off.

Comment

The markets will rarely allow you to make money unless you are willing to accept some risk. By bringing in the stop to near breakeven just one day after entry, instead of leaving the stop at the original technically significant point (approximately 75 points above the top of the prevailing consolidation), I ended up getting stopped out near the high of the rebound and missing a potentially very profitable trade. The lesson is: Don't bring a stop in closer than the closest technically significant point, especially right after entry, unless the market does something to change the technical picture.

Figure 14.11a
DECEMBER 1994 JAPANESE YEN

Trade Entry Reason

The flag consolidation formed near the top of a trading range suggested the potential for an upside breakout.

Do you agree or disagree with the analysis?
Evaluate the situation before turning page.

Figure 14.11*b*
DECEMBER 1994 JAPANESE YEN

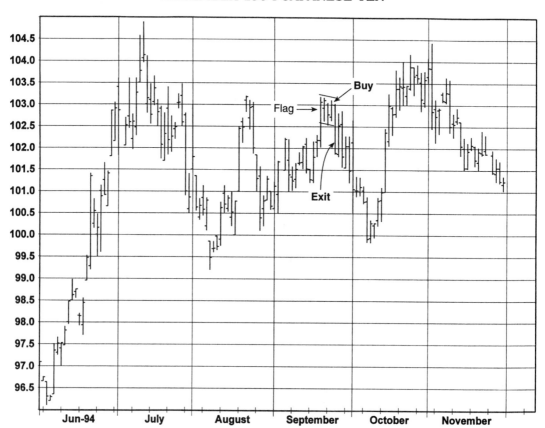

Trade Exit

The downside penetration of the flag violated the basic reason for the trade.

Comment

Generally speaking, a trade should be liquidated if the original premise for the trade is invalidated. Adherence to this principle kept the loss on this trade very small, even though a long position was implemented near a market peak.

Figure 14.12*a*
MARCH 1995 JAPANESE YEN

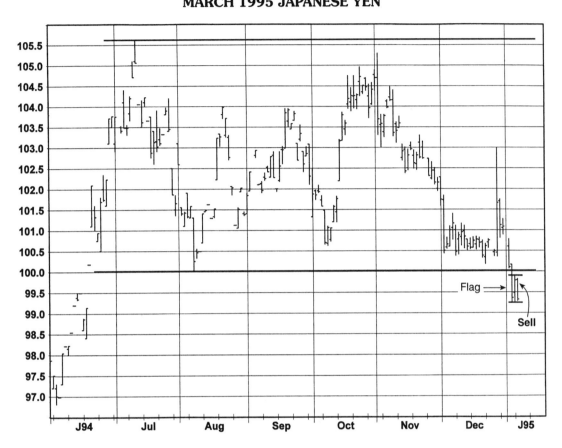

Trade Entry Reasons

The flag consolidation formed below an extended, broad trading range strongly suggested the likelihood of an impending price slide.

Do you agree or disagree with the analysis?
Evaluate the situation before turning page.

Figure 14.12*b*
MARCH 1995 JAPANESE YEN

Trade Exit

The ensuing counter-to-anticipated upside breakout of the flag pattern contradicted the trade premise.

Comment

Even reliable patterns don't work all the time. Although a flag pattern formed below an extended trading range is often an excellent sell signal, in this case, the trade was a loser. If faced with a similar situation in the future, however, I would still make the same decision, because on balance such trades should make a profit. Remember chart analysis is a game of percentages not absolutes.

Once again, note that exiting the position on the first sign that the original trade premise was violated kept the loss very small – despite, in this case, going short right near a major bottom.

Figure 14.13a
SEPTEMBER 1993 DEUTSCHE MARK

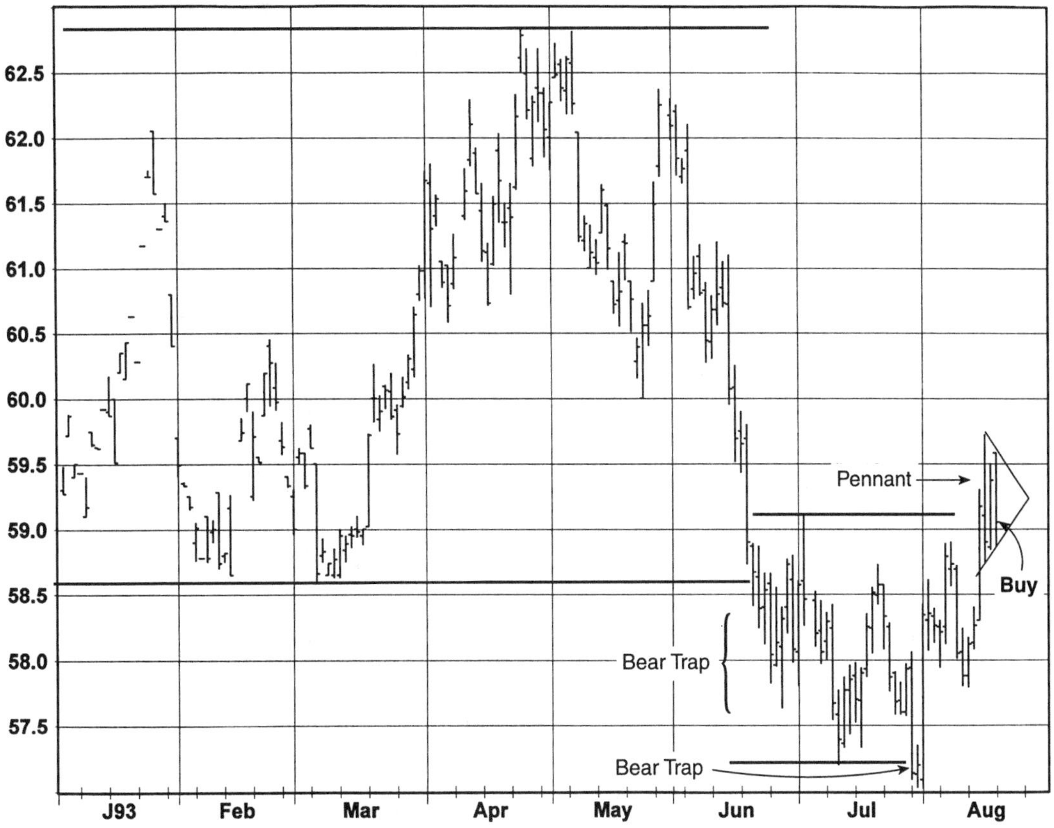

Trade Entry Reasons

1. Bear trap in terms of both the November–June broad trading range (depicted January forward) and the smaller mid-June to July range.
2. Pennant consolidation after confirmation of bear trap.

Do you agree or disagree with the analysis?
Evaluate the situation before turning page.

Figure 14.13*b*
SEPTEMBER 1993 DEUTSCHE MARK

Trade Exit

Took profits in an unbroken uptrend, in anticipation of nearby resistance based on a measured move objective and the top of a downtrend channel.

Comment

In this instance, exiting the trade without even a hint of a reversal proved to be the correct decision. (The September peak shown in chart proved to be a relative high.) However, it is difficult to draw any generalizations, since taking profits in the midst of a favorable trend can often result in exiting good trades prematurely.

Figure 14.14a
DECEMBER 1993 DEUTSCHE MARK

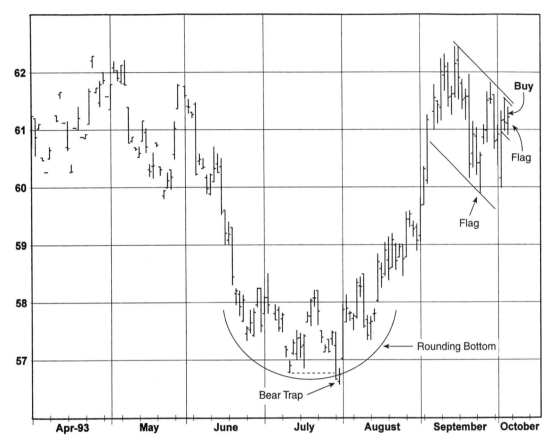

Trade Entry Reasons

1. Rounding price base and bear-trap low both suggested a major bottom was in place.

2. Both narrow flag and broader flag suggested the likelihood of an upside breakout.

Do you agree or disagree with the analysis?
Evaluate the situation before turning page.

Figure 14.14*b*
DECEMBER 1993 DEUTSCHE MARK

Trade Exit

Although the market did break out on the upside initially, there was little follow-through, and the subsequent retracement back below the midpoint of the prior flag pattern suggested a price failure.

Comment

Exit on the first sign of a technical failure kept the loss on the trade very small.

Figure 14.15a
JUNE 1994 DEUTSCHE MARK

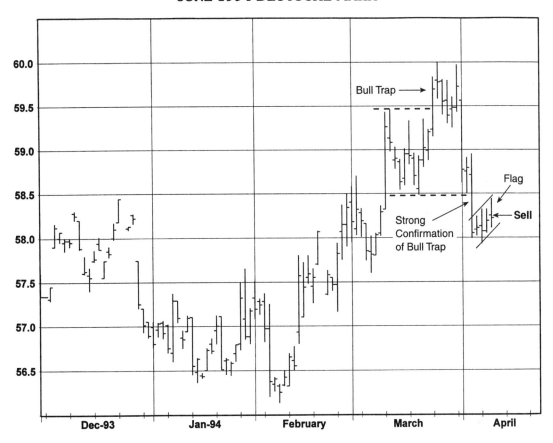

Trade Entry Reasons

1. Strong confirmation of bull trap.
2. The flag pattern formed after the downswing suggested that the next price swing would also be on downside.

Do you agree or disagree with the analysis?
Evaluate the situation before turning page.

Figure 14.15*b*
JUNE 1994 DEUTSCHE MARK

Trade Exit

Counter-to-anticipated breakout of a flag consolidation suggested an upside reversal.

Comment

Although a timely exit kept the loss small, counter-to-anticipated breakout could have been used as a signal to reverse, not merely liquidate, a short position.

Figure 14.16a
SEPTEMBER 1994 DEUTSCHE MARK

Trade Entry Reasons

1. Flag consolidation formed near top of the trading range is typically a bullish pattern.

2. Upside breakout of a flag pattern.

Do you agree or disagree with the analysis?
Evaluate the situation before turning page.

Figure 14.16b
SEPTEMBER 1994 DEUTSCHE MARK

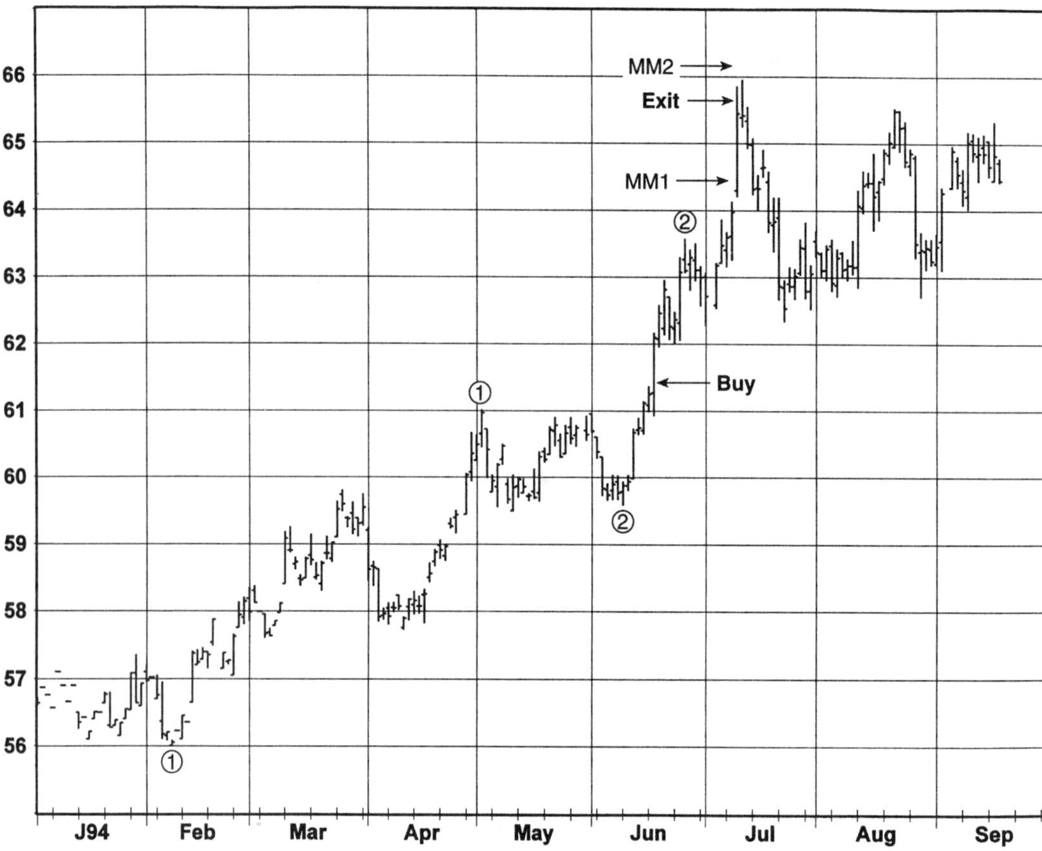

Trade Exit

Trade liquidated as profit objective reached. Profit target point selected because it was in the zone between two measured move objectives (MM1 and MM2).

Comment

Although the market eventually went well above the exit point (not shown), there is still an important advantage in taking profits if a major objective is achieved. Specifically, taking profits if an important target is attained, particularly if it is reached quickly, averts the danger of being knocked out of the trade on a temporary reversal—such as occurred here in July—even if prices eventually go higher.

Figure 14.17*a*
DECEMBER 1994 DEUTSCHE MARK

Trade Entry Reasons

1. Sustained breakout above both narrow and broad trading ranges.
2. Flag pattern formed after breakout above trading ranges.

Do you agree or disagree with the analysis?
Evaluate the situation before turning page.

Figure 14.17b
DECEMBER 1994 DEUTSCHE MARK

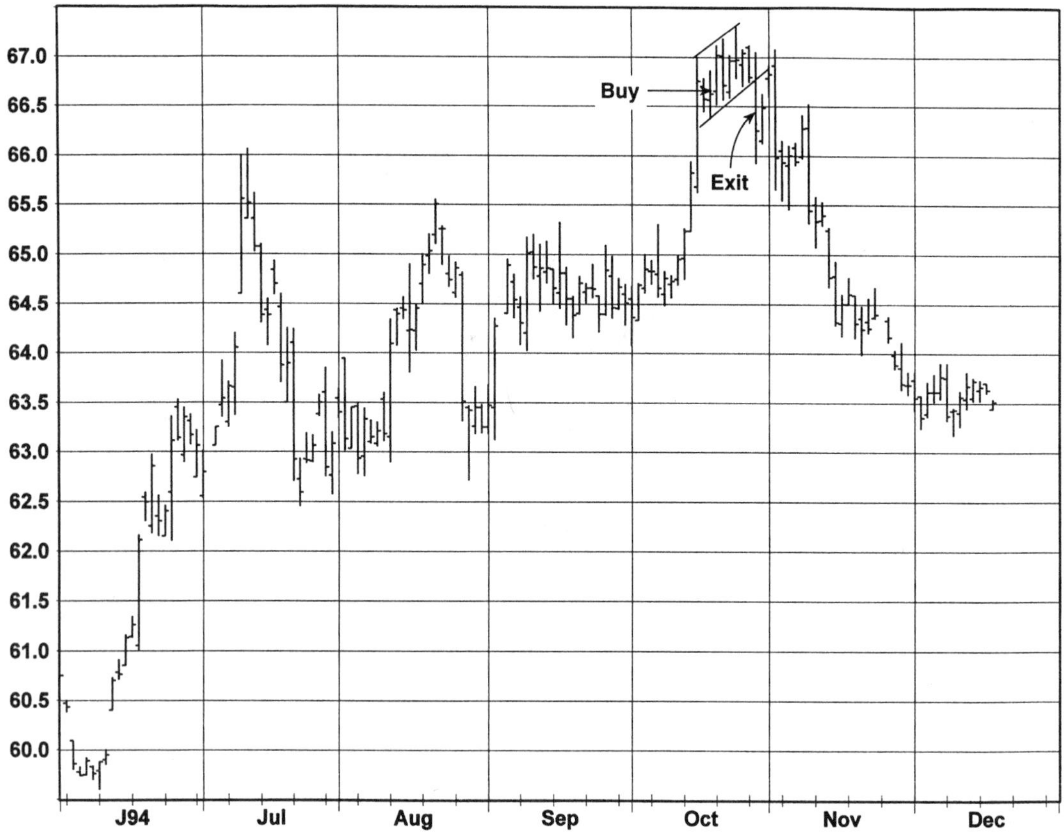

Trade Exit

Trade liquidated because a counter-to-anticipated breakout of flag consolidation suggested a downside reversal had occurred.

Comment

Note how using a short-term flag pattern as a reference point for setting the stop kept the loss on the trade small, even though a long position was implemented right near a market top.

Figure 14.18*a*
MARCH 1995 DEUTSCHE MARK

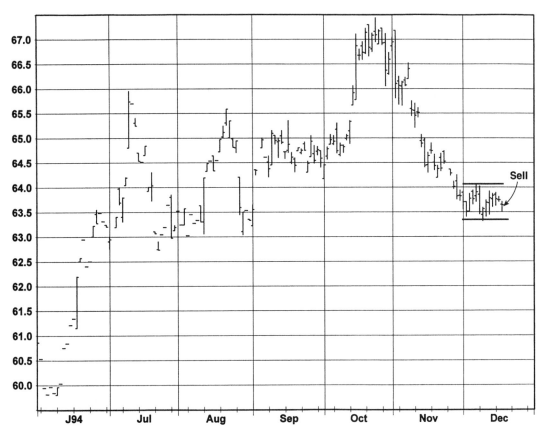

Trade Entry Reason

Narrow consolidation formed after steep price slide suggested a probable continuation of downtrend.

Do you agree or disagree with the analysis?
Evaluate the situation before turning page.

Figure 14.18*b*
MARCH 1995 DEUTSCHE MARK

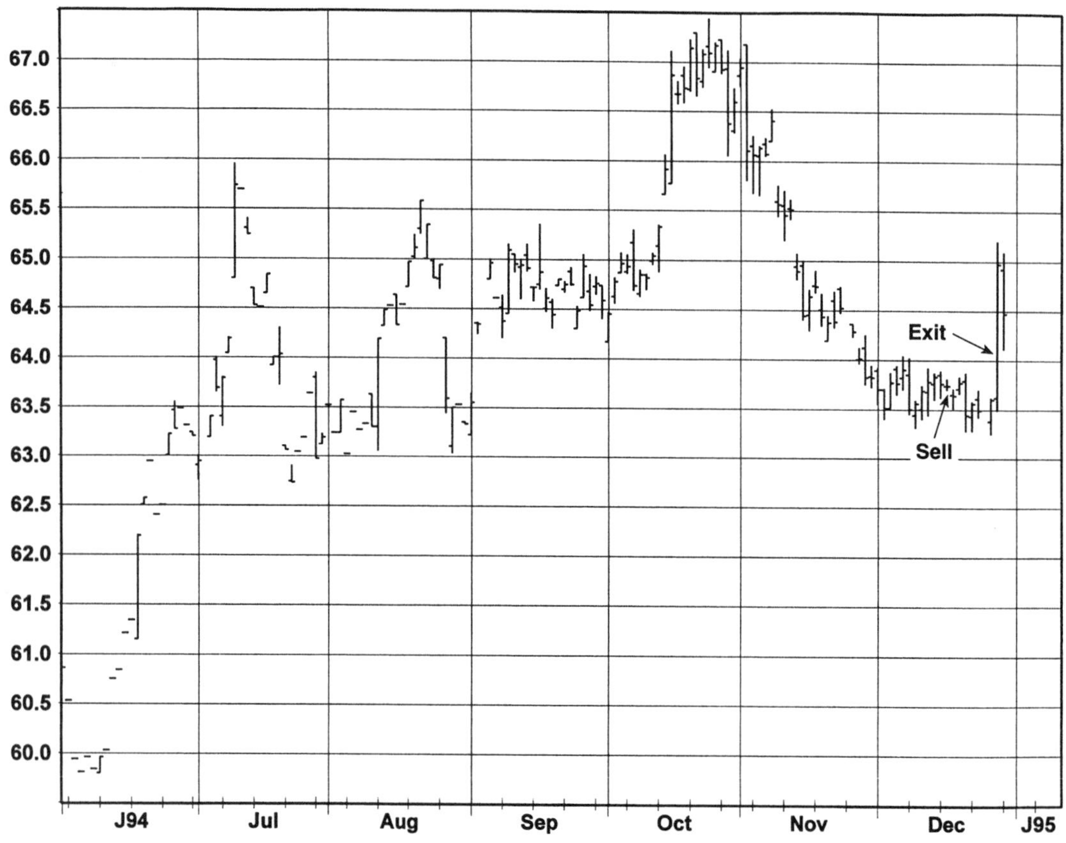

Trade Exit

Counter-to-anticipated breakout from consolidation violated a basic premise of trade.

Comment

Exit on the first sign of an invalidation of the trade premise kept the loss small.

Figure 14.19a
MARCH 1995 DEUTSCHE MARK

Trade Entry Reasons

1. Counter-to-anticipated penetration of a narrow consolidation suggested an upside reversal. (Same reason why prior trade liquidated—see Figure 14.18b.)

2. A wide-ranging day formed near a relative low is often an early sign of a trend reversal.

Do you agree or disagree with the analysis?
Evaluate the situation before turning page.

Figure 14.19b
MARCH 1995 DEUTSCHE MARK

Trade Exit

The trade was liquidated on a sharply raised stop because of the proximity of the measured move objective.

Comment

This trade provides a perfect example of the desirability of quickly reversing a trade opinion if market conditions change. Only two days before implementation of a long position in this trade, I had been bearish and short (see Figure 14.18b). However, the same factors that had suggested covering short also supported the idea of going long. Unfortunately, I am usually not this wise without the benefit of hindsight.

In this instance, getting out of a winning trade because of the proximity of an important objective sacrificed a significant further advance. Sometimes getting out near an objective is the right decision (see, for example, Figures 14.8b and 14.16b); sometimes letting the position ride is the right decision, as was the case here.

Figure 14.20a
SEPTEMBER 1993 SWISS FRANC

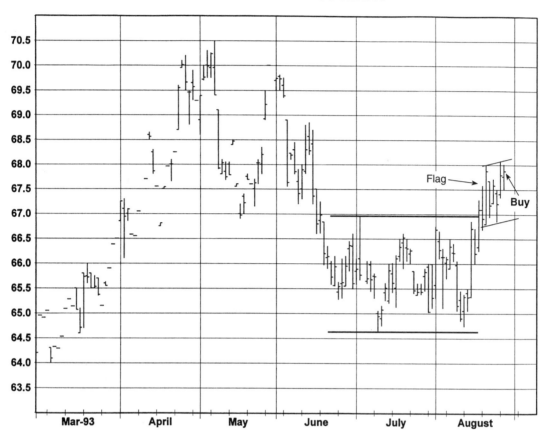

Trade Entry Reason

Flag formed above the trading range suggested the probable continuation of the advance.

Do you agree or disagree with the analysis?
Evaluate the situation before turning page.

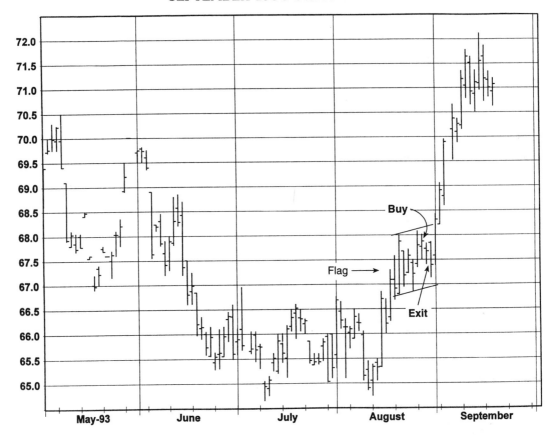

Figure 14.20b
SEPTEMBER 1993 SWISS FRANC

Trade Exit

Raised stop very close to entry shortly after trade implementation in an effort to keep a possible loss on the trade very small.

Comment

The initial stop used at the implementation of this trade was never approached. Raising the stop too close, too quickly resulted in a potentially very profitable trade being liquidated at a loss. This assessment is based on the fact that the stop was raised above the closest meaningful stop point—a price at least modestly below the prevailing flag pattern illustrated in Figures 14.20a and 14.20b—rather than a hindsight judgment reflecting the trade outcome.

The lesson is that a stop should not be raised to a point so close that its activation would still leave the original premise for the trade intact. For example, the illustrated trade was primarily based on the flag consolidation pattern that formed above a prior trading range. Since the raised stop (but not the initial stop) was within this consolidation pattern, it had no technical significance.

Figure 14.21a
JUNE 1994 SWISS FRANC

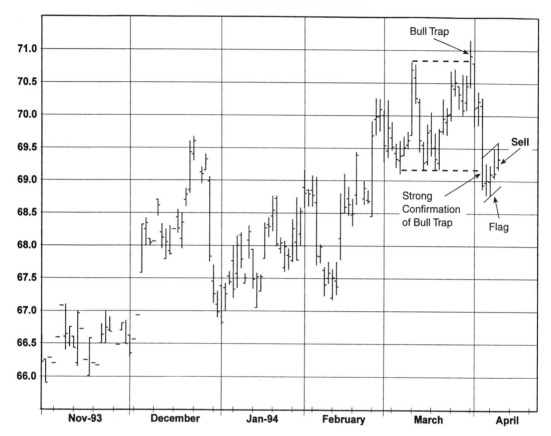

Trade Entry Reasons

1. Strong confirmation of a bull trap.
2. Flag pattern formed after a downswing from the high.

Do you agree or disagree with the analysis?
Evaluate the situation before turning page.

Figure 14.21*b*
JUNE 1994 SWISS FRANC

Trade Exit

Trade liquidated because of a counter-to-anticipated breakout from the flag pattern.

Comment

Although this trade ended up being a loser, in my view, there were no trading mistakes made either on entry or exit. The original premise for the trade still seems valid even in hindsight, while the position was exited on the first sign the trade was wrong, keeping the loss small in the process. One should not confuse losing trades with trading mistakes. Losing trades are perfectly OK—in fact, they are inevitable—as long as a *valid* trading plan was followed. Losing trades that are a consequence of following an approach that has an edge will not interfere with ultimate trading success, but trading mistakes (even on winning trades) will.

Figure 14.22a
MARCH 1995 SWISS FRANC

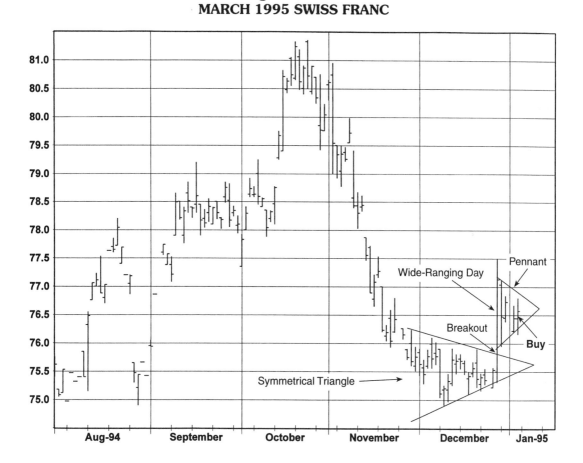

Trade Entry Reasons

1. Upside breakout of symmetrical triangle.
2. Wide-ranging up day near the low following a large downtrend.
3. Pennant consolidation after upswing.

Do you agree or disagree with the analysis?
Evaluate the situation before turning page.

Figure 14.22b
MARCH 1995 SWISS FRANC

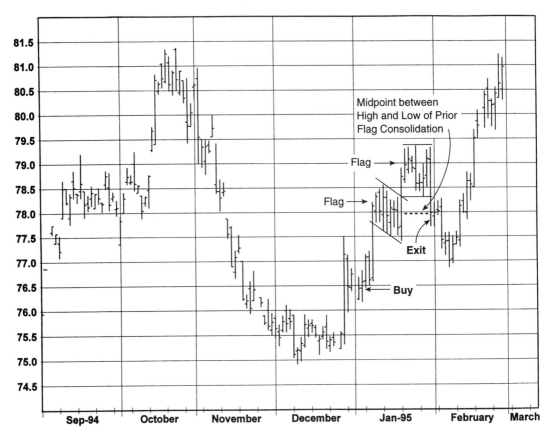

Trade Exit

Downside penetration of a flag and retracement to below the midpoint of the prior flag represented a short-term price failure.

Comment

Dramatic wide-ranging day with a close near the high of the day that occurs after an extended downtrend is often an early signal of a major trend reversal.

Figure 14.23a
MARCH 1994 CANADIAN DOLLAR

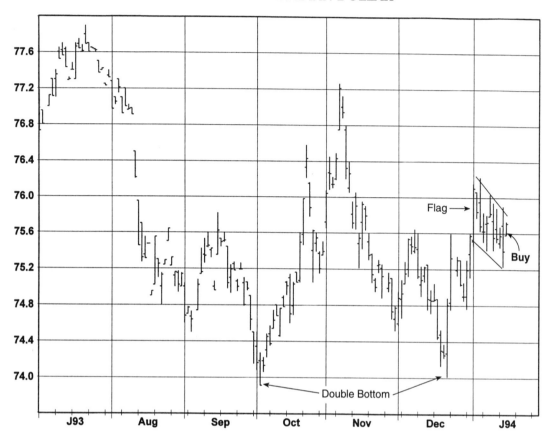

Trade Entry Reasons

1. Double bottom.
2. Flag consolidation formed after upswing.

Do you agree or disagree with the analysis?
Evaluate the situation before turning page.

Figure 14.23b
MARCH 1994 CANADIAN DOLLAR

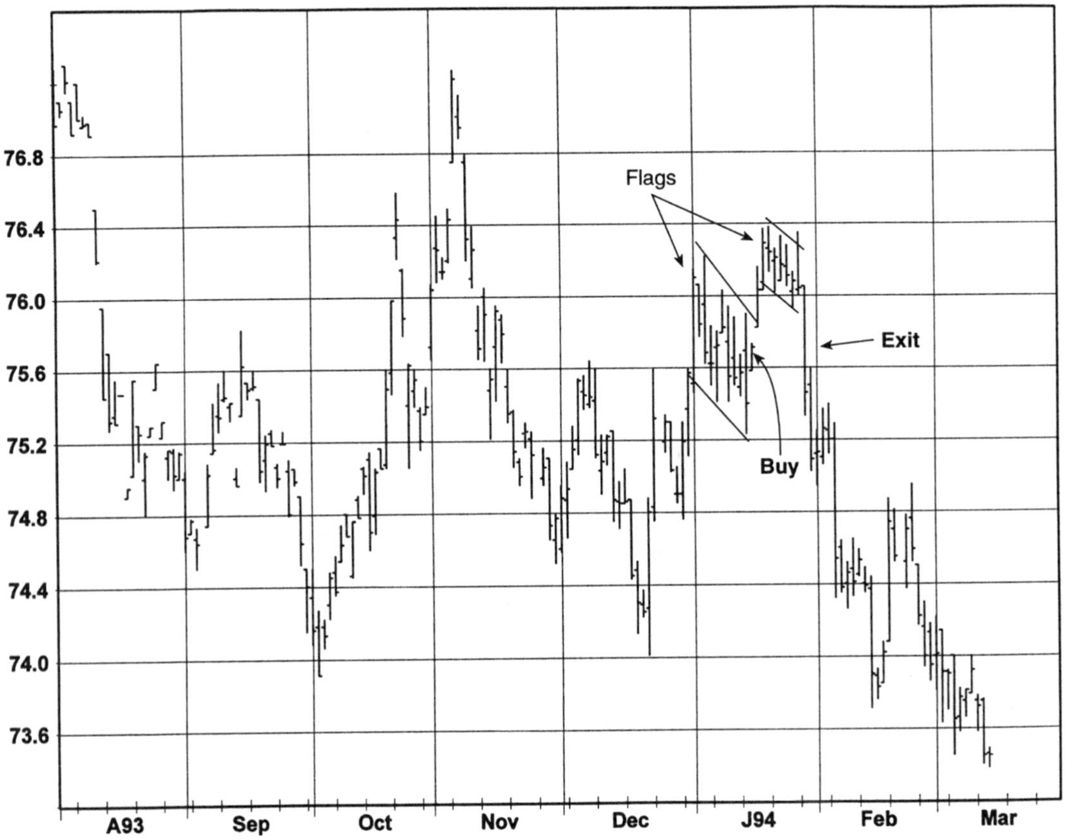

Trade Exit

Downside penetration of a flag pattern suggested a price failure.

Comment

Even though the trade idea would have been a disaster if the position was held, timing entry and exit based on short-term patterns (i.e., flags) allowed for a near break-even outcome—not bad considering the market reached a major high three days after the buy recommendation.

Figure 14.24a
SEPTEMBER 1994 CANADIAN DOLLAR

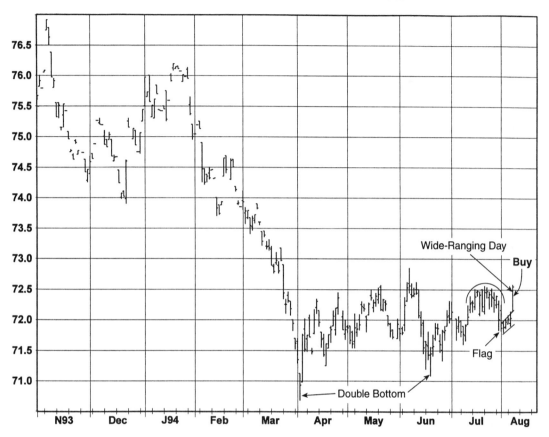

Trade Entry Reasons

1. Double bottom.
2. Curved pattern broken on upside.
3. Counter-to-anticipated breakout of flag pattern.
4. Wide-ranging up day.

Do you agree or disagree with the analysis?
Evaluate the situation before turning page.

Figure 14.24b
SEPTEMBER 1994 CANADIAN DOLLAR

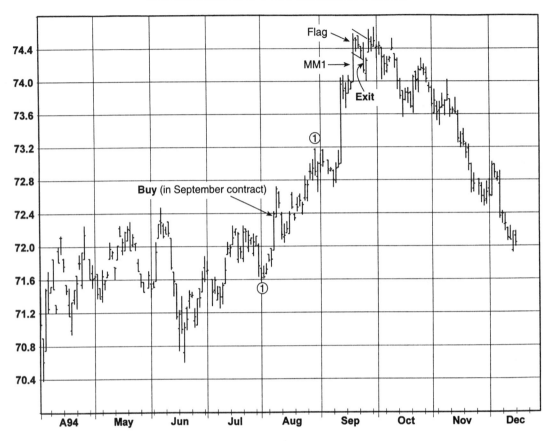

Trade Exit

1. Once the measured move objective (MM1) was reached, the stop was brought in very close.

2. Downside penetration of flag pattern provided a short-term price failure signal.

Comment

Liquidating the position on the first sign of weakness following achievement of a measured move objective allowed for exit near the top of the price move and prevented surrendering a large portion of the profits on the trade.

Figure 14.25a
OCTOBER 1993 GOLD

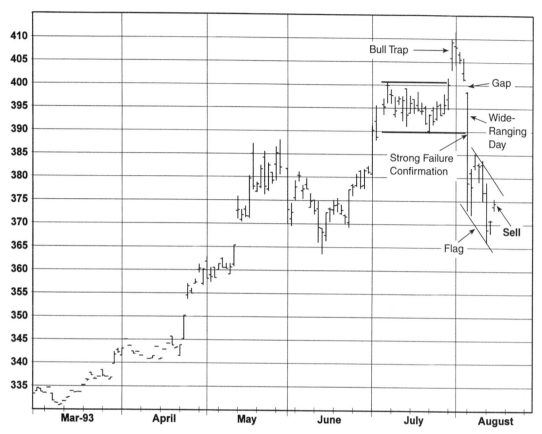

Trade Entry Reasons

1. Confirmed bull-trap top.
2. Sustained downside gap.
3. Wide-ranging down day.
4. Flag consolidation formed after downswing.

Do you agree or disagree with the analysis?
Evaluate the situation before turning page.

Figure 14.25b
OCTOBER 1993 GOLD

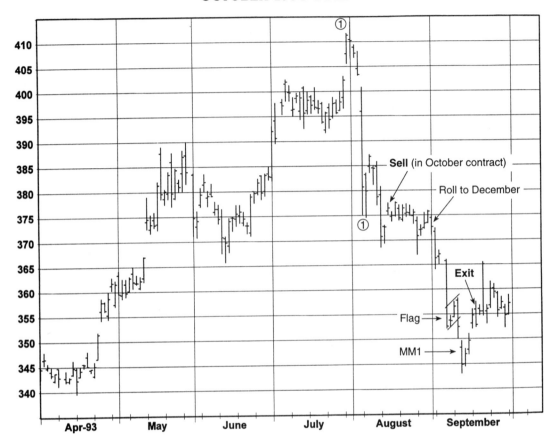

Trade Exit

1. Stop brought in very close once the measured move objective (MM1) was achieved.
2. Rebound to upper portion of prior flag provided the first sign of a possible trend reversal.

Comment

Confirmed bull-traps are among the most reliable chart signals of a major top. Also note that the achievement of a measured move objective can be used as a signal for bringing in a stop very close—an action that locks in a major portion of profits, while still leaving open the opportunity for additional profits if the price move continues uninterrupted (which, of course, was not the case here).

Figure 14.26a
DECEMBER 1993 GOLD

Trade Entry Reasons

1. Classic bull-trap top suggested a major top was in place, with the likelihood that the ensuing bear market would last much longer than two months.

2. The price rebound had carried to the resistance area implied by both an internal trend line and the approximate best-fit line of a concentration of prior relative lows.

Do you agree or disagree with the analysis?
Evaluate the situation before turning page.

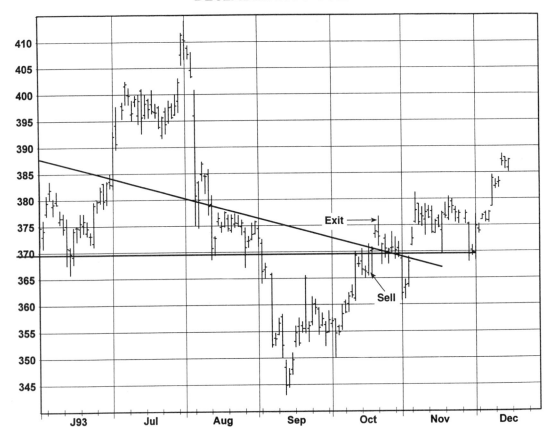

Figure 14.26b
DECEMBER 1993 GOLD

Trade Exit

The trade was liquidated following a significant upside penetration of the two aforementioned resistance lines.

Comment

Although a number of valid reasons existed for entering the trade, there was also a strong negative to the original trade: A flag consolidation suggested that the next price swing would be on the upside (see Figure 14.26a). I ignored this consideration on the assumption that the previously listed bearish factors would dominate—an assumption that proved wrong. Perhaps the lesson here is that it might be best to pass on trades where *important* pieces of the puzzle just don't fit. In other words, wait for a trade to line up so that there are no major contradictory signals from the methodology being used.

Also note that bringing in a stop on a prior short position (Figure 14.25b) because a measured move objective had been attained helped prevent surrendering a large portion of profits on that trade.

Figure 14.27a
JUNE 1994 GOLD

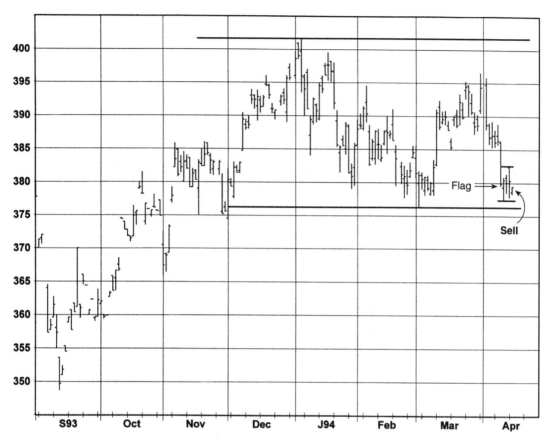

Trade Entry Reason

Flag formed near the low end of the broad trading range suggested a potential downside breakout.

Do you agree or disagree with the analysis?
Evaluate the situation before turning page.

Figure 14.27*b*
JUNE 1994 GOLD

Trade Exit

Return back to the midpoint of the flag consolidation (dashed line) after the downside breakaway gap indicated a probable upside reversal.

Comment

Note that even though the chart pattern used to implement the trade proved misleading about the ultimate long-term direction of the market, it was accurate in signaling the direction of the next price swing. This factor made it possible to use a technically meaningful stop (a price just above the midpoint of the flag consolidation used as a signal to initiate trade) that implied only a small loss on trade. This trade, as well as many others depicted in this chapter, illustrates one of the chief attributes of using flag (and pennant) consolidations as signals for trade entry and exit: Even when these patterns ultimately prove wrong, they often make it possible to keep losses small.

Figure 14.28a
JUNE 1995 GOLD

Trade Entry Reasons

1. Bear-trap bottom.
2. Upside penetration of an extended internal trend line.
3. Wide-ranging up day.

Do you agree or disagree with the analysis?
Evaluate the situation before turning page.

Figure 14.28*b*
JUNE 1995 GOLD

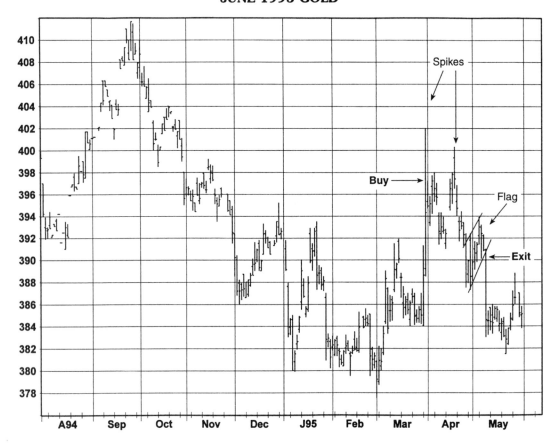

Trade Exit

1. Two spike highs suggested a possible top.
2. Downside penetration of flag pattern signaled a potential downswing.

Comment

No combination of chart patterns, regardless of how promising, works all the time. In this instance, the combination of a bear-trap after an extended decline, significant penetration of a prolonged internal trend line, and a wide-ranging up day certainly seemed like an excellent buy signal. However, the subsequent price action simply suggested the trade was wrong, which, as it turned out, it was. This trade highlights the importance of flexibility in changing a market opinion, no matter how persuasive it might have been.

Figure 14.29*a*
PLATINUM CONTINUOUS FUTURES

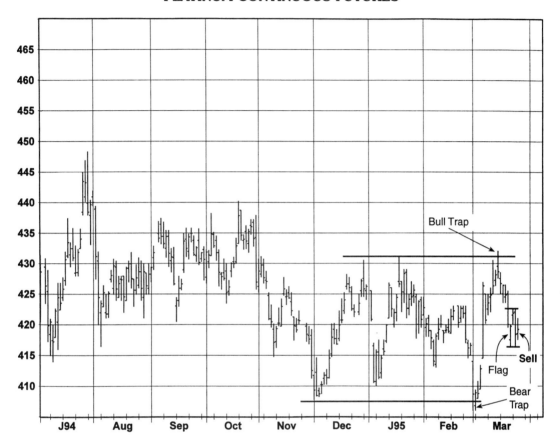

Trade Entry Reasons

1. Slight upside penetration of extended, broad trading range and immediate decline suggested a bull-trap reversal.
2. Flag formed after downswing indicated that the next price swing would probably be on the downside.

Do you agree or disagree with the analysis?
Evaluate the situation before turning page.

Figure 14.29b
PLATINUM CONTINUOUS FUTURES

Trade Exit

The subsequent upside penetration of the flag pattern violated one of the primary reasons for trade.

Comment

Although trade was truly terrible—the market went up seven straight days after the short position was implemented, gaining nearly 12 percent of the contract value in that short time—getting out on the first sign that the trade premise was wrong kept the loss exceedingly small. Keeping losses small when you are wrong—particularly dead wrong—is probably more important to ultimate trading success than an especially superior skill in picking trades.

Figure 14.30a
DECEMBER 1993 SILVER

Trade Entry Reasons

1. Confirmed bull-trap top.
2. Island reversal.
3. Wide-ranging down day.
4. Flag consolidation formed after downswing.

Do you agree or disagree with the analysis?
Evaluate the situation before turning page.

Figure 14.30*b*
DECEMBER 1993 SILVER

Trade Exit

Trade liquidated two days after entry on a sharply lowered stop.

Comment

Trade was right on target, but I was unwilling to continue to use a stop wide enough to be technically significant (which in this case would have required a stop at least about five cents above the top of the illustrated flag pattern). Certainly, the lowered stop, which was right in the midst of the ongoing flag consolidation, was totally meaningless from a technical perspective. Incidentally, similar trades in the gold market (see Figures 14.25*a* and 14.25*b*) and platinum market (not shown), which did employ meaningful stop points, proved very profitable. Lesson: The market will often make it very difficult to hold onto a good trade if you are unwilling to allow enough risk.

Figure 14.31a
MARCH 1994 SILVER

Trade Entry Reasons

1. Rally failed right below resistance implied by the top of a gap that had completed an island reversal pattern.
2. Peak of rally represented a bull trap.
3. Sell initiated on approach of minor resistance implied by prior relative highs.

Do you agree or disagree with the analysis?
Evaluate the situation before turning page.

Figure 14.31*b*
MARCH 1994 SILVER

Trade Exit

The penetration of a minor resistance line and the approach of a prior peak suggested that the assumption of a bull-trap top was invalid.

Comment

Getting out at the first sign that the initial trade premise had been violated helped keep loss relatively small.

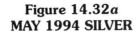

Figure 14.32a
MAY 1994 SILVER

Trade Entry Reasons

1. Normally, a flag formed above a trading range should lead to an upside breakout. The counter-to-anticipated downside breakout in this case suggested a potential trend reversal.

2. Flag formed after minor downswing suggested the next price swing would be on the downside.

Do you agree or disagree with the analysis?
Evaluate the situation before turning page.

Figure 14.32*b*
MAY 1994 SILVER

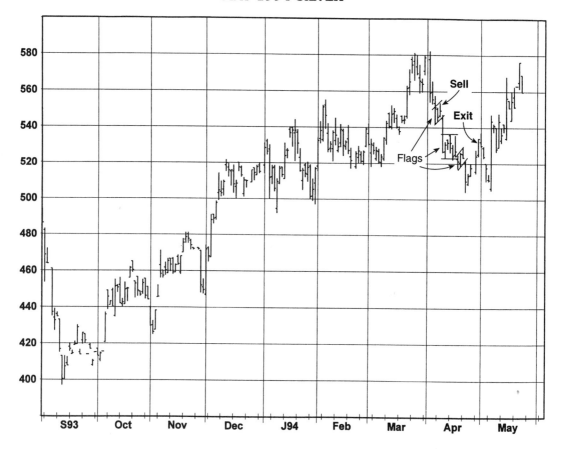

Trade Exit

Rebound above the top of the most recently formed flag pattern represented a short-term bullish signal.

Comment

This trade demonstrates how flag patterns can be used to fine-tune timing of trade entries and exits—in this case, allowing for a profitable outcome even though the original trade concept proved incorrect over the long term. This trade also illustrates the more general principle that successful chart analysis is more a matter of correctly *responding* to market price action than accurately *forecasting* market direction.

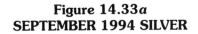

Figure 14.33a
SEPTEMBER 1994 SILVER

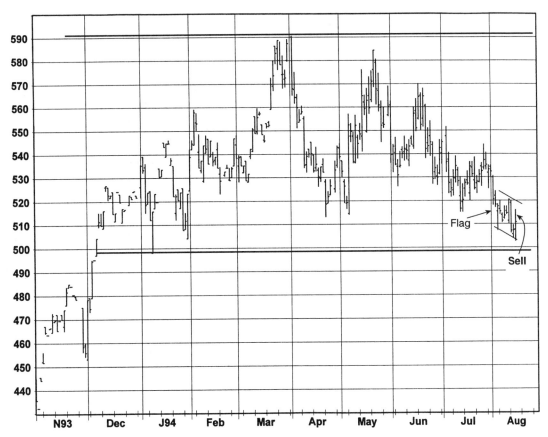

Trade Entry Reason

Flag pattern formed near the bottom of an extended, broad trading range is often an excellent sell signal.

Do you agree or disagree with the analysis?
Evaluate the situation before turning page.

Figure 14.33*b*
SEPTEMBER 1994 SILVER

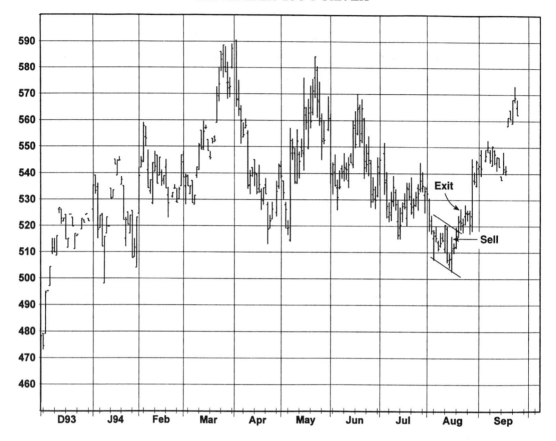

Trade Exit

Counter-to-anticipated upside breakout of flag pattern violated the trade premise.

Comment

A chart pattern does not need to be right more than 50 percent of the time—or, for that matter, even close to 50 percent of the time—to be valuable. For example, when the pattern that motivated this trade—a flag near the low end of a trading range—proves correct, it can allow the trader to capture a major downswing. On the other hand, when it is wrong, evidence of the failure is provided quickly—a modest upside penetration of the flag pattern. In other words, trading this pattern will naturally allow for much larger average gains on winning trades than average losses on losing trades. Consequently, the pattern can be a beneficial tool even if it leads to significantly more losses than gains.

In general, it is a mistake to focus on the *percentage of winning trades* generated by a system or methodology. The key factor is the *expected gain per trade*. (The expected gain per trade is equal to the percentage of winning trades times the average profit per winning trade minus the percentage of losing trades times the average loss per losing trade.)

376

Figure 14.34a
DECEMBER 1994 SILVER

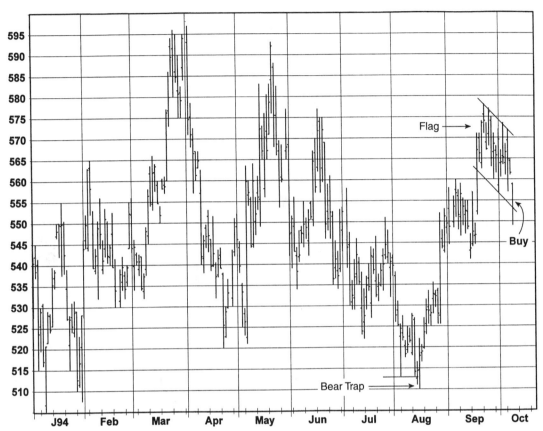

Trade Entry Reasons

1. Sustained bear trap suggested that a major low had been established.
2. Flag pattern formed following the upswing implied that the next market price swing would on the upside.
3. Buy initiated near support implied at the lower end of the broad flag consolidation.

Do you agree or disagree with the analysis?
Evaluate the situation before turning page.

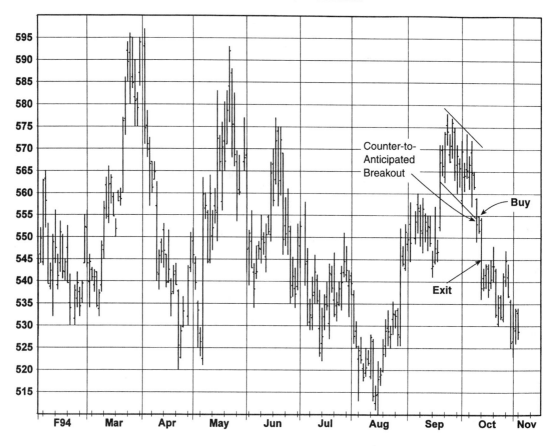

Figure 14.34*b*
DECEMBER 1994 SILVER

Counter-to-
Anticipated
Breakout

Buy

Exit

Trade Exit

Counter-to-anticipated downside penetration of the flag pattern strongly suggested the trade idea was wrong.

Comment

When the market doesn't behave as expected, get out! Although the loss on this particular trade was relatively small ($500), some readers may wonder if the loss might not have been kept even smaller by getting out closer to the counter-to-anticipated breakout point. Perhaps, but only by a marginal amount. Generally speaking, it is not a good idea to place stops too close to critical points. For example, in the case of flag patterns, the shape of the flag can change as it evolves, or the pattern may of be interrupted by a one-day spike without any follow-through. In both instances, keeping a stop very close to a breakout point can result in liquidating a position even though the flag ultimately remains intact and the original trade idea proves successful.

Figure 14.35a
DECEMBER 1994 SILVER

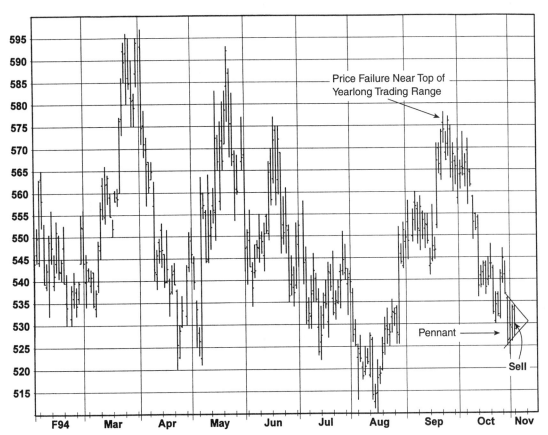

Trade Entry Reasons

1. Prior rally failed near the top of a yearlong trading range, suggesting a major peak had been established.
2. Pennant consolidation near low end of the trading range implied the potential for a downside breakout.

Do you agree or disagree with the analysis?
Evaluate the situation before turning page.

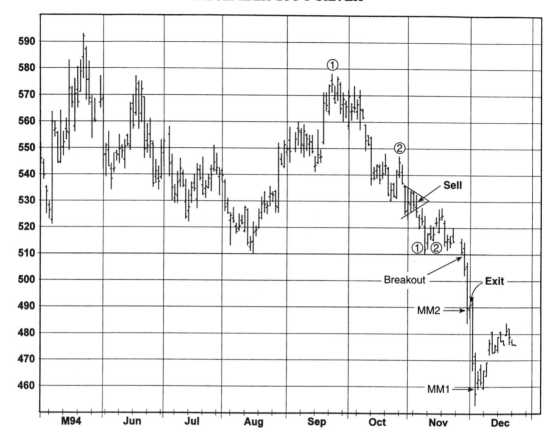

Figure 14.35*b*
DECEMBER 1994 SILVER

Trade Exit

Protective stop on the trade was brought in very close once the nearer measured move objective (MM1) was reached.

Comment

Previous illustrations contained many examples of trades that proved to be losers but did not involve any trading mistakes (at least not in my opinion). Ironically, this trade, which proved to be a significant winner, involved a major trading error. Specifically, despite the market's near unbroken movement in the anticipated direction, the stop was lowered so close that the position was liquidated on a meaningless price squiggle. Only two days later, the substantial profits on the trade would have been nearly doubled!

The reader may wonder whether the achievement of a measured move objective (MM2) didn't theoretically justify using a very close stop, notwithstanding the ultimate outcome. While this observation is generally true, there are three important exceptions here:

1. There was another more significant measured move objective (MM1) that suggested the potential for an eventual further downmove, even if the market initially stalled or reversed near the closer measured move objective (MM2).

380

2. The market had just witnessed a sharp downside penetration of a prolonged, broad trading range—a chart signal for a potential major downswing (as indeed occurred).
3. The lowered stop point had no technical significance.

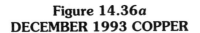

Figure 14.36*a*
DECEMBER 1993 COPPER

Trade Entry Reasons

1. Downside breakout below extended trading range.
2. Significance of breakout enhanced by the fact that it occurred on a gap.
3. A flag pattern formed just below an immediately preceding trading range represents very bearish price action.

Do you agree or disagree with the analysis?
Evaluate the situation before turning page.

Figure 14.36b
DECEMBER 1993 COPPER

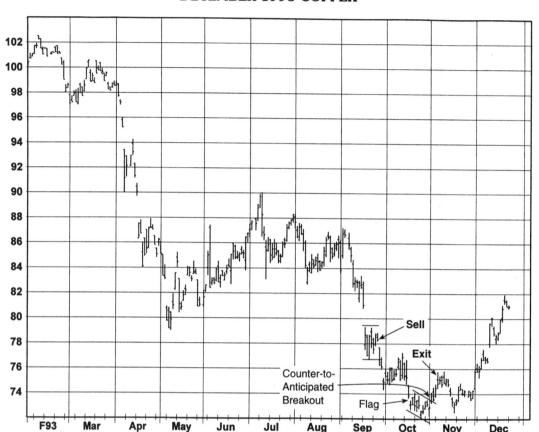

Trade Exit

Counter-to-anticipated breakout of late October flag pattern suggested a potential upside reversal.

Comment

I find flag or pennant patterns formed below extended trading ranges to be among the most valuable chart signals. In essence, the fact that the market continues to trade near or below the low end of the trading range tends to confirm the validity of the breakout.

Note that once the downside gap breakout had remained unfilled for a few days, it was possible to go short with a meaningful stop as close as the top of the gap area. The general point is that selling near lows (or buying near highs) does not necessarily require a wider risk level in order to use a meaningful stop.

Figure 14.37a
MARCH 1994 COPPER

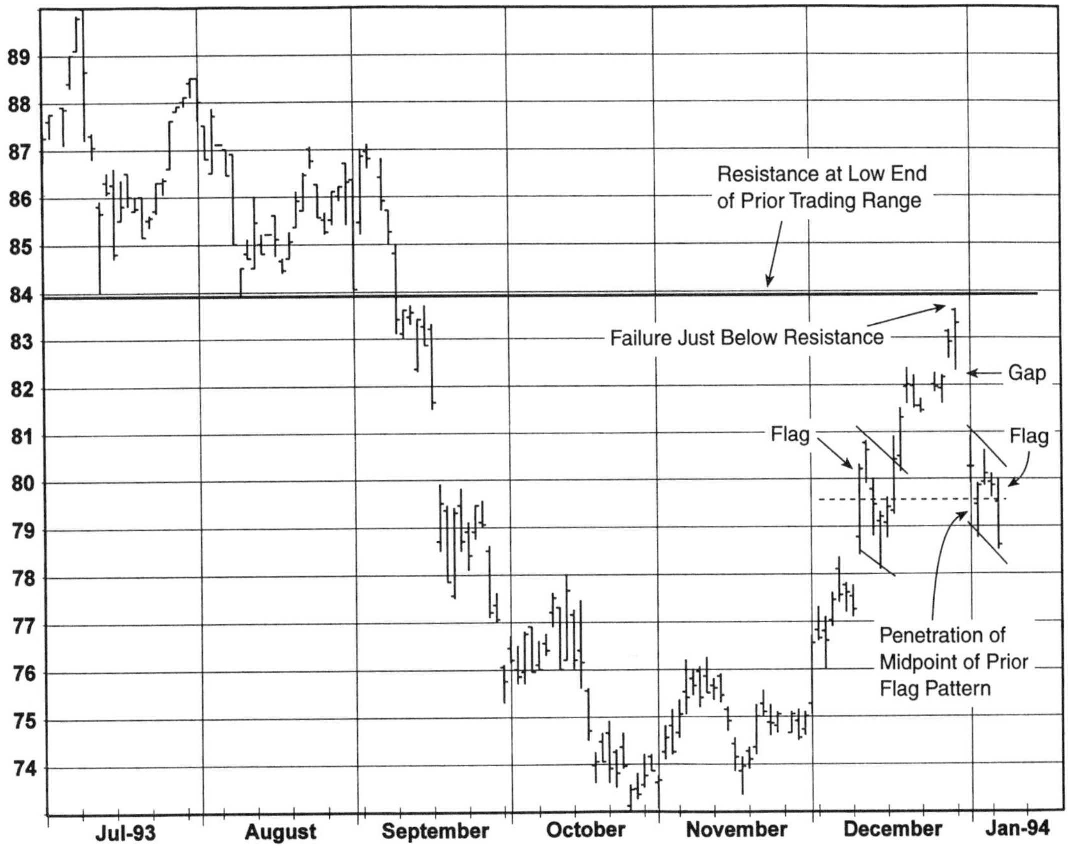

Trade Entry Reasons

1. Rally from the November low failed just below the major resistance implied by low end of the prior trading range.
2. Wide downside price gap.
3. Flag pattern formed after downswing.
4. Price break back to lower portion of prior flag pattern.

Do you agree or disagree with the analysis?
Evaluate the situation before turning page.

Figure 14.37*b*
MARCH 1994 COPPER

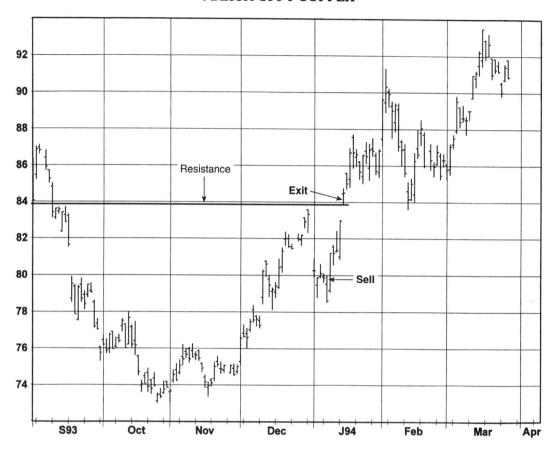

Trade Exit

The position was liquidated because the upmove on a single day provided no less than four indications contradicting trade:

1. Prior downside gap was closed.
2. New upside gap formed.
3. Market closed above major resistance line.
4. Market closed above prior relative high.

Comment

This trade seemed like a textbook case of a selling opportunity, with four chart-based factors supporting the bearish case. And, indeed, in the typical textbook, a nice downtrend would be evident immediately following the sell signal. It would all look so easy. The real world, however, doesn't work that way. No matter how compelling the reasons for a trade, remember it can always blow up in your face. In fact, this trade never even saw a single profitable day! The lesson is: Never hold a trading opinion rigidly. Flexibility in being able to change one's opinion may well be the single most important trait to the successful application of chart analysis to trading.

Figure 14.38a
MAY 1994 COPPER

Trade Entry Reasons

1. Bull-trap top.
2. Downside gap.
3. Flag pattern after downswing.
4. Sell point near resistance indicated by upper boundary of evolving flag consolidation.

Do you agree or disagree with the analysis?
Evaluate the situation before turning page.

Figure 14.38*b*
MAY 1994 COPPER

Trade Exit

Sustained upside penetration of sideways consolidation represented a bullish signal.

Comment

Another seemingly ideal trade that didn't work—and in the same market, only a few months later. Boy, the real world sure is one tough place. All the same comments of the previous trade apply here.

Figure 14.39a
DECEMBER 1994 COPPER

Trade Entry Reasons

1. Bull-trap top.
2. Nearby internal trend-line resistance.
3. Triangular consolidation after downswing more likely to be penetrated on downside.

Do you agree or disagree with the analysis?
Evaluate the situation before turning page.

Figure 14.39*b*
DECEMBER 1994 COPPER

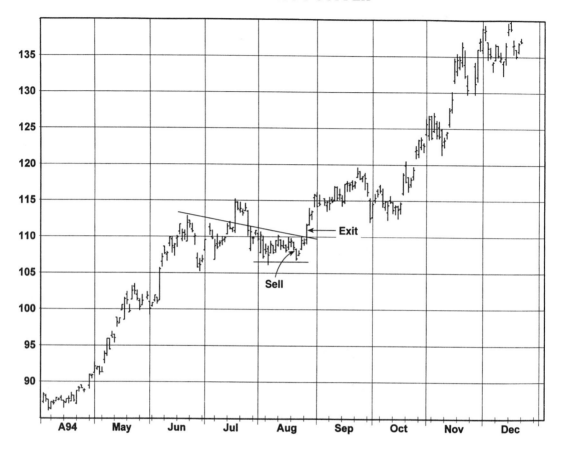

Trade Exit

Close well above the internal trend line provided a strong contradictory buy signal.

Comment

No, not again! Another seemingly attractive selling opportunity that at the minimum appeared likely to lead to a short-term downswing, but in fact proved to be a loser from day one—and, once again, in the same market, only a few months later. And, once again, the comments accompanying Figure 14.37*b* apply here as well. Also, note how much more extreme the losses could have been on these past three trades if the positions had not been liquidated relatively promptly in response to the changing market realities. Of course, if I had really been smart, I would have gone the other way.

Figure 14.40a
MARCH 1995 COPPER

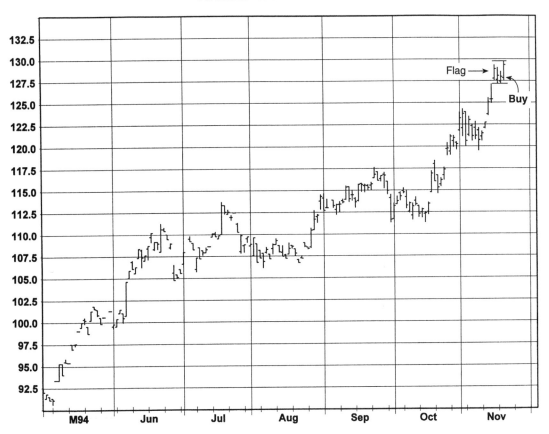

Trade Entry Reason

A flag consolidation formed in new high ground usually leads to at least a
short-term upswing.

Do you agree or disagree with the analysis?
Evaluate the situation before turning page.

Figure 14.40*b*
MARCH 1995 COPPER

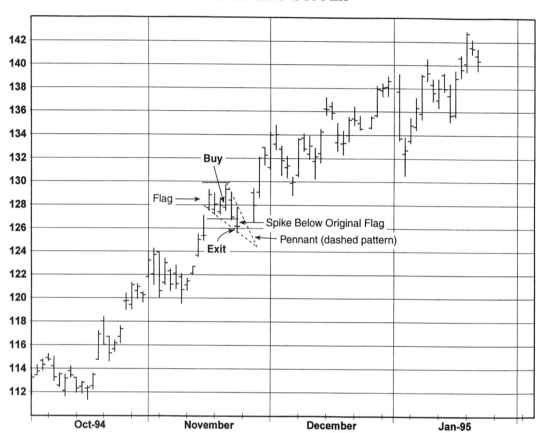

Trade Exit

Trade liquidated on a downside penetration of the flag pattern.

Comment

Although this trade idea ultimately proved correct and could have been very profitable, in reality, the trade resulted in a loss. The reason for this disappointing outcome is that I was guilty of a trading error: specifically, the stop was brought in too close. Flag and pennant consolidations frequently change their shape as they evolve. It is also quite common for such consolidations to be interrupted by one-day spikes. Consequently, it is important that stops in such trades allow for a meaningful margin beyond the existing boundary of the pattern. The illustrated trade can be viewed as either one of the aforementioned developments—that is, as either a one-day spike below the original flag pattern or a change in the shape of the consolidation (from a flag to a pennant).

Figure 14.41a
JULY 1995 COPPER

Trade Entry Reasons

1. Failure of rally near the resistance level implied by the prior peak suggested a possible double top.

2. Downside penetration of flag pattern.

Do you agree or disagree with the analysis?
Evaluate the situation before turning page.

Figure 14.41*b*
JULY 1995 COPPER

Trade Exit

Significant upside penetration of symmetrical triangle.

Comment

Although the trade did not work out as anticipated, the fact that the initial price swing was in the expected direction allowed for a small gain. The stop on this trade was probably a bit wider than it needed to be, but I leaned toward giving the market extra room, because the possibility that a double top had been formed (a chart interpretation enhanced by the fact that the pattern followed a more than yearlong advance) suggested a very large profit potential if the premise proved correct.

Figure 14.42a
NOVEMBER 1993 CRUDE OIL

Trade Entry Reasons

1. Apparent double bottom formed by a spike and secondary low.
2. Flag consolidation after upswing indicated a probable impending up-swing.
3. Upside gap.

Do you agree or disagree with the analysis?
Evaluate the situation before turning page.

Figure 14.42*b*
NOVEMBER 1993 CRUDE OIL

Trade Exit

Return to low end of the flag following the upside breakout suggested a bull trap.

Comment

Being attuned to evolving conditions *after* trade entered—bull trap, in this case—helped keep loss small in what proved to be a very wrong call.

Figure 14.43a
CRUDE OIL CONTINUOUS FUTURES

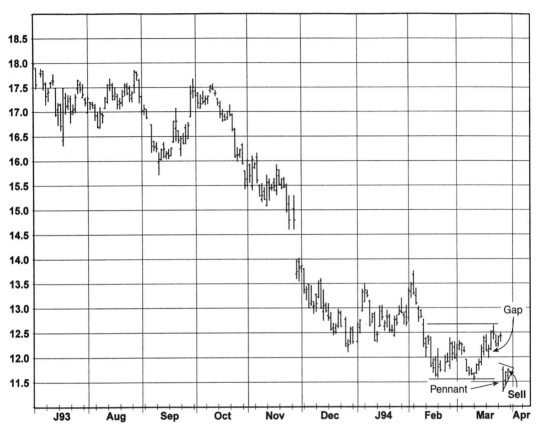

Trade Entry Reasons

1. Pennant consolidation formed near the low end of the trading range suggested the potential for another downswing.
2. Wide downside gap immediately preceding pennant consolidation.

Do you agree or disagree with the analysis?
Evaluate the situation before turning page.

Figure 14.43*b*
CRUDE OIL CONTINUOUS FUTURES

Trade Exit

Subsequent rebound back to near the top of the trading range left the low of
the pennant consolidation looking like a bear-trap reversal.

Comment

See next trade.

Figure 14.44a
CRUDE OIL CONTINUOUS FUTURES

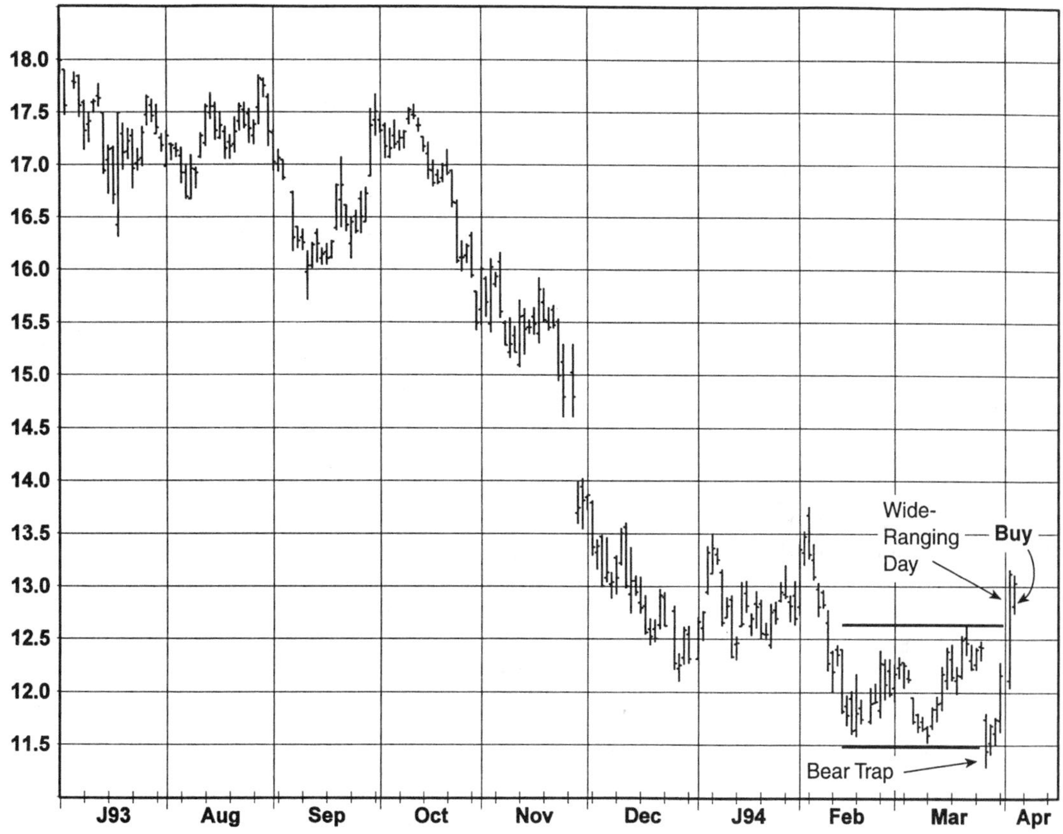

Trade Entry Reasons

1. Bear-trap low.
2. Wide-ranging up day formed near the low of an extended decline.

If this chart looks familiar, it is because the trade was implemented on the day following the activation of the stop in the prior trade.

**Do you agree or disagree with the analysis?
Evaluate the situation before turning page.**

Figure 14.44b
CRUDE OIL CONTINUOUS FUTURES

Trade Exit

Position was liquidated on a trailing stop, which at the time of exit was kept close because of large open profits.

Comment

This trade was motivated by failure signals related to the prior trade. Flexibility in recognizing a trade was wrong and reversing (not merely liquidating) the original position made it possible to capture a large gain in a trade sequence that began by going short at the virtual market bottom! (See Figure 14.43a.) This trade dramatically illustrates the concept that the ability to decisively respond to the market's constantly changing price action is a far more important attribute than skill in making market calls. (Note continuous futures charts were used to illustrate this trade because the position was rolled through several contracts.)

Figure 14.45a
JUNE 1995 CRUDE OIL

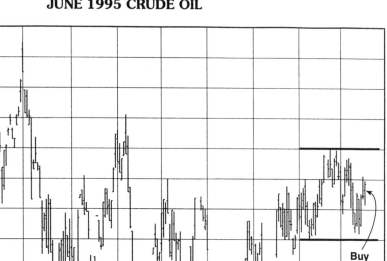

Trade Entry Reason

Narrow consolidation formed near upper portion of a broader trading range suggested the potential for an eventual upside breakout.

Do you agree or disagree with the analysis?
Evaluate the situation before turning page.

Figure 14.45*b*
JUNE 1995 CRUDE OIL

Trade Exit

The filling of a gap formed on a breakout above a pennant consolidation suggested a possible trend reversal.

Comment

Trading ranges formed near one end of broader trading ranges can signal the probable direction of the next major price swing.

Figure 14.46*a*
OCTOBER 1993 HEATING OIL

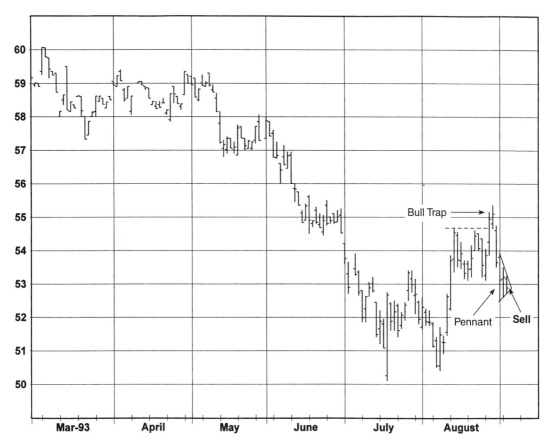

Trade Entry Reasons

1. Bull trap.
2. Pennant consolidation formed following downswing from apparent
bull trap.

Do you agree or disagree with the analysis?
Evaluate the situation before turning page.

Figure 14.46b
OCTOBER 1993 HEATING OIL

Trade Exit

The downside penetration of the July and August lows followed by a strong rebound in the same session, leaving a sharp spike low (as well as a wide-ranging day) in the process, suggested a possible trend reversal.

Comment

Sharp spikes to new lows (or highs) with closes in the opposite direction can provide a cautionary signal of a market reversal.

Figure 14.47 *a*
SEPTEMBER 1994 UNLEADED GAS

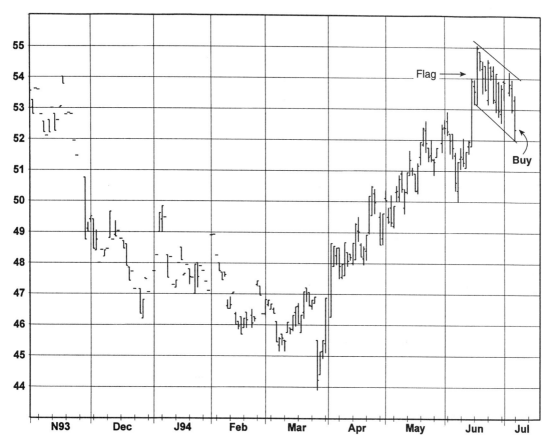

Trade Entry Reasons

1. Flag consolidation in an uptrend suggested the likelihood of another upswing.
2. Buy implemented near support implied by lower boundary of flag.

Do you agree or disagree with the analysis?
Evaluate the situation before turning page.

Figure 14.47b
SEPTEMBER 1994 UNLEADED GAS

Trade Exit

Trade was liquidated following the counter-to-anticipated penetration of a flag pattern formed after a major measured move objective had been achieved.

Comment

Counter-to-anticipated breakouts from flag patterns can sometimes provide liquidation (or reversal) signals reasonably close to major turning points—particularly when such failure signals occur after a major measured move objective has been attained.

Figure 14.48a
DECEMBER 1994 UNLEADED GAS

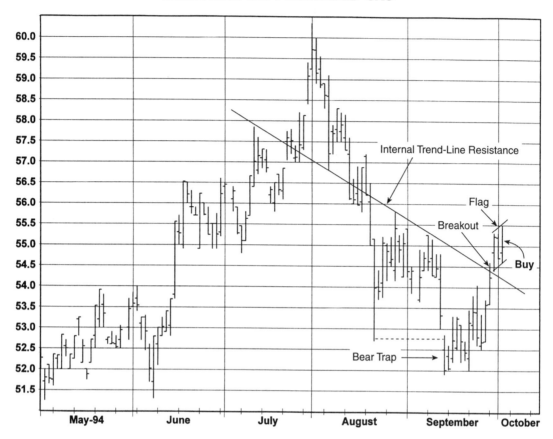

Trade Entry Reasons

1. Bear trap.
2. Upside penetration of internal trend-line resistance.
3. Flag pattern formed after upswing.

Do you agree or disagree with the analysis?
Evaluate the situation before turning page.

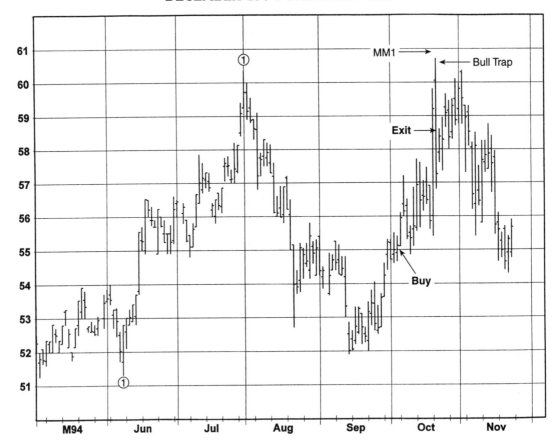

Figure 14.48b
DECEMBER 1994 UNLEADED GAS

Trade Exit

Modest penetration of prior peak, following near attainment of a major measured move objective, and subsequent sharp pullback into range suggested a possible bull-trap reversal.

Comment

Sometimes multiple indications can occur at the same time. For example, note how the peak day (day position liquidated) displayed all the following bearish characteristics:

1. High near major measured move objective;
2. Spike high;
3. Bull trap;
4. Wide-ranging down day.

Typically, such multiple simultaneous indications increase the reliability of the signal.

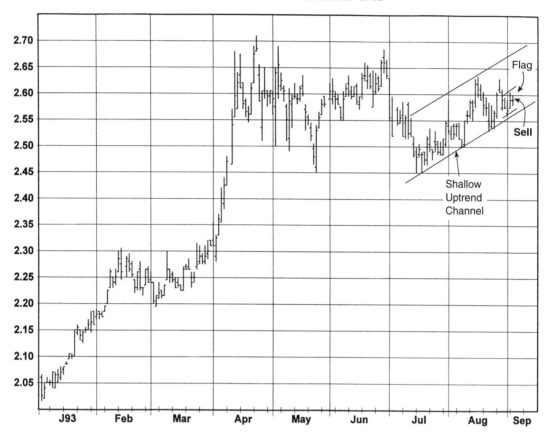

Figure 14.49a
DECEMBER 1993 NATURAL GAS

Trade Entry Reasons

1. Market appeared to be forming a broad top. The prevailing trading range was assumed to be a top pattern rather than a consolidation before an uptrend for the following reasons:

   a. Trading range preceded by large, multiple-wave price advance;
   b. Long duration of trading range (nearly five months at the time of recommendation);
   c. Broadness of trading range more characteristic of a top than a consolidation.

2. Shallow uptrend channel, despite its direction, is a bearish, not bullish, pattern—that is, it is usually broken on the downside.
3. Flag formed near the low end of the uptrend channel suggested an imminent downside breakout.

Do you agree or disagree with the analysis?
Evaluate the situation before turning page.

407

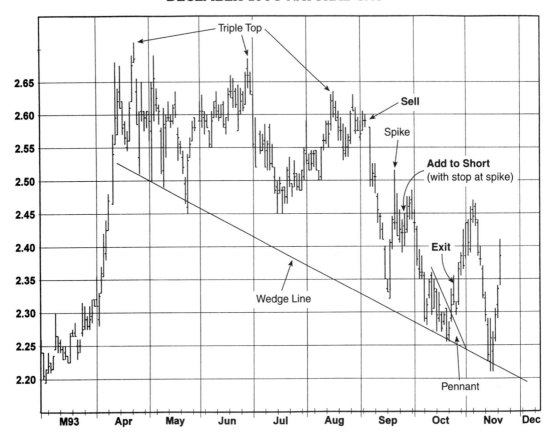

Figure 14.49*b*
DECEMBER 1993 NATURAL GAS

Trade Exit

1. The ability of the market to repeatedly hold in the vicinity of a wedge line suggested caution against the possibility of a rebound. Hence, the trailing stop was kept relatively close.
2. The sustained upside penetration of a pennant consolidation represented a short-term bullish signal.

Comment

Note addition to original position where indicated. Added short based on following two factors:

1. Apparent triple top in place.
2. Spike provided evidence of failed rally and also allowed for placement of relatively close meaningful stop on added position.

Adding to trades perceived to be major position trades is very important to enhancing profits. Such added positions should be implemented at points where it is possible to define a relatively close meaningful stop, such as the nearby spike high in this example.

This trade also illustrates the observation that if a market repeatedly holds in the vicinity of a wedge line, it suggests the potential for an abrupt rally. Therefore, evidence of an evolving wedge line can be used as a signal to tighten stops. Even though the market eventually went to a new low, relatively quick exit inspired by the reversal off the wedge line was beneficial, since a higher stop would very likely have been activated by the interim rally. Also, the short position was eventually reinstated at a higher price in a more forward contract.

Figure 14.50a
MARCH 1994 NATURAL GAS

Trade Entry Reasons

Sold into rally because:

1. Apparent broad top pattern in place.
2. Nearby resistance implied by internal trend line, lower boundary of triangle pattern, and top of breakaway gap.

Do you agree or disagree with the analysis?
Evaluate the situation before turning page.

Figure 14.50*b*
MARCH 1994 NATURAL GAS

Trade Exit

Significant penetration of each of the aforementioned resistance levels suggested the rally was part of a new bull market rather than a rebound in a bear
market.

Comment

An apparent broad top pattern (i.e., wide, extended trading range that is
followed by a downswing) whose lower boundary is significantly penetrated is
unlikely to remain intact.

Figure 14.51a
SEPTEMBER 1994 NATURAL GAS

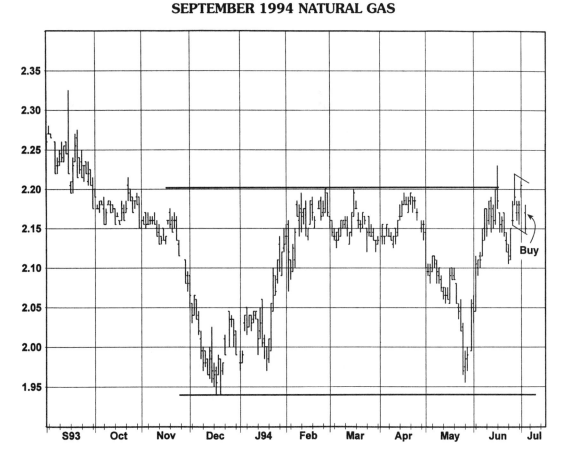

Trade Entry Reason

Flag formed near the upper end of an extended, broad trading range suggested an impending upside breakout.

Do you agree or disagree with the analysis?
Evaluate the situation before turning page.

Figure 14.51*b*
SEPTEMBER 1994 NATURAL GAS

Trade Exit

Downside penetration of flag—on a wide gap, no less—violated the basic premise of the trade.

Comment

This trade provides a striking illustration of the importance of getting out of a position immediately if the original premise of the trade is contradicted by market action. Note how adherence to this principle kept the loss on the trade small despite having implemented a long position right at the beginning of an extreme price collapse. Without such a rule, this trade could have been an absolute disaster.

Although, ostensibly, this looks like a terrible trade—a buy immediately before an extreme price slide—even in hindsight, I would still consider it a "good trade": The trade was initiated following a pattern that if traded consistently over the long-term should be profitable and liquidated on the first sign the trade was wrong.

Figure 14.52a
APRIL 1994 NATURAL GAS

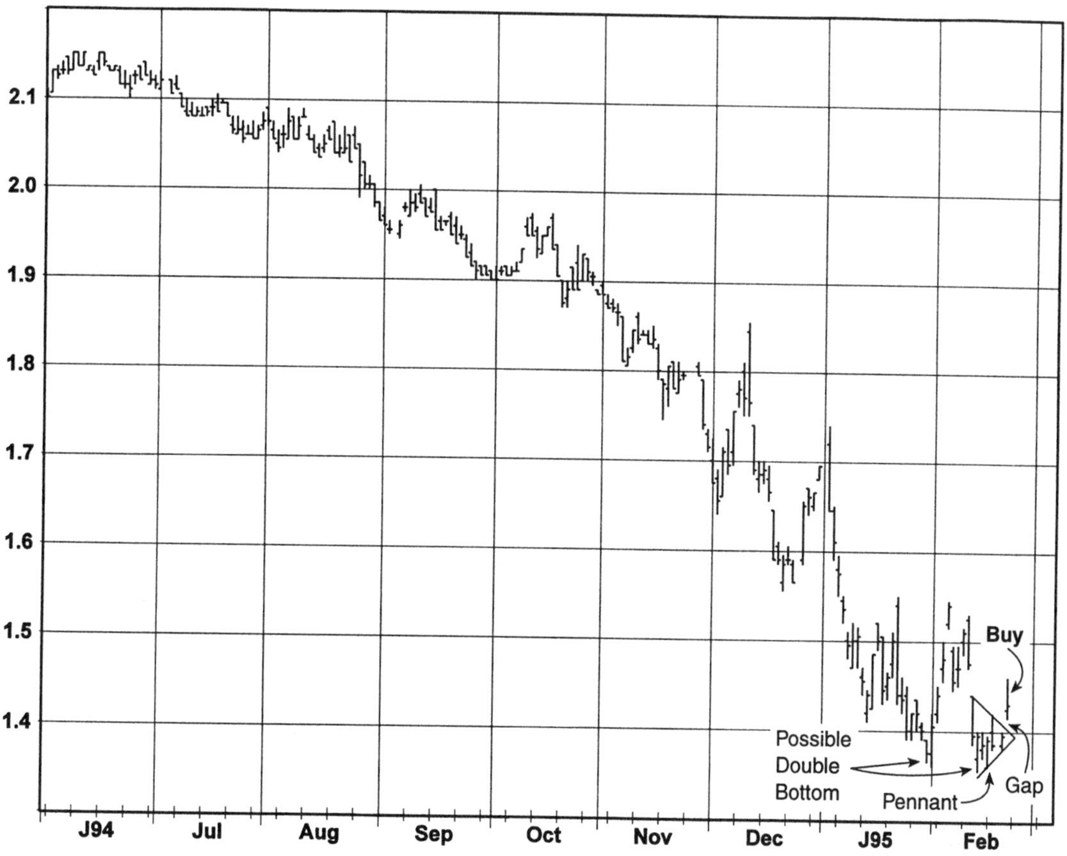

Trade Entry Reasons

1. Proximity of market to the low end of the multiyear trading range (not shown) suggested being attuned for signs of an upside reversal.
2. Counter-to-anticipated upside breakout of pennant consolidation on a gap provided the first confirmation sign of a possible double bottom.
3. Although the evidence of a double bottom was hardly persuasive, one appeal of the trade was that the implied risk based on the closest meaningful stop was relatively small. (The initial stop was placed just below the illustrated pennant consolidation.)

Do you agree or disagree with the analysis?
Evaluate the situation before turning page.

Figure 14.52*b*
APRIL 1994 NATURAL GAS

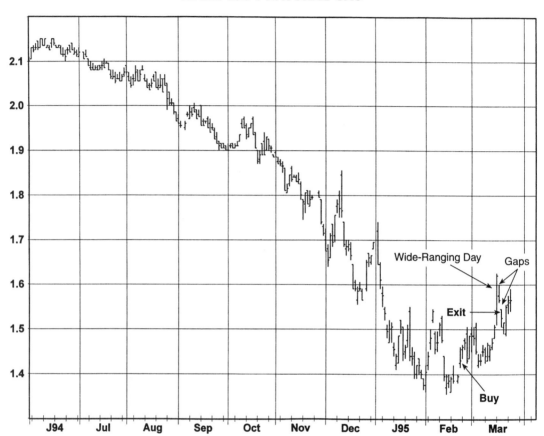

Trade Exit

The fact that the market retraced most of a wide-ranging up day on two successive days—and on downside gaps, no less—suggested a price failure.

Comment

It is not always necessary to wait for substantive proof of a bottom (or top) being in place before taking a trade based on the assumption that the trend has reversed. Sometimes, as was the case in this trade, a position can be implemented on an early sign of a reversal if the market is near a long-term support area and a meaningful, low-risk stop can be defined.

Figure 14.53a
DECEMBER 1993 CORN

Trade Entry Reasons

1. Downside breakout of huge a descending triangle.
2. Flag formed below the triangle suggested the likelihood of a continued downtrend.

Do you agree or disagree with the analysis?
Evaluate the situation before turning page.

Figure 14.53*b*
DECEMBER 1993 CORN

Trade Exit

Counter-to-anticipated breakout of flag suggested that an upside reversal had occurred.

Comment

Exiting on the first sign of violation of the trade premise kept loss very small even though the trade idea was dead wrong.

Figure 14.54a
DECEMBER 1993 CORN

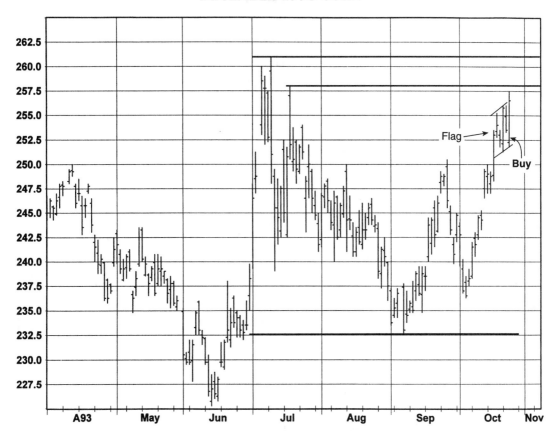

Trade Entry Reason

Flag pattern formed near the upper portion of a wide trading range suggested potential impending upmove.

Do you agree or disagree with the analysis?
Evaluate the situation before turning page.

Figure 14.54*b*
MARCH 1993 CORN

Trade Exit

Given the extent of the virtually uninterrupted advance and the proximity of the market to resistance implied by the 1990 high on the weekly nearest futures chart (not shown), the strategy was to liquidate the trade on the first hint of a price failure. This event occurred on the indicated exit day, which witnessed a downside gap and a modest downside penetration of the most recent flag pattern.

Comment

The same pattern that motivated this trade—a flag near the upper (or lower) portion of a broad trading range—was responsible for false signals in a number of previously cited illustrations. However, note how much greater the profit is on a valid signal than the typical loss when this pattern proves misleading.

Figure 14.55a
MAY 1994 CORN

Trade Entry Reasons

1. Sustained breakout below head-and-shoulders top pattern.
2. Flag consolidation formed following the breakout implied probable continuation of the downtrend.

Do you agree or disagree with the analysis?
Evaluate the situation before turning page.

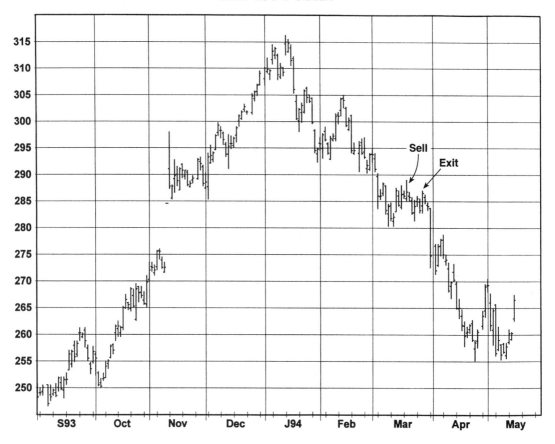

Figure 14.55*b*
MAY 1994 CORN

Trade Exit

Lowered stop shortly after entry to slightly better than breakeven.

Comment

The stop on this trade (Exit on chart) was hit at the exact high tick prior to a major price collapse! Some traders experiencing a similar turn of events would curse their luck (or the floor traders). The outcome was not a matter of bad luck, however, but rather a consequence of a trading mistake. Specifically, the stop was brought in too close, too quickly. As has been noted in a number of previous illustrations, the protective stop on a trade should not be brought in nearer than the closest technically significant point. The lowered stop in this trade was right in the midst of an ongoing consolidation and obviously had no significance whatsoever. The irony is that even a break-even stop would have remained intact. By trying to avoid any risk, a swift large profit opportunity was lost. The moral is: You can't win in trading without being willing to lose.

Figure 14.56a
MARCH 1995 CORN

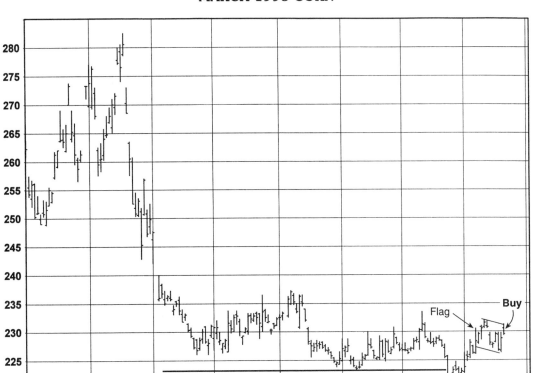

Trade Entry Reasons

1. Long-term charts (not shown) suggested the potential for a bottom being formed. Specifically, the November low was in the support zone implied by a concentration of major lows on the nearest futures chart (five major lows in the 212–222 area during the prior nine years) and right near the support level implied by the 1993 low on the continuous futures chart.
2. The one-day spike below a five-month trading range and the subsequent immediate rebound back into the range represented a classic bear-trap pattern.
3. The flag formed after an upswing implied that the next price swing would be on the upside.

Do you agree or disagree with the analysis?
Evaluate the situation before turning page.

Figure 14.56b
JULY 1995 CORN

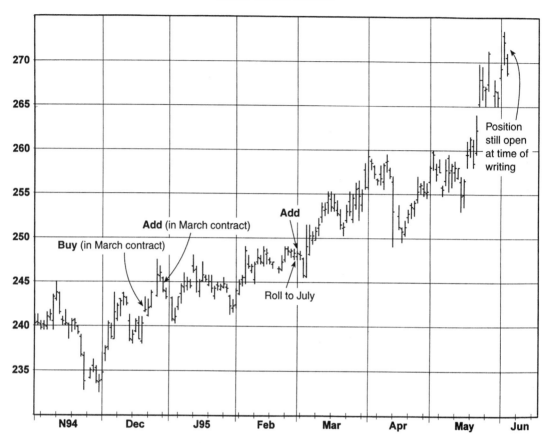

Trade Exit

This trade was still open at the time of this writing.

Comment

A bear-trap reversal that materializes near major support on long-term charts is a powerful signal of a potential market bottom. The longer the bear-trap reversal remains intact, the more reliable it is as a major trend reversal signal.

It is important to take full advantage of perceived major trading opportunities (such as the trade in this illustration) by building the position as the market trend and consolidations confirm the initial trade. Hitting home runs instead of singles in such situations is an important element of trading success. The key is that added positions are timed so that close meaningful stop points can be identified. In this manner, the risk on the total position is kept well in control.

Figure 14.57*a*
DECEMBER 1993 WHEAT

Trade Entry Reasons

1. Market held at internal trend-line support level.
2. Spike low.
3. Flag consolidation formed after upswing.

Do you agree or disagree with the analysis?
Evaluate the situation before turning page.

Figure 14.57b
DECEMBER 1993 WHEAT

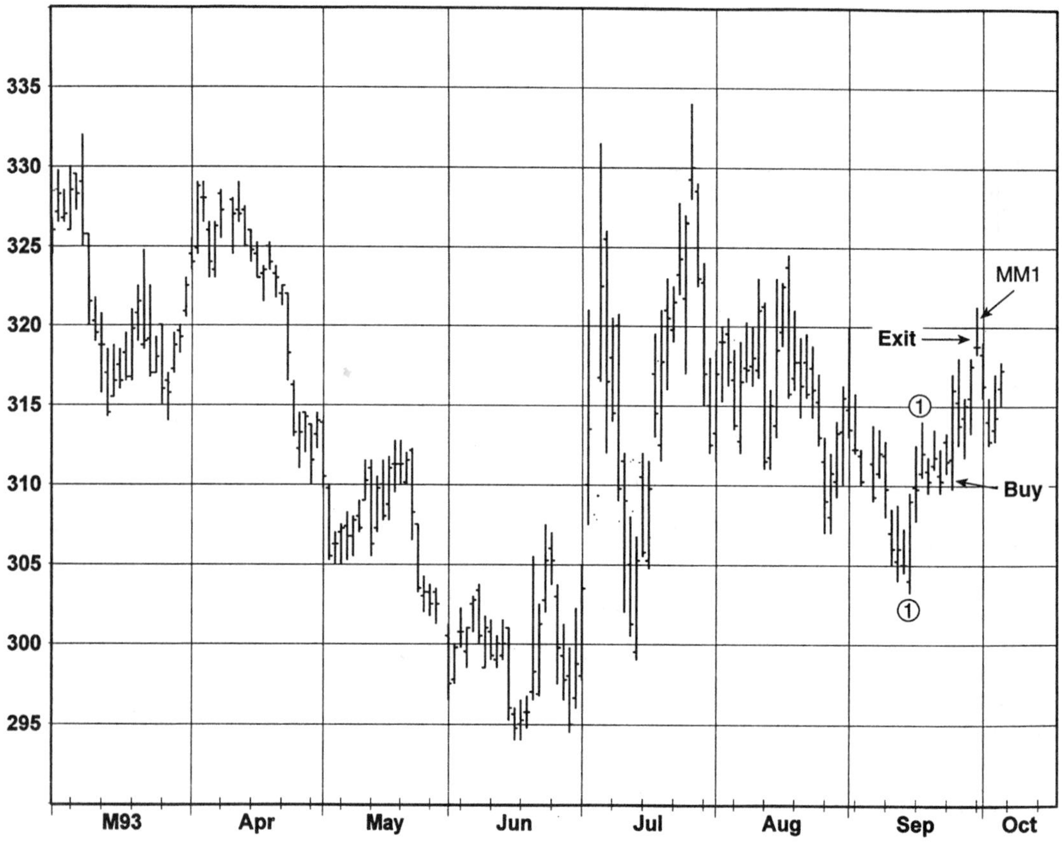

Trade Exit

Took profits on the approach of the measured move objective (MM1).

Comment

If a position is liquidated because a profit target is reached (as opposed to price action adverse to position), you need to be attuned to reentering the trade if conditions are appropriate (see next trade).

Figure 14.58a
DECEMBER 1993 WHEAT

Trade Entry Reason

Flag formed after the breakout above the trend channel suggested the likelihood of a continued price advance.

Do you agree or disagree with the analysis?
Evaluate the situation before turning page.

Figure 14.58*b*
DECEMBER 1993 WHEAT

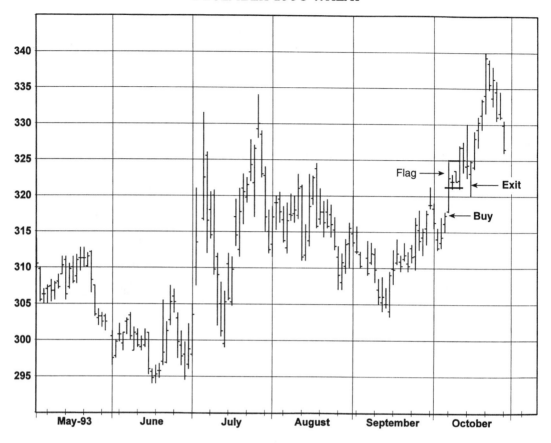

Trade Exit

Pullback to the low end of the most recent flag pattern represented a short-term failure signal.

Comment

Even though this trade was net profitable, placing the protective stop at a point representing the first sign of a market failure resulted in missing the bulk of the price move. There is a tradeoff in using stops equivalent to *closest meaningful point*: in some cases, this approach will provide very timely exits; in other instances, however, this procedure will result in the highly premature liquidation of good positions (as was the case in this illustration). There is no absolute right or wrong answer regarding the use of such stops; it is largely a matter of personal choice. One possible compromise approach is to avoid bringing the stop in closer than breakeven for the first two weeks of the trade. Such a rule would have prevented the premature exit in this trade.

Figure 14.59a
DECEMBER 1993 WHEAT

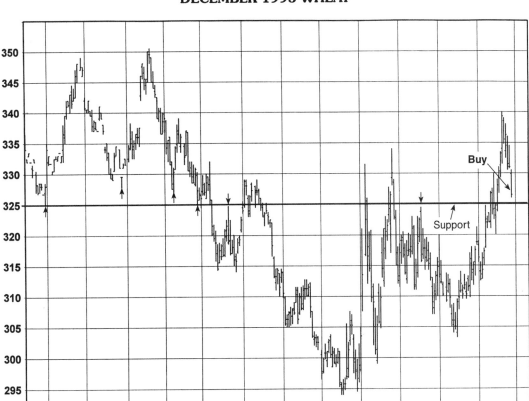

Trade Entry Reason

Long position recommended at a point near the support area implied by concentration of prior relative highs and relative lows (denoted by vertical arrows in accompanying chart).

Do you agree or disagree with the analysis?
Evaluate the situation before turning page.

Figure 14.59*b*
DECEMBER 1993 WHEAT

Trade Exit

Trade liquidated on the approach of the closer of two measured move objectives (MM2).

Comment

Even though the trade worked out exactly as planned—bought near reaction low and took profits just below a short-term high—gave up profit potential in significant extension of upmove. Note that the advance eventually carried to more major measured move objective (MM1).

Figure 14.60a
MAY 1994 WHEAT

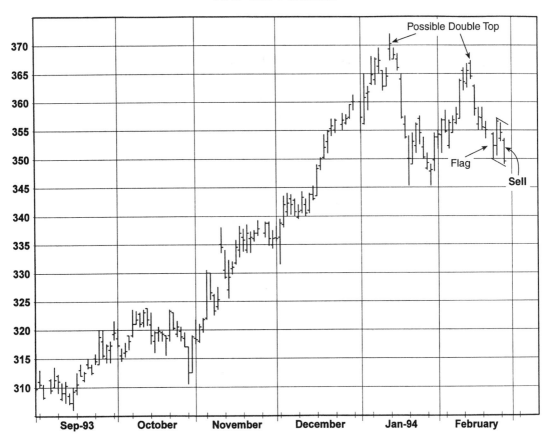

Trade Entry Reasons

1. Possible double-top formation.
2. Flag formed after downswing.

Do you agree or disagree with the analysis?
Evaluate the situation before turning page.

Figure 14.60*b*
MAY 1994 WHEAT

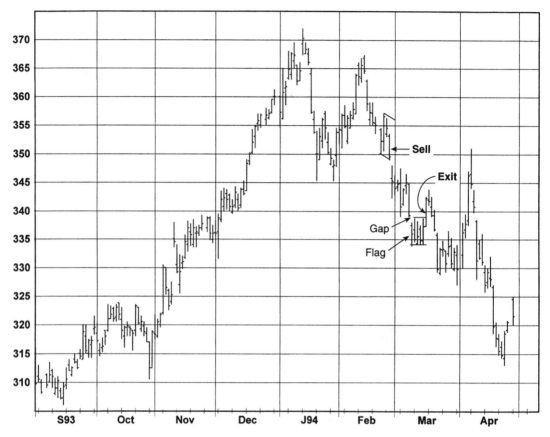

Trade Exit

Counter-to-anticipated upside penetration of flag pattern.

Comment

Note that although the market eventually went meaningfully lower, a wider stop would probably have been activated by the April rally at a worse level. Although using wide stops in an effort to ride a long-term trend is a nice concept, the reality is that some market trends are so "whippy" that using such an approach will only result in a worse exit point.

Figure 14.61a
NOVEMBER 1993 SOYBEANS

Trade Entry Reasons

1. Major spike high and bull-trap top suggested the potential for a longer-term decline.

2. Flag formed near the low end of broader consolidation suggested that the next price swing would be on the downside.

Do you agree or disagree with the analysis?
Evaluate the situation before turning page.

Figure 14.61b
NOVEMBER 1993 SOYBEANS

Trade Exit

Took profits because of proximity of major support implied by both a measured move objective and the top end of a prior trading range.

Comment

Taking profits *without any evidence of a reversal* is a reasonable strategy if the market is approaching a major support area after an extended decline (or resistance area after an extended advance). Even if a price move eventually continues, such situations are likely to witness at least temporary corrections, which could easily result in a less favorable liquidation of the position. For example, even though the market decline eventually extended below the exit level, if profits had not been taken, there is a reasonable chance that the position would have been stopped out by the interim rally in September. Also, it is always possible to reenter a trade after taking profits, if warranted by the evolving price action (see next trade).

Figure 14.62a
NOVEMBER 1993 SOYBEANS

Trade Entry Reasons:

1. Downside breakaway gap.
2. Flag formed below both a trading range and a long-term support line
suggested the probable continuation of the decline.

Do you agree or disagree with the analysis?
Evaluate the situation before turning page.

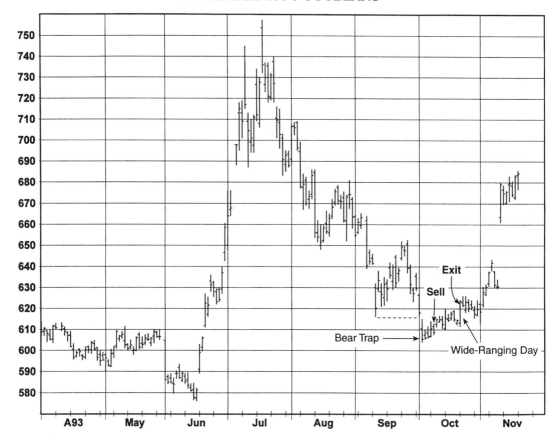

Figure 14.62b
NOVEMBER 1993 SOYBEANS

Trade Exit

1. Failure of the market to witness any follow-through on the downside in the subsequent weeks suggested a possible bear-trap reversal.
2. Wide-ranging up day formed near the market low represented a bullish signal.

Comment

This trade seemed like a shoo-in for at least a minor downswing. Yet prices witnessed only one lower close before beginning a steady advance. The point is you can never be sure of any trade—no matter how bearish or bullish the pattern. Therefore, it is important to always be willing to liquidate or reverse a position if the evolving price action fails to conform to expectations. Although this short position was implemented almost near the exact low following a long decline, the willingness to quickly liquidate a trade on contradictory price action kept the loss relatively small.

Figure 14.63*a*
MAY 1994 SOYBEANS

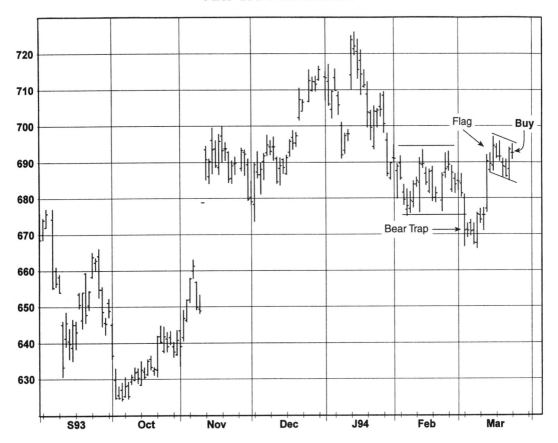

Trade Entry Reasons

1. Apparent bear trap.
2. Flag formed following an upswing.

Do you agree or disagree with the analysis?
Evaluate the situation before turning page.

Figure 14.63*b*
MAY 1994 SOYBEANS

Trade Exit

Position liquidated on a counter-to-anticipated breakout of the flag pattern.

Comment

Even with the benefit of hindsight, it is hard to fault the entry decision in this trade—the pattern still looks decisively bullish. As demonstrated in this and other examples, trading on chart patterns is a matter of percentages and keeping the average loss much smaller than the average gain. The reality, however, is that a substantial portion of all trades—even those that look most promising—will turn out to be losers. In this trade, liquidation on the first sign of trade failure kept the loss small.

Figure 14.64a
JULY 1994 SOYBEANS

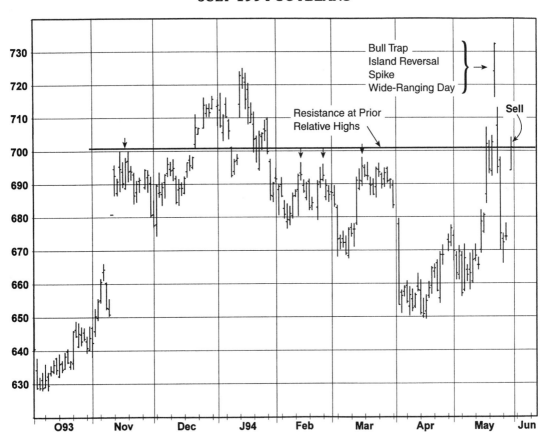

Trade Entry Reasons

1. Rebound to resistance area implied by the concentration of prior relative highs (denoted by downward-pointing arrows).
2. Apparent peak in place based on the following factors:
   a. Bull trap
   b. Island reversal
   c. Spike
   d. Wide-ranging day

It is noteworthy that all four of the listed bearish patterns occurred on a single day! (Of course, in the case of the island reversal, by definition, the pattern also included the preceding and succeeding days.)

Do you agree or disagree with the analysis?
Evaluate the situation before turning page.

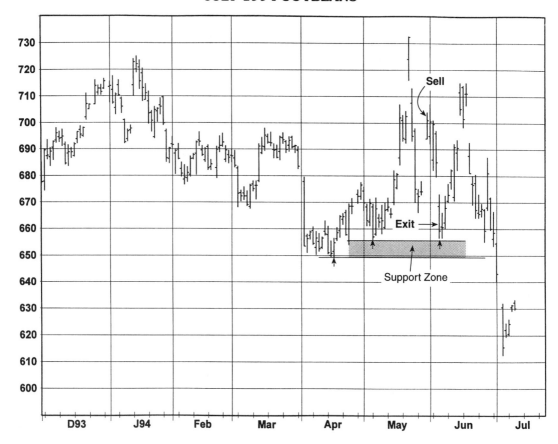

Figure 14.64b
JULY 1994 SOYBEANS

Trade Exit

Trade was liquidated on a retracement to the support zone implied by the concentration of prior relative lows (denoted by upward-pointing arrows).

Comment

Although, as a general rule, it is desirable to try to ride a trade until there is at least some sign of a reversal, a reasonable exception is provided by trades that meet the following combined conditions:

1. Very quick, *pronounced* move in anticipated direction;
2. Proximity of major support (or major resistance, in the case of long positions).

The reasoning is that these trades are particularly prone to abrupt pull-backs, and such corrective moves can easily result in trade being liquidated at a much worse price (e.g., activation of protective stop), *even if the trend eventually continues.*

438

Figure 14.65a
MAY 1995 SOYBEANS

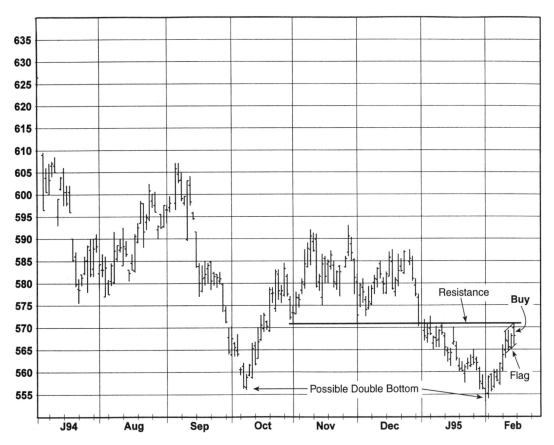

Trade Entry Reasons

1. Possible double bottom.
2. Price rebound to resistance was followed by a consolidation (flag pattern) rather than a pullback—price action indicative of a probable eventual penetration of resistance.

Do you agree or disagree with the analysis?
Evaluate the situation before turning page.

Figure 14.65*b*
MAY 1995 SOYBEANS

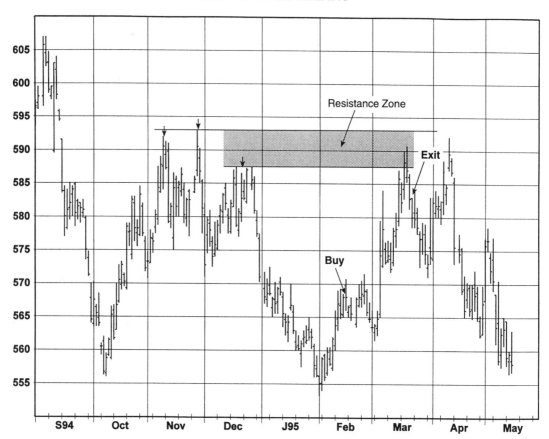

Trade Exit

Protective stop was brought in close because market had reached major resistance zone implied by prior relative highs (denoted by downward-pointing arrows).

Comment

The exit reason in this trade was very similar to that of the previous trade, except that here the same situation was used to sharply tighten the protective stop (as opposed to automatic liquidation of position). Neither of these variations is inherently better or worse than the other. The tradeoff is that tightening the stop will sometimes allow a position to be held for a further significant extension of the trend at the expense of frequently realizing a modestly worse liquidation price.

Figure 14.66a
DECEMBER 1993 SOYBEAN MEAL

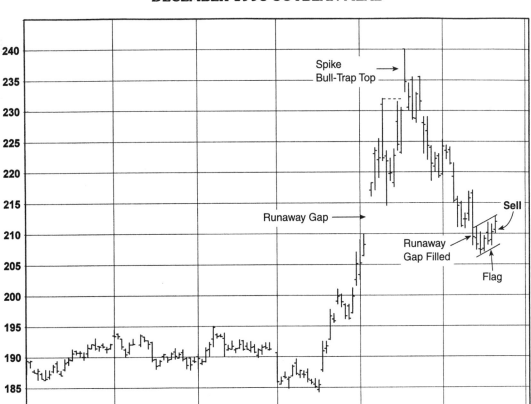

Trade Entry Reasons

1. Major peak in place as implied by both a spike and a bull trap.
2. Prior runaway gap on upside filled on decline.
3. Flag pattern formed following a downswing.

**Do you agree or disagree with the analysis?
Evaluate the situation before turning page.**

Figure 14.66b
DECEMBER 1993 SOYBEAN MEAL

Trade Exit

Counter-to-anticipated penetration of flag pattern.

Comment

Stop on this trade was simply too close. Although stop point represented a minor upside breakout of the flag pattern, it was right in the vicinity of the major resistance line implied by the low end of the broad range that formed the market top. At a minimum, the stop should have been placed at least moderately beyond this resistance level. Lesson: Placing stops too close can increase risk rather than decrease risk.

Figure 14.67a
DECEMBER 1993 SOYBEAN MEAL

Trade Entry Reasons

1. Major peak in place as implied by both a spike and bull-trap.
2. Prior runaway gap on the upside filled on decline.
3. Flag pattern formed at low end of trading range.

Do you agree or disagree with the analysis?
Evaluate the situation before turning page.

Figure 14.67b
DECEMBER 1993 SOYBEAN MEAL

Trade Exit

Trade liquidated because of the proximity of both a major support level and a measured move objective (MM1).

Comment

If this trade looks familiar, there is good reason: it is the same market as the last trade less than two weeks after that trade was liquidated. Note that the same trade was reinstated because the exit was recognized as an error. The general principle is: If market price action suggests that the liquidation of a trade was a mistake, reinstate position, *even if doing so means reentering at a significantly worse price.* This advice is more easily given than followed. Reinstating a position at a meaningfully worse price than the exit level is a particularly difficult task. Although I did the right thing here, I have to admit that my trading decisions in such circumstances are usually not as sagacious.

Figure 14.68a
DECEMBER 1993 SOYBEAN MEAL

Trade Entry Reasons

1. Flag formed after a downswing.
2. Downside gap.

Do you agree or disagree with the analysis?
Evaluate the situation before turning page.

Figure 14.68*b*
DECEMBER 1993 SOYBEAN MEAL

Trade Exit

Trade liquidated on upside penetration of the minor resistance level implied by both the low end of the September consolidation and the relative high formed following the initial rebound off the low.

Comment

Once again, this trade should look familiar as it is the same market as the last trade, one week after that position was liquidated. (Compare Figures 14.67*b* and 14.68*a*). The previous trade was liquidated because of concern that the market might rebound at least temporarily after approaching major support and reaching a measured move objective. Once the market consolidated instead of rebounding, it implied the downswing would continue, hence warranting the reinstatement of the short position. Also, it should be noted that the flag pattern formed prior to trade reentry permitted the use of a relatively close stop.

Figure 14.69a
JULY 1994 SOYBEAN MEAL

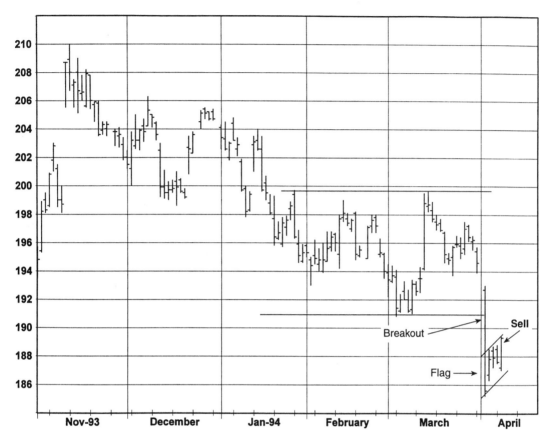

Trade Entry Reason

Flag formed following a downside breakout below a trading range represents a strong bearish signal.

Do you agree or disagree with the analysis?
Evaluate the situation before turning page.

Figure 14.69b
JULY 1994 SOYBEAN MEAL

Trade Exit

1. Transformation of the original flag into a trading range negated the key premise of the trade.

2. Penetration of the internal downtrend line suggested an upside reversal.

Comment

Even when reliable chart patterns prove misleading, subsequent price action will sometimes provide sufficient clues that a position should be liquidated in time to avoid any significant loss.

Figure 14.70a
DECEMBER 1994 SOYBEAN OIL

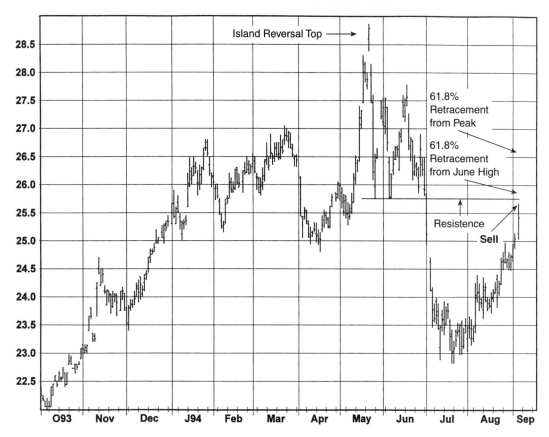

Trade Entry Reasons

1. Island reversal peak in place.
2. The proximity of both the 61.8% retracement point (relative to the June high) and the resistance level implied by the low end of the broad trading range formed during May–June suggested that prices would probably correct on the downside even if a bottom had been formed.

Do you agree or disagree with the analysis?
Evaluate the situation before turning page.

Figure 14.70*b*
DECEMBER 1994 SOYBEAN OIL

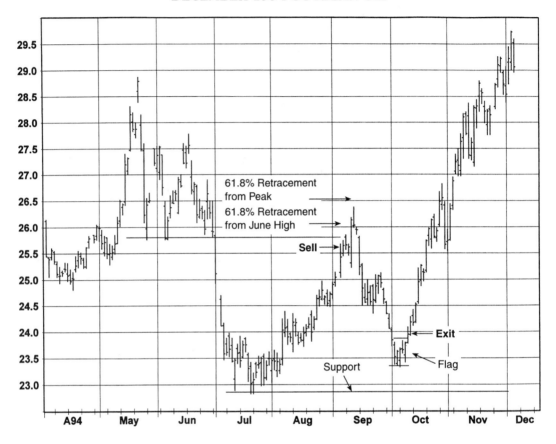

Trade Exit

1. Sharply lowered stop due to the approach of major support level.
2. Counter-to-anticipated upside breakout of the flag pattern signaled a possible upside reversal.

Comment

Although price advance moderately exceeded the anticipated resistance area, the basic trade premise proved correct. Initial stop was placed modestly above the higher of two indicated 61.8% retracement points. This trade provides a good illustration of the importance of not setting the initial protective stop too close.

Figure 14.71a
DECEMBER 1994 OATS

Trade Entry Reasons

Flag formed at low end of uptrend channel implied a potential downside breakout.

Do you agree or disagree with the analysis?
Evaluate the situation before turning page.

Figure 14.71*b*
DECEMBER 1994 OATS

Trade Exit

Protective stop brought in extremely close because of the market approach of a very major measured move objective (MM1).

Comment

If the market nearly achieves a major objective in very quick fashion, it is usually advisable to either take profits or sharply tighten stop. In such instances, the danger of at least a temporary reversal outweighs the potential for a further near-term gain.

Figure 14.72a
JUNE 1995 HOGS

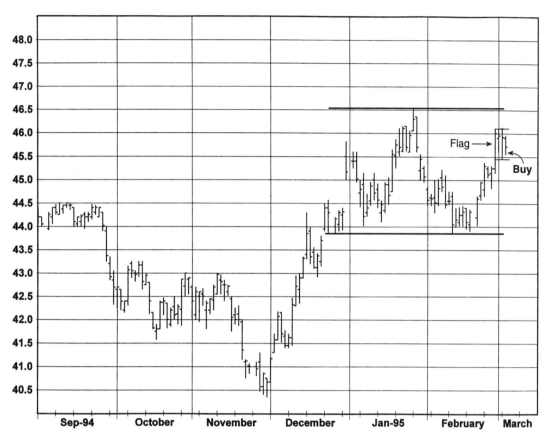

Trade Entry Reason

Flag pattern formed near the upper portion of the trading range suggested a potential upside breakout.

Do you agree or disagree with the analysis?
Evaluate the situation before turning page.

Figure 14.72*b*
JUNE 1995 HOGS

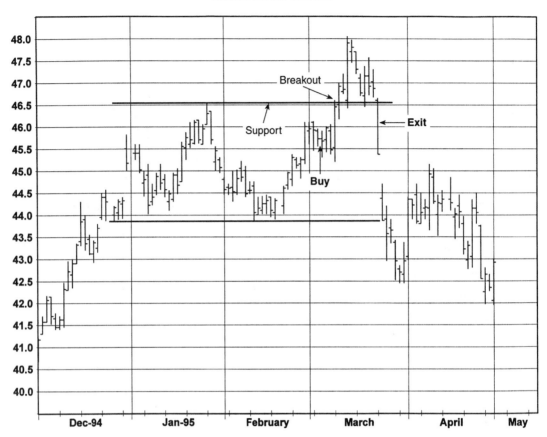

Trade Exit

The downside penetration of the consolidation that was formed after an up-side breakout above a broad trading range represented a price failure signal.

Comment

Although the chart pattern that motivated the trade ultimately proved to be a misleading indicator, the fact that it correctly anticipated the direction of the next minor price swing still allowed for a net profitable outcome on the trade.

Figure 14.73a
MAY 1994 SUGAR

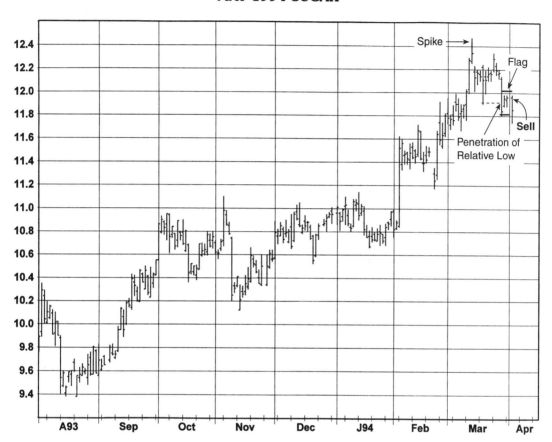

Trade Entry Reasons

1. Spike high.
2. Penetration of relative low.
3. Flag formed after a downswing suggested a greater likelihood that the next price move would also be on the downside.

Do you agree or disagree with the analysis?
Evaluate the situation before turning page.

Figure 14.73b
MAY 1994 SUGAR

Trade Exit

1. Protective stop lowered sharply following quick, large price move in the anticipated direction.
2. The fact that a wide-ranging day with a very weak close was followed by a rebound, rather than a downside follow-through, provided a preliminary warning signal of a possible upside reversal.

Comment

This trade illustrates how it is possible for the use of short-term chart patterns in timing the entry and exit of trades to sometimes result in profits even in the type of wide-swinging trading range markets that are usually disastrous for trend-following methods.

Figure 14.74a
JULY 1995 SUGAR

Trade Entry Reasons

1. Wedge top suggested the likelihood of a longer-lived bear market.
2. Narrow consolidation formed at the low end of the broader consolidation implied a probable downside breakout.

Do you agree or disagree with the analysis?
Evaluate the situation before turning page.

Figure 14.74b
JULY 1995 SUGAR

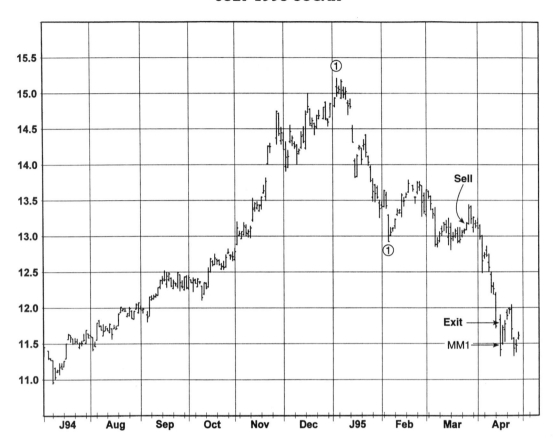

Trade Exit

Protective stop lowered sharply because of the approach of a major measured move objective (MM1).

Comment

When a trade is first put on, it is usually a good idea *not* to use an extremely close stop. For example, if the initial stop in this trade had been placed just above the narrow consolidation within the broader trading range, the trade would have resulted in a small loss instead of a quick, substantive gain. As a general rule, the stop can be brought in once a trade has been on for about one to two weeks, or once the market has moved in the anticipated direction. For example, in this trade, the stop was not lowered to near the top of the original narrow consolidation until prices had broken below the trading range.

Figure 14.75a
DECEMBER 1993 COFFEE

Trade Entry Reasons

1. The two spikes looked like relative lows in an ongoing bull market.
2. The flag pattern formed near the top of a broad trading range suggested a potential upside breakout.

Do you agree or disagree with the analysis?
Evaluate the situation before turning page.

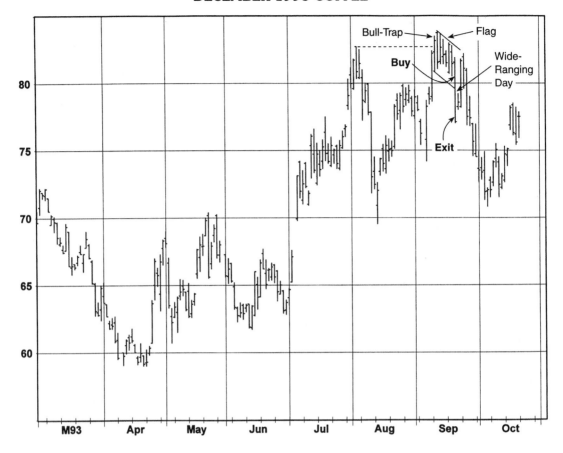

Figure 14.75*b*
DECEMBER 1993 COFFEE

Trade Exit

1. Significant downside penetration of flag pattern.
2. Wide-ranging down day.
3. Price break left the upper part of the flag looking like a possible bull-trap.

Comment

If the chart picture changes dramatically enough, a position should even be liquidated on the same day it was initiated—as was the case in this particular trade. Incidentally, there is no contradiction between this comment and the comment for the preceding trade. In this instance, the chart picture changed sufficiently to shift the chart implications from net bullish to net bearish. (In the previous trade, the original bearish chart reading was only mitigated—not reversed—by the short-term price action.) Also, the stop point in this trade was not inordinately close, even though the trade was liquidated on same day as entry.

Figure 14.76a
JULY 1994 COFFEE

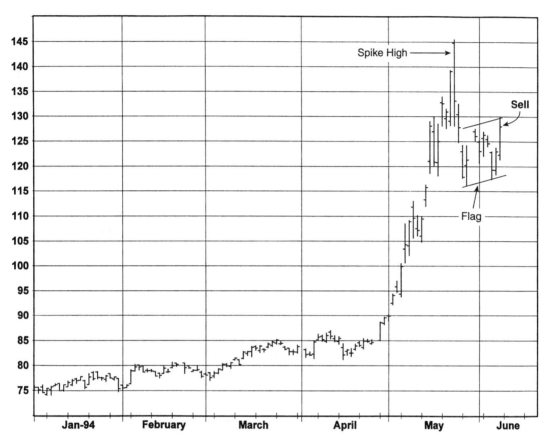

Trade Entry Reasons

1. Extreme spike high after an extended advance suggested a possible major top.
2. Flag pattern formed after downswing implied that the next price swing would also be on downside.

Do you agree or disagree with the analysis?
Evaluate the situation before turning page.

Figure 14.76b
JULY 1994 COFFEE

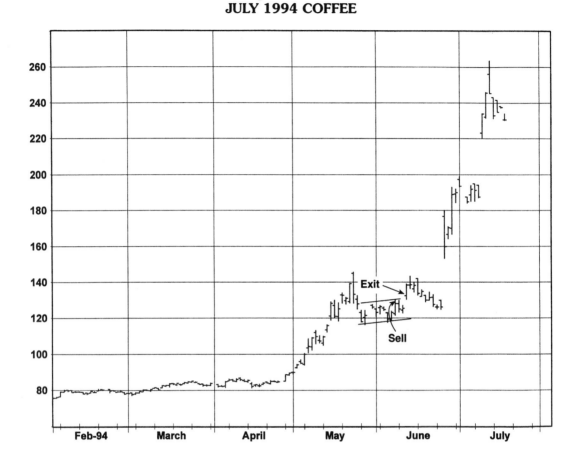

Trade Exit

The counter-to-anticipated upside breakout of the flag pattern contradicted one of the basic premises for the trade.

Comment

Sometimes what appears to be a major top proves to be only a minor peak. This trade provides a good example as to why traders who do not routinely employ a trade exit plan are unlikely to stay in the game very long.

Figure 14.77*a*
DECEMBER 1993 COCOA

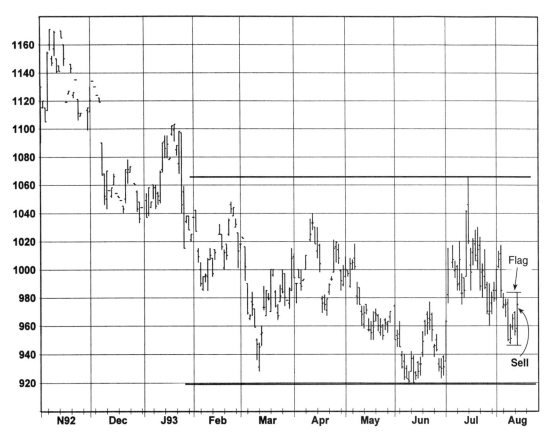

Trade Entry Reason

Flag pattern formed near the low end of an extended, broad trading range suggested a probable downside breakout.

Do you agree or disagree with the analysis?
Evaluate the situation before turning page.

Figure 14.77*b*
DECEMBER 1993 COCOA

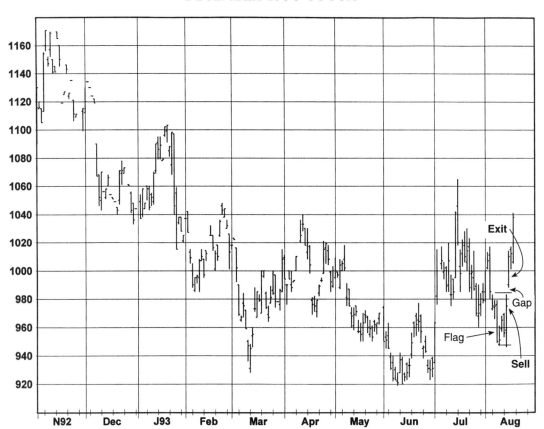

Trade Exit

Sharp upside breakout of the flag pattern—on a gap, no less—negated the trade premise.

Comment

If a trade doesn't work as expected, it is often a good idea to consider joining the other side. (See next trade.)

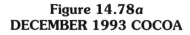
Figure 14.78a
DECEMBER 1993 COCOA

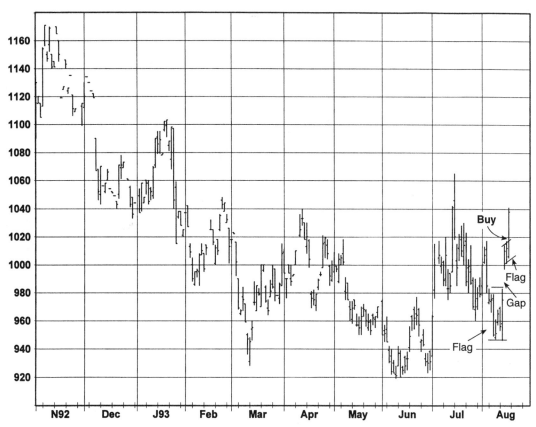

Trade Entry Reasons

1. Counter-to-anticipated upside breakout of flag pattern (same reason prior trade was liquidated).
2. Upside breakout of another flag pattern.

Do you agree or disagree with the analysis?
Evaluate the situation before turning page.

Figure 14.78b
DECEMBER 1993 COCOA

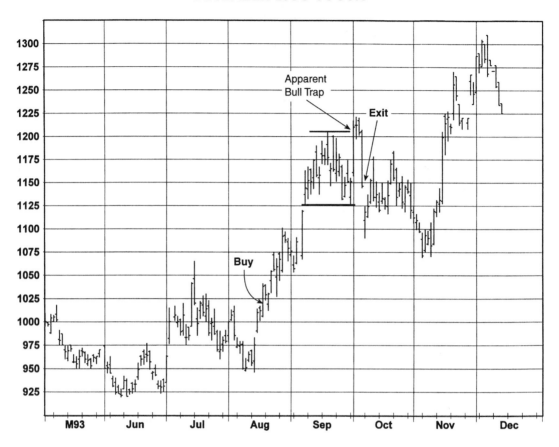

Trade Exit

Position liquidated in response to an apparent bull trap after an extended advance.

Comment

Even though the original trade idea was dead wrong (Figure 14.77b), the willingness to switch sides a few days after exiting the initial trade helped realize a significant gain in what would otherwise have been a net loss. Lack of loyalty is an important attribute for a trader.

Figure 14.79a
MAY 1994 COCOA

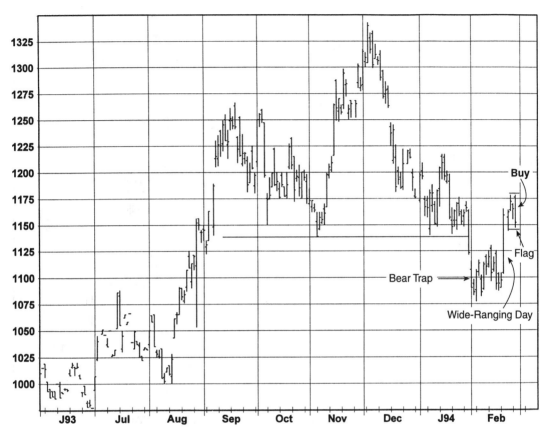

Trade Entry Reasons

1. Bear trap.
2. Wide-ranging up day.
3. Flag pattern formed after upswing.

Do you agree or disagree with the analysis?
Evaluate the situation before turning page.

Figure 14.79*b*
MAY 1994 COCOA

Trade Exit

Downside penetration of the flag pattern on a wide gap suggested at least a temporary price failure.

Comment

Note that although the original idea was wrong, in the sense that the market eventually retraced to the contract low, timing the entry and exit based on short-term chart patterns (e.g., flag consolidations) allowed for a net profit on the trade.

Figure 14.80a
JULY 1994 COCOA

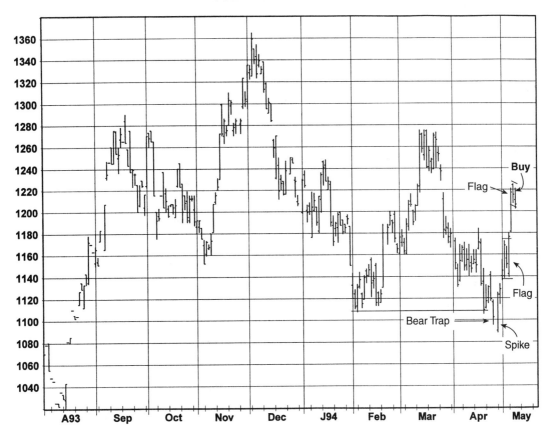

Trade Entry Reasons

1. Bear trap.
2. Spike low.
3. Flag pattern after upswing.

Do you agree or disagree with the analysis?
Evaluate the situation before turning page.

Figure 14.80*b*
JULY 1994 COCOA

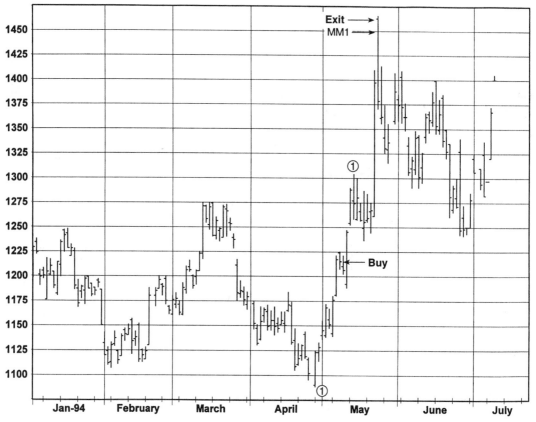

Trade Exit

Major measured move objective (MM1) achieved very shortly after trade entry.

Comment

Although the old saw about letting profits run is generally true, I would make an exception for situations in which the market reaches a *major* objective area *very quickly*. Reason: Even if the longer-term trend eventually continues—as it well may—such markets are particularly prone to corrective price moves sufficient to knock out most protective stops. (Some readers may wonder why I held out for a profit target modestly *above* the measured move objective. I didn't. The market gapped above my profit target on the opening.)

Figure 14.81a
GILT CONTINUOUS FUTURES (DAILY)

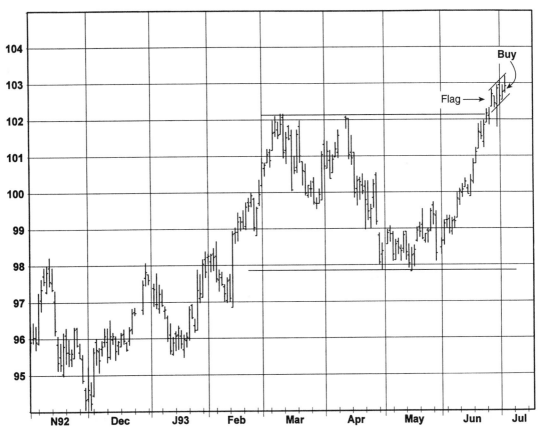

Trade Entry Reason

Flag consolidation formed above a broad trading range suggested a potential upswing.

Do you agree or disagree with the analysis?
Evaluate the situation before turning page.

Figure 14.81*b*
GILT CONTINUOUS FUTURES (DAILY)

Trade Exit

Profits were taken because of the rapid approach of an important measured move objective (MM1), with virtually no intervening corrections.

Comment

In terms of potential to risk, I consider flag patterns formed just beyond broad trading ranges to be one of the more worthwhile chart patterns for trading purposes.

The reader may note that all the trade illustrations for the gilt market use continuous futures price series. The reason for this is that gilt futures are a perfect example of a highly liquid market where virtually all the trading is concentrated in the nearest contract until near expiration. Consequently, it is usually impossible to generate individual contract charts of sufficient duration to perform an adequate chart analysis.

Figure 14.82a
GILT CONTINUOUS FUTURES (DAILY)

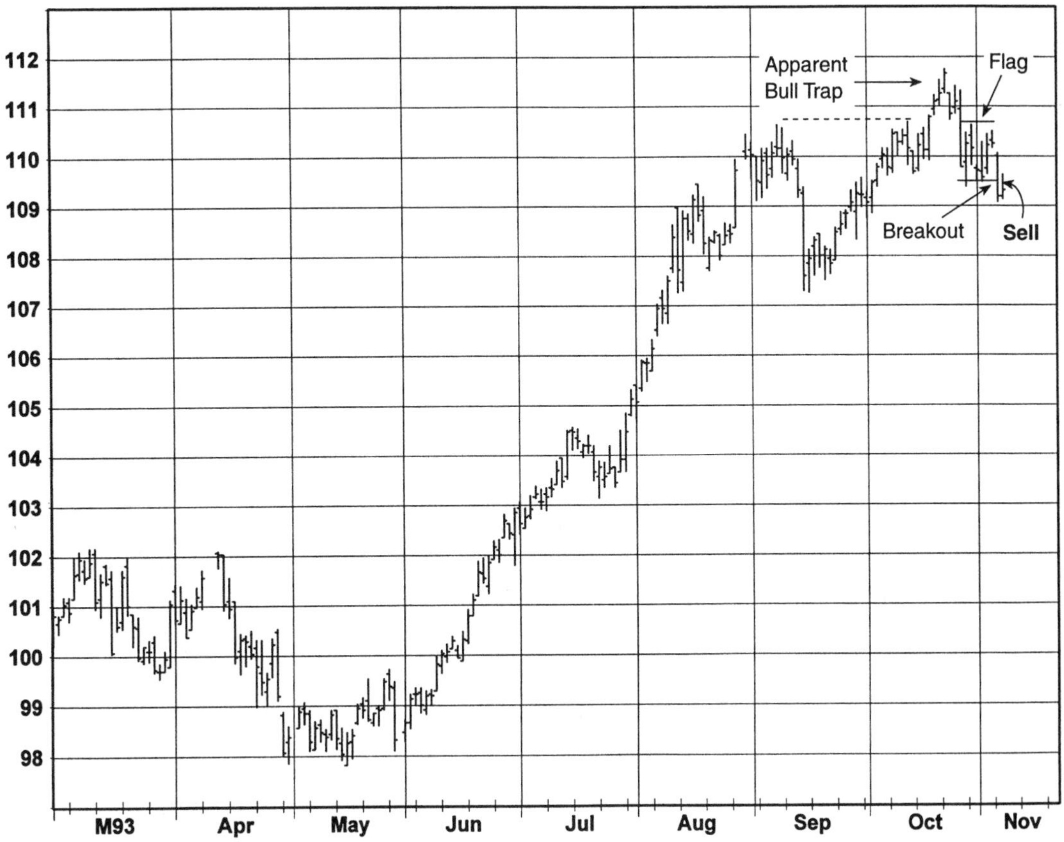

Trade Entry Reasons

1. Apparent bull trap.
2. Downside breakout of flag pattern.

Do you agree or disagree with the analysis?
Evaluate the situation before turning page.

Figure 14.82b
GILT CONTINUOUS FUTURES (DAILY)

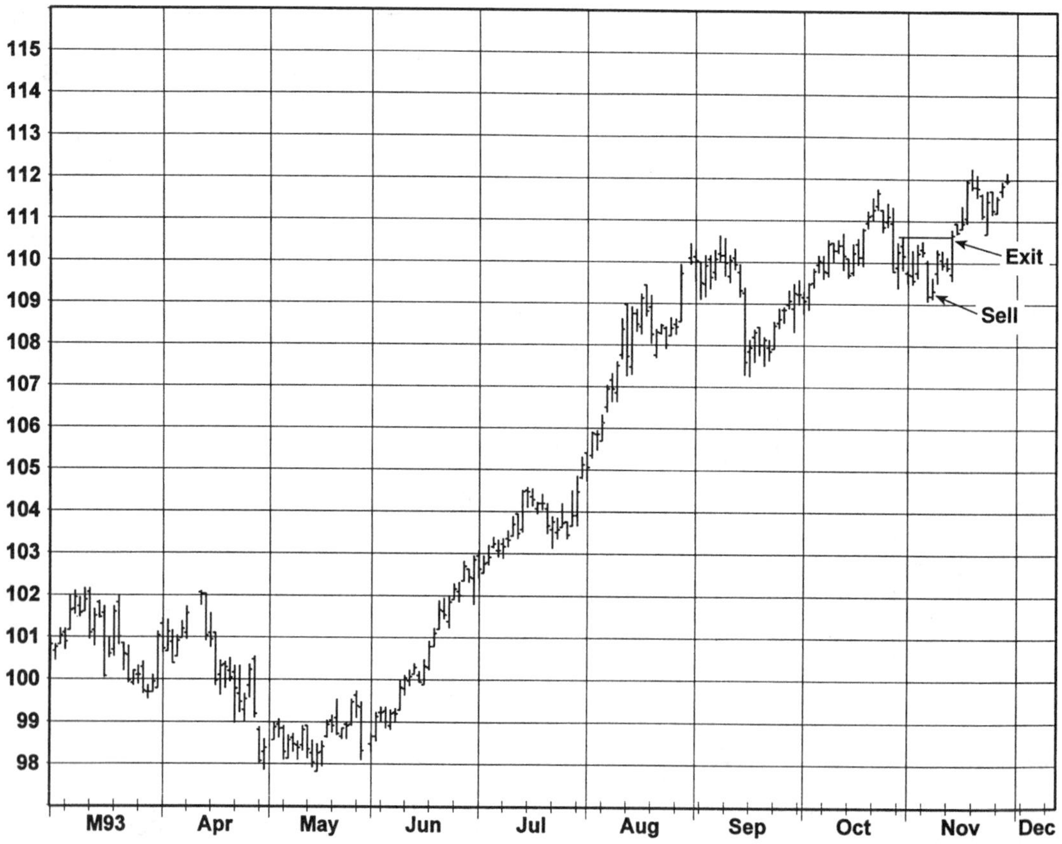

Trade Exit

Rebound back to the top of the flag pattern placed the original trade premise into question.

Comment

Ideally, one should wait four to five weeks before assuming a bull trap (or bear trap) is a valid signal. Of course, if it is a valid signal, waiting this long could result in a significantly worse trade entry price. In this trade, I knowingly jumped the gun in an effort to get a better entry price, using a very close stop to limit the risk, since adequate confirmation of the trade was lacking. As a result, the loss was small, even though the trade idea was wrong. Incidentally, waiting the minimum four weeks for confirmation of the bull-trap would have avoided the loss altogether.

Figure 14.83a
GILT CONTINUOUS FUTURES (DAILY)

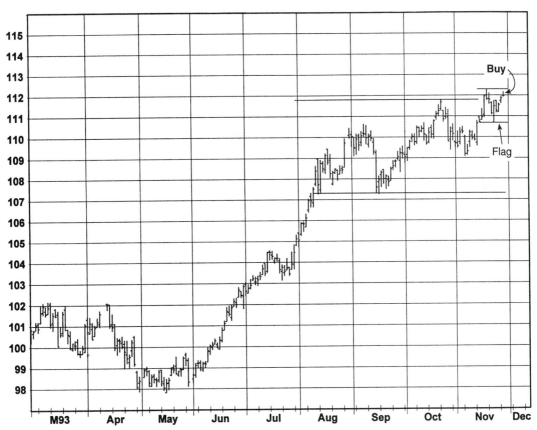

Trade Entry Reasons

Flag formed near the top of a broad trading range suggested the potential for another upswing.

Do you agree or disagree with the analysis?
Evaluate the situation before turning page.

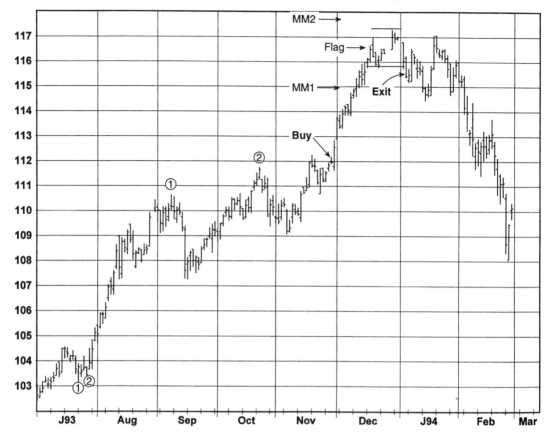

Figure 14.83*b*
GILT CONTINUOUS FUTURES (DAILY)

Trade Exit

With the market surpassing the closer measured move objective (MM1) and almost reaching the more major measured move objective (MM2), the protective stop was brought in to the closest meaningful technical point, which in this case was the downside penetration of the most recent flag pattern.

Comment

Note that this trade was entered shortly after being stopped out of trade in opposite direction (see Figure 14.82*b*). The ability to reverse one's opinion if market action proves the original premise wrong is a critical trait for trading success. Although completely wrong originally, the end result (after taking the opposite direction trade) was a significant profit, since the loss was taken quickly, while a winning trade was kept open until the first sign of market weakness.

This trade also illustrates that exiting positions on countertrend penetrations of flag patterns can be used as an effective means of limiting the surrender of open profits.

Figure 14.84*a*
GILT CONTINUOUS FUTURES (DAILY)

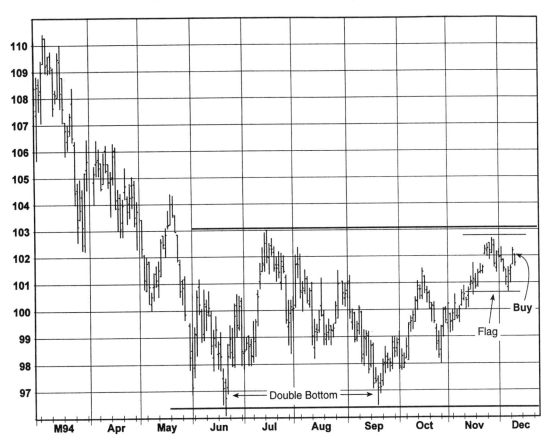

Trade Entry Reasons:

1. Double bottom.
2. Flag formed near the top of a broad trading range.

Do you agree or disagree with the analysis?
Evaluate the situation before turning page.

Figure 14.84b
GILT CONTINUOUS FUTURES (DAILY)

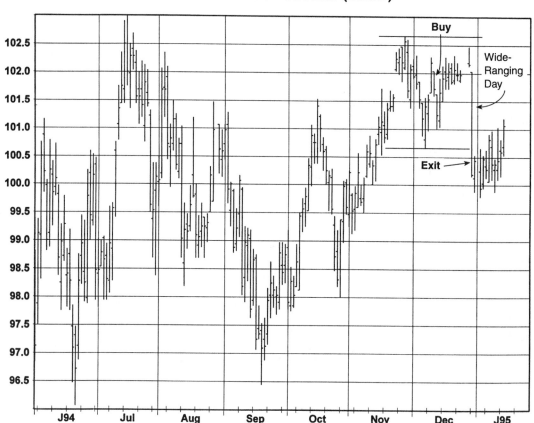

Trade Exit

Downside penetration of the flag pattern on a wide-ranging day suggested the trade was wrong.

Comment

It is instructive to compare this trade (Figure 14.84a) to the previous trade (Figure 14.83a). Both chart patterns and trade premises were quite similar. Yet the previous trade was a significant winner, while this trade was a loser. The point is that it is impossible to reliably differentiate between winning and losing chart-based trading ideas at the onset. Trading success depends not so much on correctly differentiating winners from losers in the trade selection process, as from keeping the loss on losing trades significantly smaller than the gains on winning trades.

Figure 14.85a
GILT CONTINUOUS FUTURES (DAILY)

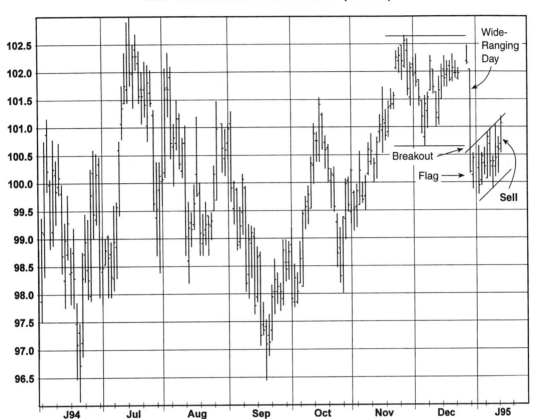

Trade Entry Reasons

1. Downside breakout of sideways consolidation.
2. Wide-ranging down day formed near relative high.
3. Flag consolidation formed after downswing.

Do you agree or disagree with the analysis?
Evaluate the situation before turning page.

Figure 14.85b
GILT CONTINUOUS FUTURES (DAILY)

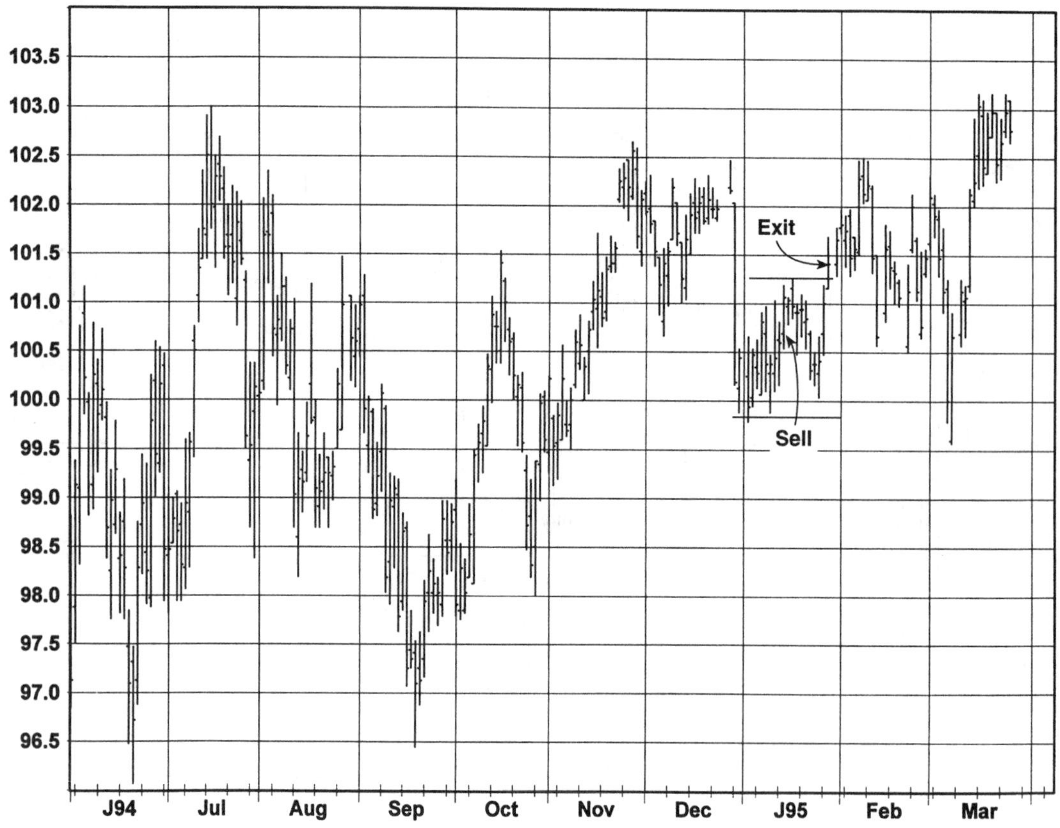

Trade Exit

Upside penetration of the flag pattern negated the trade idea.

Comment

Note that this trade was placed only about two weeks after the liquidation of the prior trade, which had been implemented in the opposite direction. In this case, the willingness to reverse the original trade only led to another loss. Nothing is infallible.

Figure 14.86*a*
GILT CONTINUOUS FUTURES (DAILY)

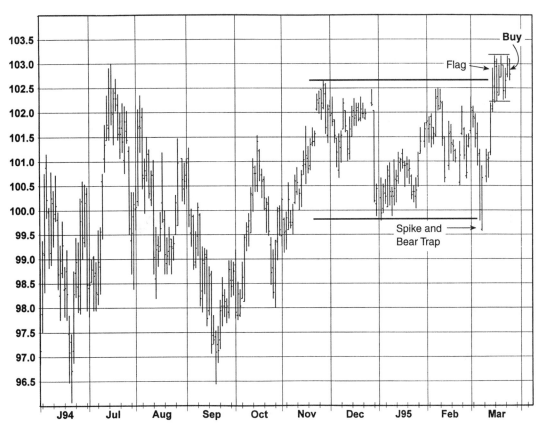

Trade Entry Reasons

1. Bear trap.
2. Spike low reversal.
3. Flag formed near the top of a broad trading range.

Do you agree or disagree with the analysis?
Evaluate the situation before turning page.

Figure 14.86*b*
GILT CONTINUOUS FUTURES (DAILY)

Trade Exit

Trade was liquidated in response to an apparent bull-trap top, which was confirmed by a significant downside penetration of the prior flag pattern.

Comment

Note that this trade essentially replaced the long position of the second previous trade (Figure 14.84*a*) at a higher price. In other words, after two whipsaw losses, the original position was replaced at a worse price. This time, however, the trade was successful, with the resulting gain more than offsetting the prior two losses. Lesson: As long as a methodology has proved itself profitable over the long run, you need the persistence to keep applying it, even if it yields several consecutive losses.

Figure 14.87a
ITALIAN BOND CONTINUOUS FUTURES (DAILY)

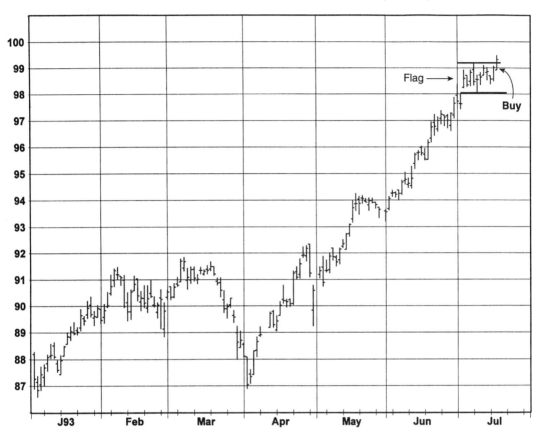

Trade Entry Reason

Flag consolidation after an uptrend suggested continuation of the uptrend.

Do you agree or disagree with the analysis?
Evaluate the situation before turning page.

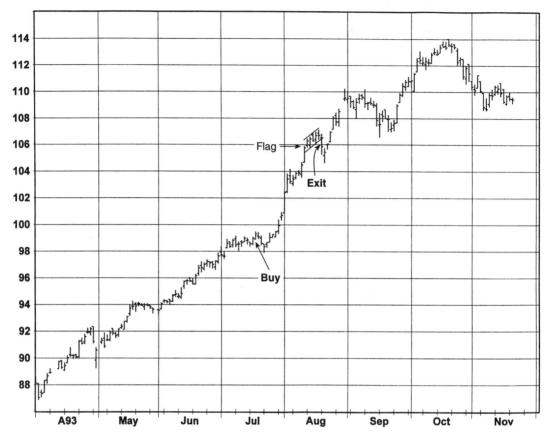

Figure 14.87*b*
ITALIAN BOND CONTINUOUS FUTURES (DAILY)

Trade Exit

Downside penetration of the flag pattern after a large advance suggested danger of at least a temporary reversal. (Continuous futures are used to depict all the Italian bond trades, because similar to the gilt, virtually all the trading in this market is concentrated in the nearest contract until near expiration, making it impossible to generate individual contract charts of sufficient duration to perform an adequate chart analysis.)

Comment

This trade provides a good illustration of two concepts:

1. Just because the market has already witnessed a large advance does not necessarily mean it's too late to buy.

2. By waiting for an appropriate chart pattern, it is possible to select a relatively close, technically *meaningful* stop, even if the market has experienced a large advance. (In this trade, the initial stop was placed moderately below the narrow consolidation formed just prior to entry.)

484

Figure 14.88a
ITALIAN BOND CONTINUOUS FUTURES (DAILY)

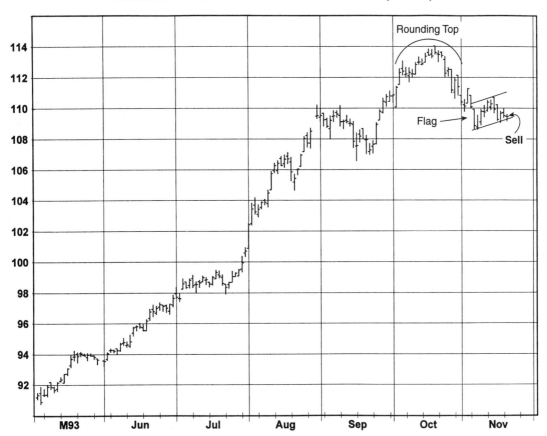

Trade Entry Reasons

   1. Rounding top pattern.
   2. Flag formed after downswing.

Do you agree or disagree with the analysis?
Evaluate the situation before turning page.

Figure 14.88*b*
ITALIAN BOND CONTINUOUS FUTURES (DAILY)

Trade Exit

Spike low and wide-ranging up day (both on the same day) suggested a possible upside reversal and prompted lowering of the stop to the break-even vicinity.

Comment

Although over the longer run the trade idea proved wrong, since the market moved sharply higher after the initial break, being attuned to the evolving chart pattern resulted in a breakeven instead of a losing trade. Also, this trade is a good example of a wide-ranging day providing an indicator of a trend reversal.

Figure 14.89a
ITALIAN BOND CONTINUOUS FUTURES (DAILY)

Trade Entry Reason

Pennant consolidation formed after a sharp upswing suggested the likelihood
of another upswing.

Do you agree or disagree with the analysis?
Evaluate the situation before turning page.

Figure 14.89*b*
ITALIAN BOND CONTINUOUS FUTURES (DAILY)

Trade Exit

The market spent too much time going sideways after the breakout above the pennant consolidation, causing the chart to lose its bullish appearance. Hence, the stop was raised to the point of entry.

Comment

Shortly after this trade was liquidated, the chart picture had deteriorated sufficiently to warrant an opposite direction position—see next trade.

Figure 14.90a
ITALIAN BOND CONTINUOUS FUTURES (DAILY)

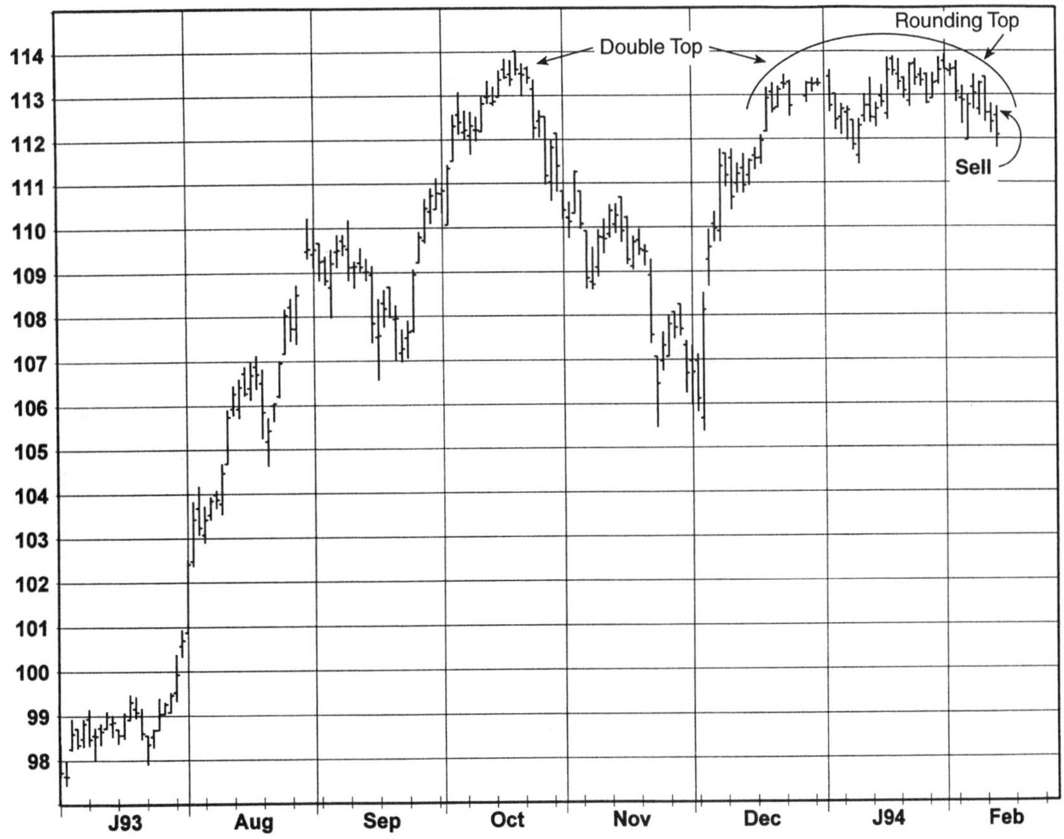

Trade Entry Reasons

1. Double top.
2. Rounding top (second half of double top).

Do you agree or disagree with the analysis?
Evaluate the situation before turning page.

Figure 14.90b
ITALIAN BOND CONTINUOUS FUTURES (DAILY)

Trade Exit

Trade liquidated because the profit target was reached. This profit target was selected because it was a point just above the support level implied by both the late-November–early-December low and a measured move objective (MM1).

Comment

Initially, less than two months earlier, I traded this market from the long side. This short position was implemented exactly one week after the long position was liquidated (see Figure 14.89b). It is important not only to cover a position when it is wrong, but ideally to trade in the other direction as well. As a result of reversing the original strategy, I ended up with a large net profit, even though the original trade (long position) was as wrong as could be.

This trade also demonstrates how a measured move objective and a prior relative low (or relative high) can be used to determine a profit target. Although the market traded sharply lower the day after exit, it moved higher thereafter. A trailing protective stop would undoubtedly have resulted in a worse exit.

As a general principal, it is often wise to take profits when a trade meets all of the following three criteria:

1. Large open profit;
2. Profit realized very quickly;
3. Major objective achieved or nearly achieved.

Reason: under such circumstances, even if a market eventually goes further in the trade direction, it will usually first correct enough to trigger most trailing stops.

Figure 14.91a
ITALIAN BOND CONTINUOUS FUTURES (DAILY)

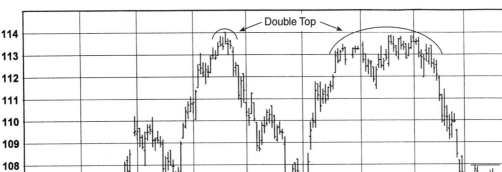

Trade Entry Reasons

1. Double top.
2. Downside breakout from consolidation pattern.

Do you agree or disagree with the analysis?
Evaluate the situation before turning page.

Figure 14.91b
ITALIAN BOND CONTINUOUS FUTURES (DAILY)

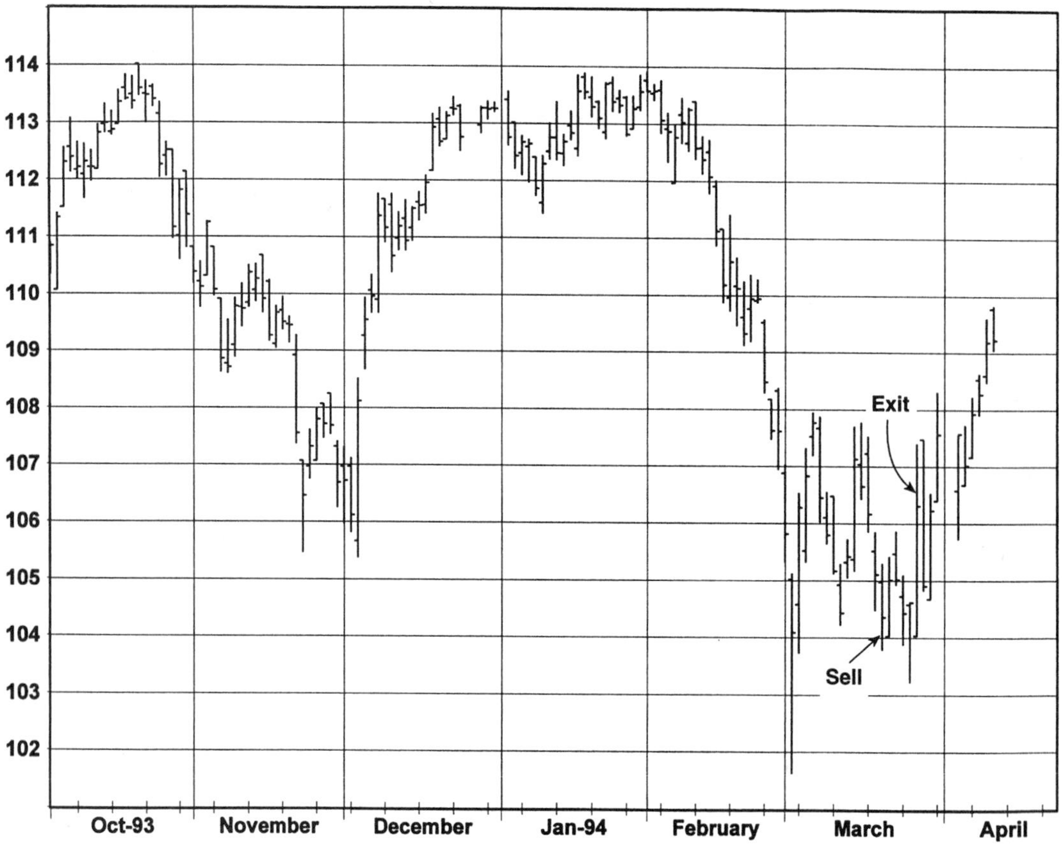

Trade Exit

Protective stop activated, as the market rebounded sharply back into consolidation.

Comment

Liquidating a losing trade does not necessarily mean giving up on the trade permanently. It may well be possible to get back into the trade at a more favorable price—as was the case in this instance (see next trade). It is a mistake to view a trade as a one-shot deal. A trade can be retried as long as it still makes sense.

Figure 14.92a
ITALIAN BOND CONTINUOUS FUTURES (DAILY)

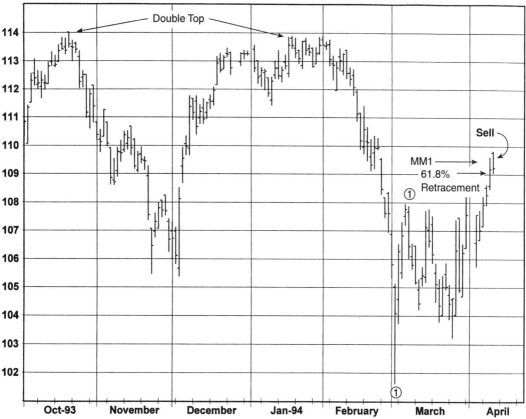

Trade Entry Reasons

1. Double top
2. Resistance anticipated based on the convergence of a measured move objective (MM1) and 61.8% retracement in the same price vicinity.

Do you agree or disagree with the analysis?
Evaluate the situation before turning page.

Figure 14.92b
ITALIAN BOND CONTINUOUS FUTURES (DAILY)

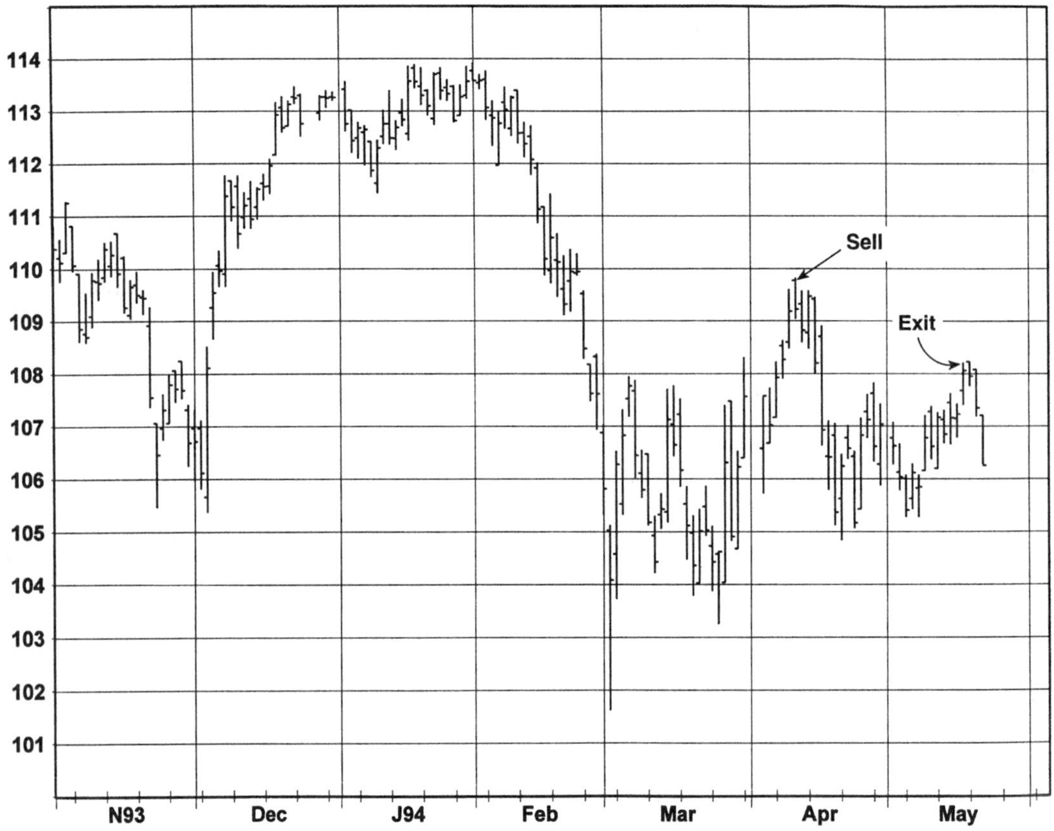

Trade Exit

Position was liquidated on lowered protective stop.

Comment

If there is a good reason to believe a major trend is still likely to be down, selling on an intermediate rally into anticipated resistance can provide a very good entry. In other words, going against the trend may be a good strategy, *as long as the long-term trend is in the opposite direction.*

   With the benefit of hindsight, I lowered the protective stop too close, too soon. See next trade, however.

Figure 14.93a
ITALIAN BOND CONTINUOUS FUTURES (DAILY)

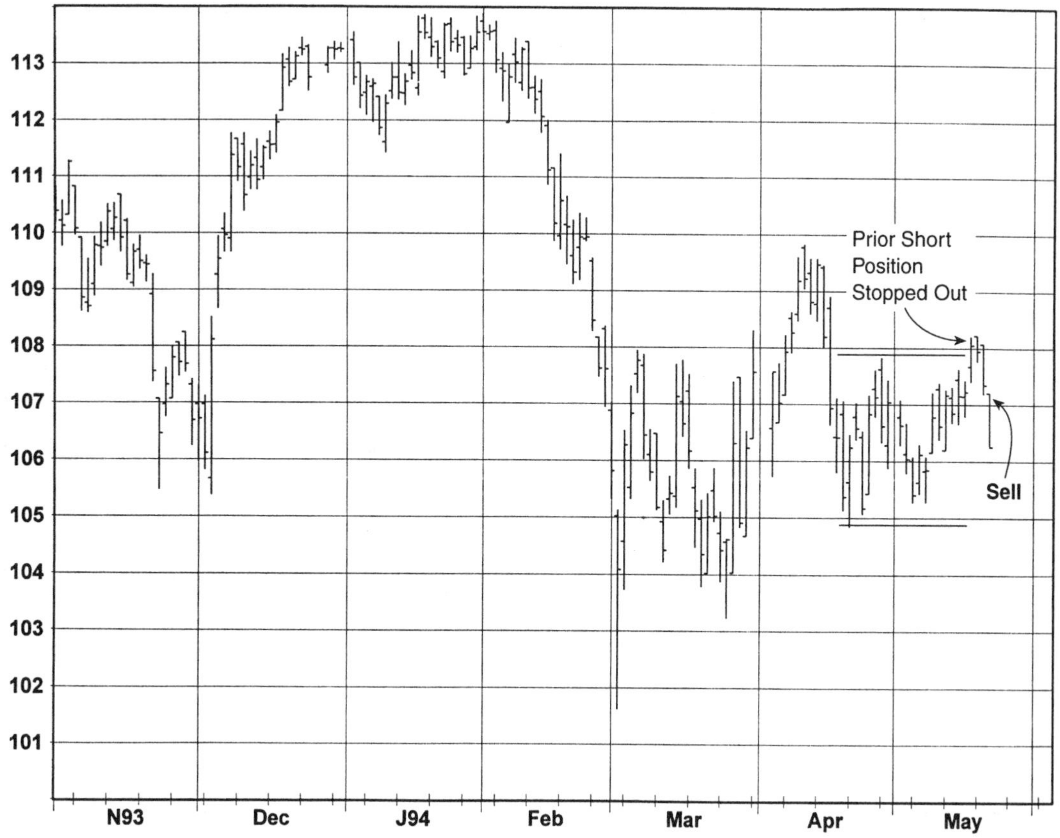

Trade Entry Reasons

This trade reentered the previous trade, because all the same reasons for the original trade still applied. The upside breakout, which triggered the lowered protective stop on the previous trade, saw no follow-through and looked like a false move. Hence reinstated position.

Do you agree or disagree with the analysis?
Evaluate the situation before turning page.

Figure 14.93*b*
ITALIAN BOND CONTINUOUS FUTURES (DAILY)

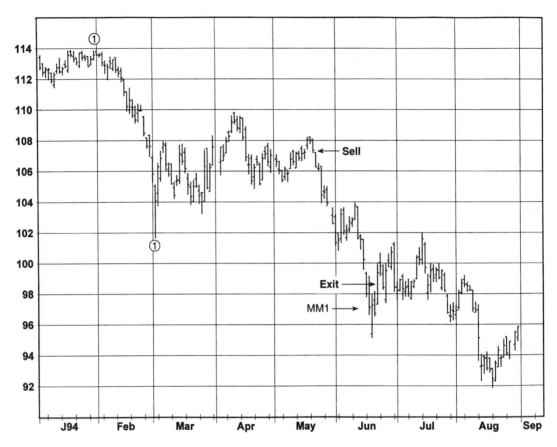

Trade Exit

The achievement of a measured move objective (MM1) was the motivation for sharply lowering the protective stop.

Comment

If you are stopped out near the extreme of a market bounce on an apparent false breakout and you still feel strongly about the trade, grit your teeth and reenter. This trade provides another illustration of the concept that a trade is an ongoing process that should not be considered over because the position is stopped out. The willingness to retry this trade after being stopped out helped salvage a large profit from what could have been a major missed trading opportunity.

Figure 14.94a
ITALIAN BOND CONTINUOUS FUTURES (DAILY)

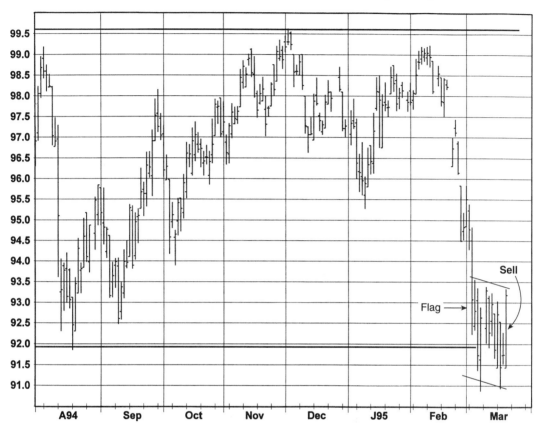

Trade Entry Reason

Flag consolidation formed near the low end of a broad trading range suggested the potential for another downswing.

Do you agree or disagree with the analysis?
Evaluate the situation before turning page.

Figure 14.94b
ITALIAN BOND CONTINUOUS FUTURES (DAILY)

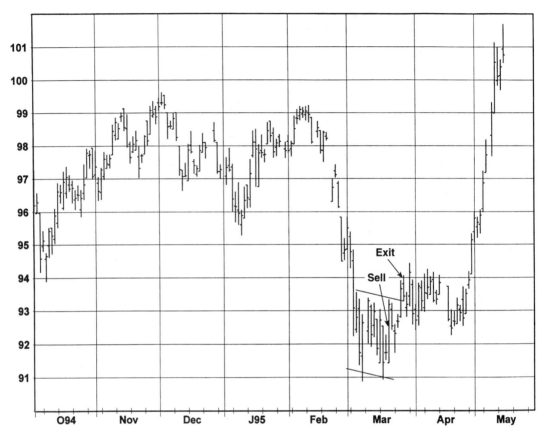

Trade Exit

Upside penetration of the flag pattern violated the trade premise.

Comment

Yet another example where getting out on the first meaningful evidence that
the trade premise was incorrect prevented a disastrous outcome.

Figure 14.95a
ITALIAN BOND CONTINUOUS FUTURES (DAILY)

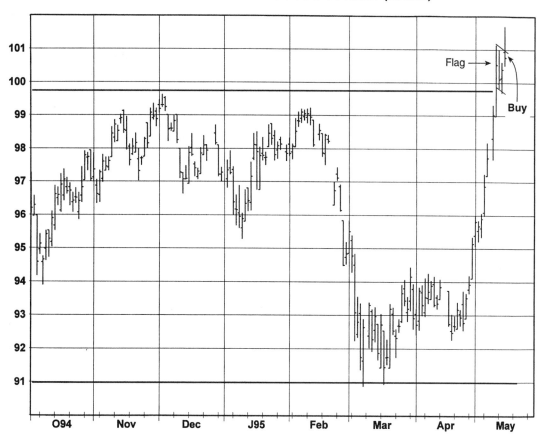

Trade Entry Reason

Narrow flag pattern formed above a broad trading range implied the advance was likely to continue.

Do you agree or disagree with the analysis?
Evaluate the situation before turning page.

Figure 14.95*b*
ITALIAN BOND CONTINUOUS FUTURES (DAILY)

Trade Exit

Return to the low end of the flag after an upside breakout from the pattern represented a short-term price failure.

Comment

One attractive feature of using flag and pennant consolidations as trading guidelines is that even when these patterns provide misleading market implications, the risk in trades based on these patterns can usually be kept relatively small.

Figure 14.96a
MATIF NOTIONAL BOND CONTINUOUS FUTURES (DAILY)

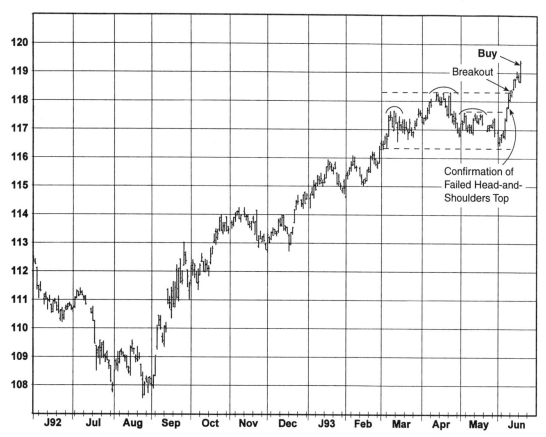

Trade Entry Reasons

1. Confirmation of failed head-and-shoulders top.
2. A sustained breakout above a prior trading range.

Do you agree or disagree with the analysis?
Evaluate the situation before turning page.

Figure 14.96b
MATIF NOTIONAL BOND CONTINUOUS FUTURES (DAILY)

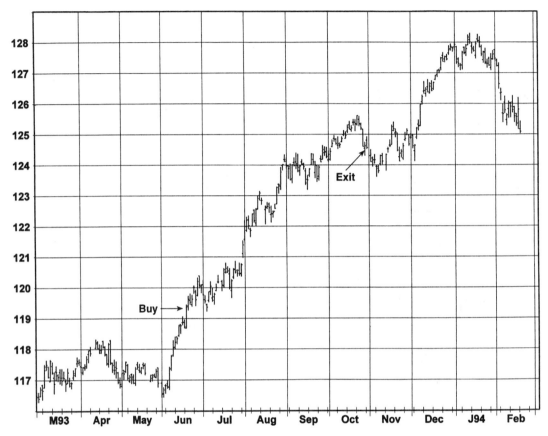

Trade Exit

Position liquidated on trailing stop, which was kept close after a large advance.

Comment

The failure of a classic chart pattern to evolve as anticipated, such as the failed head-and-shoulders pattern in this example, is often an excellent trading signal.

Figure 14.97a
MATIF NOTIONAL BOND CONTINUOUS FUTURES (DAILY)

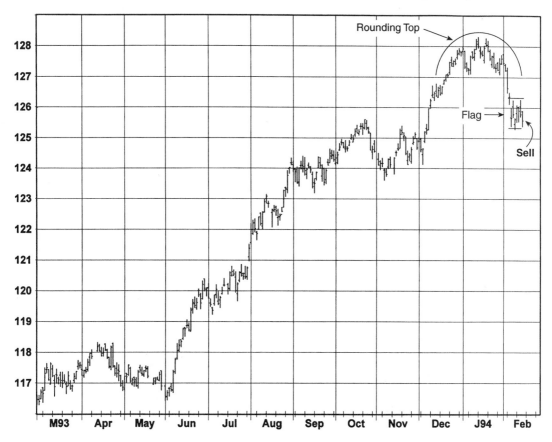

Trade Entry Reasons

1. Rounding-top pattern indicative of a possible major high.
2. Flag consolidation following the downswing suggested that the next price swing would also be on the downside.

Do you agree or disagree with the analysis?
Evaluate the situation before turning page.

Figure 14.97b
MATIF NOTIONAL BOND CONTINUOUS FUTURES (DAILY)

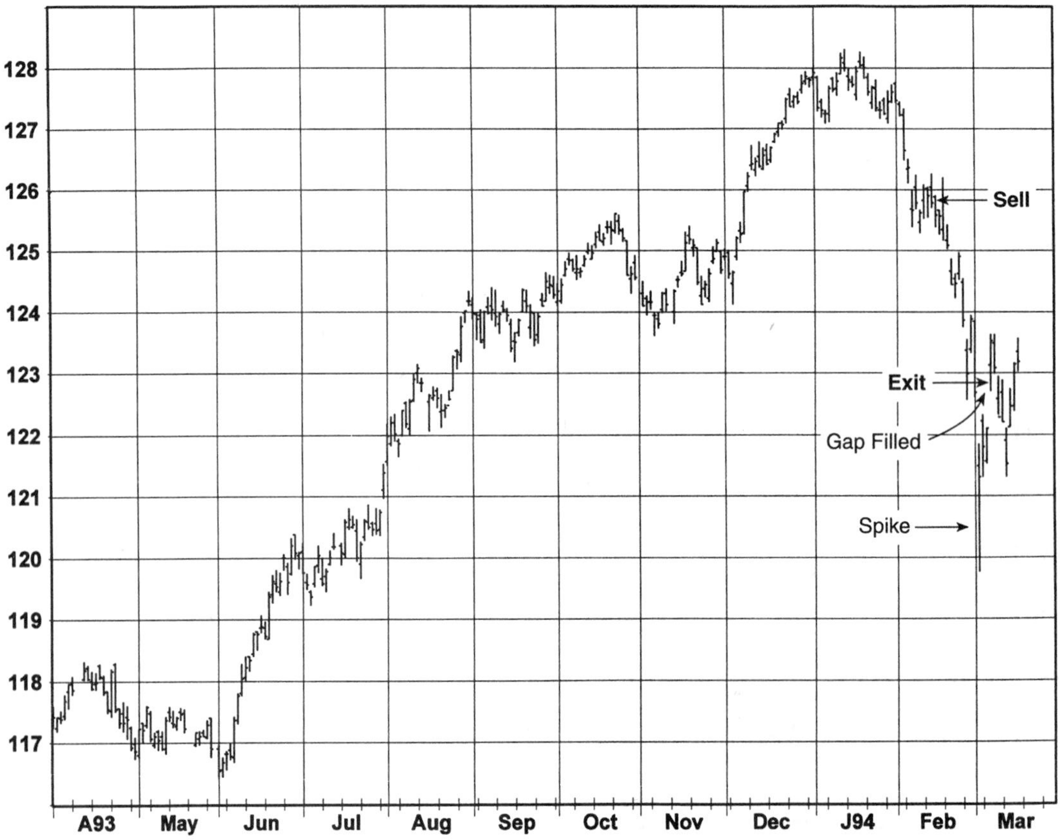

Trade Exit

The sharp spike low and the filling of a prior downside gap strongly suggested the possibility of a trend reversal.

Comment

Although the broad chart picture still suggested that a major top had been formed, the short-term action at the time of the trade exit indicated a potential temporary reversal. The idea was to lock in profits and look to reenter a short position on a further rebound.

Figure 14.98a
MATIF NOTIONAL BOND CONTINUOUS FUTURES (DAILY)

Trade Entry Reasons

1. This short position represented a reentry of the prior trade, which had been covered a little over one week earlier (see Figure 14.97b). The basic premise for the trade was still the broad rounding-top pattern—a formation that suggested that a major high had been established.

2. Viewing the chart without the spike revealed that prices had formed a flag consolidation—a formation that suggested the potential for another downswing. The sell point was selected to be near the top of this pattern.

Do you agree or disagree with the analysis?
Evaluate the situation before turning page.

Figure 14.98*b*
MATIF NOTIONAL BOND CONTINUOUS FUTURES (DAILY)

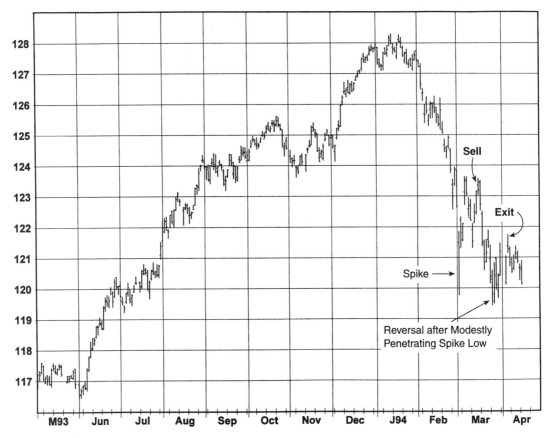

Trade Exit

Position liquidated on lowered stop in response to the reversal after the penetration of spike low.

Comment

Frequently, when sharp spikes exist, as was the case at the entry of this trade, it is also valuable to interpret the chart as if the spike did not exist. The rationale for such as interpretation is that spikes often represent aberrations due to emotional excess in the market and that as such distort the broader chart pattern.

Although with hindsight, the protective stop on this trade was obviously lowered too close, at the time, the fact that prices rebounded just after penetrating the spike low raised the possibility of an extension to the upper part of the prior month's trading range. The original game plan was to reenter the position on an upside extension. The trade was reentered, however, when the market bounce failed to extend (see next trade).

Figure 14.99*a*
MATIF NOTIONAL BOND CONTINUOUS FUTURES (DAILY)

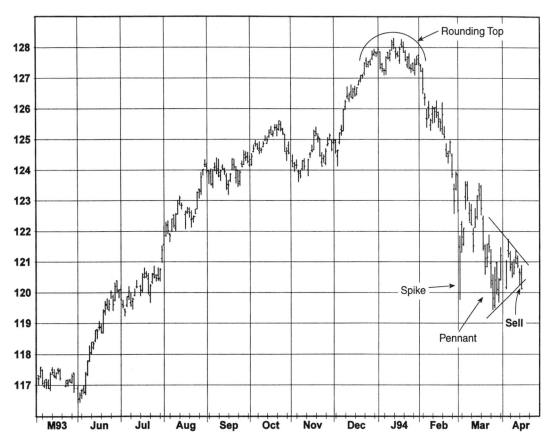

Trade Entry Reasons

1. The formation of a pennant near the low end of a trading range suggested the likelihood of a downside breakout.
2. The return to a prior spike low represented a bearish signal.
3. The long-term chart picture remained dominated by a very bearish
rounding-top pattern.

Do you agree or disagree with the analysis?
Evaluate the situation before turning page.

Figure 14.99*b*
MATIF NOTIONAL BOND CONTINUOUS FUTURES (DAILY)

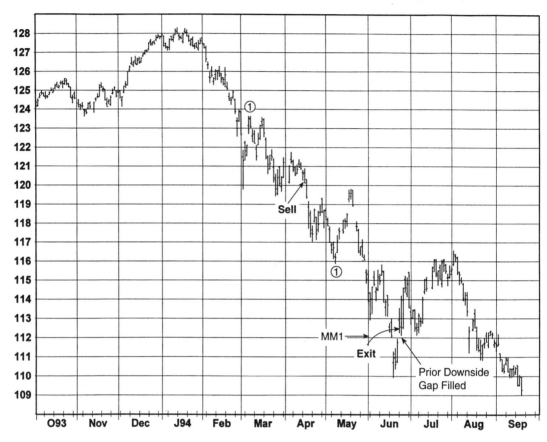

Trade Exit

The protective stop was lowered sharply following the achievement of a very major measured move objective (MM1). The short position was subsequently liquidated just above the point at which a prior downside gap was filled, a price development that provided the first sign of a possible trend reversal.

Comment

Although the downtrend ultimately resumed, lowering the stop after the market had achieved the measured move objective (MM1) helped obtain a much better exit on the trade, since the subsequent rally would have eventually stopped out the position at a much worse price. Also, the short position was reentered at a nearly equivalent price about two months later after the rally had fizzled (see next trade).

Figure 14.100a
MATIF NOTIONAL BOND CONTINUOUS FUTURES (DAILY)

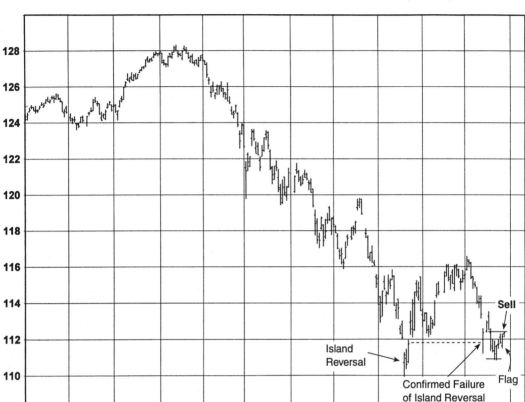

Trade Entry Reasons

1. The flag pattern formed at the low end of a broad trading range indicated the potential for a downside breakout.
2. The price decline filled the gap of a previous island reversal, providing confirmation of a failed pattern.
3. The short position was reinstated in line with the prevailing major trend.

Do you agree or disagree with the analysis?
Evaluate the situation before turning page.

Figure 14.100b
MATIF NOTIONAL BOND CONTINUOUS FUTURES (DAILY)

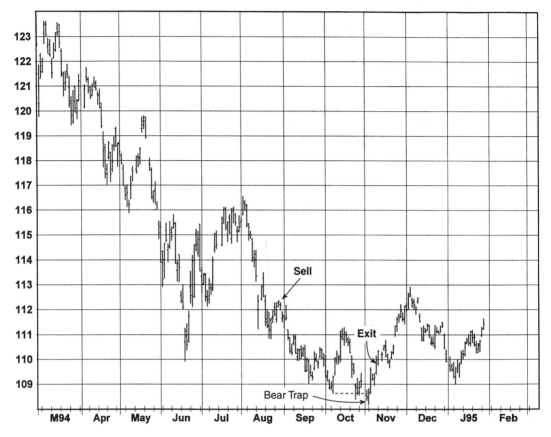

Trade Exit

Evidence of a possible bear trap—the early-November modest penetration of the prior trading range and the subsequent immediate rebound back into that range—was sufficient reason to sharply lower the protective stop. This stop was quickly activated.

Comment

Although confirmation of a bear-trap reversal requires at least three or four weeks of prices remaining above the reversal low or a rebound back to the upper portion of the preceding trading range, much less restrictive conditions can be used for the purpose of lowering protective stops on short positions. Since the market had been in a very protracted decline, even the initial signs of a bear-trap reversal were sufficient cause to bring in protective stops. Recognizing the signs of a possible bear-trap reversal allowed this position to be liquidated fairly close to the market low.

Figure 14.101*a*
SEPTEMBER 1993 PIBOR

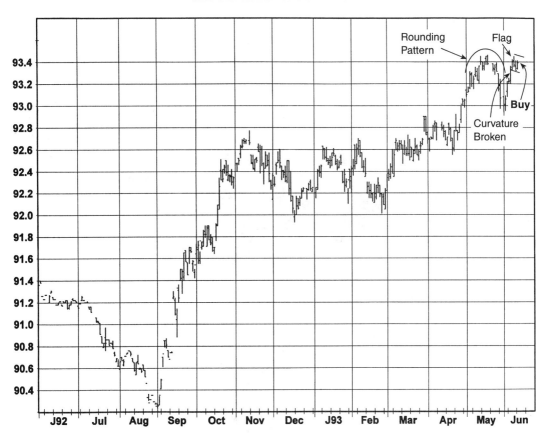

Trade Entry Reasons

1. The breaking of the downward curved pattern indicated a potential upside reversal.

2. The flag pattern formed near the upper part of the broader trading range implied that the next price swing would be on the upside.

Do you agree or disagree with the analysis?
Evaluate the situation before turning page.

Figure 14.101*b*
SEPTEMBER 1993 PIBOR

Trade Exit

The counter-to-anticipated downside breakout of the flag consolidation suggested a price failure.

Comment

Although the original trade idea proved to be a poor one, insofar as the buy point was not far from a major relative high, the flag pattern still proved reliable in terms of indicating the direction of the next minor price swing, thereby permitting the stop to be raised to near breakeven. Also, the formation of the subsequent flag pattern allowed for the selection of a relatively close meaningful stop. Note how the counter-to-anticipated price action provided the signal for a very early exit on a trade that could have resulted in a substantial loss.

Figure 14.102a
SEPTEMBER 1993 PIBOR

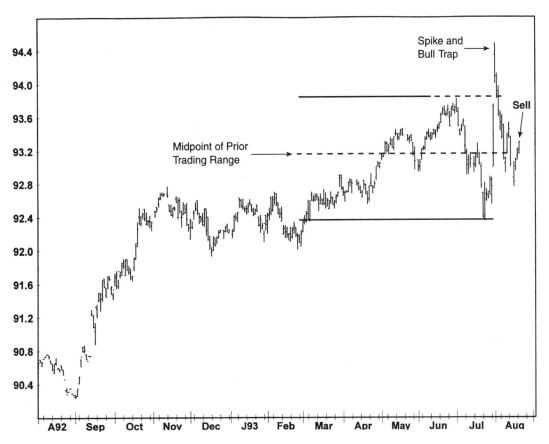

Trade Entry Reasons

1. The spike high indicated a possible reversal.
2. The subsequent price retracement back into a prior trading range suggested a bull-trap reversal, which received preliminary confirmation on the downside penetration of the midpoint of the range.

Do you agree or disagree with the analysis?
Evaluate the situation before turning page.

Figure 14.102*b*
DECEMBER 1993 PIBOR

Trade Exit

The wide-ranging day counter to the position held suggested a possible trend reversal and prompted lowering the stop to protect profits.

Comment

Once again, a bull trap, which was a primary reason for initiating the short position, provided a valuable trading signal. This trap was more evident in the September contract (see Figure 14.102*a*), which represented the initial position. The short position was subsequently rolled over to the December contract.

With the benefit of hindsight, the exit proved highly premature, as will subsequently be seen. However, the reasoning for lowering the protective stop still seems sound even in retrospect; it just didn't work well in this case.

Figure 14.103a
DECEMBER 1993 PIBOR

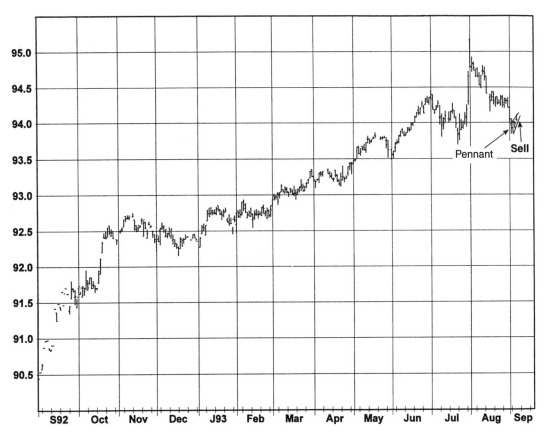

Trade Entry Reasons

The formation of a pennant consolidation provided an opportunity to add to an existing short position, using a relatively close stop. (See previous trade entry for a description of the motivation for original trade.) The basic idea was to implement the position within the pennant consolidation, anticipating a downside breakout, since the prior market swing had been down. The pennant permitted doubling the position with only a moderate increase in risk, since a meaningful stop could be placed just above the pattern.

Do you agree or disagree with the analysis?
Evaluate the situation before turning page.

Figure 14.103*b*
DECEMBER 1993 PIBOR

Trade Exit

Trade was liquidated on a lowered protective stop, when the upside penetration of a newly formed flag pattern raised the possibility of a trend reversal.

Comment

As was illustrated in this trade example, pennant and flag formations often provide a good vehicle for adding to an existing position, making it possible to use a reasonably close, technically meaningful stop on the added portion of the trade.

Figure 14.104a
MARCH 1994 PIBOR

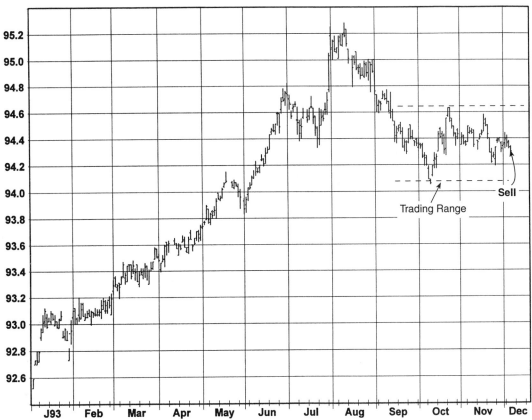

Trade Entry Reason

Trading range formed after a decline from a major peak suggested the possibility of another significant price break. Such a formation would only be considered a possible base pattern if there had been several downswings off the high (instead of only one) and if the downtrend phase had lasted much longer (at least six to nine months).

Do you agree or disagree with the analysis?
Evaluate the situation before turning page.

Figure 14.104*b*
JUNE 1994 PIBOR

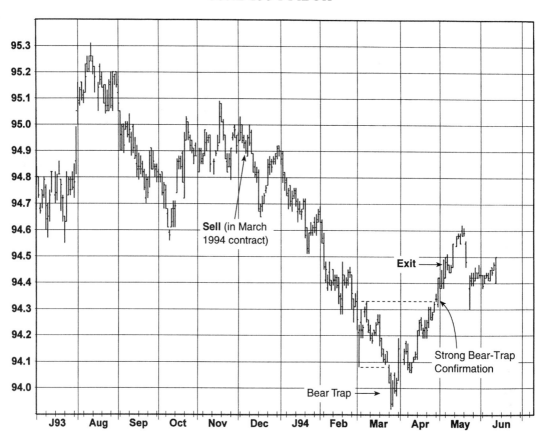

Trade Exit

Trade was exited on a trailing stop that was kept relatively wide.

Comment

Note that a bear-trap reversal was strongly confirmed by the ability of prices to return to the top of a prior trading range after breaking to new lows. Keeping the stop as wide as I did was a mistake, not because the market moved higher, but because doing so ignored an important trend-reversal signal. Thus, although the trade was a good one, insufficient attention to the exit needlessly sacrificed some of the profit potential.

Figure 14.105a
DECEMBER 1994 PIBOR

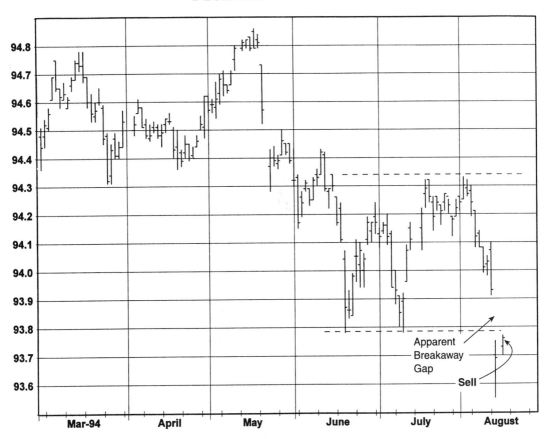

Trade Entry Reasons

1. Market was in a long-term downtrend.
2. Downside breakaway gap below the prior trading range signaled the potential beginning of a new decline.

Do you agree or disagree with the analysis?
Evaluate the situation before turning page.

Figure 14.105*b*
DECEMBER 1994 PIBOR

Trade Exit

The market rebound to the midpoint of a prior trading range suggested that a bear-trap reversal had occurred.

Comment

Although trade was terrible—selling one day away from a major low—the premise of the trade was still valid. More often than not, this type of pattern would lead to a profitable outcome; in this case, it did not. Even the most successful patterns are wrong a meaningful percentage of the time. It's all a matter of probabilities. Success depends on being right to a greater extent than one is wrong. There is a difference between a trading mistake and a trade that didn't work out. However, it is critical to have a plan to exit in case the trade is wrong. In this case, the apparent bear-trap reversal was confirmed by the penetration of the midpoint of a prior range, providing a signal to exit what proved to be a very poor trade.

Part Three

OSCILLATORS AND CYCLES

15 Oscillators

Thomas A. Bierovic

I know millions of things that won't work. I've certainly learned a lot.

—Thomas A. Edison

Oscillators are among the most valuable tools available to technical analysts, but they are also among the most misunderstood and misused. In this chapter we discuss not only the theory and construction of oscillators but also how to use them profitably.

The trend of a market is the general direction of its price fluctuations—up, down, or sideways. A market's momentum is its rate of acceleration or deceleration. An oscillator is a mathematically derived measure of a market's momentum. As early as the 1920s, technical analysts were creating oscillators to measure a market's momentum rather than limiting their efforts to determining the market's trend.

In any trend, prices are gaining, maintaining, or losing momentum. A loss of momentum in an uptrend or a downtrend—prices rising or falling at a diminishing rate—is an early warning sign that the trend might change soon. Therefore, when an oscillator shows that an uptrend is losing momentum, it is a cautionary signal that the uptrend may stall with prices either trading sideways or reversing into a downtrend. Similarly, when an oscillator indicates a loss of momentum in a downtrend, it may foreshadow a potential end to the downtrend.

Tom Bierovic is the author of *A Synergetic Approach to Profitable Trading* and the instructor on the video series *Synergetic Technical Analysis. Synergy Fax,* his daily advisory service, provides specific recommendations for the U.S. futures markets. Bierovic has presented highly rated seminars in more than 25 countries on six continents, and he also conducts private workshops for traders from novices to professionals at his office in Wheaton, Illinois.

THE DMA OSCILLATOR AND BASIC OSCILLATOR CONCEPTS

A simple oscillator can be constructed from a well-known trend-following indicator: the *dual moving average* (DMA). As a trend-following method, the DMA uses crossovers between a fast, sensitive moving average and a slow, less sensitive moving average to generate trading signals. In this discussion, we use a 5-day *exponential moving average* (EMA) for our fast line and a 20-day EMA for our slow line.

To convert the DMA from a trend-following indicator to an oscillator, subtract the slow moving average (EMA:20) from the fast one (EMA:5). This simple oscillator measures the distance between the two moving averages to determine if the trend is gaining or losing momentum (see Figure 15.1). When the fast moving average is accelerating away from the slow one, prices are gaining momentum; when the fast moving average is decelerating toward the slow one, prices are losing momentum. The oscillator's zero line corresponds to the point at which the fast and slow moving averages are equal. If the fast moving average is above the slow one, and the spread between them is increasing, the uptrend is gaining bullish momentum; if the spread is decreasing, the uptrend is losing momentum. If the fast moving average is below the slow one, and the spread between them is increasing (i.e., the oscillator is becoming more negative), the downtrend is gaining bearish momentum; if the spread is decreasing, the downtrend is losing momentum.

Overbought and Oversold Levels

An oscillator's overbought and oversold levels provide additional insight into price action. A market is considered overbought when an oscillator rallies to an extremely high level and oversold when the oscillator declines to an unusually low level. An overbought market may have risen too far too fast, and an oversold market may have fallen too far too fast. Markets with oscillators at overbought or oversold extremes are considered past due for a consolidation or a trend reversal.

Traders, however, should not automatically sell markets that are overbought or buy markets that are oversold. Although such a strategy may work well in a trading-range market, it will be disastrous in a trending market. More effective methods of using oscillators are discussed later in the chapter.

The overbought and oversold levels for our simple oscillator are drawn as horizontal lines that pass through the oscillator's highest peaks and lowest valleys. The oscillator should be in overbought or oversold territory only about 10% of the time. In other words, approximately 90% of the oscillator's values should be found between the extreme levels that the technician has determined (see Figure 15.2).

Figure 15.1
THE DUAL MOVING AVERAGE OSCILLATOR

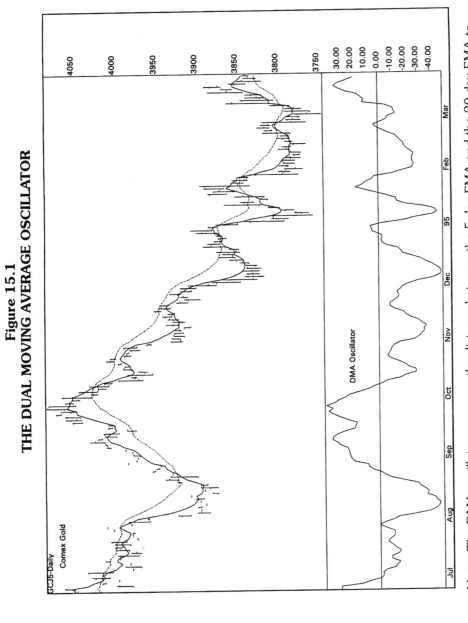

Note: The DMA oscillator measures the distance between the 5-day EMA and the 20-day EMA to provide insight into a market's momentum.

Source: FutureSource; copyright © 1986–1995; all rights reserved.

Figure 15.2
OVERBOUGHT AND OVERSOLD LEVELS

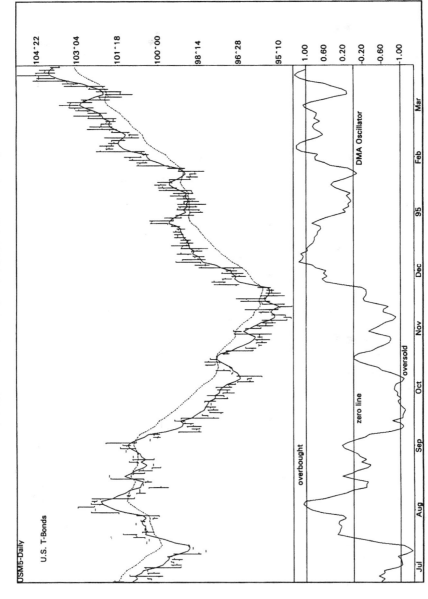

Note: The zero line of the DMA corresponds to the point at which the 5-day EMA and the 20-day EMA are equal. The overbought line has been drawn at +1.00 and the oversold line at −1.00.

Divergence

Another important feature of oscillators is *divergence* between new highs or new lows in price accompanied by an oscillator's failure to make higher highs or lower lows. Bullish divergence occurs when a market makes a low, rallies, and then declines to a lower low, while an oscillator makes a low along with the market, rallies, and then fails to decline to a new low (see Figure 15.3). Bearish divergence occurs when a market makes a high, declines, and then rallies to a higher high, while an oscillator makes a high along with the market, declines, and then fails to rally to a new high (see Figure 15.4).

Divergence is an early warning sign that a market may be in the process of changing its trend. When an oscillator-divergence signal is correct, it enables the trader to buy near a market's bottom and to sell near a market's top. Unfortunately, oscillator-divergence signals are frequently wrong. After all, oscillator-divergence signals are always in the opposite direction of the trend they are measuring, and traders are buying soon after a market declines to a lower low or selling soon after a market rallies to a higher high. During a prolonged price move, there can be two, three, or even more divergences before the trend finally reverses. However, the reliability of divergences can be greatly improved by waiting for prices to confirm the oscillator signals. The market action itself must show that the oscillator's current signal has a high probability of being correct. Trend-line penetrations (Figure 15.5), moving average penetrations (15.6), and *reversal days* (Figure 15.7) are a few of the many ways to obtain confirmation of oscillator-divergence signals. After reviewing five popular oscillators, we examine two particularly effective techniques for confirming oscillator-divergence signals: the *moving average channel* and *micro-M tops/micro-W bottoms*.

THE MOMENTUM OSCILLATOR

The *momentum* oscillator compares today's closing price with the closing price a specified number of days in the past. To calculate a nine-day momentum line, for example, subtract the close of nine days ago from today's close. If you want to create either a faster or a slower oscillator, simply decrease or increase the number of days in the calculation (see Figure 15.8). The formula for the momentum oscillator is: $M = C - C_n$, where C is the most recent closing price and C_n is the closing price n days ago.

Assuming $n = 9$, when the nine-day momentum oscillator is above its zero line and rising, nine-day price changes are positive and increasing—that is, the trend is bullish and accelerating (see Figure 15.9). If the momentum line turns flat, it implies that nine-day price changes are about equal during

Figure 15.3
BULLISH DIVERGENCE

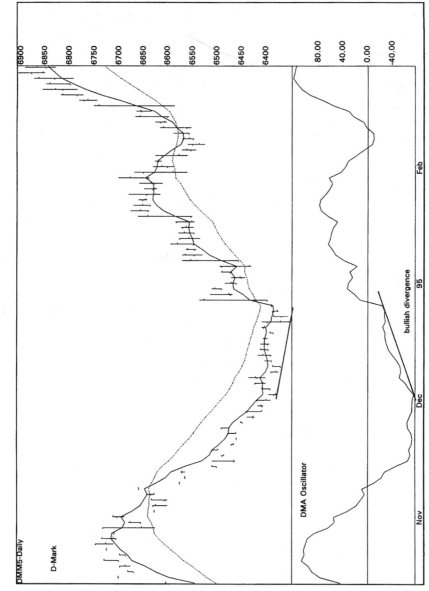

Note: Bullish divergence between a lower low in prices and a higher low in the DMA oscillator preceded the new uptrend.

Source: FutureSource; copyright © 1986–1995; all rights reserved.

Figure 15.4
BEARISH DIVERGENCE

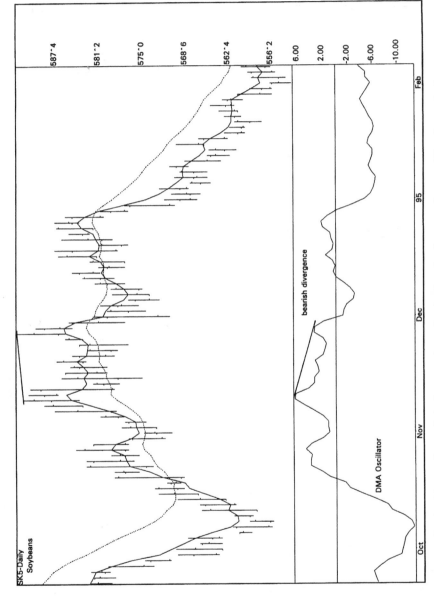

Note: The DMA oscillator failed to confirm the higher high in soybeans. This bearish divergence was followed by a new downtrend.

Source: FutureSource; copyright © 1986–1995; all rights reserved.

529

Figure 15.5
TREND LINE PENETRATION AS CONFIRMATION

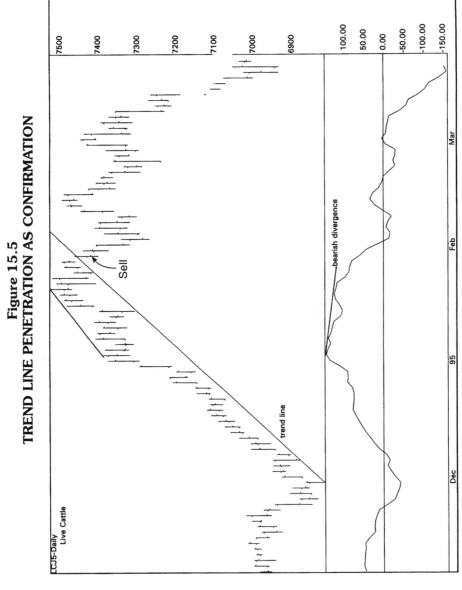

Note: After bearish divergence between prices and the DMA oscillator, the cattle market broke the bullish trend line. The trend-line penetration confirmed the oscillator signal.

Source: FutureSource; copyright © 1986–1995; all rights reserved.

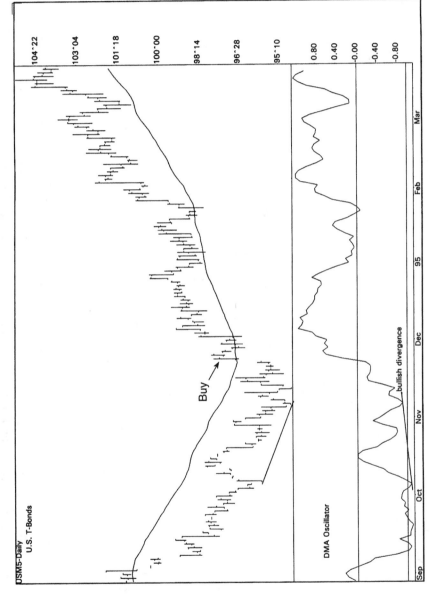

Figure 15.6
EMA PENETRATION AS CONFIRMATION

Note: The close above the 50-day EMA in November 1994 confirmed the DMA oscillator's bullish divergence signal.

Source: FutureSource; copyright © 1986–1995; all rights reserved.

Figure 15.7
REVERSAL DAY AS CONFIRMATION

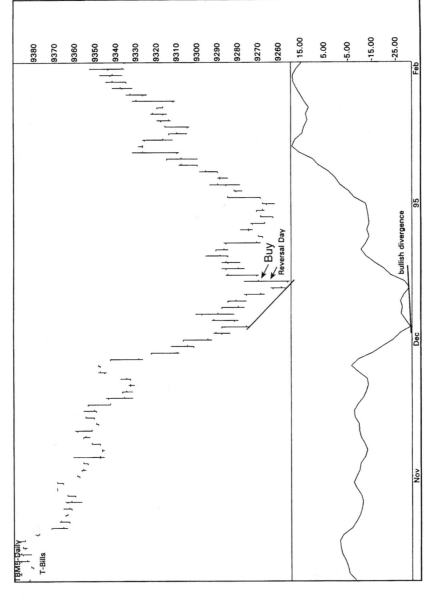

Note: In the bullish divergence environment of December 1994, T-bills made a new low for the downtrend but reversed and closed above the previous day's high. This reversal day provided additional evidence for an imminent change in trend.

Source: FutureSource; copyright © 1986–1995; all rights reserved.

Figure 15.8

COMPARING DIFFERENT *N*-VALUES FOR THE MOMENTUM OSCILLATOR

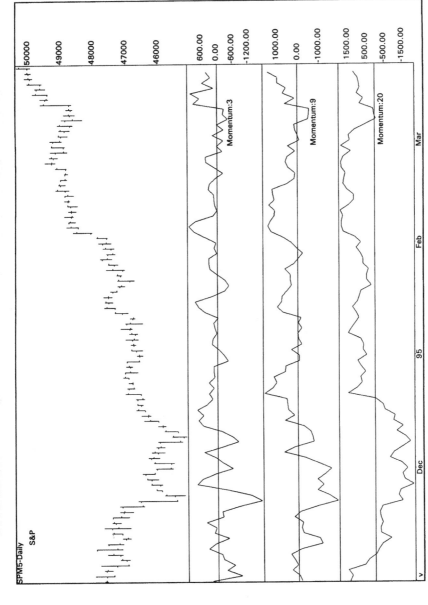

Note: This chart shows S&P futures with 3-, 9-, and 20-day momentum indicators.

Source: FutureSource; copyright © 1986–1995; all rights reserved.

Figure 15.9
THE MOMENTUM OSCILLATOR

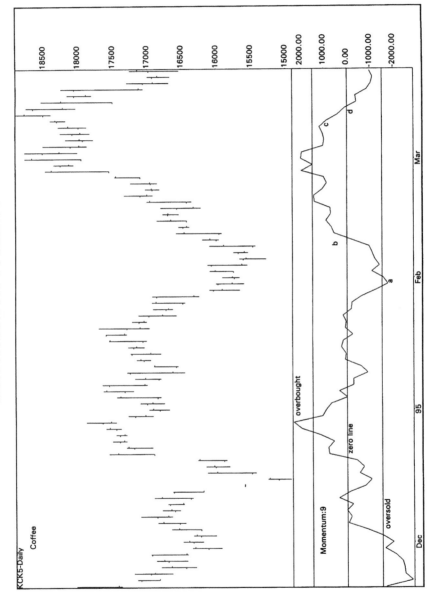

Note: After point **a** the coffee market's bearish momentum was decreasing. At point **b**, momentum turned bullish. Coffee's bullish momentum was weakening at point **c**. At point **d**, momentum became bearish.

the period of sideways movement. When the momentum oscillator begins to decline from above zero, the market's gains during the past nine days are less than the corresponding gains in the preceding days—that is, the uptrend is decelerating.

When the nine-day momentum oscillator falls below its zero line, the current close is below the close nine days ago. As the downtrend gains bearish velocity (i.e., larger nine-day declines), the momentum line accelerates downward from the zero line. An upturn of the oscillator in negative territory means that the magnitude of nine-day declines is decreasing—that is, the downtrend is decelerating.

The momentum oscillator is a leading indicator—it levels off while prices are still rising in an uptrend or falling in a downtrend, and it reverses its direction when the trend begins to slow down. Since trends generally show a decease in momentum before reversing their direction, the momentum oscillator can provide an early warning that a change in trend may be imminent.

RATE OF CHANGE

Rate of change (ROC) is another oscillator that compares today's closing price with the closing price a specified number of days in the past. It looks very similar to the momentum oscillator and is interpreted in exactly the same way (see Figure 15.10).

To calculate a nine-day ROC, divide today's close by the close nine days ago. If the current close and the close nine days ago are the same, the ROC will equal 1. If today's close is above the close nine days ago, the ROC will be greater than 1, and if today's close is below the close nine days ago, the ROC will be less than 1. The formula for the ROC oscillator is ROC = C/C_n, where C equals the most recent close and C_n equals the close n days ago.

Technical analysts monitor momentum and ROC for overbought and oversold extremes and for bullish and bearish divergences. Overbought and oversold levels for momentum and ROC are determined just as they are for the DMA oscillator. Horizontal lines pass through the highest peaks and lowest valleys so that only about 10% of the oscillator's values occur in overbought and oversold territory. Momentum and ROC indicators in their extreme zones suggest that a market is unlikely to trend much farther without a correction or consolidation. Bullish or bearish divergence provides an additional clue that the current trend is losing at least some of its power. When momentum and ROC show bullish divergence in oversold territory, watch for prices to give a buy signal (see Figure 15.11); when they show bearish divergence in overbought territory, wait for prices to confirm that it is time to sell.

Figure 15.10
COMPARING MOMENTUM AND RATE OF CHANGE

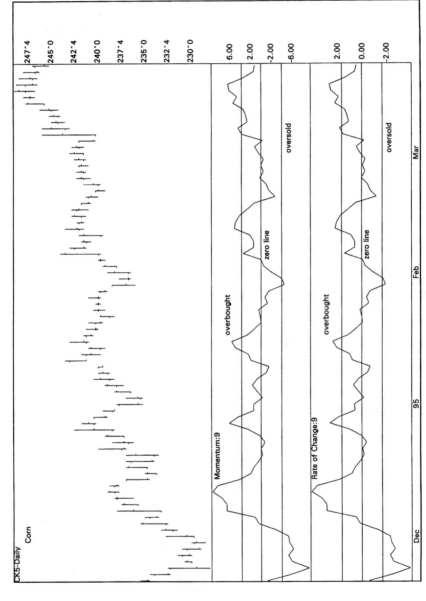

Note: Momentum and rate of change are derived from different calculations but result in very similar lines. Both are simple but logical ways to measure the velocity of price changes. Note that the scaling of the vertical axis is not the same for the two indicators but does not affect their interpretation.

Source: FutureSource; copyright © 1986–1995; all rights reserved.

Figure 15.11
BULLISH DIVERGENCE IN THE RATE OF CHANGE

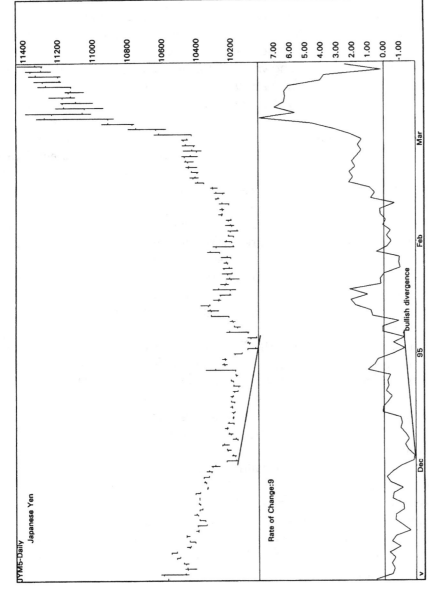

Note: The yen fell to a lower low in January 1995, but the nine-day rate of change made a higher low. The ROC's failure to penetrate its previous low was an early warning sign of a potential change in trend.

Source: FutureSource; copyright © 1986–1995; all rights reserved.

MOVING AVERAGE CONVERGENCE–DIVERGENCE

Moving average convergence–divergence (MACD), which was developed by Gerald Appel, is one of the most interesting and dependable technical indicators. It integrates positive features of both oscillators and trend-following indicators. The result is an indicator that can measure a market's momentum without losing its capability to also follow a trend.

In contrast to other well-known oscillators (such as RSI and *stochastics*), MACD is not limited to oscillating between fixed upper and lower extremes.[1] It will continue to make new highs or new lows along with prices, as long as the trend is gaining momentum (i.e., the distance between the fast and slow moving averages is increasing). In that respect, MACD also behaves as a trend-following indicator. In the respect that it measures the rate of acceleration or deceleration between two moving averages to determine if a market is gaining or losing momentum, the MACD behaves as an oscillator.

The MACD consists of two lines that are derived from three EMAs. The *MACD line* is the difference between a 12-period EMA and a 26-period EMA; the *signal line* is a nine-period EMA of the MACD line (see Figure 15.12). Many technicians adjust these parameters in an attempt to optimize MACD for specific markets, while others employ one set of values for MACD buy signals and a different set of values for MACD sell signals. My preference is to maintain a 12–26–9 MACD for all markets and for both buying and selling.

A popular variation of the MACD and signal lines is the *MACD histogram*. It is created by subtracting the signal line from the MACD line and drawing the difference as a sequence of vertical bars above and below a zero line (see Figure 15.12). Some technical analysts believe that the MACD histogram provides more timely and more profitable signals than the MACD and signal lines. I regard the MACD histogram as overly sensitive and ill-suited for most analytical purposes.

The basic method for trading with MACD is to buy when the MACD line crosses above the signal line and to sell when the MACD line crosses below the signal line. However, entering and exiting trades based solely on MACD line–signal line crossovers results in frequent whipsaw losses. To make the best use of MACD, it is advisable to wait for crossovers that are preceded by divergence and confirmed by the subsequent price action of the market (see Figures 15.13 and 15.14).

---

[1]The three oscillators discussed previously in this chapter were also not restricted by fixed boundaries.

Figure 15.12
THE MACD

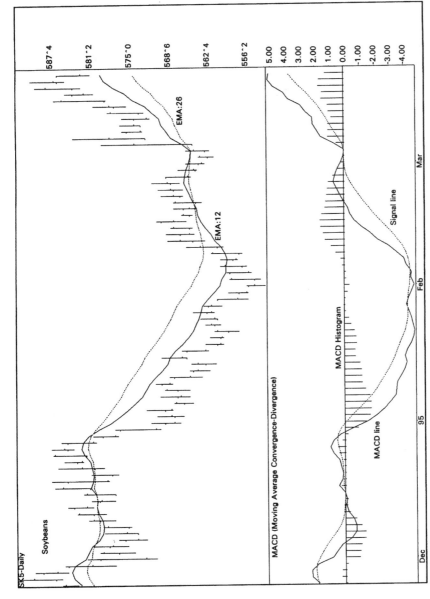

Note: The top window shows the 12- and 26-day exponential moving averages from which the MACD line is derived. In the bottom window, the MACD line is displayed as a solid line. The signal line, a 9-day EMA of the MACD, is displayed as a dotted line. Vertical bars rising above or falling below the zero line represent the MACD histogram. This variation of the MACD indicator is obtained by subtracting the signal line from the MACD line.

Source: FutureSource;

Figure 15.13
BULLISH DIVERGENCE IN THE MACD

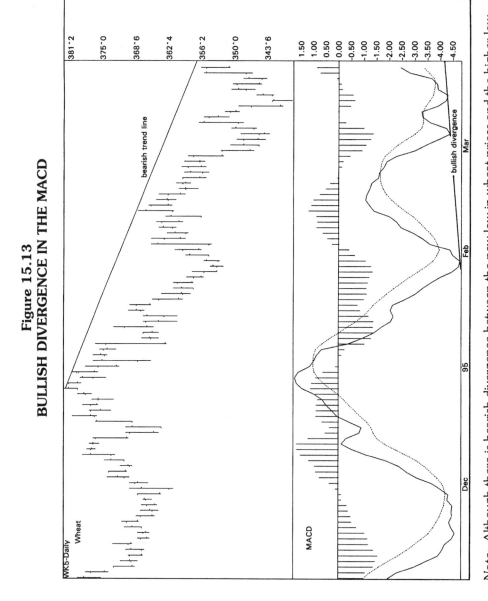

Note: Although there is bearish divergence between the new low in wheat prices and the higher low on MACD, it is advisable not to enter a long position until the market penetrates the bearish trend line.

Source: FutureSource; copyright © 1986–1995; all rights reserved.

Figure 15.14
BEARISH DIVERGENCE AND CONFIRMATION OF MACD CROSSOVER

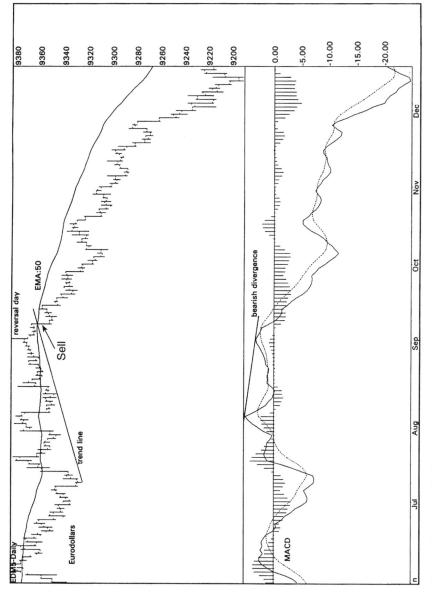

Note: In a bearish divergence environment, Eurodollars formed a reversal day, penetrated a bullish trend line, and closed below the EMA. This combination of signals confirmed the MACD sell signal and suggested a high-probability trade. The indicated sell point corresponds to the price action confirmation (i.e., penetration of trend line and close below the EMA).

Source: FutureSource; copyright © 1986–1995; all rights reserved.

RELATIVE STRENGTH INDEX

The *relative strength index* (RSI) was introduced by J. Welles Wilder, Jr., in his 1978 book, *New Concepts in Technical Trading Systems.* Of all the momentum oscillators currently in wide use, RSI responds the best to basic technical analysis methods such as trend lines, chart patterns, and support and resistance. Applying these methods to RSI in conjunction with over-bought/oversold levels and divergences can provide very valuable insight into market behavior.

RSI compares the relative strength of price gains on days that close above the previous day's close to price losses on days that close below the previous day's close. The formula for RSI is:

$$RSI = 100 - [100/1 + RS],$$

where *RS* is the average of positive closing changes for a specified number of days divided by the average of negative closing changes for the same number of days.

To calculate a nine-day RSI, for example, first add the points gained on the up days of the nine-day period and divide the total by nine. Then add the points lost on the down days of the nine-day period and divide the total by nine. Next, find the relative strength (*RS*) by dividing the up average by the down average. Finally, insert the *RS* value into the RSI formula to create an oscillator that fluctuates between zero and 100.

The RSI can be constructed for any number of days that the technical analyst considers useful. Wilder's original suggestion was 14 days, but today most technicians prefer a faster, more sensitive indicator, such as a five-, seven-, or nine-day RSI. Overbought and oversold levels are usually drawn at 70 and 30 or at 80 and 20. Some analysts attempt to optimize the number of days in the RSI calculation on a market-by-market basis or to vary the over-bought and oversold levels to adjust for each market's current trend. My pref-erence is to maintain a constant nine-day RSI with overbought and oversold levels at 70 and 30 for all markets.

The most reliable RSI buy and sell signals usually occur after RSI fails to confirm a new low or a new high in prices. Bullish divergence between a lower bottom in prices and a higher bottom in RSI sets up a potential buying opportunity (see Figure 15.15), and bearish divergence between a higher top in prices and a lower top in RSI sets up a potential selling opportunity (see Figure 15.16). When a trader identifies a bullish or bearish RSI divergence, he should then focus his attention on the price action of the market itself and wait for prices to confirm the RSI signal.

Figure 15.15
CONFIRMATION OF BULLISH DIVERGENCE IN RSI

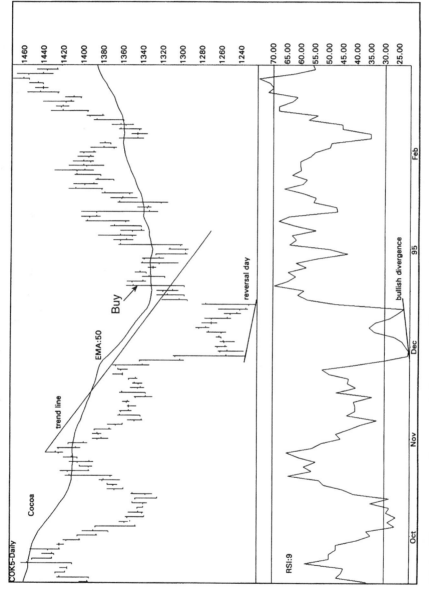

Note: The cocoa market provided a series of buy signals in December 1994: bullish divergence, a reversal day, and rallies above the trend line and the EMA.

Source: FutureSource; copyright © 1986–1995; all rights reserved.

Figure 15.16
CONFIRMATION OF BEARISH DIVERGENCE IN RSI

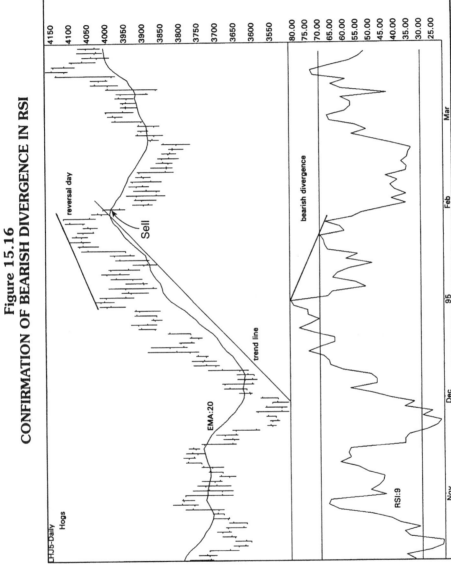

Note: Oscillator-divergence signals, even with trend-following confirmation, do not always result in spectacular trades. After bearish divergence, a reversal day and a close below the trend line and the EMA, this market traded lower for just 13 days before beginning a rally to new highs.

Source: FutureSource; copyright © 1986–1995; all rights reserved.

STOCHASTIC

The *stochastic* oscillator was developed by George Lane at Investment Educators in the late 1950s. Stochastic evaluates a market's momentum by determining the relative position of closing prices within the high–low range of a specified number of days. A 14-day stochastic, for example, measures the location of closing prices within the total high–low range of the previous 14 days. Stochastic expresses the relationship between the close and the high–low range as a percentage between zero and 100. A stochastic value of 70 or higher indicates that the close is near the top of the range; a stochastic value of 30 or lower means that the close is near the bottom of the range.

In a robust uptrend, prices generally close near the top of the recent range; in a strong downtrend, prices usually close near the bottom of the range. When an uptrend is approaching a turning point, prices begin to close farther away from the high of the range, and when a downtrend is weakening, prices tend to close farther away from the low of the range. The purpose of the stochastic oscillator is to alert technicians to the failure of bulls to close prices near the highs of an uptrend or the inability of bears to close prices near the lows of a downtrend.

The stochastic is plotted as two lines: $\%K$ and $\%D$. The formula for $\%K$ is $\%K = 100\,[(C - L_n)/(H_n - L_n)]$, where C is the current close, L_n is the low of the n-day period, and H_n is the high of the n-day period. The $\%D$ formula is $\%D = 100\,(H_3/L_3)$, in which H_3 is the three-day sum of $(C - L_n)$, and L_3 is the three-day sum of $(H_n - L_n)$.

The $\%K$ and $\%D$ formulas produce the *fast stochastic* oscillator, which is generally considered too sensitive and erratic. Fast stochastic can be subjected to a further three-day smoothing, however, which results in the *slow stochastic* that most analysts prefer. In the smoothed version of stochastic, the fast $\%D$ becomes the slow $\%K,$ and a three-day moving average of the fast $\%D$ becomes the slow $\%D$. Slow $\%K$ is usually drawn as a solid line and slow $\%D$ as a dotted or dashed line (see Figure 15.17).

I prefer to monitor a 14-day slow stochastic, with overbought/oversold levels at 70 and 30, for divergences between prices and the $\%K$ or $\%D$ lines. When stochastic fails to confirm a market's new high, wait for $\%K$ to cross below $\%D$ and to drop below 70; when stochastic fails to make a new low along with prices, wait for $\%K$ to cross above $\%D$ and to climb above 30. After identifying a bullish or bearish stochastic divergence, watch the market's price action for a confirming buy or sell signal. Figure 15.18 illustrates a buy-confirmation signal (based on a dual condition), while Figure 15.19 shows an analogous example of a sell-confirmation signal.

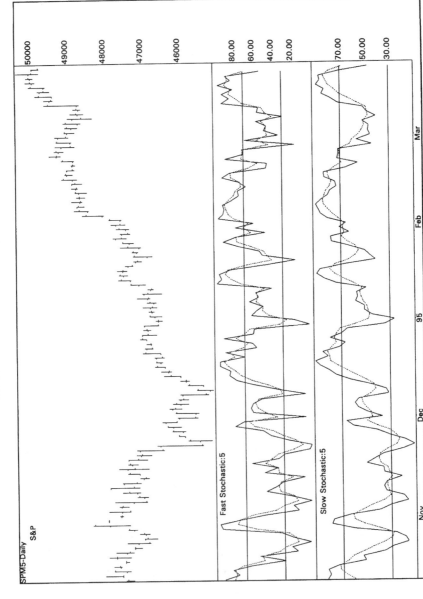

Figure 15.17
FAST AND SLOW STOCHASTIC

Note: This chart shows the difference between a five-day fast stochastic and the more widely used five-day slow stochastic.

Source: FutureSource; copyright © 1986–1995; all rights reserved.

Figure 15.18
CONFIRMATION OF BULLISH DIVERGENCE IN STOCHASTIC

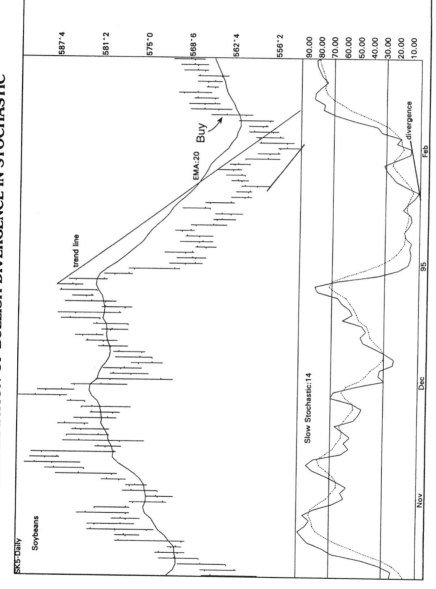

Note: A stochastic bullish divergence, a trend line break, and a close above the EMA preceded the new uptrend in soybeans.

Source: FutureSource; copyright © 1986–1995; all rights reserved.

547

Figure 15.19
CONFIRMATION OF BEARISH DIVERGENCE IN STOCHASTIC

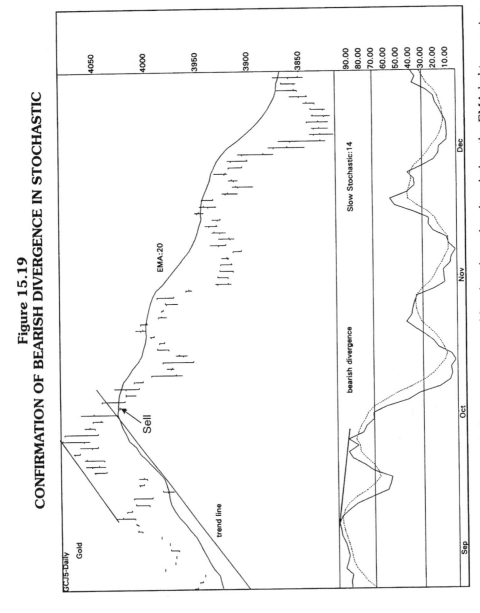

Note: A stochastic bearish divergence, a trend line break, and a close below the EMA led to a major decline in gold.

Source: FutureSource; copyright © 1986–1995; all rights reserved.

548

THE MOVING AVERAGE CHANNEL

The *moving average channel* (MAC) is a simple yet effective method for getting trend-following confirmation of oscillator divergence signals. The MAC is especially well-suited for novice traders. It provides not only a logical entry point but also an original stop-loss and a trailing stop for managing the trade.

The MAC is a price channel that consists of an *n*-day EMA of highs and an *n*-day EMA of lows. I prefer to use 28 days as the value for *n*. The channel boundaries often act as support and resistance for prices. MAC is also a good measure of volatility—it expands as volatility increases and contracts as volatility decreases.

Buying with Oscillators and the MAC

A market's rally above the MAC is a valuable trend-following confirmation of an oscillator signal (see Figure 15.20). The price action of the market is telling you that the oscillator signal has a strong probability of being correct.

The following description is intended to offer an illustration of how the MAC can be used in conjunction with divergence to enter and exit trades. After bullish divergence between price and an oscillator, place an order to buy one tick above the moving average of highs. If the market does not penetrate the top of the moving average channel on the first day after bullish divergence, continue to place your buy order one tick above the MAC until you are stopped into a long position. (If both the market and the oscillator fall to new lows without a price rally through the moving average of highs, stand aside and wait for the next divergence setup.) After entering your long position, set a sell stop one tick below the moving average of lows. Your risk on the trade (barring excessive slippage or an opening that gaps through your stop) will be only a few ticks more than the recent average daily range.

As prices move higher, maintain a trailing sell stop one tick below the MAC until the trend reverses and the market stops out the trade (hopefully, with a substantial profit). If the decline through the moving average of lows is preceded by a bearish divergence, view it as a stop-and-reverse signal, closing out your long position and simultaneously entering a new short position.

Selling with Oscillators and the MAC

A market's decline below the MAC provides a confirmation of an oscillator sell signal (see Figure 15.21). After bearish divergence, place an order to sell short one tick below the moving average of lows. If the market does not

Figure 15.20
UPSIDE PENETRATION OF MAC AS A BUY CONFIRMATION

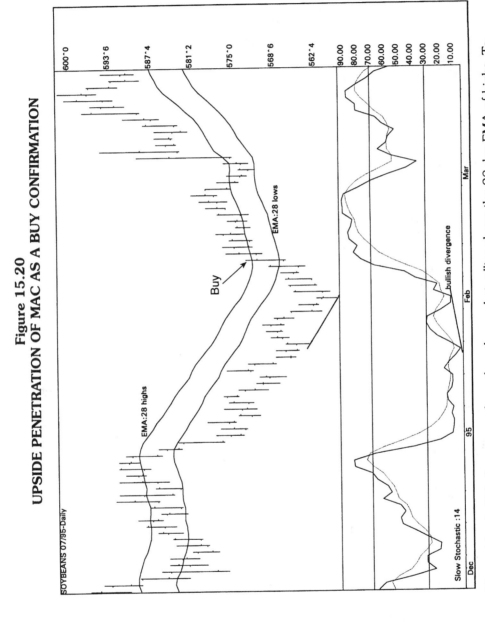

Note: After bullish divergence, buy when the market rallies above the 28-day EMA of highs. To determine your original risk and your exit, trail a sell stop one tick below the 28-day EMA of lows.

Source: FutureSource; copyright © 1986–1995; all rights reserved.

Figure 15.21
DOWNSIDE PENETRATION OF MAC AS A SELL SIGNAL

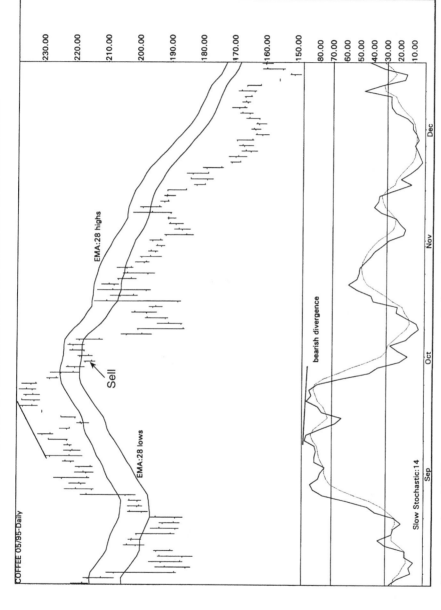

Note: In a bearish-divergence environment, sell short when prices decline below the 28-day EMA of lows. A trailing buy stop one tick above the 28-day EMA of highs provides your original risk and your exit point.

Source: FutureSource; copyright © 1986–1995; all rights reserved.

penetrate the bottom of the MAC on the first day after bearish divergence, continue to place your sell order one tick below the MAC until you are stopped into a short position. (If both the market and the oscillator rise to new highs without a price decline through the moving average of lows, stand aside and wait for the next divergence setup.) After entering your short position, set a buy stop one tick above the moving average of highs. As prices move lower, maintain a trailing buy stop one tick above the MAC until the trend reverses and the market stops you out of your short position. If the rally through the moving average of highs is preceded by a bullish divergence, close out your short position and simultaneously enter a new long position.

Additional Suggestions for the MAC

Two variations of the MAC method—one related to the oscillator component and the other one pertaining to trade management—may be of interest to MAC traders.

1. Rather than relying on a divergence signal from only one oscillator, monitor your three favorite ones and watch for divergence setups on at least two of the three indicators. For example, I follow MACD, RSI, and stochastic, which generally form similar but not identical patterns. Waiting for a divergence signal from at least two of the three oscillators leads to a higher percentage of winning trades.

2. Although holding a position until prices penetrate the farther boundary of the MAC works quite well when the market is in a strong, steady trend, orderly trends without disruptive price shocks are the exception rather than the rule. In today's choppy and volatile markets, you may want to employ a trade-management strategy of taking profits at a price objective rather than attempting to let profits run until a trend reverses.

   Consider setting objectives based on the size of the original risk on the trade. Before entering a trade, you should know where you will get out of the position if the market moves against you. The difference between your entry point and your stop-loss is the original risk on the trade. You can move your stop to breakeven when the market trades in your favor by an amount equal to or greater than the original risk, and you can take profits at an objective of two or three times the risk. If your account size and risk tolerance enable you to trade multiple contracts, you may want to exit part of your position at a price objective equal to two times the risk on the trade and to let profits run with a trailing stop on the remaining contracts.

MICRO-M TOPS AND MICRO-W BOTTOMS

Micro-M tops and micro-W bottoms are chart patterns that represent the battle between bulls and bears at market turning points and frequently provide valuable confirmation of oscillator signals. A micro-M top begins with an unconfirmed high. After a market's initial downward reaction to bearish divergence, prices start up again. If the resumption of the uptrend fails, and the market begins to trade lower, a micro-M top is completed. A micro-W bottom begins with an unconfirmed low. After the initial upward reaction to bullish divergence, prices start back down. If the resumption of the downtrend fails, and the market begins to trade higher, a micro-W bottom is completed.

The specific rules for trading with oscillators and micro-W bottoms (see Figure 15.22) are as follows:

1. When you identify a bullish-divergence low, watch for a day that closes above the previous day's close, followed immediately by a day that closes lower.
2. After the up-day/down-day sequence, buy when prices rally above the high of the up/down pattern. In other words, buy a tick above the higher of the two days in the up-day/down-day combination. The day of entry does not have to be the day immediately after the up/down pattern. The only days in a micro-W bottom that must be consecutive are the up-close/down-close days.
3. Risk to a tick below the bullish-divergence low and exit your long position when prices rally to your profit objective or decline to a trailing stop. If you trade multiple contracts, you may choose to manage your position with a combination of trailing stops and profit objectives.

The rules for micro-M tops (see Figure 15.23) are:

1. When you identify a bearish-divergence high, watch for a day that closes below the previous day's close, followed immediately by a day that closes higher.
2. After the down-day/up-day sequence, sell short when prices fall below the low of the down/up pattern. In other words, sell short a tick below the lower of the two days in the down-day/up-day combination. The day of entry does not have to be the day immediately after the down/up pattern. The only days in a micro-M top that must be consecutive are the down-close/up-close days.
3. Risk to a tick above the bearish-divergence high and exit your short position when prices decline to your profit objective or rally to a trail-

Figure 15.22
MICRO-W BOTTOM

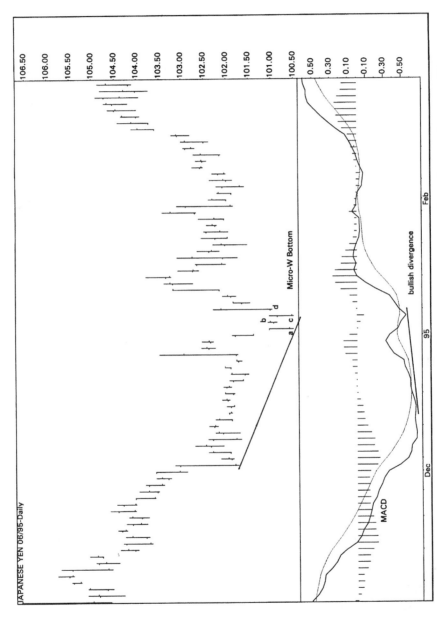

Note: MACD formed a bullish divergence by failing to make a new low along with prices. The price action (a micro-W bottom) provided trend-following confirmation of the MACD signal. The W began with a decline to point **a,** a low with bullish divergence. Points **b** and **c** were the up-day/down-day sequence. Buy on day **d,** when prices rally above the high of day **b,** and risk to a tick below the low of day **c.**

Source: FutureSource; copyright © 1986–1995; all rights reserved.

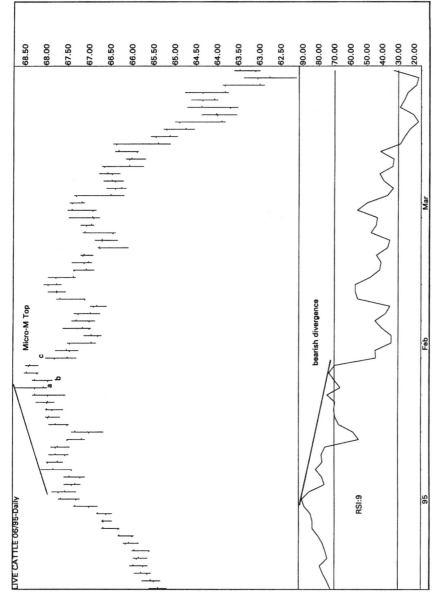

**Figure 15.23
MICRO-M TOP**

Note: RSI:9 formed a bearish divergence, and the cattle market confirmed the RSI signal by forming a micro-M top. Day **a** was *both* the divergent high and a day that closed below the previous day's close. Day **b** completed the down-day/up-day sequence. Sell short on day **c,** when prices fall below the low of day **b,** and risk to a tick above the high of day **a.**

Source: FutureSource; copyright © 1986–1995; all rights reserved.

555

ing stop. Of course, you may want to exit part of your position at a profit objective and the remaining contracts at a trailing stop.

CONCLUSION

Oscillators perform well when a market is in a trading range—that is, a sideways trend. They work poorly, however, when a market is in a strong uptrend or downtrend.

Many technical analysts attempt to determine the existing market environment—trading range or trending—and to select the most appropriate indicators for current conditions. They employ moving averages or other trend-following indicators when a market is in a good uptrend or downtrend, and they use oscillators or other countertrend indicators when a market is trading sideways. The problem with this approach is that every trend eventually fades into a trading range, and every trading range sooner or later breaks out into a trend. It is extremely difficult, or even impossible, to know in advance when the market environment is going to change from trending to nontrending or vice versa.

Fortunately, there is a better solution than trying to pick and choose technical indicators based on the current market environment. Astute technicians enter trades based on oscillators only when the signal is confirmed by the market's price action. The MAC and micro-M tops/micro-W bottoms are two of the many trend-following methods that can dramatically improve the performance of oscillators. Momentum oscillators can play an important role in the technical trader's repertoire of indicators; however, oscillators must not be allowed to upstage the price action of the market itself.

16 Cycle Analysis of the Futures Markets

Richard Mogey and Jack Schwager

The same Nature which delights in periodical repetition in the skies is the Nature which orders the affairs of the earth. Let us not underrate the value of that hint.

—Mark Twain

ARE THERE REALLY CYCLES?

Over the years, the question of the reality of cycles has been a topic of serious debate among scientists and economists. The real question, however, is not whether cycles exist—some cycles such as the transition between night and day and the changing seasons are undeniable—but to what extent physical, social, and economic phenomena are cyclical in nature. For example, there is obviously a sunspot cycle (see Figure 16.1), but are there cycles in climate? There is a clearly a business cycle, but are there cycles in the stock market?

These questions have sincere and educated proponents on both sides, and the truth probably lies in the middle: There probably are not as many cycles as cycle enthusiasts say there are, and certainly not as few as the opponents of cycle research claim. The statistical evidence that cycles exist in many economic series (such as various price data), however, is very strong. As but one example, an analysis of the stock market reveals a 40-month cycle (see Figure 16.2) that statistical testing indicates has only a 2-out-of-10,000 probability of being due to chance. Forty years ago, few people believed in cycles in either science or economics. Since that time evidence for recurring patterns has been mounting.

Richard Mogey is the executive director of the Foundation for the Study of Cycles in Wayne, Pennsylvania. He joined the foundation as research director in 1988 on a grant from Tudor Investment to study cycles in the futures markets. During his years at the foundation, Mogey conducted a complete study of cycles in all major domestic and foreign futures markets and major currencies. He has personally traded futures and stocks since 1968.

557

Figure 16.1
SUNSPOT CYCLE

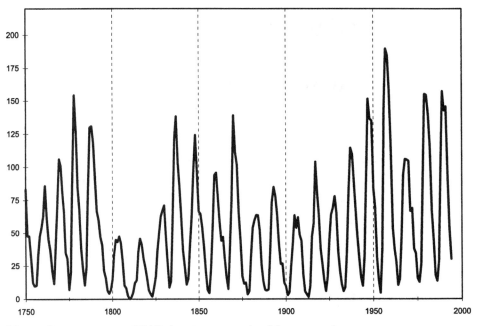

Note: Sunspots since 1749 showing a regular 11-year cycle.

Figure 16.2
FORTY-MONTH CYCLE IN STOCKS

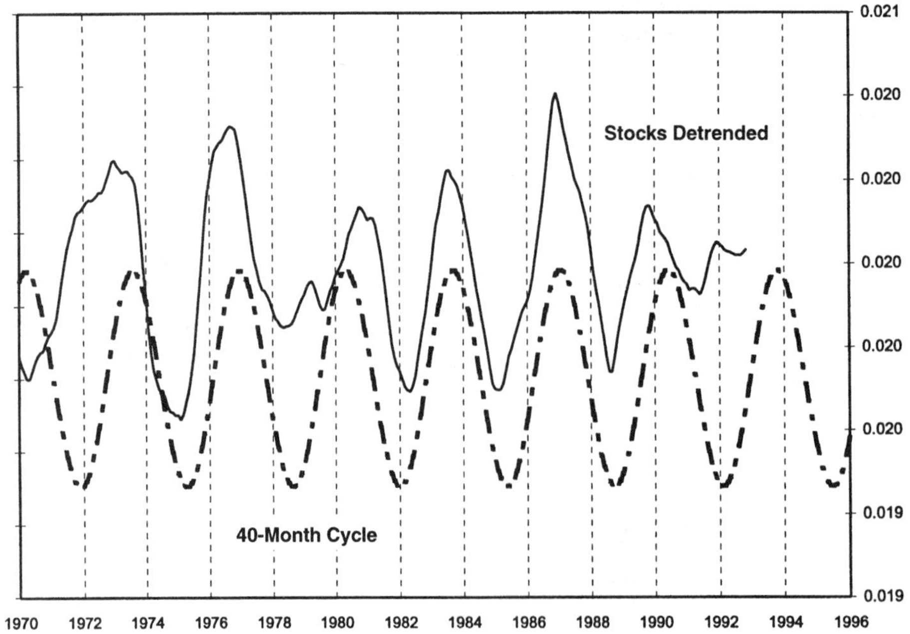

Why would cycles exist in market price data? There are two basic explanations, one fundamental and the other psychological.

1. *Fundamental: Cycles Reflect Lags that Affect Shifts in Supply and Demand.* For example, if there is a shortage of beef, causing beef prices to rise sharply, cattle producers will have the incentive to increase output. Such a decision, however, cannot be implemented instantaneously. Producers will hold back cattle from slaughter to build their breeding herds. Ironically, this action to increase supply will only accentuate the near-term shortage, driving beef prices even higher, and providing still more incentive for cattle ranchers to expand their herds. It will take several years for the offspring that result from changes in breeding decisions to reach market weight. As these lagged supplies reach the market, beef prices will begin to fall. Eventually, prices will fall enough to prompt cattle producers to reduce their breeding herds, thereby causing near-term supplies to bulge and prices to decline even further. After a lag of several years, the reduced supply of beef that results from this breeding herd liquidation will cause beef prices to rise, and the cycle will start all over again.

2. *Psychological: Cycles Reflect the Psychological Responses of Traders to Price Swings.* Markets do not move in unbroken trends. After a period of predominant movement in a given direction, the market will become increasingly vulnerable to a correction. As the trend progresses and their losses mount, more and more traders who hold positions counter to the trend will "throw in the towel," eventually leaving a paucity of buying by shorts (or selling by longs in the case of a downtrend) to propel the trend any further. Some traders will be inclined to take profits. Other traders, worried about surrendering their open profits, would be ready to liquidate their positions at the first sign of a possible trend reversal. Some traders will feel the price move is overdone and will become increasingly disposed to initiate countertrend positions. All of these factors would combine to cause periodic reactions or trend reversals.

Cyclical theory merely implies that in each market these fundamental and psychological forces will conform to approximate time patterns. Note the word *approximate*. There is no implication that market price cycles will unfold with clockwork precision. A 20-week cycle in stock prices does not imply that stock prices will set a relative low precisely every 20-weeks. If it did, one could make a quick fortune trading this pattern. The implication, however, is that there will be a tendency for stock prices to reach a relative low point *about* every 20-weeks. Sometimes the low will occur earlier, sometimes later, and sometimes the low will not occur at all, as the cycle effect is overshadowed by other price-influencing forces. The basic idea, however, is that there is enough regularity to market price cycles for this information to provide a useful input in making trading decisions.

THE BEGINNINGS OF CYCLE STUDY

Although cycles have been an important part of the world's major cultures and religions for thousands of years, the consideration of cycles as a force in economic fluctuations did not surface until the start of the nineteenth century. Ironically, the first recorded person to look for cycles as a means of understanding economic change was not an economist, but an astronomer—Sir William Herschel, the discoverer of the planet Uranus. In 1801, Herschel postulated that there could well be a relationship between the sunspot cycles and weather, which in turn could affect crop prices and ultimately the economy as a whole. At about this time, working in secret, the famous Rothschild family in Europe plotted British interest rates using three cycles, including a 40-month cycle. (More on this momentarily.)

In the 1870s, the idea of periodicity in economic data was carried forward by W. Stanley Jeavons in England and Samuel Benner, a farmer from Ohio, both of whom compared the economic data of their respective countries with sunspot records. In 1875, Benner wrote his now famous *Benner's Prophecies of Future Ups and Downs in Prices*. He too said that his cycle was due to solar activity. Benner published an interesting chart forecasting economic changes until 1895 (see Figure 16.3). Working at around the same time, Clement Juglar found a 10–12-year cycle in interest rates and the economy, a cycle that now bears his name.

The Rothchilds secretly used their cycles with great success until rumors reached New York in 1912. There a group of investors hired mathematicians to discover these curves. With the replication of the Rothschild formulas, the use of cycles in investing began in earnest. In 1923, two economists, Professors Crum and Kitchin, found an approximate 40-month cycle in economic data. Even though the Rothschilds had found this same cycle nearly a century earlier, since 1923 it has become known as the Kitchin cycle.

Figure 16.3
BENNER'S FORECAST OF ECONOMIC CYCLES

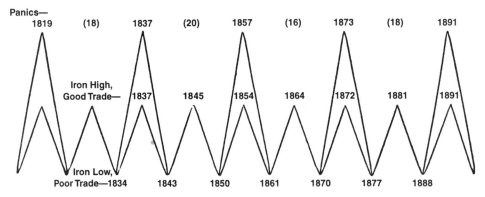

The real progress in the study of cycles needed to await mathematical advances in time-series analysis and statistics in the late nineteenth century and twentieth century. Some of these key analytical developments—the periodogram, harmonic analysis, and spectral analysis—are discussed later in this chapter.

The investment public's interest in cycles was greatly enhanced by two anonymous versions of Benner's chart that resurfaced in the 1930s, the connection with Benner having been lost. Ironically, both of these versions were purported to have been found in old desks in Pennsylvania, one in Connellsville and the other in Philadelphia. The Connellsville chart became known as the "Distillery" chart because it was found in a desk belonging to the Overholt Distilling Company. The Philadelphia version of the chart was published as "The Forecast of an Earlier Generation" by the *Wall Street Journal* on February 2, 1933. This chart became instantly famous because it purportedly forecast the depression. The *Wall Street Journal* version of Benner's original chart, however, had obviously been modified so that it would better fit the 1929 crash by showing a peak in 1929, instead of 1926, as in the original chart.

BASIC CYCLIC CONCEPTS

The Nature of the Data

Any data series can be broken down into three components: (1) growth forces, (2) periodic forces, and (3) random forces (see Figure 16.4). Cyclic analysis is concerned with finding the periodic or recurring patterns in the data.[1]

Growth forces are those influences that cause time series to increase or decrease slowly over time and are commonly referred to as *trend*. *Random* forces are factors that cause irregular fluctuations in the data that are by definition unpredictable. The cycle analyst detrends the data to remove the growth influence and smoothes the data to remove random influences in order to find the periodic patterns.

The Cycle Model

Just after the turn of the century, cycle analysts adopted a mathematical–scientific model to define cycles. The cycle became described as a sine wave

---

[1]The word *cycle* comes from the Greek word meaning "circle," which in its most general sense simply refers to a complete sequence of events, without implying any regularity of time interval. Cycle analysts, however, are concerned with periodic cycles, that is, cycles occurring over a regular time interval.

Figure 16.4
KEY COMPONENTS OF DATA

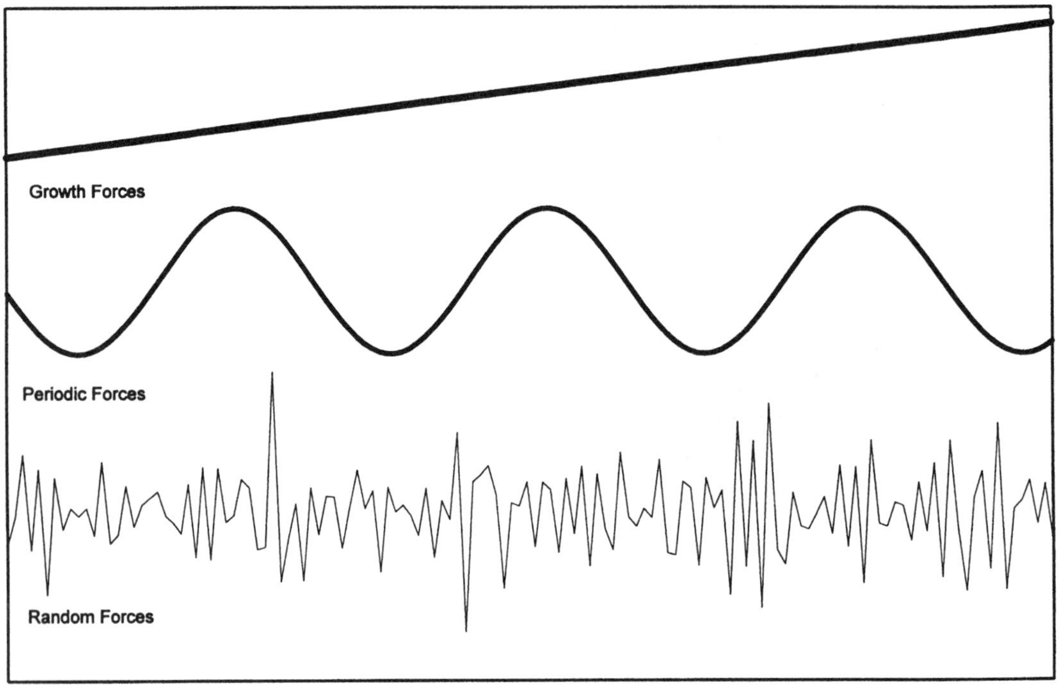

Growth Forces

Periodic Forces

Random Forces

and took the language of physics and statistics. Hence cycles were said to have *frequency, amplitude, and phase,* much like any electromagnetic wave. Because these terms are used universally to describe cycles, it is important to define them (and related terms) at the outset.

Period and Frequency

The length of a cycle is the time span from crest to crest or trough to trough and is called its *period* (see Figure 16.5). The *frequency* is the number of occurrences of a cycle in a given span of data and is inversely related to the period:

Frequency = length of data ÷ period

For example, given a series with 200 data points, a cycle whose period is 20 would have a frequency of 10 (10 = 200/20). In the two principal mathematical methods of analyzing cycles, *harmonic analysis* and *spectral analysis,* the former is based on period and the latter on frequency.

Figure 16.5
IDEAL CYCLE MODEL

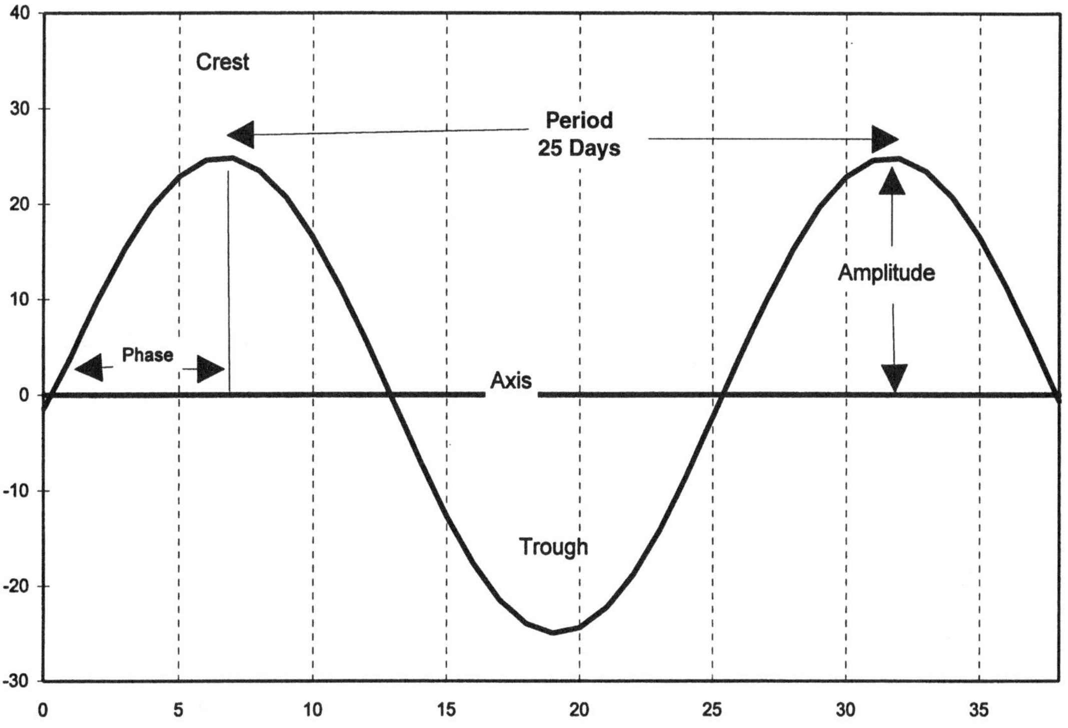

Phase, Crest, and Trough

The *phase* is the position in time of a certain point of a wave. The *crest* of a cycle is its high, and the *trough* is its low (see Figure 16.5). The phase of a cycle is normally defined by the location of the crest within the cycle. For example, if a cycle is 10 data points in length and the phase is 3, the first crest in the data comes at the third data point, with subsequent crests occurring at intervals of 10: 3, 13, 23, 33, 43, 53, and so on.

Amplitude and Axis

Amplitude is the strength of the fluctuation, or the height and depth of the wave above and below its axis. The *axis* is the straight line around which a cycle fluctuates. The amplitude in cycle analysis is measured from the axis to the crest (see Figure 16.5). The axis is often called the *inflection point* of the cycle.

EIGHT STEPS IN CONSTRUCTING A CYCLE ANALYSIS

Making a complete cycle analysis of a data series involves the following step-by-step procedure:

1. Choose the data
2. Visually inspect the data
3. Transform data into log form (initial detrending step)
4. Smooth the data
5. Find possible cycles
6. Complete detrending of data by using departures from a moving average
7. Test the cycles for statistical significance and dominance
8. Combine and project cycles into the future

These steps are examined in turn in the following sections.

Step 1: Choose the Data

Choosing the data for cycle analysis is not a trivial matter. Because of the nature of cycle analysis, different types of data—for example, futures versus cash, perpetual versus continuous, daily versus weekly—will yield different results. In addition, an analysis done on 1,000 data points can differ significantly from one using 5,000 data points. Therefore it is critical that the analyst takes care in selecting the appropriate data or else the entire analysis could prove flawed. This first step in cyclical analysis, choosing the data, can itself be broken down into four distinct steps:

A. Understand the nature of the data
B. Choose the data type
C. Choose the length of the data
D. Choose the data compression

Understand the Nature of the Data.   The nature of a data series can undergo major transitions over time, and it is important for the analyst to be familiar with such changes. An excellent example of such a change in data is provided by the crude oil market. Price data for crude oil dates back to the drilling of the first oil well in 1859 at Titusville, Pennsylvania. During the nineteenth century, crude oil was refined primarily into kerosene for use in lamps, with lubricants a secondary byproduct. After the development of the Model T and the ascendancy of the internal combustion engine, gasoline became the chief refined product of crude oil. As a result, the price patterns of crude oil before and after 1900 are strikingly different. Before 1900 and the widespread use of the automobile—a time period when crude oil was used primarily for lighting—crude oil prices behaved more like utility stocks than as a raw energy source. Hence although the data series begins in 1859, its underlying role in the economy changes after the turn of the century, and so do its cycles.

Although major data transitions are most pertinent to very long-term cycles, it should be stressed that structural changes in the nature of data are not strictly confined to the very long term. For example, soybean price cycles have changed dramatically in just the last 20 years in the aftermath of climatological and political influences. In the 1970s, El Niños caused major fish kills, drastically reducing anchovy supplies and sharply boosting demand for soybeans as a protein substitute. Once this usage shift occurred, it became permanent.

Another critical change that began around the same time was the strong growth trend in South American soybean production, which was initially spurred by President Carter's grain embargo against the Soviets. During the past 20 years, South American soybean production has more than doubled, while U.S. output has remained stagnant. The significance of this trend is that the growing season in South America is the mirror image of the U.S. season: Southern Hemisphere crops are planted in our fall and harvested in our spring. As a result of the aforementioned shifts in demand and the distribution of production, soybean price cycles have changed substantially during the past two decades.

The key point is that all the data used in a cycle analysis should be relatively homogeneous. If the nature of the data changes, then the cycles will also likely change.

Choose the Data Type.   The key principle is that the type of data chosen should reflect the actual price changes of the market and not anomalies introduced by contract rollovers or smoothing techniques. For futures traders it is best to use continuous futures, which eliminate the effects of contract rollovers. (See Chapters 12 and 19 for a detailed explanation of continuous futures, as well as the other types of price series discussed in this section.) It should be noted, however, that one consequence of using continuous futures is that it sometimes results in negative values for some historical prices. If this occurs, a constant sufficient to eliminate negative values should be added to the data (the value of the constant added will not affect the analysis) so as to allow log transformations of data, a common step in cyclical analysis, which is described later.

The least desirable data for cycle analysis—and, in fact, one that should never be used—is nearest futures, which can be subject to extreme distortions due to price gaps at contract rollovers. Cash series can sometimes be used for cycle analysis, providing interest rates are not extremely high. (Interest rates affect carrying costs and price levels, and will therefore cause larger differences between cash and futures prices when interest rates are high, as was the case in the late 1970s and early 1980s.) Perpetual futures are not as problematic as nearest futures, but insofar as this approach creates a series that never existed, it is definitely a less desirable alternative than continuous futures, which as explained in Chapter 12 parallels the market's actual price movements.

Choose the Length of the Data.   Most techniques for finding cycles have problems with too few or too many data points. Too few data points simply don't provide enough repetitions to evaluate most cycles. The basic principle is that a minimum of 10 repetitions of a cycle (but preferably 15) are required to statistically test the validity of that cycle. Hence, if one is looking for a 100-day cycle, it is necessary to have at least 1,000 points of daily data to adequately evaluate the cycle. The effective minimum is about 200 data points, regardless of the length of cycles being sought, since most mathematical algorithms will fail to work properly with fewer data points.

In cycle analysis, however, more is not necessarily better. Too many data points (for example, over 5,000) tend to obscure the phasing of the cycle, causing the statistical tests to eliminate some important cycles. The bottom line is that it is unnecessary to use more than about 2,000 data points and actually undesirable to use more than 5,000 (with the line between no benefit and an adverse impact lying somewhere in-between).

Based on experience, it is recommended that a first scan be done with 2,000 data points and a second scan with about 1,000 data points to improve the timing of the cycles. This guideline effectively means that one should limit the search for cycles in any data series to cycles with less than 100 data points, since cycles with longer periods will have fewer than 10 repetitions on the second scan. In order to find longer cycles, data compression is needed.

Choose the Data Compression.   Normally market data are summarized in time periods such as N-minute (for example, 5-, 15-, 30-, 60-, or 90-minute), daily, weekly, monthly, quarterly, or yearly intervals. In each case, all the ticks within each time period are compressed into one value, usually an average or closing value for the interval. In this sense, each time frame represents a level of data compression. Data are least compressed in five-minute intervals and most compressed in yearly intervals. All compression smoothes out changes shorter than the given interval, since it consolidates shorter-term changes into a single value.

In cycle analysis, it is important to choose the right level of compression. There are two basic guidelines in choosing the right compression: If a cycle occurs more than 250 times in the data, use a greater compression (for example, use daily data instead of hourly data). On the other hand, if a cycle occurs less than 15 times, use a smaller compression (for example, use daily data instead of weekly data). The following is a review of the attributes and drawbacks of the major types of compression:

1. Intraday Data. Although cycles can be found in intraday data, there are two problems with shorter-than-daily compressions. First, such compressions contain a great deal of random noise. (In general, compressions less than 30 minutes tend to have too much randomness.) Second, since as discussed earlier, it is best to limit data to about 2,000 points, most dominant cycles will be missed. Hourly or longer data, however, do work well on many series, and the analyst should experiment with such series. As a general principle, the greater the average daily volume, the more likely that the tick data will contain significant cycles.

2. Daily Data. Daily data are the best data for analyzing cycles. The practical minimum cycle that can be analyzed is five, since it is difficult to filter out the noise for fewer data points. The upper limit is equal to one-tenth of the data length, since as previously explained, longer cycles will contain too few occurrences to adequately test the cycle once found.

The only significant problem with using daily data is how to treat holidays. There are three basic options: (1) repeat the previous data point; (2) interpolate the missing data point; and (3) ignore the holiday. Although there is no single right answer, based on experience, our preference is to repeat the data point.

3. Weekly Data. After intraday data, weekly data are the most problematic of the data formats, because they unavoidably become out of step with any seasonal patterns. The problem arises from the fact that price changes in futures data tend to be highly affected by the seasons. In fact, many of the short- and intermediate-term cycles are seasonal. Since a month is not equal to four weeks, and a year is not actually 52 weeks long, weekly data will get out of step with seasonal changes. The main value of weekly data is that they allow one to identify cycles that are too long to be found using daily data. One plausible approach is to use a weekly analysis to find such longer cycles and then convert the cycles to days or months, which will avoid the problem of the cycle going out of phase with seasonal patterns in the data. Analogous to daily data, limit the search to cycles from a minimum of five weeks in length to a maximum equal to one-tenth of the data length.

4. Monthly Data. Along with daily data, monthly data is the best compression for cycle analysis. Monthly data have none of the problems due to randomness, since they are highly smoothed. They also perfectly harmonized with the seasonal tendencies of futures data. Monthly data can be used to find cycles ranging from 5 months to as long as 350 months. (Although this upper limit will exceed the previously stated maximum cycle length of one-tenth of the data length, this less restrictive condition is due to the smoothed nature of monthly data.)

5. Quarterly and Yearly Data. In general, for futures data these longer-term compressions don't provide enough data points for analysis. For some markets, however, cash series exist that are of sufficient duration to permit such an analysis. Usually, yearly data provide better results than quarterly data. For these longer compressions, the analyst is forced to use spliced data. For example, yearly wheat prices exist going back to 1259. A yearly wheat price series would splice together four separate series: British wheat prices prior to the existence of American data and three different American price series, reflecting changes in the prevailing most popular wheat variety (for example, hard red versus soft red). The accepted method for splicing is to have at least 10 years of overlapping data, verifying that there is a consistency of form between the two series, and then normalizing the historic data based on the most recent series.

Step 2: Visually Inspect the Data

With most cyclical analysis nowadays being done by computer, there has been a tendency to forget to look at a price chart before analyzing a new data series. This tendency is unfortunate because a visual examination serves a number of useful functions:

1. **Identify Bad Data Points.** Virtually all data contain errors. Large errors can play havoc with cycle analytic methods. Visual inspection of the data in chart form allows the analyst to quickly identify any obvious outliers, which can then be checked for accuracy.

2. **Identify Extreme Price Excursions.** The 1980 peaks in gold and silver and the October 19, 1987 crash in the stock market are examples of extraordinary price moves. Price moves such as these are so extreme that they can significantly distort the cycle analysis, making it difficult to find cycles that are present over the broad span of the data. The best approach in such situations is to make two separate analyses of the data: the first up to the anomalous movement, and the second beginning just after the price excursion. The resulting cycles found for each data set should be compared in terms of statistical tests of reliability and one set of cycles chosen.

3. **Evaluate the Trend.** A visual inspection of a chart makes it easy to spot whether there is a trend in the data and to evaluate the strength of any such trend. This knowledge is important in deciding whether the data need to be detrended and in choosing the most appropriate detrending methodology.

4. *Estimate the Average Length of Market Swings.* The eye has more insight into form than most cycle algorithms. If you can't see the swing with your eye, it probably isn't a dominant cycle. Cycles can be estimated by measuring the distance between troughs with a ruler or cycle finder.

Step 3: Transform Data into Log Form[2]

All of the mathematical routines for finding cycles assume a *static* data series, that is, a series with no trend. Therefore, to properly apply these mathematical procedures, it is necessary to detrend the data. Complete detrending of futures price data normally involves two separate steps: (1) transforming the series into log form, and (2) transforming smoothed log data into departures from a moving average. For reasons that will become evident, these steps cannot be performed consecutively. In this section, we detail the first of these detrending steps.

In a plot of an unadjusted price series, a given percentage price change will appear larger and larger as prices move higher, an undesirable quality that can lead to major distortions, particularly in series with large trends. When the data are transformed into logarithmic form (that is, when logs are taken of the data), however, equal percentage changes will show up as equal vertical movements on the chart.[3]

These data characteristics can be seen in Figure 16.6, which depicts the Dow Jones Industrial Index from 1900 through early 1995 in both raw data and log form. In the raw data plot, any given percentage price move results in a larger vertical movement as prices move higher (which is the reason for the asymptotic appearance of the raw data plot), whereas in the log chart, the vertical movement is the same at all price levels. For example, a 10 percent move in stocks is equal to 400 points at the 4,000 level, but only 10 points at the 100 level, whereas in the log plot, each 10 percent move in prices appears equal regardless of the arithmetic difference.

---

[2]For those who have forgotten their high school math, a log of a number is the value that the log base (typically 10 or the mathematical value $e = 2.718$) must be raised to yield that number. For example (assuming the log base is 10),

$$\text{If } y = \log x, \text{ then}$$
$$x = 10^y$$

The log of a number can be obtained by using any scientific calculator or from log tables.

[3]This can be demonstrated mathematically as follows:

If a number, x, is multiplied by a factor k, it will change by $(k - 1)x$:
Change in value of $x = kx - x = (k - 1)x$
Therefore, the larger x, the larger the change.
The log, however, will change by a constant, $\log(k)$, regardless of the value of x:
Change in value of $\log x = \log(kx) - \log(x) = \log(k) + \log(x) - \log(x) = \log(k)$

Figure 16.6
THE EFFECT OF A LOG TRANSFORMATION ON DATA

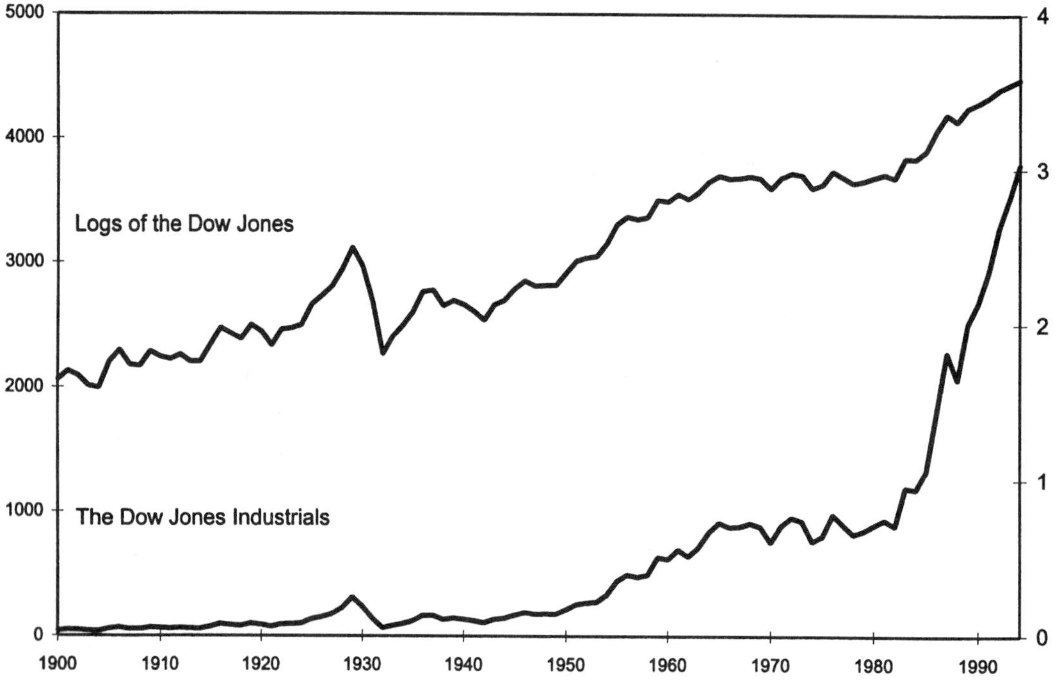

Logs should *always* be taken, *even if other detrending methods (such as departures from a moving average) are also used*. The reason for this is that logs normalize percentage price swings, which is a beneficial property even if data are detrended. If logs are not taken, a given percentage price swing at a high price level will appear larger than the same percentage swing at a lower level. Therefore, there will be a distortion in the relative amplitudes of different price swings. For example, if the stock index was detrended without taking logs, the oscillations around the resulting horizontal axis would grow progressively wider over time, as prices increased.

The discussion in this chapter assumes that cycle analysis is being applied to futures price series. For the sake of completeness, it should be noted that if cycle analysis is applied to economic series that have extremely strong trend components (for example, the consumer price index), a logarithmic transformation will be inadequate as the initial detrending step. These types of series should be detrended by one of two methods: rate of change or first differences.

The *rate of change* (ROC) is calculated by dividing the current data point by a previous data point. In monthly economic data, the previous data point is normally defined as the data point 12 months earlier. The 12-month ROC is effectively the year-to-year percentage change. *First differences* are calculated by subtracting the immediately preceding data point from each data point. First differences are one of the least used transformation techniques because this method tends to create ragged data series. Although logarithmic transformations can be combined with departures from a moving average (which is discussed later), they cannot be combined with rate of change or first difference detrending methods.

Step 4: Smooth the Data

Smoothing to Eliminate Data Errors.   This type of smoothing procedure is only necessary when the data may contain errors and can be skipped when one is using clean data. The best smoothing technique for dealing with data that may contain errors is the Tukey three-point smoothing method. This procedure involves converting the original data into a three-point moving median—the middle value of three consecutive data points is used and the higher and lower values discarded. Hence, if there are any outliers in the data, they will be eliminated. Of course, this method will remove valid outliers as well as erroneous ones. If possible, it is preferable to correct the data and avoid this technique entirely.

Smoothing to Remove Random Fluctuations.   As was discussed previously, a data series can be broken down into three basic components: trend, cycles, and random fluctuations. Therefore, to find cycles, it is necessary to remove the trend and random fluctuations from the data. If the original data series is completely detrended and random fluctuations are eliminated, the resulting series should be a cycle. Detrending has already been considered, albeit the final detrending step—departures from a moving average—is discussed later (again for reasons that will become apparent).

Smoothing to eliminate (or at least dampen) random fluctuations is achieved by taking a short-term centered moving average of the data. In contrast to the type of moving average typically used in technical analysis and trading systems, in which the moving average value for a given point is equal to the average of prices *ending* at that point (this type of moving average is detailed in Chapter 17), the moving average used in cycle analysis is *centered*, that is, it is the average of an equal number of points both before and after the given point. For example, an 11-day moving average is simply the average of the given day, previous 5 days, and succeeding 5 days. A centered moving average is always an odd number. Data points will be lost on either end of the original series, equal to half the length of the moving average rounded down. The following example shows the calculation of a three-day centered moving average:[4]

Original data	134.50	141.20	132.40	138.90
Log of data	2.1287	2.1498	2.1219	2.1427

Centered moving average calculation

$(2.1287 + 2.1498 + 2.1219)/3$ $(2.1498 + 2.1219 + 2.1427)/3$

Centered moving average value	2.1335	2.1381

When smoothing data, it is essential that the analyst choose a moving average shorter than the shortest cycle being sought. The reason for this is that if the moving average used for data smoothing is longer than any cycle being sought, it will *invert* the phase of the original cycle. This point will be explained and illustrated in the later discussion of departures from a moving average.

Step 5: Find Possible Cycles

Finding Cycles by Visual Inspection.   Perhaps the most basic way to find cycles is to count the time between similar highs and lows on a list of the data. This was the exact method researchers (e.g., Samuel Benner) used to find cycles in the nineteenth century. The major problem with this method is that it is extremely tedious. A much easier approach is to use a ruler to measure the distance between major highs and lows on a chart. One tool that greatly facilitates this procedure is the Erlich cycle finder, an accordion-like tool with nine points, which can be stretched so that the points line up under major highs or lows. One problem with all visual inspection methods is that they don't allow for the statistical testing of the cycles found. It is also difficult to combine different cycles without using the standard mathematical techniques.

The Periodogram.   The basic periodogram, which was first developed by Schuster in 1898, is one of the best known and most important tools in cycle research. The periodogram seeks to identify cycles by analyzing the data in tabular form. The available data would be chronologically segmented into columns, with the number of columns used equal to the length of the cycle being sought. A separate periodogram table would have to be constructed for

---

[4]The centered moving average calculation is shown being applied to the log of a hypothetical original data series as opposed to the data series itself because the logarithmic transformation precedes this step.

each cycle length sought. For example, if we had 135 years of annual data and wanted to check whether there was a 9-year cycle, we would segment the data into 9 columns and 15 rows. The first data point would be placed in row 1, column 1; the second data point in row 1, column 2; the ninth data point in row 1, column 9; the tenth data point in row 2, column 1. The table would be filled in this way until the 135th data point was placed in the 9th column of the 15th row. An average would then be derived for each column. If there were a nine-year cycle in the data, we would expect the column averages to show a significant peak in one column and a significant trough in another. (If there were no nine-year cycle near, the column averages would be relatively similar, excluding any trend effect in the data.)

Table 16.1 provides an example of a periodogram using logs of yearly corn prices from 1850 to 1989. (These log data were multiplied by 1,000 to avoid decimal numbers for clarity of exposition. Multiplying all the data by a constant will have no effect on a cycle analysis.) Figure 16.7 depicts a plot of the averages of all of the rows. If the data were completely detrended, the average of the rows would be relatively flat. The general uptrend in the row averages is due to the fact that taking logs only partially detrends the data.

Figure 16.8 shows the averages of the columns. The fact that there is a significant peak at column eight and a major trough at column two suggests that there may be a nine-year cycle in the data.[5] If, on the other hand, the plot of the column averages had been relatively flat, the possibility of a nine-year cycle could have been eliminated. For example, Figure 16.9 superimposes a plot of the column averages for an eight-column periodogram over the nine-column plot shown in Figure 16.8. As can be seen the variations in the eight-column averages are far more muted than their nine-column counterparts, meaning we can rule out the possibility of an eight-year cycle in the data.

The major advantage of the periodogram is that it provides an easy method for identifying all of the potential cycles in the data. The major disadvantage is that the procedure does not allow one to determine which of the possible cycles identified are statistically significant (the same major problem that existed with visual inspection). In other words, there is always some variation in the column averages. How can we judge whether the variation is statistically meaningful? In terms of the corn data example just provided, it is intuitively clear that the variation in the eight-column periodogram is not meaningful, but how do we know whether the variation in the nine-column periodogram is statistically

---

[5]The observant reader may well wonder whether the fact that a trough occurs near a lower-numbered column (2) and a peak near a higher-numbered column (8) isn't merely a consequence of the remaining trend in the data. Although the presence of trend will certainly cause a bias toward higher averages in the higher-numbered columns, the trend influence in this data is not nearly sufficient to explain the magnitude of variation present in the nine-column periodogram. This point will become apparent in a moment when we consider an eight-column periodogram.

Table 16.1
A PERIODOGRAM

Col/Row	1	2	3	4	5	6	7	8	9	Row Average
1	1,571	1,571	1,606	1,619	1,690	1,765	1,585	1,669	1,667	1,638.11
2	1,800	1,610	1,394	1,443	1,766	2,037	1,796	1,753	1,946	1,727.22
3	1,918	1,826	1,847	1,684	1,577	1,559	1,811	1,793	1,644	1,739.89
4	1,645	1,568	1,541	1,570	1,690	1,822	1,723	1,705	1,626	1,654.44
5	1,560	1,589	1,664	1,524	1,587	1,759	1,645	1,593	1,626	1,616.33
6	1,596	1,406	1,397	1,489	1,517	1,567	1,677	1,765	1,655	1,563.22
7	1,680	1,685	1,651	1,715	1,825	1,817	1,754	1,753	1,822	1,744.67
8	1,780	1,834	1,855	1,907	2,213	2,200	2,195	2,146	1,745	1,986.11
9	1,784	1,905	1,975	2,006	1,866	1,929	1,983	1,963	1,907	1,924.22
10	1,706	1,477	1,593	1,805	1,903	1,915	2,006	1,729	1,692	1,758.44
11	1,793	1,841	1,913	2,018	2,050	2,060	2,183	2,305	2,301	2,051.56
12	2,111	2,163	2,246	2,241	2,187	2,190	2,134	2,144	2,098	2,168.22
13	2,082	2,072	2,048	2,038	2,037	2,085	2,083	2,099	2,121	2,073.89
14	2,097	2,039	2,075	2,125	2,135	2,106	2,333	2,501	2,459	2,207.78
15	2,430	2,345	2,363	2,421	2,478	2,499	2,398	2,507	2,510	2,439.00
Column average	1,836.9	1,795.4	1,811.2	1,840.3	1,901.4	1,954.0	1,953.7	1,961.7	1,921.3	

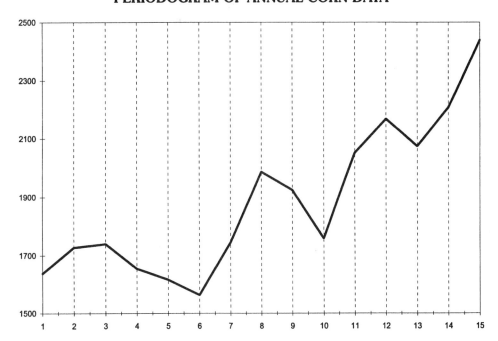

Figure 16.7
AVERAGES OF THE ROWS IN A NINE-COLUMN
PERIODOGRAM OF ANNUAL CORN DATA

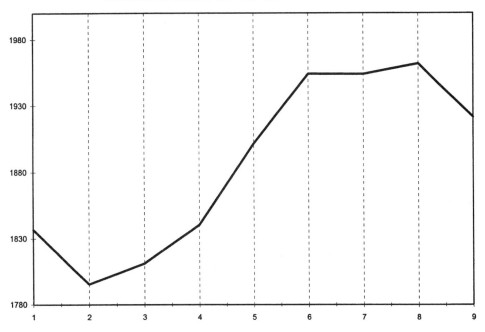

Figure 16.8
AVERAGES OF THE COLUMNS IN A NINE-COLUMN
PERIODOGRAM OF ANNUAL CORN DATA

Figure 16.9
COMPARISON OF COLUMN AVERAGES IN EIGHT-COLUMN AND
NINE-COLUMN PERIODOGRAMS

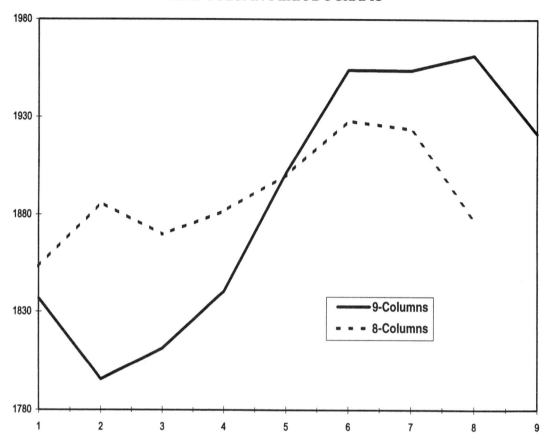

significant or still within the reasonable realm of a chance occurrence? Tests of the statistical reliability of cycles became possible with the development of harmonic analysis, which uses the periodogram as the basis for testing the statistical significance of cycles. We return to the subject of statistical testing later in this chapter.

The Fourier Series.   Nearly all mathematical algorithms in cycle analysis utilize some version of a Fourier series, an equation consisting of sines and cosines as terms. These trigonometric functions are ideally suited for fitting waves (or cycles). There are essentially two types of Fourier routines used in cycle analysis: *spectral analysis* and *harmonic analysis.* The theoretical difference between the two methods is that spectral analysis uses frequency, while harmonic analysis uses the period. (As discussed earlier, frequency and period are inversely related.) The more significant practical difference between the two approaches is that spectral analysis is best suited to *find* possible cycles, while harmonic analysis is best suited to *test* them.

Spectral Analysis.   Practically speaking, because of the magnitude of necessary computations, spectral analysis requires the use of a computer software program, such as the one provided by the Foundation for the Study of Cycles. Spectral analysis measures the strength of the cycle at each given frequency. As mentioned earlier, a minimum of 10 repetitions of a cycle (that is, frequency of 10) is needed to be able to test the statistical validity of a cycle. The maximum frequency would be equal to the number of data points divided by five, since as discussed previously, five is the practical minimum cycle length that can be measured. (Recall that frequency is equal to the number of data points divided by the length of the cycle.) Therefore, if we had a series of 1,000 points, we would perform the spectral analysis on a frequency range of 10 (10 percent of the data) to 200 (1,000 ÷ 5), which would be equivalent to a cycle length range of 100 to 5.

The output of a spectral analysis is a *power spectrum,* which indicates one value for each frequency in the frequency range analyzed. If a high value is indicated for the given frequency, it implies that the data have the form of a cycle wave of that frequency. If, however, a low value is indicated for the given frequency, it implies that the data approach a horizontal line for that frequency.

Figure 16.10 shows a power spectrum for 167 years of monthly corn data (2,000 data points). Since there are 2,000 points, we analyze a frequency range of 10 (the typical minimum) to 400 (the number of data points divided by 5). To facilitate the interpretation of the chart, the axis, which represents a frequency range of 10 to 400, has been converted to cycle length equivalents: a range of 5 (2,000 ÷ 400) to 200 (2,000 ÷ 10). Note that high values tend to cluster around given cycle lengths. The location of the peaks in each of these high-value clusters represent possible cycles. Three such relative peaks are identified as *possible* cycles in the chart. The word "possible" is intended to emphasize that statistical testing is required to determine whether the cycle lengths at which these peaks occur are genuine cycles. The results of such tests on the cycles identified by the power specrum illustrated in Figure 16.10 are detailed later in this chapter.

Although spectral analysis of partially detrended data (that is, log data) will correctly define the phase of the possible cycles found, the amplitude of these cycles will be distorted by the trend remaining in the data. This amplitude distortion will seriously bias any statistical tests of significance. Therefore, it is necessary to completely detrend the data before testing the cycles for statistical significance.

Figure 16.10
POWER SPECTRUM OF 2,000 DATA POINTS OF
MONTHLY CORN PRICES

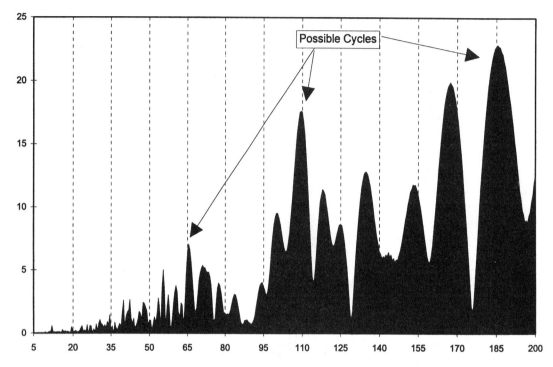

Step 6: Complete Detrending of Data by Using Departures from a Moving Average

Transforming the original data into log form, as was done in step 3, only partially detrended the data, and as just indicated, the existence of any remaining trend in the data can greatly bias tests of statistical reliability. Departures from a moving average are the best way to completely detrend data. Departures are calculated by subtracting a moving average of the data from the data. Since the moving average reflects the trend in the data, subtracting it from the data yields a detrended series (see Figure 16.11).

When a centered moving average is subtracted from the original data, the result is a new time series composed of the *departures,* or *residuals,* of the moving average. A separate departure series would be derived for each cycle being sought (that is, each potential cycle identified by the spectral analysis). The calculation of a departure series is illustrated employing the same data that was used previously to illustrate the calculation of a centered moving average:

Figure 16.11
DETRENDING DATA WITH DEPARTURES

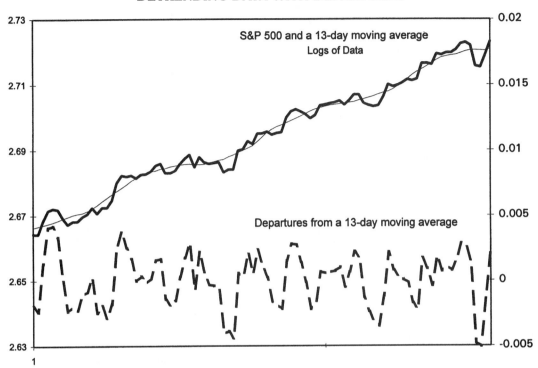

Original data	134.50	141.20	132.40	138.90
Log of data	2.1287	2.1498	2.1219	2.1427
Centered moving average value	2.1335	2.1381		
Departure (residual)	0.0163	−0.0162		

The departures-from-moving-average method must be used with care because of the effects of a moving average on periodic data. Figure 16.12 illustrates the effects of a moving average on data with a perfect 25-day cycle: a moving average smaller than the dominant period will diminish the amplitude of the cycle; a moving average of the same length will remove the cycle completely; a moving average larger than the dominant period will *reverse* the phase and reduce the amplitude of the cycle. (This latter characteristic is the reason why in the previous step of smoothing the data it was necessary to use a moving average shorter than the shortest cycle being sought.)

Since a moving average equal to the cycle length removes the cycle from the data, subtracting this moving average from the original series

Figure 16.12
THE EFFECTS OF MOVING AVERAGES ON
CYCLE AMPLITUDE AND PHASE

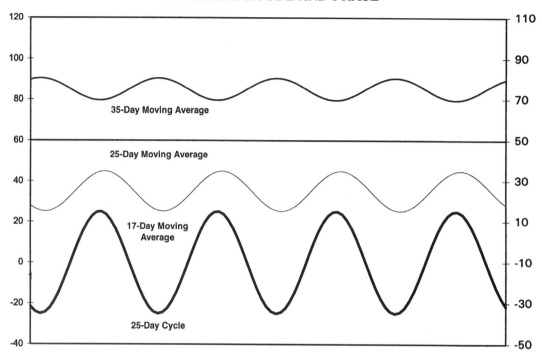

will leave only the cycle. If the moving average is significantly longer than the cycle being sought, however, it will *transform*, rather than remove, the original cycle. Consequently, subtracting such a moving average from the original series will not yield an accurate cycle. Therefore, it is essential to use a moving average approximately equal in length to the cycle being sought when using departures to detrend data. This is why it was necessary to first find the cycles (using spectral analysis) before completing the detrending process with this step. Because if the lengths of the potential cycles were not known, we would not know the moving average lengths to use in deriving the departure series.

Step 7: Test Cycles for Statistical Significance

The Need for Statistical Testing.   Once cycles are found and the data fully detrended by the preceding methods, the analyst must evaluate the cycles using various standard statistical techniques. The reason why this step is so important is that there is a tendency for the eye to believe a cycle is better than it actually is. Therefore, it is essential to use objective statistical tests. There are three important tests commonly used in cycle analysis: the Bartels test, the F-ratio, and the chi-square. Of the three, the Bartels test provides the most meaningful and reliable measure of the validity of the cycle.

General Considerations in Interpreting Statistical Test Results. Several important points should be made regarding the application and interpretation of these statistical tests:

1. All of the statistical tests used in cycle analysis will be biased by the presence of a trend, which will cause the statistical tests to understate the significance of cycles in the data. This is the reason why it was necessary to completely detrend the data before this step.
2. The level of significance yielded by these tests will depend on the number of cycle occurrences in the data. Therefore, all else being equal, shorter length cycles, which have more repetitions in the data, will tend to have better statistical results. Generally speaking, cycles that repeat fewer than 10 times in the data stream (that is, frequencies less than 10) will not tend to show high significance in statistical testing. The guidelines presented earlier, however, will avoid looking for cycle lengths corresponding to frequencies under 10.
3. The tests yield a statistical value, which corresponds to a probability. The larger the statistical value, the lower the probability—that is, the lower the probability that the cycle is due to chance, or equivalently, the higher the likelihood that the cycle is genuine. To avoid confusion, the analyst should note whether the cycle analysis software being used reports statistical test results as statistical values specific to that test or as probabilities. In the former case, the probabilities would be looked up in a statistical table for that test. At one time, it was more common for test results to be reported as statistical values due to the complexity of the probability routines. With the huge advances in processing power, however, computers can now quickly calculate the probabilities directly. Consequently, it is now more common for cycle analysis software to report probabilities, which are more directly interpretable, rather than the statistical values.
4. Generally speaking, cycles with probability scores greater than .05 (5%) are dismissed. (A probability of .05 means that there are only 5 chances in 100 that the cycle is due to randomness.) The best cycles have probabilities of .0001 (a probability of 1 out of 10,000 of being due to chance) or less.
5. One word of warning: Low probabilities on statistical tests only indicate that an apparent cycle is probably not due to chance; they do not

guarantee that the cycle is genuine. By chance, statistical tests will occasionally identify "significant" cycles even in totally random number series. Therefore, statistical tests should be viewed as a guide, not as an absolute truth to be followed without question.

The most important statistical test in cycle analysis, the Bartels test, requires that a harmonic analysis be done. This procedure is described below.

Harmonic Analysis.   Similar to spectral analysis, practically speaking, because of the magnitude of necessary computations, harmonic analysis requires the use of a computer software program. Harmonic analysis fits a trigonometric curve to the column averages of the periodogram. For example, Figure 16.13 superimposes the fitted curve derived using harmonic analysis over the plot of the column averages previously derived in the nine-column periodogram of annual corn prices and shown in Figure 16.8. Harmonic analysis can only be applied after the possible cycle lengths have been identified. That is why it was necessary to first run a spectral analysis to determine these cycle lengths. The fitted curve derived by harmonic analysis is used as the foundation for statistical tests of cycle reliability, most prominently the Bartels test, which is the most important statistical test in cycle analysis. Generally speaking, the better the fit between the harmonic curve and the plot of the periodogram column averages, the greater the statistical reliability.

Bartels Test.   The Bartels test measures the goodness of fit between the price series and the harmonic curve derived for the given cycle length being tested. The Bartels test fits the cycle curve to each occurrence of the cycle in the data, measuring the amplitude of each cycle occurrence to the amplitude expected by chance. The Bartels test measures both the amplitude (form) and phase (timing) of a cycle. The mathematical measure of cycle genuineness will be highest (that is, the probability that the cycle could be due to chance will be lowest) when there is stability in both amplitude and timing. The Bartels test was specifically designed to be used with serially correlated data (data in which the value of a data point is influenced by the value of previous data points). For this reason, the Bartels test is particularly well-suited for tests of price data, which are serially correlated.

F-Ratio.   In general, in statistics, the F-ratio is the ratio of two variances. The variance is the square of the standard deviation, which is a measure of data dispersion. A data series in which the points are widely dispersed will have a high standard deviation and variance. Conversely, a data series in which the points are closely clustered will have a low standard deviation and variance.

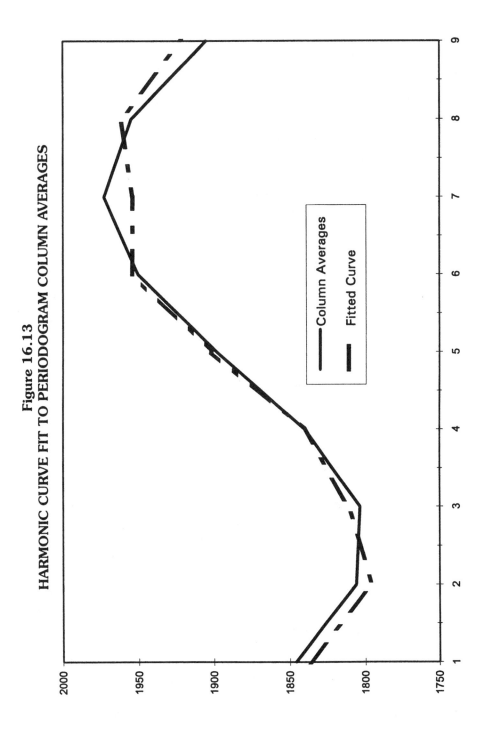

Figure 16.13

HARMONIC CURVE FIT TO PERIODOGRAM COLUMN AVERAGES

583

In cycle analysis, the F-ratio is the ratio of the variance of the column averages in the periodogram to the variance of the row averages of the periodogram. If a given length cycle does not exist in the data, the column averages of the periodogram would not show any pronounced variation (that is, there would be no salient column peaks or troughs) as, for example, was the case for the column averages in the eight-column periodogram of annual corn data (see Figure 16.9). Therefore, the variance of the column averages would not be expected to be significantly greater than the variance of the row averages, implying that the F-ratio would not be meaningfully greater than 1.0. If, on the other hand, the given cycle length was present in the data, the variance of the column averages would be significantly greater than the variance of the row averages (assuming, of course, that the data had been detrended), and the F-ratio would be substantially greater than 1.0. The higher the F-ratio, the smaller the probability that the cycle could be due to chance.

The F-ratio provides an excellent indication of whether a cycle is likely to be profitable in trading. If a cycle shows up as significant using the Bartels test and chi-square (discussed next), but has a low F-ratio (high F-ratio probability), as occasionally happens, its usefulness for trading would be suspect. The F-ratio is particularly sensitive to trend, because a trend in the data will dramatically increase the variance of the row averages in the periodogram, thereby reducing the F-ratio. Therefore, if data have not been fully detrended, the F-test might imply that the cycle is not valid, even when it is. As stated earlier, however, it is assumed that the data have been fully detrended before the cycle testing stage.

Chi-Square.   The chi-square test provides a measure of the reliability of a cycle's phase (timing), that is, whether a cycle has a tendency to make its highs and lows on time. In the chi-square test, each cycle phase (that is, row of the periodogram) is divided into seven equal sections (or bins), with the theoretical cycle peak corresponding to the center bin. The bin location of the actual peak in each cycle phase is then noted, and a count made of the number of times the cycle high occurred in each bin. If the cycle is consistent, there will be a tendency for a greater number of highs to fall in the center bin, and secondarily adjacent bins, with a much smaller number of highs resulting in bins removed from the center. Therefore, there will be a high variance (dispersion) in the number of highs in each bin. In contrast, if there were no cycle, the number of highs in each bin would tend to be evenly distributed, and the variance (dispersion) of the number of highs in each bin would be low. If the ratio of the variance of the number of highs in each bin is large relative to the variance of the highs that could be expected in a random distribution, the chi-square test would indicate that the cycle is significant, that is, that there is a low probability of the cycle being due to chance.

Summary. The chi-square test measures the reliability of a cycle's phase (timing); the F-ratio measures the reliability of a cycle's amplitude (form); and the Bartels test measures the reliability of both the phase and amplitude. Valid cycles should show up as significant on all three statistical tests, that is, have probabilities of less than .05 on each test.

In Table 16.2 we apply these statistical tests to the power spectrum derived for monthly corn data in Figure 16.10. Both the 65.7-and 109.5-month cycles show up as extremely significant on the Bartels test and F-test, and as passably significant on the chi-square. The 186.5 month cycle, however, only shows up as significant on the F-ratio. In fact, it doesn't even come close to being significant on the other two tests. Ironically, it was the 186.5 month cycle that was the most prominent on the power spectrum (see Figure 16.10). This is a perfect example of how the amplitude values in a power spectrum are badly distorted by the fact that the data are not fully detrended. (Recall that it was not possible to fully detrend the data *before* generating the power spectrum, because the final detrending step required knowledge of the possible cycle lengths, which in true Catch 22 form required the power spectrum.) The power spectrum, however, was very useful in pinpointing those cycle lengths to be detrended and tested.

Step 8: Combine and Project Cycles

Once the dominant cycles are found and validated by statistical testing, the next task is to project and plot these cycles into the future (a procedure that once again assumes the use of cycle analysis software). The typical plot will stack the dominant cycles below the historical price chart and extend the cycle repetition into the future. (See Figure 16.14 for an example.) Normally, this future projection is limited to less than one-third the length of the data series used to derive the cycles. For example, assuming the use of eight years (96 months) of daily data (slightly over 2,000 data points) in the cycle analysis, the cycle projection would extend no more than 32 months into the fu-

Table 16.2
RESULTS OF STATISTICAL TESTS
ON SPECTRAL PEAKS
(Probability Cycle Due to Chance)

Cycle Length	Bartels Test	Chi-Square	F-Ratio
65.7	.0006	.0514	.0001
109.5	.0019	.0421	.0011
186.5	.1001	.4485	.0006

Figure 16.14
CYCLE PROJECTIONS: INDIVIDUAL AND COMBINED

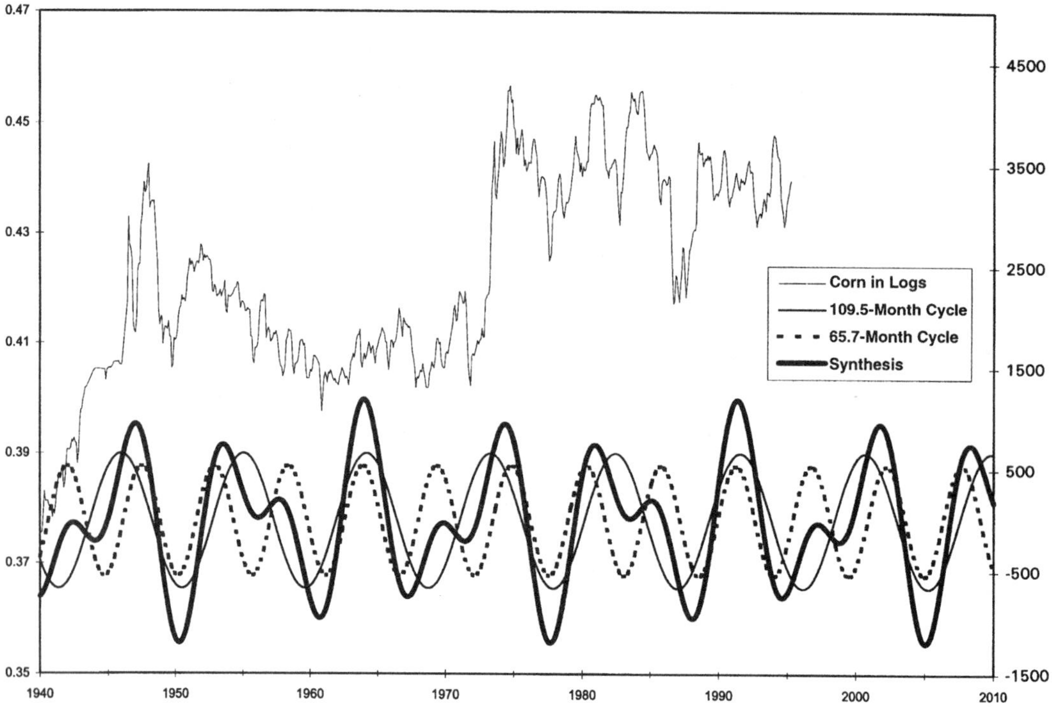

ture. The analyst should certainly perform a new analysis, incorporating new market data, well before the end point of this projection is reached.

There are two schools of thought in projecting cycles: (1) plot the cycles individually; and (2) mathematically combine the dominant cycles into a single synthesized curve. One problem with a cycle synthesis is that adding cycles can lead to amplitude distortions when two or more cycles top or bottom at approximately the same time. For example, a 20- and 30-day cycle will eventually top and bottom at the same time. This will periodically exaggerate the magnitude of the synthesized cycle and give the appearance of a major high and low when it is simply an artifact of the summation. The amplitude of any synthesis doesn't imply a larger amplitude than that of the largest dominant cycle, although combining cycles will give that impression. These problems are not meant to imply that cycles should never be combined, but rather that the trader needs to be aware of the potential pitfalls of this approach. As a generalization, cycle combinations are most useful as forecasts of future trends, while individual cycles are best suited as an aid in timing trades.

A word of caution is in order regarding cycle projections: Some traders make the mistake of viewing cycle projections as some sort of Holy Grail of trading that will provide a road map of future price activity, allowing the trader to anticipate market turning points. It should be stressed that cycle projections are probabilities, not certainties. There are two primary reasons why cycle forecasts could prove wrong:

1. Market price swings are not sinusoidal. The mathematical curves underlying cycle analysis assume that price moves are perfectly symmetrical, whereas actual price moves are asymmetrical: Price swings in the direction of the prevailing major trend will last longer than countertrend swings.
2. Cycles are not the only forces that move markets, and other price-influencing factors can often swamp the cycle effect.

Nevertheless, as long as the trader is cognizant of the limitations of cycle projections and does not rely on them as the sole source of trading decisions, they can provide a useful addition to the analytical toolkit. The incorporation of cycle projections as an input in making trading decisions is detailed in the next section.

USING CYCLES FOR TRADING

Using Cycles in the Real World

A common mistake made by many traders who attempt to use cycles as a trading tool is the assumption that market turning points will exactly conform to the cycles found. In the real world, there are two basic problems that will be encountered, *even with valid cycles that continue to work:*

1. ***Market Swings Are Not Symmetrical.*** Mathematical curves used to represent cycles are symmetrical; they implicitly assume that market upswings and downswings are of equal duration. In reality, however, market swings are usually *translated.* If upswings last longer than downswings, the cycle is termed to have a *right-hand translation;* if downswings tend to be longer, the cycle is termed to have a *left-hand translation* (see Figure 16.15).
2. ***Cycle Tops and Bottoms Can Be Early or Late.*** It is important to understand that the idealized cycles found by cycle analysis methods are actually a composite of historical occurrences of the cycle. This composite will typically consist of both early and late tops and bottoms. If even the cycles defined as the mathematically best fit to past data deviated from the timing of actual *past* tops and bottoms, there is certainly no reason to expect *future* market turning points to exactly match theoretical cycle phases.

Figure 16.15
CYCLE TRANSLATIONS

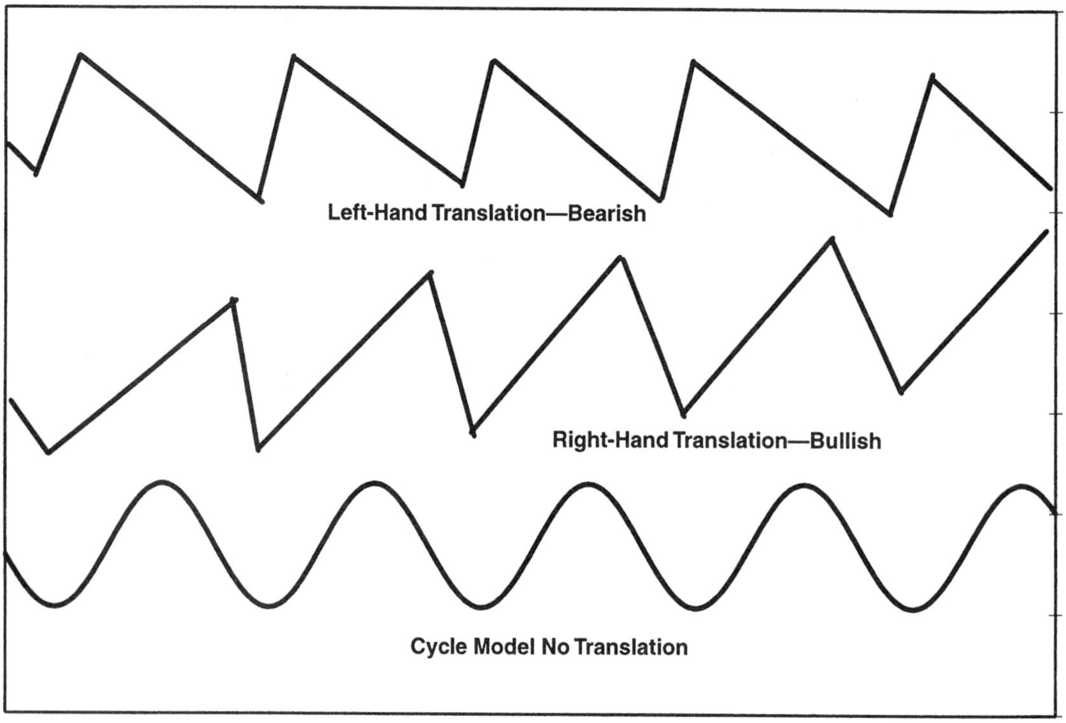

Left-Hand Translation—Bearish

Right-Hand Translation—Bullish

Cycle Model No Translation

These two problems can be dealt with by cycle translation adjustments and cycle windows. These techniques are explained in the following sections.

Cycle Translation Adjustments

Cycle translations are a function of two basic characteristics of market price movements:

1. Markets tend to rise more slowly than they decline. Another way of expressing the same idea is that bear markets tend to be shorter lived than bull markets. This behavioral pattern results in a tendency toward right-hand translation in long-term market price cycles (cycle lengths in line with the typical duration of a bull market/bear market phase).
2. For short-term to intermediate-term cycles, there will be a tendency for the cycle to be translated in the direction of the prevailing longer-

term trend (which typically will also be the direction of the longer-term cycle). In other words, within long-term downtrends, there will be a tendency for down phases in the cycle to last longer than up phases (left-hand translation), and within long-term uptrends, there will be a tendency for up phases in the cycle to last longer than down phases (right-hand translation).

The analyst should examine the location of the peaks in all past occurrences of that cycle for hints as to the probable translation in future repetitions of the cycle. Ideally, the analyst could construct a histogram of the frequency of past cycle peaks within each interval. For instance, in an 11-month cycle, such a histogram might show the number of peaks that occurred within each month of the cycle (with time being measured from the cycle low). If, for example, such an analysis showed a predominance of peaks in months seven, eight, and nine (instead of months five, six, seven, as would be expected if the cycle was symmetrical), all else being equal, the cycle projection would incorporate a right-hand translation. Such translation adjustments might be further refined by segmenting the analysis of past cycles by the prevailing direction of a given longer-term cycle. For example, one might construct separate histograms of past cycle peak locations based on the prevailing direction of a given longer-term cycle.

Cycle Windows

To allow for the fact that cycles will top and bottom earlier or later than the theoretical cycle turning points, it makes more sense to use a *cycle window* projection than a point projection. For most market data, the window should be equal to approximately 14 to 20 percent of the cycle length to either side of the theoretical cycle turning point. (Of course, if the cycle projection incorporates a translation adjustment, as was discussed in the previous section, the window would be centered at the adjusted projected turning point, as opposed to the theoretical turning point.) With shorter cycles there is little difference between these figures. For example, a 14 percent window of the 73-day cycle is 10 days on either side of the ideal turn, and the 20 percent window is 14 days. (Figure 16.16 shows a 73-day cycle with a 20 percent window.)

The trader would use windows to define time periods when a market turning point is deemed more likely. The precise use of such information would depend on the trader. Some examples of possible applications would be tightening stops on positions held counter to the projected turning point and using more sensitive trend-reversal indicators than might otherwise be employed.

Figure 16.16
CYCLE WINDOW

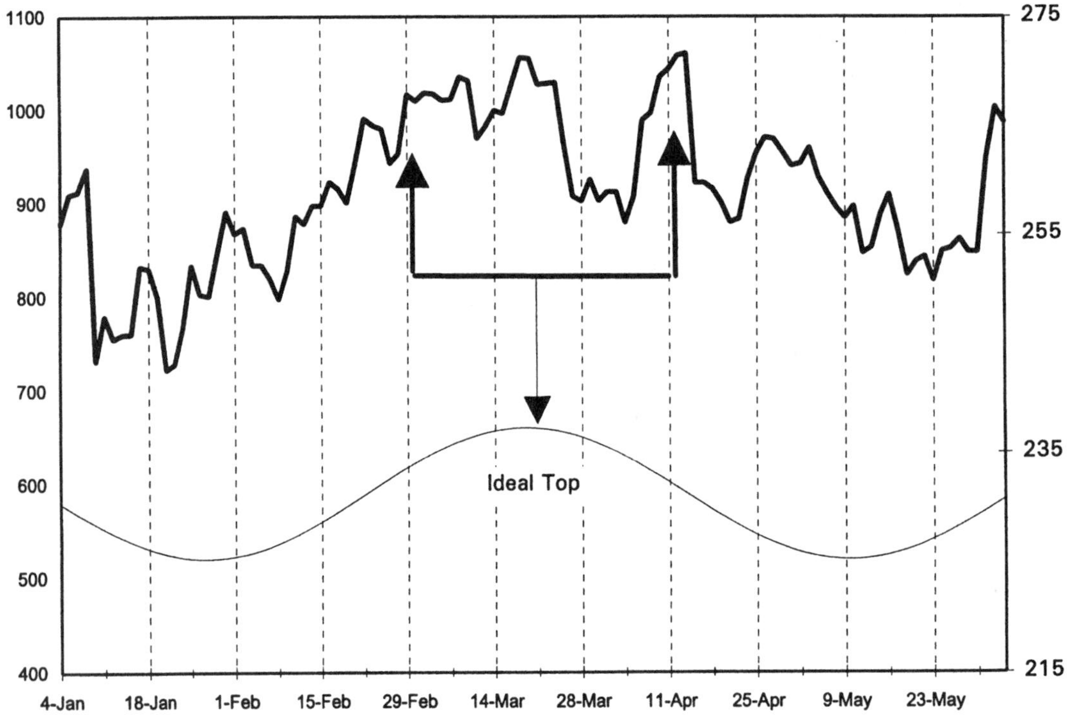

Note: This figure shows a 73-day cycle with a 20 percent window.

Trend Cycles and Timing Cycles

A trader is concerned with both market direction and timing. Cycle analysis can be a useful tool for both purposes. Conceptually, it is useful to define two types of cycles: a *trend cycle* and a *timing cycle*. The trend cycle is the cycle that would be used by the trader as a tool for forecasting the probable market *direction*. The timing cycle, as its name implies, would be used for *timing* trades. Ideally, the trader would use projected turning points (or windows) in the timing cycle to time trade entry in the direction of the trend cycle (see Figure 16.17).

The classification of any given cycle as a trend cycle or timing cycle is not inherently determined, but will depend on the individual trader. A cycle that may be well-suited as a trend cycle for one trader may be better suited as a timing cycle for a longer-term trader. Each trader, however, should choose one cycle for direction and a shorter cycle for timing. Generally speaking, the trader should choose a cycle length that is significantly longer than the intended duration of the trade as the trend cycle. For example, if the trader

Figure 16.17
TREND AND TIMING CYCLES IN THE S&P500

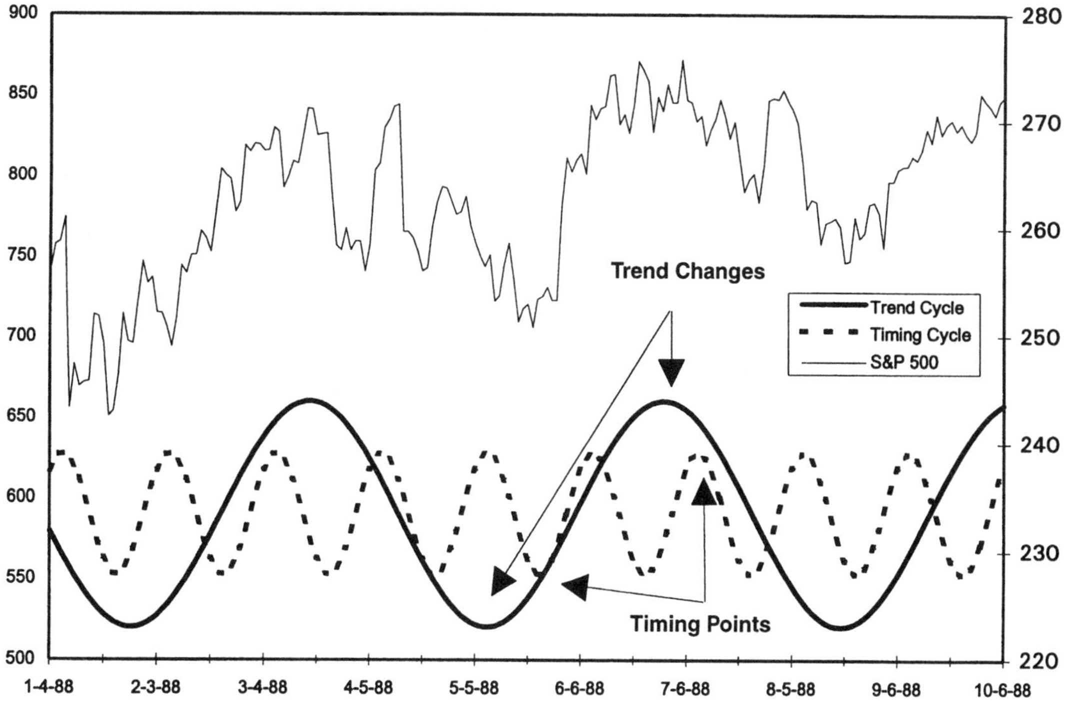

typically holds a position for about three months (assuming it is not liquidated for risk control reasons), he might choose a cycle length of about six months for the trend cycle. (Of course, the selection of a trend cycle will be limited to those cycles that showed up as significant in statistical testing.) The timing cycle, typically, would be equal to about one-half to one-third the length of the trend cycle (with the choice again restricted to statistically significant cycles).

CONCLUSION

Cycle analysis often appeals to people for the wrong reason. The desire to pick market tops and bottoms is part of human nature. Insofar as cycles can be used to project future turning points, they seem to offer a tool that can be used to fulfill this desire. The problem is that picking tops and bottoms is a trait of novice (and losing) traders, not winning traders. As has been discussed in this chapter, cycles are only one market force and can at times be swamped by other market influences. Moreover, even the most consistent cycles will deviate from their mathematical representations. Therefore, the rigid application of cycle projections in making trading decisions (to the exclusion of other methods and considerations) is a recipe for disaster. Inevitably, there will be some instances when projected cyclical lows are followed by a major downtrend and projected cyclical highs are followed by a major uptrend. The moral is that cycles can be very useful as one input in making trading decisions, but they should never be relied on as the sole source of such decisions.

Part Four

TRADING SYSTEMS AND PERFORMANCE MEASUREMENT

17 Technical Trading Systems: Structure and Design

There are only two types of trend-following systems: fast and slow.

—Jim Orcutt

WHAT THIS BOOK WILL AND WILL NOT TELL YOU ABOUT TRADING SYSTEMS

Be forewarned. If you are expecting to find the blueprint for a heretofore secret trading system that *consistently* makes 100 percent plus per year *in real life trading* with minimal risk, you'll have to look elsewhere. For one thing, I have not yet discovered such a "sure thing" money machine. But, in a sense, that is beside the point. For obvious reasons, this book will not offer detailed descriptions of the best trading systems I have designed—systems that at this writing are being used to manage about $70 million. Quite frankly, I have always been somewhat puzzled by advertisements for books or computer software promising to reveal the secrets of systems that make 100 percent, 200 percent, and more! Why are they selling such valuable information for $99, or even $2,999?

The primary goal of this chapter is to provide the reader with the background knowledge necessary to develop his or her own trading system. The discussion focuses on the following areas:

1. An overview of some basic trend-following systems
2. The key weaknesses of these systems
3. Guidelines for transforming "generic" systems into more powerful systems.
4. Counter-trend systems
5. Diversification as a means of improving performance

Chapter 18 provides additional examples of trading systems, using original systems as illustrations. The essential issues of appropriate data selection, system testing procedures, and performance measurement are discussed in Chapters 19–21.

THE BENEFITS OF A MECHANICAL TRADING SYSTEM

Is paper trading easier than real trading? Most speculators would answer yes, even though both tasks require an equivalent decision process. This difference is explained by a single factor: emotion. Overtrading, premature liquidation of good positions because of rumors, jumping the gun on market entry to get a better price, riding a losing position—these are but a few of the negative manifestations of emotion in actual trading. Perhaps the greatest value of a mechanical system is that it eliminates emotion from trading. In so doing, it allows the speculator to avoid many of the common errors that often impede trading performance. Furthermore, the removal of the implied need for constant decision making substantially reduces trading-related stress and anxiety.

Another benefit of a mechanical system is that it ensures a consistency of approach—that is, the trader follows all signals indicated by a common set of conditions. This is important, since even profitable trading strategies can lose money if applied selectively. To illustrate this point, consider the example of a market letter writer whose recommendations yield a net profit over the long run (after allowances for commissions and poor executions). Will his readers make money if they only implement trades in line with his recommendations? Not necessarily. Some subscribers will pick and choose trades, invariably missing some of the largest-profit trades. Others will stop following the recommendations after the advisor has a losing streak, and as a result may miss a string of profitable trades. The point is that a good trading strategy is not sufficient; success also depends upon consistency.

A third advantage of mechanical trading systems is that they normally provide the trader with a method for controlling risk. Money management is an essential ingredient of trading success. Without a plan for limiting losses, a single bad trade can lead to disaster. Any properly constructed mechanical system will either contain explicit stop-loss rules or specify conditions for reversing a position given a sufficient adverse price move. As a result, following signals generated by a mechanical trading system will normally prevent the possibility of huge losses on individual trades (except in extreme circumstances when one is unable to liquidate a position because the market is in the midst of a string of locked limit moves). Thus, the speculator using a mechanical system may end up losing money due to the cumulative effect of a number of negative trades, but at least his account will not be decimated by one or two bad trades.

Of course, money management does not necessarily require the use of a trading system. Risk control can also be achieved by initiating a good-till-canceled stop order whenever a new position is taken, or by predetermining the exit point upon entering a trade and sticking to that decision. However, many traders lack sufficient discipline and will be tempted to give the market just a little more time once too often.

THREE BASIC TYPES OF SYSTEMS

The number of categories used to classify trading systems is completely arbitrary. The following three-division classification is intended to emphasize a subjective interpretation of the key conceptual differences in possible trading approaches:

> **Trend-Following.** A trend-following system waits for a specified price move and then initiates a position in the same direction based on the implicit assumption that the trend will continue.
>
> **Counter-Trend.** A counter-trend system waits for a significant price move and then initiates a position in the opposite direction on the assumption that the market is due for a correction.
>
> **Pattern Recognition.** In a sense, all systems can be classified as pattern recognition systems. After all, the conditions that signal a trend or a counter-trend trade are a type of pattern (e.g., close beyond 20-day high–low). However, the implication here is that the chosen patterns are not based primarily on directional moves as is the case in trend-following and counter-trend systems. For example, a pattern-recognition system might generate signals on the basis of "spike days." In this case, the key consideration is the pattern itself (e.g., spike) rather than the extent of any preceding price move. Of course, this example is overly simplistic. In practice, the patterns used for determining trading signals will be more complex, and several patterns may be incorporated into a single system.
>
> Systems of this type may sometimes employ probability models in making trading decisions. In this case the researcher would try to identify patterns that appeared to act as precursors of price advances or declines in the past. An underlying assumption in this approach is that such past behavioral patterns can be used to estimate current probabilities for rising or declining markets given certain specified conditions. This chapter does not elaborate on this approach of trading system design since it lies beyond the scope of the overall discussion.

It should be emphasized that the division lines between the preceding categories are not always clear-cut. As modifications are incorporated, a system of one type may begin to more closely approximate the behavioral pattern of a different system category.

TREND-FOLLOWING SYSTEMS

By definition, trend-following systems never sell near the high or buy near the low, since a meaningful opposite price move is required to signal a trade. Thus, in using this type of system, the trader will always miss the first part of a price move and may surrender a significant portion of profits before an opposite signal is received (assuming the system is always in the market). There is a basic tradeoff involved in the choice of the sensitivity, or speed, of a trend-following system. A sensitive system, which responds quickly to signs of a trend reversal, will tend to maximize profits on valid signals, but it will also generate far more false signals. A nonsensitive, or slow, system will reflect the reverse set of characteristics.

Many traders become obsessed with trying to catch every market wiggle. Such a predilection leads them toward faster and faster trend-following systems. Although in some markets fast systems consistently outperform slow systems, in most markets the reverse is true, as the minimization of losing trades and commission costs in slow systems more than offsets the reduced profits in the good trades. This observation is only intended as a cautionary note against the natural tendency toward seeking out more sensitive systems. However, in all cases, the choice between fast and slow systems must be determined on the basis of empirical observation and the trader's subjective preferences.

There are a wide variety of possible approaches in constructing a trend-following system. In this chapter we focus on two of the most basic methods: moving average systems and breakout systems.

Moving Average Systems

The moving average for a given day is equal to the average of that day's closing price and the closing prices on the preceding $N - 1$ days, where N is equal to the number of days in the moving average. For example, in a 10-day moving average, the appropriate value for a given day would be the average of the 10 closing prices culminating with that day. The term *moving average* refers to the fact that the set of numbers being averaged is continuously moving through time.

Since the moving average is based upon past prices, in a rising market, the moving average will be below the price, while in a declining market, the moving average will be above the price. Thus, when a price trend reverses from up to down, prices must cross the moving average from above. Similarly, when the trend reverses from down to up, prices must cross the moving average from below. In the most basic type of moving average system, these crossover points are viewed as trade signals: a buy signal is indicated when prices cross the moving average from below; a sell signal is indicated when prices cross the moving average from above. The crossover should be determined based on closing prices. Table 17.1 illustrates the calculation of a moving average and indicates the trade signal points implied by this simple scheme.

Figure 17.1 illustrates the December 1993 T-bond contract and the corresponding 35-day moving average. The nonbordered buy and sell signals indicated on the chart are based upon the simple moving average system just described. (For now ignore the diamond-shaped signals; the meaning of these signals is explained later.) Note that although the system catches the major uptrend, it also generates many false signals. Of course, this problem can be mitigated by increasing the length of the moving average, but the tendency toward excessive false signals is a characteristic of the simple moving average system. The reason for this is that temporary, sharp price fluctuations, sufficient to trigger a signal, are commonplace events in futures markets.

One school of thought suggests that the problem with the simple moving average system is that it weights all days equally, whereas more recent days are more important and hence should be weighted more heavily. Many different weighting schemes have been proposed for constructing moving averages. Two of the most common weighting approaches are the *linearly weighted moving average* (LWMA) and the *exponentially weighted moving average* (EWMA).[1]

The LWMA assigns the oldest price in the moving average a weight of 1, the second oldest price a weight of 2, and so on. The weight of the most recent price would be equal to the number of days in the moving average. The LWMA is equal to the sum of the weighted prices divided by the sum of the weights. Or, stated as an equation:

$$
\text{LWMA} = \frac{\sum_{t=1}^{n} P_t \cdot t}{\sum_{t=1}^{n} t}
$$

where t = time indicator (oldest day = 1, 2nd oldest = 2, etc.)
  P_t = price at time t
  n = number of days in moving average

---

[1] The following two sources were used as references for the remainder of this section: (1) Perry Kaufman, *The New Commodity Trading Systems and Methods,* John Wiley & Sons, New York, 1987; (2) *Technical Analysis of Stocks and Commodities,* bonus issue 1995, sidebar, page 66.

Table 17.1
CALCULATING A MOVING AVERAGE

Day	Closing Price	10-Day Moving Average	Crossover Signal
1	80.50		
2	81.00		
3	81.90		
4	81.40		
5	83.10		
6	82.60		
7	82.20		
8	83.10		
9	84.40		
10	85.20	82.54	
11	84.60	82.95	
12	83.90	83.24	
13	84.40	83.49	
14	85.20	83.87	
15	86.10	84.17	
16	85.40	84.45	
17	84.10	84.64	Sell
18	83.50	84.68	
19	83.90	84.63	
20	83.10	84.42	
21	82.50	84.21	
22	81.90	84.01	
23	81.20	83.69	
24	81.60	83.33	
25	82.20	82.94	
26	82.80	82.68	Buy
27	83.40	82.61	
28	83.80	82.64	
29	83.90	82.64	
30	83.50	82.68	

For example, for a 10-day LWMA, the price of 10 days ago would be multiplied by 1, the price of 9 days ago by 2, and so on through the most recent price, which would be multiplied by 10. The sum of these weighted prices would then be divided by 55 (the sum of 1 through 10) to obtain the LWMA.

The EWMA is calculated as the sum of the current price multiplied by a *smoothing constant* between 0 and 1, denoted by the symbol a, and the previous day's EWMA multiplied by $1 - a$. Or, stated as an equation,

$$\text{EWMA}_t = aP_t + (1 - a)\,\text{EWMA}_{t-1}$$

Figure 17.1
DECEMBER 1993 T-BOND AND 35-DAY MOVING AVERAGE

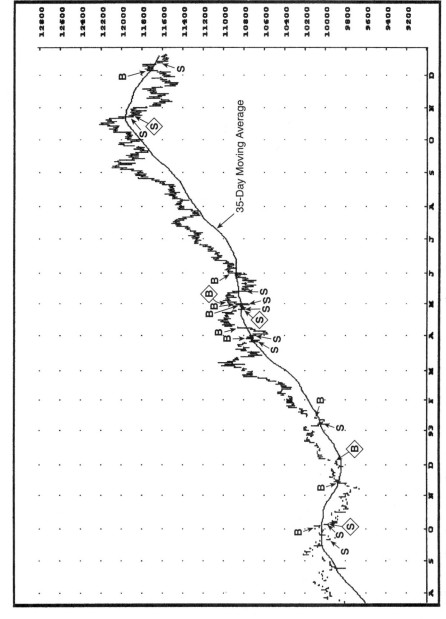

Notes: B = buy signal: prices cross moving average from below and close above line; S = sell signal: prices cross moving average from above and close below line; ⟨B⟩ = buy signal not eliminated by filter; ⟨S⟩ = sell signal not eliminated by filter.

Source: FutureSource; copyright © 1986–1995; all rights reserved.

This linked calculation wherein each day's value of the EWMA is based on the previous day's value means that *all* prior prices will have some weight, but the weight of each day drops exponentially the further back in time it is. The weight of any individual day would be:

$$a(1 - a)^k$$

where k = number of days prior to current day (for current day, $k = 0$ and term reduce to a). Since a is a value between 0 and 1, the weight of each given day drops sharply moving back in time. For example, if $a = 0.1$, yesterday's price would have a weight of 0.09, the price two days ago would have a weight of 0.081, the price 10 days ago would have a weight of 0.035, and the price 30 days ago would have a weight of 0.004.

An exponentially weighted moving average with a smoothing constant, a, corresponds roughly to a simple moving average of length n, where a and n are related by the following formula:

$$a = 2 / (n + 1)$$

or

$$n = (2 - a)/a$$

Thus, for example, an exponentially weighted moving average with a smoothing constant equal to 0.1 would correspond roughly to a 19-day simple moving average. As another example, a 40-day simple moving average would correspond roughly to an exponentially weighted moving average with a smoothing constant equal to 0.04878.

In my view, there is no strong empirical evidence to support the idea that linearly or exponentially weighted moving averages provide a substantive and consistent improvement over simple moving averages. Sometimes weighted moving averages will do better; sometimes simple moving averages will do better. The question of which method will yield better results will be entirely dependent on the markets and time periods selected, with no reason to assume that *past* relative superiority will be indicative of the probable *future* pattern. In short, experimentation with different weighted moving averages probably does not represent a particularly fruitful path for trying to improve the simple moving average system.

A far more meaningful improvement is provided by the crossover moving average approach. In this system, trade signals are based upon the interaction of two moving averages, as opposed to the interaction between a single moving average and price. The trading rules are very similar to those of the simple moving average system: a buy signal is generated when the shorter moving average crosses above the longer moving average; a sell signal is generated when the shorter moving average crosses below the longer moving average. (In a sense, the simple moving average system can be thought of as a special case of the crossover moving average system, in which the short-term moving average is equal to 1.) Since trade signals for the crossover system are based upon two smoothed series (as opposed to one smoothed series and price), the amount of false signals is substantially reduced. Figures 17.2, 17.3, and 17.4 compare trading signals indicated by a simple 12-day moving average system, a simple 48-day moving average system, and the crossover system based on these two averages. Generally speaking, the crossover moving average system is far superior to the simple moving average. (However, it should be noted that by including some of the trend-following-system modifications discussed below, even the simple moving average system can provide the core for a viable trading approach.) The weaknesses of the crossover moving average system and possible improvements are discussed later.

Breakout Systems

The basic concept underlying breakout systems is very simple: the ability of a market to move to a new high or low indicates the potential for a continued trend in the direction of the breakout. The following set of rules provides an example of a simple breakout system:

1. Cover short and go long if today's close exceeds the prior N-day high.
2. Cover long and go short if today's close is below the prior N-day low.

The value chosen for N will define the sensitivity of the system. If a short-duration period is used for comparison to the current price (e.g., $N = 7$), the system will indicate trend reversals fairly quickly, but will also generate many false signals. On the other hand, the choice of a longer-duration period (e.g., $N = 40$) will reduce false signals, but at the cost of slower entry.

A comparison of the trade signals generated by the preceding simple breakout system using $N = 7$ and $N = 40$ for soybean meal continuous futures is illustrated in Figure 17.5. The following observations, which are evidenced in Figure 17.5, are also valid as generalizations describing the tradeoffs between fast and slow breakout systems:

1. A fast system will provide an earlier signal of a major trend transition (e.g., June sell signal).
2. A fast system will generate far more false signals.

Figure 17.2
DECEMBER 1994 COTTON AND 12-DAY MOVING AVERAGE

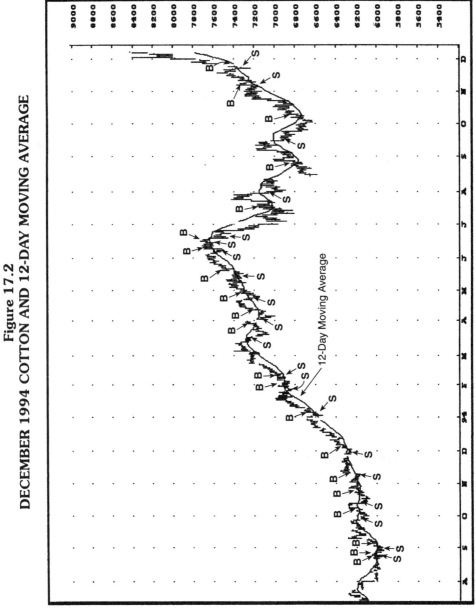

Figure 17.3
DECEMBER 1994 COTTON AND 48-DAY MOVING AVERAGE

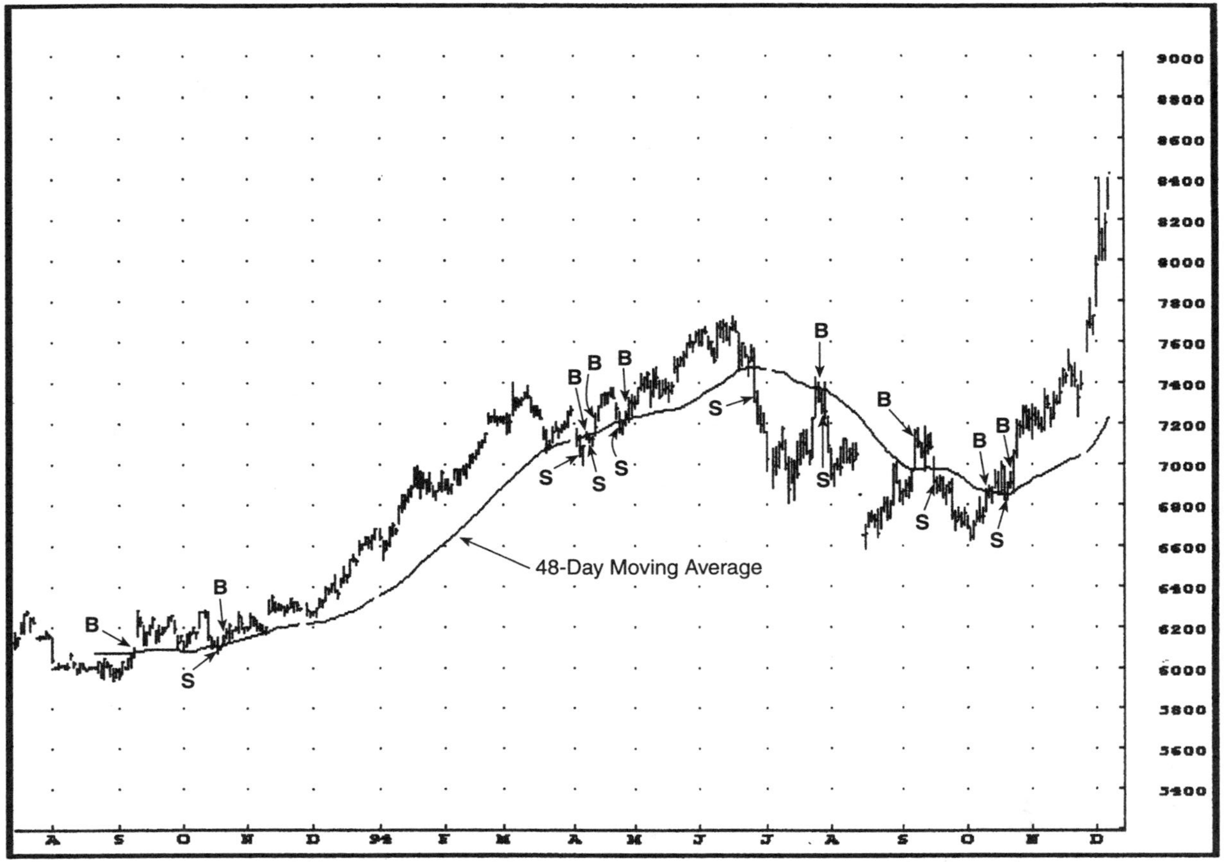

Notes: B = buy signal: prices cross moving average from below and close above line; S = sell signal: prices cross moving average from above and close below line.

Source: FutureSource; copyright © 1986–1995; all rights reserved.

605

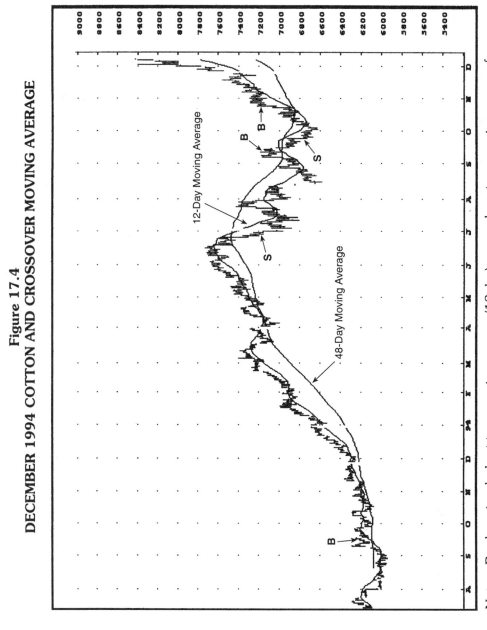

Figure 17.4
DECEMBER 1994 COTTON AND CROSSOVER MOVING AVERAGE

Notes: B = buy signal: short-term moving average (12-day) crosses long-term moving average from below; S = sell signal: short-term moving average crosses long-term moving average from above.

Source: FutureSource; copyright © 1986–1995; all rights reserved.

Figure 17.5
BREAKOUT SYSTEM SIGNALS, FAST VERSUS SLOW SYSTEMS:
SOYBEAN MEAL CONTINUOUS FUTURES

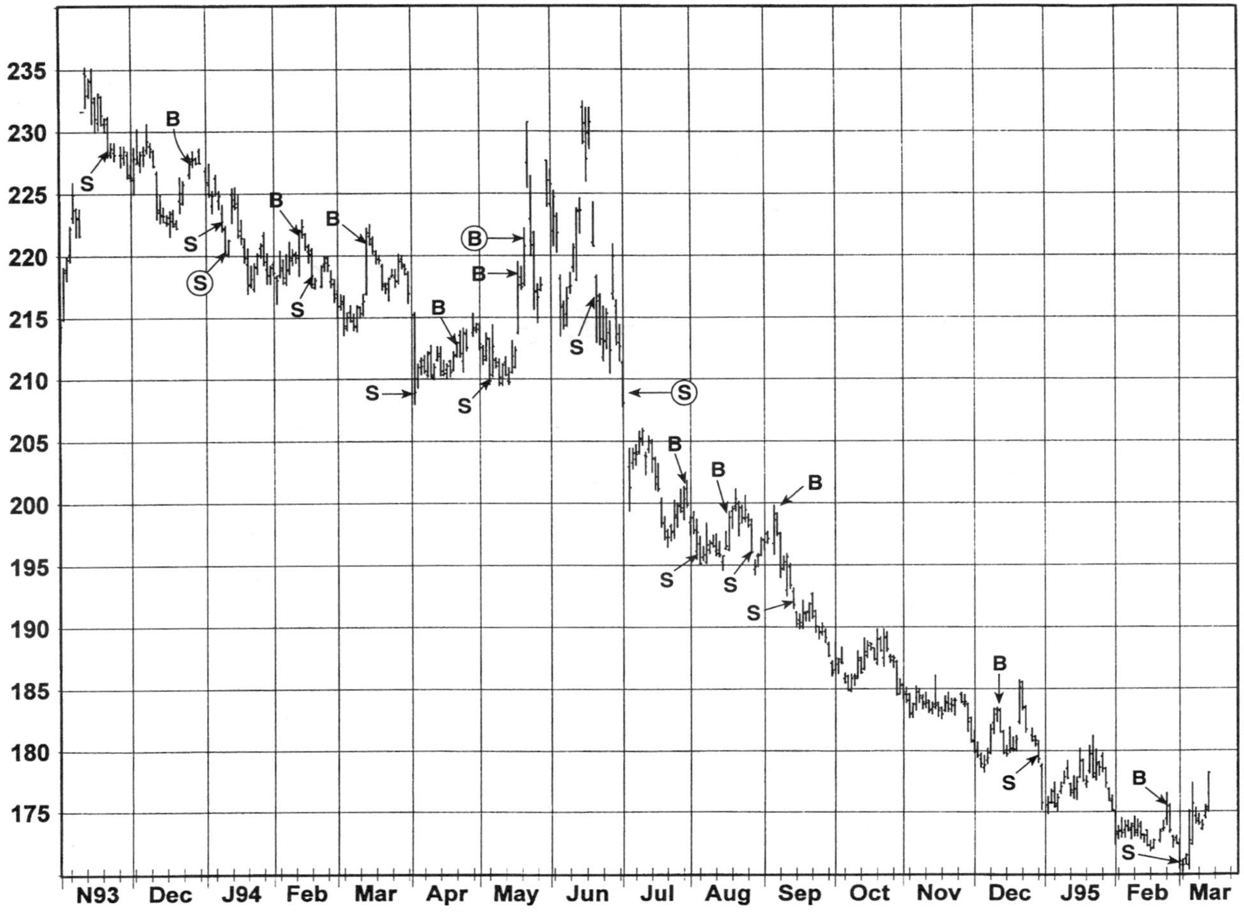

Notes: B, S = signals for N = 7; Ⓑ, Ⓢ = signals for N = 40.

607

3. The loss per trade in the slower system will be greater than the loss for the corresponding trade in the faster system. For example, the May buy signal for the $N = 40$ system results in a net loss of approximately $14. The corresponding buy signal for the $N = 7$ version results in a near break-even trade (excluding commissions). In some cases, a fast system might even realize a small profit on a minor trend, which results in a significant loss in a slower system.

As indicated by the preceding illustration, fast and slow systems will each work better under different circumstances. In the case of the chosen illustration, on balance, the slow system was much more successful. Of course, one could just as easily have chosen an example in which the reverse observation was true. However, empirical evidence suggests that, in most markets, slower systems tend to work better. In any case, the choice between a fast and slow system must be based on up-to-date empirical testing.

The previous example of a breakout system was based on the current day's close and prior period's high and low. It should be noted that these choices were arbitrary. Other alternative combinations might include current day's high or low versus prior period's high or low; current day's close versus prior period's high close and low close; and current day's high or low versus prior period's high close or low close. Although the choice of the condition that defines a breakout will affect the results, the differences between the variations just given (for the same value of N) will be largely random and not overwhelming. Thus, while each of these definitions might be tested, it probably makes more sense to focus research efforts on more meaningful modifications of the basic system.

The pitfalls of breakout-type systems are basically the same as those of moving average systems and are detailed in the following section.

TEN COMMON PROBLEMS WITH STANDARD TREND-FOLLOWING SYSTEMS

1. *Too Many Similar Systems.* Many different trend-following systems will generate similar signals. Thus it is not unusual for a number of trend-following systems to signal a trade during the same 1–5 day period. Since many speculators and futures funds base their decisions on basic trend-following systems, their common action can result in a flood of similar orders. Under such circumstances, traders using these systems may find their market and stop orders filled well beyond the intended price, if there is a paucity of offsetting orders.

2. ***Whipsaws.*** Trend-following systems will signal all major trends; the problem is that they will also generate many false signals. A major frustration experienced by traders using trend-following systems is that markets will frequently move far enough to trigger a signal and then reverse direction. This unpleasant event can even occur several times in succession; hence, the term *whipsaw*. For example, Figure 17.6 which indicates the trade signals generated by a breakout system (close beyond prior N-day high–low) for $N = 10$, provides a vivid illustration of the dark side of trend-following systems.

3. ***Failure to Exploit Major Price Moves.*** Basic trend-following systems always assume an equal-unit-size position. As a result, given an extended trend, the best such a system can do is to indicate a one-unit position in the direction of the trend. For example, in Figure 17.7 a breakout system with $N = 40$ would signal a long position in December 1993 and remain long throughout the entire uptrend. Although this is hardly unfavorable, profitability could be enhanced if the trend-following system were able to take advantage of such extended trends by generating signals indicating increases in the base position size.

4. ***Nonsensitive (Slow) Systems Can Surrender a Large Percentage of Profits.*** Although slow variations of trend-following systems may often work best, one disturbing feature of such systems is that they may sometimes surrender a large portion of open profits. For example, a breakout system with $N = 40$ catches a major portion of the late March–July price advance in unleaded gas, but then surrenders virtually the entire gain before an opposite signal is received (see Figure 17.8).

5. ***Cannot Make Money in Trading Range Markets.*** The best any trend-following system can do during a period of sideways price action is to break even—that is, generate no new trade signals. In most cases, however, trading range markets will be characterized by whipsaw losses. This is a particularly significant consideration since sideways price action represents the predominant state of most markets.

6. ***Temporary Large Losses.*** Even an excellent trend-following system may witness transitory periods of sharp equity retracement. Such events can be distressing to the trader who enjoys a profit cushion, but they can be disastrous to the trader who has just begun following the system's signals.

7. ***Extreme Volatility in Best-Performing Systems.*** In some cases, the trader may find that the most profitable trend-following systems are also subject to particularly sharp retracements, thereby implying an unacceptable level of risk.

Figure 17.6
BREAKOUT SIGNALS IN TRADING RANGE MARKET: GOLD CONTINUOUS FUTURES

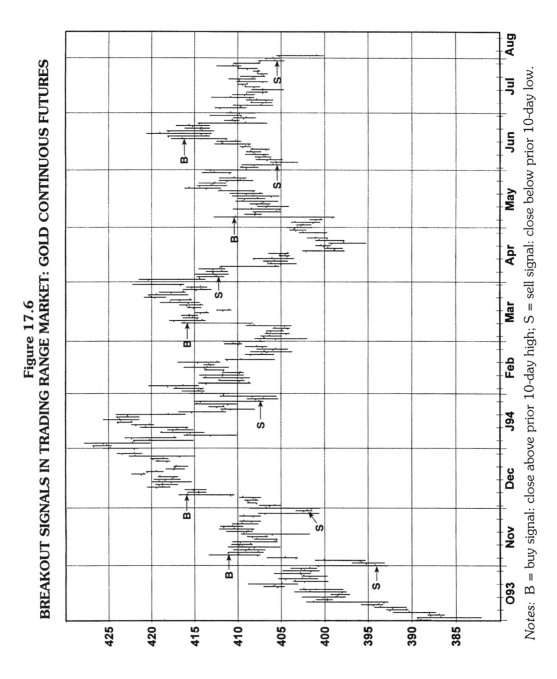

Notes: B = buy signal: close above prior 10-day high; S = sell signal: close below prior 10-day low.

Figure 17.7
FAILURE OF SYSTEM TO EXPLOIT MAJOR PRICE MOVE:
COPPER CONTINUOUS FUTURES

Note: B = buy signal: close above 40-day high.

611

Figure 17.8
SURRENDER OF PROFITS BY NONSENSITIVE SYSTEM:
UNLEADED GAS CONTINUOUS FUTURES

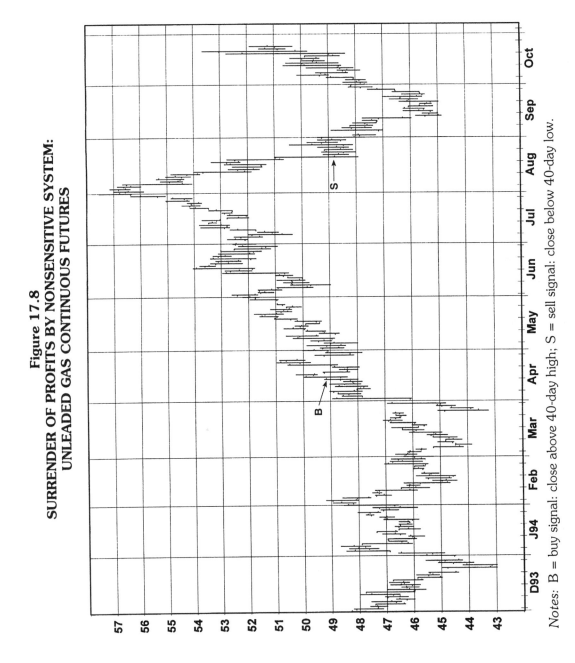

Notes: B = buy signal: close above 40-day high; S = sell signal: close below 40-day low.

8. ***System Works Well in Testing but Then Bombs.*** This is perhaps the most common tale of woe among traders who have used mechanical trading systems.

9. ***Parameter Shift.***[2] Frequently, the trader may perform an exhaustive search to find the best variation of a system based on past data (e.g., the optimum value of N in a breakout system) only to find that the same variation performs poorly (relative to other variations) in the ensuing period.

10. ***Slippage.*** Another common experience: the system generates profits on paper, but *simultaneously* loses money in actual trading. Slippage is discussed in Chapter 20.

POSSIBLE MODIFICATIONS FOR BASIC TREND-FOLLOWING SYSTEMS

Based upon the experience of the past two decades, even simple systems, such as moving average or breakout systems, will probably prove profitable if traded consistently over a broad range of markets for a sufficient length of time (e.g., 3–5 years or longer). However, the simplicity of these systems is a vice as well as a virtue. In essence, the rules of these systems are perhaps too simple to adequately account for the wide variety of possible market situations. Even if net profitable over the long run, simple trend-following systems will typically leave the trader exposed to periodic sharp losses. In fact, the natural proclivity of many, if not most, users of such systems to abandon the approach during a losing period will lead them to experience a net loss even if the system proves profitable over the longer run.

In this section, we discuss some of the primary avenues for modifying basic trend-following systems, in an effort to improve their performance. For simplicity of exposition, we base most illustrations on the previously described simple breakout system. However, the same types of modifications could also be applied to other basic trend-following systems (e.g., crossover moving average).

Confirmation Conditions

An important modification that can be made to a basic trend-following system is the requirement for additional conditions to be met before a signal is accepted. If these conditions are not realized before an opposite direction signal is received, no trade occurs. Confirmation rules are designed specifically to

---

[2]The meaning of the term *parameter* as it is used in trading systems is detailed in Chapter 20.

deal with the nemesis of trend-following systems: false signals. The idea is that valid signals will fulfill the confirmation conditions, while false signals generally will not. The range of possible choices for confirmation conditions is limited only by the imagination of the system designer. Below, we provide three examples:

1. **Penetration.** A trade signal is only accepted if the market moves a specified minimum amount beyond a given reference level (e.g., signal price). Penetration could be measured in either nominal or percentage terms. Figure 17.9 compares the trade signals generated by a standard breakout system, with $N = 12$ and the corresponding system with a confirmation rule requiring a close that penetrates the prior N-day high (low) by at least 2 percent. Note that in this example, although the confirmation rule results in moderately worse entry levels for valid signals, it eliminates all seven false signals. (The buy signals following the nonconfirmed sell signals are also eliminated, since the system is already long at that point. Similarly, the sell signals following the nonconfirmed buy signals are also eliminated, since the system is already short at that point.)

2. **Time Delay.** In this approach, a specified time delay is required, at the end of which the signal is reevaluated. For example, a confirmation rule may specify that a trade signal is taken if the market closes beyond the signal price (higher for a buy, lower for a sell) at any time six or more days beyond the original signal date. Figure 17.10 compares the signals generated by a basic breakout system with $N = 12$, and the corresponding system with the six-day time delay confirmation condition. In this case, the confirmation rule eliminates six of the seven false signals.

3. **Pattern.** This is a catch-all term for a wide variety of confirmation rules. In this approach, a specified pattern is required to validate the basic system signal. For example, the confirmation rule might require three subsequent thrust days beyond the signal price.[3] Figure 17.11 compares the signals generated by the basic breakout system, with $N = 12$ and the signals based upon the corresponding system using the three-thrust-day validation condition. The thrust day count at confirmed signals is indicated by the numbers on the chart. Here too, the confirmation rule eliminates all seven false signals.

The design of trading systems is a matter of constant tradeoffs. The advantage of confirmation conditions is that they will greatly reduce whipsaw

---

[3] A thrust day, which was originally defined in Chapter 6, is a day with a close above (below) the previous day's high (low).

Figure 17.9
PENETRATION AS CONFIRMATION CONDITION: COCOA CONTINUOUS FUTURES

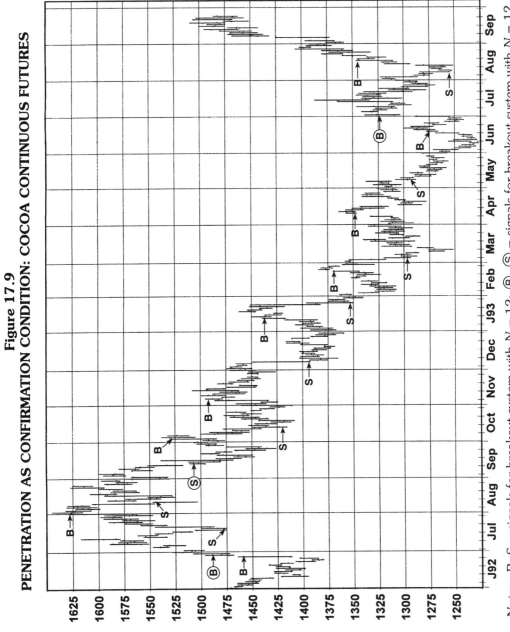

Notes: B, S = signals for breakout system with $N = 12$; ⓑ, ⓢ = signals for breakout system with $N = 12$ and 2% closing penetration confirmation.

Figure 17.10
TIME DELAY AS A CONFIRMATION CONDITION: COCOA CONTINUOUS FUTURES

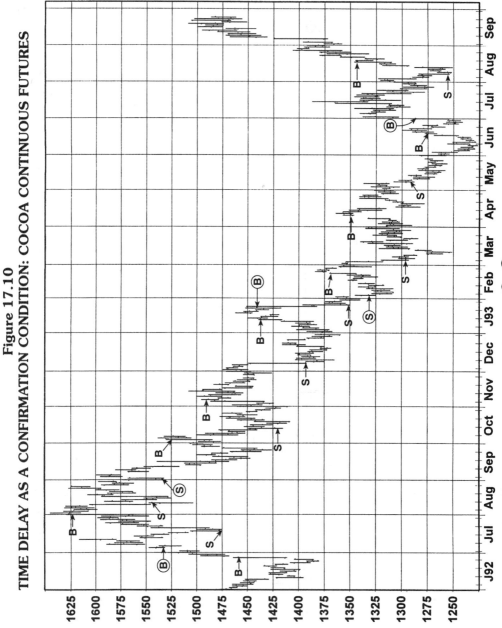

Notes: B, S = signals for breakout system with $N = 12$; Ⓑ, Ⓢ = signals for breakout system with $N = 12$ and 6-day time delay confirmation.

Figure 17.11
EXAMPLE OF A PATTERN CONFIRMATION CONDITION: COCOA CONTINUOUS FUTURES

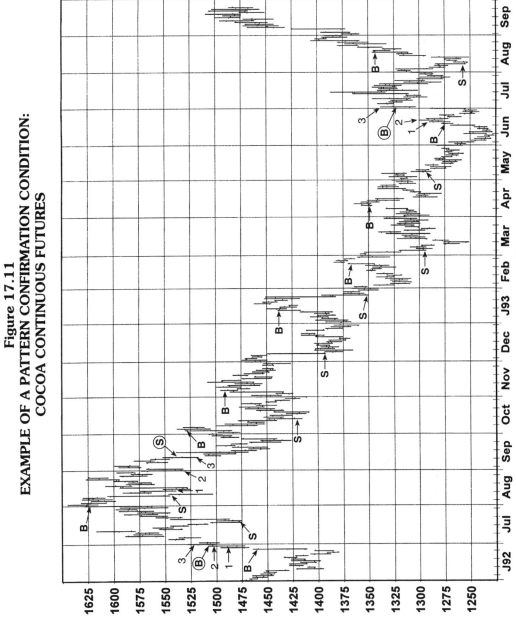

Notes: B, S = signals for breakout system with $N = 12$; Ⓑ, Ⓢ = signals for breakout system with $N = 12$ and 3 thrust day confirmation.

losses. However, it should be noted that confirmation rules also have an undesirable side effect—they will delay entry on valid signals, thereby reducing gains on profitable trades. For example, in Figures 17.9–17.11, note that the confirmation rules result in worse entry prices for the trades corresponding to the June 1992 buy signal, August 1992 sell signal, and the June 1993 buy signals in the basic system. The confirmation condition will be beneficial as long as reduced profits due to delayed entry are more than offset by avoided losses. A system that includes confirmation conditions will not always outperform its basic system counterpart, but if properly designed, it will perform significantly better over the long run.

Filter

The purpose of a filter is to eliminate those trades that are deemed to have a lower probability of success. For example, the technical system might be combined with a fundamental model that classifies the market as bullish, bearish, or neutral. Technical signals would then only be accepted if they were in agreement with the fundamental model's market designation. In cases of disagreement, a neutral position would be indicated. In most cases, however, the filter condition(s) will also be technical in nature. For example, if one could derive a set of rules that had some accuracy in defining the presence of a trading range market, signals that were received when a trading range market was indicated would not be accepted. In essence, in developing a filter, the system designer is trying to find a common denominator applicable to the majority of losing trades.

We will use the frequently unsatisfactory simple moving average system to provide a specific example of a filter condition. The nonbordered signals in Figure 17.1 illustrate the typical tendency of the simple moving average system to generate many false signals—even in trending markets. These whipsaw trades can be substantially reduced by applying the filter rule that only signals consistent with the trend of the moving average are accepted. For example, prices crossing the moving average from below and closing above the moving average would only be accepted as a buy signal if the moving average was up relative to the previous day's level. This filter condition makes intuitive sense because it adheres to the basic technical concept of trading with the major trend.

Two points should be clarified regarding the application of this rule:

1. A rejected signal could be activated at a later point, if the moving average subsequently turned in the direction of the signal *before* an opposite direction crossover of the price and moving average.

2. Signals that occur after rejected signals are ignored because the net position is already consistent with the implied trade. This is true because the simple moving average system is always in the market.

The diamond-shaped signals in Figure 17.1 indicate the trades that would have been accepted (either at the time of the crossover or after a delay) if the filter rule just described were applied. As can be seen, the rule substantially reduces the number of false signals. Although, in some cases, the application of the filter condition results in adverse trade entry delays—as, for example, the November sell signal—on balance, the benefits clearly outweigh the disadvantages. Of course, a single illustration doesn't prove anything. However, the implication of Figure 17.1 does have a more general applicability. Most empirical testing would reveal that, more often than not, the inclusion of the type of filter rule depicted in Figure 17.1 will tend to improve performance.

In fact, a crossover between price and the moving average that is opposite to the direction of the moving average trend can often provide a good signal to *add to rather than reverse* the original position. For example, in Figure 17.1, the January, March, and May penetrations of the moving average could be viewed as buy rather than sell signals because the moving average trend was still up in those instances. The rationale behind this interpretation is that in a trending market, reactions often carry to the vicinity of a moving average before prices resume their longer-term trend. Thus, in effect, such nonaccepted signals could actually provide the basis for a method of pyramiding.

It should be noted that, in a sense, the confirmation conditions detailed in the previous section represent one type of filter, insofar as signals that fulfill a subsequent set of conditions are accepted, while those that do not are eliminated. However, the distinction here is that a filter implies a set of screening rules applied *at the time* the base system signal is received. In other words, the sorting procedure occurs without any dependency on subsequent developments (although, to be perfectly accurate, subsequent developments could still permit a delayed acceptance of a rejected signal). Consequently, as we have defined the terms, a system can include both a filter and a confirmation rule. In such a system, only signals that were accepted based on the filter definition and subsequently validated by the confirmation rule(s) would actually result in trades.

Market Characteristic Adjustments

One criticism of simple trend-following systems is that they treat all markets alike. For example, in a breakout system, with $N = 20$, both highly volatile and very quiet markets will require the same conditions for a buy signal—a

20-day high. Market characteristic adjustments seek to compensate for the fact that the optimum variation of a system will depend on market conditions. For example, in the case of a breakout system, instead of using a constant value for N, the relevant value for N might be contingent on the volatility classification of the market. As a specific illustration, the average 2-day price range during the past 50-day period might be used to place the market into one of five volatility classifications.[4] The value of N used to generate signals on any given day would then depend on the prevailing volatility classification.

Volatility appears to be the most logical choice for classifying market states, although other criteria could also be tested (e.g., fundamentally based conditions, average volume level, etc.). In essence, this type of modification seeks to transform a basic trend-following system from a static to a dynamic trading method.

Differentiation between Buy and Sell Signals

Basic trend-following systems typically assume analogous conditions for buy and sell signals (e.g., buy on close above 20-day high, sell on close below 20-day low). However, there is no reason to make this assumption automatically. It can be argued that bull and bear markets behave differently. For example, a survey of a broad spectrum of historical price charts would reveal that price breaks from major tops tend to be more rapid than price rallies from major bottoms.[5] This observation suggests a rationale for using more sensitive conditions to generate sell signals than those used to generate buy signals. However, the system designer using such an approach should be particularly sensitive to the danger of overfitting the system—a pitfall discussed in detail in Chapter 20.

---

[4]A two-day price range is used as a volatility measure instead of a one-day range since the latter can easily yield a distorted image of true market volatility. For example, on a limit day, the one-day range would equal zero, in extreme contrast to the fact that limit days reflect highly volatile conditions. Of course, many other measures could be used to define volatility.

[5]The reverse statement would apply to short-term interest rate markets, which are quoted in terms of the instrument price, a value that varies inversely with the interest rate level. In the interest rate markets, interest rates rather than instrument prices are analogous to prices in standard markets. For example, there is no upper limit to a commodity's price or interest rates, but the downside for both of these items is theoretically limited. As another example, commodity markets tend to be more volatile when prices are high, while short-term interest rate markets tend to be more volatile when interest rates are high (instrument prices are low). The situation for long-term (i.e., bond) markets is ambiguous since although interest rates can fall no lower than zero, the pricing mathematics underlying these instruments result in an accelerated price advance (for equal interest rate changes) as interest rates fall.

Pyramiding

One inherent weakness in basic trend-following systems is that they automatically assume a constant unit position size under all conditions. It would seem desirable to allow for the possibility of larger position sizes in the case of major trends, which are almost entirely responsible for the success of any trend-following system. One reasonable approach for adding units to a base position in a major trend is to wait for a specified reaction and then to initiate the additional unit on evidence of a resumption of the trend. Such an approach seeks to optimize the timing of pyramid units, as well as to provide exit rules that reasonably limit the potential losses that could be incurred by such added positions. An example of this type of approach was detailed in Chapter 8. Another example of a possible pyramid strategy would be provided by the following set of rules:

Buy Case

1. A reaction is defined when the net position is long and the market closes below the prior 10-day low.

2. Once a reaction is defined, an additional long position is initiated on any subsequent 10-day high if the following conditions are met:

   a. The pyramid signal price is above the price at which the most recent long position was initiated.

   b. The net position size is less than three units. (This condition implies that there is a limit of two pyramid units.)

Sell Case

1. A reaction is defined when the net position is short and the market closes above the prior 10-day high.

2. Once a reaction is defined, an additional short position is initiated on any subsequent 10-day low if the following conditions are met:

   a. The pyramid signal price is below the price at which the most recent short position was initiated.

   b. The net position size is less than three units. (This condition implies that there is a limit of two pyramid units.)

Figure 17.12 illustrates the addition of this pyramid plan to a breakout system with $N = 40$ applied to the September 1992 coffee contract.

Risk control becomes especially important if a pyramiding component is added to a system. Generally speaking, it is usually advisable to use a more

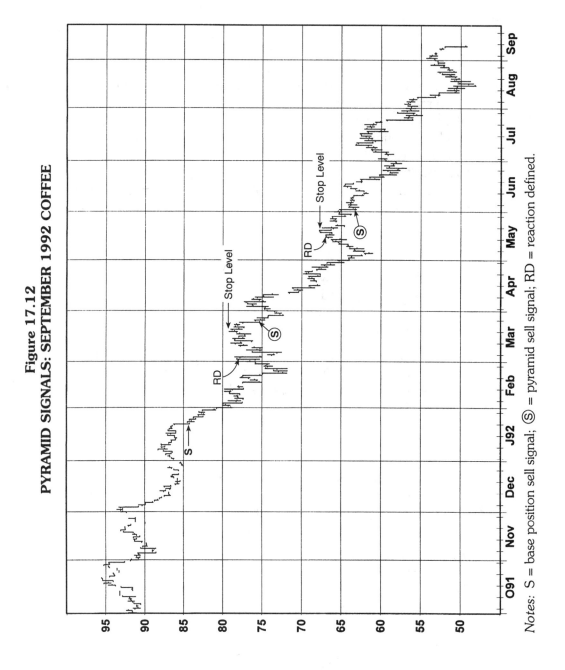

Figure 17.12
PYRAMID SIGNALS: SEPTEMBER 1992 COFFEE

Notes: S = base position sell signal; Ⓢ = pyramid sell signal; RD = reaction defined.

sensitive condition for liquidating a pyramid position than the condition required to generate an opposite signal. The following is one example of a set of stop rules that might be employed in a system that uses pyramiding. Liquidate all pyramid positions whenever either condition is fulfilled:

1. An opposite trend-following signal is received.
2. Market closes above (below) the high (low) price since the most recently defined reaction that was followed by a pyramid sell (buy). Figure 17.12 illustrates the stop levels implied by this rule in the case of September 1992 coffee.

Trade Exit

The existence of a trade exit rule in a system would permit the liquidation of a position prior to receiving an opposite trend-following signal. Such a rule would serve to limit losses on losing trades as well as limit the amount of open profits surrendered on winning trades. Although these are highly desirable goals, the tradeoff implied by using a trade exit rule is relatively severe. If a trade exit rule is used, rules must be specified for reentering the position; otherwise, the system will be vulnerable to missing major trends.

The danger in using a trade exit rule is that it may result in the premature liquidation of a good trade. Although the reentry rule will serve as a backstop, the combination of an activated trade exit rule and a subsequent reentry is a whipsaw loss. Thus, it will not be at all uncommon for the addition of a trade exit rule (and implied reentry rule) to have a negative impact on performance. Nevertheless, although it is not easy, for some systems, it will be possible to structure trade exit rules that improve performance on balance. (In terms of return, and usually in terms of return/risk measures as well, if a trade exit rule helps performance, the use of the trade exit rule as a reversal signal—as opposed to just a liquidation signal—will help performance even more.) Trade exit rules can also be made dynamic. For example, the trade exit condition can be made increasingly sensitive as a price move becomes more extended in either magnitude or duration.

COUNTER-TREND SYSTEMS

General Considerations Regarding Counter-Trend Systems

Counter-trend systems often appeal to many traders because their ultimate goal is to buy low and sell high. Unfortunately, the difficulty of achieving this goal is inversely proportional to its desirability. A critical distinction to keep in mind is that whereas a trend-following system is basically self-correcting, a counter-trend system implies unlimited losses. Therefore, it is essential to include some stop-loss conditions in any counter-trend system (unless it is traded simultaneously with trend-following systems). Otherwise, the system could end up being long for the duration of a major downtrend or short for the duration of a major uptrend. (Stop-loss conditions are optional for most trend-following systems, since an opposite signal will usually be received before the loss on a position becomes extreme.[6])

One important advantage of using a counter-trend system is that it provides the opportunity for excellent diversification with simultaneously employed trend-following systems. In this regard, it should be noted that a counter-trend system might be desirable even if it was a modest net loser, the reason being that if the counter-trend system was inversely correlated to a simultaneously traded trend-following system, trading both systems might imply less risk than trading the trend system alone. Therefore it is entirely possible that the two systems combined might yield a higher percent return (at the same risk level), even if the counter-trend system alone lost money.

Types of Counter-Trend Systems

The following are some types of approaches that can be used to try to construct a counter-trend system.

> **Fading Minimum Move.** This is perhaps the most straightforward counter-trend approach. A sell signal is indicated each time the market rallies by a certain minimum amount above the low point since the last counter-trend buy signal. Similarly, a buy signal is indicated whenever the market declines by a minimum amount below the high point since the last counter-trend sell signal. The magnitude of the price move required to generate a trade signal can be expressed in either nominal or percentage terms. Figure 17.13 illustrates the trade signals that would be generated by this type of counter-trend system for a 4 percent threshold level in the October 1993–July 1994 gold market.[7] Note that this is the same market that was previously used in this chapter to illustrate whipsaw losses for a sensitive trend-following system. This is no accident.

---

[6]Stop-loss rules, however, might be mandatory for an extremely nonsensitive trend-following system—for example, a breakout system with $N = 150$.

[7]Since Figure 17.13 depicts a continuous futures series, percentage price changes would be equal to the price changes shown on this chart divided by the corresponding nearest futures price, which is not shown. Recall from Chapter 12 that continuous futures accurately reflect price *swings* but not price *levels*. Consequently, continuous futures cannot be used as the divisor to calculate percentage changes.

Figure 17.13
COUNTER-TREND SIGNALS: GOLD CONTINUOUS FUTURES

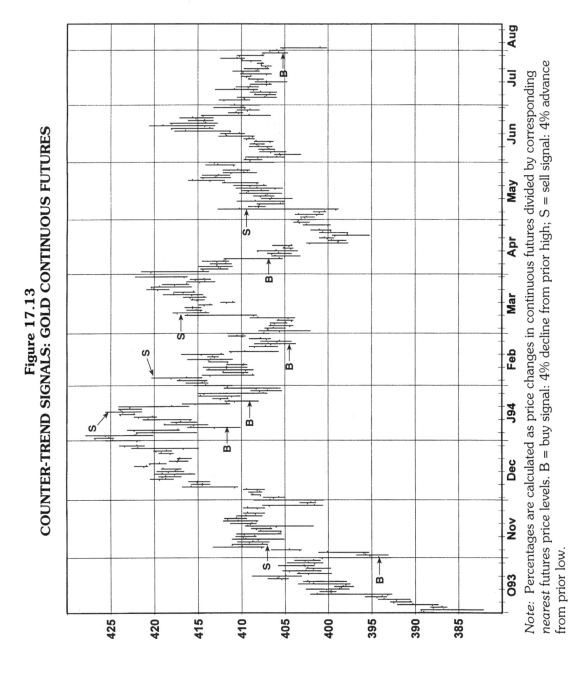

Note: Percentages are calculated as price changes in continuous futures divided by corresponding *nearest* futures price levels. B = buy signal: 4% decline from prior high; S = sell signal: 4% advance from prior low.

Counter-trend systems will tend to work best under those types of market conditions in which trend-following systems fare poorly.

Fading Minimum Move with Confirmation Delay. This is similar to the preceding counter-trend system, with the exception that some minimum indication of a trend reversal is required before the counter-trend trade is initiated. For example, a 1-thrust-day confirmation might be required to validate counter-trend signals based on fading a given percent price move.

Oscillators. A counter-trend system could use oscillators as an indicator for generating trade signals. Oscillators are fully detailed in Chapter 15. It should be noted, however, that although using oscillators to signal counter-trend trades may work well in a trading-range market, in a trending market such an approach can be disastrous. More effective methods of using oscillators are discussed in Chapter 15.

Cycles. A counter-trend system could employ cyclical analysis as a key input in timing trades. For example, during a period of an expected cyclical high, a short position would be indicated given some specified minimal evidence of weakness (e.g., an 8-day low close). See Chapter 16 for a detailed discussion of cyclical analysis.

Contrary Opinion. A counter-trend system might use contrary opinion as an input in timing trades. For example, once the contrary opinion rose above a specified level, a short position would be indicated contingent on confirmation by a very sensitive technical indicator. (Contrary opinion was discussed in Chapter 10.)

DIVERSIFICATION

The standard interpretation attached to the term *diversification* is that trading is spread across a broad range of markets. Although this is the single most important type of diversification, assuming the availability of sufficient funds, there are two additional levels of possible diversification. First, each market can be traded with several systems. Second, several variations of each system can be used. For example, if two contracts of cocoa are being traded using the breakout system, each contract can be traded using a different value of N (i.e., the number of days whose high or low must be penetrated to trigger a signal).

In the following discussion, we will use the term *single market system variation (SMSV)* to refer to the concept of a specific variation of a given system traded in a single market. Thus, the simple breakout system, with N = 20, traded in the cocoa market would be an example of an *SMSV*. In the simplest case in which a single system is used for all markets, and a single system variation is used in each market, there would be only one *SMSV* for each market traded. This simplified case represents the typical application of trading systems and employs only the standard diversification across markets. However, if sufficient funds are available, additional benefits can be obtained by also diversifying across different systems and different variations of each system.

There are three important benefits to diversification:

1. *Dampened Equity Retracements.* Different SMSVs will not witness their losses at precisely the same periods. Thus, by trading a wide variety of SMSVs, the trader can achieve a smoother equity curve. This means that trading 10 SMSVs with equivalent profit/risk characteristics would require significantly less reserve funds than trading 10 units of a single SMSV. In other words, the diversified trading portfolio would achieve a higher percent return. Or equivalently, at the same level of fund allocation, the diversified trading portfolio would achieve the same percentage return at a lower risk level. Up to a point, diversification would be beneficial even if the portfolio included SMSVs with poorer expected performance. A key consideration would be a given SMSV's correlation with the other SMSVs in the portfolio.

2. *Ensure Participation in Major Trends.* Typically, only a few of the actively traded futures markets will witness substantial price trends in any given year. Since the majority of trades in most trend-following systems will lose money,[8] it is essential that the trader participate in the large-profit trades—that is, major trends. This is a key reason for the importance of diversification across markets.

3. *Bad Luck Insurance.* Futures systems trading, like baseball, is a game of inches. Given the right combination of circumstances, even a minute difference in the price movement on a single day could have an extraordinary impact on the profitability of a specific SMSV. To illustrate this point, we consider a breakout system with a confirmation rule requiring a single thrust day that penetrates the previous day's high (low) by a minimum amount. In system A this amount is 5 points; in system B it is 10 points. This is the only difference between the two systems. Both systems compare current prices with the prior 20-day range.

Figure 17.14 compares these two systems for the July 1981 coffee market. (Although more recent illustrations could easily have been used, this particular situation provides the most striking example I have ever encountered

---

[8]Such systems can still be profitable because the average gain significantly exceeds the average loss.

Figure 17.14

SYSTEM TRADING: A GAME OF INCHES (DECEMBER 1981 COFFEE)

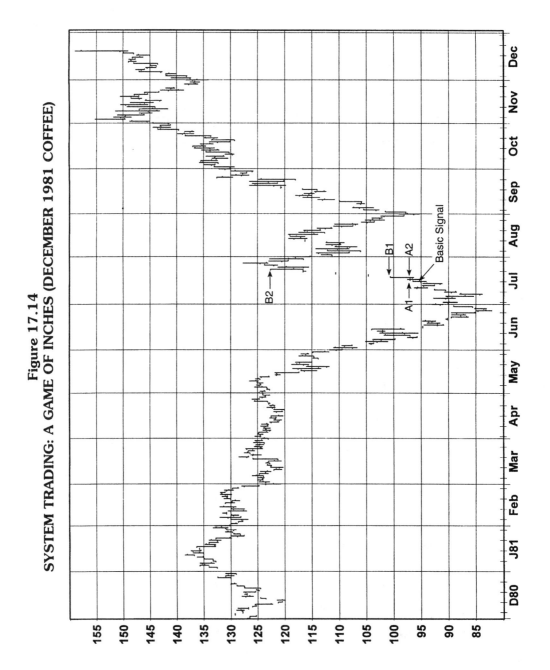

of the sensitivity of system performance to minute changes in the system values.) The basic system buy signal (i.e., close above the 20-day high) was received on July 16. This buy was confirmed by system A on July 17 as the close was 9 points above the previous day's high (point A1). System B, however, which required a 10-point penetration, did not confirm the signal until the following day (point B1).

The buy signal for system A would have been executed at approximately 97 cents (point A2). However, due to the ensuing string of limit moves, the buy signal for system B could not be filled until prices surpassed $1.22 (point B2). Thus, during this short interim, system A gained 25¢/lb ($9,375 per contract), while system B, which was unable to reverse its short position, lost a similar amount. Thus, the failure of the market to close one point higher on a given day (a price move equivalent to less than $4) resulted in an incredible $18,750 per contract difference in the performance of the two nearly identical system variations! It should be emphasized that this example reflects the randomness in commodity price movements rather than the instability of the tested system. Any system, other than a day trading system, could reflect the same degree of instability, since the performance difference was due to just a single trade in which the signals were separated by only one day.

This example should explain how it is possible for a trader to lose money in a given market using a system that generally performs well—he may just have chosen a specific variation that does much worse than most other variations (even very similar ones). By trading several variations of a system, the speculator could mitigate the impact of such isolated, abnormally poor results.[9] Of course, in so doing, the trader would also eliminate the possibility of gains far exceeding the average performance of the system. On balance, however, this prospect represents a desirable tradeoff, since it is assumed that the basic trading goal is consistent performance rather than windfall profits.

TEN COMMON PROBLEMS WITH TREND-FOLLOWING SYSTEMS REVISITED

We are now ready to consider possible solutions to the previously enumerated problems with standard trend-following systems. The problems and the possible solutions are summarized in Table 17.2.

---

[9]In the preceding example, system A and system B were deliberately chosen to be nearly identical in order to make the point about the potential impact of chance in its strongest possible form. However, in practice, the trader should choose system variations that are substantially more differentiated.

Table 17.2
PROBLEMS WITH STANDARD TREND-FOLLOWING SYSTEMS AND POSSIBLE SOLUTIONS

Problems with Standard Trend-Following Systems	Possible Solutions
1. Too many similar systems	1a. Try to construct original systems in order to avoid the problem of "trading with the crowd"
	1b. If trading more than one contract, spread out entry
2. Whipsaws	2a. Employ confirmation conditions
	2b. Develop filter rules
	2c. Employ diversification
3. Failure to exploit major moves	3. Add pyramiding component
4. Nonsensitive (slow) systems can surrender a large percentage of profits.	4. Employ trade exit rules
5. Cannot make money in trading-range markets	5. Trade trend-following systems in conjunction with counter-trend systems
6. Temporary large losses	6a. If funds permit, trade more than one system in each market
	6b. When beginning to trade a system, trade more lightly if entering positions at a point after the signal has been received
7. Extreme volatility in best performing system	7. By employing diversification, the trader can allocate some funds to a high-profit-potential system that is too risky to trade on its own
8. System works well in testing but then bombs	8. The danger of such a development can be reduced if systems are properly tested. This subject is discussed in detail in Chapter 20
9. Parameter shift	9a. If funds permit, diversify by trading several variations of each system
	9b. Experiment with systems that incorporate market characteristic adjustments
10. Slippage	10. Use realistic assumptions (discussed in Chapter 20)

18 Examples of Original Trading Systems

Nothing works at all times in all kinds of markets.

—Adam Smith

The previous chapter provided two examples of generic trading systems—moving averages and breakouts. This chapter details several original trading systems that are based on some of the patterns introduced in Chapter 6. Although the systems detailed can be used as fully automated trading strategies, the primary purpose of this chapter is not to offer specific trading systems, but rather to give the reader a feel for how technical concepts can be utilized to construct a mechanical trading approach. Studying these examples should give the reader ideas as to how to design his or her own trading systems, which is the real value of this chapter.

WHY AM I REVEALING THESE SYSTEMS?

At this point, I am sure many readers will have a number of questions in mind: Why am I revealing several original trading systems for the price of a book when systems are typically sold for hundreds or even thousands of dollars? How good can these systems possibly be if I am willing reveal them to fill a chapter in a book that is hardly short of copy to begin with? Why as a commodity trading advisor who manages substantial sums ($70 million at this writing) using trading systems would I be willing to divulge some of my systems for virtually free? Wouldn't I be concerned that the widespread use of these systems would impede their future performance?

These are all reasonable and fair questions. The basic answer to all of them is that the systems detailed in this chapter are "throwaway" systems—that is, systems too inferior in return/risk terms to other systems I have developed to bother using. This does not mean these systems are worthless. In fact, I have no doubt that these systems are probably superior to a host of systems being sold for many multiples of the price of this book. Also, I am sure that by incorporating their own revisions and enhancements, many readers will be able to use the systems in this chapter as the core of very effective computerized trading methodologies. Finally, as stated earlier, the systems in this chapter are primarily intended to provide some specific illustrations of trading system design.

THE WIDE-RANGING DAY SYSTEM

Basic Concept

A wide-ranging day, which was introduced in Chapter 3, is a day that witnesses a much wider *true range*[1] than experienced in recent trading sessions. The high volatility inherent in wide-ranging days gives these days special significance. Typically, the market will tend to extend in the direction of the initial price move beyond the boundaries of the wide-ranging day. However, situations in which the market originally penetrates one side of the wide-ranging day and then reverses to penetrate the other side also have significance.

The wide-ranging day system defines trading ranges based on wide-ranging days. Signals are generated when prices close above or below these trading ranges. In the simplest case, the trading range is defined as the wide-ranging day itself. However, we make the system more general by defining the trading range as the price range encompassing all the true highs and true lows during the period extending from $N1$ days before the wide-ranging day to $N2$ days after, where $N1$ and $N2$ are parameter values that must be defined. For example, if both $N1$ and $N2$ equal 0, the trading range would be defined by the wide-ranging day itself (i.e., the range between the true high and true low of the wide-ranging day). If $N1 = 4$ and $N2 = 2$, the trading range would be defined as the range between the highest true high and lowest true low in the interval beginning four days before the wide-ranging day and ending two days after it.

Definitions

> **Wide-Ranging Day.** A day on which the *volatility ratio* (VR) is greater than k (e.g., $k = 2.0$). The VR is equal to today's true range divided by the true range of the past N-day period (e.g., $N = 10$).

---

[1]The *true range* is equal to the *true high* minus the *true low*. The *true high* is the maximum of the current day's high and the previous day's close. The *true low* is the minimum of current day's low and the previous day's close. (The true high and true low were defined in Chapter 3.)

Price Trigger Range (PTR). The range defined by the highest true high and lowest true low in the interval between $N1$ days before the most recent wide-ranging day to $N2$ days after. Note that the PTR cannot be defined until $N2$ days after a wide-ranging day. (If $N2 = 0$, the PTR would be defined as of the close of the wide-ranging day itself.) The PTR will be redefined each time there is a new wide-ranging day (that is, $N2$ days after such an event).

Trading Signals

Buy Case. On a close above the high of the PTR, reverse from short to long.

Sell Case. On a close below the low of the PTR, reverse from long to short.

Daily Checklist

To generate trading signals, perform the following steps each day:

1. If short, check whether today's close is above the high of the PTR. If it is, reverse from short to long.
2. If long, check whether today's close is below the low of the PTR. If it is, reverse from long to short.
3. Check whether exactly $N2$ days have elapsed since the most recent wide-ranging day. If this check is affirmative, redefine the PTR.

The order of these steps is very important. Note that the check for new trading signals *precedes* the check whether the PTR should be redefined. Thus if the day a new PTR is defined also signals a trade based on the prevailing PTR going into that day, a signal would be generated. If step 3 preceded steps 1 and 2, trade signals could get delayed each time a signal occurred on the day a new PTR is defined ($N2$ days after the most recent wide-ranging day, which would be the wide-ranging day itself when $N2 = 0$). For example, assume the system is long, $N2 = 0$, and the close on a new wide-ranging day is below the low of the preceding wide-ranging day. According to the listed step order, the new wide-ranging day would signal a reversal from long to short. If steps 1 and 2 followed step 3, no signal would occur, since the PTR would be redefined, and the market would have to close below the *new* wide-ranging day to trigger a signal.

Parameters in System

N1. Number of days prior to the wide-ranging day included in the PTR period.

N2. Number of days after the wide-ranging day included in the PTR period.

k. The value the VR must exceed in order to define a wide-ranging day.

Parameter Set List

Table 18.1 provides a sample parameter set list. Readers can use this list as is or adjust it as desired.

Table 18.1
PARAMETER SET LIST

	k	N1	N2
1.	1.6	0	0
2.	1.6	3	0
3.	1.6	6	0
4.	1.6	0	3
5.	1.6	3	3
6.	1.6	6	3
7.	1.6	0	6
8.	1.6	3	6
9.	1.6	6	6
10.	2.0	0	0
11.	2.0	3	0
12.	2.0	6	0
13.	2.0	0	3
14.	2.0	3	3
15.	2.0	6	3
16.	2.0	0	6
17.	2.0	3	6
18.	2.0	6	6
19.	2.4	0	0
20.	2.4	3	0
21.	2.4	6	0
22.	2.4	0	3
23.	2.4	3	3
24.	2.4	6	3
25.	2.4	0	6
26.	2.4	3	6
27.	2.4	6	6

An Illustrated Example

To illustrate how the system works, we superimpose trading signals on sugar charts for the period January 1993 to April 1995. Note that the charts are continuous futures to coincide with the price series used to generate signals. As will be fully detailed in the next two chapters, continuous futures are usually the most suitable price series to use in trading systems. As an aid in providing visual continuity between charts, each chart overlaps one to two months of the preceding chart.

Two types of signals are indicated on the accompanying charts:

1. The nonbordered signals correspond to signals generated by the system when both $N1$ and $N2$ are set equal to zero. (In other words, the PTR is defined by the true high and true low of the wide-ranging day itself.)
2. The diamond-shaped signals correspond to signals generated by the system when $N1 = 4$ and $N2 = 2$. (In other words, the PTR is defined by the true price range encompassing the interval beginning four days before the wide-ranging day and ending two days after it.)

In many cases both sets of parameter set values will yield identical signals. In some cases, however, the second system version will trigger signals later or not at all. (The reverse can never occur, since the PTR based on $N1 = 4$ and $N2 = 2$ must be at least as wide as the PTR based on $N1 = 0$ and $N2 = 0$. Therefore any penetration of the former PTR must also be a penetration of the latter PTR, but not vice versa.)

First we examine the trading signals generated for the system version when both $N1$ and $N2$ equal zero (nonbordered signals). *Therefore for the moment ignore the diamond-shaped signals.* We subsequently examine the trades in which the two parameter sets yield different signals.

The January 1993 buy signal occurs when the market closes above the high of the January 8 wide-ranging day (Figure 18.1). None of the PTRs defined by the following four wide-ranging days are penetrated on the downside.[2] Therefore the system remains long until the low of the May 18, 1993 wide-ranging day is penetrated on the following session (Figure 18.1). In this particular instance, the system provided near perfect signals, buying near the January 1993 bottom and reversing near the May 1993 top.

The May 1993 short position is held until the market witnesses its first close above the most recent wide-ranging day, which occurs on the September 13,

---

[2]Note that although there were many days with closes below the low of the second wide-ranging day in March, these closes were not below the *true* low of that day, which was much lower. (Remember that it is the true high and true low that are used to define PTRs, since the difference between these two levels—the true range—is much more representative of volatility than the conventional range.)

Figure 18.1
WIDE-RANGING DAY SYSTEM, CHART 1:
SUGAR CONTINUOUS FUTURES

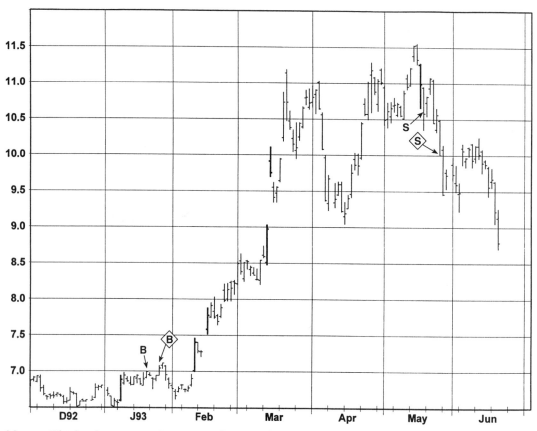

Notes: Thicker bars are wide-ranging days. B, S = buy and sell signals for $N1 = 0$ and $N2 = 0$; ⬦B, ⬦S = buy and sell signals for $N1 = 4$ and $N2 = 2$.

1993 close above the August 12, 1993 wide-ranging day (Figure 18.2). Once again the system provides a set of near perfect signals, selling reasonably close to the May 1993 top and reversing to long only moderately above the August 1993 low.

The next sell signal occurs when the market closes below the low of the November 4, 1993 wide-ranging day (which was also the November relative high) three trading sessions later (Figure 18.2). Note that the day of this sell signal was itself a wide-ranging day. This is a good example of the consequence of checking for trading signals before checking for a newly defined PTR. If the order of these steps were reversed, the sell signal would have been delayed until the November 9, 1993 wide-ranging day was itself penetrated three trading sessions later. The November 9, 1993 sell signal ends up being

Figure 18.2

WIDE-RANGING DAY SYSTEM, CHART 2: SUGAR CONTINUOUS FUTURES

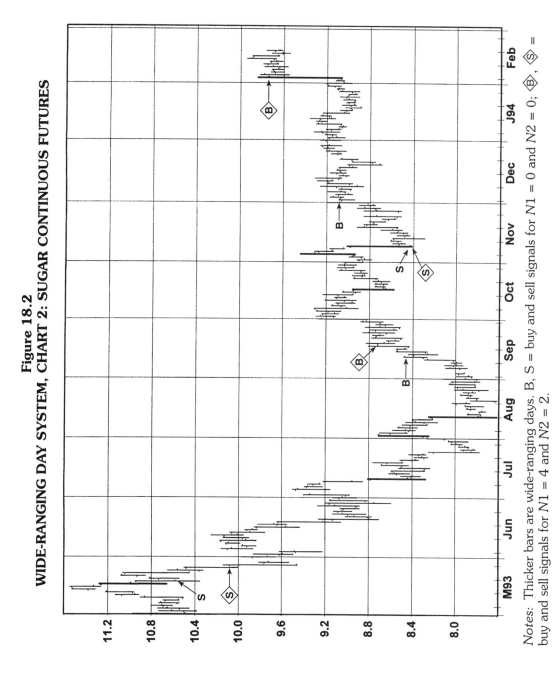

Notes: Thicker bars are wide-ranging days. B, S = buy and sell signals for $N1 = 0$ and $N2 = 0$; $\langle B \rangle$, $\langle S \rangle$ = buy and sell signals for $N1 = 4$ and $N2 = 2$.

a whipsaw trade, as a close above the true high of this wide-ranging day several weeks later results in a buy reversal signal (Figure 18.2).

The next sell signal, which is triggered by the close below the low of the March 29, 1994 wide-ranging day, is also itself a wide-ranging day (Figure 18.3). Note that although the PTR low (i.e., the March 29, 1994 low) provided a signal threshold level not far from the March 1994 high, the actual signal occurs much lower, because the first close below this level is *far* below this level. This trade, as well as the next two trades, lead to small whipsaw losses, followed by a large winning buy signal in August 1994 (Figure 18.3). The next four trades result in a string of small to moderate whipsaw losses (Figure 18.4). The final trade shown results in another large gain.

It is worth noting that the January 13, 1995 sell signal represents the *second* time a sell signal is triggered by a penetration of the November 28, 1994 wide-ranging day. The point is that a single wide-ranging day can be responsible for numerous signals if there are no intervening wide-ranging days.

Next we examine how the signals generated by the second parameter set ($N1$ = 4, $N2$ = 2) differ from those that result from the first parameter set ($N1$ = 0, $N2$ = 0). Note that the second parameter set results in a later buy signal in January 1993 (Figure 18.1), because the use of the subsequent $N2$ days in defining the PTR results in a higher value for the high of the PTR. The May 1993 sell signal also occurs later (Figure 18.1), since the PTR using the second set of parameter values is not yet defined (i.e., $N2$ days have not yet elapsed since the last wide-ranging day) at the time of the sell signal triggered by the first parameter set.

The second parameter set also results in a later buy signal in September 1993 (Figure 18.2), but for yet another reason. In this instance, the use of the prior $N4$ days in defining the PTR results in a higher value for the high of the PTR. The buy signal corresponding to the December 1, 1993 buy signal for the first parameter set occurs over two months later (February 3, 1994) for a similar reason (Figure 18.2). Similar to the May 1993 sell signal (Figure 18.1), the $N2$-day wait to define the PTR also delays the signals corresponding to the April 1994 buy signal and June 1994 sell signal for the first parameter set (Figure 18.3).

In each of the aforementioned six cases, the delay caused by using the second parameter set resulted in a less favorable or more adverse entry level. This is no accident, since the wider PTRs defined by the nonzero $N1$ and $N2$ values will always result in equal or higher buy signals and equal or lower sell signals.

The reader might well wonder why one would ever want to use nonzero values for $N1$ and $N2$, since the resulting delayed entries are invariably equal or worse than entries based on keeping $N1$ and $N2$ equal to zero. The answer lies in the fact that the broader PTRs that result from nonzero $N1$ and $N2$ values may filter out some losing signals. For example, note that the much lower low of the PTR for the case where $N1$ = 4 and $N2$ = 2 (denoted by a dashed line in Figure 18.4) avoids the losing December 1, 1994 sell signal.

Figure 18.3
WIDE-RANGING DAY SYSTEM, CHART 3: SUGAR CONTINUOUS FUTURES

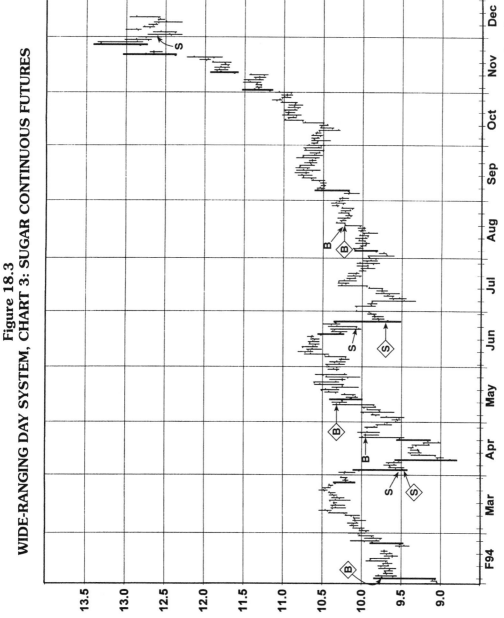

Notes: Thicker bars are wide-ranging days. B, S = buy and sell signals for $N1 = 0$ and $N2 = 0$; $\langle\!B\!\rangle$, $\langle\!S\!\rangle$ = buy and sell signals for $N1 = 4$ and $N2 = 2$.

639

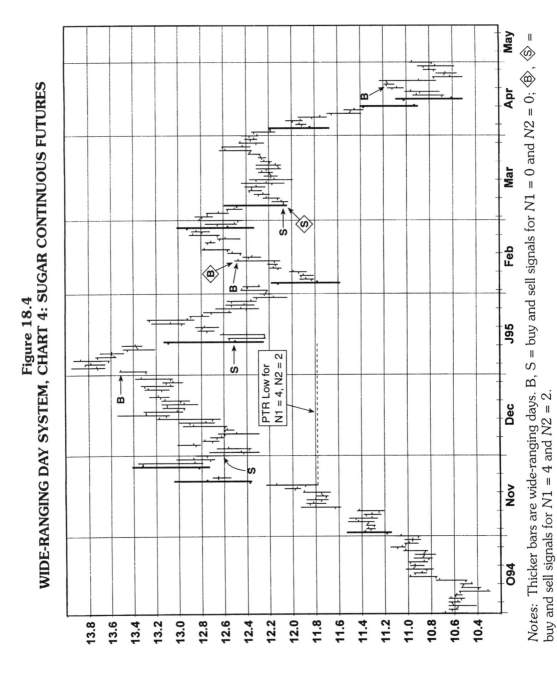

Figure 18.4
WIDE-RANGING DAY SYSTEM, CHART 4: SUGAR CONTINUOUS FUTURES

Notes: Thicker bars are wide-ranging days. B, S = buy and sell signals for $N1 = 0$ and $N2 = 0$; Ⓑ, Ⓢ = buy and sell signals for $N1 = 4$ and $N2 = 2$.

Also note that since the system is not short, the losing January 3, 1995 buy signal is avoided as well.

On balance, in this market example, the cumulative negative impact of the worse entries that resulted from using nonzero values for N1 and N2 outweighed the benefit of the filtered losing trades. Frequently, however, the reverse will be true.

It should be emphasized that the selected example was intended to illustrate the mechanics of the wide-ranging day system, not to put the system in the best light. Therefore, this example deliberately contained both intervals of strong wins as well as whipsaw losses. Note that I could easily have made the system look like a virtual holy grail by restricting the illustration to the January 1993–October 1993 period—a time interval in which the system bought near the bottom, sold near the top, and then bought near the bottom again. Such cherry-picked illustrations are all too common in books, magazine articles, and especially advertisements. We return to this subject in the discussion of "the well-chosen example" in Chapter 20.

RUN DAY BREAKOUT SYSTEM

Basic Concept

Up and *down run days* were defined in Chapter 6. As was explained in Chapter 6, run days tend to occur in strongly trending markets. In this system, buy reversal signals are generated when the market closes above the maximum true high of a specified number of prior down run days. Similarly, sell reversal signals are generated when the market closes below the minimum true low of a specified number of prior up run days. The idea is that the ability of the market to close opposite the extreme point defined by one or more such strongly trending days implies that a trend reversal has occurred.

Trading Signals

Buy Case. Reverse to long whenever *both* of these conditions are met:

1. The close is above the maximum true high among the most recent N2 down run days. (*Note:* Only the run day true highs are considered; not the true highs on the interim days.)
2. The most recent run day is an *up* run day. (Without this second condition, in some cases, the first condition in the sell case would result in an automatic reversal back to a short position.)

Sell Case. Reverse to short whenever *both* of the following conditions are met:

1. The close is below the minimum true low among the most recent N2 up run days. (*Note:* Only the run day true lows are considered; not the true lows on the interim days.)
2. The most recent run day is a *down* run day. (Without this second condition, in some cases, the first condition in the buy case would result in an automatic reversal back to a long position.)

Daily Checklist

To generate trading signals, perform the following steps each day:

1. Check whether the trading day N1 days prior to the current day can be defined as an up or down run day.[3] (Recall that a run day cannot be defined until the close N1 days after the run day.) Keep track of all run days and their true highs and true lows.
2. If short, check whether today's close is above the maximum true high of the past N2 down run days. If it is, check whether the most recent run day was an up run day. If it was, reverse from short to long.
3. If long, check whether today's close is below the minimum true low of the past N2 up run days. If it is, check whether the most recent run day was a down run day. If it was, reverse from long to short.

Parameters

N1. The parameter used to define run days. For example, if $N = 3$, a day would be defined as an up run day if its true high was greater than the maximum true high of the prior three days and its true low was less than the minimum true low of the following three days.

N2. The number of prior down run days used to compute the maximum true high that must be exceeded by a close for a buy signal. (Also, the number of prior up run days used to compute the minimum true low that must be penetrated by a close for a sell signal.)

Parameter Set List

Table 18.2 provides a sample parameter set list. Readers can use this list as is or adjust it as desired.

---

[3]Although uncommon, a day can be *both* an up run day and down run day. This unusual situation will occur if a day's true high is greater than the true highs during the prior and subsequent N1 days, and its true low is lower than the true lows during the prior and subsequent N1 days. Days that fulfill both the up and down run day definitions are not considered run days.

Table 18.2
PARAMETER SET LIST

	N1	N2
1.	3	2
2.	3	3
3.	3	4
4.	3	5
5.	5	2
6.	5	3
7.	5	4
8.	7	2
9.	7	3
10.	7	4

An Illustrated Example

To illustrate the mechanics of the run day breakout system, in Figures 18.5–18.9 we indicate the buy and sell signals generated by the system for the parameter set $N1 = 5$ and $N2 = 4$. Down run days are denoted by downward-pointing arrows and up run days by upward-pointing arrows. A close above the maximum true high of the four most recent down run days triggers a buy signal in December 1992 (Figure 18.5). Note the second condition for a buy signal—that is, the most recent run day is an up run day—is also fulfilled.

At first glance, it may appear that there should be a sell signal at the low close in mid-May 1993 (Figure 18.5). After all, this close is below the minimum true low of the four most recent up run days and the most recent run day is a down run day. The catch is that the latter statement is only known to be true in hindsight. At the time the low close occurs, the most recent *defined* run day is still the May 4, 1993 up run day. Remember that a run day cannot be defined until $N1$ days later, or five days later in the current example. By the time the first of the three May 1993 down run days is defined, all the market closes are above the minimum true low of the four most recent up run days.

In fact, there is no sell signal until November 2, 1993 (Figure 18.6)—over 10 months and 16 T-bond points ($16,000 per contract) after the buy signal! In this particular instance (market, period, and parameter set), the system worked magnificently, capturing nearly two-thirds of a huge price advance without any intervening losing trades. It should be noted, however, that the choice of a lower value for $N2$ (i.e., 1, 2, or 3) would have resulted in at least one false signal during the massive late-1992–late-1993 bull market.

The short position implemented in November 1993 is liquidated nearly unchanged in January 1994 (Figure 18.7). Note that the January 1994 buy signal seems to occur later and at a lower price than might be assumed at first

Figure 18.5
RUN DAY BREAKOUT SYSTEM (*N2* = 4), CHART 1:
T-BOND CONTINUOUS FUTURES

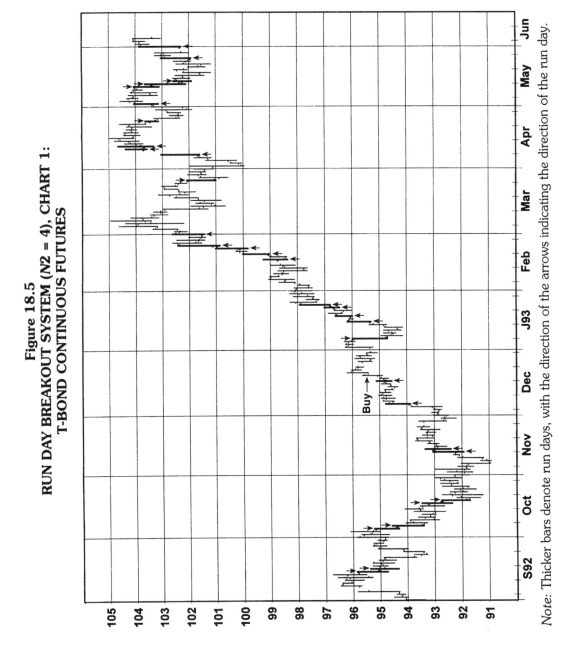

Note: Thicker bars denote run days, with the direction of the arrows indicating the direction of the run day.

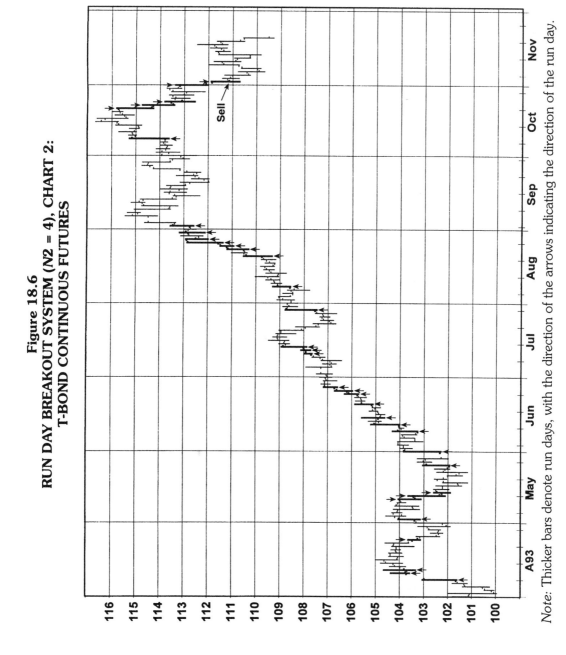

Figure 18.6
RUN DAY BREAKOUT SYSTEM ($N2 = 4$), CHART 2:
T-BOND CONTINUOUS FUTURES

Note: Thicker bars denote run days, with the direction of the arrows indicating the direction of the run day.

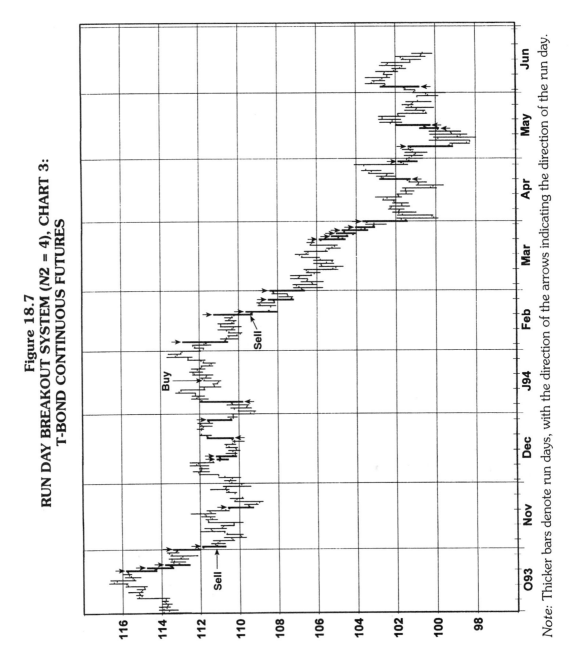

Figure 18.7
RUN DAY BREAKOUT SYSTEM (N2 = 4), CHART 3:
T-BOND CONTINUOUS FUTURES

Note: Thicker bars denote run days, with the direction of the arrows indicating the direction of the run day.

646

glance at the chart. Once again, the explanation lies in the fact that an up run day is not *defined* until after the initial January peak is set. The indicated buy point on the chart was the first day in January 1994 on which the close exceeded the maximum true high of the prior four down run days *and* the most recent *defined* run day was an up run day.

The long position is reversed about a month later at a moderate loss (Figure 18.7). Note that in this instance the four most recent up run days used to calculate the sell point span back nearly a half year prior to the sell signal and are interspersed with numerous down run days (Figures 18.6 and 18.7). This sell signal results in another huge gain, with the system staying short throughout the February–March 1994 decline, April–August trading range, and September–October decline (Figures 18.7 and 18.8). The position is finally reversed nearly 10 months and over 11 T-bond points later (Figure 18.8). The resulting long position was held throughout the subsequent large advance, which was still in progress at the time of this writing (Figure 18.9).

For the 3½ year period shown, the system performed remarkably well, registering three huge winning trades, one moderate loss, and one approximately break-even trade. Readers, however, are cautioned against generalizing the system's performance based on this single market/single parameter set example. In most cases, the system will not attain the stellar performance exhibited in this illustration. As but one example, if *N2* were set equal to 3 instead of 4, two whipsaw losses would be created without any commensurate benefits (see Figure 18.10, which is the counterpart of Figure 18.6, and Figure 18.11, which is the counterpoint of Figure 18.8).

RUN DAY CONSECUTIVE COUNT SYSTEM

Basic Concept

This system also uses run days as the key input in generating trading signals. In this system, reversal signals occur whenever there are a specified number of up run days without any intervening down run days, or vice versa.

Definitions

Up and down run days were defined in Chapter 6. In addition, the following definitions are employed in the system description:

> **Buy Count.** The buy count is activated whenever a sell signal is received. The count starts at zero and increases by one whenever a new

Figure 18.8
RUN DAY BREAKOUT SYSTEM (N2 = 4), CHART 4:
T-BOND CONTINUOUS FUTURES

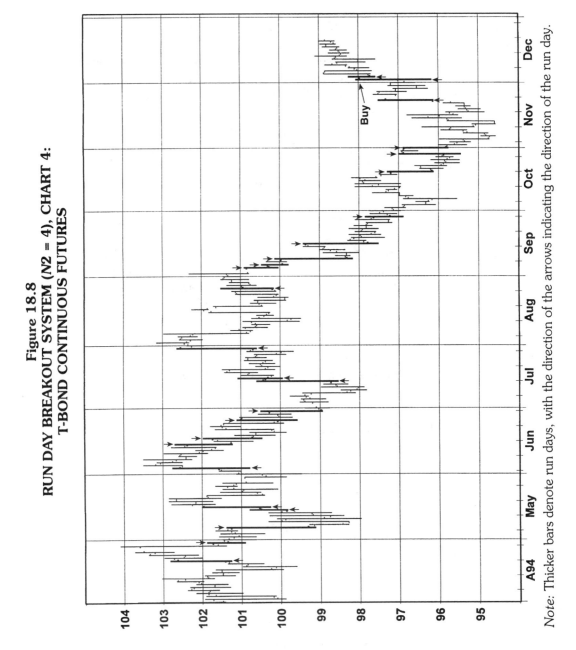

Note: Thicker bars denote run days, with the direction of the arrows indicating the direction of the run day.

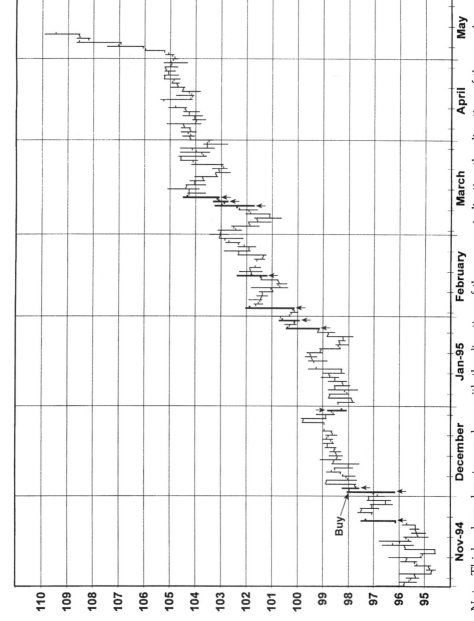

Figure 18.9
RUN DAY BREAKOUT SYSTEM (*N2* = 4), CHART 5:
T-BOND CONTINUOUS FUTURES

Note: Thicker bars denote run days, with the direction of the arrows indicating the direction of the run day.

649

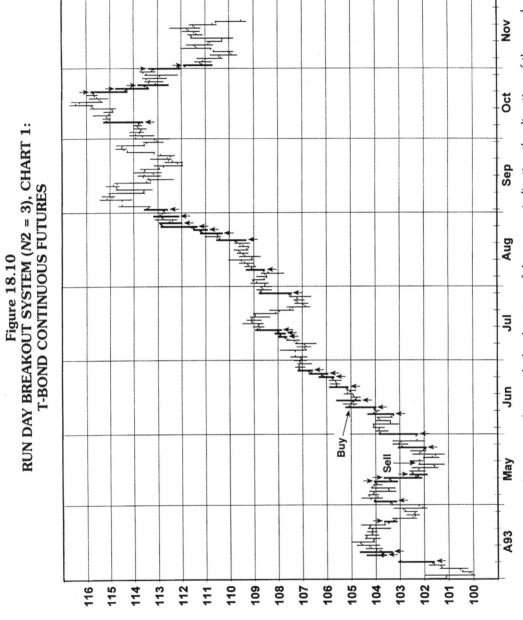

Figure 18.10
RUN DAY BREAKOUT SYSTEM (*N2* = 3), CHART 1:
T-BOND CONTINUOUS FUTURES

Notes: Thicker bars denote run days, with the direction of the arrows indicating the direction of the run day.
Sell and buy signals shown are those generated in *N2* = 3 *having no counterpart signals if N2 = 4.*

Figure 18.11
RUN DAY BREAKOUT SYSTEM (N2 = 3), CHART 2:
T-BOND CONTINUOUS FUTURES

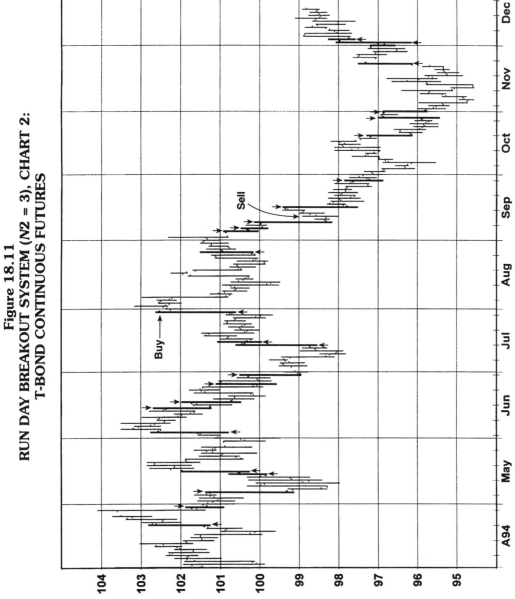

Notes: Thicker bars denote run days, with the direction of the arrows indicating the direction of the run day. Buy and sell signals shown are those generated in *N2 = 3 having no counterpart signals if N2 = 4.*

up run day is defined. The count is reset to zero whenever there is a down run day. In effect, the buy count represents the number of up run days witnessed without any intervening down run days. The buy count is closed when a buy signal is received.

Sell Count. The sell count is activated whenever a buy signal is received. The count starts at zero and increases by one whenever a new down run day is defined. The count is reset to zero whenever there is an up run day. In effect, the sell count represents the number of down run days witnessed without any intervening up run days. The sell count is closed when a sell signal is received.

Trading Signals

Buy Case. Reverse to long whenever the buy count reaches $N2$. Keep in mind that the fulfillment of this condition will not be known until $N1$ days after the $N2$th *consecutive* up run day. (Consecutive here means that there are no intervening down run days; not that the up run days occur on consecutive days.)

Sell Case. Reverse to short whenever the sell count reaches $N2$. Keep in mind that the fulfillment of this condition will not be known until $N1$ days after the $N2$th *consecutive* down run day. (Consecutive here means that there are no intervening up run days; not that the down run days occur on consecutive days.)

Daily Checklist

To generate trading signals, perform the following steps each day:

1. Check whether the trading day $N1$ days prior to the current day can be defined as an up or down run day (see footnote 3, page 642). (Recall that a run day cannot be defined until the close $N1$ days after the run day.) If the day is defined as an up run day, increase the buy count by one if the buy count is active (i.e., if the current position is short); otherwise, reset the sell count to zero. (Either the buy or sell count is always active, depending on whether the current position is short or long.) If the day is defined as a down run day, increase the sell count by one if the sell count is active (i.e., if current position is long); otherwise, reset the buy count to zero.

2. If the buy count is active, check whether it is equal to $N2$ after step 1. If it is, cover short, go long, close buy count, and activate sell count.

3. If the sell count is active, check whether it is equal to $N2$ after step 1. If it is, cover long, go short, close sell count, and activate buy count.

Parameters

N1. The parameter used to define run days.
N2. The number of *consecutive* run days required for a signal.

Parameter Set List

Table 18.3 provide a sample parameter set list. Readers can use this list as is or adjust it as desired.

An Illustrated Example

Figures 18.12–18.16 illustrate the signals generated by the run day consecutive count system for $N1 = 5$ and $N2 = 3$. In other words, the system reverses from long to short whenever there are three consecutive down run days and from short to long whenever there are three consecutive up run days. (Consecutive here means that there are no intervening run days in the opposite direction; not consecutive days.) *Keep in mind that the actual trade signal will not be received until the fifth close after the third consecutive run day, since a run day is not defined until N1 days after its occurrence (N1 = 5 in this example).*
     The first signal shown—a sell in October 1992—is not far from the major low set in the following month (Figure 18.12). This position is reversed two months later at a moderate loss (Figure 18.12). The December 1992 buy signal results in a substantial gain, but the position is reversed to short near the low of the price dip in May 1993 (Figures 18.12 and 18.13).

Table 18.3
PARAMETER SET LIST

	N1	N2
1.	3	1
2.	3	2
3.	3	3
4.	3	4
5.	5	1
6.	5	2
7.	5	3
8.	7	1
9.	7	2
10.	7	3

Figure 18.12
RUN DAY CONSECUTIVE COUNT SYSTEM, CHART 1:
T-BOND CONTINUOUS FUTURES

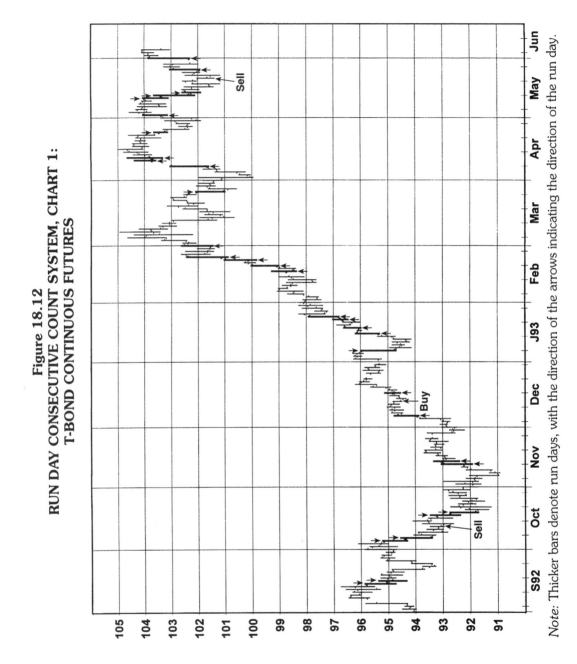

Note: Thicker bars denote run days, with the direction of the arrows indicating the direction of the run day.

Figure 18.13
RUN DAY CONSECUTIVE COUNT SYSTEM, CHART 2:
T-BOND CONTINUOUS FUTURES

Note: Thicker bars denote run days, with the direction of the arrows indicating the direction of the run day.

655

Figure 18.14
RUN DAY CONSECUTIVE COUNT SYSTEM, CHART 3:
T-BOND CONTINUOUS FUTURES

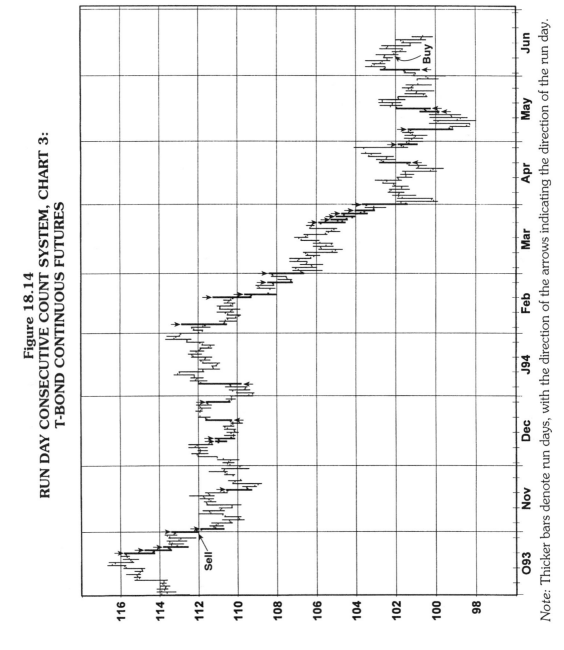

Note: Thicker bars denote run days, with the direction of the arrows indicating the direction of the run day.

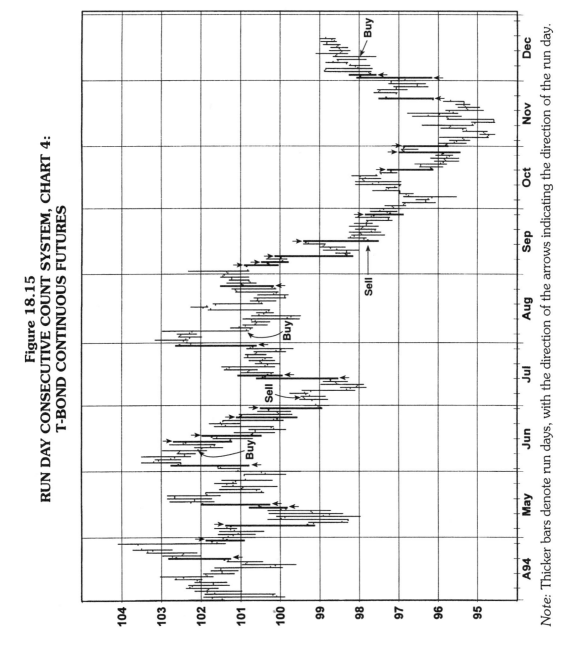

Figure 18.15
RUN DAY CONSECUTIVE COUNT SYSTEM, CHART 4:
T-BOND CONTINUOUS FUTURES

Note: Thicker bars denote run days, with the direction of the arrows indicating the direction of the run day.

657

Figure 18.16
RUN DAY CONSECUTIVE COUNT SYSTEM, CHART 5:
T-BOND CONTINUOUS FUTURES

Note: Thicker bars denote run days, with the direction of the arrows indicating the direction of the run day.

The ill-timed but short-lived May 1993 sell signal is reversed at a moderate loss in June 1993 (Figure 18.13). The system then stays long throughout the remainder of the bull move, reversing to short about two weeks after the October 1993 peak on November 1 (Figure 18.13). Note that although it looks like the November 1993 sell signal is shown occurring on the fourth down run day, this point is actually the day on which the third down run day is *defined*.

The November 1993 sell signal results in another large gain, as the system remains short throughout the entire decline to the May 1994 low, reversing to long in June 1994 (Figure 18.14). This trade, as well as the following two trades, which occur in a trading-range period, result in small to moderate losses (Figure 18.15). The end of this trading range coincides with a break-even sell signal in September 1994 (Figure 18.15). The final trade shown is a buy in December 1994 that catches the ensuing large advance (Figure 18.16).

CONCLUSION

In this chapter we have introduced some original systems. Although these systems are viable as described, readers may wish to experiment with modifications that use the concepts of these systems as the core of more complex approaches. The ultimate goal of this chapter, however, was not to present specific trading systems, but to illustrate how basic chart concepts can be transformed into trading systems. The number of possible systems that can be constructed from the technical patterns and concepts already discussed in this volume are limited only by the imagination of the reader.

19 Selecting the Best Futures Price Series for Computer Testing

Garbage in, garbage out.

—Anonymous

System traders wishing to test their ideas on futures prices have always faced a major obstacle: the transitory life span of futures contracts. In contrast to the equities market, where a given stock is represented by a single price series spanning the entire test period, in futures, each market is represented by a string of expiring contracts. Proposals for a solution to this problem have been the subject of many articles and a great deal of discussion. In the process, substantial confusion has been generated, as evidenced by the use of identical terms to describe different types of price series. Even worse, so much misinformation has been provided on this subject that many market participants now believe the equivalent of "the earth is flat" theory.

There are four basic types of price series that can be used. The definition, advantages, and disadvantages of each are discussed in turn.

ACTUAL CONTRACT SERIES

At a surface glance, the best route might seem to be to simply use the actual contract series. However, there are two major problems with this approach. First, if you are testing a system over a meaningful length of time, each market simulation will require a large number of individual price series. For example, a 15-year test run for a typical market would require using approximately 60–90 individual contract price series. Moreover, using the individual contract series requires an algorithm for determining what action to take at the rollover points. As an example of the type of problem that may be encountered, it is entirely possible for a given system to be long in the old contract and short in the new contract or vice versa. These problems are hardly insurmountable, but they make the use of individual contract series a somewhat unwieldy approach.

The awkwardness involved in using a multitude of individual contracts is not, however, the main problem. The primary drawback in using individual contract series is that the period of meaningful liquidity in most contracts is very short—much shorter than the already limited contract life spans. To see the scope of this problem, examine a cross section of futures price charts depicting the price action in the one-year period prior to expiration. In most markets, trading activity is sparse or even nonexistent until contracts approach to within at least six to eight months of expiration. In many markets, contracts don't achieve meaningful liquidity until the final five or six months of trading, and sometimes even less. This problem was illustrated in Chapter 12 (Figures 12.1–12.3). The limited time span of liquid trading in individual contracts means that any technical system or method that requires looking back at more than about six months of data—as would be true for a whole spectrum of longer-term approaches—cannot be applied to individual contract series. Thus, with the exception of short-term system traders, the use of individual contract series is not a viable alternative. It's not merely a matter of the approach being difficult, but, rather, impossible because the necessary data simply do not exist.

NEAREST FUTURES

The problems in using individual contract series as just described has led to the construction of various linked price series. The most common approach is almost universally known as "nearest futures." This price series is constructed by taking each individual contract series until its expiration and then continuing with the next contract until its expiration, and so on. This approach may be useful for constructing long-term price charts for purposes of chart analysis, but it is worthless for providing a series that can be used in the computer testing of trading systems.

The problem in using a nearest futures series is that there are price gaps between expiring and new contracts—and quite frequently, these gaps can be very substantial. For example, assume that the July corn contract expires at $3.00 and that the next nearest contract (September) closes at $2.50 on the same day. Assume that on the next day September corn moves limit-up from $2.50 to $2.62. A nearest futures price series will show the following closing levels on these two successive days: $3.00, $2.62. In other words, the nearest futures contract would imply a 38-cent loss on a day on which longs would have enjoyed (or shorts would have suffered) a limit-up price gain of 12 cents. This example is by no means artificial. In fact, it would be easy to find a plethora of similar extreme situations in actual price histories. Moreover, even if the typical distortion at rollover is considerably less extreme, the point is that there is virtually always some distortion, and the cumulative effect of these errors would destroy the validity of any computer test.

Fortunately, few traders are naive enough to use the nearest futures type of price series for computer testing. The two alternative linked price series described below have become the approaches employed by most traders wishing to use a single price series for each market in computer testing.

CONSTANT-FORWARD ("PERPETUAL") SERIES

The constant-forward (also known as "perpetual") price series consists of quotes for prices a constant amount of time forward. The interbank currency market and the London Metals Exchange markets provide actual examples of constant-forward price series. For example, the three-month forward price series for the Swiss franc represents the quote for the Swiss franc three months forward from each given day in the series. This is in contrast to the standard U.S. futures contract, which specifies a fixed expiration date.

A constant-forward series can be constructed from futures price data through interpolation. For example, if we were calculating a 90-day constant-forward (or perpetual) series, and the 90-day forward date fell exactly one-third of the way between the expirations of the nearest two contracts, the constant-forward price would be calculated as the sum of two-thirds of the nearest contract price and one-third of the subsequent contract price. As we moved forward in time, the nearer contract would be weighted less, but the weighting of the subsequent contract would increase proportionately. Eventually, the nearest contract would expire and drop out of the calculation, and the constant-forward price would be based on an interpolation between the subsequent two contracts.

As a more detailed example, assume one wishes to generate a 100-day forward price series based on Swiss franc futures. Swiss franc futures contracts are traded for March, June, September, and December. To illustrate the method for deriving the 100-day constant forward price, assume the current date is January 20. In this case, the date 100 days forward is April 30. This date falls between the March and June contracts. Assume the last trading dates for these two contracts are March 14 and June 13, respectively. Thus, April 30 is 47 days after the last trading day for the March contract and 44 days before the last trading day for the June contract. To calculate the 100-day forward price for January 20, an average price would be calculated using the quotes for March and June Swiss franc futures on January 20, weighting each quote in inverse proportion to its distance from the 100-day forward date (April 30). Thus, if on January 20 the closing price of March futures is 51.04 and the closing price of June futures is 51.77, the closing price for the 100-day forward series would be

$$\frac{44}{91}(51.04) + \frac{47}{91}(51.77) = 51.42$$

Note that the general formula for the weighting factor used for each contract price is

$$W_1 = \frac{C_2 - F}{C_2 - C_1} \qquad W_2 = \frac{F - C_1}{C_2 - C_1}$$

where C_1 = number of days until the nearby contract expiration
C_2 = number of days until the forward contract expiration
F = number of days until forward quote date
W_1 = weighting for nearby contract price quote
W_2 = weighting for forward contract price quote

So, for example, the weightings of the March and June quotes that would be used to derive a 100-day forward quote on March 2 would be as follows:

$$\text{Weighting for March quote} = \frac{103 - 100}{103 - 12} = \frac{3}{91}$$

$$\text{Weighting for June quote} = \frac{100 - 12}{103 - 12} = \frac{88}{91}$$

As we move forward in time, the nearer contract is weighted less and less, but the weighting for the subsequent contract increases proportionately. When the number of days remaining until the expiration of the forward contract equals the constant forward time (100 days in this example), the quote for the constant forward series would simply be equal to the quote for the forward contract (June). Subsequent price quotes would then be based on a weighted average of the June and September prices. In this manner, one continuous price series could be derived.

The constant forward price series eliminates the problem of huge price gaps at rollover points and is certainly a significant improvement over a nearest futures price series. However, this type of series still has major drawbacks. To begin, it must be stressed that one cannot literally trade a constant-forward series, since the series does not correspond to any real contract. An even more serious deficiency of the constant-forward series is that it fails to reflect the effect of the evaporation of time that exists in actual futures contracts. This deficiency can lead to major distortions—particularly in carrying-charge markets.

To illustrate this point, consider a hypothetical situation in which spot gold prices remain stable at approximately $400/ounce for a one-year period, while forward futures maintain a constant premium of 1.0%, per two-month spread. Given these assumptions, futures would experience a steady downtrend, declining \$24.60/ounce[1] (\$2,460 per contract) over the one-year period (the equivalent of the cumulative carrying-charge premiums). Note, however, that the constant-forward series would completely fail to reflect this bear trend because it would register an approximate constant price. For example, a two-month constant-forward series would remain stable at approximately \$404/ounce ($1.01 \times \$400 = \$404$). Thus, the price pattern of a constant-forward series can easily deviate substantially from the pattern exhibited by the actual traded contracts—a highly undesirable feature.

CONTINUOUS (SPREAD-ADJUSTED) PRICE SERIES

The spread-adjusted futures series, which we term "continuous futures," is constructed in such a way as to eliminate distortions due to the price gaps between expiring and subsequent futures contracts at transition points. In effect, the continuous futures price will precisely reflect the fluctuations of a futures position that is continuously rolled over to the subsequent contract N days before the last trading day, where N is a parameter that needs to be defined. Naturally, a trader would select a value of N that corresponds to her actual trading. For example, if a trader normally rolls a position over to a new contract approximately 20 days before last trading day, N would be defined as 20. The scale of the continuous futures series is adjusted so that the current price corresponds to a currently traded futures contract.

Table 19.1 illustrates the construction of a continuous futures price for the gold market. For simplicity of exposition, this illustration employs only two contract months, June and December; however, a continuous price could be formed using any number of traded contract months. For example, the continuous futures price could be constructed using the February, April, June, August, October, and December COMEX gold contracts.

For the moment, ignore the last column in Table 19.1 and focus instead on the unadjusted continuous futures price (column 6). At the start of the period, the actual price and the unadjusted continuous futures price are identical. At the first rollover point, the forward contract (December 1992) is trading at a \$5.90 premium to the nearby contract. All subsequent prices of the December 1992 contract are then adjusted downward by this amount (the addition of a negative nearby/forward spread), yielding the unadjusted continuous futures prices indicated in column 6. At the next rollover point,

---

[1]This is true since, given the assumptions, the one-year forward futures price would be approximately \$424.60 ($1.01^6 \times \$400 = \$424.60$) and would decline to the spot price (\$400) by expiration.

the forward contract (June 1993) is trading at a $4.10 premium to the nearby contract (December 1992). As a result, all subsequent actual prices of the June 1993 contract must now be adjusted by the cumulative adjustment factor—the total of all rollover gaps up to that point (–$10.00)—in order to avoid any artificial price gaps at the rollover point. This cumulative adjustment factor is indicated in column 5. The unadjusted continuous futures price is obtained by adding the cumulative adjustment factor to the actual price.

The preceding process is continued until the current date is reached. At this point, the final cumulative adjustment factor (which is a negative number) is subtracted from all the unadjusted continuous futures prices (column 6), a step that sets the current price of the series equal to the price of the current contract (December 1994 in our example) without changing the shape of the series. This continuous futures price is indicated in column 7 of Table 19.1. Note that although actual prices seem to imply a net price rise of $55.00 during the period surveyed, the continuous futures price indicates only a $24.30 advance—the actual price gain that would have been realized by a constant long futures position.

In effect, the construction of the continuous series can be thought of as the mathematical equivalent of taking a nearest futures chart, cutting out each individual contract series contained in the chart, and pasting the ends together (assuming a continuous series employing all contracts and using the same rollover dates as the nearest futures chart).

In some markets, the spreads between nearby and forward contracts will range from premiums to discounts (for example, cattle). However, in other markets, the spread differences will be unidirectional. For example, in the gold market, the forward month always trades at a premium to the nearby month.[2] In these types of markets, the spread-adjusted continuous price series will become increasingly disparate from actual prices.

It should be noted that in markets in which nearby premiums at contract rollovers tend to swamp nearby discounts, it is entirely possible for the series to eventually include negative prices for some past periods as cumulative adjustments mount. For example, during 1987–1991, there was a strong pro-

---

[2]The reason for this behavioral pattern in gold spreads is related to the fact that world gold inventories exceed annual usage by many multiples, perhaps even by as much as a hundredfold. Consequently, there can never actually be a "shortage" of gold—and a shortage of nearby supplies is the only reason why a storable commodity would reflect a premium for the nearby contract. (Typically, for storable commodities, the fact that the forward contracts embed carrying costs will result in these contracts trading at a premium to more nearby months.) Gold prices fluctuate in response to shifting perceptions of gold's value among buyers and sellers. Even when gold prices are at extremely lofty levels, it does not imply any actual shortage, but rather an upward shift in the market's perception of gold's value. Supplies of virtually any level are still available—at some price. This is not true for most commodities, in which there is a definite relevant limit in total supplies.

Table 19.1

CONSTRUCTION OF A CONTINUOUS FUTURES PRICE USING JUNE AND DECEMBER GOLD ($/OZ)*

(1)	(2)	(3)	(4)	(5)	(6)	(7)
Date	Contract	Actual Price	Spread at Rollover (Nearby-Forward)	Cumulative Adjustment Factor	Unadjusted Continuous Futures [Col. (3) + Col. (5)]	Continuous Futures Price [Col. (6) + 30.70]
5/27/92	June 1992	338.20			338.20	368.90
5/28/92	June 1992	337.00			337.00	367.70
5/29/92	June 1992	336.40			336.40	367.10
6/1/92	Dec 1992	343.60	-5.90	-5.90	337.70	368.40
6/2/92	Dec 1992	345.20		-5.90	339.30	370.00
• • • •						• • •
11/27/92	Dec 1992	334.00		-5.90	328.10	358.80
11/30/92	Dec 1992	334.30		-5.90	328.40	359.10
12/1/92	June 1993	339.00	-4.10	-10.00	329.00	359.70
12/2/92	June 1993	339.80		-10.00	329.80	360.50

Date	Contract	Price				
5/27/93	June 1993	381.40		−10.00	371.40	402.10
5/28/93	June 1993	378.30		−10.00	368.30	399.00
6/1/93	Dec 1993	374.70	−5.60	−15.60	359.10	389.80
6/2/93	Dec 1993	374.10		−15.60	358.50	389.20
• • •						
11/29/93	Dec 1993	369.40		−15.60	358.80	384.50
11/30/93	Dec 1993	369.80		−15.60	354.20	384.90
12/1/93	June 1994	380.30	−5.80	−21.40	358.90	389.60
12/2/93	June 1994	379.30		−21.40	357.90	388.60
• • •						
5/27/94	June 1994	384.70		−21.40	363.30	394.00
5/31/94	June 1994	387.10		−21.40	365.70	396.40
6/1/94	Dec 1994	392.70	−9.30	−30.70	362.00	392.70
6/2/94	Dec 1994	393.20		−30.70	362.50	393.20

*Assumes rollover on last day of the month preceding the contract month.

clivity for nearby months in copper futures to trade at premiums to more forward contracts, often by wide margins. As a result, the price gain that would have been realized by a continuously held futures position during this period far exceeded the net price gain implied by nearest futures, and the subtraction of the cumulative adjustment factor from current (1995) prices would result in negative prices for the early-to-mid-1980s (see Figure 19.1). Such an outcome is unavoidable if the continuous futures price series is to reflect the net gain in a continually held long position and if the series is shifted by the constant factor necessary to set the current continuous futures price equal to the current contract actual price.

Although the fact that a continuous futures price series could include negative prices may sound disconcerting, it does not present any problems in using the series for testing systems. The reason for this is that in measuring the profits

Figure 19.1
"NEGATIVE" PRICES IN A CONTINUOUS FUTURES CHART:
COPPER CONTINUOUS FUTURES

or losses of trades, it is critical that the price series employed accurately reflects price *changes,* not price *levels.* However, it also will often be useful to generate the actual prices that correspond to the continuous futures prices in order to facilitate such applications as checking trading signals against actual contract charts.

It should also be noted that the transition between contracts need not occur on the last trading day as is the conventional assumption in the nearest futures price series. In fact, because contracts are particularly vulnerable to distortions in their final weeks of trading due to technical concerns regarding delivery, it probably makes sense to avoid these prices in constructing a series. It follows then that one should use a rollover date before the last trading day (for example, 20 days prior to the last trading day).

COMPARING THE SERIES

It is important to understand that a linked futures price series can only accurately reflect either price *levels,* as does nearest futures, or price *moves* as does continuous futures, but not both—much as a coin can either land on heads or tails, but not both. The adjustment process used to construct continuous series means that past prices in a continuous series will not match the actual historical prices that prevailed at the time. However, the essential point is that the continuous series is the only linked futures series that will *exactly* reflect price swings and hence equity fluctuations in an actual trading account. Consequently, it is the only linked series that can be used to generate accurate simulations in computer testing of trading systems.

Now the preceding is an absolutely critical point! Mathematics is not a matter of opinion. There is one right answer and many wrong answers. The simple fact is that if a continuous futures price series is defined so that rollovers occur on days consistent with rollovers in actual trading, results implied by using this series will precisely match results in actual trading (assuming, of course, accurate commission and slippage cost estimates). In other words, the continuous series will exactly parallel the fluctuations of a constantly held (that is, rolled over) long position. All other types of linked series will not match actual market price movements.

To illustrate this statement, we compare the implications of various price series using the sideways gold market example cited earlier in this chapter (i.e., gold hovering near \$400 and a forward/nearby contract premium equal to 1.0% per two-month spread). A trader buying a one-year forward futures contract would therefore pay approximately \$424.60 ($1.01^6 \times \$400 = \$424.60$). The spot price would reflect a sideways pattern near \$400. As previously seen, a 60-day constant-forward price would reflect a sideways pattern near \$404 ($1.01 \times \$400$). A nearest futures price series would exhibit a general sideways pattern, characterized by extended minor downtrends (reflecting the gradual evaporation of the carrying charge time premium as each nearby contract approached expiration), interspersed with upward gaps at rollovers between expiring and subsequent futures contracts.

Thus the spot, constant-forward, and nearest futures price series would all suggest that a long position would have resulted in a break-even trade for the year. In reality, however, the buyer of the futures contract pays $424.60 for a contract that eventually expires at $400.00. Thus, from a trading or "real-world" viewpoint, the market actually witnesses a downtrend. The continuous futures price is the only chart that reflects the market decline—and real dollar loss—that would actually have been experienced by the trader.

I have often seen comments or articles by industry "experts" arguing for the use of constant-forward (perpetual) series instead of continuous series in order to avoid distortions. This is exactly backwards. Whether these proponents of constant-forward series adopt their stance because of naiveté or self-interest (that is, they are vendors of constant-forward-type data), they are simply wrong. This is not a matter of opinion. If you have any doubts, try matching up fluctuations in an actual trading account with those that would be implied by constant-forward-type price series. You will soon be a believer.

Are there any drawbacks to the continuous futures time series? Of course. It may be the best solution to the linked series problem, but it is not a perfect answer. A perfect alternative simply does not exist. One potential drawback, which is a consequence of the fact that continuous futures only accurately reflect price swings, not price levels, is that continuous futures cannot be used for any type of percentage calculations. This situation, however, can be easily remedied. If a system requires the calculation of a percentage change figure, use continuous futures to calculate the nominal price change and nearest futures for the divisor. Also, there is some unavoidable arbitrariness involved in constructing a continuous series, since one must decide which contracts to use and on what dates the rollovers should occur. However, this is not really a problem since these choices should merely mirror the contracts and rollover dates used in actual trading. Moreover, there is arbitrariness involved in the use of any of the price series discussed. Finally, in some markets, the contracts being linked together may have very different past price patterns (for example, this is often the case in livestock markets). However, this problem would exist in any kind of linked series.

CONCLUSION

For the purpose of computer testing of trading systems, there are only two types of valid price series: (1) individual contract series, and (2) continuous futures series. Individual contract series are only a viable approach if the methodologies employed do not require looking back more than four or five months in time (a restriction that rules out a vast number of technical approaches). In addition, the use of individual contract series is far clumsier. Thus, for most purposes, the continuous futures price series provides the best alternative. As long as one avoids using continuous prices for percentage calculations, this type of price series will yield accurate results (that is, results that parallel actual trading) as well as provide the efficiency of a single series per market. Again, I would strongly caution data users to avoid being misled by those who argue for the use of constant-forward-type series in computer testing applications. If your goal is a price series that will accurately reflect futures trading, the constant-forward series will create distortions rather than avoid them.

20 Testing and Optimizing Trading Systems

Every decade has its characteristic folly, but the basic cause is the same: people persist in believing that what has happened in the recent past will go on happening into the indefinite future, even while the ground is shifting under their feet.

George J. Church

THE WELL-CHOSEN EXAMPLE[1]

You've plunked down your $895 to attend the tenth annual "Secret of the Millionaires" futures trading seminar. At that price, you figure the speakers will be revealing some very valuable information.

The current speaker is explaining the Super-Razzle-Dazzle (SRD) commodity trading system. The slide on the huge screen reveals a price chart with "B" and "S" symbols representing buy and sell points. The slide is impressive: All of the buys seem to be lower than the sells.

This point is brought home even more dramatically in the next slide, which reveals the equity stream that would have been realized trading this system—a near-perfect uptrend. Not only that but the system is also very easy to keep up.

As the speaker says, "All it takes is 10 minutes a day and a knowledge of simple arithmetic."

You never realized making money in futures could be so simple. You could kick yourself for not having attended the first through ninth annual seminars.

Once you get home, you select 10 diversified markets and begin trading the SRD system. Each day you plot your equity. As the months go by, you notice a strange development. Although the equity in your account exhibits a very steady trend, just as the seminar example did, there is one small difference: The trend on your equity chart is down. What went wrong?

---

[1]The following section is adapted from an article that first appeared in *Futures* magazine in September 1984.

672

The fact is you can find a favorable illustration for almost any trading system. The mistake is in extrapolating probable future performance on the basis of an isolated and well-chosen example from the past.

A true life example may help illustrate this point. Back in 1983, when I had only been working on trading systems for a couple of years, I read an article in a trade magazine that presented the following very simple trading system:

1. If the six-day moving average is higher than the previous day's corresponding value, cover short and go long.
2. If the six-day moving average is lower than the previous day's corresponding value, cover long and go short.

The article used the Swiss franc in 1980 as an illustration. Without going into the details, suffice it to say that applying this system to the Swiss franc in 1980 would have resulted in a profit of $17,235 per contract (assuming an average round-turn transaction cost of $80). Even allowing for a conservative fund allocation of $6,000 per contract, this implied an annual gain of 287 percent! Not bad for a system that can be summarized in two sentences. It is easy to see how traders, presented with such an example, might eagerly abandon their other trading approaches for this apparent money machine.

I couldn't believe such a simple system could do so well. So I decided to test the system over a broader period—1976 to mid-1983[2]—and a wide group of markets.

Beginning with the Swiss franc, I found that the total profit during this period was $20,473. In other words, excluding 1980, the system made only $3,238 during the remaining 6½ years. Thus, assuming that you allocated $6,000 to trade this approach, the average annual percent return for those years was a meager 8 percent—quite a comedown from 287 percent in 1980.

But wait. It gets worse. Much worse.

When I applied the system to a group of 25 markets from 1976 through mid-1983, the system lost money in 19 of the 25 markets. In 13 of the markets—more than half of the total survey—the loss exceeded $22,500 or $3,000 per year, per contract! In five markets, the loss exceeded $45,000, equivalent to $6,000 per year, per contract!

Also, it should be noted that, even in the markets where the system was profitable, its performance was well below gains exhibited for these markets during the same period by most other trend-following systems.

---

[2]The start date was chosen to avoid the distortion of the extreme trends witnessed by many commodity markets during 1973–1975. The end date merely reflected the date on which I tested this particular system.

There was no question about it. This was truly a bad system. Yet, if you looked only at the well-chosen example, you might think you had stumbled upon the trading system Jesse Livermore used in his good years. Talk about a gap between perception and reality.

This system witnessed such large, broadly based losses that you may well wonder why fading the signals of such a system might not provide an attractive trading strategy. The reason is that most of the losses are the result of the system being so sensitive that it generates large transaction costs. (Transaction costs include commission costs *plus* slippage. The concept of slippage is discussed later in this chapter.) This sensitivity of the system occasionally is beneficial, as was the case for the Swiss franc in 1980. However, on balance, it is the system's major weakness.

Losses due to transaction costs would not be realized as gains by fading the system. Moreover, doing the opposite of all signals would generate equivalent transaction costs. Thus, once transaction costs are incorporated, the apparent attractiveness of a contrarian approach to using the system evaporates.

The moral is simple: Don't draw any conclusions about a system (or indicator) on the basis of isolated examples. The only way you can determine if a system has any value is by testing it (without benefit of hindsight) over an extended time period for a broad range of markets.

BASIC CONCEPTS AND DEFINITIONS

A *trading system* is a set of rules that can be used to generate trade signals. A *parameter* is a value that can be freely assigned in a trading system in order to vary the timing of signals. For example, in the basic breakout system, N (the number of prior days whose high or low must be exceeded to indicate a signal) is a parameter. Although the operation of the rules in the system will be identical whether $N = 7$ or $N = 40$, the timing of the signals will be vastly different. (For an example, see Figure 17.5 in Chapter 17.)

Most trading systems will have more than one parameter. For example, in the crossover moving average system there are two parameters: the length of the short-term moving average and the length of the long-term moving average. Any combination of parameter values is called a *parameter set*. For example, in a crossover moving average system, moving averages of 10 and 40 would represent a specific parameter set. Any other combination of moving average values would represent another parameter set. In systems with only one parameter (e.g., breakout), the parameter set would consist of only one element.[3]

---

[3]Note that the terms *parameter set* and *system variation* (the latter was used in Chapter 17) refer to identical concepts. The introduction of the term *parameter set* was merely deferred until this chapter because doing so appeared to allow for a more logically ordered presentation of the material.

Most "generic" systems are limited to one or two parameters. However, the design of more creative and flexible systems, or the addition of modifications to basic systems, will usually imply the need for three or more parameters. For example, adding a confirmation time delay rule to the crossover moving average system would imply a third parameter: the number of days in the time delay. One problem with systems that include many parameters is that it becomes increasingly cumbersome to test more than a small portion of all reasonable combinations. For example, if each parameter can assume 10 values, there would be 1,000 parameter sets if the system included three parameters, and 1,000,000 parameter sets if there were six parameters!

Quite clearly, practical considerations dictate the need for limiting the number of parameter sets. Of course, the simplest means of achieving this goal is to restrict the number of parameters in the system. In fact, as a general principle, it is wise to use the simplest form of a system (i.e., least number of parameters) that does not imply any substantial deterioration in performance relative to the more complex versions. However, one should not drop parameters that are deemed important simply to reduce the number of implied parameter sets. In this case, a more reasonable approach would be to limit the number of parameter sets actually tested.

It should be noted that even in a simple one- or two-parameter-set system, it is not necessary to test all possible combinations. For example, in a simple breakout system in which one wishes to test the performance for values of $N = 1$ to $N = 100$, it is not necessary to test each integer in this range. A far more efficient approach would be to first test the system using spaced values for N (e.g., $10, 20, 30, \ldots, 100$), and then, if desired, the trader could focus in on any areas that appeared to be of particular interest. For example, if the system exhibited particularly favorable performance for the parameter values $N = 40$ and $N = 50$, the trader might want to also test some other values of N in this narrower range. Such an additional step, however, is probably unnecessary, since as is discussed later in this chapter, performance differences in parameter set values—particularly values in such close proximity—are probably a matter of chance and lack any significance.

As a more practical real-life example, assume we wish to test a crossover moving average system that includes a time-delay confirmation rule. If we were interested in the performance of the system for parameter values 1–50 for the shorter-term moving average, 2–100 for the longer-term moving average, and 1–20 for the time delay, there would be a total of 74,500 parameter sets.[4] Obviously, it would be impractical to test, let alone evaluate, all of these combinations. Note that we cannot reduce the number of parameters

---

[4]To avoid double counting, each "short-term" moving average can only be combined with a "long-term" moving average for a longer period. Thus the total number of combinations is given by $(99 + 98 + 97 + \cdots + 50)(20) = 74{,}500$.

without severely damaging the basic structure of the system. However, we can test a far more limited number of parameter sets, which would provide a very good approximation of the system's overall performance. Specifically, we might use spacings of 10 for the shorter-term moving average (10, 20, 30, 40, and 50), spacings of 20 for the longer-term moving average (20, 40, 60, 80, and 100), and three selected values for the time delay (e.g., 5, 10, and 20). This approach would limit the number of parameter sets to be tested to 57.[5] Once these parameter sets are tested, the results would be analyzed, and a moderate number of additional parameter sets might be tested as suggested by this evaluation. For example, if a time delay of 5—the smallest value tested—seemed to work best for most favorable performing parameter sets, it would also be reasonable to test smaller values for the time delay.

Conceptually, it might be useful to define four types of parameters:

Continuous Parameter. A continuous parameter can assume any value within a given range. A percentage price penetration would be an example of a continuous parameter. Because a continuous parameter can assume an infinite number of values, it is necessary to specify some interval spacing in testing such a parameter. For example, a percent penetration parameter might be tested over a range of 0.05 percent to 0.50 percent, at intervals of 0.05 (i.e., 0.05, 0.10, . . . , 0.50). It is reasonable to expect performance results to change only moderately for an incremental change in the parameter value (assuming a sufficiently long test period).

Discrete Parameter. A discrete parameter can assume only integer values. For example, the number of days in a breakout system is a discrete parameter. Although one can test a discrete parameter for every integer value within the specified range, such detail is often unnecessary, and wider spacing is frequently employed. As with continuous parameters, it is reasonable to expect performance results to change only moderately for a small change in the parameter value.

Code Parameter. A code parameter is used to represent a definitional classification. Thus, there is no significance to the cardinal value of a code parameter. As an example of a code parameter, assume we wish to test a simple breakout system using three different definitions of a breakout (buy case): *close* above previous N-day *high, high* above previous N-day *high,* and *close* above previous N-day *high close.* We could test each of these systems separately, but it might be more efficient to use a parameter to specify the intended definition. Thus, a parameter value of 0 would indicate the first definition, a value of 1 the second definition, and a value of 2 the third definition. Note that there

---

[5](5 + 4 + 4 + 3 + 3) (3) = 57

are only three possible values for this parameter, and that there is no significance to incremental changes in parameter values.

Fixed or Nonoptimized Parameter. Normally, a parameter (of any type) will be allowed to assume different values in testing a system. However, in systems with a large number of parameters, it may be necessary to fix some parameter values in order to avoid an excessive number of parameter sets. Such parameters are called *nonoptimized parameters.* For example, in a nonsensitive (slow) trend-following system, we might wish to include a backup stop rule to prevent catastrophic losses. By definition, in this situation, the stop rule would only be activated on a few occasions. Consequently, any parameters implicit in the stop rule could be fixed, since variation in these parameter values would not greatly affect the results.

CHOOSING THE PRICE SERIES

The first step in testing a system in a given market is choosing the appropriate price series. The issues related to this selection have already been fully detailed in Chapter 19. Generally speaking, a continuous futures series is the preferred choice, although actual contract data could be used for short-term trading systems.

CHOOSING THE TIME PERIOD

Generally speaking, the longer the test period, the more reliable the results. If the time period is too short, the test will not reflect the system's performance for a reasonable range of market situations. For example, a test of a trend-following system on the cotton market that used only the two most recent years of data (April 1993–March 1995 at this writing)—a period dominated by a huge, protracted bull market (see Figure 20.1)—would yield highly misleading results in terms of the system's probable long-term performance.

On the other hand, if too long a period is used for testing a system, the earlier years in the survey period might be extremely unrepresentative of current market conditions. For example, it would probably be better not to extend the test period back far enough to include 1973–1976—a time interval that witnessed unprecedented, massive price advances and subsequent steep price collapses in a number of commodity markets. An inclusion of this highly unrepresentative period would tend to greatly exaggerate the potential performance of most trend-following systems. In other words, the enormous profits realized by most trend-following systems during this period would be unlikely to be duplicated in the future.

Although it is impossible to provide a decisive answer as to the optimum

Figure 20.1
MAJOR TRENDING PHASE AS UNREPRESENTATIVE PRICE
SAMPLE: COTTON CONTINUOUS FUTURES

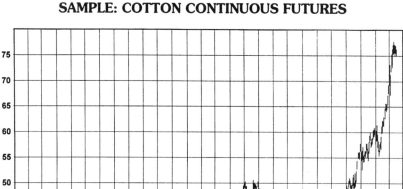

number of years to be used in testing, 10–20 years seems to be a reasonable range. For short-term trading systems (average duration of trades equal to a few weeks or less), a shorter test period (e.g., 5–10 years) would probably be sufficient. Trading system test results based on time periods significantly shorter than these guidelines should be suspect. In fact, it is rather incredible that some published studies on trading systems were based on test periods of two years or less.

Ideally, one should test a system using a longer time period (e.g., 15 years) and then evaluate the results for the period as a whole and various shorter time intervals (e.g., individual years). Such an approach is important in determining the degree of *time stability* in the system—the relative consistency of performance from one period to the next. Time stability is important because it enhances confidence regarding a system's potential for maintaining consistent favorable performance in the future. Most people would be quite hesitant about using a system that generated significant net profits over a 15-year period due to three spectacular performing years, but then witnessed losses or near break-even results in the remaining 12 years—and rightly so. In contrast, a system that registered moderate net gains during the 15-year period and was profitable in 14 of the 15 years would undoubtedly be viewed as more attractive by most traders.

REALISTIC ASSUMPTIONS

Users of trading systems often discover that their actual results are substantially worse than the paper trading results implied by the system. In fact, this situation is so common that it even has its own name: *slippage*. Assuming that the divergence in the results is not due to errors in the program, slippage is basically a consequence of a failure to use realistic assumptions in testing the system. Basically there are two types of such faulty assumptions:

1. *Transaction Costs*. Most traders don't realize that merely adjusting for actual commission costs in testing a system is not a sufficiently rigid assumption. The reason for this is that commissions only account for a portion of transaction costs. Another less tangible, but no less real, cost is the difference between the theoretical execution price and the actual fill price. For example, if one is testing a system assuming order entry on the close, the use of the midpoint of the closing range might not be a realistic assumption. For some reason, buys near the upper end of the closing range and sells near the lower end of the closing range seem to be far more common than their reverse counterparts. There are two ways of addressing this problem. First, use the worst possible fill price (e.g., high of the closing range for buys). Second, use a transaction cost per trade assumption much greater than the actual historical commission costs (e.g., $100 per trade). The latter approach is preferable because it is more general. For example, how would one decide the worst possible fill price for an intraday stop order?

2. *Limit Days*. Unless it is programmed otherwise, a computerized trading system will indicate executions on the receipt of each signal. However, in the real world things are not quite so simple. Occasionally, execution will not be possible because the market is locked at the daily permissible limit. If one assumes execution in such a situation, the paper results may dramatically overstate actual performance. Although it is possible to provide a plethora of illustrations, one example should suffice. Figure 20.2 indicates hypothetical trading signals and the corresponding implied execution prices. Note that whereas the signal prices suggest a profit of 42.4¢ ($15,900 per contract), the actual trade would have resulted in a loss of 16.2¢ ($6,075 per contract).

The potential systems trader may find that seemingly attractive trading systems disintegrate once realistic assumptions are employed. This is particularly true for very active systems, which generate very large transaction costs. However, it is far better to make this discovery in the analytical testing stage than in actual trading.

Figure 20.2
WIDE GAP BETWEEN SIGNAL PRICE AND
ACTUAL ENTRY: IMPACT OF LIMIT DAYS
(DECEMBER 1994 COFFEE)

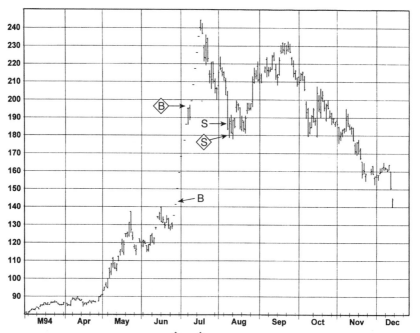

Notes: B, S = signal prices; Ⓑ, Ⓢ = execution prices.

OPTIMIZING SYSTEMS

Optimization refers to the process of finding the best performing parameter set(s) for a given system applied to a specific market. The underlying premise of optimization is that parameter sets that worked best in the past have a greater probability of superior performance in the future. (The question of whether this assumption is valid is addressed in the next section.)

A basic question that must be considered in optimization is what criteria should be used for defining best performance. Frequently, best performance is simply interpreted as largest equity gain. However, such a definition is incomplete. Ideally, four factors should be considered in performance comparisons:

1. ***Percent Return.*** Return measured relative to funds needed to trade the system. The importance of using percent return rather than nominal gain is detailed in Chapter 21.
2. ***Risk Measure.*** In addition to percent gain, it is also important to employ some measure of equity fluctuations (e.g., variability in rate of gain,

retracements in equity). Besides the obvious psychological reasons for wishing to avoid parameter sets and systems with high volatility, a risk measure is particularly significant because one might pick an unfavorable starting date for trading the system. Chapter 21 discusses several performance measures that incorporate both percent return and risk.

3. **Parameter Stability.** It is not sufficient to find a parameter set that performs well. It is also necessary to ascertain that the parameter set does not reflect a fluke in the system. In other words, we wish to determine that similar parameter sets also exhibit favorable performance. In fact, the goal of optimization should be to find broad regions of good performance rather than the single best performing parameter set.

For example, if in testing a simple breakout system one found that the parameter set $N = 7$ exhibited the best percent return/risk characteristics but that performance dropped off very sharply for parameter sets $N < 5$ and $N > 9$, while all sets in the range $N = 25$ to $N = 54$ performed relatively well, it would make much more sense to choose a parameter set from the latter range. Why? Because the exceptional performance of the set $N = 7$ appears to be a peculiarity of the historical price data, which is not likely to be repeated. The fact that surrounding parameter sets performed poorly suggests that there is no basis for confidence in trading the parameter set $N = 7$. In contrast, the broad range of performance stability for sets in the region $N = 25$ to $N = 54$ suggests that a set drawn from the center of this range would have a better prospect for success.

Determining profit regions for single parameter systems requires nothing more than scanning a column of numbers. In a two-parameter system, one would form an array of performance measures in which columns corresponded to increasing values for the first parameter and rows corresponded to increasing values for the second parameter. In this way, one could literally search for profitable performance areas. In the case of a three-parameter system, the same procedure could be used if one of the parameters only assumed a small number of alternative values. For example, in a crossover moving-average system with a time delay confirmation rule in which three values for the time delay are tested, one could form three two-dimensional arrays of performance—one for each value of the time delay. Finding profit regions for more complex systems, however, would require computerized search procedures.

4. **Time Stability.** As detailed in a previous section, it is important to ascertain that favorable performance for the period as a whole is truly representative of the total period rather than a reflection of a few isolated intervals of extraordinary performance.

Although incorporating various performance measures in the optimization procedure will provide a much more complete picture, it also greatly complicates the task. Realistically speaking, many traders will find such elaborate performance evaluation impractical. In this regard, the trader can draw solace from the fact that for comparisons involving different parameter sets for the *same* system, the preceding factors tend to be highly correlated. Generally, the parameter sets with the best gain will also be the sets that exhibit the smallest equity retracements. Consequently, for the optimization of a single system, the use of a basic return/risk measure (e.g., Sharpe ratio), or even a simple percent return measure will usually yield similar results to a complex performance evaluation that incorporates a number of performance measures. Thus, although the multifactor performance evaluation is theoretically preferable, it is often not essential. However, if one is comparing parameter sets from completely different systems, the explicit consideration of risk, parameter stability, and time stability is more important.

The foregoing represents a theoretical discussion of optimization concepts and procedures, and implicitly assumes that optimization enhances a system's *future* performance. As discussed in the next section, however, the viability of optimization is open to serious question.

THE MYTH OF OPTIMIZATION

It is ironic that optimization receives so much attention while its underlying premise is rarely considered. In other words, do the better performing parameter sets of the *past* continue to exhibit above-average performance in the *future*?

As an empirical test of the validity of optimization we examine the historical rankings of a range of parameter set values for a breakout system: reverse from short to long if today's close is higher than the highest close during the past N days; reverse from long to short if today's close is lower than the lowest close during the past N days. Nine values of N for this system were tested: 20, 30, 40, 50, 60, 70, 80, 90, and 100.

Tables 20.1–20.10 compare the profit/loss rankings of these parameter sets in 10 markets for 3 two-year test periods (1989–1990, 1991–1992, and 1993–1994), with parameter sets listed in the order of their performance during the respective *prior* eight-year periods. In other words, the top performing parameter set of the prior eight-year period is listed first, the second best parameter set of the prior period is listed second, and so on. For example, if the top number in a column is 6, it means that the best performing parameter set for that market in the prior eight-year period was the sixth ranked parameter set (out of nine) during the given test period.

As a visual aid to help see if there is any consistency between past and

Table 20.1
BREAKOUT SYSTEM (T-BONDS): COMPARISON
OF PARAMETER SET RANKINGS IN TWO-YEAR
TEST PERIODS VERSUS RANKINGS IN PRIOR
EIGHT-YEAR PERIODS

Parameter Set Rank Prior 8-Year Period	Rank of Same Parameter Set in 1989–1990	Rank of Same Parameter Set in 1991–1992	Rank of Same Parameter Set in 1993–1994
1	(9)	6	(8)
2	(8)	(9)	5
3	(1)	(8)	4
4	7	5	6
5	5	3	(9)
6	(2)	(2)	(2)
7	6	4	(1)
8	3	(1)	3
9	4	7	7

Table 20.2
BREAKOUT SYSTEM (DEUTSCHE MARK):
COMPARISON OF PARAMETER SET RANKINGS IN
TWO-YEAR TEST PERIODS VERSUS RANKINGS
IN PRIOR EIGHT-YEAR PERIODS

Parameter Set Rank Prior 8-Year Period	Rank of Same Parameter Set in 1989–1990	Rank of Same Parameter Set in 1991–1992	Rank of Same Parameter Set in 1993–1994
1	(9)	(9)	5
2	(1)	6	3
3	(2)	4	(8)
4	4	7	7
5	5	3	6
6	(8)	5	(9)
7	7	(8)	(2)
8	6	(2)	(1)
9	3	(1)	4

Table 20.3
BREAKOUT SYSTEM (JAPANESE YEN):
COMPARISON OF PARAMETER SET RANKINGS IN
TWO-YEAR TEST PERIODS VERSUS RANKINGS
IN PRIOR EIGHT-YEAR PERIODS

Parameter Set Rank Prior 8-Year Period	Rank of Same Parameter Set in 1989–1990	Rank of Same Parameter Set in 1991–1992	Rank of Same Parameter Set in 1993–1994
1	4	3	(2)
2	(8)	(2)	3
3	(1)	(1)	(8)
4	(2)	6	7
5	(9)	4	5
6	3	5	4
7	5	(9)	(1)
8	6	7	6
9	7	(8)	(9)

Table 20.4
BREAKOUT SYSTEM (GOLD): COMPARISON
OF PARAMETER SET RANKINGS IN TWO-YEAR
TEST PERIODS VERSUS RANKINGS IN PRIOR
EIGHT-YEAR PERIODS

Parameter Set Rank Prior 8-Year Period	Rank of Same Parameter Set in 1989–1990	Rank of Same Parameter Set in 1991–1992	Rank of Same Parameter Set in 1993–1994
1	4	(2)	6
2	7	5	7
3	(9)	6	(9)
4	(1)	3	3
5	5	(9)	5
6	(2)	(8)	(2)
7	3	7	(1)
8	6	4	(8)
9	(8)	(1)	4

**Table 20.5
BREAKOUT SYSTEM (SILVER): COMPARISON
OF PARAMETER SET RANKINGS IN TWO-YEAR
TEST PERIODS VERSUS RANKINGS IN PRIOR
EIGHT-YEAR PERIODS**

Parameter Set Rank Prior 8-Year Period	Rank of Same Parameter Set in 1989–1990	Rank of Same Parameter Set in 1991–1992	Rank of Same Parameter Set in 1993–1994
1	2	7	7
2	3	1	8
3	5	2	4
4	1	3	6
5	4	8	5
6	7	9	1
7	6	5	2
8	9	4	9
9	8	6	3

**Table 20.6
BREAKOUT SYSTEM (HEATING OIL):
COMPARISON OF PARAMETER SET RANKINGS IN
TWO-YEAR TEST PERIODS VERSUS RANKINGS
IN PRIOR EIGHT-YEAR PERIODS**

Parameter Set Rank Prior 8-Year Period	Rank of Same Parameter Set in 1989–1990	Rank of Same Parameter Set in 1991–1992	Rank of Same Parameter Set in 1993–1994
1	8	9	1
2	9	1	8
3	7	7	9
4	3	5	2
5	4	2	6
6	1	8	7
7	5	6	3
8	6	3	5
9	2	4	4

Table 20.7
BREAKOUT SYSTEM (CORN): COMPARISON OF PARAMETER SET RANKINGS IN TWO-YEAR TEST PERIODS VERSUS RANKINGS IN PRIOR EIGHT-YEAR PERIODS

Parameter Set Rank Prior 8-Year Period	Rank of Same Parameter Set in 1989–1990	Rank of Same Parameter Set in 1991–1992	Rank of Same Parameter Set in 1993–1994
1	8	7	1
2	6	3	5
3	5	5	6
4	4	1	8
5	7	9	3
6	1	4	2
7	2	6	4
8	3	8	7
9	9	2	9

Table 20.8
BREAKOUT SYSTEM (SOYBEANS): COMPARISON OF PARAMETER SET RANKINGS IN TWO-YEAR TEST PERIODS VERSUS RANKINGS IN PRIOR EIGHT-YEAR PERIODS

Parameter Set Rank Prior 8-Year Period	Rank of Same Parameter Set in 1989–1990	Rank of Same Parameter Set in 1991–1992	Rank of Same Parameter Set in 1993–1994
1	9	9	3
2	4	8	1
3	8	6	2
4	5	4	5
5	6	3	9
6	7	5	6
7	3	1	4
8	1	7	7
9	2	2	8

Table 20.9
BREAKOUT SYSTEM (LIVE CATTLE):
COMPARISON OF PARAMETER SET RANKINGS IN
TWO-YEAR TEST PERIODS VERSUS RANKINGS
IN PRIOR EIGHT-YEAR PERIODS

Parameter Set Rank Prior 8-Year Period	Rank of Same Parameter Set in 1989–1990	Rank of Same Parameter Set in 1991–1992	Rank of Same Parameter Set in 1993–1994
1	5	4	4
2	3	7	7
3	6	②	⑨
4	①	5	5
5	4	3	6
6	②	⑨	⑧
7	7	⑧	②
8	⑧	6	3
9	⑨	①	①

Table 20.10
BREAKOUT SYSTEM (SUGAR): COMPARISON
OF PARAMETER SET RANKINGS IN TWO-YEAR
TEST PERIODS VERSUS RANKINGS IN PRIOR
EIGHT-YEAR PERIODS

Parameter Set Rank Prior 8-Year Period	Rank of Same Parameter Set in 1989–1990	Rank of Same Parameter Set in 1991–1992	Rank of Same Parameter Set in 1993–1994
1	②	⑧	②
2	⑧	4	7
3	3	7	5
4	①	5	6
5	4	6	⑧
6	7	①	①
7	6	3	3
8	5	②	⑨
9	⑨	⑨	4

future performance, the two top performing parameter sets in each test period are denoted by unshaded circles and the two bottom parameter sets by shaded circles. If the basic premise of optimization were valid—that is, that the best performing parameter sets of the *past* were likely to be the best performing parameter sets in the *future*—then Tables 20.1–20.10 should reflect a pattern of unshaded circles near column tops and shaded circles near column bottoms. Clearly, this is not the case. Both unshaded and shaded circles are sometimes near column tops, sometimes near column bottoms, and sometimes near column midpoints. The apparent randomness in the vertical placement of the unshaded and shaded circles in Tables 20.1–20.10 implies that the correlation between past and future performance is highly tenuous.

The instability in the values of the best performing parameter sets from period to period means that gauging a system's performance by the best *past* parameter sets will grossly overstate the system's performance potential. To illustrate this point, Tables 20.11–20.14 compare the performance of the best parameter set in each test period versus the average of all parameter sets and the performance of the parameter sets that had the best and worst results in the *prior* period. In this particular example, based on the all-market totals, selecting the worst parameter set in the prior period would actually have outperformed a strategy of picking the best past parameter set in two of the three test periods, as well as the three-period total!

This observation is not intended to imply that the prior-period worst performing parameter set is likely to outperform the prior-period best performing set. If similar empirical tests were conducted for other systems, the prior-period best performing parameter set would probably outperform the prior-period worst performing set more often than the other way around (although the type of results witnessed in our example are far from uncommon). The key point, however, is that invariably, as was the case in Tables 20.11–20.14, the prior-period best performing parameter sets would fall far short of the actual best performing parameter sets for the given periods and would often fail to provide any statistically significant improvement over the average of all parameter sets.

Our example used a very small list of only nine parameter sets. Many system developers run optimizations across hundreds or even thousands of parameter sets. Imagine the degree of performance overstatement that would occur by representing a system's performance by the best parameter sets in these cases!

Although optimization seemed to have little, if any, value when applied market by market, as in Tables 20.1–20.10, optimization does appear to be a bit more useful if applied to a portfolio. In other words, instead of picking the best past parameter set for each market, the best past single parameter set applied across all markets is selected. Table 20.15 shows the two-year test period parameter set rankings for a portfolio consisting of all 10 markets

Table 20.11
PROFIT/LOSS ($) COMPARISONS FOR 1989–1990
TEST PERIOD: ACTUAL BEST PARAMETER SET VERSUS
PERIOD AVERAGE AND BEST AND WORST PARAMETER
SETS IN PRIOR PERIOD

Market	Actual Best Parameter Set in *Given* Period	Best Parameter Set in *Prior* Period	Average of all Parameter Sets	Worst Parameter Set in *Prior* Period
T-bond	6,670	−9,090	−2,180	1,420
Deutsche mark	7,780	3,020	5,390	6,340
Japanese yen	11,840	9,240	8,130	8,420
Gold	3,390	1,700	1,080	−320
Silver	5,850	5,330	3,050	1,630
Heating oil	7,650	1,760	3,380	6,430
Corn	1,640	−2,190	−590	−2,730
Soybeans	4,970	−7,160	−740	4,740
Cattle	2,090	850	−20	−3,290
Sugar	4,240	4,170	−840	−5,560
Total	**56,120**	**7,630**	**16,030**	**17,080**

Table 20.12
PROFIT/LOSS ($) COMPARISONS FOR 1991–1992
TEST PERIOD: ACTUAL BEST PARAMETER SET VERSUS
PERIOD AVERAGE AND BEST AND WORST PARAMETER
SETS IN PRIOR PERIOD

Market	Actual Best Parameter Set in *Given* Period	Best Parameter Set in *Prior* Period	Average of all Parameter Sets	Worst Parameter Set in *Prior* Period
T-bond	3,710	−1,820	−420	−2,920
Deutsche mark	9,180	1,680	4,770	9,180
Japanese yen	3,340	−240	−1,670	−3,620
Gold	1,370	90	−1,050	1,370
Silver	−720	−1,890	−1,640	−1,780
Heating oil	5,510	−980	1,540	4,290
Corn	560	−480	−440	340
Soybeans	−2,420	−6,090	−4,650	−3,190
Cattle	1,380	−160	−340	1,380
Sugar	810	−1,690	−1,410	−1,850
Total	**22,700**	**−11,570**	**−5,010**	**3,200**

Table 20.13
PROFIT/LOSS ($) COMPARISONS FOR 1993–1994
TEST PERIOD: ACTUAL BEST PARAMETER SET VERSUS
PERIOD AVERAGE AND BEST AND WORST PARAMETER
SETS IN PRIOR PERIOD

Market	Actual Best Parameter Set in *Given* Period	Best Parameter Set in *Prior* Period	Average of all Parameter Sets	Worst Parameter Set in *Prior* Period
T-bond	11,600	3,500	7,180	7,910
Deutsche mark	6,210	–3,660	–3,300	–1,410
Japanese yen	3,620	2,460	260	–3,060
Gold	490	–1,900	–1,460	–930
Silver	1,600	–3,650	–2,690	–790
Heating oil	2,200	2,200	–1,700	–890
Corn	1,910	1,910	640	–1,030
Soybeans	2,120	1,570	–240	–2,060
Cattle	1,600	950	500	1,600
Sugar	880	570	–550	–240
Total	**32,230**	**3,950**	**–1,360**	**–900**

Table 20.14
PROFIT/LOSS ($) COMPARISONS FOR THREE TEST
PERIODS COMBINED: ACTUAL BEST PARAMETER SETS
VERSUS PERIOD AVERAGES AND BEST AND WORST
PARAMETER SETS IN PRIOR PERIODS

Market	Total of Actual Best Parameter Sets in Test Periods	Total of Best Parameter Sets in *Prior* Periods	Total of Period Parameter Set Averages	Total of Worst Parameter Sets in *Prior* Periods
T-bond	21,980	–7,410	3,950	6,410
Deutsche mark	23,170	1,040	6,860	14,110
Japanese yen	18,800	11,460	6,720	1,740
Gold	5,250	–110	–1,430	120
Silver	6,730	–210	–1,280	–940
Heating oil	15,360	2,980	3,220	9,830
Corn	4,110	–760	–390	–3,420
Soybeans	4,670	–11,680	–5,330	–510
Cattle	5,070	1,640	140	–310
Sugar	5,930	3,060	–2,800	–7,650
Total	**111,070**	**10**	**9,660**	**19,380**

depicted in Tables 20.1–20.10.[6] The one striking correlation between past and future performance is that the worst parameter set in the prior eight-year period is also the worst parameter set in the subsequent two-year period in all three test intervals!

Although the worst past parameter set also seems likely to be the worst future parameter set, other past ranking placements seem to imply little predictive value. The average ranking for all three test periods of the remaining eight prior-period ranking placements (i.e., all rankings excluding the worst one) is 4.5. While the average test period ranking of the best parameter set in the prior eight-year period is somewhat better than the average at 3.3, the fourth-ranked parameter set in the prior period has by far the best average ranking in the future test periods: 2.3. Also note that the second best prior-period parameter set has an average test period rank almost identical to the corresponding average for the second worst prior-period parameter set: 4.7 versus 5.0.

To gain some insight as to why the worst prior-period ranking seems to be such an excellent predictor of future performance (namely, continued poor performance for that parameter set), while other ranking placements seem to have little predictive value, we examine performance rankings based on parameter set value. Table 20.16 indicates parameter set rankings in each of the three tests periods based on parameter set values (as opposed to prior period rankings as was the case in Table 20.15). The parameter set values are listed in ascending order.

Table 20.16 reveals that the worst performing parameter set in each of the test periods was actually the same parameter set! (Since Table 20.15 indicated that the test period worst parameter set was the same as the prior period worst parameter set in all three cases, the implication is that this same parameter set was also the worst performing parameter set in all three prior eight-year periods.) This consistently worst performing parameter set is at one extreme end of the parameter set range tested: $N = 20$.

Although $N = 20$—the most sensitive parameter set value tested—is consistently the worst performer (when applied across a portfolio), the other values tested ($N = 30$ to $N = 100$) show no consistent pattern. It is true that the parameter set $N = 80$ was by far the best performing set with an incredible average rank of 1.3. However, the average rankings of the two surrounding N values (6.7 and 3.3) suggest that the stellar performance of $N = 80$ was probably a statistical fluke. As was explained earlier in this chapter, a lack of *parameter stability* suggests that the past superior performance of a parameter set probably reflects a peculiarity in the historical data tested rather than a pattern that is likely to be repeated in the future.

---

[6]The portfolio consists of one contract in each market, with the exception of corn, which is assumed to trade two contracts because of its low volatility.

Table 20.15
BREAKOUT SYSTEM (PORTFOLIO): COMPARISON OF
PARAMETER SET RANKINGS IN TWO-YEAR TEST PERIODS
VERSUS RANKINGS IN PRIOR EIGHT-YEAR PERIODS

Parameter Set Rank Prior 8-Year Period	Rank of Same Parameter Set in 1989–1990	Rank of Same Parameter Set in 1991–1992	Rank of Same Parameter Set in 1993–1994	Average Rank
1	1	7	2	3.3
2	5	1	8	4.7
3	3	6	4	4.3
4	2	4	1	2.3
5	4	8	6	6.0
6	6	3	7	5.3
7	7	5	3	5.0
8	8	2	5	5.0
9	9	9	9	9.0

Table 20.16
BREAKOUT SYSTEM (PORTFOLIO): COMPARISON
OF PARAMETER SET RANKINGS IN TWO-YEAR TEST
PERIODS BASED ON *N*-VALUES

Parameter Set N-Value	Rank of Parameter Set in 1989–1990	Rank of Parameter Set in 1991–1992	Rank of Parameter Set in 1993–1994	Average Rank
20	9	9	9	9.0
30	8	2	5	5.0
40	7	5	3	5.0
50	6	3	1	3.3
60	4	6	6	5.3
70	5	7	8	6.7
80	1	1	2	1.3
90	2	4	4	3.3
100	3	8	7	6.0

It is instructive to review the observations revealed by the foregoing optimization experiment:

- Optimization appeared to have no value whatsoever when applied on a market-by-market basis.
- When applied to a portfolio, however, optimization appeared useful in predicting the parameter set most likely to witness inferior future performance, although it still showed no reliable pattern in predicting the parameter set most likely to witness superior future performance.
- Upon closer examination it appeared the pattern of consistent inferior performance was not so much a consequence of the prior period ranking as the parameter value. In other words, the parameter set range tested began at a value that was clearly suboptimal for the given system: $N = 20$. Although not indicated in the parameter set ranking tables, lower values of N would have shown even worse performance—in fact, strikingly worse—as the value of N was decreased.
- Once the suboptimal extreme of a parameter set range was eliminated ($N = 20$ or lower in this example), there was little stability in the value of the best performing parameter set within a broad range of parameter set values ($N = 30$ to $N = 100$ in this example).

These observations, which are consistent with the results of other similar empirical tests I have conducted in the past, suggest the following key conclusions regarding optimization:[7]

1. Any system, repeat any system, can be made to be very profitable through optimization (that is, over its past performance). If you ever find a system that can't be optimized to show good profits in the past, congratulations, you have just discovered a money machine (by doing the opposite, unless transaction costs are exorbitant). Therefore, a wonderful past performance for a system that has been optimized may be nice to look at, but it doesn't mean very much.

2. Optimization will always, repeat always, overstate the potential future performance of a system—usually by a wide margin (say, three trailer trucks' worth). Therefore, optimized results should never, repeat never, be used to evaluate a system's merit.

3. For many if not most systems, optimization will improve *future* performance only marginally, if at all.

---

[7]Although a single empirical experiment cannot be used to draw broad generalizations, I am willing to do so here because the results of the optimization test just described are fairly typical of many similar tests I have conducted in the past. In this sense, the optimization test detailed in the text is not intended as a *proof* of the severe limitations of optimization, but rather as an *illustration* of this point.

4. If optimization has any value, it is usually in defining the broad boundaries for the ranges from which parameter set values in the system should be chosen. Fine-tuning of optimization is at best a waste of time and at worst self-delusion.

5. In view of the preceding items, sophisticated and complex optimization procedures are a waste of time. The simplest optimization procedure will provide as much meaningful information (assuming that there is any meaningful information to be derived).

In summary, contrary to widespread belief, there is some reasonable question as to whether optimization will yield meaningfully better results over the long run than randomly picking the parameter sets to be traded. Lest there be any confusion, let me explicitly state that this statement is not intended to imply that optimization is never of any value. First, as indicated previously, optimization can be useful in defining the suboptimal extreme ranges that should be excluded from the selection of parameter set values (for instance, $N \leq 20$ in our breakout system example). Also, it is possible that for some systems, optimization may provide some edge in parameter set selection, even after suboptimal extreme ranges are excluded. However, I do mean to imply that the degree of improvement provided by optimization is far less than generally perceived and that traders would probably save a lot of money by first proving any assumptions they are making about optimization rather than taking such assumptions on blind faith.

TESTING VERSUS FITTING

Perhaps the most critical error made by users of commodity trading systems is the assumption that the performance of the optimized parameter sets during the test period provides an approximation of the potential performance of those sets in the future. As was demonstrated in the previous section, such assumptions will lead to grossly overstated evaluations of a system's true potential. It must be understood that futures market price fluctuations are subject to a great deal of randomness. Thus, the "ugly truth" is that the question of which parameter sets will perform best during any given period is largely a matter of chance. The laws of probability indicate that if enough parameter sets are tested, even a meaningless trading system will yield some sets with favorable past performance. Evaluating a system based on the optimized parameter sets (i.e., the best performing sets during the survey period) would be best described as fitting the system to past results rather than testing the system. If optimization can't be used to gauge performance, how then do you evaluate a system? The following sections describe two meaningful approaches.

Blind Simulation

In the blind simulation approach the system is optimized using data for a time period that deliberately excludes the most recent years. The performance of the system is then tested using the selected parameter sets for subsequent years. Ideally, this process should be repeated several times.

Note that the error of fitting results is avoided because the parameter sets used to measure performance in any given period are selected entirely on the basis of prior rather than concurrent data. In a sense, this testing approach mimics real life (i.e., one must decide which parameter sets to trade on the basis of past data).

The optimization tests of the previous section used this type of procedure, stepping through time in two-year intervals. Specifically, system results for the 1981–1988 period were used to select the best performing parameter sets, which were then tested for the 1989–1990 period. Next, the system results for the 1983–1990 period were used to select the best performing parameter sets, which were then tested for the 1991–1992 period. Finally, the system results for the 1985–1992 period were used to select the best performing parameter sets, which were then tested for the 1993–1994 period.

The essential point is that simulation and optimization periods should not be allowed to overlap. Simulations that are run over the same period as the optimization are worthless.

Average Parameter Set Performance

Finding the average parameter set performance requires defining a complete list of all parameter sets that one wishes to test *before* running any simulations. Simulations are then run for all the parameter sets selected, and the average of all sets tested is used as an indication of the system's potential performance. This approach is valid because you could always throw a dart to pick a parameter from a broad range of parameter set values. If you throw enough darts, the net result will be the average. The important point is that this average should be calculated across all parameter sets, not just those sets that prove profitable. Note that the trader might still choose to trade the optimized parameter sets for the future (instead of randomly selected ones), but the evaluation of the system's performance should be based on the average of all sets tested (which is equivalent to a random selection process).

The blind simulation approach probably comes closest to duplicating real-life trading circumstances. However, the average parameter set performance is probably as conservative and has the advantage of requiring far less calculation. Both approaches represent valid procedures for testing a system.

One important caveat: in the advertised claims for given systems, the term "simulated results" is often used loosely as a euphemism for optimized results (instead of implying that the results are based on a blind simulation process). If this is the case, the weight attached to the results should equal the amount of money invested in the system: zero. The commonplace misuse and distortion of simulated results is examined in detail in the next section.

THE TRUTH ABOUT SIMULATED RESULTS

Although the value of optimization in improving a system's future performance is open to debate, there is absolutely no question that the use of optimized results will greatly distort the implied future performance of a system. The reason for this is that, as was demonstrated earlier in this chapter, there is very little, if any, correlation between the best performing parameters in a system for one period and the best performing parameters in a subsequent period. Hence, assuming that the performance implied by the best performing parameters could have been achieved in the past is totally unrealistic.

After years of experience, my attitude toward simulated results is summarized by what I call Schwager's corollary of simulations to Gresham's law of money. As readers may recall from Economics 101, Gresham's proposition was that "bad money drives out good." Gresham's contention was that if two types of money were in circulation (e.g., gold and silver) at some arbitrarily defined ratio (e.g., 16:1), the bad money (i.e., the money overvalued at the fixed rate of exchange) would drive out the good. Thus, if gold were worth more than 16 ounces of silver, a 16:1 ratio would result in silver driving gold out of circulation (as people would tend to hoard it).

My corollary is: "bad simulations drive out good." The term "bad" means simulations derived based on highly tenuous assumptions, not bad in terms of indicated performance. On the contrary, truly "bad" simulations will show eye-popping results.

I frequently get flyers hawking systems that supposedly make 200 percent, 400 percent, or even 600 percent a year. Let's be conservative—and I use the term loosely—and assume a return of *only* 100 percent per year. At this level of return, $100,000 would grow to over $1 *billion* in just over 13 years! How can such claims possibly be true, then? The answer is that they can't. The point is that, given enough hindsight, it is possible to construct virtually any type of past-performance results. If anyone tried to sell a system or a trading program based on truly realistic simulations, the results would appear laughably puny relative to the normal promotional fare. It is in this sense that I believe that bad (unrealistic) simulations drive out good (realistic) simulations.

How are simulated results distorted? There are a number of primary means including:

1. **The Well-Chosen Example (Revisited).** In constructing a well-chosen example, the system promoter selects the best market, in the best year, using the best parameter set. Assuming a system is tested on 25 markets for 15 years and uses 100 parameter set variations, there would be a total of 37,500 ($25 \times 15 \times 100$) one-year results. It would be difficult to construct a system in which at least one of these 37,500 possible outcomes did *not* show superlative results. For example, if you tossed a group of ten coins 37,500 times, don't you think you would get 10 out of 10 heads sometimes. Absolutely. In fact, you would get 10 out of 10 heads on the average of one out of 1,024 times.

2. **Kitchen Sink Approach.** By using hindsight to add parameters and create additional system rules that conveniently take care of past losing periods, it is possible to generate virtually any level of past performance.

3. **Ignoring Risk.** Advertised system results frequently calculate return as a percent of margin or as a percent of an unrealistically low multiple of margin. This one item alone can multiply the implied returns severalfold. Of course, the risk would increase commensurately, but the ads don't provide those details.

4. **Overlooking Losing Trades.** It is hardly uncommon for charts in system brochures or advertisements to indicate buy and sell signals at the points at which some specified rules were met, but fail to indicate other points on the same chart where the same conditions were met and the resulting trades were losers.

5. **Optimize, Optimize, Optimize.** Optimization (i.e., selecting the best performing parameter sets for the *past*) can tremendously magnify the past performance of a system. Virtually any system ever conceived by man would look great if the results were based on the best parameter set (i.e., the parameter set that had the best past performance) for each market. The more parameter sets tested, the wider the selection of past results, and the greater the potential simulated return.

6. **Unrealistic Transaction Costs.** Frequently, simulated results only include commissions but not slippage (the difference between the assumed entry level and the actual fill that would be realized by using a market or stop order). For fast systems, ignoring slippage can make a system that would wipe out an account in real life look like a money machine.

7. **Fabrication.** Even though it is remarkably easy to construct system rules with great performance for the past, some promoters don't even bother doing this much. For example, one infamous individual keeps

on emerging with promotions for various $299 systems that are out-right frauds. Bruce Babcock of *Commodity Traders Consumers Report* has labeled this fellow appropriately enough the "$299 man."

The preceding is not intended to indict all system promoters or those using simulated results. Certainly, there are many individuals who construct simulated results in appropriately rigorous fashion. However, the sad truth is that the extraordinary misuse of simulations over many years has virtually made simulated results worthless. Advertised simulated results are very much like restaurant reviews written by the proprietors—you would hardly expect to ever see a bad review. I can assure you that you will never see any simulated results for a system that shows the system long the S&P as of the close of October 16, 1987. Can simulated results ever be used? Yes, if you are the system developer *and* you know what you're doing (e.g., use the simulation methods detailed in the previous section), or equivalently, if you have absolute faith in the integrity and competence of the system developer.

MULTIMARKET SYSTEM TESTING

Although it is probably unrealistic to expect any single system to work in all markets, generally speaking, a good system should demonstrate profitability in a large majority of actively traded markets (e.g., 85 percent or more). In fact, the selection of systems to be traded in a given market should depend on the performance of the systems over the broad range of markets as well as their performance in that market. There are, of course, some important exceptions. A system employing fundamental input would, by definition, only be applicable to a single market. In addition, the behavior of some markets is so atypical (e.g., stock indexes) that systems designed for trading such markets might well perform poorly over the broad range of markets.

In testing a system for a multimarket portfolio, it is necessary to predetermine the relative number of contracts to be traded in each market. This problem is frequently handled by simply assuming that the system will trade one contract in each market. However, this is a rather naive approach for two reasons. First, some markets are far more volatile than other markets. For example, a portfolio that included one contract of coffee and one contract of corn would be far more dependent on the trading results in coffee. Second, it may be desirable to downgrade the relative weightings of some markets because they are highly correlated with other markets (e.g., deutsche marks and Swiss francs).[8]

---

[8]For purposes of future trading (as opposed to historical testing), historical performance might be a third relevant factor in determining contract weightings. However, this factor cannot be included as an input in the testing procedure because it would bias the results.

In any case, the percentage allocation of available funds to each market should be determined prior to testing a system. These relative weightings can then be used to establish the number of contracts to be traded in each market. Note that as long as gain is measured in percentage rather than in nominal terms, the total number of contracts assumed to be traded in each market is irrelevant—only the contract ratios between markets will be important.

NEGATIVE RESULTS

One should not overlook the potential value of negative results. Analyzing the conditions under which a system performs poorly can sometimes reveal important weaknesses in the system that have been overlooked and thus provide clues as to how the system can be improved. Of course, the fact that the implied rule changes improve results in the poorly performing case does not prove anything. However, the validity of any suggested rule changes would be confirmed if such revisions generally tended to improve the results for other parameter sets and markets as well. The potential value of negative results as a source of ideas for how a system can be improved cannot be overstated. The concept that disorder is a catalyst for thought is a general truth that was perfectly expressed by the late novelist John Gardner: "In a perfect world, there would be no need for thought. We think because something goes wrong."

The idea of learning from poor results is basically applicable to a system that works in most markets and for most parameter sets, but performs badly in isolated cases. However, systems that exhibit disappointing results over a broad range of markets and parameter sets are likely to be lost causes, unless the results are spectacularly poor. In the latter case, a system that exactly reverses the trade signals of the original system might be attractive. For example, if tests of a new trend-following system reveal that the system consistently loses money in most markets, the implication is that one might have accidently stumbled upon an effective countertrend system. Such discoveries may be difficult on the ego, but they should not be ignored.

Of course, the fact that a system exhibits stable poor performance does not imply that the reverse system would perform favorably. The reason for this is that transaction costs often account for a significant portion of losses. Thus, the reverse system might also perform badly once these costs are taken into account. This was the case for the aforementioned *well-chosen example* described at the start of this chapter. As another example, at surface glance, reversing the signals generated by a system that loses an average of $3,000 per year may appear to be an attractive strategy. If, however, two-thirds of the loss can be attributed to transaction costs, fading the signals of this system will result in a loss of $1,000 per year, assuming a continuation of the same performance. (The preceding assumptions imply that transaction costs equal

$2,000 per year and that the trades lose $1,000 per year net of these costs. Thus, reversing the signals would imply a $1,000-per-year gain on the trades, but the $2,000-per year transaction costs would imply a net loss of $1,000 per year.) Moral: If you are going to design a bad system, it should be truly terribly if it is to be of value.

STEPS IN CONSTRUCTING AND TESTING A TRADING SYSTEM

1. Obtain all data needed for testing. Again, with the exception of short-term trading systems, which may be able to use actual contract data, the use of continuous futures (not to be confused with nearest futures or perpetual prices) is highly recommended.
2. Define the system concept.
3. Program rules to generate trades in accordance with this concept.
4. Select a small subset of markets and a subset of years for these markets.
5. Generate system trading signals for this subset of markets and time for a given parameter set.
6. Generate continuous futures charts for these markets and years and make several photocopy sets.
7. Denote trading signals on these charts. (Be sure the same price series was used to generate charts as to test the system.) This is an important step. I find it is much easier to debug a system by visually inspecting signals on charts than by working only with data printouts.
8. Check to see that the system is doing what was intended. Almost invariably, a careful check will reveal some inconsistencies due to either or both of the following reasons:

   a. errors in program;
   b. rules in program do not anticipate some circumstances or create unforeseen repercussions.

   Some examples of the latter might include the system failing to generate a signal, given an event at which a signal is intended; system generating a signal when no signal intended; system rules inadvertently creating a situation in which no new signals can be generated or in which a position is held indefinitely. In essence these types of situations arise because there will always be some missed nuances.

   The system rules need to be modified to correct both programming errors as well as unforeseen inconsistencies. It should be emphasized that corrections of the latter type are only concerned with making the system operate consistently with the intended concept and should be made *without any regard as to whether the changes help or hurt performance in the sample cases used in the developmental process.*

9. After making necessary corrections, repeat steps 7–8. Pay particular attention to changes in indicated signals versus previous run for two reasons:

a. to check whether the program changes achieved the desired fix;
b. to make sure the changes did not have unintended effects.

10. Once the system is working as intended, and all rules and contingencies have been fully defined, *and only after such a point,* test the system on the entire defined parameter set list across the full data base. (Be sure the intended trading portfolio has been defined before this test is run.)

11. As detailed earlier in this chapter, evaluate performance based on the average of all parameter sets tested or a blind simulation process. (The former involves far less work.)

12. Compare these results with the results of a generic system (e.g., breakout, crossover moving average) for the corresponding portfolio and test period. The return/risk of the system should be *measurably* better than that of the generic system, or equivalent and diversified versus generic system, if it is to be deemed to have any real value.

The preceding steps represent a rigorous procedure that is designed to avoid generating results that are upwardly biased by hindsight. As such, expect most system ideas to fail the test of merit in step 12. Designing a system with a truly superior performance is more difficult than most people think.

OBSERVATIONS ABOUT TRADING SYSTEMS

1. In trend-following systems, the basic method used to identify trends (e.g., breakout, crossover moving average) may well be the least important component of the system. In a sense, this is merely a restatement of Jim Orcutt's observation that there are only two types of trend-following systems: fast and slow. Thus, in designing trend-following systems, it may make more sense to concentrate on modifications (e.g., filters and confirmation rules to reduce bad trades, market characteristic adjustments, pyramiding rules, stop rules) than on trying to discover a better method for defining trends.

2. Complexity for its own sake is no virtue. Use the simplest form of a system that does not imply a meaningful sacrifice in performance relative to more complex versions.

3. The well-publicized and very valid reason for trading a broad range of markets is risk control through diversification. However, there is a very important additional reason for trading as many markets as possible: insurance against not missing any of the sporadic giant price moves in the futures markets. The importance of catching all such major trends cannot be overstressed—it can make the difference between mediocre performance and great performance. The 1994 coffee market (see Figure 1.2 in Chapter 1 and the 1979–1980 silver market (see Figure 1.1 in Chapter 1) are two spectacular examples of markets that were critical to portfolio performance.

4. If trading funds are sufficient, diversification should be extended to systems as well as markets. Trading several systems rather than a single system could help smooth overall performance. Ideally, the greatest degree of diversification would be achieved if the mix of systems included countertrend and pattern-recognition systems as well as trend-following systems. (However, this goal may be difficult to achieve because countertrend and pattern-recognition systems are generally significantly harder to design than trend-following systems.)

5. If sufficient funds are available, it is better to trade a number of diversified parameter sets than to trade a single optimized set.

6. Generally speaking, the value of parameter optimization is far overstated.

7. The previous observation strongly suggests that optimized results should never be used for evaluating the relative performance of a system. Two meaningful methods for testing systems were discussed in the text.

8. So-called *simulated* results are frequently *optimized* results (i.e., derived with the benefit of hindsight) and, as such, virtually meaningless. This caveat is particularly pertinent in regards to advertisement or direct mail promotions for trading systems, which invariably use very well-chosen examples.

9. An analysis of the results of successful systems will almost invariably reveal the presence of many markets with one or more years of very large profits, but few instances of very large single-year losses. The implication is that a key reason for the success of these systems is that their rules adhere to the critical, albeit hackneyed, principle of letting profits run and cutting losses short.

10. A market should not be avoided because its volatility increases sharply. In fact, the most volatile markets are often the most profitable.

11. Isolating negative results for a system that performs well on balance can provide valuable clues as to how the system can be improved.

12. A frequently overlooked fact is that trading results may often reflect more information about the market than the system. For example,

Figure 20.3
TRADING RESULTS REFLECT MARKET, NOT SYSTEM:
SHORT STERLING CONTINUOUS FUTURES

in Figure 20.3, the fact that a system that is short in early September 1992 surrenders all of its open profits before the position is reversed would not necessarily reflect inadequate risk control. Any trend-following system would have experienced the same fate. By the time the first sign of price strength was received, the market had already exceeded the entire prior 14-month trading range. In fact, only one day earlier the market had been trading below the low end of the prior 14-month trading range!

This example illustrates how the value of a system cannot be judged in a vacuum. In some cases, poor performance may reflect nothing more than the fact that market conditions would have resulted in poor results for the vast majority of systems. Similarly, favorable results may also reflect the conditions of the market rather than any degree of superiority in the tested system. These considerations suggest that a meaningful assessment of a new system's performance should include a comparison to a benchmark (e.g., the corresponding performance of standard systems, such as a crossover moving average or a simple breakout, during the same period for the same markets).

13. Use continuous futures prices for testing systems.

14. Use only a small portion of the data base (i.e., some markets for only a segment of the full time period) for developing and debugging a system.

15. Use charts with superimposed signal annotations as an aid to debugging systems.

16. In checking the accuracy and completeness of the signals generated by a system, make changes dictated by deviations from the intended operation of the system (due to oversights related to the full implications of the rules employed or unforeseen situations) with complete disregard whether such changes increase or decrease profits in the sample tests.

21 Measuring Trading Performance

For every complex problem there is a solution that is simple, neat and wrong.

—H. L. Mencken

THE NEED TO NORMALIZE GAIN[1]

Too many investors make the mistake of focusing solely on return when they evaluate money managers.[2] It is critical to also incorporate some measure of risk as part of the evaluation process.

Consider the equity streams of the accounts of Manager A and Manager B in Figure 21.1.[3] Although Manager A produces the larger return for the period as a whole, he can hardly be considered the superior performer—note the many sharp retracements in equity.

This is not a negative feature merely because investors with Manager A will have to ride out many distressing periods. Even more critical is the consideration that investors who start with Manager A at the wrong time—and that is not hard to do—will actually have significant losses. In fact, assuming that accounts will be closed once 25–50 percent of the initial equity is lost, there is a significant chance investors with Manager A will be knocked out of the game before the next rebound in performance.

It seems reasonable to assume that most investors would prefer Manager B to Manager A because the modestly lower return of Manager B is more than compensated by the apparent much lower risk. Moreover, if Manager B had used a modestly higher margin-equity ratio, she could have exceeded

---

[1]The following section is adapted from J. Schwager, "Alternative to Sharpe Ratio Better Measure of Performance," *Futures,* pp. 56–57, March 1985.

[2]In the futures industry, most money managers (i.e., those registered with the Commodity Futures Trading Commission) are called "commodity trading advisors" (CTAs), an unfortunately inappropriate choice of names. In this chapter, the more generic term "money managers" is used and can be read as interchangeable with CTAs.

[3]Although the examples of this chapter are based on evaluating money manager performance, similar examples would also apply to trading systems. Distinctions between money manager and system performance evaluation are noted where appropriate.

Figure 21.1
THE NEED TO NORMALIZE GAIN

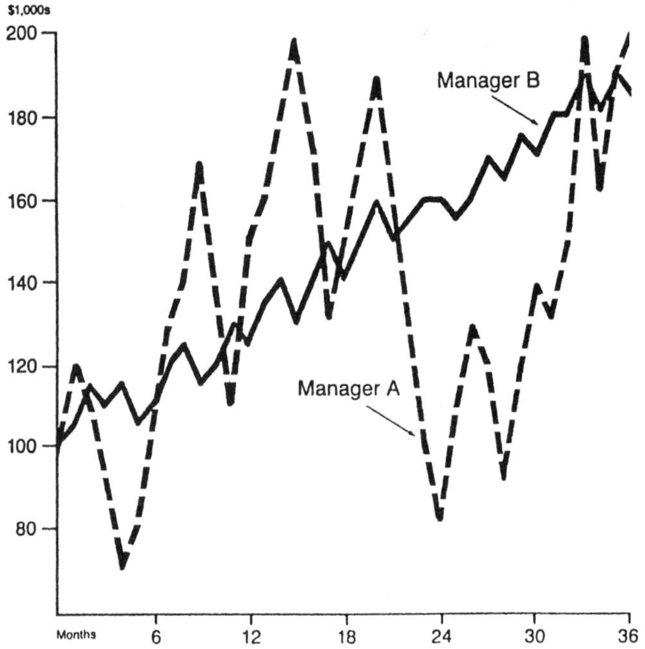

Source: J. Schwager, "Alternative to Sharpe Ratio Better Measure of Performance," *Futures,* p. 56, March 1985.

Manager A's return while still having much smaller retracements. (For money management reasons, all managers will limit the number of positions so that total margin requirements are well below total available equity; typically, the margin–equity ratio will be approximately 0.15–0.35.)

Clearly, Manager B has the better performance record. As illustrated by this example, any performance evaluation method must incorporate a risk measure to be meaningful.

THE SHARPE RATIO

The need to incorporate risk in evaluating performance has long been recognized. The classic return–risk measure is the Sharpe Ratio, which can be expressed as follows:

$$SR = \frac{E - I}{sd}$$

where E = the expected return
         I = risk-free interest rate
      sd = standard deviation of returns

E is typically stated in terms of percent return. Normally, the expected return is assumed to equal the average past return. In view of this fact, although E always refers to the expected return (i.e., applies to a future period), we will use it synonymously with the average past return.

The incorporation of I in the Sharpe Ratio recognizes that an investor could always earn a certain return *risk free*—for example, by investing in T bills. Thus, the return in excess of this risk-free return is more meaningful than the absolute level of the return.

The standard deviation is a statistic that is intended to measure the degree of dispersion in the data. The formula for the standard deviation is:

$$\text{sd} = \sqrt{\frac{\sum_{i=1}^{N}(X_i - \overline{X})^2}{N-1}}$$

where $\overline{X}$ = mean
      X_i = individual data values
      N = the number of data values

In the Sharpe Ratio application, N is equal to the number of time intervals. For example, if monthly time intervals are used for a three-year survey period, $N = 36$.

In calculating the standard deviation, it is always necessary to choose a time interval for segmenting the total period equity data (e.g., weekly, monthly). If, for example, the percent return data for a given year were broken down into weekly figures, the standard deviation would be very high if the return of many of the individual weeks deviated sharply from the average for the period. Conversely, the standard deviation would be low if the individual weeks tended to cluster around the average. Figure 21.2 illustrates two sets of data with the same average weekly return but substantially different standard deviations.

The basic premise of the Sharpe Ratio is that the standard deviation is a measure of risk. That is, the more widespread the individual returns from the average return, the riskier the investment. In essence, the standard deviation measures the ambiguity of the return. It should be intuitively clear that if the standard deviation is low, it is reasonable to assume that the actual return will be close to the expected return (assuming, of course, that the expected return is a good indicator of actual return). On the other hand, if the standard deviation is high, it suggests that there is a good chance that the actual return may vary substantially from the expected return.

Figure 21.2
COMPARISON OF TWO MANAGERS WITH EQUAL AVERAGE
RETURNS BUT DIFFERENT STANDARD DEVIATIONS

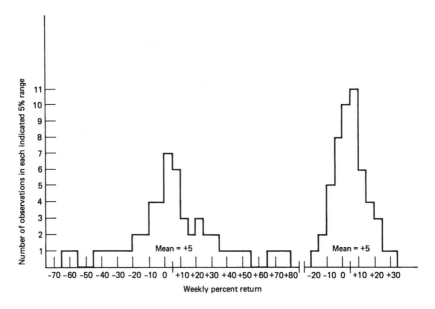

The Sharpe Ratio can be calculated rather directly for a money manager because we know the amount of funds on which percent return is based. This is not the case for a trading system. In applying the Sharpe Ratio to a trading system, we have one of two options:

1. Estimate the funds required to trade the system and use this figure to calculate a percent return.
2. Simplify the Sharpe Ratio by deleting the risk-free return I. (As is explained below, if this form of the Sharpe Ratio is used, it is not necessary to estimate the funds required to trade the system.) Thus, the Sharpe Ratio would reduce to

$$SR = \frac{E}{\text{sd}}$$

The second approach can be justified on the basis that, except for small accounts, the bulk of commodity margin requirements can be met by T-bill deposits. Thus, in contrast to the buyer of securities, the commodity trader does not sacrifice the risk-free return in order to participate in the alternative investment. The reduced form of the Sharpe Ratio also has a theoretical justification in the case of money managers: Whereas the Sharpe Ratio will increase if a manager increases her leverage—an undesirable feature—the reduced form will be unaffected by changes in leverage.

In the form $E/$sd, the Sharpe Ratio would be the same whether E were expressed in terms of dollar gain or in percent return. The reason for this is that the same unit of measurement would be used for the standard deviation. Thus, the funds requirement figure would appear in both the numerator and denominator and would cancel out.[4] To help clarify the exposition, the examples provided in the remainder of this chapter assume the reduced form of the Sharpe Ratio. This simplifying assumption does not meaningfully alter any of the theoretical or practical points discussed.

THREE PROBLEMS WITH THE SHARPE RATIO

Although the Sharpe Ratio is a useful measurement, it does have a number of potential drawbacks:[5]

1. *The Gain Measure of the Sharpe Ratio.* This measure—the annualized average monthly (or other interval) return is more attuned to assessing the probable performance for the next interval than the performance for an extended period. For example, assume that a fund manager has six months of 40 percent gains and six months of 30 percent losses in a given year. The annualized average monthly return would be 60 percent ($12 \times 5\%$). However, if position size is adjusted to existing equity, as is done by most managers, the actual return for the year would be −11 percent. That is because, for each dollar of equity at the start of the period, only $0.8858 would remain at the end of the period—$(1.40)^6 \times (0.70)^6 = 0.8858$.

As this example illustrates, if you are concerned about measuring the potential performance for an extended period rather than just the following month or other interval, then the gain measure used in the Sharpe Ratio can lead to extreme distortions. This problem can be circumvented, however, by using an annualized geometric (as opposed to arithmetic) mean rate of return for the numerator of the Sharpe Ratio, as is frequently done. The annualized geometric return is precisely equivalent to the average annual compounded return, which is discussed in the section on the return retracement ratio later in this chapter.

---

[4]The implicit assumption here is that trading funds are constant (i.e., profits are withdrawn and losses replenished). In other words, there is no compounding (i.e., reinvestment of gains, reduction of investment in the event of losses). Generally speaking, although a compounded return calculation is preferable, this consideration is more than offset by the critical advantage of not having to estimate fund requirements for a trading system. Furthermore, in comparing two systems, the system with the higher noncompounded return will often exhibit the higher compounded return.

[5]This section is adapted from J. Schwager, "Alternative to Sharpe Ratio Better Measure of Performance," *Futures*, pp. 57–58, March 1985.

2. The Sharpe Ratio Does Not Distinguish between Upside and Downside Fluctuations. The Sharpe Ratio is a measure of volatility, not risk. The two are not necessarily synonymous.

In terms of the risk calculation employed in the Sharpe Ratio—that is, the standard deviation of return—upside and downside fluctuations are considered equally bad. Thus, the Sharpe Ratio would penalize a manager who had sporadic sharp increases in equity, even if the equity retracements were small.

Figure 21.3 compares the hypothetical equity streams of Manager C, who has intermittent surges in equity and no equity retracements, and Manager D, who experiences several equity retracements. Although both managers realize equal gains for the period as a whole and Manager D goes through several retracements while Manager C doesn't have any, the Sharpe Ratio would rate Manager D higher (see Table 21.1). This outcome is a direct consequence of the fact that the Sharpe Ratio penalizes upside volatility exactly the same as downside volatility.

3. The Sharpe Ratio Does Not Distinguish between Intermittent Losses and Consecutive Losses. The risk measure in the Sharpe Ratio (the standard deviation) is independent of the order of various data points.

Figure 21.4 depicts the hypothetical equity streams of $100,000 accounts handled by Manager E and Manager F. Each earns a total of $48,000 or $24,000 per year. However, Manager E alternates $8,000 monthly gains with

Figure 21.3
**COMPARISON OF MANAGER WITH LARGE UPSIDE
VOLATILITY AND NO RETRACEMENTS TO A
MANAGER WITH RETRACEMENTS**

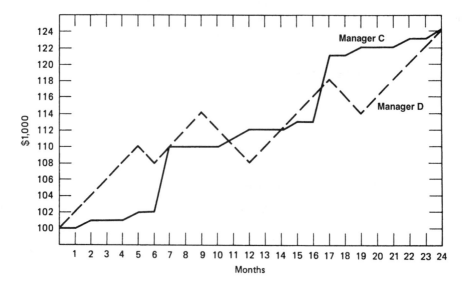

Table 21.1
COMPARISON OF MONTHLY RETURNS FOR TWO MANAGERS

Month	Manager C		Manager D	
	Equity Change	Cumulative Equity Change	Equity Change	Cumulative Equity Change
1	0	0	2,000	2,000
2	1,000	1,000	2,000	4,000
3	0	1,000	2,000	6,000
4	0	1,000	2,000	8,000
5	1,000	2,000	2,000	10,000
6	0	2,000	-2,000	8,000
7	8,000	10,000	2,000	10,000
8	0	10,000	2,000	12,000
9	0	10,000	2,000	14,000
10	0	10,000	-2,000	12,000
11	1,000	11,000	-2,000	10,000
12	1,000	12,000	-2,000	8,000
13	0	12,000	2,000	10,000
14	0	12,000	2,000	12,000
15	1,000	13,000	2,000	14,000
16	0	13,000	2,000	16,000
17	8,000	21,000	2,000	18,000
18	0	21,000	-2,000	16,000
19	1,000	22,000	-2,000	14,000
20	0	22,000	2,000	16,000
21	0	22,000	2,000	18,000
22	1,000	23,000	2,000	20,000
23	0	23,000	2,000	22,000
24	1,000	24,000	2,000	24,000

Average monthly return = 1,000   Average monthly return = 1,000

$$SR_C = \frac{E}{sd} = \frac{\dfrac{24,000}{2}}{\sqrt{12} \cdot \sqrt{\dfrac{14(1000-0)^2 + 8(1000-1000)^2 + 2(1000-8000)^2}{23}}} = 1.57$$

$$SR_D = \frac{\dfrac{24,000}{2}}{\sqrt{12} \cdot \sqrt{\dfrac{18(1000-2000)^2 + 6(1000+2000)^2}{23}}} = 1.96$$

The expected return, E, is equal to total equity gain for the period divided by the number of years, or equivalently, the average monthly return multiplied by 12. The *annualized* standard deviation is equal to the standard deviation of the monthly returns multiplied by $\sqrt{12}$.[a]

[a]To annualize an interval expected (average) return, it is necessary to multiply by the number of intervals in a year (12 for monthly data). To annualize an interval-based standard deviation, it is necessary to multiply by the square root of the number of intervals in a year ($\sqrt{12}$ for monthly data). This standard deviation conversion is a consequence of the fact that if the intervals are independent, the *variance* of return for longer interval data (e.g., year) would be equal to the variance of return for a shorter interval (e.g., month) times the number of shorter intervals in each longer interval (e.g., 12). Thus, the *standard deviation* of return for the longer interval would be equal to the standard deviation of return for the shorter interval times the *square root* of the number of shorter intervals in a longer interval (since the standard deviation is defined as the square root of the variance).

Figure 21.4
COMPARISON OF TWO MANAGERS WITH EQUAL
RETURNS AND STANDARD DEVIATIONS BUT
DIFFERENT SEQUENCE OF MONTHLY GAINS

Source: J. Schwager, "Alternative to Sharpe Ratio Better
Measure of Performance," *Futures,* p. 56, March 1985.

$4,000 monthly losses, while Manager F first loses $48,000 in the initial 12
months and subsequently gains $96,000 during the remainder of the period.

Both managers would have identical Sharpe Ratios. Despite this fact, few
traders would consider the two performance records equivalent in risk. Virtually all traders would agree that Manager F's performance implies a much
greater risk level.

RETURN RETRACEMENT RATIO

The return retracement ratio (RRR) provides a return/risk measure that avoids
the drawbacks of the Sharpe Ratio detailed in the previous section and also
comes closer to defining risk in a manner consistent with the way most traders
actually perceive risk. The RRR represents the average annualized compounded
return (R) divided by an average maximum retracement (AMR) measure:

$$RRR = \frac{R}{AMR}$$

R is that return that when compounded annually for a period coinciding with
a manager's (or system's) equity stream will yield the same ending equity,
given the starting equity. The AMR is equal to the average of the maximum
retracement (MR) for each data point (e.g., month), where the MR is equal to
the greater of the following two measures:

1. Maximum retracement from a prior equity peak (MRPP); or

2. Maximum retracement to a subsequent low (MRSL).

As the name implies, the MRPP measures the percent decline in equity from the prior high point in equity. In effect, for each data point (e.g., month end) the MRPP reflects the worst retracement that theoretically could have been experienced *by any investor* with an account at that time. The MRPP would be equal to the cumulative loss that would have been realized by an investor starting at the worst possible prior time (i.e., the prior equity peak). Note that if a new equity peak is set in a given month, the MRPP for that point will be equal to 0. One problem with the MRPP is that for early data points the drawdown measure may be understated because there are few prior points. In other words, if more prior data were available, the MRPP for those points would very likely be larger.

As the name implies, the MRSL measures the percent decline in equity to the subsequent lowest equity point. In effect, for each data point (e.g., month end), the MRSL measures the worst retracement that would be experienced *at any time* by investors starting in that month—that is, the cumulative loss that would be realized by such investors at the subsequent low point in equity. Note that if equity never decreases below a level for a given month, the MRSL for that point will be equal to 0. One problem with the MRSL is that for latter data points this drawdown measure is likely to be understated. In other words, if more data were available, there is a good chance the MRSL would be greater—that is, the subsequent equity low may not yet have been realized.

The MRPP and MRSL complement each other. Note that each measure is most likely to be understated when the other measure is least likely to be understated. For this reason the MR for each point is defined as the greater of the MRPP and MRSL. In this sense, the MR provides a true worst-case scenario for each point in time (e.g., month end). The AMR simply averages these worst-case values. This approach is far more meaningful than methods that employ only the single worst case—the maximum drawdown.

The mathematical derivation of the RRR is summarized below:

$$RRR = \frac{R}{AMR}$$

where R = average annual compounded return (see below for derivation),

$$AMR = \frac{1}{n}\sum_{i=1}^{n} MR_i$$

where n = number of months in survey period,

$$MR_i = \max(MRPP_i, MRSL_i)$$

where

$$MRPP_i = \frac{PE_i - E_i}{PE_i}$$

$$MRSL_i = \frac{E_i - ME_i}{E_i}$$

where E_i = equity at end of month i
 PE_i = peak equity on or prior to month i
 ME_i = minimum equity on or subsequent to month i

Note that $MRPP_i$ will be equal to 0 for first month and $MRSL_i$ will be equal to 0 for last month.

R, the average annual compounded return, is derived as follows:[6]

$$S(1 + R)^N = E$$

where S = starting equity
 E = ending equity
 N = number of years
 R = annualized compounded return (in decimal terms)

This equation can be reexpressed in terms of the annualized return (R):

$$R = \sqrt[N]{\frac{E}{S}} - 1$$

To facilitate solving this equation for R, it is necessary to reexpress it in terms of logarithms:

$$R = \text{antilog}\left[\frac{1}{N}(\log E - \log S)\right] - 1$$

For example, if a $100,000 account grows to $285,610 in four years, the annualized compounded return would be 0.30 or 30%:

$$R = \text{antilog } [\tfrac{1}{4}(\log 285,610 - \log 100,000)] - 1$$
$$R = \text{antilog } [\tfrac{1}{4}(5.4557734 - 5)] - 1$$
$$R = \text{antilog}[0.11394335] - 1 = 0.30$$

---

[6]The following derivation of R through the example where R = 0.30 is from J. Schwager, "Alternative to Sharpe Ratio Better Measure of Performance," *Futures,* p. 58, March 1985.

The calculation for the RRR can be applied directly in evaluating a money manager's performance, because the equity size of the account is known for each data point. However, a moment's reflection will reveal that in the case of trading systems, the equity size is not known; only the dollar gain/loss in each interval is available. How can percent return and retracements be calculated if we don't know the amount of funds needed to trade the system? The answer is that since the RRR value will be independent of the size of the funds assumed to be needed to trade the system,[7] any number can be used. Although it won't affect the calculation, as a means of selecting a plausible number, the trader can assume that the funds needed to trade the system are equal to four times the maximum dollar loss. For example, if the system's worst loss is $50,000, the funds needed to trade the system could be assumed to be $200,000.

Once the figure for the funds needed to trade the system (i.e., the assumed account size) is selected, monthly equity figures for the trading system can be generated as follows:

1. Divide all the monthly profit/loss figures by the *same* account size to generate monthly percent return figures.[8]
2. Use a chain multiple of the assumed account size and the monthly percent return numbers to generate monthly equity levels. For example, if the assumed account size is $200,000 and the percent returns for the first four months are +4%, −2%, −3%, and +6%, then the corresponding equity levels would be calculated as follows:

$$\text{Start} = \$200,000$$
$$\text{End of month } 1 = (\$200,000)\,(1.04) = \$208,000$$
$$\text{End of month } 2 = (\$200,000)\,(1.04)\,(0.98) = \$203,840$$
$$\text{End of month } 3 = (\$200,000)\,(1.04)\,(0.98)\,(0.97) = \$197,725$$
$$\text{End of month } 4 = (\$200,000)\,(1.04)\,(0.98)\,(0.97)\,(1.06) = \$209,588$$

Once the monthly equity levels are obtained, the derivation of the R and AMR values in the RRR calculation would be exactly analogous to the money manager case.

---

[7]Since the assumed account size is used as a divisor in both the numerator of the RRR (to divide dollar gain/loss in the return calculation) and the denominator of the RRR (to divide dollar retracements), the figure will cancel out. For example, doubling the size of the assumed account size would halve both the average annual compounded return and the average maximum retracement, leaving the RRR value unchanged.

[8]Note that the implicit assumption is that the system trading results were based on a fixed portfolio. In other words, the test of the system doesn't increase the number of contracts traded when the system makes money and decrease the number when the system loses. (In actual trading, of course, such adjustments would be made.) Hence, using a *constant* account size as the divisor to transform monthly profit/loss figures into percent return figures is the appropriate procedure.

It should be noted that in actual trading, the individual would adjust the funds used for trading based on personal risk preferences. The actual level used could be greater or smaller than the four times maximum loss figure used as a starting assumption in calculating the RRR for a system. The RRR value of the system, however, would be unaffected by the specific choice of the account size assumed needed to trade the system.

ANNUAL GAIN-TO-PAIN RATIO

The annual gain-to-pain ratio (AGPR) represents a simplified type of return/retracement measure. The AGPR is defined as follows:

$$AGPR = AAR \div AAMR$$

where AAR = arithmetic average of annual returns
       AAMR = average annual maximum retracement, where the maximum retracement for each year is defined as the percent retracement from a prior equity high (even if it occurred in a previous year) to that year's equity low

The RRR is a better return/retracement measure than the AGPR insofar as each data point is incorporated in the risk calculation and the measure does not artificially restrict the data (e.g., calendar year intervals). However, some traders may prefer the AGPR because it requires less computation and the resulting number has an easy-to-grasp intuitive meaning. For example, an AGPR of 3 would mean that the average annual return is three times as large as the average annual worst retracement (measured from a primary peak).

MAXIMUM LOSS AS A RISK MEASURE

One number of particular interest is the worst-case possibility in a given system. In other words, the largest retracement that would have been experienced during the entire survey period if trading was initiated on the worst possible start date. The maximum loss (ML) is merely the largest $MRSL_i$ (or largest $MRPH_i$, the two would be equivalent) and can be expressed as

$$ML = max(MRSL_i)$$

See the section, "Return Retracement Ratio" for derivation of $MRSL_i$.

The ML is not recommended as a sole risk measure or the risk component in a return/retracement ratio because it depends on only a single event and hence may be very unrepresentative of the overall performance of a system. Furthermore, because of this characteristic, the value of the ML may be highly contingent on the choice of the survey period. As a related consideration, the use of ML introduces a negative bias for managers with longer track records. However, the ML does provide important information and should be consulted in conjunction with the RRR.

TRADE-BASED PERFORMANCE MEASURES

In addition to the performance measures just discussed, the following measures may also merit supplemental attention:

1. **_The Expected Net Profit per Trade._** The expected net profit per trade (ENPPT) can be expressed as:

$$\text{ENPPT} = (\% \text{ P})(\text{AP}) - (\% \text{ L})(\text{AL})$$

   where   % P = percent of total trades that are profitable
   % L = percent of total trades that result in net losses
   AP = average net profit of profitable trade
   AL = average net loss of losing trade

   The usefulness of this indicator is that a low ENPPT figure will highlight systems that are vulnerable to a serious deterioration of profits given poor executions, increased commissions, or any other form of increased transaction cost. For example, if a system had an ENPPT of $50, its validity would be highly suspect, no matter how favorable the other performance measures. The critical disadvantage of the ENPPT is that it does not incorporate a risk measure. In addition, the ENPPT has the intrinsic drawback that it may unfairly penalize active systems. For example, a system that generated one trade with a net gain of $2,000 would rate better than a system that, during the same period, generated 100 trades with an ENPPT of $1,000 (with similar equity fluctuations).

2. **_Trade-Based Profit/Loss Ratio._** The trade-based profit/loss ratio (TBPLR) can be expressed as follows:

$$\text{TBPLR} = \frac{(\%\text{P})(\text{AP})}{(\%\text{L})(\text{AL})}$$

This measure indicates the ratio of dollars gained to dollars lost in all trades. The appeal of the TBPLR is that it deflates profits by a measurement of total pain suffered. There are three drawbacks to the TBPLR: (1) Similar to the ENPPT, it is severely biased against systems with a higher frequency of trades. For example, consider the following two systems:

System	Average Profit ($)	Average Loss ($)	Percent Profitable Trades	Percent Losing Trades	TBPLR
A	400	200	75	25	6
B	200	100	50	50	2

Superficially, it might appear that System A is better (three times better to be exact). However, suppose you are now provided with the following additional information: system B generated 100 trades per year and system A only 10, while both systems had similar risk levels (e.g., AMR), and hence required equivalent funds to trade. In this case, system B's percent return would actually be double that of system A.[9] (2) The TBPLR gives no weight to open position losses. Thus, a trade that witnesses a huge loss before it is finally closed at a slight profit would have the same effect on the TBPLR as a trade that is immediately profitable and closed at the same slight profit. The two trades, however, would hardly be equivalent in the eyes of the trader. (3) The TBPLR does not distinguish between intermittent and consecutive losses—a potentially serious flaw there is if a tendency for losing trades to be clustered.

WHICH PERFORMANCE MEASURE SHOULD BE USED?

By using drawdowns (the worst at each given point in time) to measure risk, the risk component of the RRR (the AMR) comes closer to describing most people's intuitive sense of risk than does the standard deviation in the Sharpe Ratio, which makes no distinction between sudden large gains and sudden sharp losses—two events that are perceived very differently by traders (and investors). The RRR also avoids the Sharpe Ratio's failure to distinguish between intermittent and consecutive losses. For these reasons, the RRR is probably a superior return/risk measure to the Sharpe Ratio.

Even so, the RRR is being proposed as an additional rather than replace-

---

[9]Percent return = $(ENPPT \times N)/F$, where N = number of trades and F = funds traded (assumed equal for each system). System A's percent return = $(250 \times 10)/F$, while system B's percent return = $(50 \times 100)/F$.

ment return/risk measure to the Sharpe Ratio. Reason: the Sharpe Ratio is a very widely used return/risk measure, whereas, at this writing, the RRR is not used at all. Hence, the trader or the system designer would still need to calculate a Sharpe Ratio for the purpose of comparing his results to CTA track records, industry indexes, or alternative investments. Together the Sharpe Ratio and the RRR provide a very good description of a system's or trader's relative performance.

In addition to these return/risk measures, the ENPPT should be calculated to make sure that the validity of the system would not be threatened by a moderate increase in transaction costs or a small deterioration in the average profit per trade. The maximum loss (ML) figure should be checked to make sure there was no catastrophic losing streak. Finally, the AGPR might be calculated as a supplemental measure, which yields a figure that is intuitively meaningful.

THE INADEQUACY OF A RETURN/RISK RATIO FOR EVALUATING MONEY MANAGER TRADING PERFORMANCE

In the case of evaluating trading systems, the selected return/risk measure would yield the same ranking order of systems as the *estimated* percent return. This observation, which is a consequence of the fact that fund requirements for trading a system can only be estimated basis risk, can be proved as follows:

$$\text{Selected return/risk measure} = \frac{G}{R}$$

$$\text{Estimated percent return for a system in a given market} = \frac{G}{F}$$

where G = average annual gain per contract
R = chosen risk measure (e.g., sd, AMR, ML)
F = total funds allocated for trading

The only practical way to estimate F is as a function of risk. Most directly, F might be estimated as some multiple of the chosen risk measure. That is,

$$F = kR$$

where k = multiple of risk measure (determined subjectively). Thus, the estimated percent return for a system could be expressed as

$$\frac{G}{F} = \frac{G}{kR} = \frac{1}{k}\left(\frac{G}{R}\right)$$

Note that G/R is the selected return/risk measure. Consequently, the percent return for a system will merely be equal to some constant times the return/risk measure. Although different traders will select different risk measures and values for k, once these items are specified, the return/risk measure and the estimated percent return would yield the same ranking order of systems. Also note that in the case of evaluating systems, the *percent risk*, which we define as the risk measure divided by fund requirements, is a constant (percent risk $= R/F = R/kR = 1/k$).

Whereas in the case of evaluating trading systems a higher return/risk ratio *always* implies higher percent return, this is not true for the evaluation of money managers. Also, the percent risk is no longer a constant, but instead can vary from manager to manager. Thus, it is entirely possible for a money manager to have a higher return/risk ratio than another manager, but to also have a lower percent return or a higher percent risk. (The reason for this is that in the money manager case, the link between fund requirements and risk is broken—that is, different money managers will differ in the level of risk they will assume for any given level of funds.) Consequently, a return/risk ratio is no longer a sufficient performance measure for choosing between alternative investments. We illustrate this point by using the Sharpe Ratio, but similar conclusions would apply to other return/risk measures. (In the following discussion, we assume that management fees are based entirely on profits and that interest income is not included in money manager return figures, but is received by investors. Consequently, the simplified form of the Sharpe Ratio, which deletes the riskless interest rate, is appropriate.)

Assume we are given the following set of *annualized* statistics for two money managers:

	Manager A	Manager B
Expected gain	$ 10,000	$ 50,000
Standard deviation of gain	$ 20,000	$ 80,000
Initial investment	$100,000	$100,000
Sharpe Ratio	.50	.625

Although Manager B has the higher Sharpe Ratio, not all traders would prefer Manager B, because he also has a higher risk measure (i.e., higher standard deviation). Thus, a risk-averse investor might prefer Manager A, gladly willing to sacrifice the potential for greater gain in order to avoid the substantially greater risk. For example, if annual trading results are normally distributed, for any given year, there would be a 10 percent probability of the return falling more than 1.3 standard deviations below the expected rate. In such an event, an investor would lose $54,000 with Manager B [$50,000 – (1.3 × $80,000)], but only $16,000 with Manager A. For a risk-averse investor, minimizing a loss under negative assumptions may be more important than maximizing gain under favorable conditions.[10]

Next, consider the following set of statistics for two other money managers:

	Manager C	Manager D
Expected gain	$ 20,000	$ 5,000
Standard deviation of gain	$ 20,000	$ 4,000
Initial investment	$100,000	$100,000
Sharpe Ratio	1.0	1.25

Although Manager D has a higher Sharpe Ratio, Manager C has a substantially higher percent return. Investors who are not particularly risk-averse might prefer Manager C even though he has a lower Sharpe Ratio. The reason for this is that for the major portion of probable outcomes, an investor would be better off with Manager C. Specifically, in this example, the investor will be better off as long as return does not fall more than .93 standard deviations below the expected rate—a condition that would be met 82 percent of the time (assuming trading results are normally distributed).[11]

Even more striking is the consideration that there are circumstances in which virtually all investors would prefer the money manager with the lower Sharpe Ratio. Consider the following two money managers:[12]

---

[10]Implicit assumption in this example: The investor can't place a fraction of the stated initial investment with Manager B. In other words, the minimum unit size of investment is $100,000. Otherwise, it would always be possible to devise a strategy in which the investor would be better off with the manager with the higher Sharpe Ratio. For example, placing $25,000 with Manager B would imply the same standard deviation as is the case for a $100,000 investment with Manager A but a higher expected gain ($12,500).

[11]Implicit assumption in this example: Borrowing costs for the investor are significantly greater than the interest income return realized by placing funds with a money manager. This assumption prohibits the alternative strategy of borrowing funds and placing a multiple of the initial $100,000 investment with the manager with the higher Sharpe Ratio. If borrowing costs and interest income were equal (an assumption not likely to be valid in the real world), it would always be possible to devise a strategy in which the investor would be better off with the manager with the higher Sharpe Ratio. For example, the strategy of borrowing an additional $400,000 and placing $500,000 with Manager D would imply the same standard deviation as is the case for a $100,000 investment with Manager C, but a higher expected gain ($25,000).

[12]The Sharpe Ratios used in this example are considerably higher than the levels likely to be found in the real world. However, the assumption of such higher Sharpe Ratios ellucidates the intended theoretical point.

	Manager E	Manager F
Expected gain	$ 10,000	$ 50,000
Standard deviation of gain	$ 2,000	$ 12,500
Initial investment	$100,000	$100,000
Sharpe Ratio	5.0	4.0

In this example, virtually all investors (even those that are risk-averse) would prefer Manager F, despite the fact that he has a lower Sharpe Ratio. The reason is that the percent return is so large relative to the ambiguity of that return (standard deviation), that even under extreme adverse circumstances, investors would almost certainly be better off with Manager F. For example, once again assuming that trading results are normally distributed, the probability of a gain more than three standard deviations below the expected gain is only 0.139 percent. Yet even under these extreme circumstances, an investor would still be better off with Manager F: Gain = $12,500/year (12.5 percent) compared with $4,000/year (4 percent) for Manager E. This example illustrates, even more dramatically the fact that, by itself, a return/risk ratio does not provide sufficient information for evaluating a money manager.[13] (This conclusion applies to all return/risk measures, not just the Sharpe Ratio.)

The key point is that in evaluating money managers, it is also important to consider the percent return and risk figures independently rather than merely as a ratio.

GRAPHIC EVALUATION OF TRADING PERFORMANCE

Graphic depictions can be particularly helpful in comparing the performance of different money managers. Below we consider two types of charts:

1. Net Asset Value. The net asset value (NAV) indicates the equity at each point in time (typically, month-end) based on an assumed beginning equity of $1,000. For example, an NAV of 2,000 implies that the original investment was doubled as of the indicated point in time. By definition, the NAV at the start of the survey period is equal to 1,000. Subsequent values would be derived as follows:

---

[13]Comments analogous to footnote 11 also apply here.

End of Month	Monthly Dollar Return Divided by Equity at Start of Month	NAV
1	r_1	$(1,000)(1 + r_1)$
2	r_2	$(1,000)(1 + r_1)(1 + r_2)$
3	r_3	$(1,000)(1 + r_1)(1 + r_2)(1 + r_3)$
.	.	.
.	.	.
.	.	.
n	r_n	$(1,000)(1 + r_1)(1 + r_2)(1 + r_3) \cdots (1 + r_n)$

For example, if a money manager witnesses a + 10 percent return in the first month, a −10 percent return in the second month, and a +20 percent return in the third month, the NAV at the end of the third month would be:

$$(1,000)(1 + 0.1)(1 - 0.1)(1 + 0.2) = 1,188$$

Figure 21.5 illustrates the NAV for two money managers during the January 1991–February 1995 period. Figure 21.6 presents the same information using a logarithmic scale for the NAV values. The representation in Figure 21.6 is preferable because it will assure that equal percentage changes in equity will result in equal magnitude vertical movements. For example, in Figure 21.6, a 10 percent decline in equity when the NAV value equals 2,000 would appear equivalent to a 10 percent decline in equity when the NAV equals 1,000. In Figure 21.5, however, the former decline would appear twice as large. In any case, regardless of the type of scale used to depict NAV curves, it should be stressed that only comparisons based on exactly the same survey period are meaningful.

Although the NAV is primarily a return measure, it also reflects risk. All else being equal, the more volatile a money manager's performance, the lower the NAV. For example, consider the five money managers below who, during a given year, witness the following monthly gains and losses:

Manager	Six Months of Percentage Gains Equal to:	Six Months of Percentage Losses Equal to:	NAV at End of Year
1	+11%	−1%	$(1,000)(1.11)^6(.99)^6 = 1,760$
2	+21%	−11%	$(1,000)(1.21)^6(.89)^6 = 1,560$
3	+31%	−21%	$(1,000)(1.31)^6(.79)^6 = 1,230$
4	+41%	−31%	$(1,000)(1.41)^6(.69)^6 = 850$
5	+51%	−41%	$(1,000)(1.51)^6(.59)^6 = 500$

Figure 21.5
NAVS FOR TWO MANAGERS

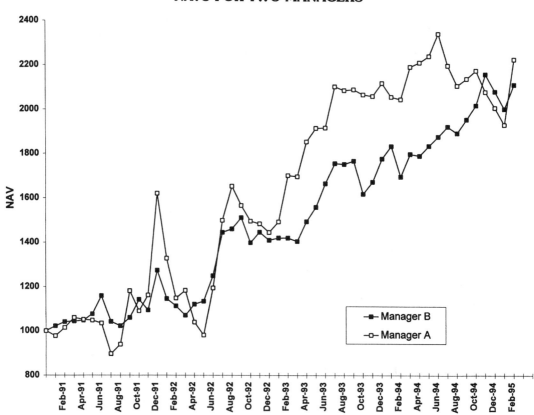

Note the dramatic differences between the ending NAV values despite the equal absolute differences between the percentage gains in winning months and percentage declines in losing months.

The degree to which the NAV incorporates risk may not be sufficient for risk-averse investors. For example, although Manager A witnesses a greater ending NAV than Manager B (see Figure 21.6), many investors might still prefer Manager B because her performance is less volatile. Clearly a more explicit depiction of risk, such as the "underwater" chart described below, would be helpful as a supplement to the NAV chart.

2. Underwater Curve.[14] The underwater curve depicts the percent drawdown as of the end of each month, measured from the previous equity peak. In other words, assuming beginning-of-month trading start dates, the underwater curve reflects the largest percentage loss as of the end of each

---

[14]The term "underwater curve" was first coined by Norman D. Strahm.

Figure 21.6
NAVS FOR TWO MANAGERS (LOG SCALE)

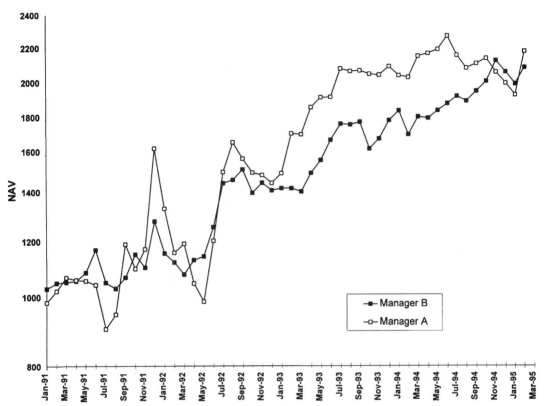

month, assuming an account had been initiated at the worst possible prior entry point (i.e., prior equity peak). Insofar as it reflects the maximum possible equity retracement at each point, the underwater curve is conceptually similar to the previously described MRPP in the RRR calculation. Figures 21.7 and 21.8 illustrate the underwater curves for the two money managers depicted in Figures 21.5 and 21.6. (The vertical bars above the zero line indicate that the given month witnessed a new equity high.) These charts clearly demonstrate the greater degree of risk implied by Manager A's performance.

Which manager (A or B) has the better performance? The answer must unavoidably be subjective because Manager A achieves the higher end of period NAV value, but also exhibits more extreme drawdowns.[15] However, the key point is that by using both the NAV and underwater charts, each

---

[15]Although this statement is theoretically true, for the example given, it is likely that the vast majority of investors would prefer Manager B because Manager A's marginally higher return hardly seems worth the substantial increase in risk.

Figure 21.7
UNDERWATER CURVE: MANAGER A

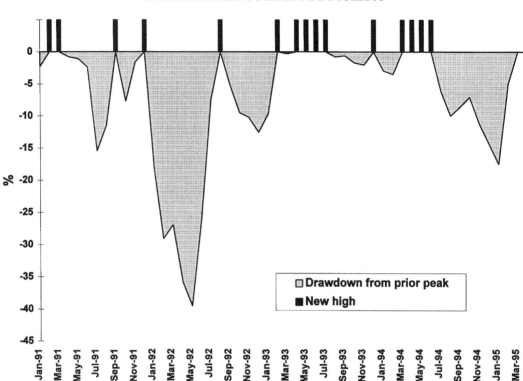

investor should have sufficient information to choose the money manager he prefers, given his personal return/risk preferences. In fact, given the relative ease with which the NAV and underwater charts can be derived, and the depth of the information they provide, for many investors, the combination of these charts may offer the ideal methodology for money manager performance comparisons.

Although this section was described in terms of depicting money manager performance, the same types of charts could be generated for trading systems. The trader would merely have to transform the system's dollar profit/loss figures into percent return figures based on the account size the trader deems necessary to trade the system. The NAV for the system could then be derived by creating a chain multiple of 1,000 and these percent return numbers.

CONCLUSIONS

1. By itself, dollar gain per unit time is an insufficient measure for evaluating the performance of a trading system or money manager.

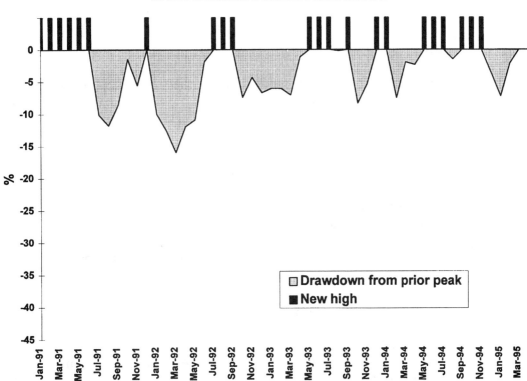

Figure 21.8
UNDERWATER CURVE: MANAGER B

2. In evaluating the performance of a system, a return/risk measure serves a dual role:

   a. It incorporates risk;
   b. It provides a proxy percent return measure.

3. The Sharpe Ratio has several potential drawbacks as a trading performance measure:

   a. Failure to distinguish between upside and downside fluctuations;
   b. Failure to distinguish between intermittent and consecutive losses;
   c. Potential distortions in the gain measure in assessing performance for an extended period.

4. The RRR is an alternative performance measure that seems to be preferable to the Sharpe Ratio in that it appears to reflect more closely the behavioral preferences of the trader (that is, traders are generally concerned about *downside* volatility in equity rather than volatility in equity). However, the Sharpe Ratio should still be considered as a supplemental measure because it is the most used return/

risk measure and hence is essential for comparing one's own track record or system to industry money managers.

5. The AGPR is a useful supplemental measure insofar as it has a clear intuitive interpretation, and requires far less computation than the RRR.

6. The ENPPT should be calculated to make sure that a system's performance is not overly dependent on transaction cost assumptions.

7. Although not suitable as a sole risk measure, the ML provides important additional information.

8. In the case of trading systems, return/risk measures will yield the same rankings as estimated percent return. Therefore, a higher return/risk ratio would always imply higher percent return. This linkage breaks down in the case of money managers because different money managers will differ in the level of risk they will assume for any given level of funds, whereas for systems, fund requirements can only be defined in terms of risk.

9. In the case of money managers, a return/risk ratio is no longer an adequate performance measure. Rather, return and risk should also be evaluated independently. The specific ordering of managers on the basis of these figures will be subjective (i.e., dependent on the individual investor's risk/reward preferences).

10. The net asset value (NAV) and underwater curve are two types of charts that are particularly helpful for money manager performance comparisons.

Part Five

PRACTICAL TRADING GUIDELINES

22 The Planned Trading Approach

If making money is a slow process, losing it is quickly done.

—Ihara Saikaku

If the amount of money you risk in futures trading represents a minuscule fraction of your net worth, and your major motivation for speculation is entertainment, the shoot-from-the-hip approach might be fine. However, if your major objective in futures trading is to make money, an organized trading plan is essential. This is not just a platitude. Search out successful futures speculators, and you will no doubt find that they all use a systematic, disciplined trading approach.

The following seven steps provide general guidelines for constructing an organized trading plan.

STEP ONE: DEFINE A TRADING PHILOSOPHY

How do you plan to make your trading decisions? If your answer is something vague like, "When my friend gets a hot tip from his broker," "When I get a trade idea from reading the newspaper," or "On market feel while watching the quote machine," you're not ready to begin trading. A meaningful strategy would be based on either fundamental analysis, chart analysis, technical trading systems, or some combination of these approaches. The same method will not necessarily be used in all markets. For example, in some markets the trader may use a synthesis of fundamental and chart analyses to make trading decisions, while in other markets decisions may be based on chart analysis only.

The more specific the trading strategy, the better. For example, a trader who plans to base his trades on chart analysis should be able to specify the types of patterns that would signal trades, as well as other details, such as confirmation rules. Of course, the most specific trading strategy would be one based on a mechanical trading system; however, such a fully automated approach may not appeal to a significant percentage of traders.

STEP TWO: CHOOSE MARKETS TO BE TRADED

After the speculator has decided on how he plans to pick his trades, he must choose the markets that will be followed. For most speculators, constraints related to time and available funds will significantly limit the number of markets that can be monitored and traded. Three factors might be considered in selecting markets.

Suitability to Trading Approach

A trader would choose those markets that appear to have the best potential for satisfactory performance, given his planned approach. Of course, such a determination can only be made on the basis of either past trading experience or historical testing of a specific trading strategy.

Diversification

The multiple benefits of diversification were fully discussed in Chapter 17. However, the essential point here is that diversification provides one of the most effective means of reducing risk. Diversification can be enhanced by choosing markets that are not closely related. For example, if a speculator knew that he wanted to trade gold, then silver and platinum would be poor choices for additional markets, unless his available funds were sufficient to permit him to trade many other markets as well.

Volatility

A trader with limited funds should avoid extremely volatile[1] markets (e.g., coffee), since the inclusion of such markets in his portfolio will severely limit the total number of markets that can be traded. Unless the speculator's ap-

---

[1]*Volatility* here refers to dollar volatility per contract. Consequently, high volatility could imply relatively large price swings, large-size contracts, or both.

proach is better suited to a given volatile market, he will be better off trading a wider variety of less volatile markets (diversification again).

STEP THREE: SPECIFY RISK CONTROL PLAN[2]

The rigid control of losses is perhaps the most critical prerequisite for successful trading. A risk control plan should include the following elements.

Maximum Risk per Trade

The speculator can substantially increase the probability of long-term success by restricting the percentage of total funds allocated to any given trade.[3] Ideally, the maximum risk on any trade should be limited to 3 percent or less, of total equity. For smaller accounts, adhering to such a guideline will require restricting trading to less volatile markets, minicontracts, and spreads. Speculators who find that they must risk more than about 7 percent of their equity on individual trades should seriously reconsider their financial suitability for futures trading.

The maximum risk per trade can also be used to determine the number of contracts that can be initiated in any given trade. For example, if the maximum risk per trade is 3 percent of equity, and the speculator's account size is $100,000, a corn trade that required a stop point 20¢/bu below the market would imply a maximum position size of three contracts (20¢ × 5,000 = $1,000; $1,000 = 1 percent of $100,000). In similar fashion, the maximum risk per trade would also be used in deciding whether pyramid units could be added without upsetting risk control guidelines.

Stop-Loss Strategy

Know where you're going to get out before you get in. The importance of this rule cannot be overemphasized. Without a predetermined exit point, the trader will find herself vulnerable to procrastinating in the liquidation of a losing posi-

---

[2]Risk control is typically referred to as "money management," although I believe the former represents the more descriptive label.

[3]The implicit assumption here is that the trader's expected net profit per trade (ENPPT) is positive. (The ENPPT was defined in the section "Other Supplemental Performance Measures" in Chapter 21.) If a trader's ENPPT is negative, the laws of probability will assure failure if he trades long enough. Such a situation would be analogous to the roulette player whose expected gain per bet is negative.

tion. At the wrong time, one such lapse of trading discipline could literally knock the speculator out of the game.

Ideally, the speculator should place a good-till-canceled (GTC) stop order when she enters the trade. However, if the trader is fairly certain that she can trust herself, a mental stop point can be determined at trade entry, while the actual placement of the stop order is deferred until the stop point is within a given day's permissible range. For a more detailed discussion of strategies regarding the placement of stop orders, see the chapter entitled "Choosing Stop-Loss Points" (Chapter 9).

It should be noted that the system trader does not necessarily need to employ stop-loss rules in order to achieve risk control. For example, if a trading system automatically reverses the position given a sufficient trend reversal, the system will inherently perform the major function of a stop-loss rule—the prevention of catastrophic losses on individual trades—without such a rule being explicit. Of course, large cumulative losses can still occur over many trades, but the same vulnerability would still apply if stops were used.

Diversification

Since different markets will witness adverse moves at different times, trading multiple markets will reduce risk. As a very simple example, assume that a trader with a $20,000 account uses a system that witnesses average drawdowns of $3,000 in both gold and soybeans. If she traded two contracts of either market, her average drawdown would be equal to 30 percent (6,000 ÷ 20,000), whereas if she traded one contract of each, her average drawdown would invariably be less (possibly even less than for *one* contract of a *single* market if the markets were inversely correlated). In fact, the average drawdown could only reach 30 percent (assuming average drawdowns remain at $3,000 for each market) if drawdowns in the two markets proved to be exactly synchronized, which is exceedingly unlikely. Of course, the risk-reduction benefit of diversification would increase as more unrelated markets were added to the portfolio. Also, as noted in Chapter 17, the concept of diversification applies not only to trading multiple markets but also multiple systems (or approaches) and multiple system variations (i.e., parameter sets) for each market, assuming equity is sufficient to do so.

Although our focus in this section is risk control, it should be noted that diversification can also increase return by allowing the trader to increase her average leverage in each market without increasing overall risk. In fact, the addition of markets with a lower average return than other markets in an existing portfolio can actually *increase the return* of the portfolio if the risk reduction gained by diversification is greater than the decline in return and the trader adjusts her leverage accordingly. Two other benefits of diversification—ensuring participation in major trends and "bad luck insurance"—were discussed in Chapter 17.

Reduce Leverage for Correlated Markets

Although adding markets to a portfolio allows a trader to increase leverage, it is important to make adjustments for highly correlated markets. For example, a currency portfolio, consisting of the six most active currency futures contracts (deutsche mark, Swiss franc, British pound, Japanese yen, Canadian dollar, and dollar index), would be subject to much greater risk than a more broadly diversified six-market portfolio because of the very strong correlations between some of these markets. Consequently, the leverage of such an all-currency portfolio should be adjusted downward vis-à-vis a more diversified six-market portfolio with equivalent individual market volatilities.

Market Volatility Adjustments

Trading leverage—the number of contracts traded in each market for any given equity size—should be adjusted to account for volatility differences. There are two aspects of this rule. First, fewer contracts would be traded in more volatile markets. Second, even for a single market, the number of contracts would vary in conjunction with fluctuations in volatility. Of course, since contracts can't be traded in fractions, traders with small accounts will be unable to make such volatility adjustments, which is one reason why small accounts will be subject to greater risk. (Other reasons include the unavoidability of the maximum risk per trade exceeding desired levels and an inability to diversify sufficiently.)

Adjusting Leverage to Equity Changes

Leverage should also be changed in accordance with major fluctuations in equity. For example, if a trader begins with a $100,000 account and loses $20,000, all else being equal, the leverage should be reduced by 20 percent. (Of course, if equity rose instead, the leverage should be increased.)

Losing Period Adjustments
(Discretionary Traders Only)

When a trader's confidence is shaken because of an ongoing losing streak, it is often a good idea to temporarily cut back position size or even take a complete trading break until confidence returns. In this way, the trader can keep a losing phase from steamrollering into a disastrous retracement. This advice would not apply to a system trader, however, since for most viable systems, a losing period enhances the potential for favorable performance in the ensuing period. Or to put it another way, confidence and frame of mind are critical to the performance of a discretionary trader but are not relevant to the performance of a system.

STEP FOUR: ESTABLISH A PLANNING TIME ROUTINE

It is important to set aside some time each evening for reviewing markets and updating trading strategies. In most cases, once the trader has established a specific routine, 30–60 minutes should be sufficient (less if only a few markets are being traded). The primary tasks performed during this time would be:

1. *Update Trading Systems and Charts.* At least one of these should be employed as an aid in making trading decisions. In those markets in which fundamental analysis is employed, the trader will also have to reevaluate the fundamental picture periodically after the release of important new information (e.g., government crop report).
2. *Plan New Trades.* Determine whether any new trades are indicated for the next day. If there are, decide on a specific entry plan (e.g., buy on opening). In some cases, a trading decision may be contingent on an evaluation of market behavior on the following day. For example, assume a trader is bearish on corn, and a modestly bullish crop report is received after the close. Such a trader might decide to go short *if* the market is trading lower on the day at any point within one hour of the close.
3. *Update Exit Points for Existing Positions.* The trader should review the stops and objectives on existing positions to see whether any revisions appear desirable in light of the current day's price action. In the case of stops, such changes should only be made to reduce trade risk.

STEP FIVE: MAINTAIN A TRADER'S NOTEBOOK

The planning routine discussed in the previous section implies some systematic form of record keeping. Figure 22.1 provides one sample of a format that might be used for a trader's notebook. The first four columns merely identify the trade.

Figure 22.1
SAMPLE PAGE FROM A TRADER'S NOTEBOOK

(1) Trade Entry Date	(2) Long or Short	(3) Units	Market	(4) Entry Price	(5) Stops Initial	(6) Stops Current	(7) Cumulative Implied Risk Initial	(8) Cumulative Implied Risk Current	(9) As Percentage of Equity Initial	(10) As Percentage of Equity Current	(11) Objective Initial	(12) Objective Current	(13) Exit Date	(14) Exit Price	(15) Net Profit or Loss	(16) Reasons for Entering Trade	(17) Comment

Column 5 would be used to indicate the intended stop point at time of entry. Revisions of this stop would be entered in column 6. (Some items, such as column 6, will require pencil entries, since they are subject to revision.) The reason for maintaining the initial stop point as a separate item is that this information may be useful to the trader in any subsequent analysis of her own trades. For example, she may wish to check whether her initial stops tend to be too wide or too close.

Columns 7–10 provide a summary of the implied risk on open positions. By adding these entries for all open positions, the trader can assess her current total exposure—information critical in controlling risk and determining whether new positions can be initiated. As a rough rule of thumb, the cumulative implied risk on all open positions should not exceed 25 percent–35 percent of total account equity. (Assuming the maximum risk on any given position is limited to 2 percent of equity, this constraint would not be relevant unless there were open positions in at least 13 markets.)

The use of objectives (columns 11 and 12) is a matter of individual preference. Although in some cases the use of objectives will permit a better exit price, in other circumstances objectives will result in the premature liquidation of a trade. Consequently, some traders may prefer to forgo the use of objectives, allowing the timing of liquidation to be determined by either a trailing stop or a change of opinion.

Liquidation information is contained in columns 13–15. The reason for maintaining the exit date is that it can be used to calculate the duration of the trade, information that may be useful to the speculator in analyzing her trades. Column 15 would indicate the profit or loss on the trade *after* deducting commissions.

Columns 16–17 provide room for capsule comments regarding the reasons for entering the trade (made at that time) and a hindsight evaluation of the trade. Such observations can be particularly useful in helping the trader detect any patterns in her successes and failures. Of course, the actual trader's notebook must allow more room for these comments than shown in the illustration provided by Figure 22.1. Furthermore, a more extensive description of the trade would be contained in a trader's diary, which is discussed in the next item.

The novice will usually benefit from a period of paper trading before plunging into actual trading. The trader's notebook would be ideally suited for this purpose, since it would not only provide an indication of potential trading success, but it would also get the new trader into the habit of approaching speculation in a systematic and disciplined fashion. Thus, when the transition is made to actual trading, the decision process will have become routine. Of course, the difficulty of trading decisions will increase dramatically once real money is at stake, but at least the new speculator will have a decisive advantage over her more typically ill-prepared counterparts.

STEP SIX: MAINTAIN A TRADER'S DIARY

The trader's diary would contain the following basic information for each trade:

1. ***Reasons for Trade.*** Over time, this information can help the speculator determine whether any of her trading strategies are particularly prone to success or failure.
2. ***How the Trade Turned Out.*** This basic background information is necessary for the evaluation of any trade. (Although the gist of this information can be determined from the net profit–loss column in the trader's notebook, it is also helpful to maintain this information along with each trade discussed in the trader's diary.)
3. ***Lessons.*** The speculator should itemize the mistakes or correct decisions made in the course of the trade. The mere act of keeping such a written record can greatly help a trader to avoid repeating past mistakes—particularly if repeated errors are indicated in capital letters and followed by several exclamation points. The trader's diary should be reviewed periodically to help reinforce these observations. After a while, the lessons will sink in. Speaking from personal experience, this approach can be instrumental in eradicating frequently repeated mistakes.

It may also be useful to augment the written diary with charts illustrating trade entry and exit points (as was done, for example, in Chapter 14).

STEP SEVEN: ANALYZE PERSONAL TRADING

The speculator must not only analyze the markets, but also his own past trades in order to isolate the strengths and weaknesses of his approach. Besides the trader's diary, two useful tools in such an analysis are analysis of segmented trades and the equity chart.

Analysis of Segmented Trades

The idea behind segmenting trades into different categories is to help identify any patterns of substantially above- or below-average performance. For example, by breaking down trades into buys and sells, a trader might discover that he has a predilection toward the long side, but that his short trades have a higher average profit. Such an observation would obviously imply the desirability of correcting a bias toward the long side.

As another example, after breaking down the results by market, a trader may find that he consistently loses money in certain markets. Such evidence might suggest that he could improve his overall performance by not trading these markets. The segmentation of trading results by market can be an extremely important exercise, since many speculators have a poor intuitive sense of their relative degree of success in various markets. The cessation of trading in poorer performing markets need not be permanent. The speculator could attempt to identify the reasons for his disappointing results in these markets and then research and test possible adjustments in his trading approach.

As a final example, a speculator who combines day trading and position trading might find it particularly instructive to compare the net results of each category. My own suspicion is that if such an analysis were performed by all speculators to whom the exercise is relevant, the population of day traders would shrink by 50 percent overnight.

Of course, there are other criteria that can be used to segment trades. Two other examples of relevant comparisons are fundamentally versus technically oriented trades, and trades that were in agreement with the position of a given trading system versus those that were not. In each case, the trader would be searching for patterns of success or failure. The process of analyzing segmented trades will be greatly simplified if the trader uses an electronic spreadsheet to maintain his "trader's notebook."

Equity Chart

This is a close-only type of chart in which the indicated value for each day represents the account equity (including the equity on open positions). The primary purpose of such a chart is to alert the trader when there is a precipitous deterioration of performance. For example, if after an extended, steady climb, the account equity experiences a sudden, steep decline, a trader might be well advised to lighten positions and take time to reassess the situation. Such an abrupt shift in performance might reflect a transformation of market conditions, a current vulnerability in the speculator's trading approach, or a recent predilection toward poor trading decisions. A determination of the actual cause is not essential, since any of these factors could be viewed as strong cautionary signals to reduce risk exposure. In short, the equity chart can be an important tool in mitigating equity retracements.

23 Eighty-Two Trading Rules and Market Observations

Live long enough and you will eventually be wrong about everything.

—Russell Baker

Few things are easier to ignore than trading advice. Many of the most critical trading rules have been so widely circulated that they have lost their ability to provoke any thought in the new trader. Thus, valid market insights are often dismissed as obvious cliches.

Consider the rule "Cut your losses short"—perhaps the single most important trading maxim. Lives there a speculator who has not heard this advice? Yet there is certainly no shortage of speculators who have ignored this rule. Not surprisingly, there is also no shortage of speculators whose accounts were virtually obliterated by one or two losing trades.

The truth is that most speculators will ignore advice until they have "rediscovered the wheel" through their own trading experience. Moreover, most traders will repeat a mistake many times before the lesson finally sinks in. Thus, I have no illusions that the advice presented in this and the next chapter will spare the reader from committing basic trading errors. However, it is hoped that several readings of these chapters (particularly following periods of negative trading results) will at least help some novice traders reduce the number of times these mistakes are repeated—hardly a trivial achievement.

The observations in this chapter are based on personal experience. Thus, the following list of rules should be viewed in their proper perspective: empirically based opinions as opposed to proven facts. Overall, there will be substantial overlap with other published expositions of trading guidelines. This is hardly surprising, since a wide range of rules (many of them mundane) are based on such sound principles that they are almost universally accepted as trading truths. For example, I have never met a successful speculator who did not believe that risk control was essential to profitable trading. On the other hand, some of the rules listed below reflect a subjective view that is contradicted by other writers (e.g., using market orders instead of limit orders). In the final analysis, each speculator must discover his or her own trading truths. It is hoped that the following list will help speed the process.

ENTERING TRADES

1. Differentiate between major position trades and short-term trades. The average risk allocated to short-term trades (as implied by number of contracts in position and stop point) should be significantly smaller. Also, the speculator should focus on major position trades, since these are usually far more critical to trading success. A mistake made by many traders is that they become so involved in trying to catch the minor market swings (generating lots of commissions and slippage in the process) that they miss the major price moves.

2. If you believe a major trading opportunity exists, don't be greedy in trying to get a slightly better entry price. The lost profit potential of one missed price move can offset the savings from 50 slightly better execution prices.

3. Entry into any major position should be planned and carefully thought out—never an intraday impulse.

4. *Find a chart pattern that says the timing is right—now.* Don't initiate a trade without such a confirming pattern. (Occasionally, one might consider a trade without such a pattern if there is a convergence of many measured moves and support/resistance points at a given price area and there is a well-defined stop point that does not imply much risk.)

5. Place orders determined by daily analysis. If the market is not close to the desired entry level, record the trade idea and review it each day until either the trade is entered or the trade idea is no longer deemed attractive. Failure to adhere to this rule can result in missing good trades. One common occurrence is that a trade idea is recalled once the market has moved beyond the intended entry, and it is then difficult to do the same trade at a worse price.

6. *When looking for a major reversal in a trend, it is usually wiser to wait for some pattern that suggests that the timing is right rather than fading the trend at projected objectives and support/resistance points.* This rule is particularly important in the case of a market in which the trend has carried prices to long-term highs/lows (e.g., highs/lows beyond a prior 100-day range). Remember, in most cases of an extended trend, the market will not form V-type reversals. Instead prices will normally pull back to test highs and lows—

often a number of times. Thus waiting for a top or bottom to form can prevent getting chopped to pieces during the topping or bottoming process—not to mention the losses that can occur if you are highly premature in picking the top or bottom. Even if the market does form a major V top or V bottom, subsequent consolidations (e.g., flags) can allow favorable reward/risk entries.

7. If you have an immediate instinctive impression when looking at a chart (particularly, if you are not conscious about which market you are looking at), go with that feeling.

8. *Don't let the fact that you missed the first major portion of a new trend keep you from trading with that trend* (as long as you can define a reasonable stop-loss point).

9. Don't fade recent price failure patterns (e.g., bull or bear traps) when implementing trades, even if there are many other reasons for the trade.

10. *Never fade the first gap of a price move!* For example, if you are waiting to enter a trade on a correction, and the correction is then formed on a price gap, don't enter the trade.

11. In most cases, use market orders rather than limit orders. This is especially important when liquidating a losing position or entering a perceived major trading opportunity—situations in which the trader is apt to be greatly concerned about the market getting away from her. Although limit orders will provide slightly better fills for a large majority of trades, this benefit will usually be more than offset by the substantially poorer fills, or missed profit potential, in those cases in which the initial limit order is not filled.

12. Never double up near the original trade entry point after having been ahead. Often, the fact that the market has completely retraced is a negative sign for the trade. Even if the trade is still good, doubling up in this manner will jeopardize holding power due to overtrading.

EXITING TRADES AND RISK CONTROL (MONEY MANAGEMENT)

13. Decide on a specific protective stop point *at the time of trade entry.*

14. *Exit any trade as newly developing patterns or market action are contrary to trade*—even if stop point has not been reached. Ask yourself, "If I had to have a position in this market, which way would it be?" If the answer is not the position you hold, get out! In fact, if contradictory indications are strong enough, reverse the position.

15. Always get out *immediately* once the original premise for a trade is violated.

16. If you are dramatically wrong the first day trade is on, abandon trade immediately—especially, if the market gaps against you.

17. In the event of a major breakout counter to the position held, either liquidate immediately or use a very close stop. *In the event of a gap breakout, always liquidate immediately.*

18. If a given market suddenly trades far in excess of its recent volatility in a direction opposite to the position held, liquidate your position immediately. For example, if a market that has been trading in approximate 50-point daily ranges opens 100–150 points higher, cover immediately if you are short.

19. *If selling (buying) into resistance (support) and the market consolidates instead of reversing, get out.*

20. For analysts and market advisors: *If your gut feeling is that a recent recommendation, hotline broadcast, trade, or written report is wrong, reverse your opinion!*

21. If you're unable to watch markets for a period of time (e.g., when traveling), either liquidate all positions or be sure to have GTC stop orders on all open positions. (Also, in such situations, limit orders can be used to ensure getting into the market on planned buys at lower prices or planned sells at higher prices.)

22. Do not get complacent about an open position. Always know where you are getting out even if the point is far removed from the current price. Also, an evolving pattern contrary to the trade may suggest the desirability of an earlier-than-intended exit.

23. *Fight the desire to immediately get back into the market following a stopped-out trade.* Getting back in will usually supplement the original loss with additional losses. The only reason to get back in on a stopped out trade is if the timing seems appropriate based on evolving prices patterns—that is, only if it meets all the conditions and justifications of any new trade.

OTHER RISK-CONTROL (MONEY MANAGEMENT) RULES

24. *When trading is going badly:* (a) *reduce position size (keep in mind that positions in strongly correlated markets are similar to one larger position);* (b) *use tight stop-loss points;* (c) *slow up in taking new trades.*

25. *When trading is going badly, reduce risk exposure by liquidating losing trades, not winning trades.* This observation was memorably related by Edwin Lefèvre in *Reminiscences of a Stock Operator:* "I did precisely the wrong thing. The cotton showed me a loss and I kept it. The wheat showed me a profit and I sold it out. Of all the speculative blunders there are few greater than trying to average a losing game. Always sell what shows you a loss and keep what shows you a profit."

26. Be extremely careful not to change trading patterns after making a profit:

    a. Do not initiate any trades that would have been deemed too risky at the start of the trading program.

    b. Do not suddenly increase the number of contracts in a typical trade. (However, a gradual increase as equity grows is OK.)

27. *Treat small positions with the same common sense as large positions. Never say, "It's only one or two contracts."*

28. Avoid holding very large positions into major reports or the release of important government statistics.

29. Apply the same money management principles to spreads as to outright positions. It is easy to be lulled into thinking that spreads move gradually enough so that it is not necessary to worry about stop-loss protection.

30. Don't buy options without planning at what outright price trade is to be liquidated.

HOLDING AND EXITING WINNING TRADES

31. Do not take *small,* quick profits in major position trades. In particular, if you are dramatically right on a trade, *never, never* take profits on the first day.

32. Don't be too hasty to get out of a trade with a gap in your direction. Use gap as initial stop; then bring in stop in trailing fashion.

33. Try to use trailing stops, supplemented by developing market action, instead of objectives as a means of getting out of profitable trades. Using objectives will often work against fully realizing potential of major trends. *Remember, you need the occasional big winners to offset losers.*

34. The preceding rule notwithstanding, it is still useful to set an initial objective at the time of trade entry to allow the application of the following rule: If a very large portion of an objective is realized very quickly (e.g., 50–60 percent in one week or 75–80 percent in two or three weeks), take partial profits, with the idea of reinstating liquidated contracts on a reaction. The idea is that it is OK to take a quick, *sizable* profit. Although this rule may often result in missing the remainder of the move on the liquidated portion of the position, holding the entire position, in such a case, can frequently lead to nervous liquidation on the first sharp retracement.

35. If an objective is reached, but you still like the trade, stay with it using a trailing stop. This rule is important in order to be able to ride a major trend. *Remember, patience is not only important in waiting for the right trades, but also in staying with trades that are working. The failure to adequately profit from correct trades is a key profit-limiting factor.*

36. One partial exception to the previous rule is that if you are *heavily* positioned and equity is surging straight up, consider taking scale-up profits. Corollary rule: *When things look too good to be true— watch out!* If everything is going right, it is probably a good time to begin taking scale-up (scale-down) profits and using close trailing stops on a portion of your positions.

37. If taking profits on a trade that is believed to still have long-term potential (but is presumably vulnerable to a near-term correction), have a game plan for reentering position. If the market doesn't retrace sufficiently to allow for reentry, be cognizant of patterns that can be used for timing a reentry. *Don't let the fact that the reentry point would be worse than the exit point keep you from getting back into a trade* in which the perception of both the long-term trend and current timing suggest reentering. *Inability to enter at a worse price can often lead to missing major portions of large trends.*

38. If trading multiple contracts, *avoid the emotional trap of wanting to be 100 percent right.* In other words, only take partial profits. Always try to keep at least a partial position for the duration of the move— until the market forms a convincing reversal pattern or reaches a meaningful stop-loss point.

MISCELLANEOUS PRINCIPLES AND RULES

39. *Always pay more attention to market action and evolving patterns than to objectives and support/resistance areas.* The latter can often cause you to reverse a correct market bias very prematurely.

40. When you feel action should be taken either entering or exiting a position—*act, don't procrastinate.*

41. Never go counter to your own opinion of the long-term trend of the market. In other words, don't try to dance between the raindrops.

42. Winning trades tend to be ahead right from the start.

43. Correct timing of entry and exit (e.g., timing entry on a reliable pattern, getting out immediately on the first sign of trade failure), can often keep a loss small *even* if the trade is dead wrong.

44. Intraday decisions are almost always losers. *Keep screen off intraday.*

45. Be sure to check markets before the close on Friday. Often the situation is clearer at the end of the week. In such cases, a better entry or exit can usually be obtained on Friday near the close than on the following Monday opening. This rule is particularly important if you are holding a significant position.

46. Act on market dreams (that are recalled unambiguously). Such dreams are often right because they represent your subconscious market knowledge attempting to break through the barriers established by the conscious mind (e.g., "How can I buy here when I could have gone long $2,000 lower last week?")

47. *You are never immune to bad trading habits—the best you can do is to keep them latent. As soon as you get lazy or sloppy, they will return.*

MARKET PATTERNS

48. If the market sets new historical highs and holds, the odds strongly favor a move very far beyond the old highs. Selling a market at new record highs is probably one the amateur trader's worst mistakes.

49. Narrow market consolidations near the upper end of broader trading ranges are bullish patterns. Similarly, *narrow* consolidations near the low end of trading ranges are bearish.

50. Play the breakout from an extended, narrow range with a stop against the other side of the range.

51. Breakouts from trading ranges that hold 1–2 weeks, or longer, are among the most reliable technical indicators of impending trends.

52. A common and particularly useful form of the above rule is: Flags or pennants forming right above or below prior extended and broad trading ranges tend to be fairly reliable continuation patterns.

53. Trade in the direction of wide gaps.

54. Gaps out of congestion patterns, particularly 1–2 month trading ranges, are often excellent signals. (This pattern works especially well in bear markets.)

55. If a "breakaway gap" is not filled during the first week, it should be viewed as a particularly reliable signal.

56. A breakout to new highs or lows followed within the next week or two by a gap (particularly a wide gap) back into the range is a particularly reliable form of a bull-trap or bear-trap.

57. If the market breaks out to a new high or low and then pulls back to form a flag or pennant in the prebreakout trading range, assume that a top or bottom is in place. A position can be taken using a protective stop beyond the flag or pennant consolidation.

58. A breakout from a trading range followed by a pullback deep into the range (e.g., three-quarters of the way back into the range or more) is yet another significant bull- or bear-trap formation.

59. If an apparent V bottom is followed by a nearby congestion pattern, it may represent a bottom pattern. However, if this consolidation is then broken on the downside and the V bottom is approached, the market action can be read as a sign of an impending move to new lows. In the latter case, short positions could be implemented using protective stops near the top of the consolidation. Analogous comments would apply to V tops followed by nearby consolidations.

60. V tops and V bottoms followed by multimonth consolidations that form in close proximity to the reversal point tend to be major top or bottom formations.

61. Tight flag and pennant consolidations tend to be reliable continuation patterns and allow entry into an existing trend, with a reasonably close, yet meaningful, stop point.

62. If a tight flag or pennant consolidation leads to a breakout in the wrong direction (i.e., a reversal instead of a continuation), expect the move to continue in the direction of the breakout.

63. Curved consolidations tend to suggest an accelerated move in the direction of the curve.

64. The breaking of a short-term curved consolidation, in the direction opposite of the curve pathway, tends to be a good trend-reversal signal.

65. Wide-ranging days (i.e., days with a range far exceeding the recent average range) with a close counter to the main trend usually tend to provide a reliable early signal of a trend change—particularly if they also trigger a reversal signal (e.g., filling of a runaway gap, complete penetration of prior consolidation).

66. Near-vertical, large price moves over a period of 2–4 days (coming off of a relative high or low) tend to be extended in the following weeks.

67. Spikes are good short-term reversal signals. The extreme of the spike can be used as a stop point.

68. In spike situations, look at chart both ways—with and without spike. For example, if when a spike is removed a flag is evident, a penetration of that flag is a meaningful signal.

69. The filling-in of a runaway gap can be viewed as evidence of a possible trend reversal.

70. An island reversal followed shortly thereafter with a pullback into the most recent trading range or consolidation pattern represents a possible major top (bottom) signal.

71. The ability of a market to hold relatively firm when other related markets are under significant pressure can be viewed as a sign of intrinsic strength. Similarly, a market acting weak when related markets are strong can be viewed as a bearish sign.

72. If a market trades consistently higher for most of the daily trading session, anticipate a close in the same direction.

73. Two successive flags with little separation can be viewed as a probable continuation pattern.

74. View a curved bottom, followed by a shallower, same-direction curved consolidation near the top of this pattern, as a bullish formation (cup-and-handle). A similar pattern would apply to market tops.

75. Moderate sentiment in a market that is strongly trending may be a more reliable indicator of a probable continuation of the price move than a high/low sentiment reading is of a reversal. In other words, extreme sentiment readings can often occur in the absence of major tops and bottoms, but major tops and bottoms rarely occur in the absence of extreme sentiment readings (current or recent).

76. A failed signal is more reliable than the original signal. Go the other way, using the high (low) before the failure signal as a stop. Some examples of such failure patterns are rule numbers 56, 57, 58, 62, 64, and 69.

77. The failure of a market to follow through on significant bullish or bearish news (e.g., a major USDA report) is often a harbinger of an imminent trend reversal. Pay particular attention to such a development if you have an existing position.

ANALYSIS AND REVIEW

78. Review charts every day—especially if you're too busy.

79. Periodically review long-term charts (*e.g., every 2–4 weeks*).

80. Religiously maintain a *trader's diary,* including a chart for *each* trade taken and noting the following: reasons for trade; intended stop and objective (if any); follow-up at a later point indicating how the trade turned out; observations and lessons (mistakes, things done right, or noteworthy patterns); and net profit/loss. It is important that the trade sheet be filled out when trade entered so that the reasons for trade accurately reflect your actual thinking rather than a reconstruction.

81. Maintain a *patterns chart book* whenever you notice a market pattern that is interesting and you want to note how you think it will turn out, or you want to record how that pattern is eventually resolved (in the case where you don't have any bias concerning the correct interpretation). Be sure to follow each chart up at a later date to see the actual outcome. Over time, this process may improve skills in chart interpretation by providing some statistical evidence of the forecasting reliability of various chart patterns (as recognized in real time).

82. Review and update trading rules, trader's diary, and patterns chart book on a regular schedule (e.g., three-month rotation for the three items). Of course, any of these items can be reviewed more frequently, whenever it is felt such a review would be useful.

24 Market Wiz(ar)dom

There is no such thing as being right or beating the market. If you make money, it is because you understood the same thing the market did. If you lose money, it is simply because you got it wrong. There is no other way of looking at it.

—Musawer Mansoor Ijaz

The previous chapter detailed specific trading rules and market observations. This chapter, which has been adapted from *The New Market Wizards,*[1] examines the broad principles and psychological factors that are crucial to trading success.

The methods employed by exceptional traders are extraordinarily diverse. Some are pure fundamentalists; others employ only technical analysis; and still others combine the two methodologies. Some traders consider two days to be long term, while others consider two months to be short term. Yet despite the wide gamut of styles, I have found that certain principles hold true for a broad spectrum of successful traders. After a score of years analyzing and trading the markets and two books of interviews with great traders, I have come down to the following list of forty-two observations regarding success in trading.

1. First Things First. First, be sure that you really want to trade. It is common for people who think they want to trade to discover that they really don't.

2. Examine Your Motives. Think about why you really want to trade. If you want to trade for the excitement, you might be better off riding a roller coaster or taking up hang gliding. In my own case, I found that the underlying motive for trading was serenity or peace of mind—hardly the emotional state typical of trading. Another personal motive for trading was that I loved puzzle solving—and the markets provided the ultimate puzzle. However, while I enjoyed the cerebral aspects of market analysis, I didn't particularly like the visceral characteristics of trading itself. The contrast between my

---

[1]*The New Market Wizards,* Jack Schwager, Harper Business, New York, 1989, pp. 461–478; copyright © 1989 by HarperCollins Publishers; by permission.

motives and the activity resulted in very obvious conflicts. You need to examine your own motives very carefully for any such conflicts. The market is a stern master. You need to do almost everything right to win. If parts of you are pulling in opposite directions, the game is lost before you start.

How did I resolve my own conflict? I decided to focus completely on mechanical trading approaches in order to eliminate the emotionality in trading. Equally important, focusing on the design of mechanical systems directed my energies to the part of trading I did enjoy—the puzzle-solving aspects. Although I had devoted some energy to mechanical systems for these reasons for a number of years, I eventually came to the realization that I wanted to move in this direction exclusively. (This is not intended as an advocacy for mechanical systems over human-decision-oriented approaches. I am only providing a personal example. The appropriate answer for another trader could well be very different.)

3. *Match the Trading Method to Your Personality.* It is critical to choose a method that is consistent with your own personality and comfort level. If you can't stand to give back significant profits, then a long-term trend-following approach—even a very good one—will be a disaster, because you will never be able to follow it. If you don't want to watch the quote screen all day (or can't), don't try a day-trading method. If you can't stand the emotional strain of making trading decisions, then try to develop a mechanical system for trading the markets. The approach you use must be right for you; it must feel comfortable. The importance of this concept cannot be overemphasized. Randy McKay, who met success as both an on-the-floor and off-the-floor trader, asserted: "Virtually every successful trader I know ultimately ended up with a trading style suited to his personality."

Incidentally, the mismatch of trading style and personality is one of the key reasons why purchased trading systems rarely make profits for those who buy them, even if the system is a good one. While the odds of getting a winning system are small—certainly less than 50/50—the odds of getting a system that fits your personality are smaller still. I'll leave it to your imagination to decide on the odds of buying a profitable/moderate risk system and using it effectively.

4. *It Is Absolutely Necessary to Have an Edge.* You can't win without an edge, even with the world's greatest discipline and money management skills. If you could, then it would be possible to win at roulette (over the long run) using perfect discipline and risk control. Of course, that is an impossible task because of the laws of probability. If you don't have an edge, all that money management and discipline will do for you is to guarantee that you will bleed to death gradually. Incidentally, if you don't know what your edge is, you don't have one.

5. *Derive a Method.* To have an edge, you must have a method. The type of method is irrelevant. Some of the supertraders are pure fundamentalists; some are pure technicians; and some are hybrids. Even within each group, there are tremendous variations. For example, within the group of technicians, there are tape readers (or their modern-day equivalent—screen watchers), chartists, mechanical system traders, Elliott Wave analysts, Gann analysts, and so on. The type of method is not important, but having one is critical—and, of course, the method must have an edge.

6. *Developing a Method Is Hard Work.* Shortcuts rarely lead to trading success. Developing your own approach requires research, observation, and thought. Expect the process to take lots of time and hard work. Expect many dead ends and multiple failures before you find a successful trading approach that is right for you. Remember that you are playing against tens of thousands of professionals. Why should you be any better? If it were that easy, there would be a lot more millionaire traders.

7. *Skill versus Hard Work.* Is trading success dependent on innate skills, or is hard work sufficient? There is no question in my mind that many of the supertraders have a special talent for trading. Marathon running provides an appropriate analogy. Virtually anyone can run a marathon, given sufficient commitment and hard work. Yet, regardless of the effort and desire, only a small fraction of the population will ever be able to run a 2:12 marathon (or 2:25 for women). Similarly, anyone can learn to play a musical instrument. But again, regardless of work and dedication, only a handful of individuals possess the natural talent to become concert soloists. The general rule is that exceptional performance requires both natural talent and hard work to realize its potential. If the innate skill is lacking, hard work may provide proficiency, but not excellence.

In my opinion, the same principles apply to trading. Virtually anyone can become a net profitable trader, but only a few have the inborn talent to become supertraders. For this reason, it may be possible to teach trading success, but only up to a point. Be realistic in your goals.

8. *Good Trading Should Be Effortless.* Wait a minute. Didn't I just list hard work as an ingredient to successful trading? How can good trading require hard work and yet be effortless?

There is no contradiction. Hard work refers to the preparatory process—the research and observation necessary to become a good trader—not to the trading itself. In this respect, hard work is associated with such qualities as vision, creativity, persistence, drive, desire, and commitment. Hard work certainly does not mean that the process of trading itself should be filled with exertion. It certainly does not imply struggling with or fighting against the markets. On the contrary, the more effortless and natural the trading process, the better the chances for success. One trader quoting *Zen and the Art of Archery* made the following analogy: "In trading, just as in archery, whenever there is effort, force, straining, struggling, or trying, it's wrong. You're out of sync; you're out of harmony with the market. The perfect trade is one that requires no effort."

Visualize a world-class distance runner, clicking off mile after mile at a five-minute pace. Now picture an out-of-shape, 250-pound couch potato trying to run a mile at a ten-minute pace. The professional runner glides along gracefully—almost effortlessly—despite the long distance and fast pace. The out-of-shape runner, however, is likely to struggle, huffing and puffing like a Yugo going up a 1 percent grade. Who is putting in more work and effort? Who is more successful? Of course, the world-class runner puts in his hard working during training, and this prior effort and commitment are essential to his success.

9. *Money Management and Risk Control.* Almost all the great traders I interviewed felt that money management was even more important than the trading method. Many potentially successful systems or trading approaches have led to disaster because the trader applying the strategy lacked a method of controlling risk. You don't have to be a mathematician or understand portfolio theory to manage risk. Risk control can be as easy as the following three-step approach:

1. Never risk more than 1 to 2 percent of your capital on any trade. (Depending on your approach, a modestly higher number might still be reasonable. However, I would strongly advise against anything over 5 percent.)
2. Predetermine your exit point *before* you get into a trade. Many of the traders I interviewed cited exactly this rule.
3. If you lose a certain predetermined amount of your starting capital (e.g., 10 percent to 20 percent), take a breather, analyze what went wrong, and wait until you feel confident and have a high-probability idea before you begin trading again. For traders with large accounts, trading very small is a reasonable alternative to a complete trading hiatus. The strategy of cutting trading size down sharply during losing streaks is one mentioned by many of the traders I interviewed.

10. *The Trading Plan.* Trying to win in the markets without a trading plan is like trying to build a house without blueprints—costly (and avoidable) mistakes are virtually inevitable. A trading plan simply requires combining a personal trading method with specific money management and trade entry rules. Robert Krausz, a hypnotist who has made a specialty of working with traders, considers the absence of a trading plan the root of all the principal difficulties traders encounter in the markets. Richard Driehaus, a very successful mutual fund manager I interviewed, stresses that a trading plan should reflect a personal core philosophy. He explains that without a core philosophy, you are not going to be able to hold on to your positions or stick with your trading plan during really difficult times.

11. *Discipline.* *Discipline* was probably the most frequent word used by the exceptional traders that I interviewed. Often, it was mentioned in an almost apologetic tone: "I know you've heard this a million times before, but believe me, it's really important."

There are two basic reasons why discipline is critical. First, it is a prerequisite for maintaining effective risk control. Second, you need discipline to apply your method without second-guessing and choosing which trades to take. I guarantee that you will almost always pick the wrong ones. Why? Because you will tend to pick the comfortable trades, and as Bill Eckhardt, a mathematician turned successful commodity trading advisor (CTA), explained, "What feels good is often the wrong thing to do."

As a final word on this subject, remember that you are never immune to bad trading habits—the best you can do is to keep them latent. As soon as you get lazy or sloppy, they will return.

12. *Understand that You Are Responsible.* Whether you win or lose, you are responsible for your own results. Even if you lost on your broker's tip, an advisory service recommendation, or a bad signal from the system you bought, you are responsible because you made the decision to listen and act. I have never met a successful trader who blamed others for his losses.

13. *The Need for Independence.* You need to do your own thinking. Don't get caught up in mass hysteria. Ed Seykota, a futures trader who multiplied the equity in his accounts a thousandfold over an 18-year period, pointed out that by the time a story is making the cover of national periodicals, the trend is probably near an end.

Independence also means making your own trading decisions. Never listen to other opinions. Even if it occasionally helps on a trade or two, listening to others invariably seems to end up costing you money—not to mention confusing your own market view. As Michael Marcus, a very successful futures trader, stated in *Market Wizards,* "You need to follow your own light. If you combine two traders, you will get the worst of each."

A related personal anecdote concerns another trader I interviewed in *Market Wizards.* Although he could trade better than I if he were blindfolded and placed in a trunk at the bottom of a pool, he still was interested in my view of the markets. One day he called and asked, "What do you think of the yen?"

The yen was one of the few markets about which I had a strong opinion at the time. It had formed a particular chart pattern that made me very bearish. "I think the yen is going straight down, and I'm short," I replied.

He proceeded to give me fifty-one reasons why the yen was oversold and due for a rally. After he hung up, I thought: "I'm leaving on a business trip tomorrow. My trading has not been going very well during the last few weeks. The short yen trade is one of the only positions in my account. Do I really want to fade one of the world's best traders given these considerations?" I decided to close out the trade.

By the time I returned from my trip several days later, the yen had fallen 150 points. As luck would have it, that afternoon the same trader called. When the conversation rolled around to the yen, I couldn't resist asking, "By the way, are you still long the yen?"

"Oh no," he replied, "I'm short."

The point is not that this trader was trying to mislead me. On the contrary, he firmly believed each market opinion at the time he expressed it. However, his timing was good enough so that he probably made money on both sides of the trade. In contrast, I ended up with nothing, even though I had the original move pegged exactly right. The moral is that even advice from a much better trader can lead to detrimental results.

14. Confidence. An unwavering confidence in their ability to continue to win in the markets, was a nearly universal characteristic among the traders I interviewed. Dr. Van Tharp, a psychologist who has done a great deal of research on traders and was interviewed in *Market Wizards,* claims that one of the basic traits of winning traders is that they believe "they've won the game before the start."

The trader who has confidence will have the courage to make the right decisions and the strength not to panic. There is a passage in Mark Twain's *Life on the Mississippi* that I find remarkably apropos, even though it has nothing to do with trading. In it, the protagonist—an apprentice steamboat river pilot—is tricked by his mentor and the crew into panicking in a stretch of river he *knows* to be the easiest in the entire run. The following exchange then ensues with his mentor:

> "Didn't you know there was no bottom in that crossing?"
> "Yes sir, I did."
> "Very well then, you shouldn't have allowed me or anybody else to shake your confidence in that knowledge. Try to remember that. And another thing, when you get into a dangerous place, don't turn coward. That isn't going to help matters any."

15. Losing is Part of the Game. The great traders fully realize that losing is an intrinsic element in the game of trading. This attitude seems linked to confidence. Because exceptional traders are confident that they will win over the long run, individual losing trades no longer seem horrible; they simply appear inevitable—which is what they are. As Linda Raschke, a futures trader with a particularly high ratio of winning to losing trades, explained, "It never bothered me to lose, because I always knew I would make it right back."

There is no more certain recipe for losing than having a fear of losing. If you can't stand taking losses, you will either end up taking large losses or missing great trading opportunities—either flaw is sufficient to sink any chance for success.

16. *Lack of Confidence and Time-Outs.* Trade only when you feel confident and optimistic. I have often heard traders say: "I just can't seem to do anything right." Or, "I bet I get stopped out right near the low again." If you find yourself thinking in such negative terms, it is a sure sign that it is time to take a break from trading. Get back into trading slowly. Think of trading as a cold ocean. Test the water before plunging in.

17. *The Urge to Seek Advice.* The urge to seek advice betrays a lack of confidence. As Linda Raschke said, "If you ever find yourself tempted to seek out someone else's opinion on a trade, that's usually a sure sign that you should get out of your position."

18. *The Virtue of Patience.* Waiting for the right opportunity increases the probability of success. You don't always have to be in the market. As Edwin Lefèvre put it in his classic *Reminiscences of a Stock Operator,* "There is the plain fool who does the wrong thing at all times anywhere, but there is the Wall Street fool who thinks he must trade all the time."

One of the more colorful descriptions of patience in trading was offered by well-known investor Jim Rogers in *Market Wizards:* "I just wait until there is money lying in the corner, and all I have to do is go over there and pick it up." In other words, until he is so sure of a trade that it seems as easy as picking money off the floor, he does nothing.

Mark Weinstein, a phenomenally consistent futures and stock trader (also interviewed in *Market Wizards*), provided the following apt analogy: "Although the cheetah is the fastest animal in the world and can catch any animal on the plains, it will wait until it is absolutely sure it can catch its prey. It may hide in the bush for a week, waiting for just the right moment. It will wait for a baby antelope, and not just any baby antelope, but preferably one that is also sick or lame. Only then, when there is no chance it can lose its prey, does it attack. That, to me, is the epitome of professional trading."

19. *The Importance of Sitting.* Patience is important not only in waiting for the right trades, but also in staying with trades that are working. The failure to adequately profit from correct trades is a key profit-limiting factor.

Quoting again from Lefèvre in *Reminiscences,* "It never was my thinking that made big money for me. It was always my sitting. Got that? My sitting tight!" Bill Eckhardt offered a particularly memorable comment on this subject: "One common adage . . . that is completely wrongheaded is: You can't go broke taking profits. That's precisely how many traders *do* go broke. While amateurs go broke by taking large losses, professionals go broke by taking small profits."

20. *Developing a Low-Risk Idea.* One of the exercises Dr. Van Tharp uses in his seminars is having the participants take the time to write down their ideas on low-risk trades. The merit of a low-risk idea is that it combines two essential elements: patience (because only a small portion of ideas will qualify) and risk control (inherent in the definition). Taking the time to think through low-risk strategies is a useful exercise for all traders. The specific ideas will vary greatly from trader to trader, depending on the markets traded and methodologies used. At the seminar I attended, the participants came up with a long list of descriptions of low-risk ideas. As one example: a trade in which the market movement required to provide convincing proof that you are wrong is small. Although it had nothing to do with trading, my personal favorite of the low-risk ideas mentioned was: "Open a doughnut shop next door to a police station."

21. *The Importance of Varying Bet Size.* All traders who win consistently over the long run have an edge. However, that edge may vary significantly from trade to trade. It can be mathematically demonstrated that in any wager game with varying probabilities, winnings are maximized by adjusting the bet size in accordance with the perceived chance for a successful outcome. Optimal blackjack betting strategy provides a perfect illustration of this concept.

If the trader has some idea as to which trades have a greater edge—say, for example, based on a higher confidence level (assuming that it is a reliable indicator)—then it makes sense to be more aggressive in these situations. As Stanley Druckenmiller, a highly profitable hedge fund manager, expresses it, "The way to build [superior] long-term returns is through preservation of capital and home runs. . . . When you have tremendous conviction on a trade, you have to go for the jugular. It takes courage to be a pig." For a number of Market Wizards, keen judgment as to when to really step on the accelerator and the courage to do so have been instrumental to their achieving exceptional (as opposed to merely good) returns.

Some of the traders I interviewed mentioned that they varied their trading size in accordance with how they were doing. For example, McKay indicated that it was not uncommon for him to vary his position size by as much as a factor of one hundred to one. He finds this approach helps him reduce risk during losing periods while enhancing profits during the winning periods.

22. *Scaling In and Out of Trades.* You don't have to get in or out of a position all at once. Scaling in and out of positions provides the flexibility of fine-tuning trades and broadens the set of alternative choices. Most traders sacrifice this flexibility without a second thought because of the innate human desire to be completely right. (By definition, a scaling approach means that some portions of a trade will be entered or exited at worse prices than other portions.) Some traders also noted that scaling enabled them to stay with at least a portion of long-term winning trades much longer than would otherwise have been the case.

23. *Being Right Is More Important than Being a Genius.* I think one reason why so many people try to pick tops and bottoms is that they want to prove to the world how smart they are. Think about winning rather than being a hero. Forget trying to judge trading success by how close you can come to picking major tops and bottoms, but rather by how well you can pick individual trades with favorable return/risk characteristics. Go for consistency on a trade-to-trade basis, not perfect trades.

24. *Don't Worry about Looking Stupid.* Last week you told everyone at the office, "My analysis has just given me a great buy signal in the S&P. The market is going to a new high." Now as you examine the market action since then, something appears to be wrong. Instead of rallying, the market is breaking down. Your gut tells you that the market is vulnerable. Whether you realize it or not, your announced prognostications are going to color your objectivity. Why? Because you don't want to look stupid after telling the world that the market was going to a new high. Consequently, you are likely to view the market's action in the most favorable light possible. "The market isn't breaking down, it's just a pullback to knock out the weak longs." As a result of this type of rationalization, you end up holding a losing position far too long. There is an easy solution to this problem: Don't talk about your position.

What if your job requires talking about your market opinions (as mine does)? Here the rule is: Whenever you start worrying about contradicting your previous opinion, view that concern as reinforcement to reverse your market stance. As a personal example, in early 1991 I came to the conclusion that the dollar had formed a major bottom. I specifically remember one talk in which an audience member asked me about my outlook for currencies. I responded by boldly predicting that the dollar would head higher for years. Several months later, when the dollar surrendered the entire gain it had realized following the news of the August 1991 Soviet coup before the coup's failure was confirmed, I sensed that something was wrong. I recalled my many predictions over the preceding months in which I had stated that the dollar would go up for years. The discomfort and embarrassment I felt about these previous forecasts told me it was time to change my opinion.

In my earlier years in the business, I invariably tried to rationalize my original market opinion in such situations. I was burned enough times that I eventually learned a lesson. In the preceding example, the abandonment of my original projection was fortunate, because the dollar collapsed in the ensuing months.

25. Sometimes Action Is More Important than Prudence. Waiting for a price correction to enter the market may sound prudent, but it is often the wrong thing to do. When your analysis, methodology, or gut tells you to get into a trade at the market instead of waiting for a correction—do so. Caution against the influence of knowing that you could have gotten in at a better price in recent sessions, particularly in those situations when the market witnesses a sudden, large move (often due to an important surprise news item). If you don't feel the market is going to correct, that consideration is irrelevant. These types of trades often work because they are so hard to do.

26. Catching Part of the Move Is Just Fine. Just because you missed the first major portion of a new trend, don't let that keep you from trading with that trend (as long as you can define a reasonable stop-loss point). McKay commented that the easiest part of a trend is the middle portion, which implies always missing part of the trend prior to entry.

27. Maximize Gains, Not the Number of Wins. Eckhardt explains that human nature does not operate to maximize gain but rather the chance of a gain. The problem with this is that it implies a lack of focus on the magnitudes of gains (and losses)—a flaw that leads to nonoptimal performance results. Eckhardt bluntly concludes: "The success rate of trades is the least important performance statistic and may even be inversely related to performance." Jeff Yass, a very successful options trader, echoes a similar theme: "The basic concept that applies to both poker and option trading is that the primary object is not winning the most hands, but rather maximizing your gains."

28. Learn to Be Disloyal. Loyalty may be a virtue in family, friends, and pets, but it is a fatal flaw for a trader. Never have loyalty to a position. The novice trader will have lots of loyalty to his original position. He will ignore signs that he is on the wrong side of the market, riding his trade into a large loss while hoping for the best. The more experienced trader, having learned the importance of money management, will exit quickly once it is apparent he has made a bad trade. However, the truly skilled trader will be able to do a 180-degree turn, *reversing* his position at a loss if market behavior points to such a course of action. Druckenmiller made the awful error of reversing his stock position from short to long on the very day before the October 19, 1987 crash. His ability to quickly recognize his error and, more important, to unhesitatingly act on that realization by reversing back to short at a large loss helped transform a potentially disastrous month into a net profitable one.

29. *Pull Out Partial Profits.* Pull a portion of winnings out of the market to prevent trading discipline from deteriorating into complacency. It is far too easy to rationalize overtrading and procrastination in liquidating losing trades by saying, "It's only profits." Profits withdrawn from an account are much more likely to be viewed as real money.

30. *Hope Is a Four-Letter Word.* Hope is a dirty word for a trader, not only in regards to procrastinating in a losing position, hoping the market will come back, but also in terms of hoping for a reaction that will allow for a better entry in a missed trade. If such trades are good, the hoped-for reaction will not materialize until it is too late. Often the only way to enter such trades is to do so as soon as a reasonable stop-loss point can be identified.

31. *Don't Do The Comfortable Thing.* Eckhardt offers the rather provocative proposition that the human tendency to select comfortable choices will lead most people to experience worse than random results. In effect, he is saying that natural human traits lead to such poor trading decisions that most people would be better off flipping coins or throwing darts. Some of the examples Eckhardt cites of the comfortable choices people tend to make that run counter to sound trading principles include gambling with losses, locking in sure winners, selling on strength and buying on weakness, and designing (or buying) trading systems that have been overfitted to past price behavior. The implied message to the trader is: Do what is right, not what feels comfortable.

32. *You Can't Win If You Have to Win.* There is an old Wall Street adage: "Scared money never wins." The reason is quite simple: If you are risking money you can't afford to lose, all the emotional pitfalls of trading will be magnified. Early in his career, when the bankruptcy of a key financial backer threatened the survival of his fledgling investment firm, Druckenmiller "bet the ranch" on one trade, in a last-ditch effort to save his firm. Even though he came within one week of picking the absolute bottom in the T-bill market, he still lost all his money. The need to win fosters trading errors (e.g., excessive leverage and a lack of planning in the example just cited). The market seldom tolerates the carelessness associated with trades born of desperation.

33. *Think Twice When the Market Lets You Off the Hook Easily.* Don't be too eager to get out of a position you have been worried about if the market allows you to exit at a much better price than anticipated. If you had been worried about an adverse overnight (or over-the-weekend) price move because of a news event or a technical price failure on the previous close, it is likely that many other traders shared this concern. The fact that the market does not follow through much on these fears strongly suggests that there must be some very powerful underlying forces in favor of the direction of the original position. This concept, which was first proposed in *Market Wizards* by Marty Schwartz, who compiled an astounding track record trading stock index futures, was illustrated by the manner in which Lipschutz, a large-scale currency trader, exited the one trade he admitted had scared him. In that instance, on Friday afternoon, a time when the currency markets are particularly thin (after Europe's close), Lipschutz found himself with an enormous short dollar position in the midst of a strongly rallying market. He had to wait over the weekend for the Tokyo opening on Sunday evening to find sufficient liquidity to exit his position. When the dollar opened weaker than expected in Tokyo, he didn't just dump his position in relief; rather, his trader's instincts told him to delay liquidation—a decision that resulted in a far better exit price.

34. A Mind Is a Terrible Thing to Close. Open-mindedness seems to be a common trait among those who excel at trading. For example, Gil Blake, a mutual fund timer who has made incredibly consistent profits, actually fell into a trading career by attempting to demonstrate to a friend that prices were random. When he realized he was wrong, he became a trader. In the words of Driehaus, "the mind is like a parachute—it's only good when it's open."

35. The Markets Are an Expensive Place to Look for Excitement. Excitement has a lot to do with the image of trading, but nothing to do with success in trading (except in an inverse sense). In *Market Wizards*, Larry Hite, the founder of Mint Management, one of the largest CTA firms, described his conversation with a friend who couldn't understand his absolute adherence to a computerized trading system. His friend asked, "Larry, how can you trade the way you do? Isn't it boring?" Larry replied, "I don't trade for excitement; I trade to win."

36. The Calm State of a Trader. If there is an emotional state associated with successful trading, it is the antithesis of excitement. Based on his observations, Charles Faulkner, an NLP practitioner who works with traders, stated that exceptional traders are able to remain calm and detached regardless of what the markets are doing. He describes Peter Steidlmayer's (a successful futures trader who is best known as the inventor of the Market Profile trading technique) response to a position that is going against him as being typified by the thought, "Hmmm, look at that."

37. *Identify and Eliminate Stress.* Stress in trading is a sign that something is wrong. If you feel stress, think about the cause, and then act to eliminate the problem. For example, let's say you determine that the greatest source of stress is indecision in getting out of a losing position. One way to solve this problem is simply to enter a protective stop order every time you put on a position.

I will give you a personal example. One of the elements of my job is providing trading recommendations to brokers in my company. This task is very similar to trading, and, having done both, I believe it's actually more difficult than trading. At one point, after years of net profitable recommendations, I hit a bad streak. I just couldn't do anything right. When I was right about the direction of the market, my buy recommendation was just a bit too low (or my sell price too high). When I got in and the direction was right, I got stopped out—frequently within a few ticks of the extreme of the reaction.

I responded by developing a range of computerized trading programs and technical indicators, thereby widely diversifying the trading advice I provided to the firm. I still made my day-to-day subjective calls on the market, but everything was no longer riding on the accuracy of these recommendations. By widely diversifying the trading-related advice and information, and transferring much of this load to mechanical approaches, I was able to greatly diminish a source of personal stress—and improve the quality of the research product in the process.

38. *Pay Attention to Intuition.* As I see it, intuition is simply experience that resides in the subconscious mind. The objectivity of the market analysis done by the conscious mind can be compromised by all sorts of extraneous considerations (e.g., one's current market position, a resistance to change a previous forecast). The subconscious, however, is not inhibited by such constraints. Unfortunately, we can't readily tap into our subconscious thoughts. However, when they come through as intuition, the trader needs to pay attention. As the Zen-quoting trader mentioned earlier expressed it, "The trick is to differentiate between what you *want* to happen and what you *know* will happen."

39 *Life's Mission and Love of the Endeavor.* In talking to the traders interviewed in *Market Wizards,* I had the definite sense that many of them felt that trading was what they were meant to do—in essence, their mission in life. In this context, Charles Faulkner quoted NLP cofounder John Grinder's description of mission: "What do you love so much that you would pay to do it?" Throughout my interviews, I was struck by the exuberance and love the Market Wizards had for trading. Many used gamelike analogies to describe trading. This type of love for the endeavor may indeed be an essential element for success.

40. *The Elements of Achievement.* Faulkner has a list of six key steps to achievement based on Gary Faris's study of successfully rehabilitated athletes, which appears to apply equally well to the goal of achieving trading success. These strategies include the following:

1. Using both "Toward" and "Away From" motivation;
2. Having a goal of full capability plus, with anything less being unacceptable;
3. Breaking down potentially overwhelming goals into chunks, with satisfaction garnered from the completion of each individual step;
4. Keeping full concentration on the present moment—that is, the single task at hand rather than the long-term goal;
5. Being personally involved in achieving goals (as opposed to depending on others); and
6. Making self-to-self comparisons to measure progress.

41. *Prices Are Nonrandom = The Markets Can Be Beat.* In reference to academicians who believe market prices are random, Monroe Trout, a CTA with one of the best risk/return records in the industry, says, "That's probably why they're professors and why I'm making money doing what I'm doing." The debate over whether prices are random is not yet over. However, my experience in interviewing scores of great traders left me with little doubt that the random walk theory is wrong. It is not the magnitude of the winnings registered by the Market Wizards, but the consistency of these winnings in some cases, that underpin my belief. As a particularly compelling example, consider Blake's 25:1 ratio of winning to losing months and his average annual return of 45 percent compared with a worst drawndown of only 5 percent. It is hard to imagine that results this lopsided could occur purely by chance—perhaps in a universe filled with traders, but not in their more finite numbers. Certainly, winning at the market is not easy—and, in fact, it is getting more difficult as professionals account for a constantly growing proportion of the activity—but it can be done!

42. *Keep Trading in Perspective.* There is more to life than trading.

Index